# The Developmental
# Social Psychology
# of Gender

# The Developmental Social Psychology of Gender

Edited by

**THOMAS ECKES**
*University of Dresden*

**HANNS M. TRAUTNER**
*University of Wuppertal*

LAWRENCE ERLBAUM ASSOCIATES, PUBLISHERS
Mahwah, New Jersey          London
2000

The final camera copy for this work was prepared by the editors
and therefore the publisher takes no responsibility for consistency
or correctness of typographical style. However, this arrangement
helps to make publication of this kind of scholarship possible.

Lawrence Erlbaum Associates, Inc., Publishers
10 Industrial Avenue
Mahwah, New Jersey 07430

Cover art by Andrea Eckes

**Library of Congress Cataloging-in-Publication Data**

The developmental social psychology of gender / edited by Thomas Eckes, Hanns M. Trautner.
        p. cm.
     Includes bibliographical references and index.
      ISBN 0-8058-3189-4 (cloth : alk. paper) — ISBN 0-8058-3190-8 (pbk. : alk. paper)
        1. Sex role. 2. Sex differences (Psychology) 3. Social psychology. 4. Developmental
psychology. I. Eckes, Thomas. II. Trautner, Hanns Martin, 1943–

HQ1075 .D47 2000
305.3—dc21

                                                                        99-058783

Books published by Lawrence Erlbaum Associates are printed on acid-free paper,
and their bindings are chosen for strength and durability.

Printed in the United States of America
10   9   8   7   6   5   4   3   2   1

# Contents

v

# Contributors

*Numbers in parantheses refer to the pages on which the authors' contributions begin.*

**Andrea E. Abele** (361), Department of Psychology, University of Erlangen, D-91054 Erlangen, Germany

**Danuta Bukatko** (295), Department of Psychology, College of the Holy Cross, Worcester, MA 01610, USA

**Linda L. Carli** (295), Department of Psychology, Wellesley College, Wellesley, MA 02181, USA

**Amanda B. Diekman** (123), Department of Psychology, Northwestern University, Evanston, IL 60208-2710, USA

**Alice H. Eagly** (123), Department of Psychology, Northwestern University, Evanston, IL 60208-2710, USA

**Jacquelynne S. Eccles** (333), Institute for Social Research, University of Michigan, Ann Arbor, MI 48106-1248, USA

**Thomas Eckes** (3, 419), Department of Psychology, University of Dresden, D-01062 Dresden, Germany

**Beverly I. Fagot** (65), Department of Psychology, University of Oregon, Eugene, OR 97403-1227, USA

**Susan T. Fiske** (207), Department of Psychology, University of Massachusetts, Amherst, MA 01003-7710, USA

**Carol Freedman-Doan** (333), Department of Psychology, Eastern Michigan University, Ypsilanti, MI 48197, USA

**Pam Frome** (333), Institute for Social Research, University of Michigan, Ann Arbor, MI 48106-1248, USA

**Judith L. Gibbons** (389), Department of Psychology, Saint Louis University, St. Louis, MO 63103, USA

**Peter Glick** (243), Department of Psychology, Lawrence University, Appleton, WI 54912-0599, USA

**Bettina Hannover** (177), Department of Psychology, University of Dortmund, D-44221 Dortmund, Germany

**Lori Hilt** (243), Department of Psychology, Lawrence University, Appleton, WI 54912-0599, USA

**Janis Jacobs** (333), Department of Human Development and Family Studies, Pennsylvania State University, University Park, PA 16802, USA

**Douglas T. Kenrick** (35), Department of Psychology, Arizona State University, Tempe, AZ 85287-1104, USA

**Hyun-Jeong Kim** (207), Department of Psychology, University of Massachusetts, Amherst, MA 01003-7710, USA

**Barbara Krahé** (273), Department of Psychology, University of Potsdam, D-14415 Potsdam, Germany

**Mary D. Leinbach** (65), 1017 Lake Front Rd., Lake Oswego, OR 97034, USA

**Carol L. Luce** (35), Department of Psychology, Arizona State University, Tempe, AZ 85287-1104, USA

**Carol Lynn Martin** (91), Department of Family Resources and Human Development, Arizona State University, Tempe, AZ 85287-2502, USA

**Carie S. Rodgers** (65), Department of Psychology, University of Oregon, Eugene, OR 97403-1227, USA

**Hanns M. Trautner** (3, 419), Department of Psychology, University of Wuppertal, D-42097 Wuppertal, Germany

**Wendy Wood** (123), Department of Psychology, Texas A&M University, College Station, TX 77843, USA

**Kwang Suk Yoon** (333), Institute for Social Research, University of Michigan, Ann Arbor, MI 48106-1248, USA

**Sarah E. Zemore** (207), Department of Psychology, University of Massachusetts, Amherst, MA 01003-7710, USA

# Preface

Gender research is currently one of the most active and dynamic areas in developmental and social psychology. Since the early 1970s there has been a tremendous increase in the understanding of gender and gender-related phenomena. The advances that have been made in theory and methodology, as well as the insights gained from myriads of empirical studies, are undoubtedly impressive. Yet, from its inception, the field has remained fragmented, making developmental and social psychological approaches to gender look like artificial divisions of a common subject matter. What's even worse, the relation between both psychological subdisciplines at times resembles well-documented effects of in-group/out-group differentiation: New approaches, concepts, and findings presented by in-group members are received with approval, whereas similarly important contributions to the same topic made by out-group members are largely ignored or overlooked. This volume is intended to overcome this unfortunate situation.

The time has come to strive for a synthesis of developmental and social psychology in pursuit of a common goal—the study of gender as a social category. In order to better understand the multifaceted and multi-dimensional nature of gender it seems necessary to take up and analyze issues at the intersection of both psychological disciplines, highlighting the interrelationships between developmental and social processes rather than looking at either kind of process in isolation. The objective of this book, then, is to provide a forum for setting out and elaborating an integrative perspective on gender and to offer a coherent counterpoint to the time-honored separation of gender research along disciplinary lines. Each chapter is intended to bring together relevant research and theory from both social and developmental psychology, thus attesting to the versatility of crossing disciplinary lines and, at the same time, providing fertile grounds for future cross-disciplinary research.

Because this is the first volume to advance an integration of both disciplines' perspectives on gender, there is a high degree of diversity. First of all, the contributions to this volume emerged from either a social psychological or a developmental background, promoting diversity in the conceptual approaches taken, the kinds of questions asked, and the methodology employed. Furthermore, some chapters focus on theoretical issues, whereas others present original pieces of empirical research. As stated more explicitly in the introductory chapter, the existence of multiple vantage points is particularly beneficial at this point in that it fosters cross-fertilization of ideas and allows freedom to choose from equally promising directions of gender research. In order to lend structure to this diversity, however, the approaches and findings covered in the various chapters are organized by means of a general conceptual framework rooted in a multidimensional view of gender.

Laying the groundwork for a developmental social psychology of gender appeared to be a task both overdue and challenging. Hence, we were extremely pleased at the response that our invitations to contribute to the volume received. As editors, we would like to thank the authors of the individual chapters for accepting this challenge. We are also grateful for their patience and willingness to respond to our questions and suggestions at all stages of the project. The commitment by the contributors to the integrative effort is reflected in the creativity and scholarship with which they set about answering the intriguing, and often highly intricate, issues emerging at the intersection of developmental and social psychological research on gender.

In terms of the writing level and complexity of material presented, the book is targeted at advanced undergraduates, graduate students, and professionals in social psychology, developmental psychology, and inter-disciplinary gender studies. Due to the richness and diversity of topics covered in the chapters, this volume is also of direct interest to readers in neighboring disciplines such as educational psychology, sociology, and anthropology.

We hope that the integrative approach advanced in this volume will stimulate much innovative research concerned with the joint analysis of developmental change and social influence. The time is ripe for social psychologists and developmentalists to recategorize their perceptions of group boundaries and to develop a common in-group identity—that of a developmental social psychology of gender.

*Thomas Eckes*
*Hanns M. Trautner*

# I

# INTRODUCTION

# 1

# Developmental Social Psychology of Gender: An Integrative Framework

Thomas Eckes
*University of Dresden*

Hanns M. Trautner
*University of Wuppertal*

Gender is one of the most important categories, if not the most important category, in human social life. Though at first sight distinguishing between female and male may seem straightforward, a closer look readily reveals that this fundamental categorization is fairly complex—it is imbued with a host of cultural meanings and practices pervading each and every aspect of individual, interpersonal, group, and societal processes. Thus, all known cultures provide rich and well-differentiated sets of concepts and terms to categorize and characterize boys and girls, men and women, to separate between female and male roles, rights, and responsibilities. In all known cultures, females and males meet with distinct sets of gender-related beliefs and expectations exerting powerful, and often subtle, influence on their thoughts, feelings, and behaviors.

For some time now, the construct of gender has figured prominently in psychological theory and research, attracting the attention of an ever-increasing number of researchers, in particular researchers from developmental and social psychology. Commenting on this research trend, Swann, Langlois, and Gilbert (1999) wrote: "Once the province of a small group of theorists and researchers operating on the periphery of psychological science, gender research has charged into the psychological mainstream during the last 2 decades" (p. 3). In a similar vein, Fiske (1998) identified gender as one of the top three categories (along with race and age) that form the primary foci of contemporary social psychological research on stereotyping, prejudice, and discrimination. The significance of the gender construct is also highlighted by the fact that the latest editions of both subdisciplines' standard references, *The Handbook of Social Psychology* (Gilbert, Fiske, & Lindzey, 1998) and the *Handbook of Child Psychology* (Damon, 1998), once more each include a chapter featuring gender phenomena—Deaux and LaFrance (1998) presented a social psychological view of gender, Ruble and Martin (1998) examined gender from a developmental perspective.

Given the importance of gender in human social life, the high level of research activities in the field does not come as a surprise. However, these activities are only very loosely, if at all, interconnected. Particularly, developmental and social psychological paradigms of research remain juxtaposed, and no attempt at integration is made. Unfortunately enough, developmental and social psychological approaches to gender do not seem to have very much in common. Thus, only a cursory look at Deaux and LaFrance's and Ruble and Martin's *Handbook* chapters suggests that gender in developmental perspective is something quite different from gender in social psychological perspective. How far these perspectives have evolved into separate spheres is quite easily illustrated: Of all the citations provided by Deaux and LaFrance (309 references) and those provided by Ruble and Martin (612 references), no more than 29 are common to both chapters.

The startlingly small degree of overlap between the sets of developmental and social psychological studies referred to in each subdiscipline's most representative current review is indicative of a long-standing compartmentalization in the field. As a result, the corresponding portrayals of gender phenomena often remain fragmentary in many respects, with several relevant issues simply failing to appear on the respective research agenda. Eisenberg (1995a) put it this way: "Findings in social psychology frequently raise important questions for developmentalists, or vice versa—questions that often are not recognized by investigators due to their lack of knowledge of work and ideas outside of their own perspectives" (p. vii).

The present volume aims at overcoming this highly unsatisfactory status quo. We believe that developmentalists and social psychologists can profit substantially from each other by exchanging insights, concepts, and theories. Understanding the multifaceted nature of gender, by this account, necessitates taking up and analyzing issues at the intersection of both psychological disciplines, highlighting the close and often complex interrelations between developmental and social processes.

Over the last two decades there have been several approaches crossing the boundaries between developmental and social psychology. Some of these works addressed fairly broad or heterogeneous sets of topics (see, e.g.,

Brehm, Kassin, & Gibbons, 1981; Durkin, 1995; Wozniak & Fischer, 1993); others undertook concerted efforts in the field of social development (Eisenberg, 1995b; Ruble & Goodnow, 1998); still others chose to adopt an integrative approach to more circumscribed issues like social cognition (Flavell & Ross, 1981b; Higgins, Ruble, & Hartup, 1983), cognitive development (Rogoff, 1990), aging (Blank, 1982; Pratt & Norris, 1994), the self (Staudinger & Greve, 1997), intelligence (Doise & Mugny, 1984), juvenile problem behavior (Silbereisen, Eyferth, & Rudinger, 1986), and cultural practices (Goodnow, Miller, & Kessel, 1995).

However, an explicitly integrative look focused on gender has been seriously lacking. This is all the more surprising as the widely acknowledged multifaceted nature of gender phenomena literally calls for bringing together relevant research and theory from both developmental and social psychology, perhaps even more so than applies to many other fields of study. Failing to meet the challenge of an integrative gender research would bear the risk of ending up like the blind wise men in the old Hindu fable cited by Constantinople (1979). Confronted with an elephant and asked to decide what it was, each of the men assumed that the object under study was best described by the part he happened to feel (a snake when feeling the tail, a tree when feeling the leg, etc.).

In the rest of this chapter, we first discuss potential benefits of integrating developmental and social psychological approaches to the study of gender. As it turns out, many of the strengths of one of these approaches are mirrored by weaknesses of the other, and vice versa, making it all the more worthwile to work toward an integration highlighting the merits of both. We then present a conceptual framework lending structure to the large variety of possible research questions in the emerging field of a developmental social psychology of gender. At its heart is a multidimensional conceptualization of gender development (Huston, 1983; Ruble & Martin, 1998), extended by incorporating multiple levels of social psychological analysis (Doise, 1986). Finally, we give a preview of this volume's chapters, pointing to the ways in which they contribute to the integrative effort.

# BENEFITS OF INTEGRATING DEVELOPMENTAL AND SOCIAL PSYCHOLOGICAL PERSPECTIVES ON GENDER

## Contributions of the Developmental Perspective

Looking at the typical way of doing research in social psychology, a severe limitation immediately becomes obvious, a limitation that is characteristic of most, if not all, nondevelopmental psychological disciplines: a profound neglect of issues and variables referring to *change over time*. Social psychological studies commonly do not allow for analysis of the developmental processes involved in the social phenomena under consideration. Put differently, change over time represents a "blind spot" of social psychology. It is as if gender attitudes or gender stereotypes, to take just two prominent topics studied extensively by social psychologists, would "arise out of nowhere, forming miraculously just before their subjects come to university" (Durkin, 1995, p. 3).

The point is that social processes in general, and gender-related processes in particular, have developmental histories necessitating a time course or life-span perspective for a fuller understanding. Although developmental studies can themselves be criticized for focusing on some particular age spans (Ruble & Goodnow, 1998, pp. 743–745), the vast majority of subjects in social psychological studies typically fall into a fairly narrow age group, that of young adults. Whereas in the 1940s and 1950s social psychologists often employed subject samples from a wide range of age groups, since the 1960s (and continuing to the present) social psychologists have almost exclusively conducted research with college-age students—an age group that is peculiar in many respects (Sears, 1986; see also Flavell & Ross, 1981a). For example, compared with older adults, college students typically have less crystallized attitudes, less well-formulated senses of self, and more unstable peer-group relationships. Even more substantial differences can be assumed to exist with respect to younger adolescents or children.

Clearly, working on such a narrow database restricts the set of research questions that can be asked and poses difficulties for the conclusions that can be drawn from research findings. With a focus on college-age students as the primary subject population, social psychology is generally ill-equipped to address processes of change over time, and it risks leaving out of account sources and consequences of variability in social, contextual, and cultural influences across the life span. It is precisely here that a developmental analysis can contribute substantially in gaining a more complete understanding of gender. In a thoughtful discussion of the general relation between developmental and social psychological research, Ruble and Goodnow (1998) outlined points of overlap between the two disciplines, as well as several distinctive features of a developmental analysis. These features are of particular interest here because they refer to potential benefits of a developmental perspective.

First, the developmental approach provides a time-course perspective that draws attention to the dynamic or temporal qualities of behavior; that is, gender-related behavior is seen as affected by the individual's place in history and ontogeny. Accordingly, a developmental approach entails looking for conditions influencing behavior within the history of the individual. The typical research design allows comparisons based on age differences, either cross-sectionally or longitudinally.

Second, in a developmental analysis much weight is given to the effects of early experience. Whereas social psychologists typically focus on proximal sources of influence on behavior, lending high importance to recency and frequency effects, developmentalists often study ontogenetically more remote, distal sources of influence (Costanzo, 1992). In a similar vein, developmentalists are prone to investigate periods of heightened sensitivity in an individual's life span. For example, life transitions such as reaching puberty, becoming a parent, or retiring can be conceptualized as sensitive periods systematically influencing an individual's self-construal, his or her social attitudes, interpersonal relationships, and so forth (Ruble, 1994).

Third, a developmental perspective highlights the pace and direction of change. This feature is immediately evident in research with children. Childhood is a period of rapid developmental change, leading to questions concerning the specifics of the processes involved. Thus, for example, children's acquisition of gender stereotypes, differentiation of gender-related self-knowledge, or adoption of gender roles can be analyzed with respect to issues of acceleration or deceleration. Similarly, studies of the direction of changes typically focus on content, structure, and flexibility of gender stereotypes; the relative proportion of feminine, masculine, or androgynous features contained within a child's self-concept; and the adoption of traditional versus nontraditional gender roles.

Finally, developmental analyses draw attention to the course or trajectory of change processes. Different kinds of social knowledge or behavior may be characterized by distinctly different developmental patterns, some forming part of a linear progression, others following a more curvilinear trend (e.g., U-shaped or reverse U-shaped) or an irregular decline. Taking account of the trajectory of change can help social psychologists to decide when to take dependent measures, to find out about the extent to which change processes are short-lived or tend to stabilize, and to comparatively analyze developmental trends in different domains of social cognition and behavior.

Taken together, analyzing the temporal qualities of behavior, looking at distal sources of influence, examining the pace and direction of change processes, and studying the trajectory of change represent distinctive and intriguing features of a developmental analysis. It is in these respects that the social psychological perspective on gender could profit most from a developmental approach.

## Contributions of the Social Psychological Perspective

Many developmentalists, especially those working in the area of cognitive development (and adopting a Piagetian or a Kohlberg approach), have often failed to pay sufficient attention to overt and covert variants of social influence on the processes under consideration. Formation and change of gender-typed cognitions, preferences, and behaviors, in their view, can (or even should) be analyzed as instances or consequences of more general cognitive-developmental processes, thus leaving aside, or abstracting from, the social context in which the individual is acting. In sharp contrast, social, contextual, and cultural factors influencing an individual's thoughts, feelings, and behaviors are of critical importance to a social psychological analysis; actually, it is social influence that defines the field (see, e.g., Allport, 1985). Hence, what constitutes a "blind spot" of the developmental perspective forms the focus of a social psychological approach to gender. Therefore, in principle, there similarly is a high potential for the developmental approach to benefit from gender research in social psychology.

Within contemporary social psychology "gender is considered a dynamic construct that draws on and impinges upon processes at the individual, interactional, group, institutional, and cultural levels" (Deaux & LaFrance, 1998, p. 788). At the core of this approach is the view of *gender as a social category* (Deaux, 1984; Sherif, 1982; see also Deaux, 1999). As Sherif (1982) put it: "Gender is a scheme for social categorization of individuals, and every known human society has some gender scheme. Every gender scheme recognizes biological differentiation while also creating social differentiations" (p. 376). A basic tenet of this view is that an individual's thoughts, feelings, and behaviors are heavily influenced by a host of intertwined multilevel social and cultural factors associated with the categorical distinction between female and male. These factors include the division of labor between the sexes, descriptive and prescriptive beliefs about women and men, and attitudes toward the sexes and toward gender-related issues (see, e.g., Ashmore, 1990; Eckes, 1997).

The gender-as-a-social-category view contrasts with two other research paradigms in the psychology of gender (Ashmore, 1990; Deaux, 1984; Trautner, 1993). The first is the *sex differences* (or *gender-as-a-subject-variable*) approach. In its most elementary form, this approach seeks to answer the seemingly simple question of whether, and to what degree, the sexes differ in a number of psychological measures referring to mental abilities, personality traits, social behaviors, and so forth. The sex differences approach was the earliest to be taken up, and it continues to attract a lot of attention (see, e.g., Eagly, 1995; Maccoby & Jacklin, 1974; Merz, 1979). In the second paradigm, gender is construed as a personality variable, that is, as one or a small number of stable, internal (i.e., traitlike) qualities. Key concepts of the *gender-as-a-personality-variable* approach are "masculinity," "femininity," and their derivative "androgyny." Here, a major attraction for theorizing and research concerns measurement issues and the concepts' explanatory power with respect to individual differences in mental health, social adjustment, and a variety of gender-related behaviors (see, e.g., Bem, 1974, 1993; Bierhoff-Alfermann, 1989; Morawski, 1987).

An important characteristic common to the sex differences and the gender-as-a-personality-variable paradigms is their almost exclusive focus on the individual level. Both emphasize the person rather than the situation, and both refer primarily to biological distinctions or prior socialization as explanatory principles (Deaux & Kite, 1987). The typical study carried out within either approach features static individual dispositions, leaving out of account the complex social dynamics underlying gender phenomena. Unlike these individual-centered approaches, the gender-as-a-social-category perspective focuses on fluctuating patterns of gender-typed behavior in social contexts. We do not argue here against sex differences research in general, mainly because significant insights into the context-bound and culturally transmitted nature of sex-differentiated behaviors presuppose a fine-grained analysis of their very occurrence, possibly inspired by theoretical assumptions derived from the gender-as-a-social-category view (discussed later). However, we do think that merely documenting and cataloging observed sex differences remains an incomplete, if not misguided, account of gender.

To illustrate, consider the following hypothetical example of a mixed-sex group of persons working on a particular task. The simple sex differences approach typically would compare the average performance score of the female group members to the corresponding score of the male group members, noting which sex outperforms the other if significant sex differences were found. In the gender-as-a-personality-variable approach, sex-typed group members (i.e., feminine women or masculine men) would similarly be compared to non-sex-typed or androgynous group members, identified as those persons scoring equally high on the femininity and masculinity subscales of some gender-role orientation questionnaire.

In contrast, issues exemplifying the gender-as-a-social-category view would include perceivers' categorizations and evaluations of the female and male group members' performance; the extent to which gender-typed behavior is displayed depending on the sex composition of the group; the short-term and long-term cognitive, affective, and behavioral consequences of having solo status (i.e., being the only female or male group member); the degree to which females' and males' task-relevant behavior is influenced by the sex of the addressee; the nature of the task, particularly with respect to its feminine or masculine content; and the pattern of communication and influence between and within female and male subgroups.

In other words, researchers working within the gender-as-a-social-category paradigm would not ask whether, and to what degree, the sexes (or, alternatively, feminine, masculine, and androgynous persons) differ in a specific trait, skill, or task performance. Rather, they would ask *how*, *when*, and *why* it makes a difference to be male or female.

## The Multifaceted Nature of Gender

Several theoretical proposals have been advanced exactly addressing the how, when, and why of sex differences. Among the most prominent ones are Ashmore's (1990) multiplicity model of gender identity, Deaux and Major's (1987) gender-in-context model (see also Deaux & LaFrance, 1998), Eagly's (1987) social role theory of sex-differentiated behavior (see also Eagly, Wood, & Diekman, chap. 5, this volume), Eccles (Parsons) et al.'s (1983) model of achievement-related choices (see also Eccles, Freedman-Doan, Frome, Jacobs, & Yoon, chap. 11, this volume), and Spence's (1993) multifactorial gender identity theory (see also Spence, 1999). Though differing from each other in many respects, these models share a set of core assumptions about the nature of social influence and about the way females and males relate to social contexts. These assumptions can be summarized as follows (see, for more detailed accounts, Ashmore, 1990; Ashmore & Sewell, 1998; Deaux & LaFrance, 1998).

First, it is argued that social influence can, and should be, studied at *multiple levels*. At any point in time, an individual's gender-related thoughts, feelings, and behaviors are being determined by multiple factors ranging from the broad societal level to specific interpersonal encounters and intraindividual processes. For instance, how someone cognizes, and acts toward, other people is dependent on his or her cognitive apparatus (e.g., self-concept, stereotypic beliefs, implicit or explicit attitudes), kind of interpersonal orientation (e.g., self-oriented vs. other-oriented), membership in particular social groups, as well as on the broader system of culturally shared conceptions, ideologies, or social representations concerning categories of people and their mutual relations. Second, social influence is conceived of as *heterogeneous*; that is, social influence originates from multiple sources. At any level of influence, and across levels as well, factors vary not only in their intensity, but also with respect to their origin and the direction of influence they exert. Put differently, interpersonal, group, or cultural environments, respectively, do not present homogeneous sets of neatly converging, clear-cut messages about gender. This typically leaves to the individual the formidable task of making sense out of vague and often conflicting socially transmitted gender-related information. Third, gender is construed as *multidimensional*. That is, gender is not viewed as some kind of unitary essence manifesting itself in a stable set of tightly interconnected gender-related thoughts, feelings, and behaviors. Rather, gender has many dimensions or facets that are related to each other in multiple ways, ranging from tightly knit associations among subsets of dimensions to only loose connections or even independence. In addition, the links between facets of gender are conceived of as highly variable among people, as well as across contexts and points in time (see also Martin, chap. 4, this volume).

The mutual relations between gender, individual, and social context are highlighted by three more specific, yet closely interconnected construals of gender. These refer to the conceptualizations of *gender-as-stimulus*, *gender-as-process*, and *gender-as-product*. That is, gender is considered a complex social stimulus that influences people's perceptions, judgments, and behaviors. At the same time, gender is given concrete meaning by individuals acting in a particular social setting or cultural context, with changes in meaning possibly occurring each time people move from one interactional setting to the next. Finally, gender can be viewed as a construct that materializes in social encounters; in other words, gender is not an essential quality of an individual's psychological makeup—rather, it is an inherently *relational* category.

This general notion was expressed most clearly in Deaux and Major's (1987) gender-in-context model, according to which variability in gender-related behaviors is the rule rather than the exception. The basic components of the model are: (a) the perceiver, bringing a set of beliefs and expectations about gender to the situation (e.g., gender stereotypes and gender-related attitudes); (b) the target person, entering the situation with particular self-conceptions and interaction goals (e.g., self-presentation or self-verification concerns); and (c) features of the situation, making gender more or less salient (e.g., the proportion of women and men in the situation or cues for the appropriateness of gender-typed behavior). Whether a person will display gender-typed behavior or not depends on a complex interplay between all three components. For example, the display of gender-typed behavior of the (female) target is highly likely when the (male) perceiver holds a traditional view of the female gender role and categorizes the target as a typical female, the target conceives of herself in a feminine way, and the interaction situation is construed by both the target and the perceiver as demanding assertive behavior from the male and submissive behavior from the female.

## Basic Propositions of a Developmental
## Social Psychology of Gender

In sum, we argue that research on gender drawing solely on either a developmental or a social psychological approach will definitely fail to yield a sufficient account of the phenomena under study. Social psychologists typically ignore processes of change over time involved in the development of gender concepts, gender identity, preferences, and gender-role behavior. Developmentalists often are not interested in the way individual change varies with social or contextual factors such as self-presentation concerns, interpersonal expectations, or gender-related attitudes, nor are they prone to address the outcome of developmental processes in adulthood.

Furthermore, it is important to note that an integrative approach to the study of gender must not confine itself to simply adding to the first perspective what the second has to offer and vice versa. Quite the contrary, at the intersection of developmental and social psychology many issues will emerge that pose new kinds of challenges for theorizing and research. Thus, for example, contexts do not stay the same over an individual's life course; instead, they are continually changing in terms of strength of influence, direction of influence, range of opportunities for satisfying individual needs, and threats to personal growth. What at one point in time may be a perfect or near-perfect match between females' or males' needs and the opportunities afforded them by their social environments, at some later point in time can become the cause of stressful or maladaptive behavior patterns (see, e.g., Eccles et al., 1993). In short, contextual and individual dynamics interrelate in complex ways. Hence, both perspectives on gender, the develomental and the social psychological, can benefit greatly from each other. This reciprocation of benefits seems to be a promising starting point for an integrative endeavor.

As suggested here, the basic propositions of a developmental social psychology of gender are:

1. Gender is subject to developmental processes throughout an individual's life span; that is, each type and each process of social influence on gender-based cognitions, attitudes, and behaviors has a developmental history and dynamics.

2. Gender is subject to social influence at any point in time; that is, each type and each process of change in gender-based cognitions, attitudes, and behaviors is dependent on the social or cultural context.

3. Developmental processes and social influence are closely linked to each other; that is, gender development cannot be adequately studied without considering social processes; analogously, the social psychological analysis of gender must not be restricted to a particular age group (i.e., young adults).

In his general critique of the traditional boundaries between developmental and social psychology, Durkin (1995) aptly concluded: "the preserve of the developmentalist is not some period prior to the point at which the social psychologist takes over. Instead, developmental change is one of life's few constants" (p. 4). Taking up this conclusion we would like to add that the preserve of the developmentalist is not the process of change over time, leaving the variety of ways in which an individual relates to, and is influenced by, other individuals, groups, or cultures to the social psychologist. Indeed, social influence is another one of life's few constants.

In the next section we present a conceptual framework for addressing issues of developmental change and issues of social influence simultaneously. It is intended to serve as a kind of guideline on the way toward a developmental social psychology of gender.

# A CONCEPTUAL FRAMEWORK
# FOR AN INTEGRATIVE APPROACH

## Ruble and Martin's (1998) Revision of the "Huston Matrix"

The developmental literature of the 1960s and 1970s was characterized by a lot of blurring conceptual distinctions concerning dimensions or features of sex typing (sex-role identity, sex-role orientation, sex-role adoption, etc.). Based on a multidimensional view, Huston (1983) was the first to advance a more principled, taxonomic approach to the developmental analysis of gender. She distinguished between *constructs*—concepts or beliefs, identity or self-perception, preferences or attitudes, and behavioral enactment—and *content areas*—biological gender, activities and interests, personal-social attributes, gender-based social relationships, and stylistic and symbolic characteristics. Arranging constructs and content areas in a matrix yielded 20 distinct kinds of issues relevant to sex-typing research.

Recently, Ruble and Martin (1998) presented a modified version of the so-called Huston matrix. Herein, the four constructs remained essentially the same, but one more content area was added—values. From a social psychological point of view, this addition is highly welcome since values (or, more generally, attitudes) are of central importance for a comprehensive analysis of gender as a social category. In the following, we first present a short outline of content areas and constructs using Ruble and Martin's terminology. Then we extend the two-dimensional taxonomic scheme by a third dimension representing the different levels at which gender as a social category can be analyzed.

The six content areas can be characterized as follows.

1. *Biological/categorical sex:* biological attributes (e.g., gonadal, hormonal, or morphological distinctions), as well as physical and material attributes that need not have a clear biological basis (e.g., bodily features of one's gender such as clothing or hair style).

2. *Activities and interests:* toys, play and leisure activities, occupations and work, household roles, tasks.

3. *Personal-social attributes:* personality traits, social behaviors, and abilities.

4. *Gender-based social relationships:* sex of peers, friends, lovers, preferred parent or attachment figure, and models (i.e., persons he or she wants to imitate or identify with).

5. *Styles and symbols:* nonverbal behaviors (e.g., facial expressions, gestures, body positions and movement), speech patterns (e.g., tempo, pitch), play styles, fantasy.

6. *Gender-related values:* evaluations of sex categories, valuing masculine and feminine attributes, gender-role attitudes, in-group favoritism and out-group derogation.

These content areas are combined with four constructs yielding 24 classes of issues potentially relevant to sex-typing research. The constructs within this scheme are:

1. *Concepts or beliefs:* an individual's gender-related knowledge or knowledge structures (i.e., gender stereotypes). In the order of the aforementioned content areas, this construct refers to (a) gender labeling and constancy; (b) knowledge of gender-typed toys, activities, and so forth; (c) knowledge of gender-typed traits or role-behaviors; (d) beliefs about gender-appropriate social relations; (e) awareness of gender-typed nonverbal behaviors and symbols; and (f) knowledge of different values attached to the sexes and to gender-related issues.

2. *Identity or self-perception:* an individual's perception of him- or herself as masculine or feminine or as possessing gender-typed attributes. Relevant topics are (a) inner sense of maleness or femaleness; (b) self-perception of activities and interests; (c) perceptions of own traits, abilities, and behaviors; (d) perception of self as relating to others (peers, friends, parents, etc.); (e) self-perception of nonverbal, stylistic, and symbolic features; and (f) perception of self in terms of one's membership in positively or negatively valued social groups.

3. *Preferences:* an individual's desire to possess gender-related attributes. The topics falling into this construct category are (a) wish to be male or female; (b) preference for toys, activities, occupations; (c)

preference for particular traits, abilities, and behaviors; (d) preference for particular others to relate with on the basis of gender; (e) preference for stylistic or symbolic objects; and (f) in-group or out-group biases, gender-related attitudes, sexist prejudice.

4. *Behavioral enactment:* an individual's pattern of gender-typed behavioral display. The topics exemplifying the content areas pertaining to this construct are (a) displaying gender-typed bodily attributes; (b) engaging in gender-typed play or leisure activities, occupations, or achievement tasks; (c) displaying gender-typed traits and abilities; (d) building, maintaining, or ending social relationships on the basis of gender; (e) displaying gender-typed stylistic or symbolic features and fantasy; and (f) discriminating against others on the basis of gender.

From a developmental point of view, at least three questions have to be addressed within each and every cell of the matrix. First, how do children acquire the respective developmental attributes (e.g., gender constancy, toy preferences, awareness of gender-typed symbols)? Second, when does the acquisition process start, and which course does it take? And, third, what is the relationship between developmental changes across content areas and constructs? The multidimensional nature of gender-typing processes implied by these research questions marks an important point of overlap with the social psychological view of gender. Moreover, in the Ruble and Martin (1998) revision of the Huston matrix there are some important cross-references to recent research and theorizing in social psychology. This particularly applies to gender stereotypes and gender-related attitudes, though the authors' review of developmental research explicitly focuses on developmental changes in children and adolescents.

## Multiple Levels of Analysis

In order to broaden the perspective, it seems crucial to specify the *levels* at which research questions are being raised and explanations of gender phenomena sought. The general levels-of-analysis notion has been around in social psychology at least since the 1980s (see, e.g., Ashmore & Del Boca, 1986; Doise, 1984, 1986, 1997; Lorenzi-Cioldi & Doise, 1990; Ragins & Sundstrom, 1989). Following these converging proposals, and adapting the specifics to the present context, we want to suggest that the sexes relate to each other at four different but interconnected levels. These are the individual level, the interpersonal (or interactional) level, the group (or role) level, and the cultural (or societal) level. It should be noted that no single level, nor single set of factors located at a given level, is adequate to account for the full range of gender phenomena. In addition, each level can be ordered along a dimension of inclusiveness or generality, with the individual level as the most specific and the cultural level as the most general or inclusive one. In the following a short characterization of each level is provided:

At the *individual level* the focus is on the way individuals organize their experience of the social environment. The intraindividual processes studied include cognitive, affective, and motivational functions. It is at this level that the developmental and the social psychological analysis of gender traditionally have the highest degree of overlap. Cognitive functions include the use of categorization schemes like gender stereotypes in impression formation and social judgment. Affective functions refer to the influence of feelings or moods on formation and change of gender stereotypes and gender-related attitudes. Finally, motivational functions comprise the need to identify with positively valued social groups or cultures, as well as the desire to reduce the complexity of the social world by the use of a small set of fairly simple and familiar cognitive categories.

The second, and more inclusive, *interpersonal level* concerns dyadic (i.e., two-person) relationships and corresponding interactional processes. A typical example of explanatory principles involved at this level are behavioral confirmation processes or self-fulfilling prophecies. Thus stereotypes induce certain kinds of expectations about the traits or abilities of other persons, and these expectations may lead to confirmatory perception–interaction sequences producing the very behavior or trait that the perceiver had originally expected. Further pertinent topics concern the display of gender-typed behavior in the presence of an attractive partner holding traditional gender-role attitudes; the activation and use of interactional scripts (e.g., dating scripts); and discriminatory behavior toward another person, for example, overtly distancing verbal or nonverbal behavior based on the interactant's membership in social categories such as gender, age, race, or a combination of these.

The *group level* deals with the relation between females and males as group members or as occupants of different social positions. At this level commonalities, as well as differences, between female–male relations and other forms of intergroup relations come to the fore. Particularly important here are power and status differences between females and males and the consequences these differences have for stability and change in gender-role distributions. A closely related group-level issue concerns the traditional division of labor between the sexes and its influence on the emergence and perpetuation of gender stereotypes, as well as on the acquisition of gender-typed skills and attitudes. Further intriguing research questions exemplifying this level address antecedents and consequences of the salience of an individual's sex-category membership, effects of holding power over others on the activation and use of stereotypes and prejudices, and gender roles as determinants of gender-segregated play behavior in children.

At the most inclusive level of analysis, the *cultural level*, gender is studied in relation to systems of socially shared beliefs, representations, norms, and values. These systems are cultural products that not only help to define an individual's place within society but also serve to maintain or foster social differentiations between females and males. Among relevant research areas are social constructions of gender showing up in stereotypic portrayals of females and males in the media, subtle forms and practices of institutional or organizational gender discrimination, as well as social support for public policies that aim at reducing prejudiced beliefs and behaviors within society. Also, studies of the content, structure, and acquisition of gender-typed beliefs and ideologies across cultures or nations become relevant at this level of analysis.

## An Extended Multidimensional Matrix of Gender Issues

The combination of content areas, constructs, and levels of analysis yields a three-dimensional matrix that forms the basis for studying gender from a developmental social psychological perspective. This 96-cell matrix is visually displayed in Fig. 1.1. For ease of presentation, the *time* axis, actually constituting a fourth dimension needed to account for processes of developmental change, is only symbolically shown as a sequence of discrete measurement points within a single arbitrary cell. Note that each cell in this matrix refers to a distinct set of research issues emerging at the intersection of a particular content area with a particular construct and level of analysis.

Making use of such a taxonomy that tries to capture the gist of developmental and social psychological approaches, as well as their interconnections, has several advantages. Among the most important features of the present framework are (a) providing a broad, general conceptual scheme for undertaking a concerted effort in gender research; (b) identifying topics that have been largely neglected or less intensely researched than others; (c) highlighting the multilevel, multidimensional nature of developmental change; (d) allowing for divergent and convergent developmental courses or trajectories within and across cells; and (e) drawing attention to the relations existing between various dimensions of the matrix, that is, identifying not only main effects, but also two- or multiway interactions between content areas, constructs, levels of analysis, and time.

Though at first glance the taxonomic organization of the field presented in Fig. 1.1 may seem bewildering, it is well worth dwelling on, thinking about the kinds of research issues associated with various cells of the matrix. To illustrate, consider the content area "gender-related values" combined with the constructs and levels-of-analysis dimensions. The resulting set of 16 cells (i.e., the bottom layer of the matrix depicted in Fig. 1.1) refers to various manifestations and representations of attitudes toward the sexes and toward gender-related issues. Although this topic is one that has been largely neglected by developmentalists (with some notable exceptions, see e.g., Lutz & Ruble, 1995), it has been at the fore of social psychological research over the last 20 years or so. Since gender-related attitudes will be dealt with by Glick and Hilt (chap. 8, this volume), in the remainder of this section the values area is picked out solely to exemplify the rich set of research questions emerging at the intersection of the developmental and social psychological perspectives embodied in our multidimensional framework. Some of these issues have already begun to be studied, whereas others are still awaiting attention.

A first set of issues concerns the *concepts* involved in the development of gender-related values. At the individual level of analysis it may be asked when and how children acquire knowledge about "better" or higher valued gender-typed traits, symbols, and activities. Regarding the interpersonal level, the structure of evaluative beliefs about same-sex and cross-sex interactions, romantic attractions, or close relationships would be studied, including the cognitive representation of the typical event sequences in face-to-face interaction (e.g., beliefs about "good" and "bad" dates). At the group level, illustrative research issues concern the evaluation and attribution of feminine or masculine behavior as it relates to the sex composition of a particular social group or to the power difference existing between female and male group members. Analyzing knowledge about gender-related values at the cultural level would include studies of stereotypic images of females and males as conveyed in the mass media, as well as studies of these images' functions in confirming or justifying shared beliefs about the sexes and traditional gender roles.

Concerning *gender identity* (or gendered self-perception), pertinent issues studied at the individual level relate to the changes in a person's self-esteem depending on his or her perception of differential evaluations of gender roles within society. In social interactions, self-evaluations may covary with the perceived gender-role orientation of the interaction partner, the partner's behavioral expectations, and the gender-typed nature of the interactional context. At the group level of analysis, theories of social identification provide a wealth of hypotheses about the dynamic evaluation of feminine and masculine components of the self; that is, membership in low- or high-valued groups is predicted to have systematic short-term and long-term effects on the kind of gendered identities that boys and girls, men and women develop or strive for. Looking at the cultural forces that may exert influence on gender-related self-evaluations, research issues refer to a given culture's view of femininity and masculinity, including comparisons between the attitudes toward gender roles in collectivistic and individualistic societies.

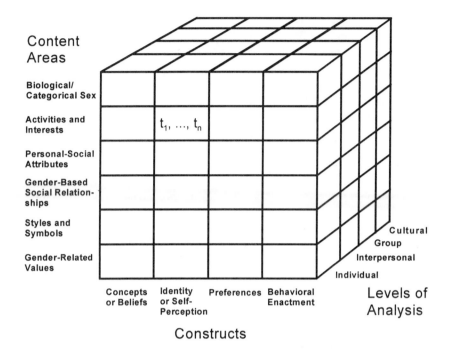

FIG. 1.1   Multidimensional matrix of research issues in a developmental social psychology of gender. ($t_1$, ..., $t_n$ = Measurement points indicating the time axis.)

The *preferences* construct directs attention to the analysis of prejudiced beliefs about the sexes and gender-related issues. At the individual level, relevant questions include the cognitive, affective, and motivational processes (e.g., the need to evaluate other persons' behavior on the basis of gender) that are involved in the formation, elaboration, and, possibly, reduction of gender biases. An interpersonal analysis would highlight the influence of evaluative beliefs on the course and outcome of social interactions, the deliberate choice of interaction partners adopting traditional or egalitarian gender-role behavior, and the thoughts and feelings of the target person when being confronted with an actor's prejudiced gender beliefs. From a group-level point of view research issues include the development of in-group biases, stability and change of attitudes toward traditional gender roles, and the degree of favor or disfavor with which gender segregation in various contexts (e.g., at school, in the family, or in the workforce) is evaluated. A cultural-level analysis would address the cultural specifics and universals of valuing feminine and masculine traits, activities, interests, and so forth.

When combined with values, *behavioral enactment* in the present scheme refers to the behavioral or conative component of gender attitudes. Here, the prime issue at all four levels of analysis is the antecedents, symptoms, and consequences of discrimination, that is, of any behavior toward members of a group that denies these persons the equal treatment they desire. Focusing on the individual level, studies may analyze factors governing distancing, overtly negative responses or, alternatively, subjectively positive or benevolent responses toward the other sex, each serving to promote or maintain an actor's status or power. In social interactions, attitudes, besides their impact on discriminatory behavior, also function as guiding schemes or heuristics for planning and regulating interpersonal behaviors, such as matching one's self-presentational style to the perceived traditionality of an interactant's gender-role attitude. A group-level perspective would draw attention to various forms of structural sexism, for example, the selection and identification of leaders on the sole basis of gender. Finally, analyzing the enactment of gender-related values at the cultural, most inclusive level points to the general social practices that serve to create and foster gender hierarchies within society.

The chapters in this volume flesh out various parts of the conceptual framework and thus demonstrate the versatility of a developmental social psychological perspective on gender. Using the multidimensional matrix shown in Fig. 1.1 as a general ordering system, the issues dealt with in each chapter can be located within a frame of reference binding issues of developmental change and social influence. It should be noted, however, that this scheme is by no means intended to exhaust the set of research questions that could possibly be asked in the field; it is all too common in the social and behavioral sciences that the set of questions in a given area of research is virtually infinite. Nor is our scheme meant to be prescriptive, telling researchers what they should put on top of their agenda and what to dismiss as irrelevant or uninteresting. Our multidimensional matrix is basically meant to serve as a guideline or heuristic that stimulates research in as many and diverse fields as possible and draws attention to their interconnections. In other words, developmental social psychological research on gender will not be finished as soon as each and every cell in our matrix has been filled with some kind of answers. Each answer given to a concrete question will by necessity produce new ones, expanding this framework in directions that are presently difficult, if not impossible, to foresee.

## THEMES AND ORGANIZATION OF THE BOOK

As explained previously, the central theme of this book is the fundamental interrelatedness of developmental change and social influence in producing the rich variety of gender phenomena. In order to present a coherent view of the complex issues involved, this volume is organized into three main parts (parts II through IV) with four chapters each, complemented by the present introductory chapter (part I) and a concluding chapter (part V).

Part II, Theoretical Approaches, comprises currently influential, yet still somewhat disparate, perspectives on gender. When viewed together, however, these theories promise to contribute substantially to a fuller understanding of gender phenomena. It would be highly counterproductive at this stage of the integrative endeavor to focus on a single theoretical position or school of thought. Eclecticism has much to recommend it when consensually accepted criteria for preferring one theory over the other are out of reach. Furthermore, narrowing down the spectrum of theoretical foci would almost inevitably bear the risk of neglecting important processes and hence lead to a severely impoverished look at the field. Only by widening the analytical lens will it be possible to account for the complex, multilevel, multidimensional nature of gender (see Maccoby, 1998, for a similar point). Consequently, the theories included in part II postulate a broad range of powerful explanatory principles that should eventually prove to complement each other. The major concepts addressed in these chapters refer to evolutionary life history, sex-differentiated socialization practices, cognitive schemas, and social roles.

Thinking about gender in evolutionary terms, as is done in chapter 2, provides an intriguing look at long-standing controversies in the field. Specifically, Kenrick and Luce advance an evolutionary life-history model of gender development, accounting for phenomena as diverse as mate choice, aggression, sexuality, and child care. The model's focus is on the developmental trajectories of an organism in terms of the differential allocation of energy to survival, growth, and reproduction across the life span. The authors show that life-history theory provides a dynamic evolutionary framework that can help unravel some of the mysteries in the realm of human sex differences and similarities, for example, those that exist in each of the behavioral domains mentioned earlier. Throughout the chapter, special emphasis is given to the interconnections between evolutionary constraints, human culture, and cognition. Kenrick and Luce particularly reject attempts to pit evolutionary, cultural, and cognitive accounts of gender against each other. Indeed, these diverse perspectives should not be construed as conflicting, nor as competing. Rather, they are interdependent, needing each other for a complete understanding of gender-typed social behaviors and their change across developmental stages (see Kenrick & Simpson, 1997, for a principled statement of this view). The concept of preparedness is a case in point. Building on the general assumption of complex gene–environment interactions, this concept implies that the sexes are biologically predisposed to experience slightly different events. Human cultures, in turn, tend to foster or accentuate these differential learning experiences in multiple and possibly highly specific ways.

Focusing on the environmental influences of family, school, and peer group, Fagot, Rodgers, and Leinbach (chap. 3) address the question of differential socialization of boys and girls. The authors consider gender development from infants' earliest recognition of sex-related differences through the acquisition of gender knowledge and gender-typed behavior during early and middle childhood. Following a careful examination of extant research and reviewing their own program of research, Fagot et al. argue that the socialization pressures and environmental input to which boys and girls are subjected are often more subtle and, at the same time, more powerful than has been asserted. It is shown how parents, teachers, and peers provide information about the importance of gender, through their reactions to the child, but also in terms of family organization, structuring of school activities, and peer group pressure for gender segregation, respectively. These environmental factors have differential effects on boys and girls at different ages, possibly coinciding with changes in cognitive development. The chapter also presents more recent evidence on the functions of metaphorical cues in gender socialization, showing that there is more to children's stereotyping than accumulating knowledge about who has or does what. Fagot et al. conclude that the child's inherent capacities and the multiple forms of environmental input interact dynamically. They agree with current cognitive developmental theory that children construct their own understanding of the world, but they also stress that gender-related environmental input provided by socializing agents and cultural practices are among the building blocks used in this construction.

Rather than focusing on the nature and consequences of environmental input, the cognitive perspective adopted by Martin (chap. 4) highlights mental structures and processes as critical determinants of gender-related thought and behavior. Martin starts with a review of cognitive developmental and gender schema approaches, discussing major propositions and relevant empirical research. Based on the assumption of multidimensionality among aspects of gender, the author goes on to examine the extent to which gender-related cognitions shape gender-related behavior. She argues for a domain-specific view of gender schemas that is better able to represent the flexibility of human thinking. For example, in this view gender cognitions would be expected to differ when thinking about others versus the self, when interacting with familiar versus unfamiliar persons, or when using narrow and specific versus broad and abstract gender concepts. To account for developmental changes in the structure of gender stereotypes, Martin argues in favor of a component model in which stereotypes are viewed as having a hierarchical structure, with gender labels at the top level and associated attributes at the lower levels. Going beyond the currently dominant cognitive approaches, the author discusses the versatility of two more recent theoretical accounts, the "theory of theories" and the "dynamic systems" perspectives. Looking at the development of gender concepts from the first perspective, the focus is on individuals' naive social psychology of gender (i.e., intuitive theories about social influence), whereas the second perspective provides a coherent way to think about conceptual change and dynamism, incorporating both long-term and short-term effects of gender concepts.

More than a decade ago, Eagly (1987) advanced a social role account of sex differences in human behavior. Since then social role theory has stimulated a large body of empirical research, the results of which have contributed to a number of refinements of the theory's propositions. In chapter 5, Eagly, Wood, and Diekman present a state-of-the-art review of social role theory, its major assumptions, empirical evidence concerning its explanatory and predictive power, and lines of corresponding conceptual developments. Adopting a social structural perspective, the authors argue that sex differences in social behavior arise from the contrasting distributions of men and women into social roles. These differing role assignments are described in terms of a sexual division of labor (i.e., women performing more domestic work than men and spending fewer hours in paid employment) and gender hierarchy (i.e., women having less power and status than men and controlling fewer resources). Eagly et al. postulate that the impact of sex-differentiated social roles on behavior is mediated by a variety of psychological and social processes. One set of processes concerns the formation of gender roles (i.e., the shared expectations that apply to individuals on the basis of their socially identified sex) and their impact on behavior in social interaction. Gender roles emerge from the activities carried out by members of each sex in their sex-typical occupational and family roles; that is, the characteristics required by these activities become stereotypic of women and men. Another set of processes refers to the acquisition of different skills and beliefs by men and women, mainly through their participation in relatively sex-segregated social roles across their life spans.

In part III, Gender Categorization and Interpersonal Behavior, the primary focus is on the individual and interpersonal levels of analysis (though, of course, the other levels are not precluded). It is shown how tightly interwoven developmental and social processes are in bringing about gender-related thoughts, feelings, and behaviors. The chapters deal with multiple facets of gender within a person's self-concept, the nature of gender stereotypes and their variable influences on interpersonal encounters, the development of gender prejudice and discriminatory behavior, and, finally, the acquisition and enactment of sexual scripts, including the occurrence of heterosexual aggression.

An issue of long-standing interest to developmentalists concerns how children come to view themselves in terms of femininity and masculinity. Hannover (chap. 6) presents an integrative approach to this issue drawing on recent findings and insights from developmental and social psychological studies of the self. She conceptualizes the self as an associative network that builds up under the permanent influence of two kinds of contextual factors, that is, factors inherent in the situation an individual encounters at a given moment, and cumulative experiences with social situations over extended periods of time. Hannover argues that knowledge of being male or female, as well as frequent exposure to gender-typed contexts promoting the activation of gender-congruent aspects of the self, gradually makes it more likely that individuals will incorporate gender-congruent knowledge into their selves. Thus, contextual priming is viewed as a fundamental mechanism accounting for gendered self-perception, preferences, and behaviors. To substantiate this claim, extant research is reviewed showing how contextual variables prime gender-congruent self-knowledge. For instance, the author discusses influences of the sex composition of social groups, the kinds of social interaction accentuating sex differences, the gender-typedness of tasks, and acting in gender-appropriate or gender-inappropriate ways. Referring to Ruble's (1994) phase model of transitions, Hannover is able to show that contextual priming of self-knowledge helps to account for developmental changes and individual differences in the propensity to integrate gender-incongruent information into the self.

Gender stereotypes, commonly defined as cognitive structures or schemas that contain socially shared knowledge about the characteristic features of women and men, are among the core constructs of the gender-as-a-social-category view. In chapter 7, Zemore, Fiske, and Kim examine content, change, and functioning of gender stereotypes in social interaction, with a focus on developmental change and stability. Building on recent research and theorizing in the adult stereotyping literature, the authors argue that children's persistent use of gender as a basis for social categorization eventually leads to the automatization of gender stereotypes; that is, by practicing gender stereotypes in early stages of development children ensure that activation and use of stereotypic gender knowledge will become effortless and often unconscious when reaching adulthood. Following a thorough discussion of cognitive, social role, social identity, and power-based accounts of people's pervasive reliance on stereotypic beliefs, Zemore et al. highlight several self-perpetuating functions of gender stereotypes. These functions include constraining the perceiver's acquisition of social knowledge (e.g., when encoding stimulus information or forming inferences and evaluations) as well as constraining the target person's behavior (e.g., through subtle processes involving behavioral confirmation, stereotype threat, or attributional ambiguity). The authors suggest that a developmental social psychological account of gender stereotypes may help devise strategies for counteracting the automatization of stereotyping processes. For them, intervening at early developmental stages seems more promising than controlling well-practiced gender stereotypes in adulthood.

As mentioned earlier, the development of gender prejudice is a prime example of the great wealth of new gender issues emerging at the interface between developmental and social psychological research activities. Although developmentalists have accumulated a huge body of data dealing with the ways in which boys and girls relate to each other in different contexts, they have typically lacked the conceptual and methodological tools needed to systematize these data and to detect regularities in the developmental change of children's prejudiced beliefs, feelings, and behaviors, if they have addressed issues like these at all. Building on recent social psychological theorizing and research, Glick and Hilt (chap. 8) present an intriguing account of how gender prejudice develops from childhood to adulthood. The conceptual basis is provided by ambivalent sexism theory (Glick & Fiske, 1996). This theory suggests that sexist attitudes are inherently ambivalent, having both a hostile and a benevolent component. Whereas hostile sexism encompasses a wide range of negative affect or antipathy toward the other sex, benevolent sexism involves subjectively positive feelings and favorable stereotypic beliefs regarding the other sex. Glick and Hilt's model posits a developmental transition from predominantly hostile, as well as cognitively simple, gender prejudice exhibited by both prepubertal boys and girls toward the other sex to a complex and ambivalent form of prejudice that begins to emerge during adolescence. The model accounts for this critical transition by adolescents' tendency to reconcile their growing interests in the other sex as potential romantic partners with their well-developed hostile attitudes.

The fundamental ambivalence of gender attitudes is epitomized in the ways heterosexual romantic relationships build up in adolescence. Indeed, it can be considered a major challenge confronting young females and males to establish, and engage in, satisfying sexual relationships (see Leaper & Anderson, 1997, for an overview). Romantic attraction and positively valued sexual contacts are, however, typically only part of the story. The experience of hostility and aggression is another significant constituent of adolescent sexuality. In chapter 9, Krahé presents a fine-grained analysis of the links between the development of sexual relationships and the problem of unwanted sexual experiences and sexual aggression in adolescence. Her focus is on the role of sexual scripts, that is, on cognitive representations of event sequences characterizing particular kinds of sexual encounters. Scripts are assumed to exert significant influence on the choice and enactment of sexual behavior. Krahé reviews research on sex-differentiated scripts (e.g., the male and the female dating script, the casual sex script) and relates these scripts to gender roles prescribing male behavior to be assertive and female behavior to be passive. Since sexual intentions are frequently communicated implicitly through nonverbal cues, misunderstandings are common in heterosexual interactions. The author thoroughly examines the influence of various types of misunderstandings, in particular the consequences of token resistance, on the likelihood of sexual victimization. Finally, Krahé discusses recent research on rape scripts, including the "real rape" script and differences in the perception of stranger versus acquaintance rape, pointing out implications for intervention and prevention.

In part IV, Gender, Group, and Culture, the focus is shifted away from individual and interpersonal processes so as to include accounts of gender phenomena at the role/group and sociocultural levels. The rationale underlying this is that a complete understanding of gender categories presupposes a perspective broad enough to embrace role-, group-, and societal-level forces continually impinging on the individual. Specifically, the chapters are concerned with the complex interplay between gender, communication, and influence, with processes of gender-role socialization in the context of the family, with antecedents and consequences of sex-differentiated career development, and, finally, with cross-cultural issues, highlighting cultural differences and similarities in gender development.

Though communication can be viewed as one of the primary means by which individuals influence one another, social psychologists have traditionally shown little interest in how precisely this influence occurs. As a result, they have typically failed to appreciate the particular ways in which the communication situation affects social behavior (see Krauss & Fussell, 1996, for an in-depth treatment of this issue). In recent years, increased research efforts directed at sex differences in verbal and nonverbal communication have contributed to overcoming this lacuna. Carli and Bukatko (chap. 10) present a thoughtful discussion of relevant research and theorizing in the field. Specifically, they examine those gender effects in communication that have been found to relate to sex differences in social influence. Throughout their chapter, the authors adopt a life-span perspective, addressing patterns of sex differences in communication and social influence in both children and adults. Having reviewed extant research on sex-differentiated communication styles and styles of interaction in groups, Carli and Bukatko come to the conclusion that females' communications are more other-directed, warm, and mitigated, and less dominant, status-asserting, and task-oriented than males'. When it comes to influencing others, both males and females are more successful when using a communication style that is stereotypically associated with their sex than when using a style associated with the other sex. Overall, the sex-differentiated patterns of communication and influence displayed by women and men, and by girls and boys as well, appear to be expedient and effective, given their power, social roles, and relative position in their interactions with others.

One area in which gender stereotypes have been particularly resistant to change concerns sex differences in mathematics and verbal ability. Yet, meta-analytic syntheses of the relevant research literatures clearly show that sex differences in both domains are so small as to be negligible (see Hyde & Frost, 1993, for a review). At the same time, participation in high-level, intensive math and English courses as well as applied fields has remained highly gender segregated. Eccles, Freedman-Doan, Frome, Jacobs, and Yoon (chap. 11) closely examine the factors contributing to children's sex-differentiated self-perceptions, interests, and performance in these and other activity domains, highlighting parents' gender-related beliefs and stereotypes. Consequently, the chapter focuses on the mechanisms of gender-role socialization in the context of the family. Mainly drawing on data from two large-scale longitudinal studies, Eccles et al. present evidence that parents' perceptions of their children's competence in math, reading/English, and sports are influenced by the children's sex, independently of their actual performance in these domains. In addition to overt performance, two factors seem to influence the formation of these sex-differentiated perceptions: (a) parents' causal attributions for their children's successes, and (b) parents' stereotypic beliefs about which sex is naturally more talented in these domains. Furthermore, it is suggested that the media strengthen parents' stereotypic views of their children's ability. Finally, the authors address the question of how parents' gender-stereotypic beliefs influence their children's self- and task-perceptions, building on a self-fulfilling prophecy framework. They conclude that one promising route to intervention is to change parents' beliefs and perceptions.

In chapter 12, Abele takes a closer look at the antecedents and consequences of the traditionally high degree of gender segregation in the workforce and in career development. In order to elucidate the psychological mechanisms responsible for the status quo, she presents a dual-impact model of gender and career-related processes. According to this model, men's and women's gendered self-conceptualization (or gender-role orientation) influences a number of career-related psychological variables (e.g., career motivation, self-efficacy) that, in turn, have impact on career-related behaviors and outcomes (e.g., income, occupational status); at the same time, being female or male elicits gender-related expectations or stereotypes, leading to differential career opportunities for women and men. In addition, it is hypothesized that career development has a reciprocal impact on females' and males' gender-role orientation. Abele reports on a series of cross-sectional and longitudinal studies aimed at testing these assumptions. Findings from large-sample studies, including student samples from Germany and the United States, reveal that gender-role orientation is a more

important determinant of   career-related psychological variables than
respondents' sex, whereas respondents' sex is a more powerful predictor of
career-related outcomes (i.e., career success) than gender-role orientation.
Moreover, career progress or stagnation influences individuals' gender-role
orientation, with differential effects for women and men; that is, career
progress more strongly enhances instrumentality in women than in men,
whereas failing to progress reduces instrumentality in men but not in
women.

In recent years it has become increasingly clear that in order to
understand an individual's place and functioning in the social world it is
necessary to look closely at the complex interplay between cultural systems
and psychological processes: Cultural practices and meanings complement
and inform individual and interpersonal processes, which in turn feed back
on cultural meanings and practices (see Fiske, Kitayama, Markus, & Nisbett,
1998, for a detailed analysis). The social category of gender is a case in
point. Cultural images, ideologies, and models of gender pervade each and
every aspect of social life; at the same time, individual beliefs and behaviors,
as well as social interactions and group life constrain, reproduce, and
transform gender at the cultural level. In chapter 13, Gibbons explores the
potential of cross-cultural and cross-national studies to advance our
knowledge about gender development. Throughout the chapter the author
stresses the importance of doing cross-cultural research on gender
development that incorporates conceptual clarity and methodological rigor.
She reviews three areas of research showing that there are both pancultural
commonalities and culture-specific findings in each of them. First, gender
constancy appears to develop in the same sequence cross-culturally, yet the
age of attaining each stage varies. Second, stereotype knowledge increases
with age cross-culturally, but the content of stereotypic beliefs has both
culture-general and culture-specific components. Third, adolescents from
different cultures share an ideal that women and men should possess
prosocial qualities, but their endorsement of nontraditional gender roles in
the ideal person varies systematically with other cultural values.

Finally, part V summarizes major advances, arguments, and perspectives
presented in the preceding chapters and points to directions for future
research. It deals with theoretical and conceptual progress that has been
made and with difficulties still facing researchers who try to study gender
issues at the intersection of developmental and social psychology. Two main
themes are discussed in some detail. First, the striking convergence of
evolutionary constraints, environmental input, cognitive processes, and
social-structural variables in producing gender-typed thought and behavior,
and, second, the fundamental interdependence of developmental change and
social dynamics in processes of gender differentiation. It is concluded that
much further progress can be made when social psychologists and

developmentalists cross disciplinary boundaries and cooperate even more closely to tackle the intricate nature of issues involved in the study of gender.

## ACKNOWLEDGMENT

We would like to thank Kay Deaux, Leo Montada, and Diane N. Ruble for helpful comments on an earlier draft of this chapter.

## REFERENCES

Allport, G. W. (1985). The historical background of social psychology. In G. Lindzey & E. Aronson (Eds.), *The handbook of social psychology* (3rd ed., Vol. 1, pp. 1–46). New York: Random House.
Ashmore, R. D. (1990). Sex, gender, and the individual. In L. A. Pervin (Ed.), *Handbook of personality: Theory and research* (pp. 486–526). New York: Guilford.
Ashmore, R. D., & Del Boca, F. K. (1986). Toward a social psychology of female–male relations. In R. D. Ashmore & F. K. Del Boca (Eds.), *The social psychology of female–male relations: A critical analysis of central concepts* (pp. 1–17). Orlando, FL: Academic Press.
Ashmore, R. D., & Sewell, A. D. (1998). Sex/gender and the individual. In D. F. Barone, M. Hersen, & V. B. Van Hasselt (Eds.), *Advanced personality* (pp. 377–408). New York: Plenum.
Bem, S. L. (1974). The measurement of psychological androgyny. *Journal of Consulting and Clinical Psychology, 42*, 155–162.
Bem, S. L. (1993). The lenses of gender: Transforming the debate on sexual inequality. New Haven, CT: Yale University Press.
Bierhoff-Alfermann, D. (1989). *Androgynie: Möglichkeiten und Grenzen der Geschlechterrollen* [Androgyny: Chances and limitations of gender roles]. Opladen, Germany: Westdeutscher Verlag.
Blank, T. O. (1982). A social psychology of developing adults. New York: Wiley.
Brehm, S. S., Kassin, S. M., & Gibbons, F. X. (Eds.). (1981). *Developmental social psychology: Theory and research*. New York: Oxford University Press.
Constantinople, A. (1979). Sex-role acquisition: In search of the elephant. *Sex Roles, 5*, 121–133.
Costanzo, P. R. (1992). External socialization and the development of adaptive individuation and social connection. In D. N. Ruble, P. R. Costanzo, & M. E. Oliveri (Eds.), *The social psychology of mental health: Basic mechanisms and applications* (pp. 55–80). New York: Guilford.
Damon, W. (Ed.). (1998). *Handbook of child psychology* (5th ed., Vols. 1–4). New York: Wiley.
Deaux, K. (1984). From individual differences to social categories: Analysis of a decade's research on gender. *American Psychologist, 39*, 105–116.
Deaux, K. (1999). An overview of research on gender: Four themes from 3 decades. In W. B. Swann, Jr., J. H. Langlois, & L. A. Gilbert (Eds.), *Sexism and stereotypes in modern society: The gender science of Janet Taylor Spence* (pp. 11–33). Washington, DC: American Psychological Association.

Deaux, K., & Kite, M. E. (1987). Thinking about gender. In B. B. Hess & M. M. Ferree (Eds.), *Analyzing gender: A handbook of social science research* (pp. 92–117). Newbury Park, CA: Sage.

Deaux, K., & LaFrance, M. (1998). Gender. In D. T. Gilbert, S. T. Fiske, & G. Lindzey (Eds.), *The handbook of social psychology* (4th ed., Vol. 1, pp. 788–827). Boston: McGraw-Hill.

Deaux, K., & Major, B. (1987). Putting gender into context: An interactive model of gender-related behavior. *Psychological Review, 94*, 369–389.

Doise, W. (1984). Social representations, inter-group experiments, and levels of analysis. In R. M. Farr & S. Moscovici (Eds.), *Social representations* (pp. 255–268). Cambridge, England: Cambridge University Press.

Doise, W. (1986). *Levels of explanation in social psychology.* Cambridge, England: Cambridge University Press.

Doise, W. (1997). Organizing social-psychological explanations. In C. McGarty & S. A. Haslam (Eds.), *The message of social psychology: Perspectives on mind in society* (pp. 63–76). Cambridge, MA: Basil Blackwell.

Doise, W., & Mugny, G. (1984). *The social development of the intellect.* Oxford, England: Pergamon Press.

Durkin, K. (1995). Developmental social psychology: From infancy to old age. Cambridge, MA: Basil Blackwell.

Eagly, A. H. (1987). *Sex differences in social behavior: A social-role interpretation.* Hillsdale, NJ: Lawrence Erlbaum Associates.

Eagly, A. H. (1995). The science and politics of comparing women and men. *American Psychologist, 50*, 145–158.

Eccles, J. S., Midgley, C., Wigfield, A., Buchanan, C. M., Reuman, D., Flanagan, C., & Mac Iver, D. (1993). Development during adolescence: The impact of stage–environment fit on young adolescents' experiences in schools and in families. *American Psychologist, 48*, 90–101.

Eccles (Parsons), J., Adler, T. F., Futterman, R., Goff, S. B., Kaczala, C. M., Meece, J. L., & Midgley, C. (1983). Expectancies, values, and academic behaviors. In J. T. Spence (Ed.), *Achievement and achievement motives: Psychological and sociological approaches* (pp. 75–146). San Francisco: Freeman.

Eckes, T. (1997). *Geschlechterstereotype: Frau und Mann in sozialpsychologischer Sicht* [Gender stereotypes: Woman and man in social psychological perspective]. Pfaffenweiler, Germany: Centaurus.

Eisenberg, N. (1995a). Editor's introduction. In N. Eisenberg (Ed.), *Review of personality and social psychology: Vol. 15. Social development* (pp. vii–xiii). Thousand Oaks, CA: Sage.

Eisenberg, N. (Ed.). (1995b). Review of personality and social psychology: Vol. 15. Social development. Thousand Oaks, CA: Sage.

Fiske, A. P., Kitayama, S., Markus, H. R., & Nisbett, R. E. (1998). The cultural matrix of social psychology. In D. T. Gilbert, S. T. Fiske, & G. Lindzey (Eds.), *The handbook of social psychology* (4th ed., Vol. 2, pp. 915–981). Boston: McGraw-Hill.

Fiske, S. T. (1998). Stereotyping, prejudice, and discrimination. In D. T. Gilbert, S. T. Fiske, & G. Lindzey (Eds.), *The handbook of social psychology* (4th ed., Vol. 2, pp. 357–411). Boston: McGraw-Hill.

Flavell, J. H., & Ross, L. (1981a). Concluding remarks. In J. H. Flavell & L. Ross (Eds.), *Social cognitive development: Frontiers and possible futures* (pp. 306–316). Cambridge, MA: Cambridge University Press.

Flavell, J. H., & Ross, L. (Eds.). (1981b). *Social cognitive development: Frontiers and possible futures.* Cambridge, England: Cambridge University Press.

Gilbert, D. T., Fiske, S. T., & Lindzey, G. (Eds.). (1998). *The handbook of social psychology* (4th ed., Vols. 1–2). Boston: McGraw-Hill.

Glick, P., & Fiske, S. T. (1996). The Ambivalent Sexism Inventory: Differentiating hostile and benevolent sexism. *Journal of Personality and Social Psychology, 70*, 491–512.

Goodnow, J. J., Miller, P. J., & Kessel, F. (Eds.). (1995). *Cultural practices as contexts for development*. San Francisco: Jossey-Bass.

Higgins, E. T., Ruble, D. N., & Hartup, W. W. (Eds.). (1983). *Social cognition and social development: A sociocultural perspective*. Cambridge, MA: Cambridge University Press.

Huston, A. C. (1983). Sex-typing. In P. H. Mussen (Ed.), *Handbook of child psychology* (4th ed., Vol. 4, pp. 387–467). New York: Wiley.

Hyde, J. S., & Frost, L. A. (1993). Meta-analysis in the psychology of women. In F. L. Denmark & M. A. Paludi (Eds.), *Psychology of women: A handbook of issues and theories* (pp. 67–103). Westport, CT: Greenwood.

Kenrick, D. T., & Simpson, J. A. (1997). Why social psychology and evolutionary psychology need one another. In J. A. Simpson & D. T. Kenrick (Eds.), *Evolutionary social psychology* (pp. 1–20). Mahwah, NJ: Lawrence Erlbaum Associates.

Krauss, R. M., & Fussell, S. R. (1996). Social psychological models of interpersonal communication. In E. T. Higgins & A. W. Kruglanski (Eds.), *Social psychology: Handbook of basic principles* (pp. 655–701). New York: Guilford.

Leaper, C., & Anderson, K. J. (1997). Gender development and heterosexual romantic relationships during adolescence. In S. Shulman & W. A. Collins (Eds.), *Romantic relationships in adolescence: Developmental perspectives* (pp. 85–103). San Francisco: Jossey-Bass.

Lorenzi-Cioldi, F., & Doise, W. (1990). Levels of analysis and social identity. In D. Abrams & M. A. Hogg (Eds.), *Social identity theory: Constructive and critical advances* (pp. 72–88). London: Harvester Wheatsheaf.

Lutz, S. E., & Ruble, D. N. (1995). Children and gender prejudice: Context, motivation, and the development of gender conceptions. *Annals of Child Development, 10*, 131–166.

Maccoby, E. E. (1998). *The two sexes: Growing up apart, coming together*. Cambridge, MA: Harvard University Press.

Maccoby, E. E., & Jacklin, C. N. (1974). *The psychology of sex differences*. Stanford, CA: Stanford University Press.

Merz, F. (1979). *Geschlechtsunterschiede und ihre Entwicklung* [Sex differences and their development]. Göttingen, Germany: Hogrefe.

Morawski, J. G. (1987). The troubled quest for masculinity, femininity, and androgyny. In P. Shaver & C. Hendrick (Eds.), *Review of personality and social psychology: Vol. 7. Sex and gender* (pp. 44–69). Beverly Hills, CA: Sage.

Pratt, M. W., & Norris, J. E. (1994). *The social psychology of aging: A cognitive perspective*. Cambridge, MA: Basil Blackwell.

Ragins, B. R., & Sundstrom, E. (1989). Gender and power in organizations: A longitudinal perspective. *Psychological Bulletin, 105*, 51–88.

Rogoff, B. (1990). Apprenticeship in thinking: Cognitive development in social context. New York: Oxford University Press.

Ruble, D. N. (1994). A phase model of transitions: Cognitive and motivational consequences. In M. P. Zanna (Ed.), *Advances in experimental social psychology* (Vol. 26, pp. 163–214). San Diego, CA: Academic Press.

Ruble, D. N., & Goodnow, J. J. (1998). Social development in childhood and adulthood. In D. T. Gilbert, S. T. Fiske, & G. Lindzey (Eds.), *The handbook of social psychology* (4th ed., Vol. 1, pp. 741–787). Boston: McGraw-Hill.

Ruble, D. N., & Martin, C. L. (1998). Gender development. In W. Damon (Series Ed.) & N. Eisenberg (Vol. Ed.), *Handbook of child psychology: Vol. 3. Social, emotional, and personality development* (5th ed., pp. 933–1016). New York: Wiley.

Sears, D. O. (1986). College sophomores in the laboratory: Influences of a narrow data base on social psychology's view of human nature. *Journal of Personality and Social Psychology, 51*, 515–530.

Sherif, C. W. (1982). Needed concepts in the study of gender identity. *Psychology of Women Quarterly, 6*, 375–398.

Silbereisen, R. K., Eyferth, K., & Rudinger, G. (Eds.). (1986). *Development as action in context: Problem behavior and normal youth development.* Berlin, Germany: Springer.

Spence, J. T. (1993). Gender-related traits and gender ideology: Evidence for a multifactorial theory. *Journal of Personality and Social Psychology, 64*, 624–635.

Spence, J. T. (1999). Thirty years of gender research: A personal chronicle. In W. B. Swann, Jr., J. H. Langlois, & L. A. Gilbert (Eds.), *Sexism and stereotypes in modern society: The gender science of Janet Taylor Spence* (pp. 255–289). Washington, DC: American Psychological Association.

Staudinger, U. M., & Greve, W. (Eds.). (1997). Das Selbst im Lebenslauf: Sozialpsychologische und entwicklungspsychologische Perspektiven [The self across the life span: Social psychological and developmental perspectives]. *Zeitschrift für Sozialpsychologie, 28* (Special Issue 1/2).

Swann, W. B., Jr., Langlois, J. H., & Gilbert, L. A. (1999). Introduction. In W. B. Swann, Jr., J. H. Langlois, & L. A. Gilbert (Eds.), *Sexism and stereotypes in modern society: The gender science of Janet Taylor Spence* (pp. 3–7). Washington, DC: American Psychological Association.

Trautner, H. M. (1993). Geschlechtszugehörigkeit als individuelles Merkmal oder als soziale Kategorie [Gender as an individual feature or as a social category]. In L. Montada (Ed.), *Bericht über den 38. Kongreß der Deutschen Gesellschaft für Psychologie in Trier 1992* (Vol. 2, pp. 760–770). Göttingen, Germany: Hogrefe.

Wozniak, R. H., & Fischer, K. W. (Eds.). (1993). *Development in context: Acting and thinking in specific environments.* Hillsdale, NJ: Lawrence Erlbaum Associates.

# II

# THEORETICAL APPROACHES

# 2

# An Evolutionary Life-History Model of Gender Differences and Similarities

Douglas T. Kenrick
Carol L. Luce
*Arizona State University*

Consider four areas where large sex differences have been found in social behavior and development within particular cultures:

*Mate choice*:   For 1,511 marriages recorded on the small isolated Philippine island of Poro between 1913 and 1939, average age differences between men and their wives changed dramatically over the life span. Men in their 20s married women who were, on average, only about 2 or 3 years younger; whereas men over 40 married women who were, on average, more than 15 years younger than themselves (Kenrick & Keefe, 1992). Women at all ages, on the other hand, married men who were, on average, a few years older than themselves.

*Aggression*:   Among the Belo Horizonte, who live in the remote reaches of Brazil's Amazon basin, men committed 97% of the 234 same-sex homicides recorded between 1961 and 1965 (Daly & Wilson, 1988).

*Sexuality*:   On the culturally isolated island of Inis Beag during the 1950s, men masturbated frequently and were, compared to women, reputed to be more interested in sex. Local residents attributed the difference to men's greater consumption of potatoes (Messenger, 1971).

*Child care*:   Among the Aka pygmies, a hunter–gatherer group living in Central Africa, mothers hold their young children 8.6 minutes for every 1 minute the fathers do (Hewlett, 1988).

# GENDER DIFFERENCES

What causes the sex differences found in these remote cultural groups? Is it
socialization into the sex-role norms of these particular societies or cognitive
adherence to an arbitrary sex-role schema? There is ample evidence that sex-
role norms vary somewhat from society to society—men in traditional
Scotland wore kilts; American women during the 1970s began to wear pants
and hold jobs traditionally assigned to men. And within a given culture,
there is substantial evidence of situational and individual variation in
adherence to sex-role schemas (Bem, 1981; Cross & Markus, 1993; Eagly,
1987). Some people are generally more sex typed than others, and some
situations elicit more sex-typed behaviors than others. Yet evolutionary
psychologists do not think that traditional social science accounts provide,
by themselves, a complete explanation of many important gender differences
in social behavior (e.g., Buss & Kenrick, 1998; Daly & Wilson, 1983;
Geary, 1998; Kenrick & Trost, 1993).

To begin with, traditional social scientific accounts have difficulty with
the cross-cultural and cross-historical robustness of many sex differences.
For example, despite numerous variations in marital customs and marital
ages across cultures, older men in all societies thus far examined show, like
the older men on the isolated island of Poro, a much stronger preference for
younger mates than do young men. And women across cultures generally
prefer older partners, and change those preferences little as they age. This
life-span pattern has been found in numerous data sets from the United
States, Germany, the Netherlands, India, Africa, remote island cultures
around the world, and Europe several centuries ago (Harpending, 1992;
Kenrick & Keefe, 1992; Kenrick, Nieuweboer, & Buunk, 1995).

Likewise, despite wide variations in homicide rates around the world, the
sex difference found among Brazil's Belo Horizonte is mirrored in other
times and places. Men have committed over 85% of murders in societies
throughout history, from medieval England to remote hunter–gatherer
villages (Daly & Wilson, 1988). Since the liberalization of sex-role norms in
the United States, this gender difference might be expected to decrease. It
has not. Instead, it has actually increased. Men committed about 85% of
American homicides during the 1960s but more than 90% during the 1990s.

Similarly, the gender differences in sexuality found on the isolated island
of Inis Beag are not unique to that time and place. Large differences in
sexual fantasy, masturbation, and willingness to engage in casual sex have
been repeatedly found in North American society, and those differences
remained robust even through the years of the "sexual revolution" (Ellis &
Symons, 1990; Kenrick, Sadalla, Groth, & Trost, 1990; Oliver & Hyde,
1993). During the 1970s, for example, student experimenters at Florida State

University approached strangers of the opposite sex and invited them to go on a date, to their apartment, or to bed. Although more than 50% of both sexes accepted an invitation for a date, more than 70% of men, but exactly 0% of women, were interested in jumping into bed with the friendly stranger (Clark & Hatfield, 1989). Margaret Mead reported Polynesian societies in which boys and girls alike enjoyed unrestricted sexuality, free of the "double standard" characterizing North American society (Mead, 1928, 1935). However, Mead had insufficient firsthand experience with these societies, and more intensive anthropological studies of those same societies later found the usual differences, with female sexuality markedly more restricted than that of males (Freeman, 1983).

The tendency of women to devote more energy to child care is also robust across human societies, even those with very nontraditional norms. Indeed, the fact that Aka men hold their newborns 10% as frequently as Aka women makes that society unusually egalitarian in this regard; in most societies men hold their children much less frequently (Geary, 1998). Even among nontraditional Swedish couples in which the husband takes leave from work to be the child's primary caretaker, women still devote more time to child care (Lamb, Frodi, Hwang, & Frodi, 1982).

There are variations within and between the sexes and within and between cultures in mating choices, aggressiveness, sexual restrictiveness, and parenting behaviors. However, powerful evolutionary pressures tend to pull human males and females in different directions regardless of societal particulars. An evolutionary account of gender roles does not deny socialization or cognitive influences on human behavior, but it does assume that human thought and human learning unfold within a wider biological context. The evolutionary history of the human species is such that ancestral males and females reliably faced different survival and reproductive tasks. As a consequence of those recurring differences in ecological pressure over eons, our ancestors passed on a slightly different array of psychological mechanisms to modern males and females. Understanding the evolutionary history of our species helps us make sense of current differences in cognition and behavior over the life span.

# GENDER SIMILARITIES

Although an evolutionary perspective has often been used to explain salient gender differences, evolutionary theorists do not expect men and women to be different on every possible psychological and behavioral dimension. Instead, differences are expected only on dimensions where ancestral males and females regularly faced different adaptive problems (e.g., direct care of young or within-sex competition for mates). Indeed, we suspect that a list of similarities between the two sexes would be much longer than a list of differences. Where males and females faced similar problems, as in maintaining a parental bond or getting along with in-group members, the sexes should share similar adaptive mechanisms.

Consider several examples of robust gender similarities in behavior. Across human cultures, men and women alike form deep long-lasting emotional bonds to one another and to their children (Daly & Wilson, 1983; Jankowiak & Fischer, 1992; Miller & Fishkin, 1997; Zeifman & Hazan, 1997). In contrast, males and females in most mammalian species do not bond, and males do not develop attachments to their offspring (Daly & Wilson, 1983; Geary, 1998). Likewise, male and female humans are similar in that both are highly selective about choosing long-term mates (Kenrick et al., 1990; Kenrick, Groth, Trost, & Sadalla, 1993). Again, this is in contrast to most mammalian species, in which only females are very choosy about the qualities of a desirable mate (Daly & Wilson, 1983; Gould & Gould, 1989).

Even to discuss differences and similarities as separate categories is an oversimplification. In many domains, one finds a pattern of shared human adaptations, with slight variations between the sexes. Both male and female humans have an extraordinarily long maturational delay before sexual maturation, for example. However, females reach puberty about 2 years earlier than males. Males also continue to grow into their 20s, whereas most females are fully mature by age 16 (Tanner, 1990). An evolutionary perspective helps us understand the general similarity—why both sexes delay sexual maturity so long—and the slight variation on that theme—why males delay longer (Geary, 1998). Similarly, both human males and females are highly selective in choosing long-term mates. Many of the criteria for long-term mates are similar for men and women—both sexes desire agreeable and attractive partners, for example (Buss, 1989; Kenrick et al., 1990). However, there is again a variation on the shared theme of choosiness—women across societies are relatively more interested in older, higher status men, whereas men across societies are relatively more interested in partners who are physically attractive and often younger (Buss, 1989; Kenrick & Keefe, 1992). We will show how an evolutionary perspective can help us understand the gender similarities as well as the differences in social behavior.

This chapter proceeds in several sections. First, we review the general assumptions of an evolutionary approach to behavior. Second, we review how differences and similarities in behavior within and across species can be understood in the light of an evolutionary life-history model. A life-history model considers the developmental trajectory of an organism in terms of the differential allocation of effort across the life span (Alexander, 1987; Kenrick, Gabrielidis, Keefe, & Cornelius, 1996; Kenrick & Keefe, 1992; Partridge & Harvey, 1988; Stearns, 1976). Third, we revisit the topic of human sex differences and similarities in light of these evolutionary models of life-history development. Finally, we consider the interconnections between evolutionary constraints, human culture, and cognition, addressing why we think it is a mistake to conceptualize these different factors as *alternative* accounts of sex-role development.

# GENERAL ASSUMPTIONS OF AN EVOLUTIONARY APPROACH TO BEHAVIOR

Evolutionary psychology has its roots in Darwin's (1872) well-known treatment of human emotions. Darwin observed that certain emotional expressions (such as the angry snarl) seem to be shared by humans and other animals. He hypothesized that such expressions had been inherited from common ancestors because they served to promote the animal's survival. In addition to studying emotional expression across species, Darwin also collected some early cross-cultural data, surveying field anthropologists and missionaries about emotional expressions in remote cultures. If certain emotional expressions were inherited from common nonhuman ancestors, one would expect to find them universally across human societies.

Darwin's (1872) approach to emotional expression foreshadowed several features of modern evolutionary psychology. Evolutionary psychologists assume that, just as the forces of natural selection can shape morphological features—a whale's flipper, a bat's wing, or a monkey's hand—so can those forces shape psychological and behavioral tendencies. To operate a whale's body requires a different program than that required to operate a bat's body or a monkey's body. Imagine a whale trying to swing from branches and peel bananas, for instance. Because they must locate moving prey in the dark, bats have a large portion of their brains dedicated to analyzing the sonarlike echoes of the specialized sounds they emit. Whales likewise have specialized auditory mechanisms for communicating under water. On the other hand, monkeys have brain mechanisms specially designed to analyze binocular color vision, to enable them to accurately gauge the distance of the branches they are jumping toward, or the ripeness of fruit on a distant limb.

Despite the very different ecological demands on whales, bats, and monkeys, they also share some behavioral programs by virtue of common descent and of common ecological pressure. In all of these species, for example, females nurse and care for their young, a feature of their common mammalian heritage. Most species of whales, bats, and monkeys also congregate in large groups, a behavioral adaptation common to many animal species, including insects, fish, and birds, but not found in all mammals (many cats are solitary for large portions of their lives, for example).

Congregation into large groups has some adaptive advantages—avoiding predators or searching for scattered food sources, for example—but also some disadvantages—such as increased intraspecies competition, disease, and so on (Alcock, 1993). Seeking the company of groups, like all behavioral tendencies, is expected to be found only when the advantages outweigh the disadvantages (more likely in prey than in predator species, for example, and less likely in species that subsist on food sources that are distributed and can be defended in small territories).

Evolutionary psychologists thus assume that animals inherit brains and bodies equipped to behave in ways that are adaptive—that are fitted to the demands of the environments within which their ancestors evolved. Some of those behavioral adaptations are shared by common descent, some are shared by common ecological demands, and some are uniquely designed to solve the particular problems encountered by a given species (flying ability in bats, but not in other mammals, for example). Evolutionary psychologists apply the same logic to Homo sapiens, making the assumption that many features related to human cognition, motivation, and behavior were designed by natural selection. Just as human morphological features—opposable thumbs, larynxes, noses, and upright postures—have been shaped by evolutionary pressures, evolutionary psychologists assume that humans inherited brains specially designed to solve recurrent problems in the ancestral world. For example, along with the larynx, humans also inherited a brain apparently designed to easily learn to communicate using language (Pinker, 1994).

From an evolutionary perspective, the first question one asks about a physical or behavioral feature is: What is its function? A baby's crying would have served to alert its mother to the child's immediate needs, and its smiling and cooing to cement the mother–infant bond, for example. From the mother's perspective, the bond would have served to increase the survival rates of her offspring (Bowlby, 1969; Zeifman & Hazan, 1997). It is assumed that many features of human cognition and behavior were designed to solve the problems of living in hominid social groups (e.g., Kenrick, Sadalla, & Keefe, 1998; Pinker, 1997; Tooby & Cosmides, 1992). For example, humans around the world have well-articulated vocabularies for describing the extent to which another person is cooperative or dominant, and' it has been suggested that this is because our ancestors' survival and reproduction would have been served by knowledge of who were reliable allies or leaders (White, 1980). Similarly, people are very good at solving normally difficult logical problems when they are framed in terms of detecting cheaters in social situations, and it has been suggested that this ability was likewise well fitted to the demands of living in human ancestral groups (Tooby & Cosmides, 1992).

It is important to note that evolutionary psychologists do not assume that humans or other organisms inherit some capacity to determine in advance which behavioral strategy will be adaptive and thereby proceed through life as "fitness-maximizing" machines. This mistaken assumption underlies the sociobiological fallacy (Buss, 1995). Instead, evolutionary psychologists assume that organisms inherit specific behavioral mechanisms designed to increase the probability of solving recurrent problems confronted during the ancestral past. For example, animals whose ancestors ate fruit are sensitive to the taste of sweetness and find it reinforcing; animals whose ancestors were purely carnivorous do not. Generally, the sweetness sensitivity mechanism led our human ancestors to eat ripe, rather than unripe, fruit (the latter having less nutritional value and higher toxin content). For a diabetes-prone individual with unlimited access to chocolate bars and ice cream in the modern world, that mechanism might shorten his or her life span; however, it would, on average, have helped his or her ancestors survive to reproductive age.

A closely associated point is that evolutionary psychologists assume the brain is designed in a modular fashion, with a number of independent mechanisms, each fashioned to solve particular problems (Kenrick et al., 1998; Pinker, 1997; Tooby & Cosmides, 1992). A *module* is a specific cognitive mechanism that is sensitive to distinct inputs and that operates according to specific decision-making rules (Sherry & Schacter, 1987). As an example, birds have completely different mechanisms for learning song, learning to avoid poisonous foods, and learning and remembering where they have stored food. A bird may learn the song of its species during a brief critical period, it may learn an irreversible food aversion on a single trial at any time in its life, and it learns and forgets where it stores food caches on a daily basis over its entire life span.

An evolutionary perspective offers some of its clearest predictions about the development of psychological sex differences, for reasons we discuss in the next section.

# LIFE-HISTORY STRATEGIES:
# EVOLUTION AND DEVELOPMENTAL SEQUENCES

A life history is a genetically organized developmental plan—a set of general strategies and specific tactics by which an organism allocates energy to survival, growth, and reproduction (Crawford & Anderson, 1989; Partridge & Harvey, 1988; Stearns, 1976). How long should an animal or plant develop before beginning to allocate resources to reproduction? Once mature, should it devote all its resources to one short reproductive burst, or should it spread its reproductive efforts over several episodes spanning months or years? Should it allocate resources to caring for its offspring after they are born, and if so, how much care should be invested before leaving the offspring to fend for themselves?

Life histories can be divided into two broad categories: *somatic effort* and *reproductive effort* (Alexander, 1987). Somatic effort is the energy expended to build the body. It is analogous to building a bank account. Reproductive effort is analogous to spending that bank account in ways that will replicate the individual's genes. Reproductive effort can be further divided into mating, parental care, and investment in other relatives (Alexander, 1987). Investment in other relatives can have a genetic payoff because siblings, nieces, nephews, or cousins, like one's own offspring, share common genes.

Organisms show an amazing array of life-history patterns. One species of tenrec, a small mammal from Madagascar, reaches sexual maturity 40 days after birth (Quammen, 1996). Elephants, on the other hand, take a hundred times that long to reach sexual maturity, and then carry the fetus for over a year, though they may nevertheless produce several offspring in their long life spans (Daly & Wilson, 1983). Pacific salmon likewise take several years to mature, but then expend all their reproductive effort in a brief period—traveling great distances to return to the place of their birth and laying several thousand eggs before dying, never again to reproduce.

Organisms that reproduce only once—in a single suicidal burst—are called semelparous; those that reproduce several times are iteroparous. These variations in rate and timing of maturity, and relative amount of effort invested in somatic versus reproductive effort, are related to ecological conditions. For example, animals whose newborns are subject to heavy predation, like wildebeests, may reproduce en masse on one day of each year, thus reducing their individual risk of losing individual offspring to predators—hyenas, for example, cannot eat all of the newborn wildebeests, born together in huge herds, who are only vulnerable for several days after they are born.

Several interesting life-history questions surround animals' frequent restraint in reproduction. From an evolutionary perspective, the name of the game is reproduction—those animals around today are descendants of a long unbroken chain of ancestors who reproduced more rapidly and efficiently than their competitors. It may thus seem puzzling why animals would ever delay reproduction, sometimes waiting several years after they have reached full size before mating. One species, the fulmar petrel, reaches full size in one season, but typically waits 9 years to begin nesting (Ollason & Dunnet, 1978). Likewise, it may seem puzzling why animals severely limit the size of their families, as they often do. For example, many smaller birds lay up to a dozen eggs in a season, but petrels reliably lay only one. The solution to such puzzles is the realization that rampant reproduction is not always successful reproduction. In many bird species, the probability of raising any of the offspring in a clutch drops if the clutch goes above a critical size (Lack, Gibb, & Owen, 1957). Along the same lines, animals that begin reproducing too early in life often do not have the requisite experience to provide for their young, and their efforts may be wasted if the offspring do not survive (Daly & Wilson, 1983).

Recall that reproductive effort is like spending a bank account. The efforts involved in caring for young can often be counted directly in weight loss and decreased longevity of the parents. Lizards who produce high numbers of offspring in one season are less likely to survive until the next, for example (Tinkle, 1969). Among elephant seals, females lose body fat in direct proportion to that gained by their pups (Reiter, Panken, & Le Boeuf, 1981). On the other side, male and female fruit flies that are experimentally prevented from mating survive longer than those that are given free access to mates (Maynard Smith, 1958; Partridge & Farquhar, 1981). Effort wasted on premature reproduction can thus reduce the probability of more successful reproduction later. Compared with younger females, older experienced female seals are more successful in rearing their pups (Reiter et al., 1981).

## Different Life-History Strategies Within the Same Species

Animals within the same species sometimes adopt different life-history strategies. For example, male sunfish may take two adult forms (Gross & Charnov, 1980). One type is a large territorial male who builds nests and attracts females with a colorful display. These males take approximately 7 years to mature. Another type, referred to as sneak copulators, take only 2 years to mature, are much smaller, and have much larger internal testes. These smaller individuals do not try to attract females but instead dart into a nest and spray sperm after a large male induces a female to lay her eggs. When the smaller "sneakers" get larger, they become "satellites," taking on the size and coloration of females and mimicking the movements of females to confuse the nesting males. Among the most fascinating developmental phenomena in nature are a number of fish species called protogynous hermaphrodites. In species such as the Nassau grouper, for example, the males are large and have harems of smaller females. All young individuals are females. When a large territorial male dies, the largest female in his harem goes through a series of hormonal changes, grows in size and coloration, and becomes a male (Warner, 1984).

It is very common for the males and females of a species to adopt different life-history strategies. In one Australian marsupial, for example, the male is semelparous, devoting all his efforts to competition within one mating season, then dying (Lee, Bradley, & Braithwaite, 1977). The female, on the other hand, is iteroparous and often survives to mate in more than one season. Such distinctions are highly pronounced in one species of fly in which the male, but not the female, dies in the very act of mating (Parker, 1970). After depositing his genitalia in the female to prevent other males from mating with her, the male fly contributes the rest of his body to her as a post-copulatory meal, thus making a substantial personal offering to the nutritional support of the offspring. Although the extremity of sex-differentiation in these examples is uncommon, some degree of sex difference in life history is common. For example, males in many species reach sexual maturity at a later age than do females (Geary, 1998). This is one of many sex differences in life-history strategy that has been linked to sexual selection and differential parental investment, two topics to which we now turn.

## Sexual Selection

*Sexual selection* was a concept advanced by Darwin (1859/1958) to explain the development of characteristics that did not seem to make sense from the perspective of *natural selection*. If selection favors characteristics that are well suited to survival, how could a peacock's feathers or the enormous antlers on certain hoofed mammals have ever evolved? Large colorful male animals are likely to die earlier for a number of reasons; one of which is that their showy displays are physiologically costly to maintain, another of which is that those displays are like neon signs that draw the attention of hungry predators. And why would male rams purposely run on full-speed collision courses only to smash their bony heads against one another?

The answer to these puzzles is that evolutionary "success" is measured not simply by survival, but ultimately by reproduction. Genes predisposing an individual to live long without reproducing do not get replicated. Thus, characteristics that enhance successful mating, even if they impose a potential survival cost, can be selected if the mating enhancement is enough to compensate for their costs on longevity. The genes of animals that live shorter but sexually active lives will, in future generations, outrepresent those of individuals who lived long safe, but celibate, existences.

Darwin (1859/1958) originally described the process of sexual selection in *The Origin of Species:*

> I believe, that when the males and females of any animal have the same general habits of life, but differ in structure, colour, or ornament, such differences have been mainly caused by sexual selection: that is, by individual males having had, in successive generations, some slight advantage over other males, in their weapons, means of defence, or charms, which they have transmitted to their male offspring alone. (p. 95)

Sexual selection can be further divided into *intrasexual selection*—based on advantages in competition within one's own sex (encompassing features such as large size and weapons of defense such as large antlers)—and *epigamic selection*—based on advantages in attracting members of the opposite sex. Darwin (1859/1958) described one species example thus:

> The rock-thrush of Guiana, birds of paradise, and some others, congregate; and successive males display with the most elaborate care, and show off in the best manner, their gorgeous plumage: they likewise perform strange antics before the females, which standing as spectators, at last choose the most attractive partner. (p. 94)

It is obvious from these quotes that Darwin believed sexual selection most commonly results from *female choice* of males. Evidence since has supported that general belief. However, there are circumstances under which male choice may have important influences in shaping the characteristics of females, which we discuss in the next section.

***Sexual Selection and Development.*** Sexual selection may account for a number of developmental sex differences found throughout the animal kingdom (Geary, 1998). For example, we mentioned that males in some species mature later than females. Among songbirds, males may mature within a year, but commonly wait until they are 2 years old to develop adult plumage (Daly & Wilson, 1983). This seems to be linked to two features of sexual selection in an interrelated way: Younger males are less able to defend valuable territories and they are, consequently, less able to attract females. Even if they can defend a territory, young male buntings are less likely to attract females than are older more experienced males, who are better equipped to win the more desirable pieces of real estate (Carey & Nolan, 1979). In addition, the surge of testosterone as males develop secondary sex characteristics suppresses the immune system, thereby further increasing mortality risks (e.g., Folstad & Karter, 1992). For these reasons, it may be a waste of effort for a male to mature too early. Territorial defense, development of antlers, or a loud colorful display all drain resources that could be directed toward bodily development and thus increase the male's chances of survival until, and reproduction in, the next season.

This phenomenon of sexual bimaturation (one sex maturing at a later age) is often pronounced in species in which one sex is highly selective about mate choice. As a consequence, members of the "selected" sex need to compete with one another for access to choosy mates. For example, males in polygynous species (where only a small percentage of males get to mate, dependent on female selectivity) mature at a later age than females (Wiley, 1974). In contrast, males and females in monogamous grouse species (where each male pairs with one female) mature at about the same age. As we noted, Darwin observed that males are more likely to be shaped by female choice than vice versa. Why? Later evolutionary theorists linked this sex difference to differential parental investment by males and females (Trivers, 1972; Williams, 1966). We turn next to this topic.

## Differential Parental Investment

Parental investment is the contribution a parent makes to its offspring, at a cost to its ability to invest in other offspring (Trivers, 1985). That investment can include direct physiological investment before birth, such as the nutrition invested in making an egg or carrying a living fetus inside the mother's body. After birth, parental investment can include the provision of food or other resources (such as protection from predators).

In most species, there is an initial difference in parental investment stemming from the fact that eggs are more nutritionally expensive than sperm. In reptiles, birds, and mammals, those initial differences are exaggerated by the expense of producing a large nutritionally rich egg (in reptiles, birds, and a few mammals) or of allowing the fertilized egg to develop inside the mother's body (in most mammals). After birth, mammalian females invest further by nursing their young for some time—a year or more in some species. In more than 95% of mammalian species, males invest no more direct nutritional resources than the calories required to produce and deposit sperm (Clutton-Brock, 1991). In many birds and a few mammalian species, males contribute nutritional resources and other indirect support, such as nest building, egg incubation, and protective care.

Evolutionary theory in general and life-history theory in particular are based on economic considerations. For example, an underlying assumption is that animals are designed to invest resources in ways that will maximize potential payoffs (replicated genes) while minimizing expenditures. Producing offspring begins with unequal investment between the parents in many animal species. That imbalance is pronounced in mammalian species. Female mammals, if they are to raise successful offspring, are obligated by their physiological structures to make large investments. Male mammals are not.

Of course, male mammals do not therefore get to reproduce without making any investment. Because females are obliged to invest more, they are more demanding shoppers in the mating marketplace. Let's return to the idea of spending money from bank accounts as an analogy for investing resources in reproduction. Imagine that men and women each have bank account balances of $1,000 when they reach reproductive age. Women are required to spend at least $100 on every child they bear. Men, on the other hand, can determine for themselves how much they will invest in a child, spending as little as 10 cents or as much as $100.

For a man, the low cost (or 10-cent) option involves only as much energy as it takes to have sex. Under conditions of such low investment, a male need not be selective about partners, because he has almost nothing to lose by mating with anyone. Contrast this with the woman, whose minimum required investment is $100, which is a significant portion of her total bank account. She won't likely spend that $100 on just anyone. In return for her higher investment, she will demand a mate of high quality, to ensure that her few precious offspring will have a good chance at survival and reproduction. When men decide to invest more than the minimum in their offspring, their choices follow the same pattern as women: Men desire a high-quality partner in return for larger investments.

If a male was going to make the minimum investment in the offspring, he could afford to be relatively less selective in choosing partners. But without increasing the size of their offers, most men will find few takers. Because females are selective, the male must demonstrate that he has qualities that make him a better deal than other males. These might be better genes than his competitors, which would be signaled by a relatively more healthy, robust, and symmetrical physical appearance, or the ability to demonstrate special coordinated movements (Gangestad & Thornhill, 1997; Miller, 1998). Or the male might demonstrate a willingness to match some of the female's investments with investments of his own, such as nest building, providing her with nutrition, and demonstrating a willingness to invest in their future offspring.

There are species in which males invest in the offspring as much as, if not more than, females. Among seahorses, the tables are turned in comparison to humans. The male seahorse cares for the young after they are born, freeing the female to invest energy in a new family. Like male humans who invest $100 rather than a dime, male seahorses are more selective about the females with which they will mate, and females in such species may compete with one another for the male's attentions (Daly & Wilson, 1983).

Thus, parental investment leads to at least two general regularities in animal behavior. First, there is a direct link between the amount of resources invested by a given sex and that sex's selectiveness in choosing mates. Second, to the extent that the members of one sex make investments, and are therefore selective, the members of the other sex will compete with one another, and hence show sexually selected traits.

Related to this is another interesting link between parenting and sexual selection. In monogamous species, males and females tend to be similar in size and appearance. In polygynous species, where one male mates with several females, males tend to be larger and to possess decorative or defensive features, such as peacocks' feathers or bucks' antlers. The reason for this is related to the principles we discussed earlier. Males in monogamous species make high investments of effort and resources in the offspring, often matching those of the females. Males in polygynous species make less direct investment in any given female or her offspring and hence are subject to strong sexual selection pressures, as females pick males with traits suggesting superior genes. Polygynous males must therefore make higher investments in features that females find attractive.

# SEX DIFFERENCES IN HUMAN LIFE-HISTORY PATTERNS

The interrelated theories of life-history development, sexual selection, and differential parental investment were derived from observations of numerous species across numerous habitats (Daly & Wilson, 1983; Trivers, 1985). What do these theories imply about human sex differences and similarities? Consider first some clear differences in physical maturation. Adult male and female humans differ in size, with males about 30% heavier. The difference in weight is accounted for largely by the development of larger upper body muscles and longer bodies in adult males (males are about 10% taller).

Male and female humans also mature at different rates. Although both sexes delay maturity for more than a decade, males typically reach puberty later than do females and continue to grow for several years longer. Beginning at puberty, males produce about 10 times as much testosterone as do females, and females produce much greater quantities of estrogen. At the other end of the developmental spectrum, females' reproductive life cycle ends earlier than males'. Fertility even in healthy, well-fed females declines after the mid-30s and disappears entirely around age 50. Healthy males continue to produce sperm and testosterone well into their 80s.

Knowing nothing else about this particular species, a biologist would observe these physical differences as the marks of some degree of sexual selection (Geary, 1998). The degree to which human males are larger and mature later than females suggests a species whose ancestors were somewhat polygynous and in which males competed with one another for females. However, human males are not immensely larger than females, as is found in highly polygynous species, such as elephant seals and baboons, where males are several times larger. The degree of difference instead suggests a species that was only mildly polygynous (Daly & Wilson, 1983).

## A Reexamination of Gender Differences
## and Similarities in Social Behavior

From an evolutionary perspective, sex differences in human physical development and reproductive life history are directly linked to the sex differences and similarities in social behavior we reviewed earlier. Let us reconsider those differences and similarities in light of our discussion of life-history theory.

*Mate Preference.*   As was noted earlier, men and women differ in their age preferences in mates and in the size of that difference over the life span (Kenrick & Keefe, 1992). Studies of singles' advertisements in the United States and Europe, of marital advertisements in India, and of marriage ages in different parts of the world consistently find that women seek men who are, on average, older than themselves. Those same studies find that older men seek partners who are substantially younger than themselves.

Previously, social scientists explained the sex difference in terms of a sex-typed norm of Western society—that men should seek younger, less powerful partners, whereas women should seek older, taller, more powerful partners (e.g., Cameron, Oskamp, & Sparks, 1977; Presser, 1975). There are two problems with that explanation, the first being that the pattern is not limited to Western society but is found all around the world. Even more problematic, however, is the fact that young men, who generally tend to be more sex typed than older men, do not show a clear preference for younger partners at all. Men in their 20s are interested in women around their own age, with a range from a few years younger to a few years older. More interestingly, teenage boys are actually interested in primarily older women (ranging from about a year younger to about 7 or 8 years older; Kenrick et al., 1996). Indeed, when teenage boys are asked to consider the most attractive date they could imagine, without regard to their own desirability to her, they describe not younger girls, but college-age women.

These findings, though problematic for traditional normative accounts, fit neatly with a life-history model. Female fertility is low in the early teenage years and peaks in the 20s. It remains high into the 30s, and then drops as women approach age 40, until disappearing completely at menopause. It appears that younger men, like older men, are most attracted to women in their peak years of fertility (younger for old men, older for young men). This would also explain why men in their 20s are attracted to women around their own age.

It is important to note that we are not suggesting that men consciously set out to find partners that they think of as reproductively fertile or whose birth certificate indicates a particular calendar age. Instead, men are attracted to proximate cues that were, in ancestral environments, likely to have led their ancestors to experience greater reproductive success. The proximate cues might have included features such as facial maturity, skin tone, and body-fat distribution typical of women who have reached sexual maturity but not yet borne children (e.g., Cunningham, Druen, & Barbee, 1997; Singh, 1993).

Female attraction to older men throughout the life span has been linked to a preference for men who have had more time to establish a position of status, to acquire resources, or both. Experimental studies have demonstrated that human females, like females in many other mammalian species, find dominance a sexually attractive characteristic (Sadalla, Kenrick, & Vershure, 1987), particularly when it is combined with a pleasant personality that would indicate a cooperative mate (Jensen-Campbell, Graziano, & West, 1995). Apparently, females want males who are successful in competition with other males but who are not likely to demonstrate hostility in their personal relationships.

*Aggression.*   We noted earlier that men have committed the vast majority of homicides across cultures and historical epochs. In an extensive series of studies on this topic, Daly and Wilson (1988) observed a number of other sex differences in homicides. Men and women commit homicide for different reasons. Men are much more likely to kill other men who challenge their position in the dominance hierarchy, for example, whereas women who do kill are more likely to kill in self-defense, murdering male sexual partners who have been physically abusing and threatening them. Wilson and Daly (1985) also observed an interesting age-linked feature of homicides—male homicides shoot up around puberty, peak around the early 20s, and then drop. Indeed, the life-span pattern of male homicides follows the life-span pattern of testosterone and is apparently linked to reproductive status. Men who kill are most likely to be younger males in the peak years of reproductive competition. Men who lack mates or the resources to attract mates are at highest risk for such competition (Wilson & Daly, 1985; Palmer, 1993). This life pattern of male violence is indicative of intrasexual competition linked to sexual selection. As we noted earlier, human females are attracted to males who can establish social dominance over other males.

It is important to note that females are probably not directly attracted to violence in men (Sadalla et al., 1987). Charismatic men who are able to acquire resources and express their social dominance through conventional means are likely most attractive to women. Intramale violence may simply be a by-product of competition for status, most likely to appear in men with high levels of reproductive hormones whose conventional paths to status are blocked or who are confronted by other desperate males (Dabbs & Morris, 1990; Mazur & Booth, 1998; Wilson & Daly, 1985).

*Sexuality.*   We already mentioned that males are distinctly more eager to engage in casual sexual liaisons and more likely to fantasize about sex frequently (Clark & Hatfield, 1989; Ellis & Symons, 1990; Oliver & Hyde, 1993). These findings fit with the evolutionary model of differential parental investment—female mammals have more investment to lose by being careless about sexual partners. Indeed, even in hunter–gatherer societies, where women have no access to birth control, it is rare for a woman to have more than 10 children, and the average number is less than 5 (Daly & Wilson, 1983). Human offspring are particularly helpless and traditionally survived better when there were two parents to care for them. Women in traditional societies who bear children without a committed male to assist in raising those children are more likely to lose those children (Geary, 1998).

Note that the parental-investment model specifies that the more one invests in one's offspring, the more selective one will be in choosing a mate. Because human males, unlike most mammals, often contribute substantial resources and effort to raising their offspring, it is to be expected that men will also be careful in choosing mates. A sex difference in selectivity would therefore only be expected for casual sexual opportunities (where male and female investments are potentially most discrepant). As male commitment increases, so should male selectivity. Results of several studies are consistent with this more complex view of human parental investment (Kenrick, Groth, Trost, & Sadalla, 1993; Kenrick et al., 1990; Regan, 1998). For example, men and women in one series of studies were asked to specify their minimum standards for partners along several dimensions (e.g., intelligence, status, attractiveness, etc.). Those minimum standards were stated for several different levels of involvement, ranging from single dates through one-night sexual encounters and up to committed long-term relationships and marriage. Both sexes generally demanded little in a single date but much in a marriage partner. The sexes differed in their criteria for casual sexual partners, however, with females generally demanding more and males often specifying lower standards for a casual sexual partner than for a "date" (Kenrick et al., 1990, 1993).

*Child Care.*    Gender differences in child care are direct manifestations of the inherent mammalian sex difference in parental investment. Human females, like other mammals, carry their fetuses inside their bodies and nurse the newborns after giving birth. Across human societies, direct care from a child's mother has been more closely related to infant and child survival than has care from a father (Geary, 1998). Traditionally, the investment made by human males has included the provision of protection and indirect resources, such as food and shelter. However, paternal care has also been clearly linked to offspring survival, as we discuss in the next section.

*Gender Similarities.*    At the beginning of this chapter, we noted a number of gender similarities, including the apparently cross-culturally robust tendency to form strong emotional bonds to one's lover and to one's children, found in men as well as women. Because human infants are immobile, slow-developing, and completely dependent on parental care, men and women who cooperated in caring for the young were more likely to see those young survive to reproductive age. A cooperative bond between two parents is still important for survival in remaining hunter–gatherer groups and was likely crucial for our ancestors (Geary, 1998).

Note that the same series of studies that demonstrated large sex differences in criteria for a one-night stand also uncovered similarities across the sexes in criteria for long-term relationships (Kenrick et al., 1990, 1993; Regan, 1998). When male investment is high, so is male selectiveness. For many criteria, the two sexes have very similar requirements in mates. Both sexes, for example, place similarly high value on characteristics likely to be associated with cooperativeness in a long-term relationship, such as kindness, a good personality, and a sense of humor (Buss & Barnes, 1986; Kenrick et al., 1990, 1993; Jensen-Campbell et al., 1995). Yet just as males and females contribute somewhat different resources to the offspring, so the criteria for mate selection are somewhat different for the two sexes—women place more emphasis on social status and resources in male partners, men place more emphasis on youth and physical attractiveness in female partners (Kenrick, Neuberg, Zierk, & Krones, 1994). Those different emphases seem in fact to be linked to the different resources contributed to the offspring. Women seek men who demonstrate capacity and willingness to invest resources and effort in the offspring; men seek women who demonstrate the youthful mature features associated with fertility. At the same time, both sexes seek partners who demonstrate characteristics associated with success in long-term cooperative relationships (Green & Kenrick, 1994).

## GENE–CULTURE–COGNITION INTERACTIONS

Several findings emerging from cross-cultural and comparative research pose problems for the idea that sex differences are the result of arbitrary cultural norms. We have discussed parallels in gender differences across cultures, for example, that are unlikely to be rooted in the norms of North American or European society. We have also discussed parallels across species that could not be rooted in the norms of any human society.

Perhaps because of a general tendency to think in black-and-white terms, evolutionary accounts for behavior are often mistakenly pitted directly against cultural accounts. When evolutionary theorists argue that arbitrary norms cannot provide a *full* explanation of human gender differences, that is sometimes misinterpreted to mean that evolutionary theorists believe human culture is therefore unimportant, uninteresting, or unvarying. But this is a misconception. Instead, evolutionary theorists assume that the action lies in a complex interaction between human genes, human cultures, and human cognition (e.g., Barkow, Cosmides, & Tooby, 1992; Kenrick, 1987; Lumsden & Wilson, 1981).

What are some of the ways that cultures, genes, and cognition interact? How does a consideration of culture enrich an evolutionary understanding of human sex differences?

## Evolution and Culture

A more textured view of culture enriches our understanding of evolved human characteristics. First, it is important to highlight the fact that human biology and culture are not isolated from each other. Accordingly, a complete perspective on human behavior would not claim that either biology or culture operates in a mutually exclusive fashion. Quite the contrary, biology and culture are inextricably interwoven (Fiske, Kitayama, Markus, & Nisbett, 1998; Kenrick, 1987; Kenrick & Trost, 1993). Culture has provided important features of the environment in which humans have evolved. Likewise, humans have created and refined the cultures in which the species resides.

***Cultural Variations in Evolutionary Perspective.***   Although cross-cultural studies reveal remarkable similarities across cultures, they virtually always reveal some cultural variations on the expression of those similarities. Two points are important to keep in mind in this regard. First, some individual variation *within* cultures is to be expected from an evolutionary perspective. An evolutionary perspective does not claim that there should be complete uniformity within (or across) cultures. Second, some differences *between* cultures are also completely consistent with an evolutionary perspective. Variations in local environments can trigger different strategies within people and result in varying manifestations of the same underlying motive. These points are expanded here.

Individuals within cultures often vary considerably. This fact does not run contrary to an evolutionary view. For example, for some characteristics, selection pressures favor the existence of two or more distinct behavioral proclivities within a population (recall the different types of sunfish). Such differences often operate according to frequency-dependent selection—the adaptiveness of one strategy depends on its frequency in comparison to the other (if most males were sneak copulators the strategy would be useless; if most were territorial males, sneaking would have a higher payoff). In the domain of sexuality, Gangestad and Simpson (1990) documented two distinct sociosexual strategies among men and women: restricted and unrestricted. Though women are on average more sexually restrictive than men, there is, at the same time, more than one strategy played by women in a population. When women adopt an unrestrictive strategy, their criteria for mates may change accordingly (Buss & Schmitt, 1993).

The second point is that some cross-cultural fluctuation can be explained as variations on the same adaptive theme. In terms of the criteria for choosing mates, all societies thus far examined have demonstrated a tendency for an age discrepancy between men and women that becomes more pronounced with age (Kenrick & Keefe, 1992). However, the size of that difference is more pronounced in more traditional societies. Older men on the remote island of Poro married much younger women than did older men in Holland or the United States. Such cultural variations are sometimes taken as evidence against an evolutionary perspective (Eagly, 1998). Unfortunately, such interpretations encourage a fundamental misunderstanding of the relationship between culture and evolved mechanisms. That relationship is undoubtedly a complex one, but it is certainly not a case in which genes are somehow an alternative to culture.

The fact that age differences in mate preference are more pronounced in traditional societies may be related to a regular link between a biological mechanism and the social environment. In traditional societies, women begin to bear children at an earlier age, and hence the women themselves age much more rapidly (Kenrick & Keefe, 1992; Symons, 1992). In modern American and European society, birth control and delayed marriage have slowed the aging process in women. In addition, women in modern industrialized societies have access to cosmetic enhancements of youthful features (makeup, hair dye, face-lifts, and figure-enhancing bras). Since men respond more to those proximal features of fertility and youth than to the official date on a woman's birth certificate, it makes eminent biological sense that relatively older women in Western societies are more attractive than women of equivalent age in traditional societies.

***Bidirectional Influences of Biology and Culture.*** This does not mean that culture has overridden biology. What it suggests is that variable features of culture and of the potentialities embedded in the human genome are interwoven with and constructed around one another. If one takes a long enough view, it is a completely two-way street. Culture is a crucial part of the environment in which humans evolved. Common human adaptations based on strong genetic inclinations are designed around recurring features of human culture, including marriages, leadership hierarchies, kinship networks, and enforced moral codes against cheating other group members.

Variation between cultures reminds us that, like the human proclivity for language, any innate inclination combines with inputs from the experienced environment. Evolutionary theorists assume that genetic influences incline human beings to develop in certain ways. Some of those genetic inclinations may be main effects, features designed to develop on the assumption of a standard set of environmental events. The suckling response in a newborn assumes that the newborn will encounter a milk-producing breast. Some newborns, whose mothers died in childbirth or shortly thereafter, did not encounter such an environmental input, but they also did not survive long enough to develop alternative nutrition-seeking mechanisms.

Other genetic inclinations may predispose very simple interactions with the environment. All humans inherited the inclination to demonstrate an angry facial expression, or to cry, but they only demonstrate those behaviors when they encounter particular environments. In animals such as the Nassau grouper, some gene–environment interactions involve more complex developmental divergences—as when a female changes into a male only if the appropriate opportunity arises (death of the local male, and her having attained sufficient size to outcompete the other females for his role).

Evolutionary theorists assume that some cultural variations in behavior reflect interactions between a flexible genetic program and a variable environment. Societal variations in the way marriage is practiced (i.e., monogamy, polygyny, or polyandry) provide good examples of how cultural features reflect evolutionary mechanisms. These variations, rather than being completely arbitrary, often reveal evolutionarily sensible correlations with other features of the physical or social environment.

For example, polyandry (one female marrying more than one male) is a marriage pattern that generally works against male interest. Among humans, polyandry is found in less than 1% of societies (Daly & Wilson, 1983). The circumstances within which it is found are revealing: where resources are quite scarce. Under these harsh conditions, brothers may pool their wealth into one family rather than taking a chance that, by dividing efforts, none of their offspring will survive. On the other side, extreme polygyny (one male marrying several females) has been found in environments that are rich enough for one family to acquire great resources but in which occasional famines make it difficult for the very poor to survive (Crook & Crook, 1988). Similar economic considerations also seem to determine switching between monogamy and polygamy in other animals (Pleszczynska & Hansell, 1980). Along the same lines, variations in the sex ratio of marriage-age men and women have been found to correlate with variations in mating strategies (Geary, 1998; Guttentag & Secord, 1983).

According to Geary (1998), childhood is the period during which flexible evolved modules are adapted to local environments. Geary argues that a long childhood (delayed maturation) enables individuals to develop complex behavioral, social, and cognitive competencies needed for success at mating and survival. For example, all humans are born with a propensity to learn language (Pinker, 1994). Whether an infant learns Japanese or Portuguese is completely determined by the individual's cultural context. The fact that an infant can learn language at all, however, is permitted by structures in the brain evolved for communication. Adaptation of modules to features of local environments is not limited to language. In cultures where adult males engage in direct conflict with spears, for example, boys' play involves throwing spears as opposed to playing tackle football (Geary, 1998).

## Cognition, Evolution, and Social Construction

Explanations of gender differences have often included an assumption that gender roles are based on cognitive constructs (e.g., Beall, 1993; Bem, 1981; Cross & Markus, 1993; Hare-Mustin & Marecek, 1988). From this perspective, the features of masculinity and femininity are usually viewed as somewhat arbitrary, and thus children in different cultures, and individuals within a particular culture, may learn to label sex-typed behaviors in different ways. For example, whether an earring, body tattoo, skirt, or painted face is viewed as appropriate to the masculine or feminine role varies from culture to culture and from time to time within a culture. Such relativity is completely compatible with sociocultural role views of gender (e.g., Beall, 1993). But because many salient features of gender roles seem so arbitrary, some consider a social constructivist view and a biological view to be in opposition to each other (e.g., Hyde, 1996).

   If one wishes to adopt the extreme position that gender roles are completely arbitrary, then evolutionary theorists would disagree, citing as evidence the consistency of many gender differences (e.g., in aggression or sexual selectivity) across species as well as cultures. However, from an interactionist perspective, we would view social role constructs and evolved psychological mechanisms as inherently connected, according to the same logic as we developed earlier in this chapter. Indeed, it appears that people's cognitive constructions of gender roles are based not on unrestrained imagination or on blind acceptance of arbitrary societal schemas, but on observations of fairly reliable differences in the behaviors of the two sexes. As with many cognitive schemas, gender schemas act as stereotypes that may lead people to exaggerate the size of the actual differences (Martin, 1987). Despite this tendency toward cognitive magnification, people are fairly accurate in guessing which behavioral sex differences are large and which are small, matching the results of statistical meta-analyses (Eagly, 1995; Swim, 1994).

   Why are constructions often similar across human societies? Some social constructivists have acknowledged that they are traceable, in part, to the inherent sex differences in size and physical strength (Hyde, 1996). Presumably, societal structures emphasizing male power were built around those simple physical differences. That is partially correct, but it leaves unanalyzed why human males and females are different in size to begin with and why those size differences are correlated with other biological differences discussed earlier. An evolutionary perspective helps us understand where those otherwise arbitrary differences come from and why sex differences are so perennially salient to people.

Adopting a biosocial interactionist perspective also helps us understand how the schemas likely to be activated on a moment-to-moment basis are sometimes linked to sex differences in mating strategies. In making self-judgments of one's own desirability as a mate, for example, women are more schematic for beauty than status (Gutierres, Kenrick, & Partch, 1999). In making decisions about one's commitment to one's current mate, on the other hand, women are more schematic for the availability of highly successful and dominant men than for the availability of physically attractive men (Kenrick et al., 1994). Men show the reverse patterns in both of these domains.

Again, the suggestion is that sex-role schemas are not an alternative to evolved mechanisms but are one manifestation of particular cognitive sensitivities, the details of which are no doubt developed as a function of one's culture—for example, dominance is defined by the standards of one's culture, and beauty is partially linked to styles and trends. However, both also have some deep structure—beauty is everywhere linked to symmetry, a high waist-to-hip ratio, and mature sexual development; social dominance means being above the competitors in whatever the local game happens to be.

## Preparedness and Gene–Environment Interactions

For decades, experimental psychologists were mired in the nature–nurture controversy, wed to the idea that learning and instinct were alternatives to each other—that animals either learned their habitual behaviors or inherited them in programs written before birth. Researchers in the field of learning and cognition have, in recent decades, shed these old dichotomous ways of thinking.

One of the most useful constructs to emerge from this controversy is the notion of *preparedness*—the idea that animals are frequently genetically predisposed to learn some associations more easily than others (e.g., Rozin & Kalat, 1971; Seligman & Hager, 1972). The best known example comes from research on food aversion. Rats exposed to novel foods and later made nauseous learn in one trial to avoid the tastes of those foods in the future (Garcia & Koelling, 1966). This aversive learning is difficult to extinguish and does not follow normal principles of classical conditioning. For example, it does not require multiple trials, and it can occur when the novel taste stimulus and the nausea response are separated by hours (rather than the usual milliseconds required for "normal" classical conditioning). Furthermore, rats cannot learn to associate nausea with visual stimuli but only with taste stimuli. Human beings likewise are subject to such one-trial conditioning to novel tastes followed by later nausea, and the phenomenon has been dubbed the Sauce Béarnaise Syndrome. The features of the syndrome suggest that animals like rats and humans, who sample widely from a range of potentially toxic plant substances, are "prepared" to learn quickly associations between novel tastes and nausea, in order to protect them from eating potentially poisonous foods more than once.

Humans are likewise prepared to learn a language in a different way from that in which they learn to avoid poisonous foods. Infants are born especially sensitive to human vocal patterns and predisposed to emit all the sounds of human language. During the first few years of life, despite their generally backward state of cognitive development and lack of formal training in grammar, they learn the local argot to a level of perfection that will not be possible at any later time in life (Pinker, 1997). Highly intelligent adult Americans who move to Germany still speak the new language with noticeable imperfections decades later, while their 4-year-old children, barely able to tie their own shoelaces or learn simple addition and subtraction, manage to converse in complex and fluent German prose.

As in the case of language, evolution-based differences between male and female animals need not be "hard-wired" at birth. Instead, the sexes may simply be "prepared" to have different learning experiences. Some of that preparation stems from simple differences in size, upper body development, and testosterone levels, which combine to make aggressiveness more appealing and rewarding for males than for females. And some may be linked to differences in estrogen and oxytocin levels, which may make parental nurturance more rewarding for females. Thus, it is not necessary to presume that gender differences arise independent of experience. The sexes may simply enter the world biologically prepared to experience slightly different events, and the societies constructed by adult members of their species may further reinforce, channel, and facilitate those differential learning experiences.

## CONCLUSION

An evolutionary life-history perspective helps us understand a number of cross-cultural and cross-species gender differences and gender similarities in behavior. A consideration of reproductive life spans, parental investment, and sexual selection ties together a number of human findings with a wide literature on animal behavior and helps us see beyond the constraints of our own culture and time. As shown in this chapter, an evolutionary perspective does not imply that human culture or human cognition is irrelevant. Instead, it provides part of a broader biosocial interactionist framework by which we can integrate the observations taken from many different theoretical vantage points.

Most of the questions about the interactions between evolved mechanisms and human development remain to be asked. There are intriguing questions about exactly how societies and genes mutually influence one another and how human cognition is constrained by genetic influences. There is ample evidence that an understanding of evolutionary life history can only help elucidate how humans construct their views of gender roles and the societies that embody those roles.

# ACKNOWLEDGMENT

The authors wish to thank David Geary, Thomas Eckes, and Hanns Martin Trautner for their helpful comments on an earlier draft of this chapter.

# REFERENCES

Alcock, J. (1993). *Animal behavior: An evolutionary approach* (5th ed.). Sunderland, MA: Sinauer Associates.

Alexander, R. D. (1987). *The biology of moral systems*. Hawthorne, NY: Aldine de Gruyter.

Barkow, J. H., Cosmides, L., & Tooby, J. (Eds.). (1992). *The adapted mind: Evolutionary psychology and the generation of culture*. New York: Oxford University Press.

Beall, A. E. (1993). A social constructionist view of gender. In A. E. Beall & R. J. Sternberg (Eds.), *The psychology of gender* (pp. 127–147). New York: Guilford.

Bem, S. L. (1981). Gender schema theory: A cognitive account of sex typing. *Psychological Review, 88*, 354–364.

Bowlby, J. (1969). *Attachment and loss: Vol. 1. Attachment*. New York: Basic Books.

Buss, D. M. (1989). Sex differences in human mate preferences: Evolutionary hypotheses tested in 37 cultures. *Behavioral and Brain Sciences, 12*, 1–49.

Buss, D. M. (1995). Evolutionary psychology: A new paradigm for psychological science. *Psychological Inquiry, 6*, 1–30.

Buss, D. M., & Barnes, M. (1986). Preferences in human mate selection. *Journal of Personality and Social Psychology, 50*, 559–570.

Buss, D. M., & Kenrick, D. T. (1998). Evolutionary social psychology. In D. T. Gilbert, S. T. Fiske, & G. Lindzey (Eds.), *The handbook of social psychology* (4th ed., Vol. 2, pp. 982–1026). Boston: McGraw-Hill.

Buss, D. M., & Schmitt, D. P. (1993). Sexual strategies theory: An evolutionary perspective on human mating. *Psychological Review, 100*, 204–232.

Cameron, C., Oskamp, S., & Sparks, W. (1977). Courtship American style—newspaper ads. *Family Coordinator, 26*, 27–30.

Carey, M., & Nolan, V. (1979). Population dynamics of indigo buntings and the evolution of avian polygyny. *Evolution, 33*, 1180–1192.

Clark, R. D., & Hatfield, E. (1989). Gender differences in receptivity to sexual offers. *Journal of Psychology and Human Sexuality, 2,* 39–55.

Clutton-Brock, T. H. (1991). *The evolution of parental care.* Princeton, NJ: Princeton University Press.

Crawford, C. B., & Anderson, J. L. (1989). Sociobiology: An environmentalist discipline? *American Psychologist, 44,* 1449–1459.

Crook, J. H., & Crook, S. J. (1988). Tibetan polyandry: Problems of adaptation and fitness. In L. Betzig, M. Borgerhoff Mulder, & P. Turke (Eds.), *Human reproductive behavior: A Darwinian perspective* (pp. 97–114). New York: Cambridge University Press.

Cross, S. E., & Markus, H. R. (1993). Gender in thought, belief, and action: A cognitive approach. In A. E. Beall & R. J. Sternberg (Eds.), *The psychology of gender* (pp. 55–98). New York: Guilford.

Cunningham, M. R., Druen, P. B., & Barbee, A. P. (1997). Angels, mentors, and friends: Trade-offs among evolutionary, social, and individual variables in physical appearance. In J. A. Simpson & D. T. Kenrick (Eds.), *Evolutionary social psychology* (pp. 109–140). Mahwah, NJ: Lawrence Erlbaum Associates.

Dabbs, J. M., Jr., & Morris, R. (1990). Testosterone, social class, and antisocial behavior in a sample of 4462 men. *Psychological Science, 1,* 209–211.

Daly, M., & Wilson, M. (1983). *Sex, evolution, and behavior* (2nd ed.). Belmont, CA: Wadsworth.

Daly, M., & Wilson, M. (1988). *Homicide.* Hawthorne, NY: Aldine de Gruyter.

Darwin, C. (1872). *The expression of emotions in man and animals.* London: Murray.

Darwin, C. (1958). *The origin of species* (6th ed.). New York: New American Library. (Original work published 1859)

Eagly, A. H. (1987). *Sex differences in social behavior: A social-role interpretation.* Hillsdale, NJ: Lawrence Erlbaum Associates.

Eagly, A. H. (1995). The science and politics of comparing women and men. *American Psychologist, 50,* 145–158.

Eagly, A. H. (1998, August). *Do we need evolutionary psychology to explain sex differences in social behavior?* Paper presented at the meeting of the American Psychological Association, San Francisco, CA.

Ellis, B. J., & Symons, D. (1990). Sex differences in sexual fantasy: An evolutionary psychological approach. *Journal of Sex Research, 27,* 527–555.

Fiske, A. P., Kitayama, S., Markus, H. R., & Nisbett, R. E. (1998). The cultural matrix of social psychology. In D. T. Gilbert, S. T. Fiske, & G. Lindzey (Eds.), *The handbook of social psychology* (4th ed., Vol. 2, pp. 915–981). Boston, MA: McGraw-Hill.

Folstad, I., & Karter, A. J. (1992). Parasites, bright males, and the immunocompetence handicap. *American Naturalist, 139,* 603–622.

Freeman, D. (1983). *Margaret Mead and Samoa.* Cambridge, MA: Harvard University Press.

Gangestad, S. W., & Simpson, J. A. (1990). Toward an evolutionary history of female sociosexual variation. *Journal of Personality, 58,* 69–96.

Gangestad, S. W., & Thornhill, R. (1997). Human sexual selection and developmental stability. In J. A. Simpson & D. T. Kenrick (Eds.), *Evolutionary social psychology* (pp. 169–195). Mahwah, NJ: Lawrence Erlbaum Associates.

Garcia, J., & Koelling, R. A. (1966). Relation of cue to consequence in avoidance learning. *Psychonomic Science, 4,* 123–124.

Geary, D. C. (1998). *Male, female: The evolution of human sex differences.* Washington, DC: American Psychological Association.

Gould, J. L., & Gould, C. G. (1989). *Sexual selection.* New York: Scientific American Library.

Green, B. L., & Kenrick, D.T. (1994). The attractiveness of gender-typed traits at different relationship levels: Androgynous characteristics may be desirable after all. *Personality and Social Psychology Bulletin, 20*, 244–253.

Gross, M. R., & Charnov, E. L. (1980). Alternative male life histories in bluegill sunfish. *Proceedings of the National Academy of Sciences, USA*, 77, 6937–6940.

Gutierres, S. E., Kenrick, D. T., & Partch, J. J. (1999). Beauty, dominance, and the mating game: Contrast effects in self-assessment reflect gender differences in mate selection. *Personality and Social Psychology Bulletin, 25*, 1126–1134.

Guttentag, M., & Secord, P. F. (1983). *Too many women? The sex ratio question.* Beverly Hills, CA: Sage.

Hare-Mustin, R. T., & Marecek, J. (1988). The meaning of difference: Gender theory, postmodernism, and psychology. *American Psychologist, 43*, 455–464.

Harpending, H. (1992). Age differences between mates in southern African pastoralists. *Behavioral and Brain Sciences, 15*, 102–103.

Hewlett, B. S. (1988). Sexual selection and paternal investment among Aka pygmies. In L. Betzig, M. Borgerhoff Mulder, & P. Turke (Eds.), *Human reproductive behaviour: A Darwinian perspective* (pp. 263–276). New York: Cambridge University Press.

Hyde, J. S. (1996). Where are the gender differences? Where are the gender similarities? In D. M. Buss & N. M. Malamuth (Eds.), *Sex, power, conflict: Evolutionary and feminist perspectives* (pp. 107–118). New York: Oxford University Press.

Jankowiak, W. R., & Fischer, E. F. (1992). A cross-cultural perspective on romantic love. *Ethnology, 31*, 149–155.

Jensen-Campbell, L. A., Graziano, W. G., & West, S. G. (1995). Dominance, prosocial orientation, and female preferences: Do nice guys really finish last? *Journal of Personality and Social Psychology, 68*, 427–440.

Kenrick, D. T. (1987). Gender, genes, and the social environment: A biosocial interactionist perspective. In P. Shaver & C. Hendrick (Eds.), *Review of personality and social psychology: Vol. 7. Sex and gender* (pp. 14–43). Newbury Park, CA: Sage.

Kenrick, D. T., Gabrielidis, C., Keefe, R. C., & Cornelius, J. S. (1996). Adolescents' age preferences for dating partners: Support for an evolutionary model of life-history strategies. *Child Development, 67*, 1499–1511.

Kenrick, D. T., Groth, G. E., Trost, M. R., & Sadalla, E. K. (1993). Integrating evolutionary and social exchange perspectives on relationships: Effects of gender, self-appraisal, and involvement level on mate selection criteria. *Journal of Personality and Social Psychology, 64*, 951–969.

Kenrick, D. T., & Keefe, R. C. (1992). Age preferences in mates reflect sex differences in human reproductive strategies. *Behavioral and Brain Sciences, 15*, 75–91.

Kenrick, D. T., Neuberg, S. L., Zierk, K. L., & Krones, J. M. (1994). Evolution and social cognition: Contrast effects as a function of sex, dominance, and physical attractiveness. *Personality and Social Psychology Bulletin, 20*, 210–217.

Kenrick, D. T., Nieuweboer, S., & Buunk, A. P. (1995, October). *Age differences in mate choice across cultures and across historical periods.* Paper presented at joint meeting of the Society of Experimental Social Psychology and the European Association of Experimental Social Psychology, Washington, DC.

Kenrick, D. T., Sadalla, E. K., Groth, G., & Trost, M. R. (1990). Evolution, traits, and the stages of human courtship: Qualifying the parental investment model. *Journal of Personality, 58*, 97–116.

Kenrick, D. T., Sadalla, E. K., & Keefe, R. C. (1998). Evolutionary cognitive psychology: The missing heart of modern cognitive science. In C. B. Crawford & D. L. Krebs (Eds.), *Handbook of evolutionary psychology: Ideas, issues, and applications* (pp. 485–514). Mahwah, NJ: Lawrence Erlbaum Associates.

Kenrick, D. T., & Trost, M. R. (1993). The evolutionary perspective. In A. E. Beall & R. J. Sternberg (Eds.), *The psychology of gender* (pp. 148–172). New York: Guilford.

Lack, D., Gibb, J., & Owen, D. F. (1957). Survival in relation to brood-size in tits. *Proceedings of the Zoological Society of London, 128*, 313–326.

Lamb, M. E., Frodi, A. M., Hwang, C.-P., & Frodi, M. (1982). Varying degrees of paternal involvement in infant care: Attitudinal and behavioral correlates. In M. E. Lamb (Ed.), *Nontraditional families: Parenting and child development* (pp. 117–137). Hillsdale, NJ: Lawrence Erlbaum Associates.

Lee, A. K., Bradley, A. J., & Braithwaite, R. W. (1977). Corticosteroid levels and male mortality in *Antechinus stuartii*. In B. Stonehouse & D. Gilmore (Eds.), *The biology of marsupials* (pp. 209–220). London: Macmillan.

Lumsden, C. J., & Wilson, E. O. (1981). *Genes, mind, and culture: The coevolutionary process*. Cambridge, MA: Harvard University Press.

Martin, C. L. (1987). A ratio measure of sex stereotyping. *Journal of Personality and Social Psychology, 52*, 489–499.

Maynard Smith, J. (1958). The effects of temperature and of egg-laying on the longevity of *Drosophila subobscura. Journal of Experimental Biology, 35*, 832–842.

Mazur, A., & Booth, A. (1998). Testosterone and dominance in men. *Behavioral and Brain Sciences, 21*, 353–363.

Mead, M. (1928). *Coming of age in Samoa*. New York: Morrow.

Mead, M. (1935). *Sex and temperament in three primitive societies*. New York: Morrow.

Messenger, J. (1971). Sex and repression in an Irish folk community. In D. Marshall & R. Suggs (Eds.), *Human sexual behavior: Variations across the ethnographic spectrum* (pp. 3–37). New York: Basic Books.

Miller, G. F. (1998). How mate choice shaped human nature: A review of sexual selection and human evolution. In C. B. Crawford & D. L. Krebs (Eds.), *Handbook of evolutionary psychology: Ideas, issues, and applications* (pp. 87–129). Mahwah, NJ: Lawrence Erlbaum Associates.

Miller, L. C., & Fishkin, S. A. (1997). On the dynamics of human bonding and reproductive success: Seeking windows on the adapted-for human-environmental interface. In J. A. Simpson & D. T. Kenrick (Eds.), *Evolutionary social psychology* (pp. 197–235). Mahwah, NJ: Lawrence Erlbaum Associates.

Oliver, M. B., & Hyde, J. S. (1993). Gender differences in sexuality: A meta-analysis. *Psychological Bulletin, 114*, 29–51.

Ollason, J. C., & Dunnet, G. M. (1978). Age, experience and other factors affecting the breeding success of the fulmar, *Fulmarus glacialis*, in Orkney. *Journal of Animal Ecology, 47*, 961–976.

Palmer, C. T. (1993). Anger, aggression, and humor in Newfoundland floor hockey: An evolutionary analysis. *Aggressive Behavior, 19*, 167–173.

Parker, G. A. (1970). Sperm competition and its evolutionary consequences in the insects. *Biological Reviews, 45*, 525–567.

Partridge, L., & Farquhar, M. (1981). Sexual activity reduces lifespan of male fruitflies. *Nature, 294*, 580–582.

Partridge, L., & Harvey, P. H. (1988). The ecological context of life history evolution. *Science, 241*, 1449–1455.

Pinker, S. (1994). *The language instinct*. New York: Morrow.

Pinker, S. (1997). *How the mind works*. New York: Norton.

Pleszczynska, W. K., & Hansell, R. I. C. (1980). Polygyny and decision theory: Testing of a model in lark buntings *(Calamospiza malanocorys). American Naturalist, 116*, 821–830.

Presser, H. B. (1975). Age differences between spouses: Trends, patterns, and social implications. *American Behavioral Scientist, 19*, 190–205.

Quammen, D. (1996). *The song of the dodo: Island biogeography in an age of extinction.* New York: Scribner's.

Regan, P. C. (1998). What if you can't get what you want? Willingness to compromise ideal mate selection standards as a function of sex, mate value, and relationship context. *Personality and Social Psychology Bulletin, 24,* 1294–1303.

Reiter, J., Panken, K. J., & Le Boeuf, B. J. (1981). Female competition and reproductive success in northern elephant seals. *Animal Behaviour, 29,* 670–687.

Rozin, P., & Kalat, J. W. (1971). Specific hungers and poison avoidance as adaptive specializations of learning. *Psychological Review, 78,* 459–486.

Sadalla, E. K., Kenrick, D. T., & Vershure, B. (1987). Dominance and heterosexual attraction. *Journal of Personality and Social Psychology, 52,* 730–738.

Seligman, M. E. P., & Hager, J. L. (1972). *Biological boundaries of learning.* New York: Appleton-Century-Crofts.

Sherry, D. F., & Schacter, D. L. (1987). The evolution of multiple memory systems. *Psychological Review, 94,* 439–454.

Singh, D. (1993). Adaptive significance of female physical attractiveness: Role of waist-to-hip ratio. *Journal of Personality and Social Psychology, 65,* 293–307.

Stearns, S. C. (1976). Life-history tactics: A review of the ideas. *Quarterly Review of Biology, 51,* 3–47.

Swim, J. K. (1994). Perceived versus meta-analytic effect sizes: An assessment of the accuracy of gender stereotypes. *Journal of Personal and Social Psychology, 66,* 21–36.

Symons, D. (1992). What do men want? *Behavioral and Brain Sciences, 15,* 113–114.

Tanner, J. M. (1990). *Foetus into man: Physical growth from conception to maturity* (rev. ed.). Cambridge, MA: Harvard University Press.

Tinkle, D. W. (1969). The concept of reproductive effort and its relation to the evolution of life histories in lizards. *American Naturalist, 103,* 501–516.

Tooby, J., & Cosmides, L. (1992). The psychological foundations of culture. In J. H. Barkow, L. Cosmides, & J. Tooby (Eds.), *The adapted mind: Evolutionary psychology and the generation of culture* (pp. 19–136). New York: Oxford University Press.

Trivers, R. L. (1972). Parental investment and sexual selection. In B. Campbell (Ed.), *Sexual selection and the descent of man 1871–1971* (pp. 136–179). Chicago: Aldine.

Trivers, R. L. (1985). *Social evolution.* Menlo Park, CA: Benjamin/Cummings.

Warner, R. R. (1984). Mating behavior and hermaphrodism in coral reef fishes. *American Scientist, 72,* 128–134.

White, G. M. (1980). Conceptual universals in interpersonal language. *American Anthropologist, 82,* 759–781.

Wiley, R. H. (1974). Evolution of social organization and life-history patterns among grouse. *Quarterly Review of Biology, 49,* 201–227.

Williams, G. C. (1966). *Adaptation and natural selection.* Princeton, NJ: Princeton University Press.

Wilson, M., & Daly, M. (1985). Competitiveness, risk taking, and violence: The young male syndrome. *Ethology and Sociobiology, 6,* 59–73.

Zeifman, D., & Hazan, C. (1997). Attachment: The bond in pair-bonds. In J. A. Simpson & D. T. Kenrick (Eds.), *Evolutionary social psychology* (pp. 237–263). Mahwah, NJ: Lawrence Erlbaum Associates.

# 3

# Theories of Gender Socialization

Beverly I. Fagot
*University of Oregon,*
*Oregon Social Learning Center*

Carie S. Rodgers
*University of Oregon*

Mary D. Leinbach
*Oregon Social Learning Center*

Gender is a category system made up of many levels, many interwoven strands. Physiology defines the most fundamental level, designating people as male or female on the basis of their observable sexual anatomy, but every known society surrounds the basic facts of sexual form and function with a system of social rules and customs concerning what males and females are supposed to be and do. As children master and internalize this system, they learn to discriminate and label themselves and others on the basis of sex, to recognize attributes, attitudes, and behaviors that are typical of or considered appropriate for each sex, and to learn how to do what is seen as appropriate and to avoid what is not. What's more, the gender category system is infused with affect to an extent few other knowledge bases can match, making it what is perhaps the most salient parameter of social categorization for the young child.

Our focus here is upon gender development from infants' earliest recognition of sex-related differences through the acquisition of gender knowledge and sex-typed behavior during early and middle childhood. Children's own construction of gender cannot be understood without considering the socialization pressures and environmental input to which they are subjected. The environmental influences with which we are most concerned are family, peers, and caregivers. Our convictions that these influences are often more subtle and more powerful than has been assumed, and the child's gender understanding more complex and less limited to concrete objects and events, have both shaped and been shaped by the work we will report here.

Although we recognize the impact that the media has on gender development in children, we do not address this topic in this chapter. It is not an area of research that we have ourselves worked in and is not, therefore, an area in which we have particular expertise. However, many excellent articles and reviews have been written on this topic and we would refer the interested reader, for example, to Beal (1994; see also Eccles, Freedman-Doan, Frome, Jacobs, & Yoon, chap. 11, this volume).

## HISTORICAL PERSPECTIVES

For many years concern with sex-role development was centered upon the parenting process and rooted in Freud's description of the family in which the mother rightly provided feminine virtues of love and nurturance and the father the masculine strengths of rules and discipline. Freud's view of sex-role development plays out as a function of the biological sex of the child rather than socialization differences. His description of children's adoption of the roles appropriate for their sex through identification with the same-sex parent and the resolution of the Oedipus and Electra complexes has permeated our thinking to an extent far greater than the amount of support for his theory, which was derived primarily from the memories of adults rather than the observation of children. However, psychoanalytic theory focused on early childhood as a critically important period and, more than any other, recognized children's enormous emotional investment in their identities and roles as boys or girls.

Freud's theory depended upon the importance of sexual motives and was devoted to the development of sexual rather than social gender roles. This emphasis was retained by many followers, including his daughter Anna, but was modified by others. Notably, Karen Horney and Clara Thompson stressed the importance of social factors, especially in the development of the female role that Freud had considered the natural outcome of reproductive physiology. Others working from a psychoanalytic perspective or attempting to integrate its insights with views from psychology and sociology emphasized social rather than (or in addition to) biological roles in family socialization. In particular, Parsons (1955) described Freudian views on development in terms of social roles, pointing out the reciprocity of roles within the family. In Parsons' model, children learn to be male or female by playing social roles that are complementary or reciprocal to the roles of other family members. In other words, roles such as husband, wife, mother, father, son, and daughter define what is expected of the individual who occupies the role in relation to the others who enact their own roles; gender development consists of learn-by-doing mastery of the prescribed roles.

Sears and his colleagues (Sears, Maccoby, & Levin, 1957; Sears, Rau, & Alpert, 1965) reworked Freud's ideas within the framework of learning theory. Sears' notions of parenting, in which the qualities of warmth and control were made explicit, were specifically sex typed, with mothers providing warmth and emotional support and fathers discipline and control. Children's sex-role identification within this supposedly optimal assignment of family roles was thought to take place through modeling and reinforcement. The social learning approach was updated as Mischel (1966) emphasized the importance of situational variables in determining the meaning of specific activities for each sex. Mischel held that the child's social learning history could be expected to affect cognition and influence attitudes as well as behavior. Thus, both internal and external processes were seen as contributing to sex-role acquisition.

The search for differences in the socialization of boys and girls was set back by the publication of Maccoby and Jacklin's (1974) review of work involving sex differences. Tallying the numbers of studies showing sex differences or failing to find them, Maccoby and Jacklin concluded that families show few disparities in the treatment of boys and girls. This conclusion was widely accepted and was reiterated in Lytton and Romney's (1991) meta-analysis, which again failed to find many socialization differences. Although the notion that parents do not treat boys and girls very differently flies in the face of common sense as well as a great deal of feminist writing, these convictions persisted and contributed to the decline in socialization research and corresponded to the rise in interest in children's self socialization via their own cognitive processes.

The "cognitive revolution" of the 1960s brought Piaget's theory of mental development to the attention of American psychology and education, shifting emphasis from parental socialization to children's own construction of sex roles. Kohlberg and Zigler (1967) presented a theory tying sex-role understanding to Piaget's stages of early cognitive development. The tide of research generated by this theory confirmed that, in general, children do not apprehend the physiological basis for identity as male or female, nor appreciate its stability or permanence, until their thinking has reached the level of concrete operations at 6 or 7 years of age. Yet despite these apparent deficiencies in understanding, sex-typed behavior is found before the age of 2, most children know their own sex and recognize that of others by age 3, and the stereotyping of behavior is not only evident but rampant between the ages of 3 and 6. As it became evident that the level of cognitive development needed to support behavioral sex typing was not as great as Kohlberg and Zigler proposed, interest in social and parental influences on sex typing was renewed. We then saw greater concern for what the young child knows about gender, a concern which sought to define the cognitive correlates of behavioral sex typing. Because gender is a categorical system, we also find a growing concern with categorical perception and knowledge from infancy on.

Rosch's (1977) work brought changes in thinking about category structure and formation. The traditional description of categories as possessing necessary and sufficient criteria for membership and classification as a skill lying well beyond the mental capabilities of the preschool child began to give way to the view that a category exists whenever two or more discriminably different entities are treated equivalently. According to Rosch (1977; Mervis & Rosch, 1981), categorization is a basic process whose workings need not be available to consciousness and whose development is complete by the end of the sensorimotor period—categories are the result of the cognitive system's ability to organize information into manageable chunks. Seen in this way, the categorization process is within infant capabilities, at least in rudimentary form, suggesting to us that the gender category system would have its roots in the infant's earliest encounters with members of the two sexes and a sex-typed world.

In the 1980s, the power of information-processing theories was brought to bear upon the study of gender acquisition. Bem (1981) and Martin and Halverson (1981) proposed theories in which children are seen as taking in and organizing environmental input schematically by chunking or categorizing information as best they can. In the ordinary course of events, this process leads to associative rather than piecemeal retention, so that related pieces of information will tend to be recognized and recalled together. The resulting networks of associations are the basis of schemas that enable the child to organize and interpret new information and to use this information to regulate behavior. Because children cannot avoid exposure to a sex-typed world, their schemas guide the adoption or avoidance of behaviors as well as knowledge of the action patterns necessary for behaving in ways their culture considers sex appropriate. Sex-role adoption is thought to be motivated as the self-concept is assimilated to the gender schema—the child claims and learns about what is seen as "for me," avoiding and therefore learning less about what is not.

Schema theory gave new impetus to examining the content of gender schemas and asking how bits and pieces of information become "gendered." Of the various capabilities that supply information to the developing schema, the ability to perceive and respond to information categorically is especially important—this is how children recognize what goes with what. Categories can be formed by detecting correlated attributes, that is, events or characteristics that tend to co-occur (Rosch, 1977), or on the basis of perceived similarity or equivalence classification (Bornstein, 1981). These processes seem quite straightforward as long as the gender schema accurately reflects what exists in the world. Tests of gender knowledge and attitudes generally look for and find just this kind of information; girls play with dolls, boys prefer trucks, women cook and sew, men drive trucks, and so on. Although such beliefs reflect correlations that are far from perfect, there is enough concrete evidence in everyday experience to support them. But, as Bem (1981) pointed out, much of the information in people's gender schemas has no necessary connection with either sex and may be quite abstract in nature.

The content of gender schemas as well as the process of their formation needs continued investigation. A major strength of schema theory as applied to gender development is its ability to incorporate all facets of experience into the child's ongoing construction of beliefs, attitudes, roles, and behaviors.

Our theoretical approach begins with Fagot's (1977, 1981) early studies conducted within the social learning theory framework, but it has always been a work in progress. As Fagot's work showed, reinforcement and modeling contribute importantly to gender development. The environment provides the raw material from which attitudes and knowledge of sex-typed behavior and its consequences are drawn, but this is not the whole story. The child's capabilities must also be taken into account, and we have stressed the need for accurate assessment of what children know and do. Thus, we have incorporated some aspects of cognitive theory into our approach and find that schema theory provides a workable conceptualization of developing gender knowledge. Bem's (1981) views concerning the inclusion of gratuitous information in gender schemas have prompted us to include the study of conceptual metaphor as described by Lakoff and Johnson (1980); we see the recognition of nonliteral similarities or correspondences among entities as the route by which much that has no necessary connection with gender becomes gendered. Above all, our work has been guided by the belief that effects produced in the laboratory must be verified by observation of their ability to affect what happens in the real world.

## CHILD CONTRIBUTIONS AND CAPACITIES

The differentiation process by which infants are exposed to gender information begins in the newborn period. There is no lack of information with which to identify or discriminate the sexes, but when do infants come to recognize men and women as categorically distinct? Discrimination alone is not enough. The discrimination must be categorical; that is, women in general must evoke responses from the infants that are different from the responses evoked by men.

A discrimination task using men's and women's voices provided the earliest evidence in which categorical perception concerning the sexes has been demonstrated: 2-month-old infants habituated to syllables spoken by a series of talkers of one sex can detect a change to the same syllables spoken by members of the opposite sex (Jusczyk, Pisoni, & Mullennix, 1992). By 7 months, infants can readily learn to respond differentially to male and female voices (Miller, Younger, & Morse, 1982). Miller (1983) further showed that, at 6 months, infants generalized habituation to the voices of either sex to novel members of the habituated gender category, indicating that they were truly responding to male and female voices categorically rather than simply discriminating any new voice. Miller also showed that infants by 7 months are sensitive to other differences between male and female voices in addition to differences in pitch. These differences remain to be identified but may include known differences in intonation patterns (Brend, 1971) and formant frequencies (Sachs, 1975).

Habituation and visual preference studies have shown that infants well under 1 year of age can discriminate individual male and female faces (Cornell, 1974; Fagan, 1976), and that the features that define faces as male or female contribute more to 5- and 6-month-olds' ability to recognize whether or not a face is familiar than does the lack of feature similarity (Fagan & Singer, 1979). The possibility of early categorical responding to female faces was shown by Cohen and Strauss (1979). Infants of 7 months, who had been habituated to a series of female faces in various orientations, generalized habituation to a familiar face in a new orientation and to an entirely new female face as well. However, only female faces were used; thus, these infants could have been habituated to faces in general rather than to female faces as a category distinct from male faces. The possibility of categorical perception of female faces was not ruled out; had a male face been presented, it might well have been perceived as novel. The need to clarify this issue prompted us to use faces of both sexes in a partial replication and extension of Cohen and Strauss' study.

We used Cohen and Strauss' (1979) infant-controlled procedure to habituate infants at 5, 7, 9, and 12 months of age to a series of faces of one sex (familiar category), then tested them with a new face from the familiar category and, as a contrast category, a face of the opposite sex (Leinbach & Fagot, 1993). The infants saw slides showing the heads and shoulders of men and women. Clothing, hairstyle, facial expression, and orientation were varied, as they would be in the real world. On the basis of these group data, we can say with certainty only that, by 9 months, infants demonstrated categorical perception of male and female faces. However, data for individual infants indicated categorical perception of male and female faces by some infants as young as 5 months.

Single-modality studies of voice and face perception indicate early recognition of certain male and female attributes; but in the real world, faces, voices, and tactile cues are all of a piece. Therefore, we would expect that infants would respond differentially to real men and women even more readily than to the disembodied stimuli used in empirical studies.

## The Child's Use of Environmental Cues

One of the more readily discriminable cues to the sex of persons one meets in ordinary circumstances in Western cultures is hair length, especially when coupled with clothing cues. We used the habituation procedure described earlier to investigate the relative importance of hair and clothing cues in 12-month-olds' categorical discrimination of male and female faces (Leinbach & Fagot, 1993). The same stimulus materials were changed so that clothing, hair length, or both were the same for each sex. Infants habituated readily, as expected, but the group criteria for dishabituation were not met. When only hair was altered, 40% dishabituated; and when both hair and clothing were altered, 25% dishabituated. We believe that infants at the end of their first year have clearly begun the process of categorizing people according to sex, but the step from recognizing or perceiving the sexes categorically to conscious awareness of this distinction is a large one, and moves the discussion from implicit to explicit learning.

Gender labeling, the application of gender labels to their referents, signals the point at which tacit knowledge is becoming available to consciousness and children can begin to tell us what they know (Leinbach & Fagot, 1986). Mastering the labels for boys and girls seldom occurs before age 2 but is found in most children by age 3. Children in families who espoused more traditional values in terms of sex typing learned gender labels earlier and continued to know more about sex typing at 4 years of age (Fagot & Leinbach, 1995).

There is no lack of information showing the accumulation of stereotypically gendered knowledge, attitudes, and behavior in the preschool child. But as Bem (1981) noted, gender cues abound in features and attributes that are figuratively or metaphorically related to masculinity or femininity. She mentioned particularly that angularity and roundedness are differentially associated with males and females. Although these characteristics may be grounded in the perception of physiological differences, they are extended to describe abstract forms as masculine or feminine. Fagot, Leinbach, Hort, and Strayer (1997) found that adults differentially ascribe such qualities as angular, rough, and angry to nonrepresentational paintings other adults had previously identified as masculine, and their opposites to paintings identified as feminine. Moreover, characters and objects children see as male or masculine are often described by adults as sharing attributes such as dangerous, angular, rough, and angry, whereas good, happy, soft, graceful, and clean are attributed to those seen as female or feminine (Hort, Leinbach, & Fagot, 1992).

Leinbach, Hort, and Fagot (1997) used animal figures, identical but for a single attribute, to investigate children's knowledge of both conventionally (size, hair length, color) and more metaphorically (texture, contour, emotion) sex-typed attributes. Children as young as 3 identified figures that were larger, shorter-haired, blue or gray as male and their opposites as female. Although some sex-typed attributes are undoubtedly specific to particular times and places, others found in other cultures may be universal (Galvan Millan, Fagot, & Leinbach, 1994). Because we consistently find that even 3-year-olds identify an angry-looking character as male (Leinbach, 1993), we are investigating the possibility that young children sex type other emotions as well.

# THE ROLE OF THE ENVIRONMENT

The raw materials of sex-role acquisition are the child's physical makeup and inherent capacity to learn and the information and consequences provided by the environment. What the child brings and what the environment provides cannot be independent of one another. They interact, and interact dynamically. That is, each affects the other so that as the child grows neither child nor environment remain static. We agree with current cognitive-developmental theory that children construct their own understanding of the world as they go along, but we insist that the building blocks used in this construction include the information and consequences socializing agents and cultural practices provide.

## The Family's Role in the Socialization of Gender

Do parents' beliefs about gender influence their treatment of infant boys and girls? Both cursory observation and the research literature indicate that differential treatment by sex begins at birth. The newborn nursery is likely to be decked out in pink if the infant is a girl, and gifts to the newcomer are carefully selected by sex. Girls receive pastel outfits, often beruffled, whereas boys are given tiny jeans and bolder colors. Shakin, Shakin, and Sternglanz (1985), observing families in a shopping mall, were able to determine the sex of nearly all infants by the clothing worn. Yet when parents were asked about their criteria in choosing clothing and accessories for their child, sex appropriateness was almost never mentioned. It is virtually automatic to present one's child, like oneself, as male or female, signaling to the world what the newcomer's gender role will be and how she or he is to be treated. Thus is the dance of gender begun. The mother, for example, while presenting herself as both mother and female, will improvise her role against the background of her own established gender identity while treating the infant as befits its sex. The infant is responded to as if he or she were responding in sex-typical ways. As male and female infants differ very little if at all with regard to sex-typical behaviors, it is likely that the imputing of gender roles has this "as if" quality—the role is imputed on the basis of the role the child will eventually fill.

Parents of newborns appear to perceive their sons and daughters differently. Rubin, Provenzano, and Luria (1974) found that new parents, especially fathers, tended to describe their infants sex-stereotypically. Even though the infants themselves did not differ in birth length, weight, or Apgar scores, fathers of girls were more likely to describe their babies as softer, finer-featured, more awkward, less attractive, weaker, and more delicate, whereas fathers who had boys rated them as firmer, larger-featured, better coordinated, more alert, stronger, and heavier. Mothers ratings of their infants, although in the same directions, were less extreme, but, interestingly, mothers rated sons as cuddlier, whereas fathers rated daughters as cuddlier. We know very little concerning how such attitudes affect actual behavior toward the infant, but some findings suggest a predictive relationship. For example, Thoman, Leiderman, and Olson (1972) found that, while still in the hospital, mothers of sons spent more time breastfeeding whereas mothers of daughters spent more time talking to their babies. In general, mothers talk more to their daughters and imitate the infant's vocalizations, whereas they provide more physical (tactile and visual) stimulation to sons (Lewis, 1974). Especially with firstborns, fathers stimulate and talk more to sons and, as the children get older, interact in a playfully rough manner (Lamb, 1978). Both parents appear to be interacting with their babies on the basis of anticipated or imputed sex differences, because such differences are not readily apparent in the behavior and appearance of young infants.

The traditional view of the family in which the mother provides warmth and caregiving and the father provides discipline and support does not appear to describe parenting today (Parsons, 1955). Even within traditional two-parent families where mothers spend more time with their children than fathers, the roles of present-day mothers and fathers appear to have evolved somewhat differently. Mothers do most of the routine caregiving, but the fathers' role is not that of the abstract disciplinarian; instead, the father appears to have taken over many of the qualities of playmate. Lamb (1977, 1981) found that when fathers spent time with toddler-aged children it was play time. When the child needed some type of care the child was returned to the mother.

Block (1976) suggested that fathers are more important to the gender-role development of children than mothers and that fathers interact with boys and girls in very different ways, whereas mothers react to boys and girls in similar ways. She based this suggestion in part upon the *reciprocal role theory* of M. M. Johnson (1963, 1975), which predicts that the father's behavior promotes typically gender-typed behavior in both boys and girls. Both mothers and fathers are expected to encourage traditional gender typing, but fathers make greater distinctions between sons and daughters. Boys are sought out by fathers and encouraged to take on an instrumental, independent style of behavior, whereas girls are encouraged to seek help and to be more dependent. Though this viewpoint has received widespread acceptance in the psychological and lay literature, it has little empirical support. Much of our information concerning the role of fathers has come from mothers. What we know directly from fathers is biased toward well-educated fathers and concerns interactions in infancy and early childhood.

In a summary article concerning differential socialization, Siegel (1987) concluded that some support exists for the uniqueness of the father's role; however, the effects were surprisingly small and sometimes contradictory. With 1- and 2-year-old children, Weinraub and Frankel (1977) reported fathers talking more to sons, whereas Stoneman and Brody (1981) reported fathers talking more to daughters when mothers were present. Fathers may be more variable than mothers in responses to their children; however, it is equally likely that method, measurement, and setting differences have also contributed to the findings. Thus, researchers are more likely to find that fathers differ in their responses to boys and girls, but this may be a statistical artifact of greater variability rather than a finding based on a consistent paternal mode of responding. In a meta-analysis in which mother–child versus father–child dyads were examined, Collins and Russell (1991) reported that individual differences among parents outweighed the role differences between mothers and fathers.

Although mothers and fathers within individual families vary in their childrearing styles, mothers as a group spend far more time with their children and do most of the caregiving (Fagot & Leinbach, 1995; Pederson, 1980). Patterson, Reid, and Dishion (1992) found that, in most studies, mother variables tend to be stronger predictors of child outcome than father variables even in two-parent families (i.e., the behavior of the mothers differentiated children, but the behavior of the fathers did not). In addition, if the family breaks up, mothers are far more likely to rear children as single parents.

In a study that controlled for income level, Leve and Fagot (1997) found that single mothers and fathers had less traditional gender-role attitudes than mothers and fathers in two-parent families, but that children in single-parent families did not differ in gender-role preference or knowledge from children in two-parent families. Leve and Fagot also found that mothers and fathers reported more negative behavior from opposite-sex children than from same-sex children; boys in single-mother families and girls in single-father families may appear to have more problems because there is no balancing report from a same-sex parent. Interestingly enough, single parents report more positive behavior from their children than do parents in two-parent families, and they tend to use more problem-solving techniques with their children; in general, however, fathers with sons use fewer problem-solving techniques than fathers with daughters or mothers with either sex.

Stevenson and Black (1988) conducted a meta-analysis on the sex-role development of children in studies comparing father-absent and father-present families. The effects were found primarily for boys and were not easy to interpret. Preschool boys from father-absent families were less sex-stereotyped in their choice of toys and activities; however, older boys from father-absent families were more sex-stereotyped, particularly in the area of aggression. The researchers found that effect size covaried with age of child, socioeconomic status of the family, reason for father absence, and race. The study is perhaps best summarized by the authors: "Overall, the differences between father absent and father present samples were not large" (p. 805). They also make the point that father-absent families are a very heterogeneous group, as many of the children in the father-absent group had some access to their fathers and often spent a considerable amount of time with them.

There is still considerable controversy over the strength of parental differences in the socialization of the sexes. Maccoby and Jacklin (1974) concluded that parental differences, outside of socialization of specific behaviors with toys and domestic activities, were relatively minimal. Lytton and Romney (1991) examined studies of parent treatment of boys and girls and found that the only consistent sex-differentiated parental reaction was in encouragement of sex-typed behaviors. The results of the Maccoby and Jacklin study as well as the Lytton and Romney meta-analysis should convince us that to look for sex-differentiated socialization in all parent reactions will not help us understand sex-role development or differences in boys and girls.

The Lytton and Romney (1991) analysis also strongly suggests that age is a crucial variable (effect sizes were greater for younger children). Confirming the effect of age of child, Fagot and Hagan (1991) found that parents observed in the home showed considerable differences in response to 12- and 18-month-old boys and girls engaged in sex-typical activities, whereas there were few differences in parents' reactions to 5-year-old boys and girls. There is some indication that parents become more differentiated in their reactions to boys and girls at adolescence and are more likely to react to sex-typed activities (Gjerde, 1986). Reviewing the research on mother–child and father–child relationships with children in middle childhood and early adolescence, Collins and Russell (1991) reported differences for both mothers and fathers in relationships with sons and daughters. However, what differences were found were more likely to be in respect to attitudes about the differences between boys and girls than in behavior toward boys and girls. At some points in the child's development the parents may be very concerned about conformity to cultural standards of sex typing; but once such conformity is obtained, parents may behave more similarly to boys and girls.

The questions of socialization of sex differences and the differential roles of mothers and fathers are still open. When one does broadscale meta-analyses of research, effect sizes appear relatively small (Lytton & Romney, 1991; Siegel, 1987; Stevenson & Black, 1988); however, one thing that meta-analyses do make clear is that one must attend to age differences, to differences in setting, and to measurement variables. Studies using natural settings where the participants are not constrained by the experimenter have been found to have larger effect sizes, studies with young children have larger effect sizes than those with older children, and studies rated of higher quality have larger effect sizes. When studies look at more molar qualities of families, such as who does the caretaking and who takes the children if the family splits up, it is clear that mothers are more involved in child care than fathers. However, explaining gender differences only as a function of parental socialization would be foolish. What parents do is provide information about the importance of gender, both in terms of their reactions to the child and in terms of family organization. That information, along with other sources of information, will be used to help the child construct categories, labels, scripts, and theories about gender. It is also important to remember that parents are not the only source of information for even very young children.

## Gender Socialization in the Schools

Are boys and girls treated differently in schools? There are two popular positions on this issue. The first is that schools femininize boys. The second is that schools ignore girls with the consequence that girls lose interest and suffer in self-esteem. The same data are being used to support both positions in early childhood.

Do teachers favor boys or do they favor girls? The answer, as in most things in psychology, is complicated. Do boys and girls receive different treatment from teachers? Yes. Is this because teachers favor one or another? Probably not. Rather it seems to be a complicated pattern of teacher expectations and children's preferences; even preschool teachers interact more with children they see behaving in a pupil-like role (Lee & Kedar-Voivodas, 1977).

Fagot and Patterson (1969) observed two preschool classrooms and found that teachers did give boys and girls different amounts of feedback. Teachers were more likely to react to children when they were engaged in art play and in table play. As these were both activities preferred by girls, the consequence was that girls received more positive feedback from the teachers. Teachers rarely joined boys in play with transportation toys, which entailed getting down on the floor and crawling on hands and knees, nor did they join in the active motor play that boys preferred when outside. This study has often been cited as evidence that teachers femininized boys. However, Fagot and Patterson examined whether boys were influenced to change their behaviors in the direction of teacher reinforcement over the course of a year. The answer was decidedly no. Boys as a group showed a greater preference for the male-preferred behaviors by the end of the preschool year even though they were not reinforced for this behavior by teachers' attention. Teachers engage children when they are in a pupil-like role and let them play when they are engaged in more playlike behaviors.

Serbin, O'Leary, Kent, and Tonick (1973) were specifically interested in teacher responses to preacademic and problem behaviors in boys and girls. They confirmed that overall, teachers interacted more with girls than boys; however, they had carefully laid out the room so that they could measure the distance that children stayed from teachers. Boys tended to stay at greater distances from the teacher, but boys in close proximity to the teacher actually received more attention than did girls at equal distance. Teachers also spent considerably more time in managing boys' problem behaviors. Boys and girls did receive differing amounts of teacher interaction, but it was in response to differences in children's behavior. Interestingly, this study is used to support both the argument that boys are femininized by teachers due to the emphasis on problem behavior management and the argument that girls are not given appropriate treatment in classrooms due to the fact that boys get more attention from the teacher for engaging in preacademic behaviors. That girls get more reinforcement for these same preacademic behaviors because they engage in them more often is ignored.

Looking at differences in male and female teachers' reinforcement patterns, Fagot (1981) observed a group of experienced and inexperienced male and female teachers. Girls were again clustering around the teacher whereas boys played at the edges of classrooms, whether the teacher was male or female. However, experienced teachers, whether male or female, engaged in the same patterns of behavior found in the Fagot and Patterson (1969) study. They interacted more with children who were engaged in preacademic or pupil-like behavior. Because girls preferred these activities, experienced teachers interacted with girls more than boys. About the only difference shown by these teachers was that experienced male teachers engaged in a bit more large-motor activity. Both male and female inexperienced teachers tended to join ongoing activities. Therefore, they were more equal in their interaction with boys and girls. They did not attempt to shape the children's behavior to more school-appropriate activities nor to provide guidance but seemed to function more as large playmates for the children.

Carpenter and Huston-Stein (1980) examined children's preference for structured versus unstructured activities. In structured activities the teachers provided rules, whereas unstructured activities were more free-form. Children of either sex who preferred highly structured activities were more compliant and used toys in less novel ways. In contrast, children who preferred less structure tended to interact more with peers. Because more boys than girls took part in the less structured activities, boys were more likely to interact with male peers and were less likely to encounter teachers. Carpenter (1983) suggested that highly structured activities contribute to the learning of rules and the accommodation of the child to the environment, whereas less structured activities may force children to adapt in new ways to the environment. It should be noted that children who prefer greater structure are learning the rules of schooling, and this preference for higher structure may be one reason that girls outperform boys in the early school years. Additionally, high structure has been found to inhibit both aggression and rough-and-tumble play. Although this may be an indication that children— boys in particular—are learning self-control, it does not appear to generalize across situations. In unstructured situations these same children remain aggressive and boisterous (Smith & Connolly, 1980).

Although the preschool literature is fairly clear that teacher behavior is highly contingent upon children's behavioral preferences, with very young children the stereotypes of day-care providers may influence their expectations of what girls and boys are like. Fagot, Hagan, Leinbach, and Kronsberg (1985) observed children in infant classrooms looking at two sets of behaviors: assertiveness, which was defined as a physical attempt to get one's way; and communication attempts with adults, which included gestures, babbling, words, and screams. The children did not differ in these two sets of behaviors, which are highly sex typed in preschool-age children. However, teacher responses to these behaviors in the infant classroom were highly contingent upon the sex of the child. The teachers reacted quickly to girls' most tentative attempts to communicate and their interactions with girls were more positive and lasted longer than those with boys. Boys' communicative attempts had to be demanding at much higher levels to receive attention. If the child was a boy, his assertive behaviors were acted upon almost immediately. The attention was very positive in tone; usually the boy was picked up and moved to a different setting or given a new toy and distracted.

We went back to these same children a year later when they were with different teachers in a much larger peer group setting and found a very different set of circumstances. Now we saw very large sex differences in the children's behavior. Boys were more assertive, using more physical means to assert themselves, and girls engaged in far more communication with the teacher. With these older children the teachers no longer respond in sex-differentiated ways; that is, if a girl aggressed she got the same response as the boy, and if a boy attempted to communicate with the teacher he was responded to in the same fashion as girls. What had happened? Infants' behavior can be very unclear, and in ambiguous situations we tend to fall back on stereotypical information and act upon those stereotypes. We believe that the teachers were using their own expectations of children's behavior in situations that were very ambiguous.

## Gender Socialization by Peers

Many modern parents who wish their children to be free of gender constraints bemoan the effect of peer groups on children's behavior. Children who were perfectly willing to try out a broad range of behaviors, wear gender-neutral clothing, and play with children of both sexes suddenly decide that they must only play with certain toys, wear certain clothes, and play with same-sex peers. Is this due to the tyranny of the peer group, or is this development the result of a more complicated process?

By the time they are 3 years old, boys and girls around the world participate in different activities, show different behavioral styles, play more with same-sex peers, and avoid opposite-sex peers (Maccoby, 1988; Whiting & Edwards, 1988). However, the route by which this gender streaming occurs differs by culture. There are some cultures in which young boys and girls are separated by the end of infancy and gender segregation is imposed from the outside. In these cultures even toddler-age children of different sexes are never together (Whiting & Edwards, 1988). Within other cultures young children are not placed together in groups but stay within the confines of their family so that their peers include a variety of siblings of different ages; these young children often play quite happily with their mixed-age and mixed-sex siblings (Rogoff, 1990). It is only when social roles begin to take one sex or another out of the home, or the children begin school, that the sexes separate in terms of both work roles and play activities. The description of male and female differences in play behavior and peer friendships presented here parallel what we find in young children in cultures where boys and girls spend time together in groups from young ages. In these cases gender segregation takes place from within the peer group rather than being imposed from the outside.

In one of the first studies to use a microsocial coding system, Fagot and Patterson (1969) observed children over the period of a year in ongoing nursery school classes. Children's activities were coded, as well as who they were interacting with (a boy, a girl, a mixed group of children, or one of the teachers) and that person's reaction to them. Even in the beginning of the nursery school year these 3-year-olds had distinct preferences for sex-stereotyped play. Girls appeared to avoid activities most preferred by boys, and boys avoided activities preferred by girls. However, not all play was stereotyped. The children seemed to avoid the other sex even when engaged in play that both sexes enjoyed, such as digging in the sand, riding tricycles, or playing with puzzles. In fact, both sexes engaged in these behaviors an equal amount of time, but they engaged in them mostly with children of the same sex. There was very little mixed-sex play in these nursery schools, and mixed-sex play almost always occurred when teachers led a group activity such as storytelling or dramatic play.

Using the same coding system as in the Fagot and Patterson (1969) study, Fagot (1977) examined a large number of children in several preschool classes and looked at what happened to boys and girls who engaged in activities preferred by the other sex. Girls who preferred boys' activities appeared to fare quite well. They were usually allowed into boys groups, and though they received slightly less positive feedback, it appeared that they went back and forth from girl to boy groups without difficulty. Boys who preferred girls activities had a very different experience. Although girls would sometimes allow them to enter their groups, it was often in very constrained roles, and they received much more negative feedback about the way they were playing. It was the reactions from other boys, however, that really set them apart. Boys would taunt and tease them when they were engaged in play in girls' activities and groups, and even when they tried to join boys' groups they were rejected, given far more criticism, and received more physical threats. Such negative reactions continued throughout the nursery school years even though many of the boys had very quickly stopped trying to play with girls' activities or groups. The types of negative feedback these boys received was of a different quality from that received by other boys and included gender derogatory terms such as *sissy boy*, *baby boy*, and so forth, which were almost never applied to other children.

Fagot (1985a) examined the reinforcement patterns of boys, girls, and teachers to sex-typed behaviors of 3- and 4-year-old boys and girls. Boys gave most positive feedback to other boys engaged in male type activities, whereas girls simply gave most positive feedback to other girls. Boys gave negative feedback to other boys playing with girls' toys or to boys playing with girls. Girls did not vary their negative feedback by sex or toy choice. More importantly, boys ignored both the positive and negative feedback from girls and teachers. Their behavior changed only in response to boys' feedback. Girls changed their behavior in response to both teachers' and other girls' feedback. This study shows the processes by which gender segregation is maintained but not much about how it is begun, as children were already engaging in same-sex play.

***Why Gender Segregation?*** Observational studies consistently find that boys and girls play in segregated groups even at very young ages. Why? Goodenough (1934) speculated that children play with members of the same sex because they have different play interests and different behavioral styles. La Freniere, Strayer, and Gauthier (1984) developed this theory, calling it the *behavioral compatibility hypothesis.* Boys and girls do show different toy and activity preferences from a very early age, probably around 2 years (O'Brien & Huston, 1985; Trautner, 1992). However, it is sometimes overstated that boys play with boy toys and girls with girl toys. Research has shown that about 20% of boys' and girls' time is spent in same-sex toy play and 5% in opposite-sex toy play, with the rest of their time spent in neutral activities (Fagot, 1996; Fagot & Patterson, 1969). Fagot and Patterson found very little mixed-group play, except when the teacher conducted group activities. In situations where no teacher was involved, Fagot found children played with same-sex peers more than 70% of the time. This is consistent with the observational studies of Thorne (1993), who found that children often separated themselves by sex unless teachers imposed mixed-sex groupings.

A related explanation has been put forward by ethologists looking at activity levels in both human and nonhuman primates. Although there do appear to be differences in activity level in males and females after the age of 2 when they are observed in groups, such differences are difficult to find outside of peer playgroups (Eaton & Keats, 1982). The activity level difference noted in some studies may be an outcome of gender segregation rather than a trait inherent in the child as a function of gender. There is more support for a difference in preferences for rough-and-tumble play. Both in nonhuman primates and human children, males play at rough-and-tumble games at much higher rates (Blurton Jones, 1967). However, monkeys spend about 80% of their play time in rough-and-tumble play, whereas such play in human children rarely exceeds 10% of total play. Therefore, it is difficult to see how the girls' wish to avoid rough-and-tumble play would account for the avoidance of play with boys in even neutral activities that are organized around sedentary play themes.

Although the explanations based upon preference for activities, avoidance of rough-and-tumble play, or aggression have some merit—for gender segregation is undoubtedly multiply determined—it is likely that the child's developing gender schema influences the development of same-sex peer groups. In our work we have asked how the child's attempt to understand the nature of gender is interrelated with the environmental messages concerning the importance of gender. It is not that one causes the other but that, as the mind develops, children make use of cues to accelerate the acceptance of gender rules.

For the peer group, one of these gender rules is that boys play with boys and girls with girls. In a set of studies designed to understand the relation of the child's gender knowledge to peer play, we observed children in different peer play groups from 12 months to almost 4 years of age. Fagot (1985b) began this set of studies by examining the relation between peer acceptance and 3- and 4-year-old children's knowledge of gender identity and constancy (Slaby & Frey, 1975). Children followed the predicted sequence, but their levels of gender constancy were not related to other types of gender behaviors such as toy preference or play with same-sex peers. Because both play preferences and peer choices are already well established by 36 months, we designed a second study using a different type of task with 2-year-old children. The children were given a modified version of Thompson's (1975) gender labeling task, which simply consisted of pairs of opposite-sex child and adult faces that the child was asked to identify using various gender labels. In this study, children who could label genders correctly were more likely to play with same-sex toys and same-sex peers. However, there is a problem with the Thompson task. There are only a few stimuli that contain pictures of boys and girls, and there are many questions dealing with adult relationships (e.g., aunts and uncles); it was unclear whether labels for adults and children had a differential effect. Therefore, Leinbach (Leinbach & Fagot, 1986) developed a gender labeling task consisting of 12 paired pictures of adults and 12 paired pictures of children, which allowed us to distinguish between children with the ability to correctly label the gender of adults only and those who could label the genders of both adults and children. This provided a well-designed task to study the effect of children's knowledge on peer interactions.

In the first study using our gender labeling task to study peer socialization, we used a cross-sectional sample of children, half of whom had passed the gender labeling task and half of whom had not (Fagot, Leinbach, & Hagan, 1986). The children were observed in ongoing playgroups for 2 weeks after they had been given the gender labeling task. We examined three different types of behavior in relation to performance on the gender labeling task: gender-typed toy choices, same-sex peer choice, and aggressive behaviors. By 24 months, toddlers use labels for adults, but no aspects of sex typing were predicted by the use of labels for adults. We did find that the children who showed knowledge concerning the boy–girl labels were more likely to play with same-sex peers, but differences in toy choice were already well established before labeling was mastered. Finally, a rather unexpected finding was that girls who passed the boy–girl gender labeling task showed much less aggression than those who failed the task. For boys there was no effect on aggressive behavior of learning gender labels.

In the next study a group of children were followed longitudinally from the time they were 18 months until after they passed the child labeling task (Fagot, 1990). Our first goal was to determine if children who were early versus late labelers differed in their behaviors prior to labeling. Because we expected age-related changes we divided the children into two groups, those who passed gender labels by 28 months and those who passed later than that. The behavior of children who would become early versus late labelers was very similar. Neither boys nor girls nor early versus late labelers showed a significant preference for playing within same-sex groups. There was also evidence for the beginnings of preferences for early sex-typed toy play prior to the development of such labels.

The second goal concerned changes in children's behavior in the play groups as a function of change in labeling status. We examined same-sex toy play, other-sex toy play, play with same-sex peers, and level of aggression. The results in general replicated our previous study (Fagot, Leinbach, & Hagan, 1986). Toy play doesn't appear to be guided by the child's understanding gender labeling. There is undoubtedly so much available information from the environment about toys that children learn which toys are appropriate for them through association and reinforcement. Children played more with same-sex peers after they learned labels. It appears that understanding that boys and girls carry different labels is related to one's choice to play with same-sex peers. There was a sex-of-child by labeling effect for aggression, which replicated our cross-sectional results. Girls who label showed a significant drop in aggression in comparison to their aggression level prior to labeling. There was no such effect for boys. For girls, the avoidance of aggression appears strongly tied to the development of gender labeling.

Why does gender segregation appear uniformly in schools even when teachers and parents neither require it nor even deliberately support it? Both the way the environment reacts to children engaged in play with the other sex and the child's own attempt to construct an understanding about gender influence gender segregation. Environmental information can be and is learned through modeling and reinforcement. However, for gender segregation, any explanation based upon behavioral compatibility, avoidance of aggression or rough-and-tumble play, or matching of activity levels seems doomed. Certainly the findings from our previous studies (Fagot, 1977,

1989) suggest that boys who attempt to play with opposite-sex toys receive very negative peer reactions, but the tone of the emotional reactions suggests that something more than simple behavioral preferences must be involved. If one believes in a learning approach then one must accept that the most common behaviors should be the ones most commonly learned. One should see a trend toward neutral activities, toward more rather than less other-sex play, and avoidance of aggression by both sexes as the consequences are equally negative for both. This is not at all what happens, and it does seem necessary to bring in some cognitive or emotional evaluation by the child of the meaning of other-sex play and of aggression. The child's understanding that there are some children like him or her and some not is important for the child's own self-definition and motivates the adoption of sex-typed behaviors and gender segregation.

***Why Be Concerned About Gender Segregation?***   The major reason for concern about gender segregation at least within westernized societies is the recognition that to succeed in the complicated societies we have today individuals need a broad range of skills and they need to work effectively with both men and woman. The concern is that children who grow up in traditional stereotyped environments will lack the necessary skills for success. It should be noted that this is a concern among the educated middle class and that within other spheres of American society it is felt that differential socialization is necessary for preparing their children for more traditional and limited roles. There are certainly movements toward more sex-typed schools or more sex-typed schooling provided at home. However, the large majority of parents appear to give their children the broadest possible experiences to prepare them for tomorrow's world.

The focus of concerns about gender segregation and the narrowing of children's behavioral repertoire has been on implications for cognitive development. There is a good deal of evidence that the predominately male and predominately female peer groups behave in different ways. According to Block (1983), the activities boys engage in require them to change their own thinking. She suggested that boys' toys and activities force them to solve problems in new and creative ways. Girls' toys and activities on the other hand allow them to engage in activities that more clearly imitate domestic life and allow them to rehearse cultural roles. Block suggested that these difference in early play styles lead to differences in intellectual and emotional development. Girls utilize existing cognitive and social structures that are modified by incremental steps. The very toys that boys and girls use in peer groups increase the differences in the ways that they approach problems. Block was concerned that gender segregation that leads to a restricted range of activities might also lead to problems in cognitive development. The question, which remains unanswered, is whether there is any evidence to determine if restricted activity and playmate experience impairs cognitive performance.

***Attempts to Change Gender Segregation.*** If gender segregation were strictly a matter of behavioral compatibilities or learned avoidances, then we should be able to reshape children's behavior within groups in such a way that there would be more similarity in play styles and play with the other sex at more equal rates. There have been a number of attempts to modify gender-typed behavior within preschool classrooms. One of the earliest was Serbin, Tonick, and Sternglanz (1977), who instructed teachers in reinforcing cross-sex play behavior. They did not try to change the activities of the children but simply had the teacher give a positive comment to situations in which boys and girls played together. Children responded to this shaping procedure, and the percentage of cross-sex play increased dramatically. However, once the reinforcement stopped the cross-sex play immediately went back to previous levels. There was clearly no changing of the child's underlying schema, and once the external reinforcement stopped, the child's understanding of appropriate behavior was reinstated.

Feldbaum, Christenson, and O'Neal (1980) attempted to use teachers to introduce new children into play groups. Their attempts were successful with girls if they were introduced into groups of other girls, but not if they were introduced to boys' groups. For boys the introduction by the teacher did not appear to help boys enter even boys' groups. The length of time and difficulty of entry for boys did not appear to be affected by teacher behaviors, although it was for girls. This is reminiscent of Fagot's (1985a) finding that boys appeared to ignore the positive and negative reactions of teachers and only changed their behavior as a result of other boys' behavior. The attempts to change the pattern of gender segregation have not been very successful.

# NEW DIRECTIONS

Future work on the social psychology of gender would do well to consider transition points in developmental processes; there is little reason to assume that gender development and environmental input are related in monotonic fashion. Our work indicates that parental and other influences impact children differently at different stages. For example, parents and teachers show greater attention to gender specific behavior at about the time Piaget would have children moving from the sensorimotor to the preoperational developmental stage. Studies that fail to find differences in parents' and teachers' socialization efforts may simply be looking at children at the wrong times. We need also to study children more often in settings other than schools—otherwise we risk mistaking findings from one setting as the norm for all. With regard to gender segregation, for example, cross-sex play and friendship are more common in family and neighborhood settings than in the world of school and playground. We should look around.

We would particularly like to see the scope of schema theory enlarged to encompass affective as well as cognitive components. One cannot be around young children without observing their very great emotional investment in their identity as boys or girls.

Finally, greater interdisciplinary awareness is called for. As psychologists we tend to look for cause and effect relations at the level of the individual, whereas we need to pay more attention to the dynamics of group behavior. This is particularly evident in the study of gender segregation—a phenomenon for which psychological explanations are woefully inadequate. Yet if we look at the social psychology and social cognition literature on group behavior and stereotyping, it is not difficult to see gender segregation as confirmation of the in-group/out-group hypothesis (Turner, 1985), which holds that groups become polarized as part of a general tendency to identify with one's own group and distinguish oneself from others, that is, the out-group.

# REFERENCES

Beal, C. R. (1994). *Boys and girls: The development of gender roles.* New York: McGraw-Hill.

Bem, S. L. (1981). Gender schema theory: A cognitive account of sex typing. *Psychological Review, 88,* 354–364.

Block, J. H. (1976). Issues, problems, and pitfalls in assessing sex differences: A critical review of "The psychology of sex differences." *Merrill-Palmer Quarterly, 22,* 283–308.

Block, J. H. (1983). Differential premises arising from differential socialization of the sexes: Some conjectures. *Child Development, 54,* 1335–1354.

Blurton Jones, N. G. (1967). An ethological study of some aspects of social behaviour of children in nursery school. In D. Morris (Ed.), *Primate ethology* (pp. 347–368). London: Weidenfeld and Nicolson.

Bornstein, M. H. (1981). Two kinds of perceptual organization near the beginning of life. In W. A. Collins (Ed.), *Aspects of the development of competence: The Minnesota symposia on child psychology* (Vol. 14, pp. 39–91). Hillsdale, NJ: Lawrence Erlbaum Associates.

Brend, R. M. (1971). Male–female intonation patterns in American English. *Proceedings of the Seventh International Congress of Phonetic Sciences* (pp. 866–869). The Hague, Netherlands: Mouton.

Carpenter, C. J. (1983). Activity structure and play: Implications for socialization. In M. B. Liss (Ed.), *Social and cognitive skills: Sex roles and children's play* (pp. 117–145). New York: Academic Press.

Carpenter, C. J., & Huston-Stein, A. (1980). Activity structure and sex-typed behavior in preschool children. *Child Development, 51,* 862–872.

Cohen, L. B., & Strauss, M. S. (1979). Concept acquisition in the human infant. *Child Development, 50,* 419–424.

Collins, W. A., & Russell, G. (1991). Mother–child and father–child relationships in middle childhood and adolescence. *Developmental Review, 11*, 99–136.

Cornell, E. (1974). Infants' discriminations of photographs following redundant presentations. *Journal of Experimental Child Psychology, 18*, 98–106.

Eaton, W. O., & Keats, J. G. (1982). Peer presence, stress, and sex differences in the motor activity levels of preschoolers. *Developmental Psychology, 18*, 534–540.

Fagan, J. F. (1976). Infants' recognition of invariant features of faces. *Child Development, 47*, 627–638.

Fagan, J. F., & Singer, L. T. (1979). The role of simple feature differences in infant recognition of faces. *Infant Behavior and Development, 2*, 39–46.

Fagot, B. I. (1977). Consequences of moderate cross-gender behavior in preschool children. *Child Development, 48*, 902–907.

Fagot, B. I. (1981). Male and female teachers: Do they treat boys and girls differently? *Sex Roles, 7*, 263–271.

Fagot, B. I. (1985a). Beyond the reinforcement principle: Another step toward understanding sex role development. *Developmental Psychology, 21*, 1097–1104.

Fagot, B. I. (1985b). Changes in thinking about early sex role development. *Developmental Review, 5*, 83–98.

Fagot, B. I. (1989). Cross-gender behavior and its consequences for boys. *Italian Journal of Clinical and Cultural Psychology, 1*, 79–84.

Fagot, B. I. (1990). A longitudinal study of gender segregation: Infancy to preschool. In F. Strayer (Chair), *Determinants of gender differences in peer relations*. Symposium presented at the International Conference on Infant Studies, Montreal, Quebec, Canada.

Fagot, B. I. (1996, August). *Boys and girls interpret negative interactions with peers differently*. Poster presented at the International Society for the Study of Behavior Disorders, Quebec City, Quebec, Canada.

Fagot, B. I., & Hagan, R. (1991). Observations of parent reactions to sex-stereotyped behaviors: Age and sex effects. *Child Development, 62*, 617–628.

Fagot, B. I., Hagan, R., Leinbach, M. D., & Kronsberg, S. (1985). Differential reactions to assertive and communicative acts of toddler boys and girls. *Child Development, 56*, 1499–1505.

Fagot, B. I., & Leinbach, M. D. (1995). Gender knowledge in egalitarian and traditional families. *Sex Roles, 32*, 513–526.

Fagot, B. I., Leinbach, M. D., & Hagan, R. (1986). Gender labeling and the adoption of sex-typed behaviors. *Developmental Psychology, 22*, 440–443.

Fagot, B. I., Leinbach, M. D., Hort, B. E., & Strayer, J. (1997). Qualities underlying the definitions of gender. *Sex Roles, 37*, 1–18.

Fagot, B. I., & Patterson, G. R. (1969). An in vivo analysis of reinforcing contingencies for sex-role behaviors in the preschool child. *Developmental Psychology, 1*, 563–568.

Feldbaum, C. L., Christenson, T. E., & O'Neal, E. C. (1980). An observational study of the assimilation of the newcomer to the preschool. *Child Development, 51*, 497–507.

Galvan Millan, M. E., Fagot, B I., & Leinbach, M. D. (1994, June). *Understanding gender attributes in Mexico and the United States*. Presented at the 13th Biennial Meetings of the International Society for the Study of Behavioral Development, The Netherlands.

Gjerde, P. F. (1986). The interpersonal structure of family interaction settings: Parent–adolescent relations in dyads and triads. *Developmental Psychology, 22*, 297–304.

Goodenough, F. (1934). *Developmental psychology: An introduction to the study of human behavior*. New York: Appleton-Century.

Hort, B. E., Leinbach, M. D., & Fagot, B. I. (1992, March). *An investigation of the conceptual parameters underlying the metaphorical constructs of gender*. Presented at the Southwest Conference for Research on Human Development, Tempe, AZ.

Johnson, M. M. (1963). Sex role learning in the nuclear family. *Child Development*, *34*, 315–333.

Johnson, M. M. (1975). Fathers, mothers, and sex typing. *Sociological Inquiry*, *45*, 15–26.

Jusczyk, P. W., Pisoni, D. B., & Mullennix, J. (1992). Some consequences of stimulus variability on speech processing by 2-month-old infants. *Cognition*, *43*, 253–291.

Kohlberg, L., & Zigler, E. (1967). The impact of cognitive maturity on the development of sex-role attitudes in the years 4 to 8. *Genetic Psychology Monographs*, *75*, 89–165.

La Freniere, P., Strayer, F. F., & Gauthier, R. (1984). The emergence of same-sex affiliative preferences among preschool peers: A developmental/ethological perspective. *Child Development*, *55*, 1958–1965.

Lakoff, G., & Johnson, M. (1980). The metaphorical structure of the human conceptual system. *Cognitive Science*, *4*, 195–208.

Lamb, M. E. (1977). Father–infant and mother–infant interaction in the first year of life. *Child Development*, *48*, 167–181.

Lamb, M. E. (Ed.). (1978). *The role of the father in child development*. New York: Wiley.

Lamb, M. E. (1981). The development of father–infant relationships. In M. E. Lamb (Ed.), *The role of the father in child development* (Rev. ed., pp. 459–488). New York: Wiley.

Lee, P. C., & Kedar-Voivodas, G. (1977). Sex role and pupil role in early childhood education. In L. Katz (Ed.), *Current topics in early childhood education* (Vol. 1, pp. 105–118). Norwood, NJ: Ablex.

Leinbach, M. D. (1993). *Which one is the daddy? Children's use of conventionally and metaphorically gendered attributes to assign gender to animal figures*. Presented at the Biennial Meeting of the Society for Research in Child Development, New Orleans, LA.

Leinbach, M. D., & Fagot, B. I. (1986). Acquisition of gender labels: A test for toddlers. *Sex Roles*, *15*, 655–666.

Leinbach, M. D., & Fagot, B. I. (1993). Categorical habituation to male and female faces: Gender schematic processing in infancy. *Infant Behavior and Development*, *16*, 317–332.

Leinbach, M. D., Hort, B. E., & Fagot, B. I. (1997). Bears are for boys: Metaphorical associations in young children's gender stereotypes. *Cognitive Development*, *12*, 107–130.

Leve, L. D., & Fagot, B. I. (1997). Gender-role socialization and discipline processes in one- and two-parent families. *Sex Roles*, *36*, 1–21.

Lewis, M. (1974). State as an infant–environment interaction: An analysis of mother–infant interaction as a function of sex. *Merrill-Palmer Quarterly*, *20*, 195–204.

Lytton, H., & Romney, D. M. (1991). Parents' differential socialization of boys and girls: A meta-analysis. *Psychological Bulletin*, *109*, 267–296.

Maccoby, E. E. (1988). Gender as a social category. *Developmental Psychology*, *24*, 755–765.

Maccoby, E. E., & Jacklin, C. N. (1974). *The psychology of sex differences*. Stanford, CA: Stanford University Press.

Martin, C. L., & Halverson, C. F. (1981). A schematic processing model of sex typing and stereotyping in children. *Child Development*, *52*, 1119–1134.

Mervis, C. B., & Rosch, E. (1981). Categorization of natural objects. *Annual Review of Psychology*, *32*, 89–115.

Miller, C. L. (1983). Developmental changes in male/female voice classification by infants. *Infant Behavior and Development*, *6*, 313–330.

Miller, C. L, Younger, B. A., & Morse, P. A. (1982). The categorization of male and female voices in infancy. *Infant Behavior and Development*, *5*, 143–159.

Mischel, W. (1966). A social-learning view of sex differences in behavior. In E. E. Maccoby (Ed.), *The development of sex differences* (pp. 56–81). Stanford, CA: Stanford University Press.

O'Brien, M., & Huston, A. C. (1985). Development of sex-typed play behavior in toddlers. *Developmental Psychology*, *21*, 866–871.

Parsons, T. (1955). Family structure and the socialization of the child. In T. Parsons & R. F. Bales (Eds.), *Family, socialization and interaction process* (pp. 35–131). Glencoe, IL: The Free Press.

Patterson, G. R., Reid, J. B., & Dishion, T. J. (1992). *Antisocial boys.* Eugene, OR: Castalia.

Pederson, F. A. (1980). *The father–infant relationship: Observational studies in the family setting.* New York: Praeger.

Rogoff, B. (1990). *Apprenticeship in thinking: Cognitive development in social context.* New York: Oxford University Press.

Rosch, E. (1977). Human categorization. In N. Warren (Ed.), *Studies in cross-cultural psychology* (Vol. 1, pp. 1–49). London: Academic Press.

Rubin, J. Z., Provenzano, F. J., & Luria, Z. (1974). The eye of the beholder: Parents' views on sex of newborns. *American Journal of Orthopsychiatry, 44,* 512–519.

Sachs, J. (1975). Cues to the identification of sex. In B. Thorne & N. Henley (Eds.), *Language and sex: Difference and dominance* (pp. 152–171). Rowley, MA: Newbury House.

Sears, R. R., Maccoby, E. E., & Levin, H. (1957). *Patterns of child rearing.* Evanston, IL: Row, Peterson.

Sears, R. R., Rau, L., & Alpert, R. (1965). *Identification and child rearing.* Stanford, CA: Stanford University Press.

Serbin, L. A., O'Leary, K. D, Kent, R. N., & Tonick, I. J. (1973). A comparison of teacher response to preacademic and problem behavior of boys and girls. *Child Development, 44,* 796–804.

Serbin, L. A., Tonick, I. J., & Sternglanz, S. H. (1977). Shaping cooperative cross-sex play. *Child Development, 48,* 924–929.

Shakin, M., Shakin, D., & Sternglanz, S. H. (1985). Infant clothing: Sex labeling for strangers. *Sex Roles, 12,* 955–964.

Siegel, M. (1987). Are sons and daughters treated more differently by fathers than by mothers? *Developmental Review, 7,* 183–209.

Slaby, R. G., & Frey, K. S. (1975). Development of gender constancy and selective attention to same-sex models. *Child Development, 46,* 849–856.

Smith, P. K., & Connolly, K. J. (1980). *The ecology of preschool behaviour.* Cambridge, England: Cambridge University Press.

Stevenson, M. R., & Black, K. N. (1988). Paternal absence and sex-role development: A meta-analysis. *Child Development, 59,* 793–814.

Stoneman, Z., & Brody, G. H. (1981). Two's company, three makes a difference: An examination of mothers' and fathers' speech to their young children. *Child Development, 52,* 705–707.

Thoman, E. B., Leiderman, P. H., & Olson, J. P. (1972). Neonate–mother interaction during breast- feeding. *Developmental Psychology, 6,* 110–118.

Thompson, S. K. (1975). Gender labels and early sex role development. *Child Development, 46,* 339–347.

Thorne, B. (1993). *Gender play: Girls and boys in school.* New Brunswick, NJ: Rutgers University Press.

Trautner, H. M. (1992). The development of sex-typing in children: A longitudinal analysis. *German Journal of Psychology, 16,* 183–199.

Turner, J. C. (1985). Social categorization and the self-concept: A social cognitive theory of group behavior. In E. J. Lawler (Ed.), *Advances in group process: Theory and research* (Vol. 2, pp. 77–122). Greenwich, CT: JAI Press.

Weinraub, M., & Frankel, J. (1977). Sex differences in parent–infant interaction during free play, departure, and separation. *Child Development, 48,* 1240–1249.

Whiting, B. B., & Edwards, C. P. (1988). *Children of different worlds: The formation of social behavior.* Cambridge, MA: Harvard University Press.

# 4

# Cognitive Theories of Gender Development

Carol Lynn Martin
*Arizona State University*

Central to a cognitive perspective is the idea that individuals are active information processors, not passive recipients of environmental input. Cognitive theorists emphasize this type of active, top-down processing, meaning that prior expectations and cognitions play an important role in how incoming information is organized and handled. According to a cognitive view, the world of information that is available to a perceiver is not constrained by the stimuli available to the senses but rather by the abilities to process and deal with information from that world. The ways in which people process information can make order from disorder and sense from nonsense. The same processes, however, also can lead to losses of information and to distortions in memory. For this reason, cognitive theorists often gain insights into the nature of information processing by assessing misperceptions, inaccurate memories, use of heuristics, and selective attention and memory, because in those instances there may be incongruence between the environmental input and one's concepts.

Many instances of distortions and selectivity in thinking about gender are apparent in everyday life. When Erin, my 4-year-old niece, showed me a drawing she had done of the children in her preschool class, I noticed something different about some of the stick figures in the drawing and asked her about it. She told me that the ones with the eyelashes were girls and that "boys don't have eyelashes!" There are several interesting aspects of Erin's thinking. First, she felt a need to distinguish boys and girls in her drawing and the more obvious methods that adults might use would be difficult to convey with stick figures. Second, she used a characteristic—having eyelashes—that does not truly distinguish the sexes. Why did she focus on a nondistinguishing characteristic like eyelashes, especially one that is not very perceptually salient? Third, she generalized the attribute to cover one whole group—the girls—while eliminating the attribute for the entire group of boys. How can Erin disregard what she sees everyday, that boys have eyelashes just as do girls?

My goal in writing this chapter is to outline the tenets of cognitive perspectives used by developmental psychologists when studying gender development and discuss the advances that have been made in using cognitive approaches. In the first section of this chapter, the two major cognitive approaches to the study of gender development are outlined. The second section is a brief description of the major issues involved in applying a cognitive approach to gender development and how these issues are being addressed with renewed emphasis on the dynamism of gender concepts. The third section is a review of how gender concepts function in different domains and at different levels of abstraction. The fourth section considers two ways of thinking about dynamic gender concepts and how these may be useful in understanding gender development.

## COGNITIVE PERSPECTIVES ON GENDER DEVELOPMENT

Cognitive perspectives can be found in some of the earliest psychological writings on stereotypes by psychologists such as Allport (1954) and journalists such as Lippmann (1922). Lippmann, for instance, described stereotypes as "pictures in our heads" (p. 3). Allport provided a comprehensive explanation of how categorization "forms large classes and clusters for guiding our daily adjustments" (p. 19). The cognitive perspective was defined most clearly by Tajfel's (1969) early writing on stereotypes in which he argued that categorization brings coherence to the environment and that biases result from the limitations of human cognitive processing. Later, the social functions related to gender cognitions were recognized, especially how gender cognitions influence the creation and maintenance of group actions and beliefs (Stroebe & Insko, 1989). The idea that perceivers have pictures in their heads about the sexes and the usefulness of categorizing information have been underlying themes of much of the recent thinking on gender from both social psychologists and developmental psychologists. Today, most researchers accept the notion that there are both cognitive and social aspects associated with gender cognitions (Stroebe & Insko, 1989).

## Cognitive Developmental Theory

In the developmental literature, cognitive notions were overshadowed for many years by an emphasis on environmental influences. Because gendered information is so pervasive in our society, the idea that individuals passively acquire gender roles and stereotypes through observation and training has been easy to imagine, and these notions held sway in the 1960s and 1970s. Cognitive theories developed within this milieu and somewhat in response to these ideas. In the developmental literature, the book *The Development of Sex Differences* (Maccoby, 1966) contained chapters that outlined the interesting problems involved in the study of sex differences and provided comprehensive theories to explain sex differences. Maccoby's seminal book contained a theory—Kohlberg's (1966) cognitive developmental theory—that set a new course for thinking about gender development. All developmental cognitive theories today have been powerfully influenced by Kohlberg's ideas (see Maccoby, 1990).

Kohlberg (1966) used Piaget's ideas as a basis for developing a new kind of theory of gender development—a cognitively oriented theory. Rather than thinking about children as passively absorbing the gendered information from their environments, Kohlberg reversed the emphasis. He argued that children are actively involved in learning about gender and in wanting to adhere to norms for gender.

Kohlberg (1966) assumed that the child's understanding of gender emerges within the framework of general cognitive development. The most revolutionary idea of that time was that children's understanding of gender initiated gender development in contrast to the learning theorists' focus on children's behavior. For Kohlberg, gender development rapidly coalesces once children acquire understanding about the nature of gender categories. Once this understanding is reached, children become motivated to seek out information about what is appropriate for their own sex by observing the behaviors of others. As a result, they then show more gender-typed behavior and remember gender-typed information better.

Research has supported Kohlberg's (1966) idea that children undergo developmental changes in understanding the concept of gender groups. Children's gender understanding moves through three stages. First, at about 2½ years, children acquire gender identity or gender labeling, in which they can label the sexes and identify their own sex. Next, by 3½, children acquire gender stability, in which they understand the invariance of sex over time. Finally, children acquire gender consistency or constancy, meaning that they understand the permanence of sex over situations (Slaby & Frey, 1975). Although research has found that children in many parts of the world pass through these stages, results concerning when children show each type of understanding have been mixed. Specifically, the ages at which children understand gender constancy vary depending on the specific wording of the questions and on the methods of assessing gender understanding (Ruble & Martin, 1998).

Because Kohlberg (1966) did not pinpoint the exact nature of the mechanisms and processes that underlie gender development, many controversies have evolved about how to interpret and how to test some of his most central notions (Huston, 1983; Martin & Little, 1990). For instance, controversy has surrounded the issue about the nature of the central motivating force in Kohlberg's theory. Was it simply knowing one's sex or does it involve a more sophisticated level of understanding? Kohlberg hinted at both ideas: He argued that children learn some aspects of gender and show some gender-typed preferences early in life while also stressing that a critical component for motivating children to learn and adhere to gender roles was children's understanding of the unchangeability of gender.

Many researchers have tackled the issue of assessing the role of gender understanding in attention, memory, and preferences. Although measurement issues confound the interpretation of results concerning the importance of gender understanding in children's overall gender development, some broad conclusions can be drawn (see Ruble & Martin, 1998). The research on children's attention to role models shows that basic information about gender may be more important than higher levels of understanding, although higher levels may provide additional motivation for children in certain situations. Specifically, children's attention to role models, especially for boys, appears to relate to their understanding of their own sex and to knowing that sex is stable over time, but it does not relate to knowing that sex is stable over situations (e.g., Slaby & Frey, 1975). The motivation associated with having a more sophisticated level of gender understanding comes into play in conflict situations. Boys who conserve sex over situations are more likely to imitate same-sex models in situations in which the relevant behaviors requires forgoing an attractive activity associated with the other sex (Frey & Ruble, 1992).

Basic gender understanding is more motivating than sophisticated levels of understanding in explaining children's toy preferences and preferences for same-sex playmates (e.g., Carter & Levy, 1988; Lobel & Menashri, 1993). For instance, children play more with same-sex toys and have stronger preferences for these toys when they know what sex they are, even before they understand the invariance of sex over time and situation (e.g., Weinraub et al., 1984). Gender stability may add additional motivational impetus to toy selections in some circumstances (Eaton, Von Bargen, & Keats, 1981). Furthermore, sophisticated levels of understanding appear to play a motivating role in situations involving conflict between attractiveness of toys and their gender-typing (Frey & Ruble, 1992). For simple toy and modeling choices, simply knowing one's sex appears to provide all the cognitive support that is necessary for making decisions. In more complex situations involving conflicting dimensions of choice, higher levels of knowledge seem to provide additional motivational impetus to select gender-typed behaviors and toys (Ruble & Martin, 1998).

Research on gender understanding and its role in memory show that knowing one's own sex and understanding the stability of sex over time may be the most important motivators involved in children's memory. Children with basic understanding of gender have higher levels of stereotype knowledge (Kuhn, Nash, & Brucken, 1978; R. D. Taylor & Carter, 1987), and in some studies, children with higher levels of gender understanding (e.g., stability) also show more stereotype knowledge (e.g., Coker, 1984; Martin & Little, 1990; O'Keefe & Hyde, 1983).

In summary, gender constancy—a sophisticated understanding of the invariance of gender over situations—does not appear to play the major organizing role in gender development that Kohlberg (1966) suggested. Instead, lower levels of gender understanding, such as knowing one's own sex and that sex is stable over time, may be more central to gender development. Gender constancy is not unimportant but is seen to be less central to gender development. Rather than initiating responsivity to gender cues, it may increase children's responsiveness to gender information and provide a period of consolidation for conclusions about gender-appropriate activities (Ruble, 1994; Stangor & Ruble, 1987).

Cognitive developmental theory has been enormously influential in understanding how children learn about gender and in helping researchers develop other cognitively oriented approaches to gender development. Even though cognitive theories developed from a different worldview and thus have a different flavor than social learning theories in their strong emphasis on active participation, few cognitive notions are necessarily outside the realm of, and in fact many are quite compatible with, the basic ideas of other theories. The expansion of cognitive ideas into social learning theory, which resulted in the adoption of a more actively involved person in a cognitive social learning theory (Bandura, 1986; Bussey & Bandura, 1992), and the development of gender-schema theories, are each testaments to the appeal and adaptability of cognitive notions.

## Gender-Schema Theories

The zeitgeist of the 1970s and 1980s, especially with influences from the cognitive revolution, provided a fertile ground for the development of other cognitively oriented gender approaches (e.g., Ashmore & Del Boca, 1979, 1981; Constantinople, 1979; Hamilton, 1981). Social and developmental psychologists began to embrace the cognitive notions of schemas and scripts. Gender schemas were ideas whose time had come. Three groups of investigators independently developed versions of gender-schema theories in the early 1980s. These theories share common assumptions and themes but differ in emphasis.

Schema theorists assume that individuals develop naive theories about gender and these theories influence the information individuals attend to, perceive, and remember. In a sense, this is a transactional processes in which the environment, which is highly organized by gender in most societies, leads to the creation of gender theories or schemas, which then promotes the gender-related processing of newly incoming information. In turn, these highly gender-focused theories then encourage the formation and continuation of gendered ideas by members of society through many levels of influence including the socialization of children. By having a highly gender-focused society, individuals are encouraged to create and interpret information through a gendered lens (Bem, 1993).

The social psychological theory of gender schemas proposed by Bem (1981) remains a compelling account of how individuals' beliefs and cognitions about the sexes and about themselves form around salient social categories, especially gender. Emphasis was placed on the functional significance of gender categories within our society. Gender is used broadly as a classification scheme in our culture: teachers line up children by sex, clothing cues mark the sexes of infants, and people respond to males and females differently. Because of its functional significance, children develop schemas about gender (see Bigler, Jones, & Lobliner, 1997). Furthermore, these schemas incorporate extensive networks of associations that go beyond the obvious associations with gender. Bem described, for instance, the metaphoric associations that individuals develop as part of gender schemas, such as soft things being feminine and rough things being masculine. Recent studies support this notion in that even children develop beliefs about softness and roundness being associated with females and hardness and angularity with males (Leinbach, Hort, & Fagot, 1997). Because of their importance in helping people interpret everyday life through the lens of societal expectations, people develop elaborate and extensive gender schemas quickly and easily.

Bem (1981) also focused attention on individual differences in gender schemas and how the Bem Sex-Role Inventory (Bem, 1974) can be used to assess these individual differences. Individuals can be labeled as being gender schematic if they describe themselves as having many sex-typed personality characteristics and few cross-sex-typed characteristics. The nonschematic individuals were those individuals who claim both kinds of personality characteristics (i.e., they are androgynous). Several studies suggest that gender schematic individuals organize their thinking and memory according to these ideas (Bem, 1981).

Another social psychological view of gender schemas was proposed by Markus, Crane, Bernstein, and Siladi (1982). Again, the emphasis of the approach was on individual differences in gender schemas. In this gender-schema approach, both masculinity and femininity were viewed as separate forms of gender schemas, each of which influenced thinking. For instance, androgynous individuals are schematic for two gender schemas, undifferentiated individuals are not schematic, and sex-typed and cross-sex-typed individuals are schematic for one type. Consistent with this view, individuals show differential reaction times to respond to traits depending on their schematicity (Markus et al., 1982).

A developmental view of gender schemas was proposed by Charles Halverson and myself (Martin, 1991; Martin & Halverson, 1981, 1987). We considered the origins of individual differences in gender schemas and the developmental significance of children learning to recognize their own gender group. Furthermore, Halverson and I focused our attention on defining the functions of gender schemas, borrowing from previous research on social schemas (S. E. Taylor & Crocker, 1981). For instance, we discussed specific ways that gender schemas organize and bias behavior, thinking, and attention. This influence of gender schemas is summarized in the notion of schematic consistency, in which individuals act and think consistently with the schemas they hold. A number of studies provide support for this notion (Martin, 1991). We also distinguished two types of gender schemas. The superordinate schema is a listlike structure that contains information about the sexes, and the own-sex schema is a more in-depth structure that contains detailed plans of action for carrying out gender-typed actions. Similar to the social psychological approaches, developmental gender-schema theory includes explanations about self-related biases in information processing.

Schema theories have been useful for providing new perspectives and insights for understanding gender development. Rather than focusing on the nature of the environment as learning theorists did, schema theorists consider the strategies that individuals use to interpret and reconstruct information from their environment. Schema approaches have been particularly useful for guiding research on all varieties of gender concepts and on how these concepts influence attention, memory, and social judgments. Schema theories also provide explanations for findings that have been difficult to explain, such as how stereotypes are maintained in the face of disconfirming evidence, why stereotypes are resistant to change, and why gender concepts may not match environmental input.

# ISSUES AND NEW DIRECTIONS FOR COGNITIVE THEORISTS

## The Relation of Cognition and Behavor

Gender has many facets. Individuals categorize themselves according to their sex; develop ideas about what it means to be a man or woman; develop concepts about feminine and masculine behaviors, appearance, and activities; develop attitudes and values about gender; engage in gender-related activities and express gender-related preferences; and develop ideas about the nature of the relationships between the sexes. Huston (1983) outlined a matrix that illustrates the many facets of gender by describing content areas of biological/categorical sex, activities and interests, personal-social attributes, gender-based social relationships, styles and symbols, and gender-related values (made a separate area by Ruble & Martin, 1998). For each of these content areas, there are four constructs that can be applied: concepts or beliefs, identity or self-perception, preferences, and behavioral enactment/adoption. This model of gender has been very useful for illuminating the numerous and varied aspects of gender and for considering how these aspects relate to one another.

One of the major concerns in the study of gender is the extent to which different aspects of gender relate to one another. This issue has come to the forefront of attention because researchers have been encouraged to consider more carefully the relations among different aspects of gender (Huston, 1983; Spence & Helmreich, 1978). Specifically, the argument is that researchers should adopt an assumption of multidimensionality among aspects of gender. Rather than assuming unity among aspects of gender, the multidimensional approach suggests that the nature of these relations is an open question. Furthermore, once the multidimensional/multifactorial view is accepted, then we must consider the notion of different etiologies for different aspects of gender. Gender must then be examined as a complex, multifaceted, and dynamic system.

For cognitive approaches, the multidimensionality issue has mainly been interpreted as questioning the extent to which gender-related cognitions relate to gender-related behavior. If a man holds the cognition that men tend to be more assertive than women, will he be more likely to be assertive in his own behavior? If a girl believes that girls like to play with girls, will she be more likely to join a group of girls on the playground than a group of boys? Thus, the question centers on whether gender-related cognitions provide the driving force in individuals' behavior. This theoretically and practically important issue remains central to the study of gender cognitions. Based on a strong version of the multidimensionality approach, we could start with the assumption that gender cognitions are not related to behavior. However, so many powerful and pervasive gender effects exist that it is hard to imagine that individuals' beliefs do not shape some of their behaviors. And, a careful examination of the social and developmental literature suggests that gender cognitions do guide behavior, with some sorts of cognitions having a more powerful influence than others (Martin, 1999). Furthermore, the increased emphasis on how gender is constructed in social interactions and situations (e.g., Bohan, 1993; West & Zimmerman, 1987) should reenergize interest in cognitive notions because the basis for much of the construction of gender is in the minds of the participants. How people think about their own sex, what they expect males and females to do in a given situation, and what they think is appropriate for each sex in a given situation are all cognitions about gender that serve to guide thinking and behavior.

The multidimensionality concern provides challenges for cognitive gender researchers. From a cognitive perspective, the message is clear that researchers need to push the limits of their thinking to consider a  more sophisticated and finely tuned set of gender-related cognitions, ones that are more directly and intimately tied to the situations in which people find themselves. How to assess and determine the dynamism of gender cognitions is a challenge to thinking about gender cognitively. In the remainder of the chapter, some variations in gender schemas and how gender schemas function in social contexts are considered.

## Expanding the Cognitive Perspective: Dynamic and Multifaceted Gender Schemas

From the very beginning, controversy has existed about how to best define gender schemas and what it means to be schematic. The term *schema* is a fuzzy construct with many meanings. The advantage of having many meanings is that the commonalties and consistencies in findings across many areas are apparent (Fiske & Linville, 1980). Research on gender identity, gender roles, and gender stereotypes can be integrated and viewed from the same perspective as more inclusive work on prediction, concept formation, and information processing. The disadvantage is that differences among gender-related constructs have been minimized or ignored. For instance, researchers may collect information about an individual's self-reported masculine and feminine personality traits or about a child's toy preferences and then assume that any one measure captures the degree to which a person is gender schematic. The underlying assumption is that gender infuses all aspects of behavior and thinking equally and so measurement of one aspect could be used to predict all other aspects. This idea stands in contrast to the view that gender is best conceived of as being multidimensional.

Issues about how to best measure gender schemas follows naturally from the issue of how to conceive of gender schemas. Many different approaches have been taken, including assessing gender knowledge, gender-related toy choices (Levy & Carter, 1989), self-reported masculine and feminine personality characteristics (Bem, 1981), and stereotype attitudes (e.g., Signorella & Liben, 1985). In the adult literature, personality measures have been used more than other types of measures. In the developmental literature, no one method has predominated (Signorella, Bigler, & Liben, 1993).

Although a static gender-stereotype-like gender schema may be the easiest to conceive and the most straightforward to measure, gender schemas are not static, nor are they easy to conceive. The difficulty in conceiving of and operationalizing gender schemas may be due to their abstract nature and their dynamism, which also is their appeal. Rather than arguing that one kind of cognition best captures the nature of gender schemas, another approach is to take a domain-specific view of gender schemas in which the goal is to consider a variety of gender cognitions and how these cognitions function. Following this stance, it becomes useful to expand the range of cognitions that are investigated (Martin, 1999). These schemas may guide behavior and thinking, however now they are more finely tuned to the particular situations in which people experience their social lives.

The advantages to a domain-specific strategy are many. First, the strategy allows movement from a grand universal system of explanation—one based on the idea that gender is infused uniformly throughout all aspects of our thinking—to a more domain-specific, contextual view of gender that better matches present-day assumptions about gender (Huston, 1983; Ruble & Martin, 1998). Second, the domain-specific strategy suggests new ways of thinking about gender and new ways to approach the study of social cognition more generally. Third, a domain-specific view better represents the flexibility and dynamism of human thinking, especially concerning central organizing categories such as gender.

## GENDER CONCEPTS IN DIFFERENT DOMAINS AND DIFFERENT LEVELS OF ABSTRACTION

A domain-specific strategy implies that within the major domains of experience, the kinds of gender cognitions that are most relevant will be accessed. Gender cognitions would be expected to differ when thinking about others versus thinking about the self. Gender cognitions would be expected to differ depending on the particular circumstances of the situations, such as whether one is interacting with a familiar or unfamiliar person. Another important feature of thinking more flexibly about gender is considering that gender concepts also differ in their level of abstraction. Some gender concepts are likely to be quite narrow and specific, whereas others would be more broadly conceived and abstract. The next section describes the research on several different types of gender concepts.

## Development of Gender Stereotypes

Children are amazingly adept at devising their own stereotypes and learning the gender stereotypes of their culture. At an early age, they develop ideas about how the sexes look and act. Children apply these gender stereotypes when making judgments about others' behavior and preferences. Developmental researchers have focused attention on how stereotypes about others develop, what kinds of information are first associated with the sexes, and how these gender cognitions then influence children's thinking and behavior.

Children show evidence of having rudimentary gender stereotypes between the ages of 2 and 3. For instance, even toddlers believe that boys hit people and girls cry (Kuhn et al., 1978). Young children's stereotypes are quite rigid, meaning that they often link gender-related characteristics exclusively to males or females (Trautner, 1992). During early childhood, children's stereotypes develop in a number of domains associated with the sexes. For instance, whereas young children may stereotype the sexes in appearance and in power-related behaviors (Ruble & Martin, 1998), older children begin to add to their stereotypes information about occupational differences and, even later, personality differences (Serbin, Powlishta, & Gulko, 1993; Signorella, Bigler, & Liben, 1993). Key concerns of the content-focused research are what kinds of information children first develop stereotypes about and why these particular stereotypes develop at such an early age.

As children grow older, their stereotypes become less rigid and more flexible (Levy, M. G. Taylor, & Gelman, 1995; Trautner, 1992). For instance, older children acknowledge that there are exceptions to stereotypic patterns, for instance, that some girls play with trucks (Leahy & Shirk, 1984). This increased flexibility is due partly to older children having more advanced abilities to classify, especially on multiple dimensions (Bigler & Liben, 1992; Trautner, 1992), and a greater understanding of the cultural relativity of gender norms (Carter & Patterson, 1982; Damon, 1977; Levy et al., 1995; Stoddart & Turiel, 1985). Surprisingly, older children also show more extreme views about crossing gender boundaries. For example, older children respond more harshly to another child who shows cross-gender behavior than do younger children (Carter & McCloskey, 1984).

Developmental researchers also have been interested in the changing structure of gender stereotypes. Most researchers have conceived of gender stereotypes as having a very simple associative structure. Girls like dolls. Men are assertive. The pairing of a trait or characteristic with a gender category label has characterized thinking and research efforts in studying children's stereotypes. For example, the most commonly used stereotype measures involves asking children to assign an activity to a sex (e.g., Edelbrock & Sugawara, 1978). Stereotype knowledge has become more broadly conceived in both the adult literature (Deaux & Lewis, 1984; Stephan, 1989) and the child literature (Martin, Wood, & Little, 1990). Research on stereotype development suggests a more complex model would be useful, namely, a component model of gender stereotypes in which stereotypes are conceived of as having a hierarchical cognitive structure, with gender labels at the top of the hierarchy and associated attributes at the lower levels. Attributes are associated with each other through their shared relation with "masculinity" or "femininity" (Deaux & Lewis, 1984; Martin et al., 1990). One advantage to thinking about gender stereotypes in a more complex manner has been an increased ability to design measures of stereo-typing sensitive to these changes. And, better measurement has led to a better understanding of the types of developmental changes that occur in gender stereotypes during childhood (Martin, 1993).

***Using Gender Stereotypes to Make Social Judgments.*** Comparison of the research on children's and adults' use of stereotypes shows interesting similarities and differences. An important similarity is that both children and adults use information about a person's sex (i.e., categorical information) to make social judgments about attributes when they have no other information about the person (Berndt & Heller, 1986; Cowan & Hoffman, 1986; Deaux & Lewis, 1984; Lobel, Bempechat, Gewirtz, Shoken-Topaz, & Bashe, 1993; Martin, 1989; Zucker, Wilson-Smith, Kurita, & Stern, 1995). Once again, this suggests that gender is a powerful and pervasive source of information upon which social interactions are based.

Given a coherent gender structure that incorporates information about the sexes, we might expect that children's hierarchical gender structures would mimic adult schemas such that once one part of the knowledge structure is activated, other parts are likewise activated. With young children, there appear to be some constraints on this sort of activation or triggering of information. Although young children easily make inferences about others based on their sex, they are not so adept at using attributes to reason about categories. For instance, after hearing about novel attributes associated with each sex, children had little difficulty inferring the attributes associated with each sex but were less able to infer sex on the basis of the attribute (Gelman, Collman, & Maccoby, 1986).

Other developmental changes occur in how children use the associative links from one attribute to another attribute within the hierarchical structure of gender stereotypes (Martin et al., 1990). Children ages 4 and 6, who are able to use the vertical associations between category labels and attributes as described previously, have limited abilities to make horizontal attribute-to-attribute associations. In a developmental study designed to investigate the different types of associative links, 4- to 10-year-olds were given short stories about unfamiliar children and were asked to make inferences about them. When given only an attribute cue (e.g., "I know a child who likes to play with kitchen sets. How much would this child like to play with trucks?"), 4- and 6-year-old children made horizontal associations only when cued with an attribute that was relevant to their own sex. For instance, a girl told about a child who likes kitchen sets might infer that the child would also like dolls, based on some understanding of the concept of feminine interests. The girl probably would not show the same pattern, however, for a masculine interest and test item, indicating that she does not have the same level of development for her concept of masculine interests. However, even within this 2-year span of time, children show increasing understanding of other-sex concepts (Martin & Fabes, 1997) and, when given very salient cues such as appearance-related cues, may recognize these horizontal links more easily (Bauer, Liebl, & Stennes, 1998). Furthermore, by the age of 8 years, children can generate horizontal associations from attribute to attribute for both own-sex and other-sex relevant attributes (Martin et al., 1990).

Compared to older children, younger children are less likely to integrate gender-conflicting information about a person or to use only presumed masculinity or femininity to make judgments about others. For instance, consider the situation of a child who is told about an unfamiliar boy who has a feminine interest (e.g., plays with kitchen sets) and then is asked to decide how much the unfamiliar boy would like playing with several other toys, some of which are stereotyped as being for girls and some for boys. In several studies using this type of task, young children rely on a highly categorical method of reasoning and ignore individuating information (Berndt & Heller, 1986; Biernat, 1991; Martin, 1989). For instance, a child might reason that, because the unfamiliar child is a boy and boys like boys' toys, then this boy will like trucks and not like dolls. In contrast to younger children, older children use individuating information about the child's interests in conjunction with information about sex to draw inferences, although more emphasis is still given to categorical information about sex. Adults rely more heavily on individuating information in similar situations, that is, they are likely to infer that a person who is assertive in one situation is likely to be assertive in another situation, regardless of sex (Locksley, Borgida, Brekke, & Hepburn, 1980). Keep in mind, however, that these inferences, although based on individuating information, are still stereotypic because inferences are drawn using concepts of masculinity and femininity. In a meta-analysis comparing adults' tendencies to rely on all sorts of categorical stereotypes and attribute information to make inferences, attribute information had larger effects on impressions than did categorical stereotypes (Kunda & Thagard, 1996).

In summary, research suggests an interesting and not entirely straightforward developmental pattern in how children and adults use sex and gender-based concepts of masculinity and femininity. Both children and adults use sex to make inferences about others when no other information is available, and the range of possible inferences probably increases as children gain additional stereotypic information about the sexes. When asked to make judgments based on only one or several gender-based attributes, both children and adults can do this, but younger children often make stereotypic inferences when given own-sex cues and not with other-sex cues. As they grow older, their likelihood of using both types of cues increases, thereby increasing their abilities to make attribute-to-attribute inferences. When information is potentially conflicting, young children tend to rely on categorical stereotypes, older children integrate both types of information, and adults rely more on attribute-based stereotypes.

Why do developmental changes occur in the use of categories and attributes? Part of the answer may lie in changes in the associative structure of gender stereotypes, especially in how the gender concepts of masculinity and femininity change as children grow older (Biernat, 1991). As children grow older, they develop more adultlike views of what it means to be masculine and feminine and how these two concepts relate to one another. Specifically, young children meld together sex and masculinity/femininity more so than adults, such that being a boy is equivalent to being masculine. Older children begin to consider these ideas as being related but not equivalent to one another, meaning a boy could be feminine or a girl could be masculine. Older children more than younger children also more strongly assume that masculinity and femininity are negatively related to one another (Biernat, 1991). Adults may more clearly separate categorical sex from the gender concepts of masculinity and femininity, especially in thinking about other people. They may be more flexible in their applications of these concepts and more variable and sensitive to situational changes. Furthermore, adults may have more sophisticated structures including more subtypes of men and women that they can use to process information (Eckes, 1994).

***Gender Stereotypes and Behavior.***     How early do children use gender stereotypes? This question has been difficult to answer for many reasons (Martin, 1993). One roadblock has been the inability to assess stereotype knowledge in very young children. Another been the lack of sophisticated stereotype measures. Many measures involve assessing the simple category–attribute associations—which may not provide a complete picture of stereotype knowledge. Ideally, more fine-tuned assessments could be used, for instance, by ascertaining the probabilities that children associate with gender stereotypes. Only a few researchers (e.g., Trautner, 1992) have attempted to use more complex methods of assessing the probabilistic nature of children's stereotypes (e.g., many more boys than girls or a few more boys than girls engage in X). Another concern has been the wording of questions, for instance, whether stereotypes are better assessed by asking children, who usually does an activity versus who can do an activity (see Signorella et al. 1993, for discussion). Finally, the type of finding that would provide acceptable evidence of children's use of  stereotypes has been difficult to determine.

One clever strategy for assessing gender-schema use in very young children has been studies of elicited imitation. Toddlers were shown a series of actions that make up the gendered script for activities such as diapering a teddy bear and shaving a teddy bear. A week after demonstrating the actions, tendencies to model the gendered scripts were assessed by providing children with the props that were used for the actions. Girls were willing to imitate the actions they had seen, regardless of whether they were "masculine" actions such as shaving or "feminine" actions such as diapering a teddy bear. Boys, however, imitated only masculine actions and not feminine actions. Some boys even refused to touch the feminine props (Bauer, 1993). Boys may have been more likely to selectively use gender schemas because their roles are more rigidly prescribed than girls' roles. This method is useful for determining whether and how much children follow the information provided for them by gender stereotypes.

Another promising strategy for assessing dynamic gender stereotypes is to consider the nature of children's and adults' gender scripts. To what extent do children and adults understand the temporal sequencing of activities for their own sex versus the other sex? What factors influence the use and development of these scripts? Does expertise in gender influence the development of these scripts? Thus far, only one study of gender scripts in children has been conducted and the findings suggest that even preschool children develop gender scripts and can order events appropriately, especially boys (Boston & Levy, 1991). How these scripts influence behavior and how they are influenced by children's actions awaits further study.

Developmental research on stereotypes has provided interesting comparisons with research on adults. However, developmental research also has illustrated that there are a number of very interesting issues about stereotype development that potentially could provide insights into the ways that stereotypes influence information processing in both adults and children. Nonetheless, further research needs to be conducted in which the dynamism of stereotypes is considered more extensively. We need to better understand the qualities of situations and interactions that may make stereotypes more salient for young children as well as how gender salience influences use of these stereotypes.

## Children's Naive Social Psychology and Gender

Cognitive developmentalists have proposed that children develop a naive biology, which involves developing ideas about biological processes such as inheritance and photosynthesis; a naive psychology, which involves developing an understanding about others' beliefs and thoughts; and a naive physics, which involves developing ideas about physical laws and actions (Wellman & Gelman, 1998). Children also may develop a *naive social psychology* in which they formulate workable and testable ideas about the nature of humans in social situations. Although a naive social psychology incorporates some ideas from naive psychology and naive biology, it seems likely that, given the importance of people and social interactions in children's survival and development, understanding of people should be a core kind of theory within children's arsenal of knowledge. Additional research is needed to investigate how naive social psychological theories change in accuracy and interconnectedness as children develop and to assess whether the likelihood of using these theories increases as children grow older, just as do other core theories (Keil, 1989).

*Gender Theories.*     Children's naive social psychology may include abstract gender concepts. For instance, children and adults may form theories about the sexes that guide their behavior and thinking in some ambiguous situations. In an attempt to capture the elusive nature of gender schemas in my own research I have tried to imagine what kinds of abstract gender theories children might form. Children may form theories about the general nature of the sexes, a notion consistent with ideas proposed in developmental schema theory (Martin & Halverson, 1981, 1987) and with ideas from social identity theory (Tajfel & Turner, 1979). For example, children may form very abstract and general theories about the sexes that focus on similarities within a group and differences between groups. At their simplest, children may form a "within-group similarity" theory and a "between-group differences" theory, and these theories may guide their behavior and thinking in situations in which they have little information to go on other than knowing someone's sex. For instance, in the first day of preschool, a girl on the playground has to decide who she will try to play with, and this decision may be influenced by these very abstract gender theories. The girl on the playground may reason, "There's a girl. She probably likes to do what I like to do." Whether this inference truly captures the nature of the unfamiliar girl's interests matters little; what matters instead is that it primes a certain sort of action, in this case, a sex-typed choice of play partner.

One simple way to assess gender theories is to ask children to make inferences in unfamiliar situations. For instance, consider a boy who is shown an unfamiliar toy and is asked to rate how much he likes the toy and then how much he thinks other boys will like the toy and how much girls would like the toy. If this child uses a within-group similarity theory, he might reason that, "I like this toy, so other boys should also like the toy." If he uses a between-group differences theory, he might reason, "If I like this toy, girls probably won't like it."

In several studies using both highly and moderately attractive unfamiliar toys, preschool children showed that they use this type of gender-based reasoning to make predictions about other children's preferences (Martin, Eisenbud, & Rose, 1995). The findings illustrate this pattern in several ways. First, for individual toys, children had smaller absolute differences between their own liking of toys and their expectations about how much same-sex children would like the toys as compared to how much they thought other-sex children would like the toys. Second, correlations were calculated among three summary scores: children's liking ratings for all toys, their predictions about how much other-sex children would like all the toys, and their predictions about how much same-sex children would like all the toys. Children's own liking ratings were highly positively correlated with their predictions for same-sex children, $r(68) = .73$, $p < .001$, whereas their own liking ratings were unrelated to their predictions for other-sex peers, $r(68) = -.07$, $p > .05$. Third, we compared each child's profile of preferences across many different toys to their profile of expectations about same-sex children's preferences and their profile of expectations about other-sex children's preferences for the toys using $P$ correlations. The results of these analyses tend to be conservative because a number of children had to be dropped due to lack of variability in their responses (e.g., a child would say he liked all the toys "a lot" = 4, and say that girls liked all the toys "a little bit" = 1). Nonetheless, there were high positive $P$ correlations between children's own profile of liking of toys and their profiles of predictions of liking for same-sex children (for girls, $P$ correlation = .77; for boys, $P$ correlation = .87, $ps < .001$) and lower correlations with profiles of predictions of liking for other-sex children ($P$ correlations = .18, .12, $ps > .05$). For both the grouped ratings and the profile comparisons, children showed stronger evidence of using within-group similarity theories than between-group differences theories.

How do these abstract gender theories change as children grow older? As a comparison to the young children, data on undergraduate students were collected using a similar procedure (Martin et al., 1995). Even undergraduate students showed evidence of using gender theories when asked to make similar sorts of ratings for unfamiliar objects. This finding suggests that these theories may be maintained in some form over the course of development.

The abstract theories that children and adults use about gender may derive from individuals' tendencies to endow some social categories, just as they do with natural kind categories, with a core essence that is assumed to characterize every member of the group (Rothbart & Taylor, 1992; Spence, 1985).

***Children's Understanding and Expectations About Others.*** Another aspect of naive social psychology would be children's understanding of how others might respond to their own behavior. Few studies have been designed to assess children's beliefs and understanding about the social consequences of their actions. The domain of gender is particularly useful for this type of investigation because the consequences have been verified—many studies indicate that other children show disapproval of children when they play in cross-gender activities (e.g., Carter & McCloskey, 1984; Langlois & Downs, 1980). When children have been asked what other kids will think of them if they play with boys or with girls, they report strongly gender-typed beliefs, and these beliefs are stronger in older children than in younger children. Furthermore, these beliefs influence their play-partner preferences. Children who believe that other kids approve of same-sex play are more likely to prefer same-sex playmates. Children who believe that other kids will approve of other-sex play are more likely to report other-sex play partner preferences. Importantly, when children's play was observed over several months, their actual play partners confirmed their self-reported play prefer-ences (Martin, Fabes, Evans, & Wyman, in press). Furthermore, even young children can report their expectations of how their parents, day-care workers, baby-sitters and best friends would respond to their playing with different types of toys. In one study, few children believed that others will disapprove of (label as "bad") play with gender-typed toys, but boys often believed that their fathers would think cross-gender play was "bad." Especially when the gender-typing of toys was made salient, boys who thought their fathers would disapprove of cross-gender play avoided cross-gender toys (Raag & Rackliff, 1998).

***Children's and Adults' Cognitions About the Origins of Sex Differ-ences.*** Part of a child's naive biology includes developing ideas about origins, such as how babies are born, genetic inheritance, and how living things grow and change. Similarly, children's naive social psychology may include ideas about why the sexes differ. These folk beliefs about origins may influence children's and adults' attitudes about the sexes, how they perceive the sexes, and whether they believe sex differences can be modified.

Young children's folk beliefs about the causes of sex differences were assessed using a very clever and engaging task (M. G. Taylor, 1996). Children were told, for instance, about a young boy who was raised on an island only by females. Children were then asked if the boy would grow up to be malelike or femalelike across a number of dimensions, for instance, in interests and future occupations. Developmental changes were found in children's beliefs. Younger children tended to believe in biological influences. They reason that a boy raised by women is still a boy, and so he will want to play football and grow up to be a firefighter. Older children were more likely to consider that his behavior could be shaped by the social forces of being raised by women. How these folk beliefs relate to other aspects of children's gender-typed behavior and thinking is yet unclear. However, we might expect that because younger children's beliefs are biologically based, they would be more universal and extreme in their application of stereotypes and they may not recognize variability in the sexes nor expect that sex differences can change easily.

Adults' folk theories about the causes of sex and race differences were also investigated (Martin & Parker, 1995). We asked a sample of almost 500 undergraduates to rate the extent to which biological factors (e.g., hormones and genes), socialization influences (e.g., peers and families), and opportunities afforded to each sex/race contributed to group differences. In this domain, the nature–nurture issue, which is always at the forefront of gender research, becomes personalized in beliefs. For both sex and race differences, biological factors, socialization, and opportunities were each believed to play a role in the origins of differences, although socialization was considered more important for explaining the origin of sex differences and biological factors were believed to be less important for explaining race differences. Beliefs about origins related to other beliefs. First, students who held a strongly biological view were somewhat more likely to perceive differences between the sexes than students with a less biologically oriented view. Second, the findings suggested that some of the students were influenced by a belief in biological determinism. Students who held a strongly biologically based view about the origins of sex and race differences assumed that sex differences were more difficult to change. Overall, the results suggest that students have multidetermined views about the origins of differences, and that individual differences in these views tend to relate in subtle ways to other beliefs and cognitions they hold about groups. How beliefs about origins shape or are shaped by other beliefs is yet unclear.

## Developing a Gendered View of Self

Understanding the gendered self has been a great challenge to social, clinical, and developmental psychologists. Developmental psychologists have focused their attention on how children develop a sense of their own sex—how they learn to which gender group they belong, develop ideas about what it means to be a girl or boy, and come to understand that gender is stable and constant despite superficial transformations (Kohlberg, 1966). Clinical psychologists focused research efforts on studying the development of gender identity in children who were atypical either through genetic disorders or surgical accidents (Bradley, Oliver, Chernick, & Zucker, 1998; Diamond & Sigmundson, 1997; Money & Ehrhardt, 1972; Zucker & Bradley, 1995). For social psychologists, studying the self has been focused much more exclusively on personality. Although early psychologists were interested in assessing masculinity and femininity, great changes occurred in the concepts and measurement of these constructs in the 1970s. Constantinople (1973) proposed an idea that led to a conceptual breakthrough, namely that both masculinity and femininity are multidimensional constructs. Bem (1974) proposed a new method to measure these constructs and to classify people according to their levels of both kinds of characteristics, which then allowed for the possibility of identifying people with both kinds of traits—people who are androgynous. Thousands of studies have been undertaken to explore how individuals' views of their personality characteristics relate to other aspects of their behavior and functioning.

The three central and interrelated cognitive issues concerning the gendered self are (a) how the gendered self develops, (b) how and whether self-related gender cognitions influence behavior, and (c) how and whether the gendered self and other gender cognitions interrelate. Much of the research from both developmental and social psychologists concerning the gendered self fits within the framework of these issues.

***Development of the Gendered Self in Early Childhood.*** The first issue—how the gendered self develops—is an arena in which the nature–nurture controversy is central. Especially in the study of atypical children, clinical psychologists and medical researchers continue to debate whether gender assignment and rearing are more important to a child's sense of self than are genetic and biological influences. Some clinical case studies suggest that children's sense of a gendered self are determined most strongly by parental attitudes and upbringing (e.g., Bradley et al., 1998; Money & Ehrhardt, 1972), whereas other cases studies suggest that biological factors can overcome socialization pressures (e.g., Diamond & Sigmundson, 1997; Imperato-McGinley, Peterson, Gautier, & Sturla, 1979).

Studies of typical children have focused on describing the patterns of development of a gendered self and understanding how different levels of understanding relate to other aspects of gender development. For children, a fundamental aspect of gender development is recognizing one's own sex (Fagot, 1985; Martin & Little, 1990). As discussed earlier, how children's gender development is initiated or strengthened by having an even more sophisticated knowledge about gender, such as understanding that a person's sex is a stable and enduring aspect of the self, remains a controversial topic.

***Development of the Gendered Self After Early Childhood.*** Little is known about the early origins of children's gender identities; likewise little is known about development of the gendered self during childhood and adolescence. One question of interest is how categorical knowledge about sex relates to children's development of stereotype knowledge about the sexes (see Intons-Peterson, 1988). Do they develop simultaneously and provide feedback for one another? Does the recognition of group membership set the stereotype acquisition process in motion?

One possible developmental scenario involves increasing differentiation. As children grow older and develop more sophisticated cognitive processing skills, they may begin to fine-tune their self-perceptions (Intons-Peterson, 1988; Martin & Halverson, 1981) and develop a more elaborate gender-role identity (Spence, 1985). While maintaining a firm gender identity (they know which sex they are), they begin to form a more well-differentiated view of their gender-role identity—that is, a sense of themselves as masculine or feminine (Stoller, 1968). Cognitive changes may promote a more differentiated self-view. Just as children gain more insights into the variability within each sex as shown in the changes in their stereotypes, they may also see themselves in a more variable and less restrictive light. For instance, older children may develop self-concepts that relate more loosely to gender stereotypes than young children's. For instance, they may believe, "most girls like to play with dolls, but I don't" or "some girls like to play with boys and I am one of them." The loosening of the ties between stereotypes and self-perceptions may be difficult to ascertain in everyday life with older children or young adolescents because they continue to hold ideas about the negative consequences of crossing gender boundaries, and these ideas about others' expectations for their behavior may be even more powerful than they were when children were younger. Tomboys may be one group for whom the loosening is most apparent. Tomboys can be less girl-like in part because people are less restrictive of girls' gender roles than boys' (Antill, 1987; Feinman, 1984; Green, 1987; Martin, 1990).

The differences between thinking about sex as a category, about the gender concepts of masculinity and femininity, and about what it means to be masculine or feminine add to the complexity of understanding how self-concepts form. An interesting finding from the adult literature on personality is that the term *masculine* does not fit neatly into the category of supposedly masculine traits (or instrumental traits), such as assertiveness or being independent, and *feminine* does not fit neatly into the category of feminine (expressive) traits, such as being sympathetic and warm (Spence, 1993). Furthermore, the terms are negatively correlated and yet the two dimensions of masculine-associated traits and feminine-associated traits are often found to be independent of one another in self-perceptions. Maybe adults do as children do—meld together *man* with being masculine and not feminine; and *woman* with being feminine and not masculine. Aspects that are not strongly linked with these core concepts, however, are the supposedly "masculine" and "feminine" traits that psychologists have found to be associated with being male or female. These traits may not carry the same psychological impact nor are they as strikingly male-associated or female-associated as the actual words, *masculine* and *feminine*.

For adults, whatever gender-congruent characteristics they have may be sufficient for maintaining and protecting their sense of gender identity or sense of masculinity or femininity (Spence, 1985). As long as a person has an adequate representation of gender-congruent characteristics, he or she can mindlessly maintain gender identity and not have to think about or wonder about his or her own identity. Gender-incongruent characteristics may be discounted or their attributions may be changed to fit personal behaviors, that is, they may be reframed as being important for all people, not just one sex or the other. What constitutes an adequate amount of gender-relevant characteristics varies from one individual to the next. Spence (1985) cogently described a complex calculus of gender-role identity with elements that enter into the calculations varying from person to person and shifting with age and with changing roles, responsibilities, and situations (see also Ashmore, 1990). For most men, for instance, being male is equivalent to being masculine because they have developed a self-concept that includes those aspects of being masculine that are important for their self-worth.

***The Gendered Self and Gendered Behavior.*** If this description holds for most people, then gender-role identities are relatively idiosyncratic and flexible cognitions about the self. Nonetheless, these cognitions may guide behavior and thinking, all the while being susceptible to change. The nature of these cognitions and whether general patterns can be discerned in how they form, and in identifying which aspects are most likely to be emphasized and valued, are worthy of future research efforts. One approach may be to consider which characteristics are more vulnerable to social pressures or situational pressures and which are more likely to be influenced by biological factors. For some aspects of gender roles, external social pressures to conform may be quite strong and these pressures may become internalized as important aspects of gender for many individuals. For these aspects, more consistency is likely to be found across individuals. For example, external characteristics (e.g., looking feminine or masculine) may be more important for individuals' identities than internal, less observable characteristics, such as being sympathetic or having good mathematical skills. Another approach is to consider the situations that cause reevaluations of gender-role identity and gender identity. After being mistaken for a man, a woman may change her hairstyle. A divorce or loss of job may trigger reevaluation of gender-role identities (Spence, 1985). In contrast, acting appropriately for a situation, even if the behavior runs counter to stereotypes, probably will not trigger changes. A woman who takes charge of a meeting that she has been designated to run is acting appropriately for the situation, although she may be demonstrating a purportedly "masculine" personality trait.

Some aspects of gender-role identity, such as boys' tendencies to play in a rough-and-tumble style, may be less susceptible to change than other aspects. How these self-related characteristics influence and are in turn influenced by gender roles and gender identity may depend on whether the characteristics are gender-congruent or gender-incongruent. Consider, for instance, a boy who is active and likes rough-and-tumble play. He will feel comfortable playing with other boys who are also likely to be active and he is likely to develop a sense of self as being similar to other boys. As such, his "boyishness" may be taken for granted. Nonetheless, his boyishness may drive the organization of other aspects of his self-identity. He may reason that, because he is so much like other boys, he will probably really like to watch football but not ballroom dancing. Now consider a boy who is not active and does not like rough-and-tumble play. He may not feel boyish at all; in fact, in extreme cases, he may even want to be a girl because he so closely associates being a boy with doing boyish things (Zucker & Bradley, 1995). As he grows older and recognizes that there is variability in the actions of both sexes, he may develop a sense of himself as a boy who is similar to some boys but is not a "typical" boy. The development and maintenance of an androgynous or a cross-gender self-view likely requires more self-conscious reasoning about gender. Children who develop these types of gender identity should be less likely guided by traditional views of boys or girls. For instance, we might predict that a boy with cross-gender interests would be less likely to expect his behavior and preferences to fit with "boyishness."

***The Gendered Self and Cognitions About Others.*** Regardless of how the various aspects of the gendered self develop, the issues of how this self-view relates to a more general view of females and males is interesting. To what extent do gender stereotypes influence how personal preferences develop, and how do personal preferences and experiences influence the development of gender stereotypes? A certain amount of overlap would be expected given the strong societal expectations about males and females. For unfamiliar or nonstereotypic information, bidirectional influences are likely between self and other concepts. Conversely, a girl who thinks that flying kites is something girls do may assume that she would like to fly kites. Even unusual experiences may be influential. A girl who likes to fly kites may assume that this is something other girls will like, simply because she likes it. Research on gender theories using novel toys suggests that children do make this kind of judgment (Martin et al., 1995). A young child whose mother has a round face may believe that having a round face is typical of females, at least until she experiences more examples of females with a variety of face shapes. As children grow older and gain more experiences, they will lose the more idiosyncratic aspects of gender stereotypes.

The final issue about determining the predictive value of the gendered cognitions about the self depends in part on using more sophisticated methods of assessing self-cognitions. One direction to consider is that there are multiple levels of self-cognitions that may be hierarchically arranged. For instance, one level of self-cognitions involves broad categorical-level influences such as recognition of membership in a gender group. Another level involves narrow and idiosyncratic gendered aspects of the self. Most of the developmental studies have been done on categorical gender influences. For instance, many studies show that children better remember information about same-sex characters than about other-sex characters (Signorella, Bigler, & Liben, 1997). Idiosyncratic aspects that are viewed in gendered ways are seldom studied. The bidirectional interplay between idiosyncratic and categorical gender influences needs to be considered more carefully.

## PERSPECTIVES ON DYNAMIC GENDER SCHEMAS

Many gendered behaviors that people exhibit appear to reside less in individuals than in their social interactions and partners (Deaux & LaFrance, 1998; Maccoby, 1988). For this reason, a multitiered level of cognitions must be considered to capture the complexity of how people respond in social interactions that occur over many varied situations and processing constraints. Several useful models have been proposed to investigate gender in social interactions, such as the Deaux and Major's (1987) model. In this model, the target individual and the interactional partner hold beliefs that work as expectancies about the nature of the interaction and provide information about their goals and motivations for engaging in the interaction. These gendered beliefs include views of self, gender stereotypes, and gender-role attitudes. Situations also must be considered. Qualities of situations may make gender more or less salient, thereby changing the nature of the interaction. Some situations more strongly elicit gendered scripts than other situations. For adults, traditional gendered scripts may be more likely at a singles bar than while working on a project at the office. For children, traditional gendered scripts may be more likely when children are separated by sex into competing groups in the classroom.

Another powerful perspective that has potential for being used to investigate the complexity of gender and social interactions is a dynamic systems (DS) approach. The focus of the DS approach is on change (Thelen & Smith, 1998). Rather than thinking about the aspects that remain the same over time, DS theorists tend to focus on the variability in behavior (Fischer & Bidell, 1998; Thelen & Smith, 1998). Thus far, in the developmental literature, a DS approach has been applied mainly to children's behaviors such as walking, reaching, and word learning. According to a DS perspective, for instance, walking is an organized system of behavior, but the exact form of walking at any given time depends on many factors including the type of material being walked on (e.g., rug versus hard wood floor) and incline of the floor. To think about gender more dynamically, for instance, we may consider how specific aspects of gender identity vary over different types of social "surfaces."

A major goal of DS studies is to measure the dynamic trajectory of a system. Each transition to a new form or level of organization involves the loss of stability, so that systems can seek new and self-organized patterns. DS researchers ask questions about when a system changes to a new state and what factors influence those changes. Dynamic views on gender would suggest that behavior may organize itself in gender-typed forms during some parts of interactions and move to a less gender-typed form in other parts of interactions or with different partners. Situational demands may influence these sorts of changes.

Applying a DS approach to social behaviors shifts attention away from the stability of gendered behaviors and onto the variability with which behavior is played out in social situations. In addition to allowing for the many situational and other-person influences that must be considered to capture the complexity of social interactions, a DS approach provides a more coherent way to think about conceptual change and dynamism. Concepts are not ignored in favor of behavior, in fact, they become one of the many factors that influence the changes in the system during social interactions. From a DS approach, mental activities are like physical activities in that they are a product of a lifetime of activity and they are influenced by the just-previous activity and by the immediate input of the situation (Smith & Samuelson, 1997). Concepts, then, are better thought of as dynamic systems of knowing, meaning that they carry with them past and present influences.

Cognitively oriented researchers and theorists should be encouraged to develop more sophisticated ways of thinking about the dynamics of gender concepts. Studying the dynamics of gender concepts is exciting as it allows for the possibility of incorporating the long-term effects of gender concepts as well as considering short-term, fluid, and situationally variable forms of cognition. The difficulty of measuring real-time changes in cognitions is just one of the many challenges that await researchers interested in exploring the value of dynamic concepts.

# REFERENCES

Allport, G. W. (1954). *The nature of prejudice*. Reading, MA: Addison-Wesley.

Antill, J. K. (1987). Parents' beliefs and values about sex roles, sex differences, and sexuality: Their sources and implications. In P. Shaver & C. Hendrick (Eds.), *Review of personality and social psychology: Vol. 7. Sex and gender* (pp. 294–328). Newbury Park, CA: Sage.

Ashmore, R. D. (1990). Sex, gender, and the individual. In L. A. Pervin (Ed.), *Handbook of personality: Theory and research* (pp. 486–526). New York: Guilford.

Ashmore, R. D., & Del Boca, F. K. (1979). Sex stereotypes and implicit personality theory: Toward a cognitive-social psychological conceptualization. *Sex Roles, 5*, 219–248.

Ashmore, R. D., & Del Boca, F. K. (1981). Conceptual approaches to stereotypes and stereotyping. In D. L. Hamilton (Ed.), *Cognitive processes in stereotyping and intergroup behavior* (pp. 1–35). Hillsdale, NJ: Lawrence Erlbaum Associates.

Bandura, A. (1986). *Social foundations of thought and action: A social cognitive theory*. Englewood Cliffs, NJ: Prentice-Hall.

Bauer, P. J. (1993). Memory for gender-consistent and gender-inconsistent event sequences by twenty-five-month-old children. *Child Development, 64*, 285–297.

Bauer, P. J., Liebl, M., & Stennes, L. (1998). PRETTY is to DRESS as BRAVE is to SUITCOAT: Gender-based property-to-property inferences by 4-½-year-old children. *Merrill-Palmer Quarterly, 44*, 355–377.

Bem, S. L. (1974). The measurement of psychological androgyny. *Journal of Consulting and Clinical Psychology, 42*, 155–162.

Bem, S. L. (1981). Gender schema theory: A cognitive account of sex typing. *Psychological Review, 88*, 354–364.

Bem, S. L. (1993). *The lenses of gender: Transforming the debate on sexual inequality*. New Haven, CT: Yale University Press.

Berndt, T. J., & Heller, K. A. (1986). Gender stereotypes and social inferences: A developmental study. *Journal of Personality and Social Psychology, 50*, 889–898.

Biernat, M. (1991). Gender stereotypes and the relationship between masculinity and femininity: A developmental analysis. *Journal of Personality and Social Psychology, 61*, 351–365.

Bigler, R. S., Jones, L. C., & Lobliner, D. B. (1997). Social categorization and the formation of intergroup attitudes in children. *Child Development, 68*, 530–543.

Bigler, R. S., & Liben, L. S. (1992). Cognitive mechanisms in children's gender stereotyping: Theoretical and educational implications of a cognitive-based intervention. *Child Development, 63*, 1351–1363.

Bohan, J. S. (1993). Regarding gender: Essentialism, constructionism, and feminist psychology. *Psychology of Women Quarterly, 17*, 5–21.

Boston, M. B., & Levy, G. D. (1991). Changes and differences in preschoolers' understanding of gender scripts. *Cognitive Development, 6*, 412–417.

Bradley, S. J., Oliver, G. D., Chernick, A. B., & Zucker, K. J. (1998). Experiment of nurture: Ablatio penis at 2 months, sex reassignment at 7 months, and a psychosexual follow-up in young adulthood. *Pediatrics, 102*, 132–133.

Bussey, K., & Bandura, A. (1992). Self-regulatory mechanisms governing gender development. *Child Development, 63*, 1236–1250.

Carter, D. B., & Levy, G. D. (1988). Cognitive aspects of early sex-role development: The influence of gender schemas on preschoolers' memories and preferences for sex-typed toys and activities. *Child Development, 59*, 782–792.

Carter, D. B., & McCloskey, L. A. (1984). Peers and the maintenance of sex-typed behavior: The development of children's conceptions of cross-gender behavior in their peers. *Social Cognition, 2*, 294–314.

Carter, D. B., & Patterson, C. J. (1982). Sex roles as social conventions: The development of children's conceptions of sex-role stereotypes. *Developmental Psychology, 18*, 812–824.

Coker, D. R. (1984). The relationships among gender concepts and cognitive maturity in preschool children. *Sex Roles, 10*, 19–31.

Constantinople, A. (1973). Masculinity–femininity: An exception to a famous dictum? *Psychological Bulletin, 80*, 389–407.

Constantinople, A. (1979). Sex-role acquisition: In search of the elephant. *Sex Roles, 5*, 121–133.

Cowan, G., & Hoffman, C. D. (1986). Gender stereotyping in young children: Evidence to support a concept-learning approach. *Sex Roles, 14*, 211–224.

Damon, W. (1977). *The social world of the child.* San Francisco: Jossey-Bass.

Deaux, K., & LaFrance, M. (1998). Gender. In D. T. Gilbert, S. T. Fiske, & G. Lindzey (Eds.), *The handbook of social psychology* (4th ed., Vol. 1, pp. 788–827). Boston: McGraw-Hill.

Deaux, K., & Lewis, L. L. (1984). Structure of gender stereotypes: Interrelationships among components and gender label. *Journal of Personality and Social Psychology, 46*, 991–1004.

Deaux, K., & Major, B. (1987). Putting gender into context: An interactive model of gender-related behavior. *Psychological Review, 94*, 369–389.

Diamond, M., & Sigmundson, H. K. (1997). Sex reassignment at birth: Long-term review and clinical implications. *Archives of Pediatrics and Adolescent Medicine, 151*, 298–304.

Eaton, W. O., Von Bargen, D., & Keats, J. G. (1981). Gender understanding and dimensions of preschooler play choice: Sex stereotype versus activity level. *Canadian Journal of Behavioral Science, 13*, 203–209.

Eckes, T. (1994). Explorations in gender cognition: Content and structure of female and male subtypes. *Social Cognition, 12*, 37–60.

Edelbrock, C., & Sugawara, A. I. (1978). Acquisition of sex-typed preferences in preschool-aged children. *Developmental Psychology, 14*, 614–623.

Fagot, B. I. (1985). Changes in thinking about early sex role development. *Developmental Review, 5*, 83–98.

Feinman, S. (1984). A status theory of the evaluation of sex-role and age-role behavior. *Sex Roles, 10*, 445–456.

Fischer, K. W., & Bidell, T. R. (1998). Dynamic development of psychological structures in action and thought. In W. Damon (Ed.) & R. M. Lerner (Vol. Ed.), *Handbook of child psychology: Vol. 1. Theoretical models of human development* (5th ed., pp. 467–561). New York: Wiley.

Fiske, S. T., & Linville, P. W. (1980). What does the schema concept buy us? *Personality and Social Psychology Bulletin, 6*, 543–557.

Frey, K. S., & Ruble, D. N. (1992). Gender constancy and the "cost" of sex-typed behavior: A test of the conflict hypothesis. *Developmental Psychology, 28*, 714–721.

Gelman, S. A., Collman, P., & Maccoby, E. E. (1986). Inferring properties from categories versus inferring categories from properties: The case of gender. *Child Development, 57,* 396–404.

Green, R. (1987). *The "sissy boy syndrome" and the development of homosexuality.* New Haven, CT: Yale University Press.

Hamilton, D. L. (Ed.). (1981). *Cognitive processes in stereotyping and intergroup behavior.* Hillsdale, NJ: Lawrence Erlbaum Associates.

Huston, A. C. (1983). Sex-typing. In P. H. Mussen (Ed.), *Handbook of child psychology* (4th ed., Vol. 4, pp. 387–467). New York: Wiley.

Imperato-McGinley, J., Peterson, R.E., Gautier, T., & Sturla, E. (1979). Androgens and the evolution of male-gender identity among male pseudohermaphrodites with 5α-reductase deficiency. *New England Journal of Medicine, 300,* 1233–1237.

Intons-Peterson, M. J. (1988). *Children's concepts of gender.* Norwood, NJ: Ablex.

Keil, F. C. (1989). *Concepts, kinds, and cognitive development.* Cambridge, MA: MIT Press.

Kohlberg, L. (1966). A cognitive-developmental analysis of children's sex-role concepts and attitudes. In E. E. Maccoby (Ed.), *The development of sex differences* (pp. 82–173). Stanford, CA: Stanford University Press.

Kuhn, D., Nash, S. C., & Brucken, L. (1978). Sex role concepts of two- and three-year-olds. *Child Development, 49,* 445–451.

Kunda, Z., & Thagard, P. (1996). Forming impressions from stereotypes, traits, and behaviors: A parallel-constraint-satisfaction theory. *Psychological Review, 103,* 284–308.

Langlois, J. H., & Downs, A. C. (1980). Mothers, fathers, and peers as socialization agents of sex-typed play behaviors in young children. *Child Development, 51,* 1237–1247.

Leahy, R. L., & Shirk, S. R. (1984). The development of classificatory skills and sex-trait stereotypes in children. *Sex Roles, 10,* 281–292.

Leinbach, M. D., Hort, B. E., & Fagot, B. I. (1997). Bears are for boys: Metaphorical associations in young children's gender stereotypes. *Cognitive Development, 12,* 107–130.

Levy, G. D., & Carter, D. B. (1989). Gender schema, gender constancy, and gender-role knowledge: The roles of cognitive factors in preschoolers' gender-role stereotype attributions. *Developmental Psychology, 25,* 444–449.

Levy, G. D., Taylor, M. G., & Gelman, S. A. (1995). Traditional and evaluative aspects of flexibility in gender roles, social conventions, moral rules, and physical laws. *Child Development, 66,* 515–531.

Lippmann, W. (1922). *Public opinion.* New York: Harcourt & Brace.

Lobel, T. E., Bempechat, J., Gewirtz, J. C., Shoken-Topaz, T., & Bashe, E. (1993). The role of gender-related information and self-endorsement of traits in preadolescents' inferences and judgments. *Child Development, 64,* 1285–1294.

Lobel, T. E., & Menashri, J. (1993). Relations of conceptions of gender-role transgressions and gender constancy to gender-typed toy preferences. *Developmental Psychology, 29,* 150–155.

Locksley, A., Borgida, E., Brekke, N., & Hepburn, C. (1980). Sex stereotypes and social judgment. *Journal of Personality and Social Psychology, 39,* 821–831.

Maccoby, E. E. (Ed.). (1966). *The development of sex differences.* Stanford, CA: Stanford University Press.

Maccoby, E. E. (1988). Gender as a social category. *Developmental Psychology, 24,* 755–765.

Maccoby, E. E. (1990). The role of gender identity and gender constancy in sex-differentiated development. In D. Schroder (Ed.), *The legacy of Lawrence Kohlberg: New directions for child development* (pp. 5–20). San Francisco: Jossey-Bass.

Markus, H., Crane, M., Bernstein, S., & Siladi, M. (1982). Self-schemas and gender. *Journal of Personality and Social Psychology, 42,* 38–50.

Martin, C. L. (1989). Children's use of gender-related information in making social judgments. *Developmental Psychology, 25,* 80–88.

Martin, C. L. (1990). Attitudes and expectations about children with nontraditional and traditional gender roles. *Sex Roles, 22*, 151–165.

Martin, C. L. (1991). The role of cognition in understanding gender effects. In H. Reese (Ed.), *Advances in child development and behavior* (Vol. 23, pp. 113–149). San Diego, CA: Academic Press.

Martin, C. L. (1993). New directions for investigating children's gender knowledge. *Developmental Review, 13*, 184–204.

Martin, C. L. (1999). A developmental perspective on gender effects and gender concepts. In W. B. Swann, Jr., J. H. Langlois, & L. A. Gilbert (Eds.), *Sexism and stereotypes in modern society: The gender science of Janet Taylor Spence* (pp. 45–73). Washington, DC: American Psychological Association.

Martin, C. L., Eisenbud, L., & Rose, H. (1995). Children's gender-based reasoning about toys. *Child Development, 66*, 1453–1471.

Martin, C. L., & Fabes, R. A. (1997, April). *Building gender stereotypes in the preschool years.* Paper presented at the meetings of the Society for Research on Child Development, Washington, DC.

Martin, C. L., Fabes, R. A., Evans, S., & Wyman, H. (in press). Social cognition on the playground: Children's beliefs about playing with girls versus boys and their relations to sex segregated play. *Journal of Personal and Social Relationships.*

Martin, C. L., & Halverson, C. F. (1981). A schematic processing model of sex typing and stereotyping in children. *Child Development, 52*, 1119–1134.

Martin, C. L., & Halverson, C. F. (1987). The roles of cognition in sex role acquisition. In D. B. Carter (Ed.), *Current conceptions of sex roles and sex typing: Theory and research* (pp. 123–137). New York: Praeger.

Martin, C. L., & Little, J. K. (1990). The relation of gender understanding to children's sex-typed preferences and gender stereotypes. *Child Development, 61*, 1427–1439.

Martin, C. L., & Parker, S. (1995). Folk theories about sex and race differences. *Personality and Social Psychology Bulletin, 21*, 45–57.

Martin, C. L., Wood, C. H., & Little, J. K. (1990). The development of gender stereotype components. *Child Development, 61*, 1891–1904.

Money, J., & Ehrhardt, A. A. (1972). *Man and woman, boy and girl: The differentiation and dimorphism of gender identity from conception to maturity.* Baltimore: Johns Hopkins University Press.

O'Keefe, E. S. C., & Hyde, J. S. (1983). The development of occupational sex-role stereotypes: The effects of gender stability and age. *Sex Roles, 9*, 481–492.

Raag, T., & Rackliff, C. L. (1998). Preschoolers' awareness of social expectations of gender: Relationships to toy choices. *Sex Roles, 38*, 685–700.

Rothbart, M., & Taylor, M. (1992). Category labels and social reality: Do we view social categories as natural kinds? In G. R. Semin & K. Fiedler (Eds.), *Language, interaction and social cognition* (pp. 11–36). Newbury Park, CA: Sage.

Ruble, D. N. (1994). A phase model of transitions: Cognitive and motivational consequences. In M. P. Zanna (Ed.), *Advances in experimental social psychology* (Vol. 26, pp. 163–214). San Diego, CA: Academic Press.

Ruble, D. N., & Martin, C. L. (1998). Gender development. In W. Damon (Series Ed.) & N. Eisenberg (Vol. Ed.), *Handbook of child psychology: Vol. 3. Social, emotional, and personality development* (5th ed., pp. 933–1016). New York: Wiley.

Serbin, L. A., Powlishta, K. K., & Gulko, J. (1993). The development of sex typing in middle childhood. *Monographs of the Society for Research in Child Development, 58* (2, Serial No. 232).

Signorella, M. L., Bigler, R. S., & Liben, L. S. (1993). Developmental differences in children's gender schemata about others: A meta-analytic review. *Developmental Review, 13*, 147–183.

Signorella, M. L., Bigler, R. S., & Liben, L. S. (1997). A meta-analysis of children's memories for own-sex and other-sex information. *Journal of Applied Developmental Psychology*, *18*, 429–445.

Signorella, M. L., & Liben, L. S. (1985). Assessing children's gender-stereotyped attitudes. *Psychological Documents*, *15*, 7.

Slaby, R. G., & Frey, K. S. (1975). Development of gender constancy and selective attention to same-sex models. *Child Development*, *46*, 849–856.

Smith, L. B., & Samuelson, L. K. (1997). Perceiving and remembering: Category stability, variability and development. In K. Lamberts & D. Shanks (Eds.), *Knowledge, concepts and categories* (pp. 161–195). Hove, UK: Psychology Press.

Spence, J. T. (1985). Gender identity and its implications for the concepts of masculinity and femininity. In T. B. Sonderegger (Ed.), *Nebraska symposium on motivation, 1984: Psychology and gender* (Vol. 32, pp. 59–95). Lincoln: University of Nebraska Press.

Spence, J. T. (1993). Gender-related traits and gender ideology: Evidence for a multifactorial theory. *Journal of Personality and Social Psychology*, *64*, 624–635.

Spence, J. T., & Helmreich, R. L. (1978). *Masculinity and femininity: Their psychological dimensions, correlates, and antecedents.* Austin: University of Texas Press.

Stangor, C., & Ruble, D. N. (1987). Development of gender role knowledge and gender constancy. In L. S. Liben & M. L. Signorella (Eds.), *Children's gender schemata* (pp. 5–22). San Francisco: Jossey-Bass.

Stephan, W. G. (1989). A cognitive approach to stereotyping. In D. Bar-Tal, C. Graumann, A. W. Kruglanski, & W. Stroebe (Eds.), *Stereotyping and prejudice: Changing conceptions* (pp. 37–57). New York: Springer.

Stoddart, T., & Turiel, E. (1985). Children's concepts of cross-gender activities. *Child Development*, *56*, 1241–1252.

Stoller, R. J. (1968). *Sex and gender: Vol. 1. The development of masculinity and femininity.* New York: Science House.

Stroebe, W., & Insko, C. A. (1989). Stereotype, prejudice, and discrimination: Changing conceptions in theory and research. In D. Bar-Tal, C. F. Graumann, A. W. Kruglanski, & W. Stroebe (Eds.), *Stereotyping and prejudice: Changing conceptions* (pp. 3–34). New York: Springer.

Tajfel, H. (1969). Cognitive aspects of prejudice. *Journal of Social Issues*, *25*(4), 79–97.

Tajfel, H., & Turner, J. (1979). An integrative theory of intergroup conflict. In W. G. Austin & S. Worchel (Eds.), *The social psychology of intergroup relations* (pp. 33–47). Monterey, CA: Brooks/Cole.

Taylor, M. G. (1996). The development of children's beliefs about social and biological aspects of gender differences. *Child Development*, *67*, 1555–1571.

Taylor, R. D., & Carter, D. B. (1987). The association between children's gender understanding, sex-role knowledge, and sex-role preferences. *Child Study Journal*, *17*, 185–196.

Taylor, S. E., & Crocker, J. (1981). Schematic bases of social information processing. In E. T. Higgins, C. P. Herman, & M. P. Zanna (Eds.), *Social cognition: The Ontario symposium* (Vol. 1, pp. 89–134). Hillsdale, NJ: Lawrence Erlbaum Associates.

Thelen, E., & Smith, L. B. (1998). Dynamic systems theories. In W. Damon (Series Ed.) & R. M. Lerner (Vol. Ed.), *Handbook of child psychology: Vol. 1. Theoretical models of human development* (5th ed., pp. 563–634). New York: Wiley.

Trautner, H. M. (1992). The development of sex-typing in children: A longitudinal analysis. *German Journal of Psychology*, *16*, 183–199.

Weinraub, M., Clemens, L. P., Sockloff, A., Ethridge, R., Gracely, E., & Myers, B. (1984). The development of sex role stereotypes in the third year: Relationships to gender labeling, gender identity, sex-typed toy preferences, and family characteristics. *Child Development*, *55*, 1493–1503.

Wellman, H. M., & Gelman, S. A. (1998). Knowledge acquisition in foundational domains. In W. Damon (Ed.), D. Kuhn & R. S. Siegler (Vol. Eds.), *Handbook of child psychology: Vol. 2. Cognition, perception, and language* (5th ed., pp. 523–573). New York: Wiley.

West, C., & Zimmerman, D. H. (1987). Doing gender. *Gender and Society, 1,* 125–151.

Zucker, K. J., & Bradley, S. J. (1995). *Gender identity disorder and psychosexual problems in children and adolescents.* New York: Guilford.

Zucker, K. J., Wilson-Smith, D. N., Kurita, J. A., & Stern, A. (1995). Children's appraisals of sex-typed behavior in their peers. *Sex Roles, 33,* 703–725.

# 5

# Social Role Theory of Sex Differences and Similarities: A Current Appraisal

Alice H. Eagly
*Northwestern University*

Wendy Wood
*Texas A&M University*

Amanda B. Diekman
*Northwestern University*

Social role theory originated as an effort to understand the causes of sex differences and similarities in social behavior. In the 1980s when the theory emerged, many research psychologists had begun to use meta-analytic methods to aggregate research findings bearing on the issue of whether female and male behavior differs (Eagly, 1987). These researchers had to come to terms with the persisting presence of differences in these data. Although these differences were typically not large (Eagly, 1995, 1997a; Hyde, 1996), they were often large enough to be consequential, particularly in view of the substantial cumulative impact that small differences can have if repeatedly enacted over a period of time (Abelson, 1985; Martell, Lane, & Emrich, 1995). The more accurate description of sex differences and similarities produced by quantitative reviewing, compared with earlier narrative reviewing (e.g., Maccoby & Jacklin, 1974), allowed more systematic examination of important issues such as the variation of differences and similarities across situations. More valid descriptions brought a flowering of theory, as some researchers were inspired to renew their efforts to develop theories that explain the intriguing patterns of difference and similarity present in psychological findings (e.g., Ashmore & Del Boca, 1986; Beall & Sternberg, 1993; Deaux & Major, 1987).

Psychologists benefited as well from the growth of knowledge about the beliefs that people hold about women and men—work that began in the 1950s (McKee & Sherriffs, 1957; Sherriffs & McKee, 1957) and intensified in the 1970s (e.g., Broverman, Vogel, Broverman, Clarkson, & Rosenkrantz, 1972; Spence & Helmreich, 1978). This research on gender stereotypes made it clear that perceivers have a highly elaborated set of associations concerning men and women and believe in a range of overall differences between these groups. This stereotype research raised questions concerning the accuracy of these beliefs and the processes by which perceivers derive them and apply them in everyday social interaction.

As the scientific literature on sex differences and similarities began to mature in the 1980s in the wake of the prior decade's research on gender stereotypes, it became apparent that there is something of a match between the differences revealed in the scientific literature and the beliefs that perceivers hold about differences, despite the traditional depiction of stereotypes by social scientists as inaccurate portrayals of groups (Allport, 1954). Fueled by social psychologists' increasing knowledge of the power of expectancies to produce behavior that confirms them (see review by Olson, Roese, & Zanna, 1996), social role theory evolved in part from the observation of this match between the content of the ideas people have about women and men and scientifically documented sex differences in social behavior and personality. This theory argues that the beliefs that people hold about the sexes are derived from observations of the role performances of men and women and thus reflect the sexual division of labor and gender hierarchy of the society. In their abstract and general form, these beliefs constitute gender roles, which, through a variety of mediating processes, foster real differences in behavior.

Another important influence on our social role theory of sex differences and similarities is the sociological tradition of studying social roles—analyses that extend back to the classic role theorists such as Georg Simmel, George Herbert Mead, Ralph Linton, and Jacob Moreno (see Biddle, 1979, 1986). This tradition is wide ranging and encompasses many different types of research. Of specific relevance to gender roles is the functional analysis of role differentiation in the family proposed by Parsons and Bales (1955). These theorists observed a traditional division of labor between husbands and wives that they described in terms of male instrumental specialization and female expressive specialization. They also observed a presumably analogous division of responsibility in all-male groups between task leaders and social emotional leaders. Moreover, in mixed-sex groups men, more than women, tended to specialize in behaviors related to task accomplishment, and women, more than men, in behaviors related to group maintenance and other distinctively social concerns (Strodtbeck & Mann, 1956). These commonalities led these early functional theorists to reason that families and small groups produce role differentiation along instrumental and expressive lines that is functionally necessary to harmonious social interaction. This analysis has been justifiably criticized for its assumption that complementary male and female roles are necessary to a smoothly functioning society (Connell, 1995; Lopata & Thorne, 1978) and its lack of emphasis on status and power differences between the sexes (Howard & Hollander, 1997; Meeker & Weitzel-O'Neill, 1977, 1985).

In our social role theory of sex differences and similarities, the concept of gender role is stripped from its functionalist moorings by recognizing that it is not inherent in the construct of gender roles that they be complementary or have particular expressive or instrumental content. Also, our analysis does not assume that personal adjustment or harmonious social interaction require gender roles that have the content assumed by Parsons and Bales (1955). However, in the spirit of Parsons and Bales' analysis, our theory assumes that gender roles reflect a society's distributions of men and women into breadwinner and homemaker roles and into occupations. Moreover, as we argue in this chapter, expectations about women and men necessarily reflect status and power differences to the extent that women and men are positioned in a gender hierarchy. Freed from the nonessential aspects of the Parsons and Bales framework, postulating gender roles correctly recognizes that cultures feature shared expectations for the appropriate conduct of men and women and that these expectations foster sex-differentiated behavior. Moreover, social role theory treats gender roles as a dynamic aspect of culture that changes in response to alterations of the typical work and family roles of the sexes. To explicate this approach, this chapter begins with a summary of the theory and then provides detailed discussion of some of the theory's components, combined with review of relevant empirical literature.

## SOCIAL ROLE THEORY

According to social role theory, the differences in the behavior of women and men that are observed in psychological studies of social behavior and personality originate in the contrasting distributions of men and women into social roles (Eagly, 1987, 1997b). As the division of labor is realized in the United States and many other nations, women perform more domestic work than men and spend fewer hours in paid employment (Shelton, 1992). Although most women in the United States are employed in the paid workforce, they have lower wages than men, are concentrated in different occupations, and are rarely at the highest levels of organizational hierarchies (Jacobs, 1989; Tomaskovic-Devey, 1995; Valian, 1998). Also, in contemporary American society and in most other societies, women have less power, status, and resources (Rhoodie, 1989). This aspect of social structure is often denoted by terms such as gender hierarchy or patriarchy. From a social structural perspective, these features of social organization, in particular the sexual division of labor and gender hierarchy, are the root cause of sex-differentiated behavior.

The sex differences that commonly occur in social behavior follow from the typical characteristics of roles commonly held by women versus men. One principle governing these differences follows from the differing balance of activities associated with the typical roles of each sex. Women and men adjust to sex-typical roles by acquiring the specific skills and resources linked to successful role performance and by adapting their social behavior to role requirements. A variety of sex-differentiated skills and beliefs arise from the typical family and economic roles of men and women. Although in many contemporary societies, especially industrial countries, these roles can be described as resource provider and homemaker, the roles of women and men that are modal in a society have taken a wide variety of forms when they are viewed cross-culturally (Murdock & Provost, 1973). Women and men seek to accommodate to the roles that are available to them in their society by acquiring role-related skills; for example, in the presence of a homemaker–provider division of labor, women and girls learn domestic skills such as cooking and sewing, and men and boys learn skills that are marketable in the paid economy. The types of social behavior that typify the homemaker–provider division of labor have been characterized in terms of the distinction between communal and agentic characteristics (Bakan, 1966; Eagly, 1987). Thus, women's accommodation to the domestic role fosters a pattern of interpersonally facilitative and friendly behaviors that can be termed communal. Particularly important in encouraging communal behaviors is the assignment of the majority of childrearing to women, a responsibility that requires nurturant behaviors that facilitate care for children and other dependent individuals. The importance of close relationships to women's nurturing role favors the acquisition of superior interpersonal skills and ability to communicate nonverbally. In contrast, men's accommodation to the employment role, especially to male-dominated occupations, favors a pattern of relatively assertive and independent behaviors that can be termed agentic (Eagly & Steffen, 1984).

In societies with high levels of female labor force participation, such as the United States, the distribution of the sexes into occupations is another important influence on gender roles. Given the moderately strong sex segregation of the labor force (Reskin & Padavic, 1994), perceivers may infer the typical qualities of the sexes from observations of the type of paid work that they most commonly undertake. Surely paid occupations show wide variation in the extent to which they favor more masculine or feminine qualities. Yet, consistent with the agentic focus of the male gender role and the communal focus of the female gender role, occupational success is perceived to follow from agentic personal qualities to the extent that occupations are male-dominated and from communal personal qualities to the extent that they are female-dominated (Cejka & Eagly, 1999; Glick, 1991).

Although social role theory treats the differing assignments of women and men into social roles as the basic underlying cause of sex-differentiated social behavior, the impact of roles on behavior is mediated by psychological and social processes. Important among these processes is the formation of gender roles by which each sex is expected to have characteristics that equip it for its sex-typical roles. Gender roles are thus the shared expectations that apply to individuals on the basis of their socially identified sex. Gender roles are emergents from the activities carried out by individuals of each sex in their sex-typical occupational and family roles; the characteristics required by these activities become stereotypic of women or men. To the extent that women more than men occupy roles that require predominantly communal behaviors, domestic behaviors, or subordinate behaviors for successful role performance, such tendencies become stereotypic of women and are incorporated into a female gender role. To the extent that men more than women occupy roles that require predominantly agentic behaviors, resource acquisition behaviors, or dominant behaviors for successful role performance, such tendencies become stereotypic of men and are incorporated into a male gender role. These gender roles, which are an important focus of socialization, begin to be acquired early in childhood and are elaborated throughout childhood and adolescence.

Gender roles facilitate the activities typically carried out by adults of each sex. For example, the expectation that women be other-oriented and compassionate facilitates their nurturing activities within the family as well as their work in many female-dominated occupations (e.g., teacher, nurse, social worker). The expectancies associated with gender roles act as normative pressures that foster behaviors consistent with sex-typical work roles through expectancy confirmation processes and self-regulatory processes. Gender roles can thereby induce sex differences in behavior in the absence of any intrinsic, inborn psychological differences between women and men. In the remainder of this chapter, we explicate these ideas and review empirical support for them after first discussing the first component of our theory, the division of labor and gender hierarchy.

# ORIGINS OF DIVISION OF LABOR
# AND GENDER HIERARCHY

To become a convincing theory of sex differences and similarities, social role theory must face the task of explaining the sexual division of labor (see Wood & Eagly, 1999). If sex differences in human behavior originate mainly in the contrasting social roles of men and women rather than in psychological differences that are intrinsic to women and men (e.g., evolved mechanisms, see Buss & Kenrick, 1998), these role distributions must themselves be determined primarily by factors other than intrinsic psychological sex differences. If, for example, genetically controlled differences in brain structure and hormones are the principal cause of behavioral sex differences, position in the social structure and the associated gender roles would be mere by-products of these more distal causal forces. If men and women are intrinsically different psychological beings, it would hardly be surprising that they tend to occupy different social roles. However, contrary to such reasoning, a strong case can be made that the division of labor and gender hierarchy are produced by factors other than intrinsic psychological sex differences.

Any analysis of the division of labor must acknowledge impressive evidence for commonalities in this division across societies. Cross-cultural research by anthropologists has shown that all known societies established a division of labor according to sex. Within individual societies, the majority of productive activities are carried out solely or typically by one sex (Murdock, 1967; Murdock & Provost, 1973; Schlegel & Barry, 1986). Moreover, viewed cross-culturally, certain activities are typically in the province of one sex. For example, in Murdock and Provost's sample of 185 societies, a variety of specific activities were highly gender typed: Hunting of large aquatic animals, metalworking, smelting of ores, lumbering, and hunting large land animals were performed exclusively or almost exclusively by men; water carrying, laundering, cooking, and gathering and preparation of vegetal foods were performed primarily by women.

Another cross-cultural commonality is that the status and power differences that do exist within societies typically favor men (e.g., Leacock, 1978; Pratto, 1996; Rhoodie, 1989). Although this aspect of social structure has often been treated as a global feature of societies and labeled gender hierarchy or patriarchy, the dimensions of status that are linked to sex appear to vary across societies (Mukhopadhyay & Higgins, 1988) and to be relatively independent of one another in cross-cultural analyses (Whyte, 1978). Yet, sex differences on these dimensions are typically in the direction of women possessing fewer resources than men, of less value being placed on women's lives, and of greater control of women's marital and sexual behavior.

First and foremost among the causal factors implicated by anthropologists as accounting for the division of labor are physical sex differences, especially women's reproductive activities of pregnancy and lactation (see Wood & Eagly, 1999). Reproduction affects role occupancy directly as well as indirectly through facilitating or limiting other types of behaviors (Schlegel, 1977). Women's tasks thus include gestating, nursing, and caring for highly dependent infants; and these activities limit women's ability to perform tasks that require speed, uninterrupted periods of activity, or long-distance travel away from home. Therefore, women generally eschew tasks such as hunting large animals, plowing, and warfare in favor of activities that can be performed simultaneously with child care (Brown, 1970; Friedl, 1978; Murdock & Provost, 1973). Such consequences of reproduction are less important in societies with low birthrates, less reliance on lactation for feeding infants, and more nonmaternal care of young children.

Another determinant of the distribution of the sexes into social roles is men's greater size and strength. To the extent that productive tasks within a society are highly demanding of speed and of physical strength, especially brief bursts of force and upper-body strength, men, on average, are more likely to be successful at task performance than women. In foraging, horticultural, and agricultural societies, the activities especially likely to be facilitated by men's physical attributes include hunting large animals, plowing, and warfare (M. Harris, 1993; Murdock & Provost, 1973). These considerations of men's greater size and strength are less important in societies in which few occupational roles demand these attributes, such as post-industrial societies in particular.

In general, physical sex differences, in interaction with demands of the economy, technology, and local ecology, influence the roles held by men and women (see Wood & Eagly, 1999). The resulting division of labor does not necessarily produce patriarchy (see Broude, 1990). In fact, social structural accounts of male–female relations typically emphasize that relatively egalitarian relations are found in decentralized, nonhierarchical societies with limited technology and especially in simple economies that derive subsistence from foraging (e.g., Ehrenberg, 1989; Leacock, 1978; Lerner, 1986; Lévi-Strauss, 1949/1969). Yet, in more complex societies, the physical attributes of the sexes generally interact with economic and technological developments to enhance men's power and status. For example, in societies with somewhat developed economies and technology, men's greater upper-body strength and speed generally give them preference over women in performance of activities, such as warfare, that can yield decision-making power, authority, and access to resources (M. Harris, 1993; Hayden, Deal, Cannon, & Casey, 1986).

A number of specific aspects of technology and the economy have been linked to gender-typed role assignments that foster gender hierarchies. These features include (a) the development and use of plow technology in agricultural societies (Ehrenberg, 1989; M. Harris, 1993; Murdock & Provost, 1973); (b) women's increased domestic work that takes them out of the public sphere in societies with intensive agriculture (Ehrenberg, 1989; Ember, 1983); and (c) a constellation of economic factors including private property ownership, the exchange of commodities and women between tribes, and the inheritance of land through men (Coontz & Henderson, 1986; Engels, 1902/1942; Lerner, 1986; Lévi-Strauss, 1949/1969; Whyte, 1978). Common to these analyses is the idea that prior to some specific economic, technological, or social development or some complex of such developments, societies tended to be relatively egalitarian, including in relations between the sexes. A shift to male dominance occurred concurrent with one or more such developments.

In conclusion, most anthropological scholarship accounts for the division of labor and gender hierarchy by arguments that physical sex differences, particularly women's reproduction and men's size and strength, interact with the demands of socioeconomic systems. Psychological specialization of women and men is rarely explicitly postulated as a prior cause of the division of labor or gender hierarchy. It thus does not contradict the great majority of these scholars to argue that these features of social structure are for the most part a product of the sexes' accommodations to gender-typed social roles.

## GENDER STEREOTYPES AND ROLES: WHAT PEOPLE THINK ABOUT HOW MEN AND WOMEN ACTUALLY BEHAVE AND SHOULD BEHAVE

Because in social role theory the contrasting social position of the sexes produces differing gender roles, it is crucial to understand what gender roles are. As collections of beliefs about what women and men actually do and ought to do, the construct of gender role derives from the general concept of social role, which refers to the shared expectations that apply to persons who occupy a certain social position or are members of a particular social category (e.g., Biddle, 1979; Sarbin & Allen, 1968; Staines, 1986).[1] Like

---

[1]In another tradition of defining social role, the key aspect of roles is not expectations but typical patterns of behavior of persons occupying a given social position, as these behaviors are regulated by a set of rights and duties (see Biddle, 1979). Although this approach is also useful, especially in sociological scholarship, psychologists generally define roles as sets of

other social roles, gender roles encompass what Cialdini and Trost (1998) labeled *injunctive norms*, which are expectations about what people ought to do or ideally would do, as well as what they labeled *descriptive norms*, which are expectations about what people actually do.

The distinction between descriptive and injunctive norms helps explain why gender roles have the power to influence behavior. In general, observations of deviations from descriptive norms produce emotions that are imbued with surprise, whereas observations of deviations from injunctive norms produce emotions that are tinged more strongly with moral disapproval (Cialdini & Trost, 1998). Because descriptive norms describe what is normal or typical, they can provide guidance concerning what behaviors are likely to be effective in a situation. Perceivers may thus refer to others of their own sex to find out what sorts of behaviors are usual for their sex in a situation. Especially if a situation is unfamiliar, ambiguous, or confusing, perceivers very often turn to others for guidance (Festinger, 1954) and tend to conform to sex-typical behaviors. Illustrating this principle are social learning experiments performed with child participants, which have shown greater imitation of models of the child's own sex (vs. the other sex) when several same-sex models behave in a particular manner or the model behaves in a manner that is typical of his or her sex (Perry & Bussey, 1979).

Because injunctive norms describe what is desirable and proper, they can provide guidance concerning the behaviors that are likely to elicit approval from others. Consistent with the well-known concept of *normative influence* (e.g., Deutsch & Gerard, 1955) as well as the use of others' approval as a determinant of action in attitude–behavior models (e.g., Fishbein & Ajzen, 1975), people tend to engage in behaviors that they believe are approved by significant others. To the extent that norms differ for women and men, people tend to refer to what is desirable for individuals of their own sex and thereby form intentions and engage in actions that differ by sex. However, if information effectively counters a norm by which a behavior is deemed more desirable for one sex, the stereotypic sex difference in the behavior should erode. Demonstrating this principle is Grossman and Wood's (1993) research in which the general tendency for emotionality to be perceived as more desirable in women than men was countered by a manipulation that made emotional responsiveness seem generally desirable or undesirable. When normative expectations were thus made equivalent for women and men, the typical sex difference in participants' self-reports of their emotions was absent.

In contrast to specific roles based on occupations, family relationships, and membership in other groups such as volunteer organizations, gender

---

expectations or beliefs that are shared among members of a society. This more psychological definition links readily to research on stereotyping and cognitive processes more generally.

roles are diffuse because they apply to people who have membership in the extremely general social categories of men and women. Gender roles thus pertain to virtually everyone. These roles, like other diffuse roles based on demographic characteristics such as age, race, and social class,[2] have great scope or generality because they are applicable to all portions of one's daily life. In contrast, more specific roles based on factors such as family relationships (e.g., father, daughter) and occupation (e.g., kindergarten teacher, police officer) are mainly relevant to behavior in a particular group or organizational context—in the workplace, for example, in the case of occupational roles. Gender roles coexist with specific roles and are relevant to most social interactions, including encounters that are also structured by these specific roles (see subsequent section, "Multiple Roles: Gender Roles and Specific Roles"). Gender roles are thus ubiquitous in their influence. Because categorization as male or female is fundamental to social interaction, gender roles cannot be temporarily eliminated by moving to a different social context.

## People Believe in Sex Differences

At the individual level, a role encompasses a construct or knowledge structure consisting of a set of beliefs about a group of people. Empirical evidence that people have such knowledge structures about women and men follows from research on gender stereotypes, which has consistently documented that people believe that the typical traits and behaviors of men and women differ (e.g., Berndt & Heller, 1986; Broverman et al., 1972; Cejka & Eagly, 1999; Diekman & Eagly, in press; McKee & Sherriffs, 1957; Spence & Buckner, in press; Spence & Helmreich, 1978; Survey Research Consultants International, 1998; Williams & Best, 1990a). The implicit statistical model that perceivers generally hold is of differences in central tendency, with distributions of women and men overlapping to a greater or lesser extent, depending on the domain (Eagly, 1987; Swim, 1994). Factor analytic studies have shown that a substantial portion of the content of these perceived differences can be summarized in terms of personal characteristics

---

[2]Critics of the gender-role construct (e.g., Lopata & Thorne, 1978) have noted that social scientists often refer to gender (or sex) roles but seldom to race roles or class roles. Although there surely are diffuse expectations associated with race and social class, as claimed by status characteristics theorists (e.g., Berger & Zelditch, 1985), these expectations may not be as often conceptualized as roles because they may lack the prescriptive force of expectations about women and men. Whereas people thus tend to agree that it is desirable that women and men have certain sex-differentiated characteristics (e.g., agentic and communal tendencies; see Spence & Helmreich, 1978), they are no doubt far less likely to agree on the desirability of race-based and class-based patterns of behavior.

that are readily grouped into the communal and agentic categories that we noted in our description of social role theory. The communal personal characteristics that are disproportionately assigned to women, such as friendly and concerned with others, and the agentic characteristics that are assigned to men, such as independent and instrumentally competent, are generally expressed in trait terminology (Berninger & DeSoto, 1985; Deaux & Lewis, 1983). This pattern appears not only in conventional stereotype studies in which respondents describe men and women in general but also in studies in which respondents rate the characteristics of individual women and men who are presented in photographs (Feingold, 1998).

Beliefs about the sexes also include ideas about undesirable personal characteristics of each sex. Particularly ascribed to men are domineering qualities that reflect an excess of agency that is unmitigated by communion (e.g., arrogant, boastful, unprincipled); particularly ascribed to women are passive, subordinate qualities that reflect an excess of communion unmitigated by agency (e.g., spineless, servile, nagging; Fritz & Helgeson, 1998; Helgeson, 1994; Spence, Helmreich, & Holahan, 1979). Finally, people's ideas about the sexes encompass beliefs about physical characteristics, typical roles, cognitive abilities, attitudes, specific skills, and emotional dispositions (Cejka & Eagly, 1999; Deaux & Lewis, 1983, 1984; Eckes, 1994a). In general, the network of associations concerning men and women is highly elaborated, reflecting perceivers' high frequency of close contact with persons of both sexes (S. T. Fiske & Stevens, 1993).

The ubiquity of thinking about people as female and male is revealed by findings showing that sex is the personal characteristic that most readily captures perceivers' attention; it provides the strongest basis of categorizing people, even when compared with race, age, and occupation (A. P. Fiske, Haslam, & Fiske, 1991; Stangor, Lynch, Duan, & Glass, 1992; van Knippenberg, van Twuyver, & Pepels, 1994). Moreover, numerous experiments have demonstrated not merely that people hold gender-stereotypic beliefs but in addition that these beliefs are easily and automatically activated. For example, preconsciously priming gender-related words (e.g., jobs such as *nurse* or *doctor*) versus nonstereotypic words caused participants to classify gender-matched pronouns (e.g., *he* or *she*) more quickly into male and female categories (Banaji & Hardin, 1996). Also, preconsciously priming stereotypic characteristics (e.g., *sensitive* or *logical*) caused participants to more quickly identify the gender of male or female first names (e.g., *Gina* or *Gary*) that matched the primes' gender (Blair & Banaji, 1996). In addition, implicit but conscious priming induced by having participants unscramble sentences with male or female stereotypic (vs. nonstereotypic) content produced more stereotypic ratings of the gender-matched male or female target person (Banaji, Hardin, & Rothman, 1993). Other research has shown that participants classified people by occupation more quickly in stereotypic than counterstereotypic combinations of person and occupation (Zárate & Sandoval, 1995) and exhibited larger event-related brain potentials (i.e., indicating semantic incongruity) in response to sentences containing counterstereotypic occupational information (e.g., "the beautician put himself through beauty school"; Osterhout, Bersick, & McLaughlin, 1997). Such phenomena are consistent with the claim that perceivers have acquired a network of associations about men and women that are readily activated by the presentation of gender-related cues, even if that presentation is preconscious (see S. T. Fiske, 1998).

## People Approve of Many Stereotypic Sex Differences

Demonstrations that people's knowledge structures about women and men encompass injunctive norms as well as descriptive norms can be found in research showing that stereotypic ways of behaving are perceived as generally desirable for people of the congruent sex, insofar as researchers examine the evaluatively positive aspects of gender stereotypes. To identify the behaviors thought to be desirable for women versus men, researchers have investigated the beliefs that people hold about ideal women and men (Broverman et al., 1972; Spence & Helmreich, 1978; Williams & Best, 1990b) or that women and men hold about the selves that they ideally would be or ought to be (Wood, Christensen, Hebl, & Rothgerber, 1997). In general, such beliefs about the ideal traits and behaviors of women and men resemble beliefs about the positive aspects of their typical behavior. Moreover, the more sex-differentiated that behaviors and traits actually are, the more strongly they are differentially evaluated as appropriate for only one sex. This important relation was established by Hall and Carter (1998), who found a positive relation between the desirability of 77 diverse traits and behaviors for women versus men and the actual predominance of these traits and behaviors in women versus men, as established by meta-analytic reviews of sex differences. It thus appears that people tend to think that they themselves as well as women and men more generally ought to differ in gender-typed ways. This oughtness adds the essential injunctive ingredient that transforms gender stereotypes into gender roles. Moreover, the prescriptive quality of gender roles connects them to a broader ideology by which gender differentiation and inequality are viewed as the natural order of human life (see Jackman, 1994; Pratto, 1999).

The tendency for the attributes that are differentially ascribed to each sex to be valued in their behavior fits with evidence that the stereotypes of both sexes are in general evaluatively positive. Although women are typically a subordinated group in the society and thus perceived as inferior in power and status, they are not generally devalued, as shown by analyses of the evaluative content of gender stereotypes (e.g., Williams & Best, 1990a). On the contrary, the stereotype of women is even somewhat more positive than the stereotype of men, at least in some recent North American data sets, largely because of the high value placed on the positive communal characteristics that are ascribed more to women than men (Eagly & Mladinic, 1989, 1994; Eagly, Mladinic, & Otto, 1991; Haddock & Zanna, 1994).[3] These very qualities, however, contribute to patriarchal features of society because they are thought to qualify women for the domestic role (Eagly & Steffen, 1984) as well as for female-dominated occupations (Cejka & Eagly, 1999). A similar point was made by Jackman (1994) based on her survey research assessing Americans' beliefs about women and men: "Women are warmly congratulated for their distinctiveness in personal traits that are appropriate to the tasks and behaviors assigned to them and to which men have no aspirations" (p. 347).

## People Are Aware That Beliefs About Men and Women Are Shared in Society

The idea that expectations about male and female behavior are shared implies that some degree of consensus exists about typical and appropriate behaviors and that people are aware of this consensus. Despite some limited evidence that beliefs about the sexes are weakly correlated with respondents' attitudes on sexism scales (Spence & Buckner, in press; Swim, Aikin, Hall, & Hunter, 1995), these beliefs appear to be widely held. Research has thus established that largely similar beliefs are held by men and women, students and older adults, and people who differ in social class and income (e.g., Broverman et al., 1972; Diekman & Eagly, in press; Hall & Carter, 1998; Jackman, 1994). Developmentally, children even as young as 3 years of age show stereotyping of children's toys and activities and of traitlike characteristics; more complex gender-stereotypic beliefs develop steadily throughout the preschool and elementary years (Ruble & Martin, 1998). Moreover, consistent with the social cognitive research noted earlier in this section (e.g., Banaji & Hardin, 1996), it is reasonable to argue that virtually everyone has a cognitive representation of their culture's stereotypic beliefs about the sexes (see also Devine, 1989), although the possibility remains that these

---

[3]These studies obtained such findings with methods that involved explicitly asking respondents about the qualities that are typical of women and men. In addition, Mitchell (1998) obtained more positive evaluations of women than men using an implicit measure that assessed participants' reaction time for associating men or women with the adjective *pleasant* or *unpleasant*. With this task, the tendency to evaluate women more favorably than men was stronger among the female than the male participants, but significant in both sexes.

available beliefs may be more accessible among people with sexist attitudes (e.g., Dijksterhuis, Macrae, & Haddock, 1999).

This consensus does not mean that everyone approves of all evaluatively positive aspects of sex differences. Rather, as observers of their world, people become aware of the sex-differentiated aspects of behavior and the positive value placed on many of these differences, and moreover they become aware that other people are also cognizant of these differences. This awareness of an apparent consensus has been shown in research that asked respondents to report the characteristics that they think that people in their culture associate with each sex (e.g., Lunneborg, 1970; Williams & Best, 1990a). Respondents readily reported these characteristics. Although surely there are individual differences in personal evaluation of stereotypic behaviors and practices, especially in relation to the rights and roles of women and men (e.g., Glick & Fiske, 1996; Spence & Helmreich, 1978; Swim et al., 1995; Tougas, Brown, Beaton, & Joly, 1995), people would tend to expect that the typical other person endorses the norms that are modal in the culture and thus would react with surprise and disapproval to behavior that is inconsistent with them. Therefore, it is reasonable for people to assume that the most likely route to social approval in most situations is to behave consistently with their gender role or at least to avoid strongly deviating from it. However, cues that others hold nontraditional attitudes and beliefs can produce contexts in which nontraditional behaviors are likely to elicit approval (e.g., Zanna & Pack, 1975).

To the extent that role constructs are consensual—that is, shared among members of a society—they are important structures at the macrosocial level as well as the individual level. Roles are thus aspects of culture, which can be understood as "cognitive and evaluative beliefs shared among members of a social system and generally developed and maintained through processes of socialization" (House, 1995, p. 390). Roles produce constraints on behavior and therefore influence social structure, which can be understood as "persisting and bounded patterns of behavior and interaction among people or positions" (House, 1995, p. 390). Thus, people who have the same social position within a social structure such as an organization or family or who are classified in the same general societal category (e.g., as women, as immigrants) experience common prescriptive constraints that tend to maintain their characteristic patterns of behavior. These constraints arise from the shared beliefs that people in their society hold.

## WHY GENDER STEREOTYPES HAVE CERTAIN CONTENT: CORRESPONDENT INFERENCE CAUSES THESE STEREOTYPES TO REFLECT THE SOCIAL POSITION OF THE SEXES

### Perceivers Assume Correspondence Between Role-Constrained Behavior and the Personal Attributes of Role Occupants

That perceivers assume correspondence between the type of actions people engage in and their inner dispositions is a basic principle of social psychology (see Gilbert, 1998). Because people often do not give much weight to situational constraints in interpreting others' behavior, this correspondence tendency has often been interpreted as producing error and labeled, for example, the *fundamental attribution error* (Ross, 1977) or *correspondence bias* (Gilbert & Malone, 1995). Yet, regardless of whether inferring people's inner qualities from their actions produces erroneous judgments, correspondent inference is the basic psychological process that produces stereotypes of social groups that mirror the qualities that they play out in their social roles.

Supporting this point about correspondent inference, research has demonstrated that people fail to give much weight to the constraints of social roles in inferring role players' dispositions. For example, an experiment by Ross, Amabile, and Steinmetz (1977) involved encounters between undergraduates who were arbitrarily placed either in the social role of questioner who composed difficult questions based on his or her general knowledge or in the role of answerer of these questions. Failing to take account of the biasing effects of these questioner and answerer roles, participants rated the questioners as superior to the answerers in their general knowledge. Therefore, to the extent that these participants described dispositional knowledge and not merely enacted, role-bound behavior, they gave relatively little weight to role constraints. Similarly, perceivers who ascribe nurturance to women are engaging in correspondent inference that gives little weight to role requirements by which women must more frequently perform nurturant behavior in carrying out the child care aspects of the domestic role.

Reflecting this logic of correspondence bias, Schaller (1994, 1996; Schaller & O'Brien, 1992) argued that accurate inferences about group members' enduring traits require that perceivers control for situational constraints by using statistical reasoning analogous to an analysis of covariance in which these constraints would function as covariates. Schaller has shown that people generally fail to engage in such reasoning and as a consequence form erroneous impressions of groups. In a similar vein,

Hoffman and Hurst (1990) argued that gender stereotypes can function as rationalizations for role distributions and that these stereotypes can develop in the absence of any true intrinsic differences between the sexes. Providing a creative experimental demonstration using fictitious groups of city workers and child raisers who were described as not differing in their agentic and communal traits, Hoffman and Hurst showed that, even under these conditions, role-consistent agentic traits were ascribed to city workers and communal traits to child raisers. Hoffman and Hurst argued that such correspondent inferences allow stereotypes to justify role distributions, a viewpoint that was furthered by Jost and Banaji's (1994) analysis of stereotypes as providing *system justification.*

One reservation about this correspondent inference theory of stereotyping arises from perceivers' possible logic that dispositional differences between groups determine role assignment—for example, the reasoning that people who become city workers differed at the outset from people who become child rearers because they freely chose these social roles based on their preferences.[4] However, research suggests that perceivers do not give a large weight to freedom of choice versus coercion in inferring target persons' dispositions. The classic demonstration of this phenomenon is Jones and Harris' (1967) experiment, in which participants inferred the attitude of the author of an essay that either supported or opposed Castro's regime. The essayist was described as having freely chosen to support one side of this issue or as having been required to take the side by an authority figure. In general, participants demonstrated correspondent inference by indicating that the essayists endorsed the positions that they took. Although knowing that the position was coerced reduced this effect somewhat, it did not eliminate it: Participants still judged the pro-Castro essayist as more favorable to Castro than the anti-Castro essayist. Demonstrating an analogous effect in relation to family roles, Riggs (1998) described a target father or mother who anticipated either being employed or staying at home to care for his or her baby and either having choice or no choice about employment or staying at home. Participants rated persons who expected to stay at home as more communal and less agentic than persons who expected to be employed. Although the absence of choice reduced these effects, it did not eliminate them. This experiment thus demonstrates the overriding tendency for perceivers to judge that dispositions correspond to behaviors, even when these behaviors are constrained by roles that are not freely chosen.

---

[4]Hoffman and Hurst (1990) tried to restrain this inference by providing information about the equivalence of the dispositions of their child rearers and city workers.

## Correspondent Inferences About Women
## and Men Reflect Their Typical Social Roles

Underlying the principle that gender stereotypes follow from the distribution of the sexes into social roles are the insights that (a) the roles typically performed by men versus women have somewhat different requirements and demands and (b) perceivers make correspondent inferences from role behavior to the dispositions of role occupants. Yount (1986) expressed this argument especially clearly by arguing that people's knowledge about the sexes emerges from attributes that are associated with their productive activity. Because gender-stereotypic attributes reflect the social and physical conditions of this productive activity, Yount regarded these stereotypes as instances of *work-emergent traits*. The conditions of production differ for women and men in a largely sex-segregated workforce, and therefore the traits ascribed to women and men differ. It follows that sex-typical roles should be thought to require gender-stereotypic attributes. We consider the relation between the distribution of the sexes into social roles and the gender stereotyping of these roles by reviewing studies of the attributes ascribed to employees versus homemakers, job-holders in male-dominated versus female-dominated occupations, and occupants of higher status versus lower status roles.[5]

***Employees and Homemakers.*** That gender-stereotypic meaning follows from the division of labor between domestic labor and wage labor was demonstrated empirically in experiments by Eagly and Steffen (1984, 1986b, 1988), which elicited judgments of the communal and agentic attributes of people who were described in various ways. Participants thus judged women and men whose occupations were not indicated or were described as either homemaker or full-time employee. As expected, occupational role proved to be a strong determinant of judgments of communal and agentic attributes: People in the domestic role were regarded as more communal and less agentic than people in the employee role, regardless of their sex. Male and female homemakers were perceived equivalently, and male and female

---

[5]One criticism of the proposition that the division of labor and gender hierarchy produce gender roles stems from the idea that most roles are actually quite flexible in allowing for a fairly wide range of more masculine and feminine behaviors (e.g., Valian, 1998). Although there is surely some flexibility, it is likely to be sharply limited in actual practice because of the norms that grow up around occupations and foster particular ways of behaving. These norms change only gradually. Moreover, occupations do require that certain activities be carried out, and many of these activities inherently and predominantly demand styles of social interaction that are associated with one sex (e.g., taking care of infants demands communal behavior; military combat requires agentic behavior. See also subsequent discussion of "Multiple Roles: Gender Roles and Specific Roles.").

employees were perceived similarly.[6] Also, average women and men whose occupations were not mentioned were perceived stereotypically: Women were seen as higher in communion and lower in agency compared with men. According to social role theory, this gender-stereotypic perception of the sexes stems from the perceived association of women with the domestic role and of men with the provider role. The characteristics that are thought to typify providers are thus ascribed to men in general, and the characteristics that are thought to typify homemakers are ascribed to women in general. Consistent with this demonstration, in studies of the subtypes of women that people commonly identify, the overall stereotype of women resembled the subtype stereotypes of mothers and housewives (Deaux, Winton, Crowley, & Lewis, 1985; Eckes, 1994a, 1994b).

These findings showing an association between the basic division of labor between providers and homemakers and the ascription of agentic and communal qualities to people have been replicated by several other researchers who have incorporated part of Eagly and Steffen's (1984) homemaker–employee design into their experiments (e.g., Bridges & Etaugh, 1992; Bridges & Orza, 1992, 1993; Kite, 1996; Riggs, 1997, 1998). Also, given the prevalence of part-time employment, especially among women, Eagly and Steffen (1986b) extended their earlier analysis by examining perceptions of the communal and agentic attributes of part-time employees as well as homemakers and full-time employees. As expected, part-time employees were in general accorded a middle ground between these other two groups.

***Occupational Roles Differing in Sex Distributions.***    The activities that perceivers associate with agentic qualities can be described broadly as those connected with paid employment. However, certain occupational activities that are highly male-dominated may be especially important in shaping the male gender role and stereotype to emphasize agentic qualities. For example, M. Harris (1977, 1993) argued that the assignment of military roles to men

---

[6]A consistent tendency emerged for female employees to receive somewhat more extreme ratings on agentic characteristics than male employees. Perhaps, as Eagly and Steffen (1984) maintained, the perception that women have greater freedom of choice about being employed may underlie this trend. Subsequently, Biernat and Manis' shifting standards model (Biernat, 1995; Biernat & Manis, 1994) showed that implicit stereotypes can shape within-sex standards for evaluating men and women on gender-typed attributes. According to this principle, a level of agency that would be considered "somewhat agentic" for a man might be considered "very agentic" for a woman because a higher level of agency is thought to be typical of men and both sexes are judged in relation to their own group. Therefore, in Eagly and Steffen's experiments, employed women may not have been perceived as more agentic than employed men. More generally, perceived sex differences may actually be more stereotypic than those revealed by studies that present respondents with subjective rating scales that allow standards to shift between male and female targets.

fosters society's ascription of aggressiveness and other agentic qualities in men. More generally, Cejka and Eagly (1999) demonstrated that to the extent that occupational roles are male dominated, they are perceived to require agentic qualities for successful performance and to the extent that occupational roles are female dominated, they are thought to require communal qualities (see also Glick, 1991). Moreover, stereotypically masculine physical qualities (e.g., muscular, tall, brawny) are thought to be more important for success in occupations to the extent that they are male dominated, and stereotypically feminine physical qualities (e.g., sexy, dainty, pretty) are thought to be more important to the extent that they are female dominated. In addition, numerous other studies have established that occupations' sex ratios are related to the ascription of some gender-stereotypic attributes to job holders in these occupations (e.g., Kalin, 1986; McLean & Kalin, 1994; Shinar, 1978) or to the perceived masculinity versus femininity of occupations (Beggs & Doolittle, 1993; Shinar, 1975). The particular masculine qualities associated with male-dominated occupations are thus varied (e.g., physical strength in some, assertiveness and leadership qualities in others), as are the particular feminine qualities associated with female-dominated occupations (e.g., pleasing physical appearance in some, kindness and nurturance in others).

***High-Status and Low-Status Roles.*** Also important in relation to gender roles and stereotypes is the tendency for the specific roles occupied by men to be higher in hierarchies of status and authority than the roles occupied by women. The domestic role has lower status than the provider role; and in the family, husbands have an overall power advantage for both routine decision making and conflict resolution, even though there are some areas of decision making in which wives have primary authority (Scanzoni, 1979; Steil, 1997). In employment settings, women are more likely than men to be employed in positions that have relatively low status and that have little power and limited opportunity for advancement. As far as supervisory and administrative roles in organizations are concerned, there is abundant evidence that women are much scarcer at higher levels (e.g., Federal Glass Ceiling Commission, 1995; Valian, 1998; Zweigenhaft & Domhoff, 1998).

Consistent with the argument that sex differences in role status underlie gender stereotypes, status is correlated with beliefs about role occupants' agentic and communal qualities. Eagly and Steffen (1984) thus found a strong tendency for occupants of higher status roles to be perceived as more agentic than occupants of lower status roles. Illustrating one aspect of this greater agency, Eagly and Wood (1982) showed that people holding higher status roles in an organization are believed to exert influence more successfully and to be influenced less readily than people holding lower status roles, regardless of their sex. However, when Eagly and Wood's participants had no information about target individuals' roles, they judged that men were more influential and women easily influenced, presumably because of their prior observations of women's chronically lower status in natural settings. Without any information contradicting the usual covariation of sex and status within organizations, participants thus assumed that men are likely to be in higher-status roles than women; inferences about social influence followed from this assumption (see also Eagly, 1983). Substantiating this claim that status and influence are associated, Moskowitz, Suh, and Desaulniers (1994) found that occupants of organizational roles perceived themselves as less dominant and more submissive when interacting with supervisors than with subordinates.

The idea that the link between sex and status in people's minds produces an increment in men's perceived agency is consistent with the perspective and research findings of sociologists working within the tradition of *status characteristics theory*, which is one of the branches of *expectation states theory* (e.g., Berger, Wagner, & Zelditch, 1985; Berger, Webster, Ridgeway, & Rosenholtz, 1986). According to this approach, sex functions as a status cue or *diffuse status characteristic* (e.g., Meeker & Weitzel-O'Neill, 1977, 1985; Ridgeway & Diekema, 1992; P. Stewart, 1988; Wagner & Berger, 1997). People use sex as a status cue because of their prior experience in natural settings where they observed that men were likely to have greater power and status. According to this theory, in task-oriented groups people infer others' general competence from their sex because of its function as a status cue. Men are therefore thought to be more competent than women, when competence is construed in terms of the agentic qualities that are most relevant to performance in task-oriented groups.

Status also influences perceptions of communal characteristics, although this effect does not appear to be as strong as its impact on agentic characteristics. Eagly and Steffen (1984) failed to produce such an effect in two experiments in which participants rated the gender-stereotypic attributes of men and women who were described as having higher status occupations (e.g., bank vice president, physician) or lower status occupations (e.g., bank teller, X-ray technician). However, research by Conway, Pizzamiglio, and Mount (1996) showed that Eagly and Steffen's null finding reflected their nonrepresentative selection of high-status roles that are somewhat communally demanding. With more representative sampling of high-status roles, low-status occupations were indeed perceived as generally higher in terms of their interpersonal, communal demands. Moreover, fictitious groups described as having low status were perceived more communally as well as more agentically than groups described as having high status.

In agreement with this association of lower status with communal behavior, Ridgeway and Diekema (1992) argued that women display more cooperative and group-oriented behavior in group settings because, in the absence of such behavior, their attempts to gain influence tend to be perceived as illegitimate because of their low diffuse status. Women who behave in this group-oriented way achieve more influence than they otherwise would, whereas men's ability to influence is unaffected by such displays (Ridgeway, 1982; Shackelford, Wood, & Worchel, 1996). Such demonstrations suggest a relation between low status and communal behavior that is consistent with the claim that the ascription of communal attributes to women stems at least in part from their occupancy of social roles with less status and authority attached to them (see also Wood & Karten, 1986). In summary, a substantial body of research has established that the stereotypic beliefs that women are especially communal and men are especially agentic have their roots in three features of social structure: (a) the division of labor between providers and homemakers, (b) the distribution of the sexes into male-dominated and female-dominated paid occupations, and (c) the gender hierarchy by which men are more likely than women to occupy high-status roles.

Finally, the general proposition that beliefs about the attributes of members of social groups follow from their positioning in the social structure provides a general theory of the content of stereotypes of all social groups. Therefore, it is not surprising that this principle has been invoked by researchers investigating stereotypes based on ethnicity (e.g., Brewer & Campbell, 1976; LeVine & Campbell, 1972), race (Feldman, 1972; Smedley & Bayton, 1978), nationality (Eagly & Kite, 1987), and age (Kite, 1996). For example, because African Americans are more socioeconomically disadvantaged than European Americans, the content of the African American stereotype reflects the roles typically occupied by citizens who are poorer and less educated. This more general applicability of a social structural analysis strengthens its plausibility as an analysis of gender stereotypes and roles.

## WHY ACTUAL SEX DIFFERENCES MIRROR GENDER ROLES AND STEREOTYPES: THE IMPORTANCE OF EXPECTANCY CONFIRMATION AND SELF-REGULATION

After correspondent inference has shaped perceivers' ideas about the dispositions of men and women and these ideas are shared to become aspects of culture, these shared ideas are powerful influences on the self-concepts and behavior of both sexes. These ideas foster sex-differentiated behavior. The principle that actual differences between the sexes mirror gender stereotypes, which in turn mirror the positioning of the sexes in the social

structure, reaches back to the classic functional analysis of role differentiation in the family offered by Parsons and Bales (1955). Elaborating aspects
of this analysis, Williams and Best (1990a) argued that, because communal
qualities are important for good performance of domestic activities,
especially childrearing, and agentic qualities are important for good
performance of behaviors enacted in the specific roles more often occupied
by men, each sex accommodates by becoming appropriately specialized.
More generally, each sex accommodates to its unpaid and paid specific
roles. This personal participation in roles dominated by one's own sex
throughout the life cycle is critical to the socialization and maintenance of
sex differences. Females and males thereby learn different skills and acquire
different attitudes, insofar as they occupy such roles. However, social role
theory goes beyond the simple statement that people who are in particular
social roles perform in role-appropriate ways. In addition, the theory
maintains that the differing histories of women and men in sex-typical social
roles in a society and the embodiment of these histories in the culture in the
form of consensual gender roles foster general behavioral tendencies that
differ in women and men. The mechanisms that are especially important in
instilling these tendencies are the behavioral confirmation of others' gender-
stereotypic expectancies and the self-regulation of behavior based on
gender-stereotypic self-construals.

## People Behaviorally Confirm Others'
## Gender-Stereotypic Expectancies

That people often conform to others' expectancies is a social psychological
principle that extends back to classic concepts such as *self-fulfilling
prophecy* (Jussim, 1986; Merton, 1948) and *normative influence* (Deutsch &
Gerard, 1955). In general, people are assumed to communicate their
expectations to others through verbal and nonverbal behaviors and to react
positively if their expectations are confirmed. The relevant processes are
presumed to operate often at a relatively implicit or automatic level. Thus,
perceivers are not necessarily aware of their expectations or of the processes
by which they convey them to others; nor are the targets of these
expectancies necessarily aware of others' influence on them (Vorauer &
Miller, 1997). The specific processes by which one person's expectations
result in another's expectancy-confirming behavior are diverse, and the link
between expectancies and behavior is contingent on various conditions (see
Darley & Fazio, 1980; M. J. Harris & Rosenthal, 1985; Snyder, 1984).
Surely people do not always passively acquiesce by behaving consistently
with expectations and norms. Instead, individuals differ in the extent to
which they conform to norms, and situations differ in the extent to which

they elicit conformity (see review by Olson et al., 1996). Nonetheless, expectancy-confirming behavior appears to be common (Rosenthal & Rubin, 1978), and stereotypic expectancies have considerable power to produce behavior that confirms them (see Snyder, 1981).

Expectancies about women and men have yielded some of the clearest demonstrations of behavioral confirmation (e.g., Christensen & Rosenthal, 1982; von Baeyer, Sherk, & Zanna, 1981; Zanna & Pack, 1975; see review by Geis, 1993). Illustrating these demonstrations is Skrypnek and Snyder's (1982) experiment in which male–female pairs of students, located in different rooms, used a signaling system to negotiate a division of labor on a series of tasks that differed in the extent to which they were gender-stereotypic. Some male members of the pairs were not informed of their partner's sex; others received either correct (i.e., female) or incorrect (i.e., male) information about the sex of their partner. Men who believed that they were dealing with a woman assigned more feminine tasks to their partner and were less likely to yield to her preferences than men who (incorrectly) believed that they were dealing with a man. Moreover, women whose partners thought they were women chose more feminine tasks than women who partners believed they were men. Women thus acted to confirm the gender-stereotypic beliefs held by their male partner.

Deaux and Major (1987; see also Deaux & LaFrance, 1998) formulated a comprehensive model of the proximal processes that may be involved in producing behaviors that confirm gender roles. These processes involve the activation of a gender role in the perceiver's mind (i.e., *gender-related schema* in Deaux and Major's terminology), in response to target attributes and situational cues, and the initiation of action toward the target individual. This step of action encompasses the most obvious reason that people confirm others' expectancies—namely, that these others deliver penalties for nonconformity with gender roles and rewards for conformity. These penalties and rewards are often delivered without awareness of gender violations or the formation of an intention to punish them. Rather, people unwittingly and unknowingly manifest approval for conformity to gender norms and disapproval for nonconformity.

One context in which differential sanctions may be applied for behaviors congruent versus incongruent with gender roles is parental socialization. Although cross-culturally it is common that boys are encouraged to be aggressive and self-reliant and to show fortitude and that girls are encouraged to be industrious, responsible, obedient, and sexually restrained (Barry, Josephson, Lauer, & Marshall, 1976), these socialization pressures show systematic variation depending on family structure, societal stratification, and women's power and control (Low, 1989), as social role theory would predict. Although sex-differentiated parental pressures in the domains examined by Barry et al. are generally unremarkable in most contemporary data from countries such as the United States, a meta-analysis by Lytton and Romney (1991) found relatively clear-cut effects in one area, which is encouraging gender-typed activities and interests—for example, gender-typed toys, games, and chores. Yet, such differential reinforcement is more often delivered by fathers than mothers and directed toward boys rather than girls (Lytton & Romney, 1991; Ruble & Martin, 1998). Consistent with this generalization, Raag and Rackliff (1998) found the strongest evidence for encouragement of gender-typed play for fathers in relation to their sons, and the sons who reported that their fathers would have negative reactions to cross-gender play showed more play with tools and less play with dishes, relative to other children. Because such play activity frequently models adult role performances (e.g., doll play models caring for children), it provides tutelage in sex-typical adult social roles. Assigning household chores on the basis of sex similarly provides apprenticeship in sex-typical adult roles. In addition, such gender-typed activities foster children's learning of gender distinctions and stereotypes and influence their learning of cognitive and social skills. As Ruble and Martin (1998) argued, masculine toys such as vehicles and building sets may foster visual-spatial, mechanical, and exploratory skills, whereas feminine toys such as dolls may foster verbal skills.

Childhood and adolescent peer groups are also important sources of encouragement for gender-stereotypic behavior, as Maccoby (1998) argued. Each sex develops strong gender stereotypes and group cultures, enhanced by considerable voluntary sex segregation in childhood. Consistent with J. R. Harris' (1995, 1998) arguments about the importance of socialization by peer groups, the gender roles sustained by such groups may be a more powerful influence enhancing sex-differentiated behavior than parental socialization.

In social psychological research on adults, evidence abounds for negative reactions to deviations from male and female gender roles. For example, one early study demonstrated that men who were portrayed as behaving passively and women as behaving assertively were rated less favorably than men who were portrayed as behaving assertively and women as behaving passively (Costrich, Feinstein, Kidder, Marecek, & Pascale, 1975). Other research showed that when gender-role expectations were violated by mothers who were described as employed full-time after the birth of an infant or by fathers who were described as employed part-time, participants reacted more negatively than they did to the role-congruent parents (i.e., mothers employed part-time and fathers employed full-time; Etaugh & Folger, 1998). In addition, consistent with Heilman's (1983) lack-of-fit model of sex bias in work settings, job applicants whose sex is atypical of job-holders in an occupation are perceived as generally less qualified than equivalent applicants of the typical sex (e.g., Glick, 1991; Judd & Oswald,

1997). Experimental studies of hiring hypothetical candidates for management and other male-dominated occupations generally showed bias against women, even though the characteristics of the female and male candidates were equated (e.g., see meta-analysis by Davison & Burke, in press; Olian, Schwab, & Haberfeld, 1988).

Because of the contemporary change in the status of women in the United States and many other nations, many studies have examined reactions to behavior that is traditionally considered to be masculine. Much of this research has documented the negative sanctioning of women who behave in agentic or dominant ways. For example, attitudinal studies have shown that "feminists" are evaluated less favorably than "housewives" (Haddock & Zanna, 1994). In a meta-analysis of 61 experiments involving evaluations of male and female leaders whose behavior had been equated, Eagly, Makhijani, and Klonsky (1992) showed that women who adopted a male-stereotypic autocratic and directive leadership style were evaluated more negatively than men who adopted this same style, whereas women and men who adopted more democratic and participative styles were evaluated equivalently. In small-group interaction, women's competent, task-oriented contributions are more likely to be ignored and to elicit negative reactions than comparable contributions from men (Altemeyer & Jones, 1974; Ridgeway, 1982). Rudman (1998) presented evidence that self-promotion in the form of speaking directly and highlighting one's accomplishments can make a women less likable and attractive, whereas self-promoting men do not suffer these costs. In general, women tend to lose likability and influence when they behave in a dominant style by expressing clear-cut disagreement with another person, using direct rather than tentative speech, and behaving in an extremely competent manner (e.g., Carli, 1990, 1995; see review by Carli & Eagly, 1999). Such research details some of the processes involved in the norm-sending mechanism that helps produce gender-congruent behavior. People thus elicit conformity to gender-role norms by dispensing rewards such as liking, compliance, and cooperation in return for conformity and dispensing punishments such as rejection, noncompliance, and neglect in return for nonconformity. These negative reactions to gender nonconformity can be relatively subtle (e.g., facial expressions conveying disapproval; Butler & Geis, 1990).

Consistent with the idea that gender roles' power stems in part from their communication of appropriate or desirable behavior, the presence of other people can affect how gender-stereotypic behavior is. The presence of others may make gender-role norms more salient, especially under certain circumstances (e.g., when one is a numerical token in a group; Kanter, 1977). Also, the presence of others may bring self-presentational concerns to the fore, as people become more concerned about gaining others' approval. Consistent with the idea that the presence of other people often produces more stereotypic behavior was Eagly and Crowley's (1986) meta-analytic finding that the presence of an audience heightens the greater helping by men than women that is typical of situations that allow for chivalrous or heroic actions. Analogous findings have been obtained in several contexts. For example, in public but not in private, men took a more independent stance in response to group pressure, whereas women did not show this effect (Eagly, Wood, & Fishbaugh, 1981; see also Eagly & Chrvala, 1986). Also, women made more modest interpretations of their performance on laboratory tests of ability in public than in private (Berg, Stephan, & Dodson, 1981), whereas men were unaffected by this variation (Gould & Slone, 1982). Similarly, first-year college women (but not men) made more modest predictions of their first semester grade point averages in public than in private (Daubman, Heatherington, & Ahn, 1992; Heatherington et al., 1993). Also, women's (but not men's) aggression decreased when research participants were individually identified to others rather than anonymous (Lightdale & Prentice, 1994). Given the assumptions that gender roles call for men to be chivalrous, heroic, and independent in the face of group pressure and for women to be unaggressive and modest about achievements, research thus shows that behavior is typically more gender-stereotypic in the presence of others.

Because people often sanction behavior that is inconsistent with gender roles, these roles have a generally conservative impact on men and women by exacting costs from those who deviate from norms concerning male and female behavior. Weighing these negative outcomes in a cost-benefit analysis, people would hesitate to engage in nonconformity with their gender role unless it produced benefits that would outweigh these costs. Part of these perceived benefits for women, as members of a subordinate group in society, may be having some chance to gain access to rewards and opportunities formerly reserved for men. Therefore, under some circumstances, increasing the salience of gender-role norms may make women in particular react against traditional expectations. Just such an effect was observed by Cialdini, Wosinska, Dabul, Whetstone-Dion, and Heszen (1998) in a study of modest self-presentation. Gender-role norms were made accessible by having participants respond to stereotypic statements (e.g., "drink beer") by indicating if the behavior was more socially approved for females or males (vs. respond to nonstereotypic statements in a control condition). Participants then completed a self-report measure of modesty. Although when gender norms were not made accessible, the women were indeed more modest than the men, the manipulation substantially decreased women's modesty, so that women were then as immodest as the men. However, this effect was not obtained in a sample of university students in Poland. Gender roles in the United States are apparently sufficiently questioned by female university students that enhancing their awareness of them can produce a boomerang toward nontraditional behavior.

## People Regulate Their Own Behavior
## Based on Gender-Stereotypic Self-Construals

Gender roles can produce sex differences in behavior not only by affecting the rewards and punishments received from others but also by influencing the self-concepts of women and men. In forming that aspect of the self that has been termed gender identity, people thus take societal gender roles into account along with their self-categorization in terms of biological sex (Ashmore, 1990; Frable, 1997). As Spence (1993) showed, a person's gender identity does not ordinarily entail accepting all of the attributes that are generally thought to be typical and appropriate for his or her sex but accepting some portion of them. Also, gender identity is not necessarily activated in a given situation; rather, situational cues can activate aspects of gender identity (Deaux & Major, 1987). For example, Hogg and Turner (1987) showed that people thought of themselves in more gender-stereotypic terms in mixed-sex groups than in single-sex dyads, presumably because gender identity was triggered by the presence of the other sex.

Because self-definitions are important in regulating behavior (see reviews by Baumeister, 1998; Mischel, Cantor, & Feldman, 1996), gender-typed selves as well as others' expectations can underlie sex-differentiated behavior. Research showing that people's self-concepts tend to have gender-stereotypic content (e.g., Bem, 1974; Biernat, 1991; Spence, 1993; Spence & Buckner, 1998; Spence & Helmreich, 1978) suggests that gender roles influence people's ideas about themselves. Providing an analysis of sex differences in the structure of the self, Cross and Madson (1997) maintained that women's construals of themselves are oriented toward interdependence in the sense that they treat representations of others as part of their selves and that men's construals of themselves are oriented toward independence and separation in the sense that they treat representations of others as separate from the self (see also Josephs, Markus, & Tafarodi, 1992). This characterization of men has proven controversial, however. Baumeister and Sommer (1997) maintained that men's seemingly independent self-construals are oriented to connections with larger social groups rather than the dyads and intimate groups favored by women and are especially directed toward competition for status and power. Research by Gabriel and Gardner (1999) has supported the principle that women focus more on the relational aspects of interdependence and men on the collective aspects of interdependence. A male emphasis on competition for power and status in larger collectives is surely compatible with social role theory, which argues that the male gender role follows in part from men's greater access to status and power in society. As a consequence, men's self-concepts should be marked by their striving for advantaged positions in social hierarchies.

The internalization of gender-stereotypic qualities results in people adopting gender-typed norms as personal standards for judging their own behavior. They tend to evaluate themselves favorably to the extent that they conform to these personal standards and to evaluate themselves unfavorably to the extent that they deviate from these standards. In a demonstration of such processes, Wood et al. (1997) investigated normative beliefs that men are powerful, dominant, and self-assertive and that women are caring, intimate with others, and emotionally expressive. They found that to the extent that these gender-role norms were personally relevant to participants, experiences that were congruent with gender norms yielded positive feelings about the self and brought participants' actual self-concepts closer to the standards represented by their ought and ideal selves.[7] This evidence thus demonstrates that one of the processes by which gender roles affect behavior is that they are incorporated into people's self-concepts and then operate as personal standards.

The link between gender roles and self-construals helps explain why there are substantial individual differences in the extent to which women and men engage in behavior consistent with the consensual gender roles of their culture. Although everyone acquires knowledge of the gender roles of their culture, some individuals internalize and personally endorse aspects of these societal gender roles, and others do not. Moreover, people who do internalize gendered norms behave more stereotypically in the areas regulated by these norms, as Grossman and Wood (1993) demonstrated in relation to emotional expression. More generally, Taylor and Hall (1982) meta-analytically demonstrated that to the extent that people have a more communal self-concept, they have a stronger tendency to engage in communal behaviors; to the extent that they have a more agentic self-concept, they have a stronger tendency to engage in agentic behaviors. Conversely, people raised in or influenced by culturally atypical environments may not internalize conventional gender-role norms and thus may have self-construals atypical of their gender. Such individuals are less likely to show traditionally gender-typed behavior. Findings from several

---

[7]In theorizing about self-knowledge, Higgins (1987) distinguished between two types of self-guides: the ideal self, which contains ideas about the person one would like ideally to be, and the ought self, which contains ideas about the person one should try to be. Under some circumstances, the ideal self and the ought self may diverge. According to Higgins' approach, falling short of one's ideal self produces emotions of sadness and depression, whereas falling short of one's ought self produces emotions of anxiety and guilt. The distinction is relevant to gender roles to the extent that they become internalized into the self and thereby produce ideal and ought self-guides (see Wood et al., 1997).

types of studies are thus consistent with the assumption that self-regulatory processes are important causes of sex-differentiated behavior.

# THE OUTCOME: MODAL WOMEN AND MEN BEHAVE STEREOTYPICALLY

Social role theory predicts that, as general tendencies, the sex differences manifested in behavior conform to gender roles and stereotypes. As these differences are assessed by psychologists, they are behavioral tendencies that are manifested on questionnaires and other measures of abilities, traits, and attitudes as well as in laboratory settings and occasionally in field settings. To the extent that men and women actually behave stereotypically, these differences would in turn strengthen gender roles and stereotypes and channel men and women into different social roles. Thus, the forward causal sequence of social role theory—from division of labor and gender hierarchy to gender roles to behavior—should allow for a backward sequence as well. Moreover, to the extent that causes of sex differences not treated by social role theory (e.g., direct impact of sex hormones on behavior) might have some influence, their impact would also flow backward onto gender roles and role distributions.

Given the propositions of social role theory, it is important to examine the extent to which psychological research has established that actual sex differences correspond to gender stereotypes and roles. In recent years, most of the scientific discussion about psychological sex differences has centered on meta-analytic integrations (see Johnson & Eagly, in press) of relatively large numbers of studies of particular classes of behaviors (see overviews by Eagly, 1995; Hall, 1998; Hyde, 1996), although more qualitative research that is not amenable to meta-analysis remains influential (e.g., Gilligan, 1982; Tannen, 1990). These richly elaborated meta-analytic reviews have provided grist for the theoretical mill as psychologists have pondered the causes of sex differences, both as "main effect" findings that are averaged across all available studies and as "interaction" findings that are moderated by studies' characteristics.

With respect to social behavior and personality, meta-analyses were conducted in many research literatures. For example, Hall and her colleagues (Hall, 1984; Hall & Halberstadt, 1986; Stier & Hall, 1984) carried out numerous meta-analyses on sex differences in nonverbal behaviors. Also reviewed were studies of conformity and social influence (Becker, 1986; Cooper, 1979; Eagly & Carli, 1981; Lockheed, 1985), empathy (Eisenberg & Lennon, 1983), helping behavior (Eagly & Crowley, 1986), and aggressive behavior (Bettencourt & Miller, 1996; Eagly & Steffen, 1986a;

Hyde, 1984). Meta-analyses of group behavior investigated interaction styles (L. R. Anderson & Blanchard, 1982; Carli, 1982), leader emergence (Eagly & Karau, 1991), group performance (Wood, 1987), and competition and cooperation (Walters, Stuhlmacher, & Meyer, 1998). In syntheses that included both organizational and laboratory studies, meta-analysts examined whether the style and the effectiveness of leaders and managers differ according to their sex (Eagly & Johnson, 1990; Eagly, Karau, & Makhijani, 1995).

Quantitative reviewers examined whether men differ from women in the qualities they prefer in mates (Feingold, 1990, 1992), their disclosure of personal concerns to others (Dindia & Allen, 1992), and their body image (Feingold & Mazzella, 1998). Other meta-analyses concerned sexual behavior and attitudes (Kite & Whitley, 1996; Murnen & Stockton, 1997; Oliver & Hyde, 1993), subjective well-being (Wood, Rhodes, & Whelan, 1989), mental illness (Nolen-Hoeksema, 1987), personality traits (Feingold, 1994; Twenge, 1997b), and personality growth (Cohn, 1991). Also quantitatively synthesized were sex differences in attitudes and beliefs concerning other people in general (Winquist, Mohr, & Kenny, 1998), women's rights and roles (Twenge, 1997a), rape (K. B. Anderson, Cooper, & Okamura, 1997), sexual harassment (Blumenthal, 1998), computers (Whitley, 1997), science (Weinburgh, 1995), and the ethics of business (Franke, Crown, & Spake, 1997). Finally, with respect to cognitive abilities and performances, researchers provided numerous meta-analyses and summaries of large databases (e.g., Hedges & Nowell, 1995; see overviews by Halpern, 1992, 1997).

Each meta-analysis produced a complex set of findings: Conclusions about an overall difference between the sexes were accompanied by a series of conclusions about moderator variables that revealed some of the conditions under which the overall difference became larger or smaller or even sometimes reversed its usual direction. The great majority of these meta-analyses yielded evidence of consequential differences, at least under some circumstances. Although the complexity of the outcomes of typical meta-analytic reviews means that main-effect sex differences are only the beginning of the story that the reviewers told about gender in each domain of behavior, researchers have provided listings of these overall findings (e.g., Ashmore, 1990, Table 19.1). Particularly complete is Hall's (1998, Tables 7.1 and 7.2) listing of 77 traits and behaviors. Perhaps the best global description of these meta-analytic results is that they generally conform to people's ideas about the sexes, a generalization that is compatible with social role theory. This conclusion was first proposed on the basis of a thematic analysis of demonstrated sex differences in social behavior and personality (Eagly & Wood, 1991).

Considerably more formal evidence of the stereotypic quality of sex differences has emerged subsequently. The first such demonstration was Swim's (1994) study showing that student judges' estimates of differences between the sexes with respect to 17 different attributes of personality, social behavior, and cognitive abilities predicted with considerable success the mean effect sizes representing the sex differences obtained in meta-analyses of psychological research findings on these attributes. The correlation between the estimated sex differences and the meta-analytic effect sizes— the criterion provided by psychological research—was high in two studies ($rs$ = .79 and .78).[8] Using a similar procedure, Briton and Hall (1995) investigated perceptions of sex differences in 17 aspects of nonverbal communication and obtained similar correlations between perceived and meta-analytic sex differences.

In a far more extensive study examining 77 meta-analyzed traits, abilities, and behaviors, Hall and Carter (1999) found a similar correlation between student judges' estimates of sex differences and the meta-analytic effect sizes ($r$ = .70). Accuracy was similarly high for women and men, and it held across various behavioral domains. These judges displayed understanding of the relative magnitude of differences in addition to their male or female direction. Also demonstrating the sophistication of perceivers' knowledge of gender are meta-analyses that obtained judges' estimates of female and male behavior for each of the reviewed studies (Eagly & Crowley, 1986; Eagly & Karau, 1991; Eagly & Steffen, 1986a). Specifically, student judges estimated male and female behavior after reading a brief description of the particular behavior examined in each of the studies that had compared the behavior of women and men. The correlations between these estimates, which represented gender stereotypes about specific types of behaviors, and the behavioral sex differences in the studies, assessed by their effect sizes, were positive and significant (e.g., Eagly & Crowley, 1986, Table 5; Eagly & Karau, 1991, Table 6; Eagly & Steffen, 1986a, Table 5). In showing that the judges were successful in taking the particular characteristics of the behaviors and their situational contexts into account, these findings demonstrate the detail and subtlety of people's beliefs about women and men.

This research showing the rather close match between the sex differences obtained in psychological research and perceivers' beliefs about the sexes is important from several perspectives, including of course the social role

---

[8]These correlations and the others cited in this section are based on correlating judges' mean estimates of sex differences with an index of sex differences. Another strategy is to correlate the estimates and the index of differences separately for each individual judge and to average these correlations across the judges. Correlations of the first type, which are based on aggregated data, are generally larger than correlations of the second type, which are based on individual data.

proposition that gender roles help produce these very differences. Although the correlational nature of these findings limits their ability to show that gender roles are causal in relation to sex differences, they are surely consistent with the argument. Also, these findings add fuel to the debate about the accuracy of stereotypes (see Lee, Jussim, & McCauley, 1995) and weigh in generally on the side of accuracy (see Eagly & Diekman, 1997). As Hall and Carter (1999) argued based on their examination of the personality correlates of accuracy in predicting sex differences, the ability to accurately predict male and female behavior reveals a sensitivity to one's social environment or ecological sensitivity that is a product of careful observation not only of sex differences but of other features of human behavior. This point is not to deny that there are biases in perceiving the sexes (see Eagly, Diekman, & Kulesa, 1999). Moreover, accuracy at the level of differences between groups does not imply that predictions of individual behavior that are guided by these stereotypes are accurate. Instead, the categorization of people into groups tends to produce somewhat homogeneous perceptions of group members and thus results in some bias at the level of predicting individual behavior (see Brewer & Brown, 1998).

## MULTIPLE ROLES:
## GENDER ROLES AND SPECIFIC ROLES

Gender roles, viewed as shared expectations that apply to individuals on the basis of their socially identified sex (Eagly, 1987), coexist with specific roles based on factors such as family relationships (e.g., mother, son) and occupations (e.g., secretary, firefighter). In workplace settings, for example, a manager occupies a role defined by occupation but is simultaneously a man or woman and thus to some extent functions also under the constraints of his or her gender role. Similarly, in a community organization an individual who has the role of volunteer is simultaneously categorized as female or male and is thus perceived in terms of the expectations that are applied to people of that sex. According to social role theory, because specific social roles are typically very constraining, gender roles become relatively less important determinants of behavior in their presence.

Children and adults have a generally different situation with respect to the pressures of specific social roles. Whereas adults generally have constraining occupational roles and family roles as mothers and fathers, children have roles based mainly on gender and on being dependent members of a family. They lack the strong forces of other roles, especially occupational roles, that compete with gender roles for control of adult behavior. The tendencies for children to have quite rigid ideas about gender and to show pronounced gender prejudice (see reviews by Glick & Hilt, chap. 8, this volume; Ruble & Martin, 1998) may reflect the relatively greater prominence of gender roles in their lives. Among adults, other social roles exert their influence, and sex differences tend to diminish when men and women occupying the same specific social role are compared. However, gender roles ordinarily continue to have some impact on adult behavior, despite the constraints of specific roles. In agreement with this reasoning, Gutek and Morasch (1982) argued that gender roles "spill over" to workplace roles and cause people to have different expectations for female and male occupants of the same workplace role.

Experimental evidence (e.g., Hembroff, 1982) suggests that people combine or average the expectations associated with specific roles and more diffuse roles such as gender roles in a manner that weights each set of expectations according to its relevance to the task at hand. Because specific roles have more direct implications for task performance in many natural settings, they may often be generally more important than gender roles. This conclusion was foreshadowed by experimental demonstrations that stereotypic sex differences can be eliminated by providing information that specifically counters gender-based expectations. For example, Wood and Karten (1986) found that manipulating competency-based status in mixed-sex groups through false feedback that described participants as low or high in competence eliminated the usual sex differences in interaction style by which men, compared with women, showed more active task behavior and less positive social behavior (see also Shackelford et al., 1996). Also suggesting an erosion of sex differences by experimental manipulations of demands are Snodgrass' (1985, 1992) experiments investigating the moderation of sex differences in interpersonal sensitivity by superior–subordinate roles that were assigned in a laboratory task. In experiments in which teacher–learner roles (Snodgrass, 1985) or boss–employee roles (Snodgrass, 1992) were established, status differences in sensitivity were found but not the sex differences that are typically present.

The social role theory analysis of the joint impact of gender roles and specific roles on behavior was implemented by Eagly and Johnson (1990) in a meta-analytic review of studies that had compared the leadership styles of men and women. In organizational studies, because the men and women who' were compared had the same job (e.g., as middle managers in a business organization), they occupied the same specific managerial role. Because organizations have traditions of management that managers of both sexes have to learn, the constraints of the managerial role were expected to minimize sex differences in leadership style, at least compared with the differences that would occur in laboratory studies with student participants, who were merely temporary occupants of a leadership role in a group formed for an experiment. Yet, gender roles should not disappear entirely in organizations but continue to have some impact, above and beyond the managerial role. The meta-analytic findings obtained by Eagly and Johnson were generally supportive of this reasoning. Specifically, in organizational studies, male and female managers did not differ in their tendencies to adopt an interpersonally oriented style or a task-oriented style. However, college students in laboratory studies did show gender-stereotypic differences in these aspects of leadership style. Nonetheless, among the organizational managers (and the college students as well), there was one important difference between the women and men: Women tended to adopt a more participative or democratic style, compared with the more directive and autocratic style of men. This stereotypic difference may be a product of several factors, especially the effects of the diffuse gender roles that continued to influence managers, despite their occupancy of the same workplace role.

An other meta-analysis relevant to the simultaneous influence of gender roles and organizational roles concerned ethical decision making in business contexts (Franke et al., 1997). Although in general women were more likely than men to perceive questionable business practices (e.g., use of insider information) as unethical, this difference was largest in the student samples and declined with increases in the work experience of the respondent sample. This sex difference was thus quite small among nonstudents, who in the typical study were women and men in the same occupation (e.g., Fortune 1000 executives, advertising professionals) and were therefore subject to the influence of similar employment roles.

An exceptional study by Moskowitz et al. (1994) used behavioral measures to examine the simultaneous influence of gender roles and organizational roles with a sample of Canadian adults who held a wide range of jobs in a variety of organizational settings. This study used an experience-sampling method by which participants monitored their interpersonal behavior for 20 days, using an event-sampling strategy. For each event, participants indicated the gender and role of the interaction partner and chose from a list the behaviors that they had engaged in during the social interaction. These behaviors represented dominance, agreeableness, submissiveness, and quarrelsomeness, and the researchers subtracted submissive from dominant behaviors to assess agency and subtracted quarrelsome from agreeable behaviors to assess communion. With the partner's status represented in terms of the social roles of supervisor, coworker, or supervisee, the effects of participants' gender were examined. In general, agentic behavior was controlled by the relative status of the interaction partners, with participants behaving most agentically when with a supervisee and least agentically when with a boss. Yet, communal behaviors were influenced by the sex of participants, with women behaving more communally, especially in interactions with other women.

Research on physicians has also demonstrated women's more communal behavior, even in the presence of a constraining occupational role. For example, a study by Hall, Irish, Roter, Ehrlich, and Miller (1994) analyzed videotaped physician–patient interactions during 100 routine medical visits. Compared with male physicians, female physicians evidenced a more communal style of interaction, characterized by more positive statements, more statements implying partnership with the patient, more smiling and nodding, and more back-channel responses (i.e., attentive and encouraging statements emitted by a speaker who does not have the floor). More generally, Roter and Hall's (1998) meta-analysis of 19 studies of physician–patient interaction found that, in this research literature as a whole, female physicians engaged in more partnership building with the patient, more emotionally focused talk, more positive talk, more giving of psychosocial information (e.g., concerning personal habits, impact on family), and more question asking in all content areas.

Although research concerning the joint impact of gender roles and other roles is sparse and mainly centers on occupational roles, some tentative generalizations are suggested about the leveling of sex differences by the demands of other roles. It is thus likely that employment roles provide relatively clear-cut rules about the performance of particular tasks. A physician, for example, must obtain information about symptoms from a patient, provide a diagnosis, and design treatment that is intended to alleviate the patient's symptoms. Within the task rules that regulate physician–patient interactions, there is still room for some variation in behavioral styles. Physicians may behave in a warm, caring manner that focuses on producing a positive relationship or in a more remote and less personally responsive style that focuses more exclusively on information exchange and problem solving. The female gender role may foster more caring, communal behavior in physicians or a more participative style of decision making in managers. Thus, occupational roles no doubt have primary influence on how people accomplish the tasks required by their jobs, which would therefore be similarly accomplished by male and female role occupants. In contrast, gender roles may "spill over" to have their primary influence on the discretionary behaviors that are not required by the occupational role, which may sometimes be behaviors in the communal repertoire but other times be other types of behaviors. Gender roles are thus still an important factor, even if they become something of a background influence in settings in which specific roles are of primary importance. As Ridgeway (1997) wrote in relation to social interaction in the workplace, "The problems of interacting cause actors to automatically sex-categorize others and, thus, to cue gender stereotypes that have various effects on interactional outcomes, usually by modifying the performance of other, more salient identities" (p. 200).

# CHANGE IN GENDER ROLES
# AND SEX DIFFERENCES OVER TIME

The view that gender roles are rooted in the division of labor and gender hierarchy implies that these roles should change if these features of social structure change. Remarkable in the second half of the 20th century is the rapid increase in the extent to which women are employed in the paid labor force in the United States and many other nations (Reskin & Padavic, 1994). In the United States, the percentages of employed women and men were 34% and 86%, respectively, in 1950 and 60% and 75% in 1997 (U.S. Department of Labor, 1999).Women's greatly increased education, by which their rates of school and university education exceed those of men in the United States and some other nations (United Nations Development Programme, 1999), has qualified them for jobs with more status and income than the jobs that women typically held in the past. Additionally, the career plans of male and female university students showed a marked convergence from 1966 to 1996 that is accounted for mainly by changes in women's career aspirations (Astin, Parrott, Korn, & Sax, 1997). Even though the tendency for men to increase their responsibility for child care and other domestic work is modest (Shelton, 1992), these changes in the division of labor, especially women's entry into paid employment, should result in decreasing acceptance of the traditional gender roles and a redefinition of the patterns of behavior that are most appropriate to women and men. Yet, the impact of such molar social changes would be quite variable, depending on life stage (A. J. Stewart & Healy, 1989) and personality characteristics (Agronick & Duncan, 1998; Roberts & Helson, 1997).

Attitudinal changes congruent with actual changes in the roles of men and women have been documented in the form of increasingly less approval of the traditional system of divergent roles and responsibilities for women and men (R. J. Harris & Firestone, 1998; Loo & Thorpe, 1998; Sherman & Spence, 1997; Simon & Landis, 1989; Spence & Hahn, 1997). Twenge (1997a) meta-analytically demonstrated a general shift toward more egalitarian definitions of women's rights and responsibilities between 1970 and 1995, although the change in women's attitudes was somewhat larger than the change in men's attitudes. However, some portion of people in Western nations still endorse aspects of traditional gender roles, as displayed in survey data (e.g., Zuo, 1997) and individual differences in acceptance of traditional norms about male and female behavior (e.g., Glick & Fiske, 1996; Swim et al., 1995; Tougas et al., 1995). Moreover, as studies of gender stereotypes have shown (e.g., Leuptow, Garovich, & Leuptow, 1995; Spence & Buckner, in press), the tendency to ascribe differing communal and agentic personal characteristics to the sexes has shown little change when earlier and later data sets are compared.[9] However, self-reports of respondents' own communal and agentic tendencies do show change over time, primarily in the form of women viewing themselves as increasingly more agentic (Spence & Buckner, in press; Twenge, 1997b). This mix of findings suggests that gender roles are in considerable flux, at least in Western societies. Although these shifts suggest that a loss of consensus may lessen the power of gender roles to influence behavior, the traditional consensus is apparently intact in some of the more conservative segments of society, and a new consensus may have emerged or be emerging in other segments of society. Nonetheless, the new consensus may share some features with the old consensus, such as the expectation that men take the major responsibility for providing financially for their families (Riggs, 1997). Furthermore, occupational sex segregation is still prevalent with women concentrated (more than men) in occupations that are thought to require feminine qualities and men (more than women) in occupations thought to require masculine qualities (e.g., Cejka & Eagly, 1999; Glick, 1991). Given that occupational segregation currently takes this form, social role theory would not predict that either gender stereotypes or sex-differentiated behavior should have already disappeared. Instead, to the extent that the traditional sexual division between wage labor and domestic labor erodes and the sexes become similarly distributed into paid occupations, men and women should become more similar. In some psychological research literatures, this idea that sex differences are disappearing is amenable to testing, at least over a limited span of years, with meta-analytic techniques (e.g., Feingold, 1988; Nowell & Hedges, 1998; Twenge, 1997b).

Regardless of the status of scientific evidence on the convergence of the sexes, perceivers believe that men and women are becoming more similar. These beliefs have been demonstrated by Diekman and Eagly (in press), who showed that people believe that women and men have converged in their personality, cognitive, and physical characteristics during the past 50 years and will continue to converge during the next 50 years. Path analyses suggested that perceivers function like implicit role theorists by assuming that, because the roles of women and men have become more similar, their attributes converge. The demise of most sex differences with increasing gender equality, a proposition that thus fits popular beliefs about the characteristics of women and men, is a prediction of social role theory that

---

[9]This apparent lag in changes in gender stereotypes is provocative from the perspective of social cognitive theories of stereotype change (see review by Hilton & von Hippel, 1996). Although "bookkeeping" models that presume constant updating of stereotypes in response to changing reality suggest that stereotypes should change as external realities change, other models suggest mechanisms whereby stereotypes can readily be maintained (e.g., the formation of subtypes to encompass deviating cases).

will be more adequately tested as more societies produce conditions of equality or near equality.

## CONCLUSION

The social role theory of sex differences in behavior, initially proposed over a decade ago (Eagly, 1987), has been greatly enriched through empirical work that has tested its propositions and in some cases produced modifications. Fitting within a body of social psychology that maintains that social structural and cultural factors influence individual behavior (see Pettigrew, 1997), the theory maintains its initial focus on the positioning of women and men in the social structure as the root cause of sex differences in behavior. The contrasting position of the sexes yields gender roles, which have powerful effects on individuals, who strive to take these roles into account as they try to reach important goals, enhance their self-esteem, and gain approval from others. Other social roles, especially those pertaining to occupations and family relationships, are also very important, and the effects of these other roles combine with those of gender roles to influence behavior. In all social settings, people must engage in social interaction as a man or a woman and therefore must contend with their own and others' expectations concerning the behavior that is typical and appropriate for individuals of their sex. For children and adolescents, understanding gender roles and the consequences of gender conformity and deviation are a critical focus of their learning to successfully negotiate their social environment. Violating others' expectations about male or female behavior can bring a variety of negative reactions, whereas meeting their expectations can bring rewards of social approval and cooperation. In addition, living up to one's own personal expectations about gender-appropriate behavior can yield rewards of self-esteem and satisfaction. Yet, in many modern societies, because women's position in the social structure is undergoing rapid change, gender roles are in flux. Although shifting gender roles can loosen the constraints of traditional rules about how men and women should behave and thus allow more behavioral flexibility, these changes also produce ambiguity, confusion, and debates concerning what is the proper place of women and men in society.

## ACKNOWLEDGMENT

The writing of this chapter was supported by a research grant to the first author from the National Science Foundation, SBR-9729449. The chapter was written while the first author was a Visiting Scholar at the Murray Research Center of Radcliffe College and supported by a Sabbatical Award from the James McKeen Cattell Fund.

# REFERENCES

Abelson, R. P. (1985). A variance explanation paradox: When a little is a lot. *Psychological Bulletin, 97*, 129–133.

Agronick, G. S., & Duncan, L. E. (1998). Personality and social change: Individual differences, life path, and importance attributed to the women's movement. *Journal of Personality and Social Psychology, 74*, 1545–1555.

Allport, G. W. (1954). *The nature of prejudice*. Reading, MA: Addison-Wesley.

Altemeyer, R. A., & Jones, K. (1974). Sexual identity, physical attractiveness and seating position as determinants of influence in discussion groups. *Canadian Journal of Behavioural Science, 6*, 357–375.

Anderson, K. B., Cooper, H., & Okamura, L. (1997). Individual differences and attitudes toward rape: A meta-analytic review. *Personality and Social Psychology Bulletin, 23*, 295–315.

Anderson, L. R., & Blanchard, P. N. (1982). Sex differences in task and social-emotional behavior. *Basic and Applied Social Psychology, 3*, 109–139.

Ashmore, R. D. (1990). Sex, gender, and the individual. In L. A. Pervin (Ed.), *Handbook of personality: Theory and research* (pp. 486–526). New York: Guilford.

Ashmore, R. D., & Del Boca, F. K. (Eds.). (1986). *The social psychology of female–male relations: A critical analysis of central concepts*. Orlando, FL: Academic Press.

Astin, A. W., Parrott, S. A., Korn, W. S., & Sax, L. J. (1997). *The American freshman: Thirty year trends*. Los Angeles: Higher Education Research Institute, UCLA.

Bakan, D. (1966). *The duality of human existence: An essay on psychology and religion*. Chicago: Rand McNally.

Banaji, M. R., & Hardin, C. (1996). Automatic stereotyping. *Psychological Science, 7*, 136–141.

Banaji, M. R., Hardin, C., & Rothman, A. J. (1993). Implicit stereotyping in person judgment. *Journal of Personality and Social Psychology, 65*, 272–281.

Barry, H., III, Josephson, L., Lauer, E., & Marshall, C. (1976). Traits inculcated in childhood: Cross-cultural codes 5. *Ethnology, 15*, 83–114.

Baumeister, R. F. (1998). The self. In D. T. Gilbert, S. T. Fiske, & G. Lindzey (Eds.), *The handbook of social psychology* (4th ed., Vol. 1, pp. 680–740). Boston: McGraw-Hill.

Baumeister, R. F., & Sommer, K. L. (1997). What do men want? Gender differences and two spheres of belongingness: Comment on Cross and Madson (1997). *Psychological Bulletin, 122*, 38–44.

Beall, A. E., & Sternberg, R. J. (Eds.). (1993). *The psychology of gender*. New York: Guilford.

Becker, B. J. (1986). Influence again: An examination of reviews and studies of gender differences in social influence. In J. S. Hyde & M. C. Linn (Eds.), *The psychology of gender: Advances through meta-analysis* (pp. 178–209). Baltimore: Johns Hopkins University Press.

Beggs, J. M., & Doolittle, D. C. (1993). Perceptions now and then of occupational sex typing: A replication of Shinar's 1975 study. *Journal of Applied Social Psychology, 23*, 1435–1453.

Bem, S. L. (1974). The measurement of psychological androgyny. *Journal of Consulting and Clinical Psychology, 42*, 155–162.

162 EAGLY, WOOD, DIEKMAN

Berg, J. H., Stephan, W. G., & Dodson, M. (1981). Attributional modesty in women. *Psychology of Women Quarterly, 5*, 711–727.

Berger, J., Wagner, D. G., & Zelditch, M., Jr. (1985). Expectations states theory: Review and assessment. In J. Berger & M. Zelditch, Jr. (Eds.), *Status, rewards, and influence: How expectations organize behavior* (pp. 1–72). San Francisco: Jossey-Bass.

Berger, J., Webster, M., Jr., Ridgeway, C. L., & Rosenholtz, S. J. (1986). Status cues, expectations, and behaviors. In E. Lawler (Ed.), *Advances in group processes* (Vol. 3, pp. 1–22). Greenwich, CT: JAI.

Berger, J., & Zelditch, M., Jr. (Eds.). (1985). *Status, rewards, and influence: How expectations organize behavior.* San Francisco: Jossey-Bass.

Berndt, T. J., & Heller, K. A. (1986). Gender stereotypes and social inferences: A developmental study. *Journal of Personality and Social Psychology, 50*, 889–898.

Berninger, V. W., & DeSoto, C. (1985). Cognitive representation of personal stereotypes. *European Journal of Social Psychology, 15*, 189–211.

Bettencourt, B. A., & Miller, N. (1996). Gender differences in aggression as a function of provocation: A meta-analysis. *Psychological Bulletin, 119*, 422–447.

Biddle, B. J. (1979). *Role theory: Expectancies, identities, and behaviors.* New York: Academic Press.

Biddle, B. J. (1986). Recent developments in role theory. *Annual Review of Sociology, 12*, 67–92.

Biernat, M. (1991). A multicomponent, developmental analysis of sex typing. *Sex Roles, 24*, 567–586.

Biernat, M. (1995). The shifting standards model: Implications of stereotype accuracy for social judgment. In Y.-T. Lee, L. J. Jussim, & C. R. McCauley (Eds.), *Stereotype accuracy: Toward appreciating group differences* (pp. 87–114). Washington, DC: American Psychological Association.

Biernat, M., & Manis, M. (1994). Shifting standards and stereotype-based judgments. *Journal of Personality and Social Psychology, 66*, 5–20.

Blair, I. V., & Banaji, M. R. (1996). Automatic and controlled processes in stereotype priming. *Journal of Personality and Social Psychology, 70*, 1142–1163.

Blumenthal, J. A. (1998). The reasonable woman standard: A meta-analytic review of gender differences in perceptions of sexual harassment. *Law and Human Behavior, 22*, 33–57.

Brewer, M. B., & Brown, R. J. (1998). Intergroup relations. In D. T. Gilbert, S. T. Fiske, & G. Lindzey (Eds.), *The handbook of social psychology* (4th ed., Vol. 2, pp. 554–594). Boston: McGraw-Hill.

Brewer, M. B., & Campbell, D. T. (1976). *Ethnocentrism and intergroup attitudes: East African evidence.* New York: Sage.

Bridges, J. S., & Etaugh, C. (1995). College students' perceptions of mothers: Effects of maternal employment–childrearing pattern and motive for employment. *Sex Roles, 32*, 735–751.

Bridges, J. S., & Orza, A. M. (1992). The effects of employment role and motive for employment on the perceptions of mothers. *Sex Roles, 27*, 331–343.

Bridges, J. S., & Orza, A. M. (1993). Effects of maternal employment–childrearing pattern on college students' perceptions of a mother and her child. *Psychology of Women Quarterly, 17*, 103–117.

Briton, N. J., & Hall, J. A. (1995). Beliefs about female and male nonverbal communication. *Sex Roles, 32*, 79–90.

Broude, G. J. (1990). The division of labor by sex and other gender-related variables: An exploratory study. *Behavior Science Research, 24*, 29–49.

Broverman, I. K., Vogel, S. R., Broverman, D. M., Clarkson, F. E., & Rosenkrantz, P. S. (1972). Sex-role stereotypes: A current appraisal. *Journal of Social Issues, 28*(2), 59–78.

Brown, J. K. (1970). A note on the division of labor by sex. *American Anthropologist, 72*, 1073–1078.

Buss, D. M., & Kenrick, D. T. (1998). Evolutionary social psychology. In D. T. Gilbert, S. T. Fiske, & G. Lindzey (Eds.), *The handbook of social psychology* (4th ed., Vol. 2, pp. 982–1026). Boston: McGraw-Hill.

Butler, D., & Geis, F. L. (1990). Nonverbal affect responses to male and female leaders: Implications for leadership evaluations. *Journal of Personality and Social Psychology, 58*, 48–59.

Carli, L. L. (1982). *Are women more social and men more task-oriented? A meta-analytic review of sex differences in group interaction, reward allocation, coalition formation, and cooperation in the Prisoner's Dilemma game.* Unpublished manuscript, University of Massachusetts at Amherst.

Carli, L. L. (1990). Gender, language, and influence. *Journal of Personality and Social Psychology, 59*, 941–951.

Carli, L. L. (1995). Nonverbal behavior, gender, and influence. *Journal of Personality and Social Psychology, 68*, 1030–1041.

Carli, L. L., & Eagly, A. H. (1999). Gender effects on social influence and emergent leadership. In G. N. Powell (Ed.), *Handbook of gender in organizations* (pp. 203–222). Thousand Oaks, CA: Sage.

Cejka, M. A., & Eagly, A. H. (1999). Gender-stereotypic images of occupations correspond to the sex segregation of employment. *Personality and Social Psychology Bulletin, 25*, 413–423.

Christensen, D., & Rosenthal, R. (1982). Gender and nonverbal decoding skill as determinants of interpersonal expectancy effects. *Journal of Personality and Social Psychology, 42*, 75–87.

Cialdini, R. B., & Trost, M. R. (1998). Social influence: Social norms, conformity, and compliance. In D. T. Gilbert, S. T. Fiske, & G. Lindzey (Eds.), *The handbook of social psychology* (4th ed., Vol. 2, pp. 151–192). Boston: McGraw-Hill.

Cialdini, R. B., Wosinska, W., Dabul, A. J., Whetstone-Dion, R., & Heszen, I. (1998). When social role salience leads to social role rejection: Modest self-presentation among women and men in two cultures. *Personality and Social Psychology Bulletin, 24*, 473–481.

Cohn, L. D. (1991). Sex differences in the course of personality development: A meta-analysis. *Psychological Bulletin, 109*, 252–266.

Connell, R.W. (1995). *Masculinities.* Berkeley: University of California Press.

Conway, M., Pizzamiglio, M. T., & Mount, L. (1996). Status, communality, and agency: Implications for stereotypes of gender and other groups. *Journal of Personality and Social Psychology, 71*, 25–38.

Coontz, S., & Henderson, P. (1986). Property forms, political power and female labour in the origins of class and state societies. In S. Coontz & P. Henderson (Eds.), *Women's work, men's property: The origins of gender and class* (pp. 108–155). Thetford, England: Thetford Press.

Cooper, H. M. (1979). Statistically combining independent studies: A meta-analysis of sex differences in conformity research. *Journal of Personality and Social Psychology, 37*, 131–146.

Costrich, N., Feinstein, J., Kidder, L., Marecek, J., & Pascale, L. (1975). When stereotypes hurt: Three studies of penalties for sex-role reversals. *Journal of Experimental Social Psychology, 11*, 520–530.

Cross, S. E., & Madson, L. (1997). Models of the self: Self-construals and gender. *Psychological Bulletin, 122*, 5–37.

Darley, J. M., & Fazio, R. H. (1980). Expectancy confirmation processes arising in the social interaction sequence. *American Psychologist, 35*, 867–881.

Daubman, K. A., Heatherington, L., & Ahn, A. (1992). Gender and the self-presentation of academic achievement. *Sex Roles, 27*, 187–204.

Davison, H. K., & Burke, M. J. (in press). Sex discrimination in simulated employment contexts: A meta-analytic investigation. *Journal of Vocational Behavior.*

Deaux, K., & LaFrance, M. (1998). Gender. In D. T. Gilbert, S. T. Fiske, & G. Lindzey (Eds.), *The handbook of social psychology* (4th ed., Vol. 1, pp. 788–827). Boston: McGraw-Hill.

Deaux, K., & Lewis, L. L. (1983). Assessment of gender stereotypes: Methodology and components. *Psychological Documents, 13* (2) Ms. 2583 25.

Deaux, K., & Lewis, L. L. (1984). Structure of gender stereotypes: Interrelationships among components and gender label. *Journal of Personality and Social Psychology, 46*, 991–1004.

Deaux, K., & Major, B. (1987). Putting gender into context: An interactive model of gender-related behavior. *Psychological Review, 94*, 369–389.

Deaux, K., Winton, W., Crowley, M., & Lewis, L. L. (1985). Level of categorization and content of gender stereotypes. *Social Cognition, 3*, 145–167.

Deutsch, M., & Gerard, H. B. (1955). A study of normative and informational social influences upon individual judgment. *Journal of Abnormal and Social Psychology, 51*, 629–636.

Devine, P. G. (1989). Stereotypes and prejudice: Their automatic and controlled components. *Journal of Personality and Social Psychology, 56*, 5–18.

Diekman, A. B., & Eagly, A. H. (in press). Stereotypes as dynamic constructs: Women and men of the past, present, and future. *Personality and Social Psychology Bulletin.*

Dijksterhuis, A., Macrae, C. N., & Haddock, G. (1999). When recollective experiences matter: Subjective ease of retrieval and stereotyping. *Personality and Social Psychology Bulletin, 25*, 760–768.

Dindia, K., & Allen, M. (1992). Sex differences in self-disclosure: A meta-analysis. *Psychological Bulletin, 112*, 106–124.

Eagly, A. H. (1983). Gender and social influence: A social psychological analysis. *American Psychologist, 38*, 971–981.

Eagly, A. H. (1987). *Sex differences in social behavior: A social-role interpretation.* Hillsdale, NJ: Lawrence Erlbaum Associates.

Eagly, A. H. (1995). The science and politics of comparing women and men. *American Psychologist, 50*, 145–158.

Eagly, A. H. (1997a). Comparing women and men: Methods, findings, and politics. In M. R. Walsh (Ed.), *Women, men, and gender: Ongoing debates* (pp. 24–31). New Haven, CT: Yale University Press.

Eagly, A. H. (1997b). Sex differences in social behavior: Comparing social role theory and evolutionary psychology. *American Psychologist, 52*, 1380–1383.

Eagly, A. H., & Carli, L. L. (1981). Sex of researchers and sex-typed communications as determinants of sex differences in influenceability: A meta-analysis of social influence studies. *Psychological Bulletin, 90*, 1–20.

Eagly, A. H., & Chrvala, C. (1986). Sex differences in conformity: Status and gender role interpretations. *Psychology of Women Quarterly, 10*, 203–220.

Eagly, A. H., & Crowley, M. (1986). Gender and helping behavior: A meta-analytic review of the social psychological literature. *Psychological Bulletin, 100*, 283–308.

Eagly, A. H., & Diekman, A. B. (1997). The accuracy of gender stereotypes: A dilemma for feminism. *Revue Internationale de Psychologie Sociale/International Review of Social Psychology, 10*, 11–30.

Eagly, A. H., Diekman, A. B., & Kulesa, P. (1999). *Accuracy and bias in stereotypes about the attitudes of women and men.* Unpublished manuscript.

Eagly, A. H., & Johnson, B. T. (1990). Gender and leadership style: A meta-analysis. *Psychological Bulletin, 108*, 233–256.

Eagly, A. H., & Karau, S. J. (1991). Gender and the emergence of leaders: A meta-analysis. *Journal of Personality and Social Psychology, 60*, 685–710.

Eagly, A. H., Karau, S. J., & Makhijani, M. G. (1995). Gender and the effectiveness of leaders: A meta-analysis. *Psychological Bulletin, 117*, 125–145.

Eagly, A. H., & Kite, M. E. (1987). Are stereotypes of nationalities applied to both women and men? *Journal of Personality and Social Psychology, 53*, 451–462.

Eagly, A. H., Makhijani, M. G., & Klonsky, B. G. (1992). Gender and the evaluation of leaders: A meta-analysis. *Psychological Bulletin, 111*, 3–22.

Eagly, A. H., & Mladinic, A. (1989). Gender stereotypes and attitudes toward women and men. *Personality and Social Psychology Bulletin, 15*, 543–558.

Eagly, A. H., & Mladinic, A. (1994). Are people prejudiced against women? Some answers from research on attitudes, gender stereotypes, and judgments of competence. In W. Stroebe & M. Hewstone (Eds.), *European review of social psychology* (Vol. 5, pp. 1–35). New York: Wiley.

Eagly, A. H., Mladinic, A., & Otto, S. (1991). Are women evaluated more favorably than men? An analysis of attitudes, beliefs, and emotions. *Psychology of Women Quarterly, 15*, 203–216.

Eagly, A. H., & Steffen, V. J. (1984). Gender stereotypes stem from the distribution of women and men into social roles. *Journal of Personality and Social Psychology, 46*, 735–754.

Eagly, A. H., & Steffen, V. J. (1986a). Gender and aggressive behavior: A meta-analytic review of the social psychological literature. *Psychological Bulletin, 100*, 309–330.

Eagly, A. H., & Steffen, V. J. (1986b). Gender stereotypes, occupational roles, and beliefs about part-time employees. *Psychology of Women Quarterly, 10*, 252–262.

Eagly, A. H., & Steffen, V. J. (1988). A note on assessing stereotypes. *Personality and Social Psychology Bulletin, 14*, 676–680.

Eagly, A. H., & Wood, W. (1982). Inferred sex differences in status as a determinant of gender stereotypes about social influence. *Journal of Personality and Social Psychology, 43*, 915–928.

Eagly, A. H., & Wood, W. (1991). Explaining sex differences in social behavior: A meta-analytic perspective. *Personality and Social Psychology Bulletin, 17*, 306–315.

Eagly, A. H., & Wood, W. (1999). The origins of sex differences in human behavior: Evolved dispositions versus social roles. *American Psychologist, 54*, 408–423.

Eagly, A. H., Wood, W., & Fishbaugh, L. (1981). Sex differences in conformity: Surveillance by the group as a determinant of male non-conformity. *Journal of Personality and Social Psychology, 40*, 384–394.

Eckes, T. (1994a). Explorations in gender cognition: Content and structure of female and male subtypes. *Social Cognition, 12*, 37–60.

Eckes, T. (1994b). Features of men, features of women: Assessing stereotypic beliefs about gender subtypes. *British Journal of Social Psychology, 33*, 107–123.

Ehrenberg, M. (1989). *Women in prehistory.* Norman: University of Oklahoma Press.

Eisenberg, N., & Lennon, R. (1983). Sex differences in empathy and related capacities. *Psychological Bulletin, 94*, 100–131.

Ember, C. R. (1983). The relative decline in women's contribution to agriculture with intensification. *American Anthropologist, 85*, 285–303.

Engels, F. (1902/1942). *Origin of the family, private property, and the state* [Ursprung der Familie, des Privateigentums und des Staats] (in the light of the researches of Lewis H. Morgan). New York: International Publishers.

Etaugh, C., & Folger, D. (1998). Perceptions of parents whose work and parenting behaviors deviate from role expectations. *Sex Roles, 39*, 215–223.

Federal Glass Ceiling Commission. (1995). *Good for business: Making full use of the nation's human capital: The environmental scan: A fact-finding report of the Federal Glass Ceiling Commission.* Washington, DC: Glass Ceiling Commission, U.S. Department of Labor.

Feingold, A. (1988). Cognitive gender differences are disappearing. *American Psychologist, 43,* 95–103.

Feingold, A. (1990). Gender differences in the effects of physical attractiveness on romantic attraction: A comparison across five research paradigms. *Journal of Personality and Social Psychology, 59,* 981–993.

Feingold, A. (1992). Gender differences in mate selection preferences: A test of the parental investment model. *Psychological Bulletin, 112,* 125–139.

Feingold, A. (1994). Gender differences in personality: A meta-analysis. *Psychological Bulletin, 116,* 429–456.

Feingold, A. (1998). Gender stereotyping for sociability, dominance, character, and mental health: A meta-analysis of findings from the bogus stranger paradigm. *Genetic, Social, and General Psychology Monographs, 124,* 253–270.

Feingold, A., & Mazzella, R. (1998). Gender differences in body image are increasing. *Psychological Science, 9,* 190–195.

Feldman, J. M. (1972). Stimulus characteristics and subject prejudice as determinants of stereotype attribution. *Journal of Personality and Social Psychology, 21,* 333–340.

Festinger, L. (1954). A theory of social comparison processes. *Human Relations, 7,* 117–140.

Fishbein, M., & Ajzen, I. (1975). *Belief, attitude, intention, and behavior: An introduction to theory and research.* Reading, MA: Addison-Wesley.

Fiske, A. P., Haslam, N., & Fiske, S. T. (1991). Confusing one person with another: What errors reveal about the elementary forms of social relations. *Journal of Personality and Social Psychology, 60,* 656–674.

Fiske, S. T. (1998). Stereotyping, prejudice, and discrimination. In D. T. Gilbert, S. T. Fiske, & G. Lindzey (Eds.), *The handbook of social psychology* (4th ed., Vol. 2, pp. 357–411). Boston: McGraw-Hill.

Fiske, S. T., & Stevens, L. E. (1993). What's so special about sex? Gender stereotyping and discrimination. In S. Oskamp & M. Costanzo (Eds.), *Gender issues in contemporary society* (pp. 173–196). Newbury Park, CA: Sage.

Frable, D. E. S. (1997). Gender, racial, ethnic, sexual, and class identities. *Annual Review of Psychology, 48,* 139–162.

Franke, G. R., Crown, D. F., & Spake, D. F. (1997). Gender differences in ethical perceptions of business practices: A social role theory perspective. *Journal of Applied Psychology, 82,* 920–934.

Friedl, E. (1978). Society and sex roles. *Human Nature, 1,* 68–75.

Fritz, H. L., & Helgeson, V. S. (1998). Distinctions of unmitigated communion from communion: Self-neglect and overinvolvement with others. *Journal of Personality and Social Psychology, 75,* 121–140.

Gabriel, S., & Gardner, W. L. (1999). Are there "his" and "hers" types of interdependence? The implications of gender differences in collective versus relational interdependence for affect, behavior, and cognition. *Journal of Personality and Social Psychology, 77,* 642–655.

Geis, F. L. (1993). Self-fulfilling prophecies: A social psychological view of gender. In A. E. Beall & R. J. Sternberg (Eds.), *The psychology of gender* (pp. 9–54). New York: Guilford.

Gilbert, D. T. (1998). Ordinary personology. In D. T. Gilbert, S. T. Fiske, & G. Lindzey (Eds.), *The handbook of social psychology* (4th ed., Vol. 2, pp. 89–150). Boston: McGraw-Hill.

Gilbert, D. T., & Malone, P. S. (1995). The correspondence bias. *Psychological Bulletin, 117,* 21–38.

Gilligan, C. (1982). *In a different voice: Psychological theory and women's development.* Cambridge, MA: Harvard University Press.

Glick, P. (1991). Trait-based and sex-based discrimination in occupational prestige, occupational salary, and hiring. *Sex Roles, 25,* 351–378.

Glick, P., & Fiske, S. T. (1996). The Ambivalent Sexism Inventory: Differentiating hostile and benevolent sexism. *Journal of Personality and Social Psychology, 70,* 491–512.

Gould, R. J., & Sloane, C. G. (1982). The "feminine modesty" effect: A self-presentational interpretation of sex differences in causal attribution. *Personality and Social Psychology Bulletin, 8,* 477–485.

Grossman, M., & Wood, W. (1993). Sex differences in intensity of emotional experience: A social role interpretation. *Journal of Personality and Social Psychology, 65,* 1010–1022.

Gutek, B. A., & Morasch, B. (1982). Sex-ratios, sex-role spillover, and sexual harassment of women at work. *Journal of Social Issues, 38*(4), 55–74.

Haddock, G., & Zanna, M. P. (1994). Preferring "housewives" to "feminists": Categorization and the favorability of attitudes toward women. *Psychology of Women Quarterly, 18,* 25–52.

Hall, J. A. (1984). *Nonverbal sex differences: Communication accuracy and expressive style.* Baltimore: Johns Hopkins University Press.

Hall, J. A. (1998). How big are nonverbal sex differences? The case of smiling and sensitivity to nonverbal cues. In D. J. Canary & K. Dindia (Eds.), *Sex differences and similarities in communication: Critical essays and empirical investigations of sex and gender in interaction* (pp. 155–177). Mahwah, NJ: Lawrence Erlbaum Associates.

Hall, J. A., & Carter, J. D. (1998). [Gender appropriateness and gender differences]. Unpublished data.

Hall, J. A., & Carter, J. D. (1999). Gender-stereotype accuracy as an individual difference. *Journal of Personality and Social Psychology, 77,* 350–359.

Hall, J. A., & Halberstadt, A. G. (1986). Smiling and gazing. In J. S. Hyde & M. C. Linn (Eds.), *The psychology of gender: Advances through meta-analysis* (pp. 136–158). Baltimore: Johns Hopkins University Press.

Hall, J. A., Irish, J. T., Roter, D. L., Ehrlich, C. M., & Miller, L. H. (1994). Gender in medical encounters: An analysis of physician and patient communication in a primary care setting. *Health Psychology, 13,* 384–392.

Halpern, D. F. (1992). *Sex differences in cognitive abilities* (2nd ed.). Hillsdale, NJ: Lawrence Erlbaum Associates.

Halpern, D. F. (1997). Sex differences in intelligence: Implications for education. *American Psychologist, 52,* 1091–1102.

Harris, J. R. (1995). Where is the child's environment? A group socialization theory of development. *Psychological Review, 102,* 458–489.

Harris, J. R. (1998). *The nurture assumption: Why children turn out the way they do.* New York: Free Press.

Harris, M. (1977). *Cannibals and kings.* New York: Random House.

Harris, M. (1993). The evolution of human gender hierarchies: A trial formulation. In B. D. Miller (Ed.), *Sex and gender hierarchies* (pp. 57–79). New York: Cambridge University Press.

Harris, M. J., & Rosenthal, R. (1985). Mediation of interpersonal expectancy effects: 31 meta-analyses. *Psychological Bulletin, 97,* 363–386.

Harris, R. J., & Firestone, J. M. (1998). Changes in predictors of gender role ideologies among women: A multivariate analysis. *Sex Roles, 38,* 239–252.

Hayden, B., Deal, M., Cannon, A., & Casey, J. (1986). Ecological determinants of women's status among hunter/gatherers. *Human Evolution, 1,* 449–474.

Heatherington, L., Daubman, K. A., Bates, C., Ahn, A., Brown, H., & Preston, C. (1993). Two investigations of "female modesty" in achievement situations. *Sex Roles, 29*, 739–754.

Hedges, L. V., & Nowell, A. (1995). Sex differences in mental test scores, variability, and numbers of high-scoring individuals. *Science, 269*, 41–45.

Heilman, M. E. (1983). Sex bias in work settings: The Lack of Fit model. *Research in Organizational Behavior, 5*, 269–298.

Helgeson, V. S. (1994). Relation of agency and communion to well-being: Evidence and potential explanations. *Psychological Bulletin, 116*, 412–428.

Hembroff, L. A. (1982). Resolving status inconsistency: An expectation states theory and test. *Social Forces, 61*, 183–205.

Higgins, E. T. (1987). Self-discrepancy: A theory relating self and affect. *Psychological Review, 94*, 319–340.

Hilton, J. L., & von Hippel, W. (1996). Stereotypes. *Annual Review of Psychology, 47*, 237–271.

Hoffman, C., & Hurst, N. (1990). Gender stereotypes: Perception or rationalization? *Journal of Personality and Social Psychology, 58*, 197–208.

Hogg, M. A., & Turner, J. C. (1987). Intergroup behaviour, self-stereotyping and the salience of social categories. *British Journal of Social Psychology, 26*, 325–340.

House, J. S. (1995). Social structure, relationships, and the individual. In K. S. Cook, G. A. Fine, & J. S. House (Eds.), *Sociological perspectives on social psychology* (pp. 387–395). Boston: Allyn & Bacon.

Howard, J. A., & Hollander, J. (1997). *Gendered situations, gendered selves: A gender lens on social psychology.* Thousand Oaks, CA: Sage.

Hyde, J. S. (1984). How large are gender differences in aggression? A developmental meta-analysis. *Developmental Psychology, 20*, 722–736.

Hyde, J. S. (1996). Where are the gender differences? Where are the gender similarities? In D. M. Buss & N. M. Malamuth (Eds.), *Sex, power, conflict: Evolutionary and feminist perspectives* (pp. 107–118). New York: Oxford University Press.

Jackman, M. R. (1994). *The velvet glove: Paternalism and conflict in gender, class, and race relations.* Berkeley: University of California Press.

Jacobs, J. A. (1989). *Revolving doors: Sex segregation and women's careers.* Stanford, CA: Stanford University Press.

Johnson, B. T., & Eagly, A. H. (in press). Quantitative synthesis of social psychological research. In H. T. Reis & C. M. Judd (Eds.), *Handbook of research methods in social psychology.* New York: Cambridge University Press.

Jones, E. E., & Harris, V. A. (1967). The attribution of attitudes. *Journal of Experimental Social Psychology, 3*, 1–24.

Josephs, R. A., Markus, H. R., & Tafarodi, R. W. (1992). Gender and self-esteem. *Journal of Personality and Social Psychology, 63*, 391–402.

Jost, J. T., & Banaji, M. R. (1994). The role of stereotyping in system-justification and the production of false consciousness. *British Journal of Social Psychology, 33*, 1–27.

Judd, P. C., & Oswald, P. A. (1997). Employment desirability: The interactive effects of gender-typed profile, stimulus sex, and gender-typed occupation. *Sex Roles, 37*, 467–476.

Jussim, L. (1986). Self-fulfilling prophecies: A theoretical and integrative review. *Psychological Review, 93*, 429–445.

Kalin, R. (1986, August). *The role of gender in occupational images.* Poster presented at the 94th Annual Convention of the American Psychological Association, Washington, DC.

Kanter, R. M. (1977). Some effects of proportions on group life: Skewed sex ratios and responses to token women. *American Journal of Sociology, 82*, 465–490.

Kite, M. E. (1996). Age, gender, and occupational label: A test of social role theory. *Psychology of Women Quarterly, 20*, 361–374.

Kite, M. E., & Whitley, B. E. (1996). Sex differences in attitudes toward homosexual persons, behaviors, and civil rights: A meta-analysis. *Personality and Social Psychology Bulletin, 22*, 336–353.

Leacock, E. (1978). Women's status in egalitarian society: Implications for social evolution. *Current Anthropology, 19*, 247–275.

Lee, Y.-T., Jussim, L. J., & McCauley, C. R. (Eds.). (1995). *Stereotype accuracy: Toward appreciating group differences.* Washington, DC: American Psychological Association.

Lerner, G. (1986). *The creation of patriarchy.* New York: Oxford University Press.

Leuptow, L. B., Garovich, L., & Leuptow, M. B. (1995). The persistence of gender stereotypes in the face of changing sex roles: Evidence contrary to the sociocultural model. *Ethology and Sociobiology, 16*, 509–530.

LeVine, R. A., & Campbell, D. T. (1972). *Ethnocentrism: Theories of conflict, ethnic attitudes, and group behavior.* New York: Wiley.

Lévi-Strauss, C. (1949/1969). *The elementary structures of kinship.* Boston: Beacon Press.

Lightdale, J. R., & Prentice, D. A. (1994). Rethinking sex differences in aggression: Aggressive behavior in the absence of social roles. *Personality and Social Psychology Bulletin, 20*, 34–44.

Lockheed, M. E. (1985). Sex and social influence: A meta-analysis guided by theory. In J. Berger & M. Zelditch, Jr. (Eds.), *Status, rewards, and influence: How expectations organize behavior* (pp. 406–429). San Francisco: Jossey-Bass.

Loo, R., & Thorpe, K. (1998). Attitudes toward women's roles in society: A replication after 20 years. *Sex Roles, 39*, 903–912.

Lopata, H. Z., & Thorne, B. (1978). On the term "sex roles." *Signs: Journal of Women in Culture and Society, 3*, 718–721.

Low, B. S. (1989). Cross-cultural patterns in the training of children: An evolutionary perspective. *Journal of Comparative Psychology, 103*, 311–319.

Lunneborg, P. W. (1970). Stereotypic aspect in masculinity–femininity measurement. *Journal of Consulting and Clinical Psychology, 34*, 113–118.

Lytton, H., & Romney, D. M. (1991). Parents' differential socialization of boys and girls: A meta-analysis. *Psychological Bulletin, 109*, 267–296.

Maccoby, E. E. (1998). *The two sexes: Growing up apart, coming together.* Cambridge, MA: Harvard University Press.

Maccoby, E. E., & Jacklin, C. N. (1974). *The psychology of sex differences.* Stanford, CA: Stanford University Press.

Martell, R. F., Lane, D. M., & Emrich, C. (1995). Male–female differences: A computer simulation. *American Psychologist, 51*, 157–158.

McKee, J. P., & Sherriffs, A. C. (1957). The differential evaluation of males and females. *Journal of Personality, 25*, 356–371.

McLean, H. M., & Kalin, R. (1994). Congruence between self-image and occupational stereotypes in students entering gender-dominated occupations. *Canadian Journal of Behavioural Science, 26*, 142–162.

Meeker, B. F., & Weitzel-O'Neill, P. A. (1977). Sex roles and interpersonal behavior in task-oriented groups. *American Sociological Review, 42*, 91–105.

Meeker, B. F., & Weitzel-O'Neill, P. A. (1985). Sex roles and interpersonal behavior in task-oriented groups. In J. Berger & M. Zelditch, Jr. (Eds.), *Status, rewards, and influence: How expectations organize behavior* (pp. 379–405). San Francisco: Jossey-Bass.

Merton, R. K. (1948). The self-fulfilling prophecy. *Antioch Review, 8*, 193–210.

Mitchell, J. (1998). [Dissociated attitudes]. Unpublished data.

Mischel, W., Cantor, N., & Feldman, S. (1996). Principles of self-regulation: The nature of willpower and self-control. In E. T. Higgins & A. W. Kruglanski (Eds.), *Social psychology: Handbook of basic principles* (pp. 329–360). New York: Guilford.

Moskowitz, D. W., Suh, E. J., & Desaulniers, J. (1994). Situational influences on gender differences in agency and communion. *Journal of Personality and Social Psychology, 66,* 753–761.

Mukhopadhyay, C. C., & Higgins, P. J. (1988). Anthropological studies of women's status revisited: 1977–1987. *Annual Review of Anthropology, 17,* 461–495.

Murdock, G. P. (1967). *Ethnographic atlas.* Pittsburgh, PA: University of Pittsburgh Press.

Murdock, G. P., & Provost, C. (1973). Factors in the division of labor by sex: A cross-cultural analysis. *Ethnology, 13,* 203–225.

Murnen, S. K., & Stockton, M. (1997). Gender and self-reported sexual arousal in response to sexual stimuli: A meta-analytic review. *Sex Roles, 37,*135–153.

Nolen-Hoeksema, S. (1987). Sex differences in unipolar depression: Evidence and theory. *Psychological Bulletin, 101,* 259–282.

Nowell, A., & Hedges, L. V. (1998). Trends in gender differences in academic achievement from 1960 to 1994: An analysis of differences in mean, variance, and extreme scores. *Sex Roles, 39,* 21–43.

Olian, J. D., Schwab, D. P., & Haberfeld, Y. (1988). The impact of applicant gender compared to qualifications on hiring recommendations: A meta-analysis of experimental studies. *Organizational Behavior and Human Decision Processes, 41,* 180–195.

Oliver, M. B., & Hyde, J. S. (1993). Gender differences in sexuality: A meta-analysis. *Psychological Bulletin, 114,* 29–51.

Olson, J. M., Roese, N. J., & Zanna, M. P. (1996). Expectancies. In E. T. Higgins & A. W. Kruglanski (Eds.), *Social psychology: Handbook of basic principles* (pp. 211–238). New York: Guilford.

Osterhout, L., Bersick, M., & McLaughlin, J. (1997). Brain potentials reflect violations of gender stereotypes. *Memory and Cognition, 25,* 273–285.

Parsons, T., & Bales, R. F. (Eds.). (1955). *Family, socialization and interaction process.* Glencoe, IL: The Free Press.

Perry, D. G., & Bussey, K. (1979). The social learning theory of sex differences: Imitation is alive and well. *Journal of Personality and Social Psychology, 37,* 1699–1712.

Pettigrew, T. F. (1997). Personality and social structure: Social psychological contributions. In R. Hogan, J. Johnson, & S. Briggs (Eds.), *Handbook of personality psychology* (pp. 417–438). San Diego, CA: Academic Press.

Pratto, F. (1996). Sexual politics: The gender gap in the bedroom, the cupboard, and the cabinet. In D. M. Buss & N. M. Malamuth (Eds.), *Sex, power, conflict: Evolutionary and feminist perspectives* (pp. 179–230). New York: Oxford University Press.

Pratto, F. (1999). The puzzle of continuing group inequality: Piecing together psychological, social, and cultural forces in social dominance theory. In M. P. Zanna (Ed.), *Advances in experimental social psychology* (Vol. 31, pp. 191–263). San Diego, CA: Academic Press.

Raag, T., & Rackliff, C. L. (1998). Preschoolers' awareness of social expectations of gender: Relationships to toy choices. *Sex Roles, 38,* 685–700.

Reskin, B. F., & Padavic, I. (1994). *Women and men at work.* Thousand Oaks, CA: Pine Forge Press.

Rhoodie, E. M. (1989). *Discrimination against women: A global survey of the economic, educational, social and political status of women.* Jefferson, NC: McFarland.

Ridgeway, C. L. (1982). Status in groups: The importance of motivation. *American Sociological Review, 47,* 76–88.

Ridgeway, C. L. (1997). Interaction and the conservation of gender inequality: Considering employment. *American Sociological Review, 62,* 218–235.

Ridgeway, C. L., & Diekema, D. (1992). Are gender differences status differences? In C. L. Ridgeway (Ed.), *Gender, interaction, and inequality* (pp. 157–180). New York: Springer.

Riggs, J. M. (1997). Mandates for mothers and fathers: Perceptions of breadwinners and care givers. *Sex Roles, 37,* 565–580.

Riggs, J. M. (1998). Social roles we choose and don't choose: Impressions of employed and unemployed parents. *Sex Roles, 39,* 431–443.

Roberts, B. W., & Helson, R. (1997). Changes in culture, changes in personality: The influence of individualism in a longitudinal study of women. *Journal of Personality and Social Psychology, 72,* 641–651.

Rosenthal, R., & Rubin, D. B. (1978). Interpersonal expectancy effects: The first 345 studies. *Behavioral and Brain Sciences, 3,* 377–415.

Ross, L. (1977). The intuitive psychologist and his shortcomings: Distortions in the attribution process. In L. Berkowitz (Ed.), *Advances in experimental social psychology* (Vol. 10, pp. 173–220). New York: Academic Press.

Ross, L., Amabile, T. M., & Steinmetz, J. L. (1977). Social roles, social control, and biases in social-perception processes. *Journal of Personality and Social Psychology, 35,* 485–494.

Roter, D. L., & Hall, J. A. (1999). *Physician gender effects in medical communication: A quantitative review.* Manuscript under review.

Ruble, D. N., & Martin, C. L. (1998). Gender development. In W. Damon (Series Ed.) & N. Eisenberg (Vol. Ed.), *Handbook of child psychology: Vol. 3. Social, emotional, and personality development* (5th ed., pp. 933–1016). New York: Wiley.

Rudman, L. A. (1998). Self-promotion as a risk factor for women: The costs and benefits of counterstereotypical impression management. *Journal of Personality and Social Psychology, 74,* 629–645.

Sarbin, T. R., & Allen, V. L. (1968). Role theory. In G. Lindzey & E. Aronson (Eds.), *Handbook of social psychology* (2nd ed., Vol. 1, pp. 488–567). Reading, MA: Addison-Wesley.

Scanzoni, J. (1979). Social processes and power in families. In W. R. Burr, R. Hill, F. I. Nye, & I. L. Reiss (Eds.), *Contemporary theories about the family* (Vol. 1, pp. 295–316). New York: The Free Press.

Schaller, M. (1994). The role of statistical reasoning in the formation, preservation and prevention of group stereotypes. *British Journal of Social Psychology, 33,* 47–61.

Schaller, M. (1996). Training in statistical reasoning inhibits the formation of erroneous group stereotypes. *Personality and Social Psychology Bulletin, 22,* 829–844.

Schaller, M. & O'Brien, M. (1992). "Intuitive analysis of covariance" and group stereotype formation. *Personality and Social Psychology Bulletin, 18,* 776–785.

Schlegel, A. (1977). Toward a theory of sexual stratification. In A. Schlegel (Ed.), *Sexual stratification: A cross-cultural view* (pp. 1–40). New York: Columbia University Press.

Schlegel, A., & Barry, H., III. (1986). The cultural consequences of female contribution to subsistence. *American Anthropologist, 88,* 142–150.

Shackelford, S., Wood, W., & Worchel, S. (1996). Behavioral styles and the influence of women in mixed-sex groups. *Social Psychology Quarterly, 59,* 284–293.

Shelton, B. A. (1992). *Women, men, and time: Gender differences in paid work, housework, and leisure.* Westport, CT: Greenwood.

Sherman, P. J., & Spence, J. T. (1997). A comparison of two cohorts of college students in responses to the Male–Female Relations Questionnaire. *Psychology of Women Quarterly, 21,* 265–278.

Sherriffs, A. C., & McKee, J. P. (1957). Qualitative aspects of beliefs about men and women. *Journal of Personality, 25,* 457–464.

Shinar, E. H. (1975). Sexual stereotypes of occupations. *Journal of Vocational Behavior, 7,* 99–111.

Shinar, E. H. (1978). Person perception as a function of occupation and sex. *Sex Roles, 4,* 679–693.

Simon, R. J., & Landis, J. M. (1989). The polls – A report: Women's and men's attitudes about a woman's place and role. *Public Opinion Quarterly, 53*, 265–276.

Skrypnek, .B. J., & Snyder, M. (1982). On the self-perpetuating nature of stereotypes about women and men. *Journal of Experimental Social Psychology, 18*, 277–291.

Smedley, J. W., & Bayton, J. A. (1978). Evaluative race–class stereotypes by race and perceived class of subjects. *Journal of Personality and Social Psychology, 36*, 530–535.

Snodgrass, S. E. (1985). Women's intuition: The effect of subordinate role on interpersonal sensitivity. *Journal of Personality and Social Psychology, 49*, 146–155.

Snodgrass, S. E. (1992). Further effects of role versus gender on interpersonal sensitivity. *Journal of Personality and Social Psychology, 62*, 154–158.

Snyder, M. (1981). On the self-perpetuating nature of social stereotypes. In D. L. Hamilton (Ed.), *Cognitive processes in stereotyping and intergroup behavior* (pp. 183–212). Hillsdale, NJ: Lawrence Erlbaum Associates.

Snyder, M. (1984). When belief creates reality. In L. Berkowitz (Ed.), *Advances in experimental social psychology* (Vol. 18, pp. 247–305). New York: Academic Press.

Spence, J. T. (1993). Gender-related traits and gender ideology: Evidence for a multifactorial theory. *Journal of Personality and Social Psychology, 64*, 624–635.

Spence, J. T., & Buckner, C. E. (in press). Gender-related trait stereotypes and self-perceptions: What do they signify? *Psychology of Women Quarterly*.

Spence, J. T., & Hahn, E. D. (1997). The Attitudes Toward Women Scale and attitude change in college students. *Psychology of Women Quarterly, 21*, 17–34.

Spence, J. T., & Helmreich, R. L. (1978). *Masculinity and femininity: Their psychological dimensions, correlates, and antecedents*. Austin: University of Texas Press.

Spence, J. T., Helmreich, R. L., & Holahan, C. K. (1979). Negative and positive components of psychological masculinity and femininity and their relationships to self-reports of neurotic and acting out behaviors. *Journal of Personality and Social Psychology, 37*, 1673–1682.

Staines, G. L. (with Libby, P. L.). (1986). Men and women in role relationships. In R. D. Ashmore & F. K. Del Boca (Eds.), *The social psychology of female–male relations: A critical analysis of central concepts* (pp. 211–258). Orlando, FL: Academic Press.

Stangor, C., Lynch, L., Duan, C., & Glass, B. (1992). Categorization of individuals on the basis of multiple social features. *Journal of Personality and Social Psychology, 62*, 207–218.

Steil, J. M. (1997). *Marital equality: Its relationship to the well-being of husbands and wives.* Thousand Oaks, CA: Sage.

Stewart, A. J., & Healy, J. M., Jr. (1989). Linking individual development and social changes. *American Psychologist, 44*, 30–42.

Stewart, P. (1988). Women and men in groups: A status characteristics approach to interaction. In M. Webster, Jr., & M. Foschi (Eds.), *Status generalization: New theory and research* (pp. 69–85). Stanford, CA: Stanford University Press.

Stier, D. S., & Hall, J. A. (1984). Gender differences in touch: An empirical and theoretical review. *Journal of Personality and Social Psychology, 47*, 440–459.

Strodtbeck, F. L. & Mann, R. D. (1956). Sex role differentiation in jury deliberations. *Sociometry, 22*, 713–719.

Survey Research Consultants International. (1998). *Index to international public opinion, 1996–1997*. Westport, CT: Greenwood.

Swim, J. K. (1994). Perceived versus meta-analytic effect sizes: An assessment of the accuracy of gender stereotypes. *Journal of Personality and Social Psychology, 66*, 21–36.

Swim, J. K., Aiken, K. J., Hall, W. S., & Hunter, B. A. (1995). Sexism and racism: Old-fashioned and modern prejudices. *Journal of Personality and Social Psychology, 68*, 199–214.

Tannen, D. (1990). *You just don't understand: Women and men in conversation*. New York: Morrow.

Taylor, M. C., & Hall, J. A. (1982). Psychological androgyny: Theories, methods, and conclusions. *Psychological Bulletin, 92*, 347–366.

Tomaskovic-Devey, D. (1995). Sex composition and gendered earnings inequality: A comparison of job and occupational models. In J. A. Jacobs (Ed.), *Gender inequality at work* (pp. 23–56). Thousand Oaks, CA: Sage.

Tougas, F., Brown, R., Beaton, A. M., & Joly, S. (1995). Neosexism: Plus ça change, plus c'est pareil. *Personality and Social Psychology Bulletin, 21*, 842–849.

Twenge, J. M. (1997a). Attitudes toward women, 1970–1995: A meta-analysis. *Psychology of Women Quarterly, 21*, 35–51.

Twenge, J. M. (1997b). Changes in masculine and feminine traits over time: A meta-analysis. *Sex Roles, 36*, 305–325.

United Nations Development Programme. (1999). *Human development report 1999*. New York: Oxford University Press.

U.S. Department of Labor. (1999). Labor force statistics from the current population survey. Retrieved May 25, 1999 from Bureau of Labor Statistics database (series IDs LFU600001 and LFU600002), on the World Wide Web: http://146.142.4.24/cgi-bin/srgate

Valian, V. (1998). *Why so slow? The advancement of women*. Cambridge, MA: MIT Press.

van Knippenberg, A., van Twuyver, M., & Pepels, J. (1994). Factors affecting social categorization processes in memory. *British Journal of Social Psychology, 33*, 419–431.

von Baeyer, C. L., Sherk, D. L., & Zanna, M. P. (1981). Impression management in the job interview: When the female applicant meets the male "chauvinist" interviewer. *Personality and Social Psychology Bulletin, 7*, 45–51.

Vorauer, J. D., & Miller, D. T. (1997). Failure to recognize the effect of implicit social influence on the presentation of self. *Journal of Personality and Social Psychology, 73*, 281–295.

Wagner, D. G., & Berger, J. (1997). Gender and interpersonal task behaviors: Status expectation accounts. *Sociological Perspectives, 40*, 1–32.

Walters, A. E., Stuhlmacher, A. F., & Meyer, L. L. (1998). Gender and negotiator competitiveness: A meta-analysis. *Organizational Behavior and Human Decision Processes, 76*, 1–29.

Weinburgh, M. (1995). Gender differences in student attitudes toward science: A meta-analysis of the literature from 1970 to 1991. *Journal of Research in Science Teaching, 32*, 387–398.

Whitley, B. E. (1997). Gender differences in computer-related attitudes and behavior: A meta-analysis. *Computers in Human Behavior, 13*, 1–22.

Whyte, M. K. (1978). *The status of women in preindustrial societies*. Princeton, NJ: Princeton University Press

Williams, J. E., & Best, D. L. (1990a). *Measuring sex stereotypes: A multination study* (Rev. ed.). Newbury Park, CA: Sage.

Williams, J. E., & Best, D. L. (1990b). *Sex and psyche: Gender and self viewed cross-culturally*. Newbury Park, CA: Sage.

Winquist, L. A., Mohr, C. D., & Kenny, D. A. (1998). The female positivity effect in the perception of others. *Journal of Research in Personality, 32*, 370–388.

Wood, W. (1987). Meta-analytic review of sex differences in group performance. *Psychological Bulletin, 102*, 53–71.

Wood, W., Christensen, P. N., Hebl, M. R., & Rothgerber, H. (1997). Conformity to sex-typed norms, affect, and the self-concept. *Journal of Personality and Social Psychology, 73*, 523–535.

Wood, W., & Eagly, A. H. (1999). *The origins of the division of labor and gender hierarchy: Implications for sex differences in social behavior*. Manuscript in preparation.

Wood, W., & Karten, S. J. (1986). Sex differences in interaction style as a product of perceived sex differences in competence. *Journal of Personality and Social Psychology, 50*, 341–347.

Wood, W., Rhodes, N., & Whelan, M. (1989). Sex differences in positive well-being: A consideration of emotional style and marital status. *Psychological Bulletin, 106*, 249–264.

Yount, K. (1986). A theory of productive activity: The relationships among self-concept, gender, sex role stereotypes, and work-emergent traits. *Psychology of Women Quarterly, 10*, 63–88.

Zanna, M. P., & Pack, S. J. (1975). On the self-fulfilling nature of apparent sex differences in behavior. *Journal of Experimental Social Psychology, 11*, 583–591.

Zárate, M. A., & Sandoval, P. (1995). The effects of contextual cues on making occupational and gender categorizations. *British Journal of Social Psychology, 34*, 353–362.

Zuo, J. (1997). The effect of men's breadwinner status on their changing gender beliefs. *Sex Roles, 37*, 799–816.

Zweigenhaft, R. L., & Domhoff, G. W. (1998). *Diversity in the power elite: Have women and minorities reached the top?* New Haven, CT: Yale University Press.

# III

# GENDER CATEGORIZATION AND INTERPERSONAL BEHAVIOR

# 6

# Development of the Self
# in Gendered Contexts

Bettina Hannover
*University of Dortmund*

The present volume aims at bridging gaps between developmental and social psychological perspectives on gender. To promote this goal, this chapter considers the role of gender in the development of the self. We suggest that differences in the ways in which males' and females' selves change over time can account for gender-typed behavior and gender differences in various attributes.

Traditionally, developmental psychologists have focused on the prerequisite cognitive conditions for a self-categorization as male or female and for the acquisition of a particular gender-role identity (e.g., Fagot & Leinbach, 1985; Kohlberg, 1966; Martin & Halverson, 1981; Piaget, 1960), as well as on developmental changes in knowledge about gender stereotypes and their application (e.g., Berndt & Heller, 1986; Biernat, 1991; Deaux, 1984; Ruble & Martin, 1998). Social psychologists, on the other hand, have examined how gender stereotypes arise (e.g., Eagly & Steffen, 1984; Hoffman & Hurst, 1990; Swim, 1994), how they affect the processing of social information (e.g., Banaji, Hardin, & Rothman, 1993; Bem, 1981), and how they foster the development of gender-typed interests and behavior (e.g., Bussey & Bandura, 1984; Eagly, 1987; Geis, 1993; Lott & Maluso, 1993).

Eckes and Trautner (chap. 1, this volume) have pointed to the fact that whereas social psychologists have typically failed to consider variables referring to change over time, evident in their research participants almost exclusively stemming from a very narrow age group, developmental psychologists have often neglected the social influence emanating from the context in which an individual is acting. Here, we set about integrating social psychological and developmental perspectives by describing how social context variables influence individuals' self-construals over time. We start from the assumption that the self negotiates between the social environment and an individual's behavior, specifically proposing that gender-typed behavior or gender differences emerge and are maintained to the extent that males' and females' selves are being shaped differently by the social context during development (see also Cross & Madson, 1997; Deaux & LaFrance, 1998; Markus & Oyserman, 1989).

In the present contextual approach, gender is viewed as a social category. That is, we provide an answer to the question of *"how, when,* and *why* it makes a difference to be male or female" (Eckes & Trautner, chap. 1, this volume, p. 10). Specifically, we identify the mechanisms by which gender differences emerge out of an interaction between the self and the social context. To achieve this, we differentiate between two kinds of sources of contextual influences on an individual: (a) *situational sources,* that is, a particular situation's immediate influence, and (b) *chronic sources,* that is, cumulative situational influences persisting over extended periods of time. Whereas situational sources have typically been examined in social psychological studies of gender, chronic sources have traditionally been the focus of developmental gender research.

In adopting such an integrative perspective, we highlight the fact that the way in which the social context brings about gender-typed behavior or differences between the sexes can only be fully understood once we study its influence on the person's construal of his or her self. To put it in a nutshell, we argue that as individuals construe their selves during personal development, a cognitive structure about their being male or female is formed. Whenever this cognitive structure is activated by situational or chronic contextual sources, it influences the person's ongoing information processing in such a manner that the likelihood of gender-congruent behavior is increased.

Referring to Eckes and Trautner's question cited previously, in our view, it makes a difference to be male or female (a) in that depending on their sex, people either incorporate more stereotypically masculine or more stereotypically feminine knowledge into their selves (*how*), (b) whenever situational or chronic contextual sources activate gender-related self-knowledge (*when*), and (c) because people behave consistently with the content of self-knowledge being activated by situational or chronic sources (*why*).

We first turn to the question how in the course of personal development individuals construe their selves in general and their selves as male or female in particular. We then present a theoretical model that should illustrate how the self negotiates between situational and chronic contextual sources on the one hand and an individual's behavior on the other, and we describe how this model can explain the emergence and maintenance of gender-typed behavior from a developmental perspective.

# THE CONSTRUAL OF SELF AND OF GENDER-RELATED SELF-KNOWLEDGE DURING DEVELOPMENT

In this section, we try to show how individuals construe their selves during development. Special attention will be given to the question of how individuals come to understand their being male or female and how this knowledge becomes part of the self. In particular, we argue that as individuals move through childhood, knowledge related to gender contained in the self varies in predictable ways within and between the sexes.

We are working on the general principle that the self is an associative memory network that functions in the same way as other knowledge structures but is specific in that it contains only self-related information, that is, all the information about themselves that individuals encode in memory during their lives (e.g., Bower & Gilligan, 1979; Kihlstrom & Hoyt, 1988; Linville & Carlston, 1994; Markus, 1977). By implication, the self becomes more complex in the course of personal development. As a result, the self of a grown-up can be considered as the most extensive and most highly differentiated knowledge structure the person has available. As is illustrated in Fig. 6.1, in the associative network approach, the large amount of information contained in a person's self is assumed to be represented in multiple constructs, with each self-construct referring to a specific context of the respective person's life, for example "self as female," "self at the sports club," or "self as teacher."

The development of this complex knowledge structure can be considered a lifelong process. Roughly speaking, as an individual encounters new contexts and acquires new knowledge, it may be expected that corresponding new self-definitions are incorporated into the self. For instance, the differentiation *male versus female* is one of the first social categories children acquire (Kohlberg, 1966), namely at about 2 years of age (e.g., Berndt & Heller, 1986; Biernat, 1991; Ruble & Martin, 1998). Here, the child learns to categorize people according to their sex, that is, the child develops a *non-self-related knowledge construct about gender* (see also Martin & Halverson, 1981). This construct is a prerequisite condition for the acquisition of a corresponding self-definition (Bussey & Bandura, 1984; Kohlberg, 1966; Martin & Halverson, 1981). Thus, the *self-knowledge of being female or male* is formed around the age of 2 to 3 (e.g., Fagot & Leinbach, 1985; Kuhn, Nash, & Brucken, 1978), and gender constancy, that is, the realization that one's gender is constant across time and situations, is reached at 4 to 6 years of age (see Ruble, 1994, and Ruble & Martin, 1998, for reviews).

The more knowledge referring to the social category *male versus female* is acquired, the more complex the corresponding self-definition would be

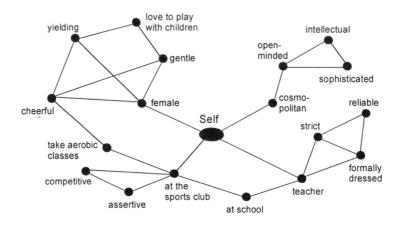

FIG. 6.1   A hypothetical example of the self as an associative memory network.

expected to become. For instance, at the age of 4, children already know about gender-typed traits, and at the age of 5 they know about gender-typed interests, preferences, or activities—for example, which professions are considered typically male or female in a given society (e.g., Golombok & Fivush, 1994; Ruble & Martin, 1998; Trautner, Helbing, Sahm, & Lohaus, 1988; Williams & Best, 1982). Such newly learned knowledge may be incorporated into the self, that is, it is checked according to its applicability to the self and, if applicable, stored as an information node linked to the already existing self-knowledge of being male or female.

As a result of this acquisition process, *gender-congruent information* corresponding to the core dimensions of gender stereotypes is linked to the information node of being male or female, establishing the person's *gender-related self-construct* (i.e., the self-concept of one's masculinity or femininity). This construct can be conceived of as an intersection in memory between the representation of gender-congruent information and the self. In Fig. 6.1, the person's gender-related self-construct consists of all pieces of information that are closely linked to the information node of being female. For females, gender-congruent information consists of attributes related to expressiveness, communion, pursuit of harmony, closeness, and interrelatedness with others; and for males, gender-congruent information consists of attributes related to instrumentality, agency, power, efficiency, competence, and independence from others (e.g., Bakan, 1966; Bem, 1981; Cross & Madson, 1997; Eagly, 1987; Parsons & Bales, 1955; Spence, 1993; Swim, 1994; Williams & Best, 1982).

To summarize, in early childhood, when gender stereotypes are acquired, individuals incorporate gender-congruent knowledge into their selves.

However, many studies have shown that reliance on gender stereotypes observed in kindergarteners and in first graders decreases with age (e.g., Berndt & Heller, 1986; Biernat, 1991; Ruble & Martin, 1998). It seems that as children grow older they come to understand the overlapping nature of females' and males' distributions in personality traits, interests, and activities.

For instance, Trautner et al. (1988) had children categorize personality traits and activities according to their occurrence in groups with different sex composition. For example, the child had to decide who helps with the housekeeping, who would play with dolls or who would role-play "cowboys and Indians"—a group made up exclusively of boys, a group with more boys than girls, a group with an equal number of boys and girls, a group with more girls than boys or an all-girl group. Results show that the percentage of children who assigned a certain activity or personality trait exclusively to one sex increased from age 4 (about 50%) to 6 (about 90%), and decreased from then on until age 10 (about 30%). These results reflect children's growing recognition of similarities between the sexes. Likewise, when comparing the use of global gender stereotypes and individuating gender-relevant information in kindergarteners, 3rd graders, 7th graders, 10th graders, and college students, Biernat (1991) found that while reliance on the use of gender labels as judgment cues remained stable developmentally, the use of individuating information increased with age.

Applied to the construal of self, these results point to the fact that as children grow older, they become more flexible in the sense that they do not necessarily apply all newly acquired knowledge about stereotypical characteristics of their own-sex group to themselves, but they may also incorporate *gender-incongruent information* into their selves. In other words, whereas gender stereotypes may first help individuals to establish a gender-related self-construct, at a later stage the self becomes more idiosyncratic or differentiated, in that gender-incongruent information is incorporated into other (non-gender-related) constructs contained in the person's self. Once this more differentiated level of development is reached, we can assume that the self of almost every individual incorporates both gender-congruent and gender-incongruent knowledge.

There is substantial convergence across different lines of research concerning the issue of how individuals acquire self-knowledge related to gender in the course of development. These lines are addressed in the following sections.

## Ruble's (1994) Phase Model of Transitions

Our assumptions concerning the construal of a gender-related self-construct are supported by the work of Ruble (1994) who described knowledge acquisition from a different developmental perspective. In particular, Ruble assumed that as individuals move through periods of major life changes, such as transition to a new school environment or transition to parenthood, their orientation toward relevant information changes in meaningful ways. Ruble identified three different phases to occur in most transitions: *construction, consolidation,* and *integration.* When an individual realizes that his or her categories or expectations are no longer applicable in a new psychological situation, he or she enters the construction phase of a transition. Since knowledge is low, the individual is actively gathering information, focusing on defining features and procedures of the new topic. Once such basic knowledge has been acquired, the individual's information seeking is focused, during consolidation, on drawing inferences about the topic's applicability and relevance to the self. Finally, the third phase of a transition aims at integrating the conclusions drawn with ongoing activities and with other aspects of knowledge about the self and the social world.

In the context of this chapter, Ruble's (1994) phase model is particularly useful in its application to the *gender transition.* Here, the model substantiates our assumption that during different phases of development, the content of self-knowledge related to gender varies in systematic and predictable ways. Specifically, we have assumed that once the child learns to categorize people according to their sex, a non-self-related knowledge construct about gender, mainly consisting of knowledge about gender stereotypes, is formed. Stated in Ruble's terms, at this stage the child enters the construction phase of the gender transition, with active information seeking being focused on defining the gender categories.

We have further assumed that the acquisition of some basic knowledge about gender is a prerequisite condition for a corresponding self-definition. Moreover, in this view, once a self-categorization as male or female is attained, the child will check newly acquired gender-related knowledge according to its applicability to the self and, as a result of this acquisition process, gender-congruent information corresponding to the core dimensions of gender stereotypes will constitute a gender-related self-construct. In terms of Ruble's (1994) transition model, this stage corresponds to the consolidation phase. In particular, the attainment of gender constancy is viewed as reflecting a shift from construction to consolidation. During this phase, as we have assumed in our model, children are expected to focus on information relevant to gender-appropriate behavior and to attach great importance to such information.

In summary, because in early childhood gender-related knowledge is first acquired without reference to the self, we can expect an unrestricted search and encoding of gender-related information, irrespective of its appropriateness to the child's own sex. However, once gender-related self-categorization or gender constancy is attained, a self-initiated focus in the search and encoding of information relevant to the child's own sex rather than the other is to be expected.

Finally, we have assumed that once a gender-related self-construct is being established, individuals become more flexible, again in the sense that they may also incorporate gender-incongruent information into their selves. In Ruble's (1994) model, this phase is described as integration. Here, the individual has reached a sufficient level of gender-related knowledge, and uncertainty with respect to its own gender identity is diminished. Accordingly, interest in information related to one's own sex is reduced and a greater flexibility in its impact on the self is displayed. As a result of integration, we should observe interindividual differences in the importance and accessibility of gender-related self-knowledge, in the use of gender as a category, and in the processing of gender-relevant information.

## Cognitive Accounts of Sex Typing

Our assumptions concerning the acquisition of gender-related self-knowledge are further supported by the work of several scholars who have proposed a cognitive account of sex typing. For instance, in their schematic processing model of gender stereotyping, Martin and Halverson (1981) suggested that as soon as children realize that gender is a salient human characteristic, they develop an *overall in-group/out-group schema* about gender, coinciding with the formation of rudimentary cognitive categories about male and female characteristics. In our theoretical approach, this stage corresponds to the acquisition of a non-self-related knowledge construct about gender. Martin and Halverson noted that children's sex typing starts with a self-categorization as male or female, leading to an increasing focus on social information relevant to their own-sex group. Thereby they establish an *own-sex schema*, that is, they become more expert with respect to what is appropriate for their own sex than for the other. In other words, as we have suggested for the gender-related self-construct, the own-sex schema in Martin and Halverson's approach is assumed to consist of gender-congruent information.

Closely related to our assumptions concerning the construal of a gender-related self-construct is the work of scholars who have focused on interindividual differences in the extent to which gender is used as a basic category of social information processing. In both Markus, Crane, Bernstein, and

Siladi's (1982) self-schema approach and in Bem's (1981) gender-schema theory it is argued that by the time children become aware of gender as a social category, they develop some basic cognitive categories of masculinity and femininity. Expressed in our theoretical terms, this stage of development corresponds to the acquisition of a non-self-related knowledge construct about gender.

Focusing on interindividual differences, however, Markus et al. (1982) went on to assume that once a network of knowledge relevant to masculinity or femininity has been acquired, only some individuals establish a highly elaborated and highly accessible cognitive structure describing the self as male or female, that is, a *self-schema about gender*, with this self-schema guiding information processing about gender in general and about the gender-related aspects of the self in particular. More specifically, depending on whether individuals think of themselves as particularly masculine or as particularly feminine, the network of knowledge relevant to masculinity or the network of knowledge relevant to femininity is expected to become part of the self.

Bem (1981) differentiated individuals according to the extent to which they spontaneously categorize and interpret social information in general with respect to the basic categories of masculinity or femininity. This tendency is measured by an individual's self-ascription of feminine and masculine personality characteristics. Specifically, whereas individuals who consider both feminine and masculine traits as self-descriptive are expected to display gender-role adaptability across situations, individuals who report relatively more attributes of one kind or the other should strongly tend to categorize social information according to its gender appropriateness and thus be limited in their behavior in accordance with their self-definition as masculine or feminine.

Empirical studies on the self-schema approach (Markus et al., 1982) and on gender-schema theory (Bem, 1981) substantiate our theoretical assumptions concerning the acquisition of gender-related self-knowledge in two different respects. First, these studies have shown that given a certain age level, the self of almost everyone includes both gender-congruent and gender-incongruent knowledge. For instance, not even 1% of the many research participants having completed self-report inventories measuring masculinity and femininity of the self (e.g., Personal Attributes Questionnaire [PAQ], Spence, Helmreich, Stapp, 1974; Bem Sex-Role Inventory [BSRI], Bem, 1974) endorsed fewer than half of the attributes from both the feminine and the masculine subscale. Second, these studies have shown that in the majority of cases, there seems to be a larger intersection between the representation of self and the network of knowledge relevant to an individual's own-sex group than between the self and the representation of the other-sex group: People tend to describe themselves in line with a general stereotype about their own sex. These results support our assumption that, in general, the gender-related self-construct consists of gender-congruent pieces of information.

## THE SELF AS NEGOTIATOR BETWEEN THE SOCIAL CONTEXT AND AN INDIVIDUAL'S BEHAVIOR

Having described different lines of research on how a gender-related self-construct is being construed in the course of personal development, we now explain why the self, conceived of as a negotiator between the social context and an individual's behavior, can account for the emergence and maintenance of gender-typed behavior. When talking about gender-typed behavior, we not only mean to account for gender differences in observable, overt action; rather, referring to the taxonomy of constructs relevant to sex-typing research described by Ruble and Martin (1998), we also want to explain gender differences in self-perceptions (e.g., of own traits or abilities), in preferences (e.g., for school subjects, occupations, leisure activities), and in behavioral enactments (e.g., course enrollment at school, subject choice for vocational training, engagement in leisure activities).

The model depicted in Fig. 6.2 describes the interaction between a person's self, the social context, and the person's behavior (Hannover, 1997a). In this model, principles described in the literature on knowledge activation and schematic processing (see Bargh, 1997, and Smith, 1998, for reviews) have been applied to the self as an associative knowledge structure. In particular, in the associative memory network model pieces of information within a certain self-construct are assumed to be more highly interconnected than constructs are among each other (see Fig. 6.1). Therefore, activation of a certain information node can be expected to mainly spread to other nodes within the same construct, and across constructs only to the extent that they are interconnected. As a result, activation should shift from one self-construct to another such that, at any given time, only a single self-construct or a small number of self-constructs is expected to be accessible. The shifting activation of different self-constructs implies that at different points in time, individuals should access different information about themselves. In our example in Fig. 6.1, when activating the gender-related self-construct, the information "I am yielding" is incorporated in the working self, whereas when the self-construct "at the sports club" is most accessible, the information "I am assertive" becomes part of the working self.

As indicated in Fig. 6.2, the configuration of temporarily activated self-constructs is called a person's *working self* (Cantor, Markus, Niedenthal, & Nurius, 1986; Higgins, 1990). Information contained in the working

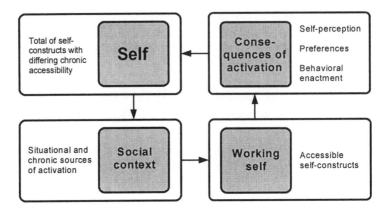

FIG. 6.2    The self as negotiator between the social context and an individual's behavior.

self can more easily be used than other information contained in the self. Accordingly, we would expect individuals to behave consistently with the information contained in their working selves. Using our example in Fig. 6.1 again, when at the sports club, the person would be more likely to perceive herself as "assertive" and to behave assertively than in a situation in which her gender-related self-construct is contained in the working self.

Which self-construct is incorporated into the working self at a particular point in time is assumed to depend on the *social context*. As is illustrated in Fig. 6.2, the context should provide sources of activation depending on which different self-constructs become part of the working self. As already mentioned, we differentiate between situational and chronic sources of activation (see also Higgins, 1990). We would expect the person's working self to contain both *situationally accessible self-constructs*, that is, self-knowledge that has most recently been primed by immediately present context factors (situational sources of activation) and *chronically accessible self-constructs*, that is, self-knowledge that has been primed frequently in the past (chronic sources of activation). Situational and chronic accessibility are mutually dependent. As can be seen from Fig. 6.2, with each situational activation, a self-construct's chronic accessibility is also increased, and the more chronically accessible it is, the more likely will it be incorporated into the working self again in the future.

Having described these priniciples, we are now able to understand how gender differences emerge and are maintained across the life span. We start out from the assumption that the self of virtually every individual encompasses both stereotypically masculine and stereotypically feminine aspects. We want to suggest, however, that during an individual's development, those aspects of the self that are gender-congruent will more likely be incorporated into the working self than gender-incongruent aspects. This is expected because individuals are typically more frequently exposed to social contexts that promote the activation of gender-congruent aspects of the self than to contexts in which gender-incongruent aspects are more applicable.

Given the assumptions about situational and chronic accessibility, we can infer that for an individual who is consistently exposed to context variables activating gender-congruent self-knowledge over extended periods of time, gender-congruent self-knowledge will become highly chronically accessible. That is, long-term individual differences in the frequency with which different self-constructs are primed may be expected to lead to individual differences in the chronic accessibility of these constructs (Higgins, 1990). Activated self-aspects, in turn, guide the individual's behavior, with gender-congruent self-aspects supporting gender-typed behavior. In this way, the emergence and maintenance of gender differences can be accounted for by differences in the social contexts that males and females are typically exposed to in the course of their development.

# DIFFERENCES IN SELF-PERCEPTION, PREFERENCES, AND BEHAVIORAL ENACTMENT BETWEEN AND WITHIN THE SEXES

The considerations presented previously can help us to explain differences in self-perception, preferences, and behavioral enactment between and within the sexes.

## Self-Perception

It has consistently been found in samples from different age groups that when describing themselves using experimenter-selected dimensions, females are more likely than males to report expressive, interdependence-related attributes (e.g., gentle, cheerful, sociable), whereas males consider instrumental, independence-related attributes (e.g., competitive, takes a stand, self-sufficient) as more self-characteristic (e.g., Bem, 1981; Lippa, 1995; Markus et al., 1982; Spence, 1993; Swan & Wyer, 1997). Similar findings have been obtained in studies using less restricted self-description measures. For example, girls freely describe themselves in terms of a greater number of other persons than do boys and are more likely to mention other specific significant persons rather than people in general (McGuire &

McGuire, 1982, 1988). Similarly, when asked to select photos that best describe one's self, females included more pictures displaying themselves together with others and fewer pictures of themselves alone than males did (Clancy & Dollinger, 1993).

Given the model depicted in Fig. 6.2, we can account for these gender differences in self-perceptions by the fact that, for both sexes, gender-congruent self-knowledge is chronically more accessible than gender-incongruent knowledge. Research on social judgment has shown that while judging an ambiguous stimulus, individuals use the categories that are most accessible, that is, categories that can most easily be retrieved from memory, with judgments being assimilated toward the content of the activated category (see Bargh, 1997, for a review). Therefore, when asked to describe themselves, individuals can be expected to use the self-constructs that most easily come to mind. If females report more expressive, interdependence-related attributes as being self-characteristic and males more instrumental, independence-related attributes, this could be due to their gender-related self-construct being more accessible than gender-incongruent knowledge contained in other, non-gender-related self-constructs.

This assumption is supported by studies that looked at the speed with which individuals rejected or endorsed certain personality attributes as self-characteristic. Here it was found that males not only endorsed more instrumental, independence-related attributes and fewer expressive, interdependence-related ones than females, but also that gender-congruent attributes were processed significantly faster than gender-incongruent ones (Hannover, 1997c). Response latencies are a reflection of the ease with which relevant information can be retrieved from memory. Correspondingly, we can expect information incorporated in the working self to be processed more quickly than other information contained in the self. Therefore, these results suggest that gender differences in self-descriptions are due to gender-congruent self-knowledge being chronically more accessible, that is, more often contained in the working self, than gender-incongruent self-knowledge.

Taken together, these assumptions may explain differences in self-perception *between* the sexes. However, the differential accessibility of gender-congruent and gender-incongruent self-knowledge can also account for variations in self-perception *within* the sexes. A huge empirical literature exists on ‧interindividual differences in the degree to which expressive, interdependence-related attributes versus instrumental, independence-related attributes are reported as self-descriptive. Thus, irrespective of their sex, individuals who report expressive (i.e., typically female) attributes to be as much self-characteristic as instrumental (i.e., typically male) attributes are considered androgynous, whereas individuals who report more attributes of one kind or the other are considered nonandrogynous (e.g., Deaux & LaFrance, 1998; Sieverding & Alfermann, 1992). Markus et al. (1982) have found that when describing themselves, androgynous individuals, no matter if male or female, endorsed both expressive, interdependence-related and instrumental, independence-related personality traits with the same speed, whereas nonandrogynous individuals needed more time to process the kind of attributes they considered as less self-characteristic. These results are congruent with our theoretical assumptions: It is only in androgynous individuals that gender-congruent and gender-incongruent aspects of self-knowledge exhibit a similar chronic accessibility.

## Preferences and Behavioral Enactment

Knowledge incorporated into the working self can more easily be accessed than other knowledge contained in the self. Therefore, self-constructs that are part of the working self will be used when newly incoming information is processed. As a result, this information will be assimilated toward the denotative and connotative aspects of the content of the working self. Because the gender-related self-construct contains predominantly gender-congruent information, we can predict that whenever this self-construct is incorporated into the working self, individuals will indicate preferences that are consistent with their gender or they will behave consistently with their gender, that is, gender-congruent preferences and behavioral enactments are most likely to occur, and gender-incongruent preferences and behavioral enactments are least likely (see Cross & Madson, 1997, for a comprehensive review of the literature on consequences of the use of gender-related self-knowledge on cognition, motivation, affect, and relationships).

Support for this assumption stems from research on androgyny. For instance, Bem and Lenney (1976) found that nonandrogynous research participants, that is, individuals for whom gender-congruent self-knowledge is chronically more highly accessible than gender-incongruent self-knowledge, preferred to have their picture taken while performing a sex-typed activity than while performing a cross-sex-typed one; whereas for androgynous participants, preferences were equally strong irrespective of the gender appropriateness of the task.

In addition, Bem (1975) found that androgynous research participants were more likely than nonandrogynous participants to engage in situationally effective behavior irrespective of the behavior being considered as more appropriate for one sex or the other. In particular, whereas androgynous subjects of both sexes displayed typically masculine behavior (resisting pressure to conform) or typically feminine behavior (playing with a kitten) according to the situational appropriateness of these behaviors, for nonandrogynous participants, behavioral deficits of one sort or another were observed.

Bem's (1975) results support the assumption that individuals indicate preferences or show behavioral enactments consistently with the content of their working selves: Individuals with equally accessible gender-congruent and gender-incongruent self-knowledge (androgynous participants) incorporated the type of self-knowledge into their working selves that was activated by the requirements of the situation. However, participants for whom gender-congruent self-knowledge was chronically more accessible than gender-incongruent self-knowledge (i.e., nonandrogynous participants) were unable to access the type of self-knowledge that would have fitted the situational requirements best. Consequently, such participants tried to avoid being photographed or displayed behavioral impairments when asked to perform gender-incongruent behavior.

## CONTEXT VARIABLES ACTIVATING GENDER-CONGRUENT AND GENDER-INCONGRUENT SELF-KNOWLEDGE ACROSS THE LIFE SPAN

Taken together, the empirical evidence suggests that in most individuals, gender-congruent self-knowledge is chronically more accessible than gender-incongruent self-knowledge. Given our assumptions about the shifting activation of different self-constructs, we are now able to explain these differences as the cumulative result of a lifelong process during which individuals are more frequently exposed to social contexts activating gender-congruent self-knowledge than to contexts in which gender-incongruent self-knowledge is most applicable. In the following, we describe in more detail the contextual sources that activate gender-congruent or gender-incongruent self-knowledge. Once we have identified such priming features, we can predict the kind of self-knowledge that will become chronically highly accessible based on the type of activating contextual sources an individual is exposed to more frequently.

### Sex Composition of Groups

Research has shown that a given personal characteristic becomes spontaneously salient in an individual's self according to the extent that this characteristic is distinctive within a given social context (see McGuire & McGuire, 1988, for a review). For instance, in a study by McGuire and Padawer-Singer (1976), spontaneous self-descriptions were elicited by presenting boys and girls from 10 different school classes a "Tell us about yourself!" probe. Consistent with the authors' hypotheses, 26% of students belonging to the minority-sex group in a given school class spontaneously mentioned their gender when describing themselves, in comparison with only 11% of students in the majority-sex group.

Cota und Dion (1986) found that the extent to which sex is salient in a person's self is also determined by the sex composition of ad hoc interaction groups. They found that 34% of participants whose sex was in the minority in a group of three mentioned their gender category, compared to only 16% of participants belonging to the majority-sex group and 17% of the students tested in single-sex groups.

These results suggest that the more salient a person's sex is in a given social context, the more likely is gender-congruent self-knowledge to be incorporated in the working self. In other words, minority sexual status in mixed-sex groups can be considered as a contextual source that activates gender-congruent self-knowledge. Accordingly, we would expect individuals to behave in a gender-typed manner to the extent that their sex is distinctive within a given situation.[1]

Analyses like these may help us to explain why, in different countries, girls from single-sex classes were found to show less reduced interest in mathematics and sciences than were girls from mixed-sex classes (e.g., Ainley, Robinson, Harvey-Beavis, Elsworth, & Fleming, 1994; Hoffmann, Häußler, & Peters-Haft, 1997). Since sex is a more distinctive personal characteristic in mixed-sex groups than in single-sex groups, students from coeducational classes can be expected to access gender-congruent self-knowledge more frequently. Indirect support for this assumption stems from a study by Hannover (1997b). Here, boys and girls from mixed-sex and single-sex schools were asked to indicate (a) their pubertal maturation status and (b) those students they most frequently interacted with in their respective school class. Results showed that whereas in mixed-sex classes students indicated those others which were most similar to themselves with respect to pubertal status, in single-sex classes choices were independent of the students' relative maturation. Since self-perception of one's pubertal status can be considered to be a part of the gender-related self-construct, these results are consistent with our assumption that in mixed-sex classes students

---

[1]This assumption is restricted to situations in which individuals are unaware of gender-congruent self-knowledge being primed. If individuals' attention is called to such activation, they may engage in attempts to correct the priming effect. As a result, priming effects are attenuated or even reversed (see Strack & Hannover, 1996, for a comprehensive discussion). For instance, Swan and Wyer (1997) found that both male and female research participants described themselves as relatively more masculine when they were the only one of their sex in a group of four than when their sex was in the majority. Swan and Wyer inferred that consciousness of their sex made women aware of their relatively low social status and motivated them to activate concepts that distinguish themselves from other members of their low-status group. These considerations may also explain why tokenism has dissimilar effects on men and women (e.g., Cohen & Swim, 1995).

more frequently access gender-congruent self-knowledge. These considerations may contribute to an explanation of why girls in coed classes are more
likely to retreat from school subjects that are regarded as stereotypically
masculine.

## Gender Stereotypes

Additional activating sources of gender-congruent self-knowledge are
provided by gender stereotypes. Self-knowledge related to gender can be
expected to become particularly relevant to a person's self-definition in
situations for which strong, culturally shared descriptive or prescriptive
gender-stereotypic beliefs exist. We therefore expect that individuals will
access gender-congruent self-knowledge whenever they are directly or
indirectly given information that is relevant to their concepts of masculinity
or femininity or that emphasizes differences between the sexes.

*Emphasizing Gender Differences.* This process was demonstrated in an
experiment by Hogg and Turner (1987). Research participants were
combined in discussion groups in such a manner that they held contradictory
attitudes toward topics such as artificial insemination or euthanasia. In a
dyad condition, two participants of the same sex were asked to discuss the
topics, whereas in a group condition, two males and two females interacted
in the discussion. Participants in the dyad condition were led to believe that
they were taking part in a study about interindividual differences in
discussion style, whereas participants in the group condition were told that
the study was about well-documented gender differences in discussion style.

Following the experimental session, participants were asked to indicate
how much they had acted like a "typical female" or like a "typical male"
during the discussion. As expected, both males and females taking part in
the group condition described their behavior as more typical of their own sex
group than those in the dyad condition. Also, subjects had to describe
themselves using adjectives from the BSRI (Bem, 1974), "as you see
yourself *now*, and not in terms of enduring personality attributes" (Hogg &
Turner, 1987, p. 329). The dependent variable, the degree of self-
stereotyping, was calculated as the difference between participants' pretest
ratings of how typical certain adjectives were for males or for females and
self-ascription of these adjectives. As expected, in the group condition both
males and females displayed stronger self-stereotyping than in the dyad
condition (however, only on positive adjectives of the scale; see Hannover,
1997a, for a discussion).

Hogg and Turner's (1987) results are consistent with our assumption that
in a situation in which gender differences are emphasized—in this case when

told the study dealt with "well-documented gender differences in discussion style"—gender-congruent self-knoweldge is incorporated into the working self and guides the person's behavior more strongly than in situations where gender differences are not emphasized.

The same mechanism can account for females' impaired performance in stereotypically masculine achievement domains. Empirical support for this assumption is provided by studies on stereotype threat. Steele (1997) suggested that when in a situation where a negative stereotype applies to a group individuals belong to, they feel threatened because they expect to be judged or treated stereotypically and because they are at risk of confirming the stereotype about their group as self-characteristic. If such a threat is experienced while working on a task, individuals' emotional reaction may directly interfere with their performance (situational threat). If the threat is chronically present, however, individuals disidentify with the domain the stereotype refers to, that is, they disengage their self-esteem from how poorly or how well they fare in that domain.

Using gender stereotypes as an example, in a study by Spencer, Steele, and Quinn (1999), women and men who were good at mathematics *and* considered themselves to be good mathematics students were given a difficult mathematics test that was expected to frustrate their skills but not totally exceed them. As expected, males outperformed their equally qualified female counterparts. In an experimental study, to prove that such gender differences in performance reflect the impairing effect of chronic stereotype threat, Spencer et al. varied the degree to which female participants were under stereotype threat while working on the test. To achieve this, participants were either led to believe that test results would typically differ between the sexes or that no such gender differences had been observed. As expected, in the condition in which the test had been characterized as being related to gender, women's underachievement was replicated; however, no sex differences in performance appeared in the condition where the test had been announced as being unrelated to gender.

The results of these studies suggest that individuals spontaneously access gender-congruent self-knowledge whenever they are given information emphasizing differences between the sexes. Correspondingly, if such information is given while working on a task, performance deficits are to be expected when the task is stereotypically gender-incongruent. From Steele's (1997) work we can also infer that girls and women disidentify with academic outcomes in stereotypically masculine subject domains because poor performance not only threatens their personal self-esteem—as is also the case in boys and men—but additionally puts them at risk of confirming the stereotype about females' inferiority on masculine tasks. In other words, by retreating from stereotypically masculine subject domains, girls or women can avoid contexts in which gender-related self-knowledge is chronically activated.

***Gender-Typed Tasks.*** In our view, the work on stereotype threat presented previously implies that the gender-typedness of a task may in itself be a subtle activating source of gender-congruent self-knowledge. We assume that whenever both sexes agree that one sex or the other is better at a task, individuals consider their sex as relevant when predicting the likelihood to succeed or when evaluating their performance outcome. Therefore, when individuals anticipate working on a task that they consider as gender-typed, gender-congruent self-knowledge can be expected to be incorporated into the working self. As a result, individuals' expectations of success and self-evaluations of performance will be distorted in a way consistent with gender stereotypes.

That individuals distort their expectations of success according to gender stereotypes was confirmed in an experiment by Hannover and Beyer (1999). Here, priming of gender-congruent self-knowledge was found to have differential effects on expectations of success in stereotypically masculine and feminine tasks. Gender-congruent self-knowledge was primed by having research participants evaluate photographs according to the physical attractiveness of the depicted person. In a control group, the same photographs had to be judged according to the mood of the person depicted. As expected, both males and females in the experimental group were less confident about their ability to succeed in gender-incongruent tasks than were control group participants. However, participants' expectations of success in gender-congruent tasks remained unchanged by the experimental treatment.

Further support for the assumption that individuals use gender-congruent self-knowledge while working on gender-typed tasks and consequently distort evaluations of their performance in stereotypic direction is provided in a study by Beyer (1990). She used multiple-choice tasks to measure the accuracy of individuals' self-evaluations of performance outcomes. Beyer's results show that participants' self-perceptions were best described by an interaction between their sex and the gender-typedness of the task. Whereas in a posttask estimation of the number of correctly answered stereotypically male questions (on political and sports figures), men's self-evaluations were accurate, women underestimated their actual performance. This gender difference in accuracy disappeared when the influence of participants' expectations was statistically controlled. In other words, participants' pretask expectations of how many correct answers they would produce were distorted in line with gender stereotypes. Similarly, in a study by Beyer and Bowden (1997), females underestimated their performance in a posttask self-evaluation of a stereotypically male task; they were less well-calibrated in their confidence statements for individual multiple-choice questions and displayed a more conservative response bias than males, that is, they were less likely to indicate high confidence and more likely to mistakenly state low confidence despite having answered a question correctly. In conclusion, these results suggest that a gender-typed task may in itself serve as an activating source of gender-related self-knowledge.

***Gender-Stereotypic Beliefs of People in an Individual's Social Environment.*** The aforementioned studies suggest that in situations in which gender stereotypes are relevant, individuals access gender-congruent self-knowledge. In these studies, experimental techniques were used in order to expose research participants to gender stereotypes. In which forms, however, do individuals encounter gender stereotypes within their social environment?

People in an individual's social milieu, in particular parents, teachers, peers, and later, in the person's life, colleagues and the person's mate(s), may act as gender-role socializers in that they convey gender stereotypes. More precisely, these socializers may personally hold gender-stereotypical beliefs or exert pressure to conform to gender stereotypes and thereby contribute to an individual's use of gender-congruent self-knowledge. In other words, the emergence of gender-typed behavior is promoted to the extent that individuals incorporate gender stereotypes conveyed by their social environment into their selves (see also Wood, Christensen, Hebl, & Rothgerber, 1997).

This process was described in detailed analyses by Eccles and her colleagues, focusing on the mediating role of parents' gender-stereotypical beliefs. In particular, Eccles (1985) proposed a model that specifies both a psychological and a socialization determinant of achievement-related behavioral choices, such as course enrollment at school (see also Eccles, Freedman-Doan, Frome, Jacobs, & Yoon, chap. 11, this volume). According to the model's psychological component, such behavioral choices can be predicted from a child's expectations of success, which in turn are directly influenced by the child's self-perception of ability and perception of task difficulty. According to the model's socialization component, a child's self-perception of ability as well as a child's estimation of task difficulty and expectation of success are strongly influenced by the parents' perceptions of their child's ability.

In a longitudinal investigation of more than 900 sixth graders and their parents, Frome and Eccles (1998) found that in stereotypically masculine domains (mathematics) and stereotypically feminine domains (English), parents' beliefs about their children's ability and about the effort needed to do well were dominant factors in predicting children's self-perception of ability, their expectation of success, and their perception of task difficulty. But what is more, parents' perceptions had a stronger effect on children's beliefs than did the children's grades. These results are intriguing given the fact that parents (in particular mothers) overestimated or underestimated their child's ability consistent with gender stereotypes: Despite girls having better mathematics grades, neither mothers nor fathers had a differential perception favoring their daughters, and mothers of daughters even assumed that their children needed more effort to do well in mathematics than did the mothers of sons. At the same time, both mothers and fathers of sons perceived their child as having lower ability in English and as needing to exert more effort to do well in English than did the parents of girls.

These results are consistent with our reasoning that parents' gender-stereotypical beliefs may activate gender-congruent self-knowledge in their children. It is conceivable that when asked to evaluate personal ability, task difficulty, and likelihood to succeed, that is, variables that influence course enrollment plans (Eccles, 1985), children of parents holding gender-stereotypical beliefs will more likely use gender-related self-knowledge than children who can infer from their parents' beliefs that gender is irrelevant with respect to these variables.[2] Conceived in this way, the well-documented gender differences in ability-related self-perceptions can be accounted for by contextual activating sources—parents' beliefs priming gender-congruent self-knowledge.

## Activities That Are Considered as More Appropriate for One Sex or the Other

In brief, gender stereotypes may activate gender-congruent self-knowledge and thus foster sex-differentiated behavior through a variety of mechanisms—by emphasizing gender differences, by tasks being perceived as gender-typed, and by socializers holding gender-stereotypical beliefs.

Additional contextual activating sources of gender-related self-knowledge are activities that are considered as being more appropriate for one sex or the other. This should be the case because mental representations of personal experiences with stereotypically masculine or feminine activities would be expected to be strongly associated with either self-knowledge about instrumental, independence-related attributes or self-knowledge about expressive, interdependence-related ones (see, e.g., Markus et al., 1982). Therefore, performance of a typically feminine activity would be expected to

---

[2]This interpretation would have been further substantiated by parents' perceptions mediating the relationship between children's gender and children's beliefs, an effect that was not found in Frome and Eccles' (1998) study. However, the correlation of gender with children's beliefs was also very low. This prompted Frome and Eccles to conclude that "at this stage in the child's development gender differentiation of self-concept of ability . . . is just beginning" (p. 446).

increase the likelihood that expressive, interdependence-related self-knowledge is activated by both males and females. While performing a typically masculine activity, on the other hand, instrumental, independence-related self-knowledge should more likely be incorporated into the working self (see also Eagly, Wood, & Diekman, chap. 5, this volume).

Support for this assumption stems from a study by Hannover (1997c). Both girls and boys were asked either to change a doll's diaper (feminine activity group) or to pound large nails into a piece of wood (masculine activity group). In a supposedly independent second study, participants were then asked to describe themselves as quickly as possible by endorsing or rejecting expressive, interdependence-related and instrumental, independence-related trait adjectives. As expected, results showed that, when compared with a control group where no gender-related activity had been carried out, both girls and boys in the feminine activity group endorsed more expressive traits and fewer instrumental traits as being self-descriptive. Furthermore, participants in this group processed expressive traits faster, and instrumental traits more slowly, than participants in the control group. On the other hand, compared to control subjects, participants in the masculine activity group described themselves using fewer expressive traits and more instrumental traits. Also as expected, participants in the masculine activity group processed expressive traits more slowly than those in the control group, whereas their processing of instrumental traits was accelerated. These results support the assumption that gender-congruent behavior serves as a contextual activating source of gender-congruent self-knowledge. While performing a gender-incongruent behavior, on the other hand, gender-incongruent knowledge will most likely be incorporated into the working self.

# INTERINDIVIDUAL DIFFERENCES IN CHRONIC ACTIVATION OF GENDER-RELATED SELF-KNOWLEDGE

## Differences in Chronic Sources of Activation Between the Sexes

We have seen that with each single activation, the respective self-knowledge becomes chronically more accessible. Therefore, chronic gender differences in the self, which can account for gender differences in social behavior, would appear to be the cumulative result of a lifelong process during which females are more frequently exposed to sources activating expressive, interdependence-related self-knowledge and males more likely encounter contexts in which instrumental, independence-related self-knowledge is primed.

Origins of such contextual variation between the sexes are manifold and have been described for many different cultures (see Alfermann, 1996, Maccoby & Jacklin, 1974, Markus & Oyserman, 1989, and Trautner, 1994, for reviews of the literature on gender-typed socialization). For instance, in a meta-analysis of 172 studies on parents' differential socialization of girls and boys, Lytton and Romney (1991) have documented that even in early childhood, children are particularly encouraged to engage in gender-typed play and activities. For instance, girls are more likely to be reinforced for playing with dolls, for helping with the housekeeping, or for making themselves look pretty, whereas boys are more often stimulated to play with tools or to be busy out of the house.

The differential encouragement of activities promoting expressiveness and interdependence in girls and of activities supporting instrumentality and independence in boys continues as children move into and through adolescence. Here, girls are more frequently assigned to care about younger siblings, whereas boys are stimulated to work at technical and craftsperson's problems (Goodnow, 1988; Ruble & Martin, 1998; Zern, 1984).

Finally, during adulthood, even if professionally employed, women spend much more time than males in raising their children and in taking care of relatives, and they take over a larger share of the housework (e.g., Biernat & Wortman, 1991). Also, in the world of professional work, occupations continue to differentially reinforce expressiveness and interdependence in women but instrumentality and independence in men (Eagly & Steffen, 1984). For instance, compared to men, women are more often found in caregiving professions and in subordinate positions, that is, in positions that promote nurturance and the ability to fit in with, or to adjust oneself to, others. Generally, the supportiveness of the environment is gender-typed such that during their lives, girls or women are more frequently exposed to contexts in which self-knowledge related to expressiveness and interdependence is primed, whereas the selves of boys and men are continually shaped by contexts in which the application of self-knowledge related to instrumentality and independence is most appropriate.

## Differences in Chronic Sources
## of Activation Within the Sexes

Differences in contexts that individuals are typically exposed to can also explain interindividual differences *within* the sexes. For instance, contexts that shape individuals' selves change historically, and cultures or societies vary in the degree to which they emphasize gender differences or foster gender stereotypical versus androgynous personal development (see Gibbons, chap. 13, this volume). For example, whereas children's socialization toward gender-appropriate behavior has long been considered an important obligation parents had to meet, today there seems to be a growing number of parents who try to convey the same norms and competencies to both their daughters and sons (Trautner, 1994).

Besides such historical trends, the combination of context variables influencing construal of the self can contribute to the emergence of interindividual differences within the sexes. As we have described in more detail earlier, we can assume that (a) the more frequently individuals are exposed to contexts in which their sex is salient, (b) the more frequently they encounter gender stereotypes, and (c) the more consistently they are encouraged to engage in gender-typed activities, the more likely is gender-congruent self-knowledge to become highly chronically accessible and the more likely is the person to display gender-congruent behavior.

For instance, we would expect interindividual differences in the degree to which expressive, interdependence-related attributes on the one hand and instrumental, independence-related attributes on the other are reported as self-descriptive (see, e.g., Bem, 1981; Markus et al., 1982) to be systematically related to the amount of relevant activating sources the person had been exposed to during development. Thus, if one compared androgynous and nonandrogynous individuals, an androgynous person would be expected to report having experienced fewer contexts priming gender-congruent self-knowledge and more contexts promoting the use of gender-incongruent self-knowledge. An empirical test of this hypothesis remains a task for future research.

## Differences in Chronic Sources of Activation Between Age Groups

Finally, we can account for *developmental changes* in the self and in social behavior by changes in the contexts that individuals experience according to their age or to developmental tasks. For instance, our theoretical assumptions can help to explain developmental shifts in the degree to which gender stereotypes influence the self and an individual's behavior. We may speculate about whether the fact that boys and girls increasingly interact in gender-segregated groups from about age 3 on (Maccoby, 1990) is in any way related to gender-related self-knowledge being less frequently primed in single-sex groups than in mixed-sex groups. As mentioned earlier, at this age level a child's self-concept typically contains almost exclusively gender-congruent information. Accordingly, whenever a situation requires gender-incongruent behavior, the activation of gender-related self-knowledge may lead to behavioral impairments. Therefore, children may prefer to interact in gender-segregated groups because here they are less limited to behave in accordance with their self-definition as masculine or feminine.

Also, we may speculate about whether the increasing impact of gender stereotypes on individuals' selves and behaviors in early adolescence is due to an age-related augmentation of contextual sources activating gender-congruent self-knowledge. Such sources may consist of pressures to conform to gender stereotypes emanating from parents and peers (Eccles & Bryan, 1994; Jussim & Eccles, 1992). For instance, Hill and Lynch (1983) found that, in order to prepare their daughters for adulthood roles, parents reinforce femininity and punish independence once girls reach adolescence. In addition, it is conceivable that the onset of puberty triggers a gender-related self-perception—with secondary sex characteristics maturing, the adolescent's self-awareness is focused on becoming a woman or a man. Therefore, it makes sense to assume that as children move into and through puberty, gender-congruent self-knowledge is particularly frequently used (Hannover, 1997b). This may explain why during this phase of development, gender differences in self-perception of abilities, preferences, and actual achievements in stereotypically masculine and feminine domains increase dramatically (see, e.g., Eccles, 1985; Hill & Lynch, 1983; Hoffmann et al., 1997; Hyde, Fennema, & Lamon, 1990).

## SUMMARY AND CONCLUSIONS

In this chapter, we illustrated the mechanisms by which gender differences emerge out of an interaction between the self and the social environment. In the first part of this chapter, we argued that as individuals move through childhood, the content of knowledge related to gender contained in their selves varies in predictable and meaningful ways (Ruble, 1994). Even before having attained a self-categorization as male or female and before having attained gender constancy, children develop basic knowledge structures about the concepts of masculinity and femininity (Bem, 1981; Kohlberg, 1966; Markus et al., 1982; Martin & Halverson, 1981). Once the child learns to categorize his or her self according to gender, the cognitive category related to the child's own sex merges with a gender-related self-construct, such that at this developmental level, the self almost exclusively contains gender-congruent information (Kohlberg, 1966; Martin & Halverson, 1981). Whereas at this age children generally focus on information relevant to their own sex, as they grow older, gender-incongruent knowledge will additionally become incorporated into different (non-gender-related) self-constructs (Bem, 1981; Markus et al., 1982; Ruble, 1994). However, as a result of this acquisition process, irrespective of age, the gender-related self-construct predominantly consists of gender-congruent information. Therefore, individuals will develop and exhibit gender-typed preferences and behaviors to the extent that their gender-related self-constructs have been activated by contextual sources.

In the second part of this chapter, we listed several context variables that can be considered sources of activation of the gender-related self-construct. We hypothesized that whenever a person's gender-related self-construct is activated in a given situation, he or she will most likely behave in a gender-congruent manner, whereas gender-incongruent behavior is least likely to occur. However, the emergence of gender-typed behavior is not only fostered by such situational activation of gender-related self-knowledge; rather, we have assumed the gender-related self-construct's chronic accessibility to increase with each situational activation. Accordingly, with each single situational activation the construct will more likely spontaneously be activated again in the future. This may explain why at later developmental stages, we can observe individual differences in the accessibility of gender-congruent and gender-incongruent self-knowledge (Ruble, 1994). As was described in more detail by Bem (1981) and Markus et al. (1982), the majority of people more easily access gender-congruent self-knowledge than gender-incongruent self-knowledge, whereas in some individuals self-knowledge of one kind or the other does not differ in its chronic accessibility.

Having described differing degrees of gender-typedness of the information contained in an individual's self at different age levels, we finally speculated that during different phases of development, the activation of gender-related self-knowledge may have a different impact on an individual's behavior. In particular, in time periods during which the person's self exclusively contains gender-congruent information (i.e., after having acquired a gender-related self-categorization but before having incorporated gender-incongruent information into the self), situational activation would be expected to foster gender-typed behavior in a particularly strong way. The same activating sources, however, should not have so strong an effect once the person has attained the phase of integration in the gender transition (Ruble, 1994), that is, once the self encompasses both feminine and masculine aspects. Finally, to the extent that individual differences in the accessibility of gender-congruent and gender-incongruent self-knowledge emerge, a particular source may activate gender-related self-knowledge only in some people. It remains a task for future research to describe in more detail such differential effects of activating sources across different stages of development.

Referring to the main theme of this volume, in the present chapter we suggested situational and chronic activation to be central mechanisms bridging the gap between social and developmental perspectives on gender.

Whereas situational sources of activation, that is, a particular situation's immediate influence on individuals' self-construals and behavior, have been focused on mostly in social psychological gender research, chronic sources, that is, cumulative effects of situational influences over extended periods of time, have traditionally been the topic of developmental studies of gender. Once we take both situational and chronic contextual influences on the construal of self into account, we may gain a better understanding of how gender-typed behavior emerges and is maintained across an individual's life span.

# REFERENCES

Ainley, J., Robinson, L., Harvey-Beavis, A., Elsworth, G., & Fleming, M. (1994). *Subject choice in years 11 and 12*. Canberra: Australian Government Publishing Service.

Alfermann, D. (1996). *Geschlechterrollen und geschlechtstypisches Verhalten* [Gender roles and gender-typical behavior]. Stuttgart, Germany: Kohlhammer.

Bakan, D. (1966). *The duality of human existence: An essay on psychology and religion.* Chicago: Rand McNally.

Banaji, M. R., Hardin, C., & Rothman, A. J. (1993). Implicit stereotyping in person judgment. *Journal of Personality and Social Psychology, 62*, 272–281.

Bargh, J. A. (1997). The automaticity of everyday life. In R. S. Wyer (Ed.), *Advances in social cognition* (Vol. 10, pp. 1–61). Mahwah, NJ: Lawrence Erlbaum Associates.

Bem, S. L. (1974). The measurement of psychological androgyny. *Journal of Consulting and Clinical Psychology, 42*, 155–162.

Bem, S. L. (1975). Sex role adaptability: One consequence of psychological androgyny. *Journal of Personality and Social Psychology, 31*, 634–643.

Bem, S. L. (1981). Gender schema theory: A cognitive account of sex typing. *Psychological Review, 88*, 354–364.

Bem, S. L., & Lenney, E. (1976). Sex typing and the avoidance of cross-sex behavior. *Journal of Personality and Social Psychology, 33*, 48–54.

Berndt, T. J., & Heller, K. A. (1986). Gender stereotypes and social inferences: A developmental study. *Journal of Personality and Social Psychology, 50*, 889–898.

Beyer, S. (1990). Gender differences in the accuracy of self-evaluations of performance. *Journal of Personality and Social Psychology, 59*, 960–970.

Beyer, S., & Bowden, E. M. (1997). Gender differences in self-perceptions: Convergent evidence from three measures of accuracy and bias. *Personality and Social Psychology Bulletin, 23*, 157–172.

Biernat, M. (1991). Gender stereotypes and the relationship between masculinity and femininity: A developmental analysis. *Journal of Personality and Social Psychology, 61*, 351–365.

Biernat, M., & Wortman, C. B. (1991). Sharing of home responsibilities between professionally employed women and their husbands. *Journal of Personality and Social Psychology, 60*, 844–860.

Bower, G. H., & Gilligan, S. G. (1979). Remembering information related to one's self. *Journal of Research in Personality, 13*, 404–419.

Bussey, K., & Bandura, A. (1984). Influence of gender constancy and social power on sex-linked modeling. *Journal of Personality and Social Psychology, 47*, 1292–1302.

Cantor, N., Markus, H., Niedenthal, P., & Nurius, P. (1986). On motivation and the self-concept. In R. M. Sorrentino & E. T. Higgins (Eds.), *Handbook of motivation and cognition: Foundations of social behavior* (Vol.1, pp. 96–121). New York: Guilford.

Clancy, S. M., & Dollinger, S. J. (1993). Photographic depictions of the self: Gender and age differences in social connectedness. *Sex Roles, 29,* 477–495.

Cohen, L. L., & Swim, J. K. (1995). The differential impact of gender ratios on women and men: Tokenism, self-confidence, and expectations. *Personality and Social Psychology Bulletin, 21,* 876–884.

Cota, A. A., & Dion, K. L. (1986). Salience of gender and sex composition of ad hoc groups: An experimental test of distinctiveness theory. *Journal of Personality and Social Psychology, 50,* 770–776.

Cross, S. E., & Madson, L. (1997). Models of the self: Self-construals and gender. *Psychological Bulletin, 122,* 5–37.

Deaux, K. (1984). From individual differences to social categories: Analysis of a decade's research on gender. *American Psychologist, 39,* 105–116.

Deaux, K., & LaFrance, M. (1998). Gender. In D. T. Gilbert, S. T. Fiske, & G. Lindzey (Eds.), *The handbook of social psychology* (4th ed., Vol. 1, pp. 788–827). Boston: McGraw-Hill.

Eagly, A. H. (1987). *Sex differences in social behavior: A social-role interpretation.* Hillsdale, NJ: Lawrence Erlbaum Associates.

Eagly, A. H., & Steffen, V. J. (1984). Gender stereotypes stem from the distribution of women and men into social roles. *Journal of Personality and Social Psychology, 46,* 735–754.

Eccles, J. (1985). Sex differences in achievement patterns. In T. B. Sonderegger (Ed.), *Nebraska symposium on motivation, 1984: Psychology and gender* (Vol. 32, pp. 97–132). Lincoln: University of Nebraska Press.

Eccles, J., & Bryan, J. (1994). Adolescence: Critical crossroad in the path of gender-role development. In M. Stevenson (Ed.), *Gender roles through the life span* (pp. 111–148). Muncie, IN: Ball State University.

Fagot, B. I., & Leinbach, M. D. (1985). Gender identity: Some thoughts on an old concept. *Journal of the American Academy of Child Psychiatry, 24,* 684–688.

Frome, P. M., & Eccles, J. S. (1998). Parents' influence on children's achievement-related perceptions. *Journal of Personality and Social Psychology, 74,* 435–452.

Geis, F. L. (1993). Self-fulfilling prophecies: A social psychological view of gender. In A. E. Beall & R. J. Sternberg (Eds.), *The psychology of gender* (pp. 9–54). New York: Guilford.

Golombok, S., & Fivush, R. (1994). *Gender development.* Cambridge, England: Cambridge University Press.

Goodnow, J. J. (1988). Children's household work: Its nature and functions. *Psychological Bulletin, 103,* 5–26.

Hannover, B. (1997a). *Das dynamische Selbst: Zur Kontextabhängigkeit selbstbezogenen Wissens* [The dynamic self: On the context-dependency of self-related knowledge]. Bern, Switzerland: Huber.

Hannover, B. (1997b). Die Bedeutung des pubertären Reifestatus für die Herausbildung informeller Interaktionsgruppen in koedukativen Klassen und in Mädchenschulklassen [Effects of pubertal maturation upon the formation of informal interaction groups in coeducational school classes and in girls' school classes]. *Zeitschrift für Pädagogische Psychologie, 11,* 3–13.

Hannover, B. (1997c). Zur Entwicklung des geschlechtsrollenbezogenen Selbstkonzepts: Der Einfluß "maskuliner" und "femininer Tätigkeiten" auf die Selbstbeschreibung mit instrumentellen und expressiven Personeigenschaften [On the development of self-concept about gender: The influence of "typically masculine" and "typically feminine" activities on the self-ascription of instrumental and expressive personality traits]. *Zeitschrift für Sozialpsychologie, 28,* 60–75.

Hannover, B., & Beyer, S. (1999). *Self-stereotyping and expectancies for success in sex typed tasks*. Unpublished manuscript.

Higgins, E. T. (1990). Personality, social psychology, and person–situation relations: Standards and knowledge activation as a common language. In L. A. Pervin (Ed.), *Handbook of personality: Theory and research* (pp. 301–338). New York: Guilford.

Hill, J. P., & Lynch, M. E. (1983). The intensification of gender-related role expectations during early adolescence. In J. Brooks-Gunn & A. C. Petersen (Eds.), *Girls at puberty: Biological and psychosocial perspectives* (pp. 201–228). New York: Plenum.

Hoffman, C., & Hurst, N. (1990). Gender stereotypes: Perception or rationalization? *Journal of Personality and Social Psychology, 58*, 197–208.

Hoffmann, L., Häußler, P., & Peters-Haft, S. (1997). *An den Interessen von Mädchen und Jungen orientierter Physikunterricht.* [Orienting physics education toward girls' and boys' interests]. Kiel, Germany: Institut für die Pädagogik der Naturwissenschaften an der Universität Kiel.

Hogg, M. A., & Turner, J. C. (1987). Intergroup behaviour, self-stereotyping and the salience of social categories. *British Journal of Social Psychology, 26*, 325–340.

Hyde, J. S., Fennema, E., & Lamon, S. J. (1990). Gender differences in mathematics performance: A meta-analysis. *Psychological Bulletin, 107*, 139–155.

Jussim, L., & Eccles, J. S. (1992). Teacher expectations II: Construction and reflection of student achievement. *Journal of Personality and Social Psychology, 63*, 947–961.

Kihlstrom, J. F., & Hoyt, I. P. (1988). Hypnosis and the psychology of delusions. In T. F. Oltmanns & B. A. Maher (Eds.), *Delusional beliefs* (pp. 66–109). New York: Wiley.

Kohlberg, L. (1966). A cognitive-developmental analysis of children's sex-role concepts and attitudes. In E. E. Maccoby (Ed.), *The development of sex differences* (pp. 82–173). Stanford, CA: Stanford University Press.

Kuhn, D., Nash, S. C., & Brucken, L. (1978). Sex role concepts of two- and three-year-olds. *Child Development, 49*, 445–451.

Linville, P. W., & Carlston, D. E. (1994). Social cognition of the self. In P. G. Devine, D. L. Hamilton, & T. M. Ostrom (Eds.), *Social cognition: Impact on social psychology* (pp. 143–193). San Diego, CA.: Academic Press.

Lippa, R. (1995). Gender-related individual differences and psychological adjustment in terms of the big five and circumplex models. *Journal of Personality and Social Psychology, 69*, 1184–1202.

Lott, B., & Maluso, D. (1993). The social learning of gender. In A. E. Beall & R. J. Sternberg (Eds.), *The psychology of gender* (pp. 99–123). New York: Guilford.

Lytton, H., & Romney, D. M. (1991). Parent's differential socialization of boys and girls: A meta-analysis. *Psychological Bulletin, 109*, 267–296.

Maccoby, E. E. (1990). Gender and relationships: A developmental account. *American Psychologist, 45*, 513–520.

Maccoby, E. E., & Jacklin, C. N. (1974). *The psychology of sex differences.* Stanford, CA: Stanford University Press.

Markus, H. (1977). Self-schemata and processing information about the self. *Journal of Personality and Social Psychology, 35*, 63–78.

Markus, H., Crane, M., Bernstein, S., & Siladi, M. (1982). Self-schemas and gender. *Journal of Personality and Social Psychology, 42*, 38–50.

Markus, H., & Oyserman, D. (1989). Gender and thought: The role of the self-concept. In M. Crawford & M. Gentry (Eds.), *Gender and thought: Psychological perspectives* (pp. 100–127). New York: Springer.

Martin, C. L., & Halverson, C. F. (1981). A schematic processing model of sex typing and stereotyping in children. *Child Development, 52*, 1119–1134.

McGuire, W. J., & McGuire, C. V. (1982). Significant others in self-space: Sex differences and developmental trends in the social self. In J. Suls (Ed.), *Psychological perspectives on the self* (Vol. 1, pp. 71–96). Hillsdale, NJ: Lawrence Erlbaum Associates.

McGuire, W. J., & McGuire, C. V. (1988). Content and process in the experience of self. In L. Berkowitz (Ed.), *Advances in experimental social psychology* (Vol. 21, pp. 97–144). San Diego, CA: Academic Press.

McGuire, W. J., & Padawer-Singer, A. (1976). Trait salience in the spontaneous self-concept. *Journal of Personality and Social Psychology, 33*, 743–754.

Parsons, T., & Bales, R. F. (Eds.). (1955). *Family, socialization and interaction process.* Glencoe, IL: The Free Press.

Piaget, J. (1960). *The psychology of intelligence.* New York: Harcourt Brace.

Ruble, D. N. (1994). A phase model of transitions: Cognitive and motivational consequences. In M. P. Zanna (Ed.), *Advances in experimental social psychology* (Vol. 26, pp. 163–214). San Diego, CA.: Academic Press.

Ruble, D. N., & Martin, C. L. (1998). Gender development. In W. Damon (Series Ed.) & N. Eisenberg (Vol. Ed.), *Handbook of child psychology: Vol. 3. Social, emotional, and personality development* (5th ed., pp. 933–1016). New York: Wiley.

Sieverding, M., & Alfermann, D. (1992). Instrumentelles (maskulines) und expressives (feminines) Selbstkonzept: Ihre Bedeutung für die Geschlechtsrollenforschung [Instrumental (masculine) and expressive (feminine) self-concepts: Their meaning for gender-role research]. *Zeitschrift für Sozialpsychologie, 23*, 6–15.

Smith, E. R. (1998). Mental representation and memory. In D. T. Gilbert, S. T. Fiske, & G. Lindzey (Eds.), *The handbook of social psychology* (4th ed., Vol. 1, pp. 391–445). Boston: McGraw-Hill.

Spence, J. T. (1993). Gender-related traits and gender ideology: Evidence for a multifactorial theory. *Journal of Personality and Social Psychology, 64*, 624–635.

Spence, J. T., Helmreich, R. L., & Stapp, J. (1974). The Personal Attributes Questionnaire: A measure of sex-role stereotypes and masculinity–femininity. *JSAS Catalog of Selected Documents in Psychology, 4*, 43–44.

Spencer, S. J., Steele, C. M., & Quinn, D. M. (1999). Stereotype threat and women's math performance. *Journal of Experimental Social Psychology, 35*, 4–28.

Steele, C. M. (1997). A threat in the air: How stereotypes shape intellectual identity and performance. *American Psychologist, 52*, 613–629.

Strack, F., & Hannover, B. (1996). Awareness of influence as a precondition for implementing correctional goals. In P. M. Gollwitzer & J. A. Bargh (Eds.), *The psychology of action: Linking cognition and motivation to behavior* (pp. 579–598). New York: Guilford.

Swan, S., & Wyer, R. S. (1997). Gender stereotypes and social identity: How being in the minority affects judgments of self and others. *Personality and Social Psychology Bulletin, 23*, 1265–1276.

Swim, J. K. (1994). Perceived versus meta-analytic effect sizes: An assessment of the accuracy of gender stereotypes. *Journal of Personality and Social Psychology, 66*, 21–36.

Trautner, H. M. (1994). Geschlechtsspezifische Erziehung und Sozialisation [Gender-specific education and socialization]. In K. A. Schneewind (Ed.), *Psychologie der Erziehung und Sozialisation* (pp. 167–195). Göttingen, Germany: Hogrefe.

Trautner, H. M., Helbing, N., Sahm, W., & Lohaus, A. (1988). Unkenntnis—Rigidität—Flexibilität: Ein Entwicklungsmodell der Geschlechtsrollen-Stereotypisierung [Unawareness—rigidity—flexibility: A developmental model of gender-role stereotyping]. *Zeitschrift für Entwicklungspsychologie und Pädagogische Psychologie, 19*, 105–120.

Williams, J. E., & Best, D. L. (1982). *Measuring sex stereotypes: A thirty-nation study.* Beverly Hills, CA: Sage.

Wood, W., Christensen, P. N., Hebl, M. R., & Rothgerber, H. (1997). Conformity to sex-typed norms, affect, and the self-concept. *Journal of Personality and Social Psychology, 73,* 523–535.

Zern, D. S. (1984). Relationships among selected child-rearing variables in a cross-cultural sample of 110 societies. *Developmental Psychology, 20,* 683–690.

# 7

# Gender Stereotypes and the Dynamics of Social Interaction

Sarah E. Zemore
Susan T. Fiske
Hyun-Jeong Kim
*University of Massachusetts at Amherst*

Children acquire basic gender categories with remarkable facility and, soon after, learn to apply gender to an extraordinary range of stimuli. Gender is, typically, the first of the top three social categories (including gender, race, and age) to be acquired (Mackie, Hamilton, Susskind, & Rosselli, 1996). At just 7 months, children who have been habituated to one female face subsequently habituate to new female faces, suggesting that they have formed an abstract category describing females (Cohen & Strauss, 1979).

In adulthood, gender continues to dominate perceivers' attention. Across several contexts, gender dominates race (A. P. Fiske, Haslam, & Fiske, 1991; Stangor, Lynch, Duan, & Glass, 1992), age (A. P. Fiske et al., 1991), and social role (van Knippenberg & van Twuyver, 1994) as a basis for categorization. In fact, it is doubtful that we can think about people at all without thinking about their gender. "Gender is, for us as social animals, part of the 'air we breathe,' a reality that is ever part of our experience" (Deaux & LaFrance, 1998, p. 788).

Is there some relation between children's early awareness of gender and adults' pervasive use of it? This chapter argues that it is no coincidence that gender dominates person perception in both childhood and adulthood. More precisely, we argue that children's persistent use of gender rapidly automatizes gender stereotypes, so that, by adulthood, gender stereotyping occurs frequently, effortlessly, and often unconsciously. Although gender stereotypes continue to serve important functions throughout development, their broad and persistent use in adulthood largely stems from their broad and persistent use in earlier stages of development.

This argument does not imply that adults can never control their tendency to stereotype by gender. Stereotyping is controllable at various levels: Factors at the level of the perpetrator, the victim, and the situation can inhibit the tendency to stereotype (see S. T. Fiske, 1998, for a review). However, the argument does imply that attempts to influence stereotyping may best be aimed at stereotyping in its earliest stages. Blocking the development of gender stereotypes reduces the need to control, through moral and legal restraints, stereotyping and its effects later in life. However, controlling stereotyping in children demands effort: It requires a thorough understanding of how stereotypes function across development.

In pursuit of this understanding, this chapter explores the forces conditioning gender stereotypes and their use at different stages of development. In each section, the chapter introduces research on adult stereotyping to frame research on children's use of gender concepts. This chapter intentionally does not supply a thorough review of the literature, aiming to identify new lines of inquiry rather than approaching definite conclusions.

The first section grounds the discussion with a review of stereotype content and an inquiry into its development. Importantly, this section highlights evidence that the core content of gender stereotypes crystallizes well before the age of 5. Next, the chapter reviews possible determinants of children's acquisition and use of gender stereotypes. These sections argue that children use gender stereotypes for the specific functions that stereotypes serve, and as a result of characteristics inherent to the operation of stereotypes. A fourth section shows that young children's broad and frequent use of gender stereotypes promotes their automatization. To conclude, a final section explores the development of stereotype-control mechanisms and poses questions for further research.

## DEVELOPMENT OF GENDER STEREOTYPES: CONTENT

What do people believe about men and women? How and when does this knowledge emerge? This section addresses these questions with an overview of stereotype content and its development.

## Gender Descriptions

In thinking about the content of gender stereotypes, researchers often distinguish between the descriptive and prescriptive components. The descriptive component consists of beliefs about the characteristics that each gender does possess, whereas the prescriptive component consists of beliefs about the characteristics that each gender should possess. So the descriptive component of the female stereotype might include beliefs that women are emotional, whereas the prescriptive component might specify that women should be submissive.

Considerable effort has detailed the descriptive component of adult gender stereotypes. In reviewing the findings, Deaux and LaFrance (1998) concluded, with Eagly (1987), that people typically describe women using communal (interpersonally oriented) attributes, whereas descriptions of men cluster around agentic (achievement-oriented) attributes. Women are described as affectionate, emotionally expressive, and responsive to others; men are described as independent, assertive, and active (Ashmore, Del Boca, & Wohlers, 1986). On the negative side, people are more likely to describe women as spineless and whiny, and men as arrogant and selfish (Spence, Helmreich, & Holahan, 1979). Gender distinctions along the dimensions of agency and communion persist steadfastly, both over time and across culture (Deaux & Kite, 1993; Ruble & Ruble, 1982; Swim, Aikin, Hall, & Hunter, 1995). In fact, agency and communion may be the fundamental distinctions underlying conceptions of masculinity and femininity (Bem, 1974).

How do adult gender stereotypes develop? According to a recent review, children acquire descriptive stereotypes in slow, incremental stages (Ruble & Martin, 1998). Gender-related knowledge accumulates steadily through-out childhood and into adolescence. At about 26 months, children first become aware of gender differences associated with adult possessions, roles, and physical characteristics. Six months later, they have learned to associate gender with children's toys and activities. At 5 years, children begin to associate high-level personality traits (the pivot of adult stereotypes) with gender, and their knowledge continues to increase until early adolescence.

Though gender stereotypes develop gradually, the fundamental distinctions of agency and communion appear to crystallize at a very early age. Children between the ages of 2 and 3 reliably distinguish between boys and girls along the agentic dimension of strength (boys are strong, girls are weak) and along the communal dimension of niceness (boys are mean, girls are nice). Toddlers also tend to see boys as faster, harder, and more prone to anger/hitting than girls, whereas girls are stereotyped as more talkative, more interested in housework, and more likely to ask for help than boys (Cowan & Hoffman, 1986; Haugh, Hoffman, & Cowan, 1980; Kuhn, Nash, & Brucken, 1978). Thus, a visual inspection of how children rate boys and girls suggests that children as young as 2 develop a bidimensional (agency, communion) attitudinal structure differentiating males and females (but see Ruble & Martin, 1998, for a slightly different interpretation of these findings). Of course, a caveat specifies that any conclusions about attitudinal structure must remain tentative until further data can be collected and analyzed—that is, until children's ratings of boys and girls can be statistically analyzed to confirm that agency and communion underlie their gender stereotypes, just as these dimensions seem to underlie adult gender stereotypes.

To summarize, although gender stereotypes develop gradually, the fundamental gender distinctions stabilize with fearful rapidity. For adults, "the typical woman is seen as nice but incompetent, the typical man is seen as competent but maybe not so nice" (S. T. Fiske, 1998, p. 377). For preschoolers, girls are sugar and spice . . . and boys are snakes and snails (Serbin, Moller, Gulko, Powlishta, & Colburne, 1993, cited in Ruble & Martin, 1998).

## Subtypes: More Informative Descriptions

Often, people want detailed information about how to behave in specific situations. People want to know how to introduce themselves to a female African American, how to eat spaghetti with a male toddler, and whether to open the door for a female hockey player. Global stereotypes cannot provide the specific information that people need. As a result, people often abandon global stereotypes in favor of the informationally richer subtypes (Stangor et al., 1992). This tendency to operate on the level of subcategories does not confine itself to gender stereotyping; rather, it extends to many other domains. People use intermediate-level categories to classify objects of many types, maximizing predictive power (Estes, 1993).

Subtypes are subcategories of the global stereotype, and they often develop in response to isolated cases that disconfirm a more global stereotype (Fiske & Taylor, 1991; Taylor, 1981).[1] Like global stereotypes, subtypes center around dimensions of agency and communion. However, they also incorporate characteristics that are inconsistent with, or unspecified by, the global stereotype, allowing people to retain their global stereotypes in the face of new evidence (Hewstone, Hopkins, & Routh, 1992; Hewstone,

---

[1]Maurer, Park, and Rothbart (1995) drew an important distinction between subtyping and subgrouping. *Subtyping* involves mentally isolating individuals who disconfirm a stereotype, whereas *subgrouping* involves dividing the superordinate category into similar but distinct subcategories. Subtypes leave the stereotype unchanged, but subgroups lead to perceptions of increased intercategory variability. Conventional treatments of social stereotyping neglect this distinction, referring to both subtyping and subgrouping as subtyping. To avoid confusion, this chapter also adopts the term *subtyping* to describe what is, more precisely, called subgrouping.

Johnston, & Aird, 1992; Johnston, Hewstone, Pendry, & Frankish, 1994; see Hewstone, 1994, for a review).

Some subtypes share many features with the superordinate stereotype, whereas others show little overlap. Thus, subtypes of mothers, White women, and middle-class women overlap substantially with the global stereotype of women, but subtypes of career women, Black women, and lower-class women overlap far less (Deaux, Winton, Crowley, & Lewis, 1985; Eckes, 1994; Landrine, 1985; Riedle, 1991). Characteristics of the situational context help determine which of the available subtypes is activated at any given moment. For example, participants viewing women in nontraditional work settings may be more likely to apply the feminist/lesbian subtype (emphasizing masculinity and power) than participants viewing women in more traditional settings (Burgess & Borgida, 1997). Interestingly, people seem to make numerous, overlapping associations between common situations and female subtypes, associating each female subtype with a relatively wide range of situations, and each situation with a relatively large number of female subtypes; conversely, male subtypes tend to be associated with narrow, more exclusively defined sets of situations (Eckes, 1996). This suggests that people have fairly consensual beliefs about precisely which kinds of men interact in which situations (e.g., only trendy types go to cafes). On the other hand, it may be easier for men than it is for women to avoid particular stereotypic labels by avoiding the associated situations.

Although much is known about the content of subtypes, relatively little is known about the timing and nature of their acquisition. By adulthood, people generally converge on four distinct subtypes of women, including house-wife, sexy woman, career woman, and feminist; adult male subtypes include business man and macho man (Deaux et al., 1985; Glick, Diebold, Bailey-Werner, & Zhu, 1997; Six & Eckes, 1991; see Deaux & LaFrance, 1998, for a review). Still, the acquisition of these subtypes remains mysterious. The fact that young children demonstrate the ability to link gender to social roles argues that subtypes develop early, perhaps contemporaneously with global stereotypes. Meanwhile, evidence that children of the same age tend to ignore variability within gender categories (Martin, 1994) argues that subtypes do not develop until middle or late childhood, as children acquire the capacity to use stereotypes more flexibly. These possibilities deserve further exploration.

## Gender Prescriptions

Gender descriptions and their subtypes connect with prescriptive beliefs. People often value men and women who fit traditional gender stereotypes, and they respond to violations of gender norms with anger, disgust, and various forms of censure. In several famous cases, employers have even fired their female employees for violating traditional female roles (S. T. Fiske & Stevens, 1993).

Recent surveys suggest that traditionally sexist beliefs about women's roles have declined significantly since the 1970s (Spence & Hahn, 1997). However, more sensitive scales reveal that prescriptive beliefs persist, albeit in modern forms. For example, the Modern Sexism Scale (Swim et al., 1995) identifies a subgroup of men who overtly reject traditional gender stereotypes, yet still report feeling negatively toward women making economic and political demands, believe that gender discrimination is no longer a problem, and believe that the government and the media pay more attention to women than is appropriate. Similarly, the Ambivalent Sexism Inventory (ASI; Glick & Fiske, 1996) reveals a related form of sexism characterized by benevolent attitudes toward women who conform to traditional gender prescriptions and hostile attitudes toward women who challenge those prescriptions. Ambivalent sexists believe that a "good woman" should be set on a pedestal, but also that women, and especially feminists, exaggerate the prevalence of discrimination and claim unreasonable favors from men. Thus, although modern and ambivalent sexists are not willing (or not able) to admit bias, their rejection of women who challenge stereotypical roles suggests that they do support traditional gender prescriptions.

Unfortunately, the available research on stereotyping in children has often failed to distinguish between gender knowledge and gender attitudes (Ruble & Martin, 1998). This makes it difficult to determine precisely when gender prescriptions develop. Nevertheless, evidence on children's reactions to gender violations hints at early development. Children as young as 4 report disliking children described as tomboys or sissies, preferring, instead, stereotypical children of their own gender (Martin, 1994). Similarly, kindergartners react negatively to gender violations in appearance—for example, they dislike boys wearing nail polish (Stoddart & Turiel, 1985). This suggests that gender descriptions are rapidly, if not immediately, transformed into gender prescriptions.

In sum, experiences prior to grade school apparently cement the core beliefs about what each gender is and should be, though questions remain about the nature of this learning process. Having introduced these basic concepts, we turn now to an exploration of why children learn gender stereotypes.

# DEVELOPMENT OF GENDER STEREOTYPES: PROCESSES OF CATEGORIZATION

Why do children acquire gender stereotypes so early and use them so frequently? The present section addresses these questions in detail.

Children acquire gender categories, and continue to use them, because gender categories are useful. To substantiate this argument, this section introduces four major approaches to the causes of social stereotyping. Among the perspectives, the cognitive approach assumes center stage, in recognition of its prominence in contemporary theory and its ability to explain both the early acquisition, and later use, of gender categories. The cognitive approach, as the dominant approach, also guides subsequent sections' treatment of the effects of gender stereotyping. However, the cognitive approach falls short of providing a complete account of gender stereotyping, primarily because it shies from questions of stereotype content. This approach cannot explain how individuals attach particular beliefs to gender categories (Mackie et al., 1996), such as the belief that women are communal or men agentic. Hence, this section introduces social role theory, social identity theory, and power-based approaches to address this limitation (see also Martin, chap. 4, this volume).

Social role theory, a variant on the cognitive approach, explains how certain associations between gender and social roles encourage the development of gender-related knowledge. Social identity theory complements this perspective with a motivationally based explanation for how stereotypes take on their particular evaluative flavor. Finally, power-based approaches combine cognitive and motivationally based explanations, predicting when people are likely to stereotype and, more recently, what the content of those stereotypes will be.

## The Cognitive Approach

The dominant approach to the causes of social stereotyping claims that stereotyping, a universal, adaptive function, makes human reasoning possible. Proponents of this (cognitive) approach assert that people stereotype because stereotypes organize information and facilitate inference. Most notably, Allport (1954) argued that stereotyping is neither abnormal nor irrational but, rather, a fundamental part of simplifying the otherwise impossibly complex social world. In a similar vein, Taylor (1981) proposed that stereotypes organize social information, permitting people to make rapid, good-enough inferences about others. These perspectives specify how cognitive constraints interact with the stimulus environment to produce social stereotyping.

Insights of the cognitive approach go far toward explaining the acquisition and use of gender categories. Cognitive approaches imply that children use gender categories for their utility in processing information. In fact, three lines of evidence suggest that children have the need, the capacity, and the tendency to use gender categories in processing information.

First, according to maturational perspectives of development, children face particularly strong limitations on their abilities to process information (Flavell, 1992). Thus, children have a particular need to organize social information, and should be motivated to seize on any category that organizes information and facilitates inference. Gender is one such category.

Second, even infants are capable of using categories to form inferences about the world (Hayne, Rovee-Collier, & Perris, 1987, cited in Gelman, 1996; Baldwin, Martin, & Maclartin, 1993, cited in Gelman, 1996). For example, children as young as 3 months can generalize the behavior of one mobile to make predictions about an unfamiliar, but perceptually similar, mobile. Gender-based inferences come later, but not by much: Preschoolers already use gender to make inferences about the characteristics of infants (Haugh et al., 1980).

Third, children's nonselective use of gender categories suggests that they are, in fact, using gender categories to facilitate information processing. Research on gender categorization (e.g., Ruble & Ruble, 1982) reveals that children apply gender distinctions liberally, to a broad range of stimuli (e.g., toys, activities, and occupations). This nonselective application suggests that gender categories function as central pegs for organizing and assimilating a diverse range of important information about the world.

The cognitive approach, by focusing on the brain and the stimulus environment, also illuminates why gender categories, relative to other social classifications, are acquired so quickly. A look at gender categories themselves reveals three distinct advantages. A first advantage is that gender categories are dichotomous, as children probably find it difficult to remember, and use, multiple classifications (Mackie et al., 1996). A further advantage is that gender categories are mutually exclusive, as children seem to learn mutually exclusive categories more quickly than overlapping categories (Markman, 1989). Last, gender categories are visually salient and, because children typically organize stimuli by their concrete, perceptual characteristics (Bruner, Olver, & Greenfield, 1966), gender categories may be particularly suited to children.

A look at the stimulus environment reveals additional characteristics that may speed the  acquisition of gender categories. Children have constant exposure to exemplars from both gender categories (Mackie et al., 1996). They live with, grow attached to, and depend on many people of both genders, quickly constructing a large database of information. Since children are more likely to form categories and concepts in domains of particular expertise (Gelman, 1996), it makes sense that they form gender categories more quickly than they form categories of other, less accessible social groups. Thus, the cognitive approach lays a solid foundation for understanding why children prefer gender categories in forming their impressions of others.

## The Social Role Approach

A second approach to stereotyping, Eagly's (1987) social role theory examines how the stimulus environment encourages the development of particular gender-related beliefs. This approach focuses explicitly on gender stereotyping, emphasizing the contribution of current social arrangements to adult conceptions of men and women (see also Eagly, Wood, & Diekman, chap. 5, this volume).

Social role theory suggests that societal divisions of labor, in which men are more likely to occupy paid positions and women are (relatively) more likely to occupy domestic roles, contribute to people's expectations of men and women. The essence of the argument runs as follows:

1. People expect paid employees to be agentic and homemakers to be communal.

2. These expectations elicit confirmatory behavior, so that paid employees demonstrate agentic behavior and homemakers demonstrate communal behavior.

3. Both the occupant of the role and surrounding observers attribute role-consistent behavior to the gender of the individual rather than to social forces.

4. Men disproportionately occupy positions as paid employees, whereas women disproportionately occupy positions as homemakers; hence, men are more often seen as agentic, whereas women are more often seen as communal.

A corollary of the argument states that gender stereotyping is best addressed by a redistribution of social roles. If men and women occupied equivalent social roles, then their behavior would look similar, and gender would become less meaningful.

The social role approach may illuminate important causes behind stereotype use in early development. For young children, role divisions correlate with gender as highly as, if not more highly than, they do in adulthood. Moving from social role theory, we can speculate on how these associations affect stereotype development.

In early childhood, then, the first woman that children usually encounter is their mother, whom they see in the role of a caretaker. Early, frequent, and intimate interaction with the mother in this role—the moment-to-moment soothing, smiling, gurgling, talking, and feeding—may teach the infant what it means to be female. This close contact may encourage the formation of female stereotypes, including the particular beliefs that women are likely to be caregivers, and that women are warm and nurturing. Meanwhile, the first man that children encounter is their father, whose primary occupation is usually outside of the home. In contrast to maternal experiences, infants typically have fewer opportunities to interact with their fathers. This means that they largely infer (rather than experience) the characteristics of men. As a result, stereotypes of men should be less well-organized than those of women, and the content should be related to achievement and competence more than to sociality—as it is.

Even as children enter school, gender roles remain distinct. Children's teachers (also caretakers) are usually female, whereas school principals and other administrators (having high-status, agentic roles) are usually male. Importantly, this is particularly true in the early grades. Children's storybooks and television shows are also highly stereotypical (Ruble & Martin, 1998). Again, these associations may reinforce stereotype development.

Social role theory, however, should not be incautiously applied to explain stereotype development in early childhood. One concern is that children do not seem to infer dispositions from behavior (i.e., they do not show the correspondence bias) until they are 7 or 8 years of age (Mackie et al., 1996). This challenges the thesis that children make gender-related inferences on the basis of their caretakers' behavior. On the other hand, good evidence suggests that a mother's social role does contribute to stereotype formation at a young age. Maternal employment correlates with less stereotyped concepts in both boys and girls as young as 3, and with less gender-typed role preferences for girls (Huston & Alvarez, 1990; J. V. Lerner, 1994). Further, when children do reach middle childhood, they become even more likely than adults to form dispositional inferences from behavior (Mackie et al., 1996). Thus, though young children process associations between gender and behavior in different ways than older children (making more concrete, behavioral inferences about men and women), such associations are probably important influences on stereotype formation across development.

## Social Identity Theory

Social identity theory (Tajfel & Turner, 1986), a third view of stereotyping, departs from cognitive perspectives by emphasizing the role of motivational factors. Moreover, this approach uniquely stresses that stereotyping can be a group process, and not only something that happens in the heads of individuals.

Social identity theory begins with the thesis that, because self-esteem depends on group identity, all people strive to achieve a positive identity for their in-group. By this view, positive social identity depends on favorable comparisons with a relevant out-group. The in-group compares favorably to an out-group only when it can demonstrate *positive distinctiveness* from the out-group. Because stereotypes accentuate intergroup differences and intragroup similarities, groups use stereotypes to achieve positive distinctiveness. This same motivation for positive distinctiveness also propels groups to assign positive qualities to the in-group and negative qualities to the out-group (Tajfel & Turner, 1986). Thus, unlike the first two approaches, social identity theory explains how group stereotypes acquire their evaluative flavor.

Social identity theory suggests that children form and use gender stereotypes to achieve a positive, distinct identity for their in-group. Several lines of evidence support this proposal. First, for older children at least, group identity does influence self-esteem. During middle school, girls become aware of the lower status of their category (Ruble & Martin, 1998); this realization is accompanied by a marked decline in self-esteem for girls, compared with no change in self-esteem for boys. A second line of support is that self-categorization is linked to behavioral strategies that differentiate males and females. In particular, the ability to label gender accurately (at 28 months) roughly coincides with the onset of gender segregation (at 27 months for girls, and 36 months for boys) (Ruble & Martin, 1998). This confirms that, as soon as children become aware of their gender, they strive to differentiate themselves from the out-group. Finally, evidence that young children make evaluative distinctions between the genders supports the thesis that social identity processes operate in children (Mackie et al., 1996). At times, girls as young as 3 show significant in-group bias, and, by 5, both boys and girls are markedly more positive about their own sex (Yee & Brown, 1994). Although the basis for this tendency remains unclear, esteem motivations constitute one possibility.

## Power-Based Approaches

As a final perspective on the causes of social stereotyping, power-based approaches suggest that stereotyping is inherently linked to power. These approaches share with social role theory an emphasis on sociostructural factors, but consider the influence of these factors on both cognition and motivation.

Power-based approaches unite in the proposal that people attribute negative characteristics to out-group members to establish, maintain, and justify superior power and status. According to these approaches, individuals and groups stereotype intentionally, by design, to further their positions relative to others (Goodwin & Fiske, 1995). Negative stereotypes confer advantage to powerholders by legitimizing both the unequal division of resources and the social system more generally (Glick & Fiske, in press; Jost & Banaji, 1994; M. J. Lerner, 1980). Such stereotypes encourage both the powerful and the powerless to fault the victim, attributing inequality to the natural inferiority (e.g., incompetence, laziness) of the powerless (Major, 1994).

In recent years, S. T. Fiske and colleagues (Goodwin & Fiske, 1995; Goodwin, Gubin, Fiske, & Yzerbyt, 1998; see Fiske & Dépret, 1996, for a review) extended these theories. Consistent with earlier approaches, they suggested that powerful people stereotype *by design*, in the interests of actively maintaining the status quo. The powerful sometimes want to suppress those with less power, and stereotypes serve this function. However, the researchers also proposed that, at times, powerful people stereotype *by default*. In this view, powerful people also stereotype unintentionally, simply because they do not care much about the people that they control. Powerful people do not necessarily want to suppress their subordinates, but neither are they particularly motivated to learn about them. As a result, they use heuristics to form their impressions rather than expending the effort to gather individuating information.

Power-based approaches make interesting predictions about gender stereotyping. They imply that both men and women should stereotype women more than men because, politically, economically, and interpersonally, men often enjoy asymmetrical control over the outcomes of women. Both genders should attend to, and individuate, the powerful: men. Supporting this prediction, research suggests that gender influences impressions of women more than it does impressions of men (see S. T. Fiske, 1998, for a review). With no other cues present, people of both genders categorize women as women more quickly than they categorize men as men (Zárate & Sandoval, 1995); moreover, both men and women tend to view women as a more homogeneous group than men (Lorenzi-Cioldi, Eagly, & Stewart, 1995).

Linking power to stereotyping in children, Glick and Hilt (chap. 8, this volume) propose that changes in the power dynamics of children's peer relationships may constrain the evaluations that they attach to gender stereotypes. More specifically, they propose that the movement from independent (segregated play) to interdependent (dating) relationships stimulates the movement from hostile to benevolent sexism. By this analysis, power is a critical determinant of the *valence* of gender stereotypes.

The exploration of power and stereotype development might take various directions from here. To mention one, researchers could extend the inquiry of Glick and Hilt (chap. 8, this volume) by investigating how power constrains the *accessibility* (or use) of gender stereotypes across development. Glick and Hilt suggest that boys and girls maintain greater independence from each other than do men and women. According to power theory, children should, as a result, make comparatively heavy use of gender stereotypes. In fact, children entering elementary school do apply gender stereotypes more rigidly than both older children and adults (see Ruble & Martin, 1998, for a review). However, no research yet demonstrates the causal nature of relationships between power and stereotyping in children. Moreover, some evidence suggests that adolescents show a resurgence in stereotype rigidity (see Ruble & Ruble, 1982, for a review), a finding inconsistent with increasing interdependence between the genders.

Following a different direction, researchers might explore the role of power in the development of gender differences in stereotyping. Maccoby (1990) suggested that, just as women have less power than men, girls have less interpersonal power than boys, who usually get their way in mixed-sex groups. Thus, children, like adults, should be more likely to stereotype girls than boys. Continuing in this vein, power theory also predicts that, given their relatively disempowered position, girls should form more individuated impressions of both genders than do boys. As predicted, girls do use gender stereotypes more flexibly than boys. In both third and sixth grades, girls accept both sexes in traditionally male occupations more frequently than do boys (Hageman & Gladding, 1983); and through adolescence, adolescent girls use gender stereotypes more flexibly than do adolescent boys (Canter & Ageton, 1984). These associations argue once more for power's influence on stereotyping. Still, a complete test of the proposed relationships requires manipulating power and observing the effects on stereotyping in children.

The preceding sections developed the argument that children and adults acquire and use gender categories because they serve important functions. However, in addition to these functions, more basic aspects of how stereotypes operate contribute to their persistence.

# DEVELOPMENT OF GENDER STEREOTYPES:
# SELF-PERPETUATING EFFECTS

This section continues to approach an answer for why children use gender stereotypes. Toward this goal, we explore the self-perpetuating mechanisms of gender stereotypes. Once again, this section extrapolates from research on stereotyping in adults to make inferences about stereotyping in children. Subsequent sections then trace the developmental path of gender stereotypes, from frequent use in childhood to rapid automatization, and from automatization to frequent use in adulthood.

## Gender Stereotypes Constrain the Acquisition of Knowledge

Gender stereotypes bias the acquisition of knowledge from the most basic levels of thought (i.e., encoding the stimulus) to the highest (i.e., forming inferences and evaluations). Biases at all levels ensure the persistence of gender stereotyping across development.

*Encoding.*    From the first moment that a stimulus is perceived, stereotypes influence how adults view the world. Among their positive effects, stereotypes allow people to rapidly identify attributes of a stimulus and organize them into meaningful patterns: They group information into digestible chunks. Stereotypes yield maximum profit when people do not have the cognitive capacity to individuate others (Macrae, Hewstone, & Griffiths, 1993) or when stimuli are degraded (Macrae, Stangor, & Milne, 1994). However, the extent to which stereotypes facilitate encoding depends on the type of information to be encoded. Stereotypes make processing most efficient when the information to be encoded relates to self-categories. Thus, women identify and remember information about other women more easily than they do information about men, whereas the reverse is true for men. Consistent with this proposal, females identify *she* as a pronoun faster than *he*, but males classify *he* more quickly than *she* (Banaji & Hardin, 1996). Similarly, people classify same-gender photographs faster than other-gender photographs (Zárate and Sandoval, 1995) and recall more individuating information about same-sex than other-sex targets (Park & Rothbart, 1982). The advantage for self-relevant information may be, in part, a result of the accessibility of self-categories. Self-categories are highly accessible to consciousness, and hence, they are more likely to influence processing than are categories weakly associated with the self.

Despite the benefits, stereotyping carries costs, costs that contribute to the self-perpetuation of stereotypes even when their utility is dubious.

Stereotypes can constrict attention to a narrow range of input, sacrificing accuracy for speed. At times, people using stereotypes attend less to information that is neutral or inconsistent than they do to stereotype-consistent information (Macrae, Milne, & Bodenhausen, 1994; Ruscher & Fiske, 1990). Under certain conditions, people are also less likely to search for (Johnston & Macrae, 1994) and remember (Macrae et al., 1993; Rothbart, 1981) stereotype-inconsistent information. The disadvantage for stereotype-inconsistent information occurs most frequently when expectations are strong (as with gender), when the information to be processed is complex and processing time is limited (as in daily interactions), and when the information concerns a social group (e.g., women) rather than an individual (e.g., a woman). (In the absence of these conditions, the effect may disappear, or even reverse; see Smith, 1998, for a review.) Recent evidence suggests a mechanism for these effects, demonstrating that stereotypes can actually inhibit the assimilation of potentially disconfirming material (Dijksterhuis & van Knippenberg, 1996). All of these effects can bolster gender stereotypes by limiting the availability of disconfirming information.

Fortunately, relevant experience sometimes mitigates the negative effects of stereotyping. As people become experts in a domain, they attend more to, and remember better, the inconsistent information (Bargh & Thein, 1985; Borgida & DeBono, 1989). With practice, the identification and organization of consistent information becomes relatively automatic, freeing capacity for the consideration of inconsistent information (S. T. Fiske, Kinder, & Larter, 1983). When inconsistent information receives attention, stereotypes may change. However, unless people actively strive to form accurate impressions, they may avoid changing their stereotypes by forming subtypes or by explaining away the irregularities (Hewstone, Hopkins, & Routh, 1992). Thus, increasing experience may or may not produce stereotype change.

Based on the research to date, children fall prey to encoding biases at least as often as do adults. Children are just as likely to show the positive effects of gender stereotyping (see Ruble & Martin, 1998, for a review). They pay more attention to, and then later remember, information that fits their gender stereotypes (Ruble & Stangor, 1986); further, they show the equivalent facilitation effect as adults for information related to their own gender categories (Stangor & Ruble, 1987). Children above the age of 5 also display the negative effects of gender stereotyping. When presented with information that does not match their stereotypes, these children tend to encode it inaccurately, if they encode it at all. Interestingly, children younger than 5 show better recall of stereotype-inconsistent than stereotype-consistent information, supporting the hypothesis that, when expectations are weak or developing, the disadvantage for stereotype-inconsistent information disappears or reverses (Stangor & Ruble, 1989). One of the more intriguing questions addresses the conditions under which children change their established stereotypes of men and women. As expert models predict, children generally become more flexible in stereotype use with age (Martin, 1989). The unanswered question is if, and when, real changes in the global stereotype occur (as opposed to the generation of subtypes, or increases in perceived variability, while the central tendency is maintained).

**Inference and Evaluation.**    Gender stereotypes also affect inference and evaluation, with further implications for their persistence. Ashmore and Del Boca (1979) def ned gender stereotypes as "the structured sets of *inferential relations* [italics added] that link personal attributes to the social categories female and male" (p. 225). This definition puts inference at the heart of gender stereotyping, and with good reason.

People use gender to make inferences about a person's personality traits (Friedman & Zebrowitz, 1992), social roles (Wood & Karten, 1986), and physical characteristics (Biernat, 1993). Even when the behavior is equivalent, people are more willing to attribute confidence, influence, analytic skills, and respect to a man, and sensitivity and warmth to a woman (Taylor, 1981). Inferential biases frequently operate at a subtle level. Demonstrating this point, Banaji and Greenwald (1995) found that people who were asked to judge the fame associated with various names (none of which actually belonged to a famous person) judged familiar male names as more famous than familiar female names. Because fame is stereotypically associated with men, participants were more likely to view male targets as famous, even though they were probably unaware of gender's effect on their decisions. Biases like these maintain gender stereotypes by slanting the evidence in a confirmatory direction.

Gender stereotypes also bias people's evaluations of others. Categorization, in general, causes people to evaluate the out-group less positively than the in-group (Brewer, 1979). For gender groups, however, the picture is slightly more complex. Men's attitudes toward women seem to be characterized by ambivalence more than negativity. On self-report measures of sexism, men endorse both hostile and benevolent attitudes toward women, and, in undergraduates, hostility and benevolence are correlated. Conversely, women's attitudes toward men are more purely hostile: Antimale scales show that women usually deny benevolent feelings toward men (Glick & Fiske, 1996; Glick & Hilt, chap. 8, this volume). Despite the differences, both men and women can experience some degree of residual hostility. This hostility may perpetuate gender stereotypes by encouraging groups to avoid contact, severing, thereby, access to stereotype-inconsistent information.

Last, gender stereotypes affect people's perceptions of the variability within each group. Simply categorizing people into two groups accentuates intergroup difference and enhances intragroup similarity (Allport, 1954; Taylor, 1981; Wilder, 1981). Mere categorization also makes the out-group seem more homogeneous than the in-group (Mullen & Hu, 1989). For women, men are all alike, and they are all different from women; for men, women are all alike, and they are all different from men: Men are from Mars, and women are from Venus (Gray, 1992). Like encoding biases, biases in perceptions of variability contribute to stereotype persistence by creating a false sense that one's stereotypes truly comprehend the data.

Gender categorization affects adults' inferences about men and women, their evaluations of men and women, and their perceptions of the variability within each group. Research on young children finds a parallel for each of these effects. To illustrate, children use gender to make inferences about the competence of others on sex-typed tasks (Cann & Palmer, 1986) and whether or not they will like them (Martin, 1989). By 5 years of age, children also evaluate the other sex more negatively than their own (Yee & Brown, 1994). Finally, through and until the age of 8, children dramatically underestimate the variability in gender groups (Martin, 1989). Children often fail to realize that individuals may deviate from group norms, frequently relying on gender, rather than individual attributes, to make inferences about others. These findings imply that, from a young age, gender stereotypes have self-perpetuating effects that are at least as strong as they are for adults. They also suggest that biases in inference and evaluation are a part of group perception at its most basic level.

To this point, we have argued that gender categories ensure their own persistence because of their functions for, and effects on, the (young) perpetrator. However, stereotypes also affect their targets in ways that, once again, ensure the continued use of gender stereotypes.

## Gender Stereotypes Constrain the Behavior of the Target

Gender stereotypes affect targets in various ways. All of these effects encourage people to match their behavior to gender stereotypes. Behavioral confirmation (described next) encourages targets to behave in ways that confirm gender stereotypes, whereas stereotype threat and attributional ambiguity (described later) both encourage confirmation and deter disconfirmation. The consequence is that, across development, gender stereotypes continue to seem like accurate characterizations of their targets, perhaps even more so as we grow older and are increasingly shaped by the forces attached to stereotyping.

***Behavioral Confirmation.*** One of the most powerful processes sustaining gender stereotypes is behavioral confirmation (Snyder, 1981). Behavioral confirmation occurs when the perceiver's stereotypic expectations induce the target of these expectations to behave in a way that confirms the stereotype (Claire & Fiske, 1998). Examples of this process pepper the literature. For example, when a man expects a female coworker to enjoy feminine tasks, she chooses those tasks in a joint activity (Skrypnek & Snyder, 1982); when a man believes a woman to be unattractive, he elicits unfriendly and uninteresting responses in conversation with her (Snyder, Tanke, & Berscheid, 1977).

Behavioral confirmation suits lazy perceivers well, permitting them to resist the work of modifying well-worn stereotypes. The process is less comfortable for targets, who, by confirming expectations, face constraints on identity development, acquisition of skills, and, ultimately, access to societal resources.

Targets may confirm the expectations of others for various reasons. In some cases, the behavior of others provides subtle, nonverbal cues that elicit the expected behavior. Word, Zanna, and Cooper's (1974) classic investigation illustrates this process. In the first of two studies, experimenters observed the verbal and nonverbal behavior of White participants asked to interview Black and White job applicants. In a second study, experimenters trained White confederates to approximate the interview styles of participants in the first study. A panel of judges rating the applicants judged those applicants interviewed using the "Black applicant" style as more nervous and less competent than applicants treated to the alternative, "White applicant" style, confirming the racial stereotype. These data suggest that subtle differences in interaction styles can elicit stereotype-confirming behavior, often to the detriment of the stereotyped. Behavioral confirmation of gender stereotypes probably operates in analogous fashion.

In other cases, people provide more overt cues that gender-typed behavior is expected, and this also encourages confirmatory behavior. People explicitly demand or reinforce stereotype-consistent behavior, and they punish stereotype-inconsistent behavior (S. T. Fiske & Stevens, 1993). In an experimental demonstration of this process, female undergraduates described themselves to an attractive male partner whose prototype of the ideal woman either conformed or did not conform to the traditional female stereotype. When the partner expressed a traditional ideology, women presented themselves (on a self-report questionnaire) as highly conventional; when the partner expressed a nontraditional ideology, the women described themselves in much less conventional terms (Zanna & Pack, 1975).

Through both subtle and overt cues, stereotypic expectations encourage confirmatory behavior. If expectations were limited to a single interaction between strangers, then confirmatory pressures might be less powerful. However, outside of the lab, people's interactions are embedded in a wider social, political, and temporal context, a context that probably accentuates the pressure to conform.

In natural contexts, targets of social stereotypes frequently attach high importance to their relationships with perceivers. Real targets may be particularly prone to go along with stereotypic expectations, if only to get along with valued others. Consistent with this reasoning, a discussion partner's attitudes exert greater influence on people operating under the goal of having a positive interaction than they do on people trying to form accurate opinions (S. Chen, Shechter, & Chaiken, 1996). At a broader level, targets of negative stereotypes (e.g., women and minorities) also tend to occupy less powerful positions than perceivers. In consequence, they may be especially unwilling, or even unable, to disconfirm perceivers' stereotypes (Claire & Fiske, 1998). Finally, targets of social stereotypes typically engage in extended interaction with multiple perceivers sharing the same stereotype. Targets encounter repeated pressures to behave in identical, stereotypic ways, and this may increase the subjective plausibility of the stereotype and, hence, the likelihood of internalization (Claire & Fiske, 1998; Snyder, 1981). Although researchers have not studied internalization over extended time periods, some evidence indicates that targets do repeat behaviors that were elicited by perceivers in previous situations (Fazio, Effrein, & Falender, 1981).

How do stereotypic expectations affect children? The indirect route to answering this question explores how parents treat boys and girls. Assuming that differential socialization reflects gender-linked expectations, and given evidence that differential socialization prompts behavioral change, one can conclude that behavioral confirmation operates in children. This route is a bit rocky, as reviews and meta-analyses of the literature on parental socialization arrive at different conclusions on the prevalence and effects of differential socialization. Huston's (1983) review identified numerous forms of differential treatment, such as encouragement of motor activity for boys and nurturance play for girls; Huston also linked differential socialization to the development of gender-typed personality traits in children. Eight years later, Lytton and Romney's (1991) meta-analysis found little consistent evidence of differential socialization practices, except in the domains of play activities and household chores, where parents reinforced traditional gender stereotypes. These results pose a striking contrast to the earlier review, but methodological limitations suggest that the analysis underestimated the pervasiveness of differential treatment (Ruble & Martin, 1998). By broadly grouping heterogeneous data sets, the reviewers may have masked important associations. In support of this proposal, more detailed analyses revealed that several factors moderated the degree to which the child's gender affected parental treatment. Importantly, differential socialization was strongest for fathers and when children were younger. Thus, young children may face compounded pressures to conform to stereotypic expectations: Just when children are most dependent on their parents for emotional support, guidance, and self-knowledge, parents are most likely to emphasize gender stereotypes.

The more direct route to exploring behavioral confirmation in children links parental expectations directly to their children's behavior. In a series of studies of this type, Eccles et al. (1993) found that parents who held stronger stereotypes regarding the capabilities of boys and girls in English, math, and sports had more gender-stereotypic expectations regarding their own children's abilities in these subjects, which were, in turn, related to children's self-perceived competence, even when actual ability levels were controlled. Separate studies revealed that both children's self-perceived competence and parental expectations influenced children's exposure to enriching experiences. Children who believed they were good at math or sports enrolled in high school math classes or joined sports teams, respectively; and parents confident in their children's abilities within a domain were likely to encourage participation in that domain. Thus, according to Eccles et al., differential expectations propel boys and girls into different domains, and the experiences that they gain (or miss) there account for gender differences in skill development (see also Eccles, Freedman-Doan, Frome, Jacobs, & Yoon, chap. 11, this volume).

For both adults and children, behavioral confirmation appears to sustain gender stereotypes in the course of the interaction at the same time as it makes future confirmation more likely. Behavioral confirmation, however, is not the only process to affect personality development, as the next section shows.

***Stereotype Threat.***      People sometimes become aware that they might confirm, through their behavior, a negative social stereotype. This awareness creates a predicament for the stereotyped that has been called stereotype threat (Steele, 1998; Steele & Aronson, 1995). Stereotype threat is a complicated concept but worth elaborating for the predictions it makes about the development of gender stereotypes.

The definition of stereotype threat is quite narrow. *Stereotype threat* describes the temporary state of awareness and anxiety that is activated by a particular kind of situation. Stereotype threat does not occur as the result of global feelings of inferiority or internalized self-hatred. Rather, it occurs only in specific situations, when people become aware that the content of a negative stereotype could provide a plausible explanation for their behavior or experiences in their own eyes, in the eyes of others, or both. As a further qualification, stereotype threat occurs only when the activating situation carries evaluative relevance for the self, when the outcomes really matter.

To illustrate, a girl who generally worries that she is a failure at math would not be called stereotype-threatened. In contrast, a girl who, approaching a math test, worries that she may fail, and confirm the stereotype, is called stereotype-threatened. The difference is that, in the latter example, the feeling is temporary: It is a state of anxiety cued by the specific situation of taking the test rather than by an internalized sense of inferiority. Of course, a girl who does not care about math would never be called stereotype-threatened with regard to math because, for her, math is not self-relevant.

Stereotype threat may affect the performance of women in ways that confirm gender stereotypes. Here, again, is another case of behavioral confirmation, but by a different route. For women, performance in settings where negative stereotypes apply takes on special meaning. When the stereotype of incompetence becomes a threat, women may feel strongly pressured to succeed. Ironically, the anxiety created by this pressure can cause women to perform more poorly than they otherwise would have, thus confirming the stereotype. Illustrating these points, research shows that, controlling for initial interest and ability, women given testing instructions that emphasize gender differences perform worse than men on challenging math tests (e.g., the Advanced Graduate Record Examination). However, when the test is described as one on which there are no gender differences—an instruction that reduces stereotype threat by making gender an implausible interpretation of performance—women perform as well as men (Spencer, Steele, & Quinn, 1999).

The previous section suggested that behavioral confirmation effects perseverate over time. Similarly, stereotype threat may spur processes that bolster stereotypes over development. Steele (1998) argued that, as a reaction to stereotype threat, targets may *disidentify* with threatening domains. Disidentification means detaching self-esteem from one's performance in a specific domain. Disidentification has the temporary effect of buffering self-esteem, but, once again, it encourages confirmation of negative stereotypes (or, at least, discourages disconfirmation) by deterring people from applying themselves in gender-atypical domains. To make this concrete, a woman may convince herself that math is boring if she is made anxious by the thought that she might fail. By convincing herself that math does not matter, she might stop doing her homework, deteriorate in her abilities, and confirm the stereotype of incompetence. Research on disidentification is in its early stages, but there is some support for threat-driven disidentification in African American and female students (see Crocker, Major, & Steele, 1998).

Stereotype threat and threat-induced disidentification have not been explicitly addressed in a developmental context. However, research has detailed the more general process of disidentification in girls, with disturbing results. Academic disidentification appears to set in by the first grade: At this age, math is relevant for boys' self-concept, but not for girls' (Entwisle, Alexander, Pallas, & Cadigan, 1987). Later in elementary school, girls continue to think that math is less important, less useful, and less enjoyable than do boys, and these evaluations mediate their lower enrollment in advanced math and physics classes in high school (Eccles, 1994). Still, the role of stereotype threat in this process remains an open question. Early disidentification may be prompted by gender socialization or genetic/hormonal influences rather than by stereotype threat. We do not have precise knowledge of when, and in which situations, children become aware that their behavior may be interpreted according to a negative stereotype. The theory of stereotype threat opens a new line of inquiry and suggests new possibilities for counteracting disidentification.

Efforts to counteract disidentification should be guided by the recognition that, in all likelihood, stereotype threat functions differently for boys and girls. In a reversal of the usual understanding of stereotype threat, boys seem to fear violating male stereotypes rather than confirming them. Put another way, boys worry about confirming the female stereotype, because behaving astereotypically carries social costs. Meanwhile, girls may fear both violating norms for femininity and, paradoxically, confirming female stereotypes. As a result of societal devaluation of "female" characteristics, girls fear being—and not being—feminine.

In support of these proposals, evidence argues that attraction to the female role rapidly declines, for both boys and girls, as age increases. At 2 or 3 years old, boys, but not girls, show stable avoidance of cross-gender play (Powlishta, Serbin, & Moller, 1993). This trend continues through preschool, where boys continue to avoid cross-gender behavior more than girls (Bussey & Bandura, 1992). From preschool to middle school, the preference for male activities only increases: Girls' preference for same-sex activities peaks at about 4, whereas boys' preferences become increasingly sex-typed (Maccoby & Jacklin, 1974). For girls, a cultural preference for maleness apparently weakens the trend toward in-group favoritism, at least on behavioral measures of gender-related attitudes.

At the same time, children may punish girls who pursue male activities and ideals. Thorne's (1993) observational studies of school-age children revealed that boys who violate gender norms are teased, shunned, and referred to as "girls," whereas girls who violate gender norms also suffer peer ridicule, though to a lesser extent than boys. These findings highlight the contrast between children's acceptance of stereotypic prescriptions for boys and their ambivalence about stereotypic prescriptions for girls. Boys go wrong by acting like girls, but girls go wrong by acting too much like girls, or, too little like girls.

When and why stereotype threat first occurs, and how children cope with it, constitute intriguing questions for future research. In the meantime, current evidence hints that stereotype threat, and the accompanying disidentification, develop surprisingly early. The next section explores a related influence on the targets of stereotyping which, once again, ensures the persistence of gender stereotypes.

*Attributional Ambiguity.*    In some cases, the awareness that people's judgments and behavior are influenced by stereotypes can create a second dilemma for the stereotyped, a dilemma called attributional ambiguity (Crocker & Major, 1989; Crocker, Voelkl, Testa, & Major, 1991; Major & Crocker, 1993). *Attributional ambiguity* refers to the uncertainty that stereotyped groups confront in attempting to understand the causes of their outcomes.

For the targets of social stereotypes, positive and negative outcomes can often be attributed either to internal causes, or to people's reactions to their social categories. The case is clearest for negative experiences. Targets may attribute the experience of failure either to personal deficiencies, such as lack of ability or poor effort, or to prejudice and discrimination. Less obviously, positive experiences can also be attributionally ambiguous. When stereotyped individuals succeed, they may attribute their success to personal merit; in fact, the attribution to merit may actually be augmented if individuals see themselves as having succeeded in spite of discrimination. Nevertheless, targets may also attribute their success to false feedback or the "benevolent" intervention of others who believe that they, as members of a particular social group, need help. This concern over the meaning of positive feedback is well founded. As Deaux and LaFrance (1998) proposed, people may respond more positively to members of stereotyped groups as a result of ambivalent feelings toward the group, the wish to avoid appearing prejudiced, or the desire to demonstrate their egalitarian values.

The inability to determine the true causes of goal-relevant feedback can have wide-ranging effects on men and, especially, women (see Crocker, Major, & Steele, 1998, for a review). On the one hand, attributional ambiguity can protect self-esteem from the implications of negative outcomes. Ambiguity provides the targets of social stereotypes an opportunity to shift blame for their failures to external causes, whether failures are generated by internal deficiencies or by discrimination (Crocker et al., 1991). On the other hand, ambiguity can threaten self-competence by making it hard for individuals to take credit for their successes (Crocker et al., 1991). Worse, ambiguity may undermine intrinsic motivation by weakening the link between personal efforts and outcomes. This damage to motivation could, in turn, impair performance (Major & Crocker, 1993). Finally, it has been suggested that ambiguity impairs performance in another way, by making it difficult to accurately assess one's abilities and potential (Major & Crocker, 1993). When people cannot obtain or trust feedback relevant to their goals, they find it difficult to make progress. Because people stereotype women more frequently than men, and because women's stereotypes involve a dimension of general incompetence, these effects should endanger women more than men.

Like stereotype threat, attributional ambiguity may encourage the confirmation of stereotypes, both by influencing temporary attributions for behavior and by shaping behavior in subsequent interactions. Attributional ambiguity may increase the likelihood that women confirm stereotypes of incompetence (or at least lessen the likelihood that they disconfirm such stereotypes) both in their own minds and in reality.

Children's realization that their outcomes may, or may not, be influenced by other people's reactions to their gender probably occurs in stages. Such a realization undoubtedly calls for a high level of cognitive sophistication, but there may be precursors long before children can articulately describe their predicaments. Again, given the importance of attributional ambiguity to psychological adaptation, a richer understanding of how and when children begin to cope with the predicament would prove invaluable.

## DEVELOPMENT OF GENDER STEREOTYPES: AUTOMATIZATION

To this point, this chapter has proposed two explanations for why children use gender stereotypes. First, the chapter suggested that children, like adults, use gender stereotypes because stereotypes are functional. In this context, we introduced several approaches to stereotyping, including the cognitive, social role, social identity, and power-based perspectives. Second, the chapter proposed that children use gender stereotypes because stereotypes are self-perpetuating. Under these sections, we argued that stereotypes self-perpetuate because of the effects they have on both perpetrators and targets; we argued that stereotypes constrain the acquisition of knowledge and constrain how targets behave in ways that reinforce gender stereotypes. Throughout, the discussion emphasized that even very young children are as susceptible as adults—if not more so—to processes that ensure the use and perpetuation of gender stereotypes. This section suggests that, merely by using stereotypes in early stages of development, children ensure that gender stereotypes will persist into adulthood. To begin, the concept of automaticity is introduced.

## Dual-Component Models of Social Stereotyping

Current models of stereotyping suggest that stereotypes have two components: a controlled component and an automatic component (e.g., Brewer, 1988; Devine, 1989; S. T. Fiske & Neuberg, 1990; Gaertner & Dovidio, 1986; see S. T. Fiske, 1998, for a review). The common theme of these models is that, at some level, people can control the tendency to stereotype others, at least after the first moments of interaction. People can engage in controlled processes—effortful, intentional, and conscious strategies—to reduce or exaggerate the stereotypicality of their impressions. People can seek out individuating information, they can actively suppress their stereotypes, or they can seek out information confirming their stereotypes. Nevertheless, the execution of these strategies requires time, motivation, and cognitive resources. Moreover, controlled processes only attenuate or amplify what is happening at a more fundamental level.

At a more fundamental level, stereotyping is driven by automatic processes, by the effortless, unintentional, and unconscious process of social categorization (see Wegner & Bargh, 1998, for a review). People categorize others within milliseconds of perceiving them, and this simple act can, by itself, elicit the thoughts and emotions that underlie prejudice. Categorization makes stereotypic perceptions, inferences, and evaluations more likely.

Researchers sometimes use priming studies to explore the influence of automatic processes on cognition. The classic paradigm exposes participants to a stereotype-related stimulus (i.e., prime) so quickly that they do not report seeing it. Although participants have no conscious recollection of the prime, the prime does affect their responses to subsequent measures, suggesting that they have processed it unconsciously. The nature of participants' responses reveals unconscious associations with the stimulus, along with their effects. For example, in a variant of this paradigm, Blair and Banaji (1996) demonstrated that preconsciously priming people with gender-stereotypic physical traits, activities, roles, and objects speeds their responses to gender-matched names (e.g., "John" vs. "Jane"). In general, studies like these confirm that automatic processes influence how adults perceive and evaluate others.

Priming studies also suggest that the automatic components of stereotypes influence how people behave. People base both inferences and behavior on stereotypic knowledge, even if they do not intend to (Wegner & Bargh, 1998). To illustrate, a recent experiment primed race-related concepts in White participants by exposing them to pictures of African Americans. Following a bogus computer crash, participants who had been primed with pictures of African Americans expressed more hostility than participants primed with control pictures (Bargh, M. Chen, & Burrows, 1996).

Importantly, similar effects occur when gender categories are primed. Rudman and Borgida (1995) found that male participants who had watched sexist ads (priming the category of *women as sexual objects*) responded more quickly to sexist words and more slowly to nonsexist words than did participants who watched control ads. When asked to interview a female confederate later in the study, participants primed with sexist ads also asked more stereotyped questions and showed more sexist behavior than did controls. Thus, merely activating gender categories can have durable and meaningful effects on behavior.

## Automatization of Gender Stereotypes

Despite the importance of automatic components in social stereotyping, few have explored how these components develop. Devine (1989) suggested that repeated use of racial stereotypes prompts their automatization. Ruble and Ruble (1982) used different language to make similar claims about gender stereotypes, asserting that "knowledge of both sex stereotypes and sex-typed behavior is acquired by preschool children. Thus, children may become essentially restricted toward a sex-linked way of viewing and behaving in the world (and flexibility of choice may be concomitantly reduced) at a strikingly early age" (p. 214). The current section develops this argument in detail.

We propose that adult gender stereotyping is largely driven by automatic processes, and that gender stereotypes become automatic because they are practiced frequently in early stages of development. This argument draws on repetition priming research, which suggests that the frequent activation of a mental construct makes that construct more accessible on future occasions (see Smith, 1998, for a review). Repetition priming drives learning: When people are exposed to information (e.g., nonsense syllables) at one point in time, that information becomes easier to recall or to relearn at a later point in time. Repetition priming operates on social information (e.g., traits) as well as on nonsocial information, and the effects can endure, undiminished, at length. One brief exposure to a word list facilitates performance on word-completion tasks across a 7-day retention interval, and without appreciable decline (Tulving, Schacter, & Stark, 1982). In short, repetition priming constitutes a central influence on cognitive functioning, and, as such, it probably plays a central role in gender stereotyping. Previous sections detailed why children use gender stereotypes so frequently. Repetition priming research suggests that this repeated use automatizes gender stereotypes, with the result that, in adulthood, gender stereotypes dominate person perception.

Actually, particular aspects of how repetition priming operates may magnify priming's effects on stereotype accessibility. Importantly, the effects of repetition priming depend on the degree of overlap between the context of encoding and the context of retrieval: High overlap produces the most significant increase in construct accessibility. This is because contextual information is encoded along with the target construct, so that contextual information serves as a retrieval cue for the target (Smith, 1998). Because children typically extend gender classifications to numerous domains, as discussed, gender constructs should be linked to a broad range of contexts, any one of which could serve as a retrieval cue. That is, children's nonselective application of gender constructs should ensure that such constructs are activated particularly often in the future, making them especially persistent.

The proposal that practice leads to automatization, though simple, makes interesting predictions about how the precocity of category acquisition affects later stereotype strength. Early acquisition should lead to stronger stereotypes for two reasons. Most obviously, the earlier the acquisition, the more time an individual has to practice application of the stereotype. Further, early acquisition may give social categories a "leg up" over other categories. If stereotypes actually inhibit the recognition of information that does not fit the stereotype (Dijksterhuis & van Knippenburg, 1996), then categories that are acquired first should delay recognition of alternative strategies for grouping people and information. These proposals help explain why gender is preferred as a basis for categorization. Gender is typically acquired before all other social categories, ensuring relatively greater practice and more rapid automatization.

# FUTURE DIRECTIONS

This chapter has argued that gender stereotyping is a predominantly automatic response acquired from children's propensity to chunk information by gender. Gender stereotypes attract children because stereotypes are useful, and because stereotypes make information fit their predictions. So children use gender stereotypes a lot. Repeated use causes the application of gender stereotypes to become automatic, so that, as adults, we stereotype men, and especially women, within seconds, without meaning to, and without even realizing what we are doing.

If this argument is correct, then we cannot understand adult stereotyping without understanding how stereotypes develop and function early in life. Thus, a comprehensive theory of gender stereotyping demands an integration between developmental and social psychology. The construction of more complete theories of gender stereotyping would also have clear practical benefits. Precise knowledge of how stereotypes develop would permit society to obstruct, at an early age, the automatization of negative gender stereotypes. Such early intervention is bound to be more successful than trying to control stereotypes at later stages. When adults try to suppress their stereotypes, they may, ironically, use their stereotypes more than if they had not attempted suppression in the first place (Bodenhausen & Macrae, 1996; Macrae, Bodenhausen, Milne, & Jetten, 1994; Wegner, 1994). Meanwhile, external pressures to avoid stereotyping may prove ineffective, and, in the worst cases, they anger the perpetrator (Devine, Monteith, Zuwerink, & Elliot, 1991). Efforts to control well-practiced stereotypes exact heavy costs. So much the better to start young.

Counteracting gender stereotypes depends, in part, on intensifying children's exposure to stereotype-inconsistent information. Among adults, exposure to stereotype-inconsistent information undermines group stereotypes—particularly when the information is dispersed over numerous cases rather than concentrated in a small number of extreme cases (Weber & Crocker, 1983; see Hewstone, 1994, for a review). Similarly, children given frequent exposure to people who do not quite fit gender stereotypes should be less likely to rely on such stereotypes than children growing up in more traditional environments.

Exposure to stereotype-inconsistent information alone, however, may not be enough. Children face particular limitations on their ability to process information, limitations that may hinder the assimilation of inconsistent information. To mention one, children under age 10 cannot reliably classify stimuli along multiple dimensions. An example clarifies the problem: If children cannot classify a man as both a man and a housekeeper (or florist or secretary or nurse . . .), then they may ignore one of his two identities, with the result that the male stereotype persists, unchanged. Consistent with this thinking, researchers (Bigler, 1995; Bigler & Liben, 1992; Leahy & Shirk, 1984) found that the inability to classify stimuli along multiple dimensions is associated with more gender-stereotypic responses in 5- to 10-year-olds. Fortunately, though, the problem is not insoluble, as training in multiple classification with social stimuli apparently reduces gender stereotyping (Bigler & Liben, 1992). Another effective remedy requires training children to use alternative bases (i.e., not gender) for categorization. For example, Bigler and Liben trained children to use job qualifications rather than gender as a basis for assigning people to occupations, prompting a significant reduction in gender-stereotyping irrespective of change in multiple classification skills. Sometimes, then, offering children other strategies for grouping people may suffice.

Perhaps a more serious obstacle to stereotype reduction in children is that the mere use of gender categories strengthens gender stereotypes. Just hearing adults use gender categories—even when such categories are not explicitly associated with stereotypes—can stimulate children to develop stronger stereotypes (Bigler, 1995). This means that weakening stereotypes may require attacking societal emphasis on gender more globally.

Despite their challenges, early interventions promise unique gain. By the time children enter elementary school, gender stereotypes have set their claws: The course becomes difficult to reverse, and the consequences are already serious. For girls, academic disidentification occurs as early as age 6. From there, girls disproportionately suffer declines in self-esteem, lowered expectations for success, and maladaptive reactions to failure (see Ruble & Martin, 1998, for a review). Girls increasingly face power imbalances in personal relationships and, as they enter the workforce, discrimination and lower pay. It is clearly important to intervene, and to intervene early. The work of tomorrow includes further exploration of gender stereotyping throughout development. It also includes the negotiation of more balanced identities for men and women, and for this, we depend on society at large.

# REFERENCES

Allport, G. W. (1954). *The nature of prejudice.* Reading, MA: Addison-Wesley.

Ashmore, R. D., & Del Boca, F. K. (1979). Sex stereotypes and implicit personality theory: Toward a cognitive–social psychological conceptualization. *Sex Roles, 5,* 219–248.

Ashmore, R. D., Del Boca, F. K., & Wohlers, A. J. (1986). Gender stereotypes. In R. D. Ashmore & F. K. Del Boca (Eds.), *The social psychology of female–male relations: A critical analysis of central concepts* (pp. 69–119). Orlando, FL: Academic Press.

Banaji, M. R., & Greenwald, A. G. (1995). Implicit gender stereotyping in judgments of fame. *Journal of Personality and Social Psychology, 68,* 181–198.

Banaji, M. R., & Hardin, C. (1996). Automatic stereotyping. *Psychological Science, 7,* 136–141.

Bargh, J. A., Chen, M., & Burrows, L. (1996). Automaticity of social behavior: Direct effects of trait construct and stereotype activation on action. *Journal of Personality and Social Psychology, 71,* 230–244.

Bargh, J. A., & Thein, R. D. (1985). Individual construct accessibility, person memory, and the recall–judgment link: The case of information overload. *Journal of Personality and Social Psychology, 49,* 1129–1146.

Bem, S. L. (1974). The measurement of psychological androgyny. *Journal of Consulting and Clinical Psychology, 42,* 155–162.

Biernat, M. (1993). Gender and height: Developmental patterns in knowledge and use of an accurate stereotype. *Sex Roles, 29,* 691–713.

Bigler, R. S. (1995). The role of classification skill in moderating environmental influences on children's gender stereotyping: A study of the functional use of gender in the classroom. *Child Development, 66,* 1072–1087.

Bigler, R. S., & Liben, L. S. (1992). Cognitive mechanisms in children's gender stereotyping: Theoretical and educational implications of a cognitive-based intervention. *Child Development, 63,* 1351–1363.

Blair, I. V., & Banaji, M. R. (1996). Automatic and controlled processes in stereotype priming. *Journal of Personality and Social Psychology, 70,* 1142–1163.

Bodenhausen, G. V., & Macrae, C. N. (1996). The self-regulation of intergroup perception: Mechanisms and consequences of stereotype suppression. In C. N. Macrae, C. Stangor, & M. Hewstone (Eds.), *Stereotypes and stereotyping* (pp. 227–253). New York: Guilford.

Borgida, E. & DeBono, K. G. (1989). Social hypothesis testing and the role of expertise. *Personality and Social Psychology Bulletin, 15*, 212–221.

Brewer, M. B. (1979). In-group bias in the minimal intergroup situation: A cognitive-motivational analysis. *Psychological Bulletin, 86*, 307–324.

Brewer, M. B. (1988). A dual process model of impression formation. In T. K. Srull & R. S. Wyer (Eds.), *Advances in social cognition* (Vol. 1, pp. 1–36). Hillsdale, NJ: Lawrence Erlbaum Associates.

Bruner, J. S:, Olver, R. R., & Greenfield, P. M. (1966). *Studies in cognitive growth.* New York: Wiley.

Burgess, D., & Borgida, E. (1997). Sexual harassment: An experimental test of sex-role spillover theory. *Personality and Social Psychology Bulletin, 23*, 63–75.

Bussey, K., & Bandura, A. (1992). Self-regulatory mechanisms governing gender development. *Child Development, 63*, 1236–1250.

Cann, A., & Palmer, S. (1986). Children's assumptions about the generalizability of sex-typed abilities. *Sex Roles, 15*, 551–558.

Canter, R. J., & Ageton, S. S. (1984). The epidemiology of adolescent sex-role attitudes. *Sex Roles, 11*, 657–676.

Chen, S., Shechter, D., & Chaiken, S. (1996). Getting at the truth or getting along: Accuracy-versus impression-motivated heuristic and systematic processing. *Journal of Personality and Social Psychology, 71*, 262–275.

Claire, T., & Fiske, S. T. (1998). A systemic view of behavioral confirmation: Counterpoint to the individualist view. In C. Sedikides, J. Schopler, & C. A. Insko (Eds.), *Intergroup cognition and intergroup behavior* (pp. 205–231). Mahwah, NJ: Lawrence Erlbaum Associates.

Cohen, L. B., & Strauss, M. S. (1979). Concept acquisition in the human infant. *Child Development, 50*, 419–424.

Cowan, G., & Hoffman, C. D. (1986). Gender stereotyping in young children: Evidence to support a concept-learning approach. *Sex Roles, 14*, 211–224.

Crocker, J., & Major, B. (1989). Social stigma and self-esteem: The self-protective properties of stigma. *Psychological Review, 96*, 608–630.

Crocker, J., Major, B., & Steele, C. (1998). Social stigma. In D. T. Gilbert, S. T. Fiske, & G. Lindzey (Eds.), *The handbook of social psychology* (4th ed., Vol. 2, pp. 504–553). Boston: McGraw-Hill.

Crocker, J., Voelkl, K., Testa, M., & Major, B. (1991). Social stigma: The affective consequences of attributional ambiguity. *Journal of Personality and Social Psychology, 60*, 218–228.

Deaux, K., & Kite, M. E. (1993). Gender stereotypes. In F. L. Denmark & M. A. Paludi (Eds.), *Psychology of women: A handbook of issues and theories* (pp. 107–139). Westport, CT: Greenwood.

Deaux, K., & LaFrance, M. (1998). Gender. In D. T. Gilbert, S. T. Fiske, & G. Lindzey (Eds.), *The handbook of social psychology* (4th ed., Vol. 1, pp. 788–827). Boston: McGraw-Hill.

Deaux, K., Winton, W., Crowley, M., & Lewis, L. L. (1985). Level of categorization and content of gender stereotypes. *Social Cognition, 3*, 145–167.

Devine, P. G. (1989). Stereotypes and prejudice: Their automatic and controlled components. *Journal of Personality and Social Psychology, 56*, 5–18.

Devine, P. G., Monteith, M. J., Zuwerink, J. R., & Elliot, A. J. (1991). Prejudice with and without compunction. *Journal of Personality and Social Psychology, 60*, 817–830.

Dijksterhuis, A., & van Knippenberg, A. (1996). The knife that cuts both ways: Facilitated and inhibited access to traits as a result of stereotype activation. *Journal of Experimental Social Psychology, 32,* 271–288.

Eagly, A. H. (1987). *Sex differences in social behavior: A social-role interpretation.* Hillsdale, NJ: Lawrence Erlbaum Associates.

Eccles, J. S. (1994). Understanding women's educational and occupational choices: Applying the Eccles et al. model of achievement-related choices. *Psychology of Women Quarterly, 18,* 585–609.

Eccles, J. S., Jacobs, J. E., Harold, R. D., Yoon, K. S., Arbreton, A., & Freedman-Doan, C. (1993). Parents and gender-role socialization during the middle childhood and adolescent years. In S. Oskamp & M. Costanzo (Eds.), *Gender issues in contemporary society* (pp. 59–83). Newbury Park, CA: Sage.

Eckes, T. (1994). Features of men, features of women: Assessing stereotypic beliefs about gender subtypes. *British Journal of Social Psychology, 33,* 107–123.

Eckes, T. (1996). Linking female and male subtypes to situations: A range-of-situation-fit effect. *Sex Roles, 35,* 401–426.

Entwisle, D. R., Alexander, K. L., Pallas, A. M., & Cadigan, D. (1987). The emergent academic self-image of first graders: Its response to social structure. *Child Development, 58,* 1190–1206.

Estes, W. K. (1993). Models of categorization and category learning. In G. V. Nakamura, D. L. Medin, & R. Taraban (Eds.), *The psychology of learning and motivation* (Vol. 29, pp. 15–56). San Diego, CA: Academic Press.

Fazio, R. H., Effrein, E. A., & Falender, V. J. (1981). Self-perception following social interaction. *Journal of Personality and Social Psychology, 41,* 232–242.

Fiske, A. P., Haslam, N., & Fiske, S. T. (1991). Confusing one person with another: What errors reveal about the elementary forms of social relations. *Journal of Personality and Social Psychology, 60,* 656–674.

Fiske, S. T. (1998). Stereotyping, prejudice, and discrimination. In D. T. Gilbert, S. T. Fiske, & G. Lindzey (Eds.), *The handbook of social psychology* (4th ed., Vol. 2, pp. 357–411). Boston: McGraw-Hill.

Fiske, S. T., & Dépret, E. (1996). Control, interdependence, and power: Understanding social cognition in its social context. In W. Stroebe & M. Hewstone (Eds.), *European review of social psychology* (Vol. 7, pp. 31–61). New York: Wiley.

Fiske, S. T., Kinder, D. R., & Larter, W. M. (1983). The novice and the expert: Knowledge-based strategies in political cognition. *Journal of Experimental Social Psychology, 19,* 381–400.

Fiske, S. T., & Neuberg, S. L. (1990). A continuum of impression formation, from category-based to individuating processes: Influences of information and motivation on attention and interpretation. In M. P. Zanna (Ed.), *Advances in experimental psychology* (Vol. 23, pp. 1–74). San Diego, CA: Academic Press.

Fiske, S. T., & Stevens, L. E. (1993). What's so special about sex? Gender stereotyping and discrimination. In S. Oskamp & M. Costanzo (Eds.), *Gender issues in contemporary society* (pp. 173–196). Newbury Park, CA: Sage.

Fiske, S. T., & Taylor, S. E. (1991). *Social cognition* (2nd ed.). New York: McGraw-Hill.

Flavell, J. H. (1992). Cognitive development: Past, present, and future. *Developmental Psychology, 28,* 998–1005.

Friedman, H., & Zebrowitz, L. A. (1992). The contribution of typical sex differences in facial maturity to sex role stereotypes. *Personality and Social Psychology Bulletin, 18,* 430–438.

Gaertner, S. L., & Dovidio, J. F. (1986). The aversive form of racism. In J. F. Dovidio & S. L. Gaertner (Eds.), *Prejudice, discrimination, and racism* (pp. 61–89). Orlando, FL: Academic Press.

Gelman, S. A. (1996). Concepts and theories. In R. Gelman & T. K.-F. Au (Eds.), *Perceptual and cognitive development* (pp. 117–150). San Diego, CA: Academic Press.

Glick, P., Diebold, J., Bailey-Werner, B., & Zhu, L. (1997). The two faces of Adam: Ambivalent sexism and polarized attitudes toward women. *Personality and Social Psychology Bulletin, 23*, 1323–1334.

Glick, P., & Fiske, S. T. (1996). The Ambivalent Sexism Inventory: Differentiating hostile and benevolent sexism. *Journal of Personality and Social Psychology, 70*, 491–512.

Glick, P., & Fiske, S. T. (in press). Ambivalent stereotypes as legitimizing ideologies: Differentiating paternalistic and envious prejudice. In J. T. Jost & B. Major (Eds.), *The psychology of legitimacy: Emerging perspectives on ideology, justice, and intergroup relations.* New York: Cambridge University Press.

Goodwin, S. A., & Fiske, S. T. (1995). *Power and motivated impression formation: How powerholders stereotype by default and by design.* Manuscript submitted for publication, University of Massachusetts at Amherst.

Goodwin, S. A., Gubin, A., Fiske, S. T., & Yzerbyt, V. (1998). *Power can bias impression formation: Stereotyping subordinates by default and by design.* Manuscript submitted for publication, University of Massachusetts at Amherst.

Gray, J. (1992). *Men are from Mars, women are from Venus: A practical guide for improving communication and getting what you want in your relationship.* New York: HarperCollins.

Hageman, M. B., & Gladding, S. T. (1983). The art of career exploration: Occupational sex-role stereotyping among elementary school children. *Elementary School Guidance and Counselling, 17*, 280–287.

Haugh, S. S., Hoffman, C. D., & Cowan, G. (1980). The eye of the very young beholder: Sex typing of infants by young children. *Child Development, 51*, 598–600.

Hewstone, M. (1994). Revision and change of stereotypic beliefs: In search of the elusive subtyping model. In W. Stroebe & M. Hewstone (Eds.), *European review of social psychology* (Vol. 5, pp. 69–109). New York: Wiley.

Hewstone, M., Hopkins, N., & Routh, D. A. (1992). Cognitive models of stereotype change: (1) Generalization and subtyping in young people's views of the police. *European Journal of Social Psychology, 22*, 219–234.

Hewstone, M., Johnston, L., & Aird, P. (1992). Cognitive models of stereotype change: (2) Perceptions of homogeneous and heterogeneous groups. *European Journal of Social Psychology, 22*, 235–249.

Huston, A. C., & Alvarez, M. M. (1990). The socialization context of gender role development in early adolescence. In R. Montemayor, G. R. Adams, & T. P. Gullotta (Eds.), *From childhood to adolescence: A transitional period?* (pp. 156–179). Newbury Park, CA: Sage.

Johnston, L. C. & Hewstone, M., Pendry, L., & Frankish, C. (1994). Cognitive models of stereotype change: (4) Motivational and cognitive influences. *European Journal of Social Psychology, 24*, 237–265.

Johnston, L. C., & Macrae, C. N. (1994). Changing social stereotypes: The case of the information seeker. *European Journal of Social Psychology, 24*, 581–592.

Jost, J. T., & Banaji, M. R. (1994). The role of stereotyping in system-justification and the production of false consciousness. *British Journal of Social Psychology, 33*, 1–27.

Kuhn, D., Nash, S. C., & Brucken, L. (1978). Sex role concepts of two- and three-year-olds. *Child Development, 49*, 445–451.

Landrine, H. (1985). Race × class stereotypes of women. *Sex Roles, 13*, 65–75.

Leahy, R. L., & Shirk, S. R. (1984). The development of classificatory skills and sex-trait stereotypes in young children. *Sex Roles, 10*, 281–292.

Lerner, J. V. (1994). *Working women and their families.* Thousand Oaks, CA: Sage.

Lerner, M. J. (1980). *The belief in a just world: A fundamental delusion.* New York: Plenum.

Lorenzi-Cioldi, F., Eagly, A. H., & Stewart, T. L. (1995). Homogeneity of gender groups in memory. *Journal of Experimental Social Psychology, 31*, 193–217.

Lytton, H., & Romney, D. M. (1991). Parents' differential socialization of boys and girls: A meta-analysis. *Psychological Bulletin, 109*, 267–296.

Maccoby, E. E. (1990). Gender and relationships: A developmental account. *American Psychologist, 45*, 513–520.

Maccoby, E. E., & Jacklin, C. N. (1974). *The psychology of sex differences.* Stanford, CA: Stanford University Press.

Mackie, D. M., Hamilton, D. L., Susskind, J., & Rosselli, F. (1996). Social psychological foundations of stereotype formation. In C. N. Macrae, C. Stangor, & M. Hewstone (Eds.), *Stereotypes and stereotyping* (pp. 41–78). New York: Guilford.

Macrae, C. N., Bodenhausen, G. V., Milne, A. B., & Jetten, J. (1994). Out of mind but back in sight: Stereotypes on the rebound. *Journal of Personality and Social Psychology, 67*, 808–817.

Macrae, C. N., Hewstone, M., & Griffiths, R. J. (1993). Processing load and memory for stereotype-based information. *European Journal of Social Psychology, 23*, 77–87.

Macrae, C. N., Milne, A. B., & Bodenhausen, G. V. (1994). Stereotypes as energy-saving devices: A peek inside the cognitive toolbox. *Journal of Personality and Social Psychology, 66*, 37–47.

Macrae, C. N., Stangor, C., & Milne, A. B. (1994). Activating social stereotypes: A functional analysis. *Journal of Experimental Social Psychology, 30*, 370–389.

Major, B. (1994). From social inequality to personal entitlement: The role of social comparisons, legitimacy appraisals, and group membership. In M. P. Zanna (Ed.), *Advances in experimental social psychology* (Vol. 26, pp. 293–355). San Diego, CA: Academic Press.

Major, B., & Crocker, J. (1993). Social stigma: The consequences of attributional ambiguity. In D. M. Mackie & D. L. Hamilton (Eds.), *Affect, cognition, and stereotyping: Interactive processes in group perception* (pp. 345–370). San Diego, CA: Academic Press.

Markman, E. M. (1989). *Categorization and naming in children: Problems of induction.* Cambridge, MA: MIT Press.

Martin, C. L. (1989). Children's use of gender-related information in making social judgments. *Developmental Psychology, 25*, 80–88.

Martin, C. L. (1994). Cognitive influences on the development and maintenance of gender segregation. In B. Damon (Series Ed.) & C. Leaper (Vol. Ed.), *New directions for child development: The development of gender relationships* (pp. 35–51). San Francisco: Jossey-Bass.

Maurer, K. L., Park, B., & Rothbart, M. (1995). Subtyping versus subgrouping processes in stereotype representation. *Journal of Personality and Social Psychology, 69*, 812–824.

Mullen, B., & Hu, L. (1989). Perceptions of ingroup and outgroup variability: A meta-analytic integration. *Basic and Applied Social Psychology, 10*, 233–252.

Park, B., & Rothbart, M. (1982). Perception of out-group homogeneity and levels of social categorization: Memory for the subordinate attributes of in-group and out-group members. *Journal of Personality and Social Psychology, 42*, 1051–1068.

Powlishta, K. K., Serbin, L. A., & Moller, L. C. (1993). The stability of individual differences in gender typing: Implications for understanding gender segregation. *Sex Roles, 29*, 723–737.

Riedle, J. E. (1991). Exploring the subcategories of stereotypes: Not all mothers are the same. *Sex Roles, 24*, 711–723.

Rothbart, M. (1981). Memory processes and social beliefs. In D. L. Hamilton (Ed.), *Cognitive processes in stereotyping and intergroup behavior* (pp. 145–181). Hillsdale, NJ: Lawrence Erlbaum Associates.

Ruble, D. N., & Martin, C. L. (1998). Gender development. In W. Damon (Series Ed.) & N. Eisenberg (Vol. Ed.), *Handbook of child psychology: Vol. 3. Social, emotional, and personality development* (5th ed., pp. 933–1016). New York: Wiley.

Ruble, D. N., & Ruble, T. L. (1982). Sex stereotypes. In A. G. Miller (Ed.), *In the eye of the beholder: Contemporary issues in stereotyping* (pp. 188–252). New York: Praeger.

Ruble, D. N., & Stangor, C. (1986). Stalking the elusive schema: Insights from developmental and social-psychological analyses of gender schemas. *Social Cognition, 4*, 227–261.

Rudman, L. A., & Borgida, E. (1995). The afterglow of construct accessibility: The behavioral consequences of priming men to view women as sexual objects. *Journal of Experimental Social Psychology, 31*, 493–517.

Ruscher, J. B., & Fiske, S. T. (1990). Interpersonal competition can cause individuating processes. *Journal of Personality and Social Psychology, 58*, 832–843.

Six, B., & Eckes, T. (1991). A closer look at the complex structure of gender stereotypes. *Sex Roles, 24*, 57–71.

Skrypnek, B. J., & Snyder, M. (1982). On the self-perpetuating nature of stereotypes about women and men. *Journal of Experimental Social Psychology, 18*, 277–291.

Smith, E. R. (1998). Mental representation and memory. In D. T. Gilbert, S. T. Fiske, & G. Lindzey (Eds.), *The handbook of social psychology* (4th ed., Vol. 1, pp. 391–445). Boston: McGraw-Hill.

Snyder, M. (1981). On the self-perpetuating nature of social stereotypes. In D. L. Hamilton (Ed.), *Cognitive processes in stereotyping and intergroup behavior* (pp. 183–212). Hillsdale, NJ: Lawrence Erlbaum Associates.

Snyder, M., Tanke, E. D., & Berscheid, E. (1977). Social perception and interpersonal behavior: On the self-fulfilling nature of social stereotypes. *Journal of Personality and Social Psychology, 35*, 656–666.

Spence, J. T., & Hahn, E. D. (1997). The Attitudes Toward Women Scale and attitude change in college students. *Psychology of Women Quarterly, 21*, 17–34.

Spence, J. T., Helmreich, R. L., & Holahan, C. K. (1979). Negative and positive components of psychological masculinity and femininity and their relationships to self-reports of neurotic and acting out behaviors. *Journal of Personality and Social Psychology, 37*, 1673–1682.

Spencer, S. J., Steele, C. M., & Quinn, D. M. (1999). Stereotype threat and women's math performance. *Journal of Experimental Social Psychology, 35*, 4–28.

Stangor, C., Lynch, L., Duan, C., & Glass, B. (1992). Categorization of individuals on the basis of multiple social features. *Journal of Personality and Social Psychology, 62*, 207–218.

Stangor, C., & Ruble, D. N. (1987). Development of gender role knowledge and gender constancy. In L. S. Liben & M. L. Signorella (Eds.), *Children's gender schemata* (pp. 5–22). San Francisco: Jossey-Bass.

Stangor, C., & Ruble, D. N. (1989). Differential influences of gender schemata and gender constancy on children's information processing and behavior. *Social Cognition, 7*, 353–372.

Steele, C. M. (1998). A threat in the air: How stereotypes shape intellectual identity and performance. In J. L. Eberhardt & S. T. Fiske (Eds.), *Confronting racism: The problem and the response* (pp. 202–233). Thousand Oaks, CA: Sage.

Steele, C. M., & Aronson, J. (1995). Stereotype threat and the intellectual test performance of African Americans. *Journal of Personality and Social Psychology, 69*, 797–811.

Stoddart, T., & Turiel, E. (1985). Children's concepts of cross-gender activities. *Child Development, 56*, 1241–1252.

Swim, J. K., Aikin, K. J., Hall, W. S., & Hunter, B. A. (1995). Sexism and racism: Old-fashioned and modern prejudices. *Journal of Personality and Social Psychology, 68*, 199–214.

Tajfel, H., & Turner, J. C. (1986). The social identity theory of intergroup behavior. In S. Worchel & W. G. Austin (Eds.), *Psychology of intergroup relations* (2nd ed., pp. 7–24). Chicago: Nelson-Hall.

Taylor, S. E. (1981). A categorization approach to stereotyping. In D. L. Hamilton (Ed.), *Cognitive processes in stereotyping and intergroup behavior* (pp. 83–114). Hillsdale, NJ: Lawrence Erlbaum Associates.

Thorne, B. (1993). *Gender play: Girls and boys in school.* New Brunswick, NJ: Rutgers University Press.

Tulving, E., Schacter, D. L., & Stark, H. A. (1982). Priming effects in word-fragment completion are independent of recognition memory. *Journal of Experimental Psychology: Learning, Memory, and Cognition, 8*, 336–342.

van Knippenberg, A., & van Twuyver, M. (1994). Factors affecting social categorization processes in memory. *British Journal of Social Psychology, 33*, 419–431.

Weber, R. & Crocker, J. (1983). Cognitive processes in the revision of stereotypic beliefs. *Journal of Personality and Social Psychology, 45*, 961–977.

Wegner, D. M. (1994). Ironic processes of mental control. *Psychological Review, 101*, 34–52.

Wegner, D. M., & Bargh, J. A. (1998). Control and automaticity in social life. In D. T. Gilbert, S. T. Fiske, & G. Lindzey (Eds.), *The handbook of social psychology* (4th ed., Vol. 1, pp. 446–496). Boston: McGraw-Hill.

Wilder, D. A. (1981). Perceiving persons as a group: Categorization and intergroup relations. In D. L. Hamilton (Ed.), *Cognitive processes in stereotyping and intergroup behavior* (pp. 213–257). Hillsdale, NJ: Lawrence Erlbaum Associates.

Wood, W., & Karten, S. J. (1986). Sex differences in interaction style as a product of perceived sex differences in competence. *Journal of Personality and Social Psychology, 50*, 341–347.

Word, C. O., Zanna, M. P., & Cooper, J. (1974). The nonverbal mediation of self-fulfilling prophecies in interracial interaction. *Journal of Experimenal Social Psychology, 10*, 109–120.

Yee, M., & Brown, R. (1994). The development of gender differentiation in young children. *British Journal of Social Psychology, 33*, 183–196.

Zanna, M. P., & Pack, S. J. (1975). On the self-fulfilling nature of apparent sex differences in behavior. *Journal of Experimental Social Psychology, 11*, 583–591.

Zárate, M. A., & Sandoval, P. (1995). The effects of contextual cues on making occupational and gender categorizations. *British Journal of Social Psychology, 34*, 353–362.

# 8

# Combative Children to Ambivalent Adults: The Development of Gender Prejudice

Peter Glick
Lori Hilt
*Lawrence University*

*Questioner: "Is it better to be single or married?"*
*Kenny (age 7): "It gives me a headache to think about that stuff. I'm just a kid. I don't need that kind of trouble."*

At some point in your life you probably acted as though playing with members of the other sex would contaminate you with a germlike substance (we called them "cooties"). Though perhaps you realized that some day you might be attracted to other-sex peers, your daily interaction with them was probably less frequent, and characterized by more teasing, name calling, and hostility than were interactions with same-sex peers—especially in group settings unsupervised by adults (e.g., on the school playground). Chances are that your attitudes about and interactions with members of the other sex have become more complex, your emotions toward them sometimes quite positive, though often ambivalent. This chapter charts the development of gender prejudice in terms of two general modes of intergroup prejudice, *hostile* and *benevolent*. Our main contention is that children's attitudes toward the other sex fit well into the standard social psychological model of hostile intergroup relations, but that the dependencies that develop between the sexes during puberty as romantic sexual attraction comes into play foster a "benevolent" form of prejudice (Glick & Fiske, 1996).[1] The newer benevolent mode may coexist with continued hostile competition, creating ambivalent attitudes and polarized behavior in adult cross-sex interactions.

# DEFINING PREJUDICE

How can prejudice be benevolent? According to standard social psychological definitions of prejudice, it cannot. Allport (1954) defined prejudice as "an antipathy based on a faulty and inflexible generalization" (p. 9). Although some aspects of Allport's definition have been rejected by other prejudice theorists, most continue to define prejudice as an antipathy (e.g., see Brown, 1995). Definitions of gender prejudice or sexism have followed suit, though they typically specify that gender prejudice is hostility directed toward women (e.g., Lott, 1995; Lutz & Ruble, 1995). Other work (particularly in the area of gender prejudice), however, has forced a reexamination of the equation of prejudice with antipathy. Eagly and Mladinic (1994) showed that stereotypes and evaluations of women (as a group) are usually more favorable than are stereotypes and evaluations of men, even among men who embrace traditional attitudes about gender roles. Glick and Fiske (1996) argued that these subjectively positive attitudes about women nevertheless serve to justify and perpetuate women's subordination. This position is consistent with Jackman's (1994) analysis that dominant groups tend to avoid hostile relations with members of subordinate groups, preferring sweeter forms of coercion to keep subordinates in line. Jackman argued that high-status groups tend to adopt what they believe to be benevolent attitudes that are affectionate but patronizing toward disadvantaged groups. Such paternalism serves as a more effective means of control as members of the low-status group are thereby motivated to avoid direct challenges to the authority of the high-status group, for to do so would risk the affection and incur the wrath of the more powerful group.

The work described thus far suggests a need for a revised definition of prejudice, the key to which can be found in an afterthought by Allport (1954). "The net effect of prejudice," Allport wrote, ". . . is to place the object of prejudice at some disadvantage not merited by his own conduct" (p. 9). Rather than seeing disadvantage as merely an effect of prejudice, we propose that seeking to place another group at a disadvantage should be at

---

[1] We use the term *benevolent* to indicate a patronizing, paternalistic form of prejudice in which prejudiced perceivers believe that their attitudes are favorable to the target group, but which treat the targeted group as inferior. We have chosen to use *benevolent* rather than *paternalistic* as we believe that women sometimes exhibit this form of prejudice toward men (e.g., the belief that men can't take care of themselves at home).

the core of any definition of prejudice. If this criterion is accepted as the sine qua non of prejudice, the notion of benevolent prejudice can now be understood. For example, the subjectively favorable belief that women are wonderful at caring for children (and men are not) is a form of prejudice against women if it is part and parcel of a system of beliefs that justify confining women to domestic roles and excluding them from powerful roles outside the home. This aim need not be consciously held. Indeed, part of the point of benevolent prejudices is a form of self-deception in which the prejudiced perceiver constructs a nonprejudiced self-image. Apologists for slavery and colonialism who invoked the "white man's burden" disguised their exploitation of subordinate groups as a magnanimous beneficence ("They are happier and better off when we govern them"). Subtle, modern forms of prejudice often involve related self-deceptions that allow prejudiced individuals to claim they are egalitarian (see, for example, Gaertner & Dovidio's, 1986, analysis of racism; or Swim, Aikin, Hall, & Hunter's, 1995, work on modern sexism). Fortunately, even if such self-deception is successful, the nonegalitarian motives behind these ideologies can be uncovered empirically by demonstrating links to more overt forms of prejudice and to a desire for social dominance (Sidanius, Pratto, & Bobo, 1994).

We therefore define prejudice as *the implicit or explicit attitude that a group deserves inferior social status.* The cognitive, emotional, and behavioral aspects of prejudiced attitudes may (for the prejudiced perceiver) be subjectively favorable, unfavorable, or ambivalent in their orientation toward the target group, yet they all serve to promote or maintain that group's subordination. That prejudice may be "implicit" recognizes that the desire to subordinate another group may not be consciously recognized, may be covert or hidden. Also, this definition permits the possibility of prejudice directed at one's own group. For example, some women may believe that members of their sex are less competent than men and ought not to pursue positions of power. In general, however, we will focus on prejudice directed by members of each sex toward the other.

By this definition, prejudice can be directed "upward" toward groups that have higher status, but who are viewed as *deserving* a status lower than one's own group. Whether prejudice is directed upward (from a lower status group to one of higher status) or downward (from a higher status group toward a lower status group) strongly affects the subjective nature of the prejudice (Glick & Fiske, 1999b, in press). Prejudice directed upward is more likely to be *envious*, mixing an implicit admiration for the powerful group with envy, fear, and a desire to undermine the other group's status. We argue that adult women's prejudice toward men is of this type. In contrast, high- status groups are likely to exhibit a *paternalistic* form of prejudice toward lower status groups, characterized by hostile condescension but also patronizing affection (the type of prejudice adult men often exhibit toward women). Each of these forms of prejudice can be *ambivalent*, with benevolent and hostile components, particularly when groups are interdependent (as is the case with men and women).

Defining prejudice as an *attitude* follows a tradition that links prejudice to a central social psychological construct. An attitude is defined as "*a psychological tendency that is expressed by evaluating a particular entity with some degree of favor or disfavor*" (Eagly & Chaiken, 1993, p. 1). These evaluations may be manifested in cognition, affect, and behavior (Eagly & Chaiken, 1993). The cognitive aspect of prejudice includes stereotypes, which are beliefs about group members' characteristics (e.g., men are more assertive), and ideologies (e.g., believing that women ought to have different roles than men). The affective component of prejudice includes subjectively positive (e.g., patronizing affection) and/or negative emotions (e.g., revulsion) directed toward the targeted group. The behavioral aspects of prejudice involve discriminatory actions, including acts that seem to be prosocial but which are designed to reinforce a group's subordination (e.g., helping women in ways that imply they are incapable of accomplishing certain tasks on their own).

Although attitudes have cognitive, emotional, and behavioral components, it is important to keep in mind that these components may be relatively independent of each other. It has been well established that although beliefs, emotions, and behavior are often related, they are distinct aspects of attitudes (see Eagly & Chaiken, 1993). Thus, in intergroup relations, it has been found that stereotypes (cognitions) may not (as many stereotype researchers have assumed) necessarily reveal the overall affective evaluation of a group or predict discriminatory behavior (Smith, 1993). The quasi-independence between attitude components has important implications for the measurement of gender prejudice.

## DEFINING AND MEASURING GENDER PREJUDICE

We use the term *gender prejudice* or *sexism* to refer to prejudiced attitudes (i.e., the attitude that a group deserves lower social status) based on gender-related categorization of people. Gender prejudice is the more precise term in that we mean to include not just the basic sex categories of male and female but a much wider array of categories that include all sorts of subtypes of women and men. Women, in particular, tend to be subtyped (e.g., as feminists, homemakers, babes, career women, etc.) and may be treated quite differently based on whether they are placed in one subgroup or another (e.g., Glick, Diebold, Bailey-Werner, & Zhu, 1997). These subcategories, however, are predominantly a gender-based phenomenon as they distinguish between types of women who fulfill versus defy conventional gender roles (Ashmore, Del Boca, & Titus, 1984; Six & Eckes, 1991). Although the term *sexism* implies a narrower focus on the two overall sex categories, we use this term interchangeably with gender prejudice and mean it to refer to the same phenomena. Gender prejudice or sexism, in our view, can be directed at men as well as at women, though the history of power differences favoring men means that more attention has been given to attitudes directed at women. These power differences also mean that the prejudice exhibited by women toward men has a different psychological quality to it (an envious ambivalence) than does prejudice that men direct toward women (a paternalistic ambivalence). In this chapter we consider the conventional gender prejudices of each sex toward the other.

Gender prejudice has been studied in a wide variety of ways. Unfortunately, conceptual and methodological confusions have plagued much of the research on gender-related attitudes. Prominent social and developmental researchers (e.g., Ashmore, Del Boca, & Bilder, 1995; Bigler, 1997; Spence, 1993) have recently urged greater care in defining and measuring gender-related constructs, as it is increasingly clear that these attitudes are multidimensional and complex, not homogenous and monolithic as often has been assumed. For example, assigning gender-congruent traits to oneself is largely independent of the tendency to stereotype others (Bigler, 1997; Spence, 1993), knowledge of general sex-stereotypes is unrelated to endorsement of these stereotypes as prescriptions that men and women ought to follow (Bigler, 1997), and implicit stereotypes (stereotyped assumptions made without conscious reflection) may be unrelated to consciously endorsed sexist attitudes (Banaji & Hardin, 1996).

Lack of conceptual clarity concerning gender-related attitudes has spawned methodological and interpretational confusión in both social and developmental psychology, though these problems are manifested differently in each field. In social psychology, the absence of a good conceptual framework has resulted in a profusion of scales, tests, and measures (see Beere, 1990, for a compilation), often purporting to measure something similar when they may be tapping distinctly different constructs. Thus, one study of "sex typing" (to take a prominent methodological example) may measure the tendency to assign sex-typed personality traits to the self, whereas another may examine knowledge of general sex stereotypes about men and women, and still another might assess prescriptive attitudes about appropriate roles for men and women, all of which are wrongly lumped into the same conceptual category. To some extent, research by developmental psychologists has suffered the same problem (see Bigler, 1997, for a discussion). Developmentalists, however, have tended to use a more limited set of tests and measures. Lutz and Ruble (1995) pointed out that developmental researchers have focused mainly on cognitive variables, such as gender constancy or knowledge about men's and women's roles, and given much less attention to general emotional appraisals of gender groups. As we argue later, some of these cognitive measures, such as knowledge (or even endorsement) of gender stereotypes, though interesting in their own right, may be poor indexes of gender prejudice in children. Further, what is measured is often confounded with the age of participants (though often for sound developmental reasons). Studies of young children, for example, are more likely to assess behavior, such as the tendency toward sex-segregation in play, whereas studies of adolescents are more likely to assess ideologies, such as attitudes about women's rights. Such differences in methodological approaches to studying children, adolescents, and adults may not be particularly problematic if a sound theoretical framework suggests that different measures are getting at similar underlying constructs. For example, attachment is measured quite differently in young children than it is in adolescents and adults, yet there are sound theoretical reasons for suggesting that the different, age-appropriate methodologies are tapping the same construct. In the absence of such a framework, however, these methodological differences in measuring gender-related attitudes only add to the confusion.

In this chapter, we suggest a developmental sequence that will direct researchers' attention to the likely ways in which hostile and benevolent gender prejudices are (or are not) manifested in young children, adolescents, and adults. This framework may help researchers to think about how measures used at different ages relate (or fail to relate) to each other, and we will suggest hypotheses about how gender prejudice may manifest itself in different ways at different points in development. For example, among young children, hostile prejudice may be more evident in overall emotional evaluations of the other sex ("Who is better, boys or girls?") than in complex stereotypes about which sex possesses which traits (Powlishta, 1995a; see also Tajfel & Jahoda, 1966). In contrast, among adolescents (who have greater cognitive abilities and for whom sexual relations are suddenly more salient), hostility may be more evident in attitudes about specific subtypes of men and women or in attitudes about heterosexual relationships (e.g., toward sexual violence).

Our central thesis is that past research and theory have failed to capture a critical developmental transition from a wholly hostile, as well as cognitively simple, gender prejudice that is typical of young children to a volatile, complex, and ambivalent form of prejudice that begins to emerge during puberty. This transition is driven by sexual interdependence, which fuels a benevolent form of sexism (particularly for boys toward girls), even as the earlier hostile form of prejudice that both sexes evince toward the other remains (though with further developments and mutations that accommodate the new modes of interaction between the sexes). During and after adolescence, gender prejudice is an increasingly complex phenomenon for which benevolent as well as hostile attitudes are critical to legitimating and perpetuating a system that disadvantages girls and women.

## AMBIVALENT SEXISM THEORY

Glick and Fiske (1996, 1999a) suggested that structural aspects of adult male–female relations create ambivalent attitudes on the part of each sex toward the other. Panculturally, men possess significantly greater structural power—control over economic, political, religious, and social institutions (Guttentag & Secord, 1983). This power difference has resulted in male attitudes of hostile sexism, a legitimizing ideology that casts women as inferior to men. Women, even those who do not consider themselves feminists, may resent men's greater power and exhibit a reflected hostility toward men. At the same time, heterosexual reproduction has created strong interdependencies between the sexes. Men's dependence on women as wives, mothers, and romantic objects fosters benevolent sexism, a set of subjectively positive (for the sexist) beliefs about women. These beliefs reflect a benevolent, paternalistic mode of group relations in which women are idealized as objects of men's affections and viewed as weak but wonderful creatures who ought to be protected by men. Because the dependencies created by heterosexuality work both ways, women too are likely to develop benevolent attitudes toward men, such as an admiration for men's greater power (from which a woman may benefit if a man serves as her protector) and the belief that a woman is happier when romantically involved with a man.

Glick and Fiske (1996, 1999a) proposed that the hostile and benevolent attitudes exhibited by each sex toward the other encompass three dimensions: *gender differentiation, power,* and *heterosexuality.*[2] The hostile aspects of gender differentiation are the attempts by both men and women to establish positively differentiated definitions of their groups (i.e., gender stereotypes that favor one's own sex and derogate the other sex). Hostile attitudes on the power dimension include men's desires to retain greater power and women's resentment of this power. Hostile forms of heterosexuality encompass male attitudes that characterize women purely as sexual objects and hostile female reactions to such male attitudes. In contrast, benevolent gender differentiation includes favorable stereotypes about the other sex (e.g., women believing that men are more analytical and men believing that women are more nurturant). Benevolent attitudes on the

---

[2]This model is designed presuming heterosexuality and may not apply well to the attitudes of homosexual individuals.

power dimension include men's protective paternalism toward women (e.g., that women ought to be rescued first in disasters) and women's maternalism toward men. Like protective paternalism (which presumes women are weak and therefore in need of protection), maternalism is also patronizing as it presumes men's incompetence in the domestic sphere (e.g., that men can't take care of themselves at home, which is why women must care for them). Finally, benevolent beliefs about heterosexuality emphasize the notion that men and women are, romantically speaking, two halves of a whole and that individuals need to be involved in a heterosexual romantic relationship to be happy. Glick and Fiske created measures of men's ambivalent prejudice toward women, the Ambivalent Sexism Inventory (ASI; Glick & Fiske, 1996), and of women's ambivalent prejudice toward men, the Ambivalence Toward Men Inventory (AMI; Glick & Fiske, 1999a).

Ambivalent sexism theory suggests that both men and women who endorse the conventional attitudes described earlier are exhibiting ambivalent gender prejudice toward the other sex. The type of ambivalent prejudice men hold toward women is a *paternalistic* form of prejudice, characteristic of high-status groups toward lower status groups on whom they depend (Glick & Fiske, in press). The subjectively benevolent side of this type of prejudice consists of patronizing attitudes that cast the lower status group as incapable of holding the most powerful roles in society, and which are accompanied by feelings of affection and behaviors designed to "protect" the subordinate group in a manner that reinforces their lower power. In short, men's paternalistic prejudice toward women, though subjectively ambivalent, is a coordinated set of beliefs—all presuming women's inferiority—that helps to maintain the status quo in gender relations. The benefits that the benevolent aspects of this prejudice offer to women (e.g., protection and affection if they fulfill traditional roles) in combination with the hostile aspects of men's prejudice, which are directed at women who fail to conform, create a powerful system of incentives that has successfully kept women subordinated for centuries. Thus, the subjectively hostile and benevolent ideologies described here are a form of prejudice against women, as both serve to justify women's subordination (which is why endorsement of one predicts endorsement of the other, even though they represent different valences in attitudes toward women; Glick & Fiske, 1996; Glick et al., 1997).

Women's conventional ambivalent prejudice toward men represents an attempt by women to gain positive differentiation for their own group within a system in which women have less status and power. This form of prejudice is not paternalistic but envious of men's power and control and thus has a different psychological quality (Glick & Fiske, in press). It too is nevertheless ambivalent and qualifies as a form of prejudice. The ambivalence lies in the underlying respect accorded to men (e.g., admiration for men's greater power) that accompanies resentment of men's status and power. Such feelings need not qualify as prejudice if they are motivated by egalitarianism. An honest recognition of patriarchy and a desire to attain equality are not a form of prejudice. The conventional attitudes of women toward men described previously are not, however, a form of egalitarian-minded feminism. Rather, they represent an attempt by women to gain power over men in a highly conventional way and within a very restricted domain that corresponds to conventional gender roles. Thus, the benevolence toward men described here is one that presumes men's incompetence in the domestic arena and women's covert control over men in domestic and romantic relationships (e.g., a benevolent AMI item states that "Women ought to take care of their men at home, because men would fall apart if they had to take care of themselves"). This form of maternalism is quite similar to men's paternalism—both presume an incompetence on the part of the other sex. Other benevolent items suggest a highly instrumental orientation toward men (e.g., " Men are mainly useful to provide financial security for women"; see the appendix of Glick & Fiske, 1999a, for a list of AMI items).

The picture that emerges in this ambivalent ideology is one of women attempting to control and "use" men through covert manipulation, in ways that are compatible with conventional gender roles (e.g., gaining power within the home). The attitudes expressed are a form of prejudice engaged in by the less powerful toward the more powerful that looks for weaknesses of the powerful group to exploit. Ironically, however, this form of prejudice merely serves to perpetuate a social system in which men maintain structural power because women who endorse these ideologies seek power in the domains in which men are dependent on them—romantic relationships and domestic life—and cede the powerful roles outside the home to men.

This ambivalent sexism model, and the corresponding measures of these attitudes, were constructed with adult gender relations in mind. This model presumes that greater structural power on the part of men is coupled with interdependence between the sexes, both for sexual gratification and a division of labor in the household. Although this is the case for adult men and women, the structure of childhood gender relations are quite different. In the remainder of this chapter, we consider the ambivalent sexism model in a developmental perspective. What are the developmental origins of hostile and benevolent gender prejudices? How do relations between the sexes change over time on the dimensions of gender differentiation, power, and heterosexuality?

# CHILDHOOD:
# HOSTILITY WITHOUT BENEVOLENCE

The issue of childhood sexuality is a controversial one. But whether children possess a latent form of sexuality or not, overtly (at least) they do not seem to suffer from an excessive attraction to members of the other sex. Rather, the dimensions specified by ambivalent sexism theory that are most relevant to prepubertal children are the hostile aspects of *gender differentiation* and *power differences*. In the absence of the dependence of each sex on the other that heterosexual romantic impulses introduce, childhood gender relations are predominantly hostile. Indeed, the overwhelming finding of developmental researchers is that sex segregation and antipathy toward the other sex are powerful, cross-cultural phenomena that resist egalitarian-minded interventions by adults (e.g., Bukowski, Gauze, Hoza, & Newcomb, 1993; Hayden-Thompson, Rubin, & Hymel, 1987; Powlishta, Serbin, Doyle, & White, 1994; Yee & Brown, 1994; see Maccoby, 1990, for a review). The hostile gender prejudice evident in children may be related to some of the hostile components of adult ambivalence, yet this hostility seems to be reflected in a fun-house mirror in a child's world characterized by an exaggerated dislike of the other sex. This process begins relatively mildly when children learn at around 2½ to 3 years of age to categorize themselves and others as boys and girls (Fagot & Leinbach, 1993; Miller, 1983; Thompson, 1975), but it soon develops into a hostile form of *competitive gender differentiation* by age 5 and seems to continue in this mode until about age 11.

Although the early-learned ability to categorize oneself and others as boy or girl is a necessary condition for gender prejudice (as all definitions of prejudice presume some form of group categorization), it is not (logically speaking) sufficient. For instance, we may classify others as blue-eyed and brown-eyed, yet not have different evaluations of these groups or see one as deserving higher status. To understand how gender categorization creates prejudice, some developmental theorists (Bigler, Jones, & Lobliner, 1997; Lutz & Ruble, 1995; Maccoby, 1988) have imported the most prominent general theory of prejudice used by social psychologists, social identity theory (Tajfel, 1981). Social identity theory states that categorization of people implicates self-relevant motivations because the individual perceiver is or is not a member of any given group, resulting in "in-groups" (groups in which I am a member) and "out-groups" (groups to which I do not belong). In-groups become an extension of the self, particularly when membership in a group is salient or deemed to be important to self-identity. As a result, one's self-esteem is increased when one's group is positively evaluated (Oakes & Turner, 1980). All group evaluations involve at least implicit intergroup comparisons—that is, my group is only "good" to the extent that it is better than alternative groups (just as I am only "smart" if I am intelligent relative to other people). Thus, belonging to a group motivates individuals to evaluate their group more positively than other groups. When young children learn that there are two sexes and that they belong to one sex or the other, they are (according to social identity theory) motivated to evaluate their sex more positively than the other sex as a way of feeling good about themselves.

In-group favoritism need not create overt hostility (e.g., a boy may think that girls are fine, but boys are better), but even such mild favoritism sows the seeds of a competitive orientation in which one of the easiest ways to boost one's own self-image is to elevate one's own group by disparaging the out-group. Tajfel (1981) showed that this tendency can even override objective self-interest. When given a choice, people often prefer to allocate less money to their own group if this choice means that the out-group will be hit worse (i.e., what matters is how well the in-group does relative to the out-group, not how well the in-group does on an absolute scale).

Gender prejudice among children is more severe than a mild in-group bias, as evidenced by their behavior toward and feelings about the other sex. Behaviorally, from 2 to 3 years of age until puberty, children prefer to play with same-sex others, a preference that only strengthens with age (until about 11). In Maccoby and Jacklin's (1987) longitudinal study, 4-year-olds spent about three times as much time playing with children of the same, as compared to the other, sex. This increased to 11 times as much play with same-sex partners when these children were 6 years old. It is important to note that gender segregation increases when children play without adult supervision, suggesting that segregation is at least partly maintained as a matter of children's choice. The feelings and beliefs children direct toward the other sex confirm that relations are predominately hostile. Powlishta and her colleagues (Powlishta, 1995b; Powlishta et al., 1994) found strong gender prejudice among boys and girls from kindergarten to sixth grade using multiple measures of feelings toward and beliefs about each gender group. General evaluations of the other sex as a group demonstrate a rejection of the other sex, not merely a bias in favor of the same sex (see also Yee & Brown, 1994). Children attributed more negative and fewer positive traits to the other sex; they also expressed greater dislike for other-sex peers and more liking for same-sex peers. In contrast to the increase in behavioral segregation, Powlishta et al. (1994) found that increased age was associated with greater flexibility in elementary school children's gender-related attitudes and with a lessening of gender prejudice. Yee and Brown (1994), however, found an increase in prejudice against the other sex when comparing 3-year-olds with 5-year-olds, with prejudice remaining at similarly high levels among 5-, 7-, and 9-year-olds. Interestingly, several researchers (Powlishta et al., 1994; Yee & Brown, 1994; Zalk & Katz, 1978) have independently found that girls exhibit more hostile attitudes toward boys than vice versa (although both sexes exhibit strong in-group favoritism). Both behaviorally and emotionally, then, boys and girls alike are prejudiced against the other sex.

Why, however, does gender identity become so overwhelmingly important to children? Lutz and Ruble (1995) reviewed evidence suggesting that gender prejudice is intensified by the development of gender constancy, defined as *"the understanding that gender is unchanging over time and despite superficial changes in appearance"* (p. 134; italics added). Gender constancy is most likely achieved between the ages of 5 and 7 (see Lutz & Ruble, 1995), though some have placed it as early as 3½ years (e.g., Bem, 1989). Lutz and Ruble suggested that the development of gender constancy—the realization that being male or female is an unchanging part of one's identity that continues into an adult life that is structured by male and female roles—motivates children to identify more strongly with their gender category, resulting in heightened gender prejudice.

In addition to gender constancy, the attention adults pay to categorization by sex can affect how salient and important this category is to children. Thus parents' tendency to dress boys and girls in ways that make gender distinctions more visible and to enforce different norms of behavior for girls and boys, media portrayals that reinforce gender distinctions (such as television commercials that pitch certain toys to girls and others to boys), and children's observation of an adult world in which there is considerable segregation of male and female roles (such as the tendency for day-care workers and elementary teachers to be female and firefighters to be male) are all likely to enhance the importance of gender distinctions in children's minds, making gender identity chronically salient and important to self-definition. Because gender identity is perhaps the first form of social identity (other than family membership) that children learn, they are likely to place inordinate importance on it. Once group identification begins, social identity concerns motivate children to develop a strong degree of in-group favoritism and gender prejudice toward the other sex. Although cultural forces may be largely responsible for the origins of childhood gender prejudice, the motivational forces described by social identity theory may account for the vehemence of childhood gender prejudice (Brown, 1995) and its resistance to interventions by adults (Bigler, 1999).

Social identity concerns may also be intensified because gender classification among young children involves a simple male–female dichotomy (rather than the multiple groups of, for example, ethnic classification). Thus, all evaluations of one's gender in-group involve direct comparisons with the other sex. As a result, the sexes are seen as "opposites" in every way, creating exaggerated childhood gender prejudices. Although multiple gender classifications may blossom as cognitive abilities develop and gender subtypes are recognized (e.g., "tomboys" vs. "chicks"), young children are likely to seize onto the simpler two-group classification and make overgeneralized comparisons in which their own sex is "good" and the other sex is "bad."

Early in childhood, then, complex beliefs about the characteristics of the in-group and the out-group may not exist, even though identification with the in-group and an overall devaluation of the out-group may be quite strong. For example, Tajfel and Jahoda (1966) showed that young English children have strong, consensual overall emotional evaluations of national out-groups, seeing Americans, for example, as better than Russians, well before they have any agreed-upon stereotypes about what characteristics actually distinguish these groups (e.g., that Americans are rich). From a social identity perspective, this makes perfect sense because the crucial motivation is to see the in-group (or groups identified as compatible with the in-group) as better than out-groups. Specific stereotypes develop later and help to support the overall emotional appraisals of groups, but they may be quite irrelevant in explaining young children's emotions about out-groups (see Aboud, 1988). For 3- to 5-year-olds, categories may mainly consist of verbal labels associated with simplistic, but strong "good/bad" emotional evaluations (Allport, 1954).

Direct support for this view in the realm of gender relations comes from Powlishta's (1995a) study in which 8- to 10-year-olds rated personality traits as masculine or feminine, as well as rating these traits as positive or negative. Both boys and girls showed strong in-group biases, assigning more positive traits to their own sex and negative traits to the other sex. Crucially (with a few important exceptions reviewed later), this in-group favoritism had little to do with whether traits were traditionally masculine or feminine according to adult stereotypes. For example, girls saw "strong" (a positive trait) as being feminine, whereas boys claimed it as masculine. And boys claimed the positive trait "gentle" as masculine, whereas girls predictably saw it as feminine. For highly sex-stereotyped traits, such as the previous examples, some degree of sex typing was still evident—for example, "strong" was seen as highly masculine by boys and only as slightly feminine by girls (with "gentle" showing the reverse pattern). Still, there was only weak evidence of conventional sex stereotypes about boys and girls on most traits, but strong evidence of a general bias favoring one's own gender—the best predictor of whether children would claim a trait for their own sex was the trait's perceived positivity. This suggests that developmental psychologists' emphasis on cognitive measures as an indication of gender prejudice is, ironically, developmentally inappropriate for young children. The much less frequently used technique of asking for overall emotional appraisals of girls and boys may more accurately reveal the hostile prejudice of younger girls and boys. These children may not know (or may not care) which traits are thought by adults to be associated with each sex, yet they strongly feel that their sex is better than the other one. Such prejudice tends to peak at around 7 years of age—both for gender and for ethnic prejudices (Allport, 1954; Brown, 1995). The 5- to 7-year-old period is when children have developed a sense of gender constancy that motivates hostile prejudice toward the other sex. At this period, children are prone to total rejection of out-groups and overgeneralized stereotypes that assign all good traits to in-groups and all bad traits to out-groups. Young boys and girls tend very simply to think that their own sex is "the best" in every way.

Although we have focused on social identity concerns, there are other forces that may inflate the importance of gender categorization among children. In particular, Maccoby (1990) suggested two likely causes for children's desire to segregate by sex: (a) a gender-linked preference for different styles of play, and (b) a concern for dominance and competition among boys that girls find aversive. Both of these tendencies may stem from biological differences between the sexes. Even if the choice to segregate is not caused initially by hostile intergroup attitudes, however, segregation is likely to contribute to hostility as it makes gender a more salient part of children's social world and lends gender categorization a great deal of social utility in daily life, such as by helping to decide with whom it might be fun to play. Indeed, Brown (1995) noted that the tendency spontaneously to use sex as a principle of categorization in sorting tasks (in which children sort pictures of other children into groups) is much stronger when decisions about who would be good to play with are involved.

The differences in style that contribute to child-initiated sex segregation implicate another dimension that ambivalent sexism theory specifies as important in understanding gender relations: *power*. Gender-related power differences may seem to be a trivial issue in young children as it is only in adulthood that men gain greater control than women over economic, political, and social institutions. Nevertheless, Maccoby (1990) suggested that early gender differentiation is related to interpersonal power. Recall that one reason why girls may choose not to associate with boys is that the latter value competition and dominance. Young girls learn that they are unable to exert influence over boys, who tend only to respond to direct demands, rather than the polite suggestions that girls typically use (Serbin, Sprafkin, Elman, & Doyle, 1984). As a result, in mixed-sex groups, boys tend to get their way (Powlishta, 1987). In groups, boys also seem to exert more power, tending to take up much more playground space and being more likely to interrupt the activity of girls (Thorne, 1986). Thus, gender segregation may be caused by the different styles of interaction girls and boys develop (as girls find boys' style aversive and avoid interacting with boys). This segregation, in turn, reinforces the development of gender differences in interaction styles as boys and girls virtually come to live in two different worlds of peer interaction. Whatever the reasons (perhaps biological as well as social) for these differing styles of influence that lend boys greater power, the evidence suggests that gender-related power differences, like gender differentiation, begin early (perhaps around 3 years of age).

Power differences are evident not only in children's behavior, but in the shared beliefs or stereotypes about what girls and boys are like. As we already reported, Powlishta (1995a) found that children have a general tendency to assign positive traits to their own sex and negative traits to the other, regardless of whether the traits are stereotypically male or female, with a few crucial exceptions. The exceptions (i.e., those few traits that boys and girls agree are definitely masculine or definitely feminine) are highly suggestive of boys' greater power. Out of 48 traits rated, both boys and girls (ages 8 to 10) agreed in their feminine–masculine ratings of 13 traits. Of these traits, 6 were classified neutrally, leaving only 7 that were consensually classified as masculine or feminine: "crude," "loud," and "fights," were agreed to be masculine traits, whereas "shy," "steady," "dependent," and "sorry for self" were classified as feminine by both boys and girls. Clearly these traits are strongly suggestive of male power and female submissiveness. Children's agreement on the masculinity and femininity of these traits suggests that they recognize power-related differences between the sexes. Perhaps girls' tendency to exhibit stronger prejudice toward boys than boys do toward girls (Powlishta et al., 1994; Yee & Brown, 1994; Zalk & Katz, 1978) is a reflection of this power gap. If boys typically get their way in cross-sex interactions, they may view girls as inferior but not feel particularly resentful toward them. Girls, on the other hand, may experience a childhood version of the resentment of male power that Glick and Fiske (1999a) found to be one of the components of women's hostility toward men.

In summary, childhood is marked by hostile emotions, beliefs, and behaviors that anticipate hostile forms of gender prejudice that the ASI and AMI tap in adults. *Competitive gender differentiation* is strongly evident in both boys' and girls' attitudes toward the other sex and is perhaps the most important single motivation in explaining gender prejudice in childhood. An additional factor is the power difference that seems to favor boys, anticipating the *dominative paternalism* of adult men. Girls' dislike of this power difference anticipates the *resentment of paternalism* that is one component of women's hostility toward men. The final factor suggested by the ambivalent sexism approach is heterosexuality. Although heterosexual romantic impulses may affect children before puberty, this dimension of male–female relations is undoubtedly of considerably less importance before pubescence. In any event, studies of heterosexual romantic beliefs, emotions, and behavior among younger children are rare. Some authors (Maccoby,

1990; Thorne, 1997), however, noted that young children actively inhibit expression of heterosexual affection through teasing (e.g., that cross-sex interaction gives one "cooties"), which is entirely in keeping with the overall hostility of childhood gender prejudice. This situation changes radically at the onset of puberty, with profound consequences for the nature of gender prejudice among adolescents and adults. It is to this crucial adolescent transition that we now turn.

## ADOLESCENCE:
## BENEVOLENCE AS WELL AS HOSTILITY

The gender-segregated, hostile, and competitive intergroup relations of boys and girls are turned topsy-turvy by the powerful new form of interdependence that budding sexuality creates. Younger children are well aware that sexual interdependence will, at some point, change how they interact. Maccoby (1988) noted that young boys and girls "are intensely aware of one another as future romantic partners, but they appear to be following a pattern of avoidance of sexuality—one that is monitored through the vigilance and teasing of other children" (p. 756). This behavior fits well with our perspective on the development of gender relations. Children's awareness of gender constancy and the fact that they, one day, will be adult men and women relating in adult ways poses a challenge to their more purely hostile attitudes about the other sex. One way boys and girls deal with this knowledge is to tease each other about heterosexual attraction. This not only defuses the situation by turning sexuality and romance into a joke, but redefines sexually tinged interactions as being hostile, not affectionate. For example, chasing with the threat to kiss the target if captured (a common form of sexual teasing) may be seen as a hostile competition with winners and losers; and kissing is defined as a form of punishment for losing, rather than a consequence of attraction. This borderwork reinforces segregation and gender differentiation as children avoid cross-sex friendships, or at least do not publicly acknowledge them, for fear of being teased (Best, 1983; Maccoby, 1988; Thorne, 1997). Furthermore, when boys permit girls who are typed as tomboys to join their activities, any tinge of sexuality in these relationships is denied as such girls are defined as "buddies" and "one can't be a 'buddy' and 'goin' with' [a girl] at the same time" (Thorne, 1997, p. 195).

During adolescence, however, sexual attraction can no longer be denied. Cross-sex interactions and friendships increase (Petersen, Leffert, & Graham, 1995), though friendships still tend mainly to be with same-sex peers (Bukowski et al., 1993; Maccoby, 1990). How does this new form of dependency affect attitudes toward the other sex? In particular, how do heterosexual adolescents reconcile their formerly hostile group relations with this newfound dependence on members of the other sex? Research on ambivalent sexism suggests that the hostile prejudice of childhood does not simply disappear but becomes melded with new intergroup attitudes that promote some degree of benevolence, at least on the part of boys toward girls. Despite the conflict in the valence of hostile and benevolent sexist attitudes about the other sex, these attitudes (as measured by the ASI and the AMI) are positively correlated among adolescents, presumably because both represent conventional gender attitudes (Glick & Fiske, 1996, 1999a). Because benevolently sexist attitudes may often be viewed as more socially desirable than hostile gender attitudes (indeed, Kilianski & Rudman, 1998, found that college-aged women liked a man described as being a benevolent sexist), these highly traditional attitudes may serve to entrench gender roles more effectively (and, not coincidentally, more insidiously) than do their hostile counterparts.

The effects of sexual interdependency on gender attitudes and behavior are, of course, most evident in dating. It is here that benevolent sexism (in attitudes concerning power, gender differentiation, and sexuality) most clearly comes into play and its behavioral manifestations are most easily seen. Research on dating scripts reveals that adolescents today remain very traditional in their conceptions of appropriate dating behavior (Rose & Frieze, 1989, 1993). Benevolently sexist "courtly" or chivalrous male behavior (e.g., opening doors) has not gone out of style. In addition, Rose and Frieze (1993) found that both ideal and actual dating scripts cast boys in an active role, as initiators and planners of the date and of sexual behavior, whereas girls are expected to react and to serve as gatekeepers for sex. These roles reflect a strong degree of gender differentiation and of power difference between the groups.

The ASI, which was developed with participants in the later stages of adolescence (college undergraduates), shows clear evidence of benevolent sexism in men's attitudes toward women. Glick and Fiske (1996) found that although college men endorse hostile sexism items (concerning women as targets) at a significantly higher rate than do women, they endorse benevolently sexist beliefs about women at a similarly high rate, suggesting a sea change in male attitudes toward women, from the purely hostile attitudes of childhood to an ambivalent stance that includes both hostile and benevolent sexism.

The AMI, which taps attitudes toward men, suggests that adolescent female college students, at least, do not become particularly benevolent toward men. Female, as compared to male, respondents score significantly higher on hostility and significantly lower on benevolence toward men (Glick & Fiske, 1999a). The lack of benevolence toward men is striking, with women in both community and college-student samples showing a strong unwillingness to endorse these items (e.g., that women need romantic relationships with men to be happy).

Findings from the AMI and the ASI are consistent with research by Eagly and Mladinic (1994) on the evaluative content of stereotypes about men and women. The stereotypes admitted by college undergraduates differentiate men and women, but contrary to the claim that such stereotypes evaluate women less favorably, Eagly and Mladinic find that stereotypes of women are significantly more favorable than stereotypes about men. The content of these stereotypes is instructive for they suggest that men are viewed less favorably because they are attributed negative (as well as positive) traits associated with power, such as being arrogant, egotistical, and dictatorial. In contrast, both men and women associate low-power, but highly likable, traits with women, such as helpfulness, sensitivity to others, and nurturance.

As in childhood, then, gender differentiation remains strong and the content of stereotypically male and female traits reflects men's greater power. The difference between childhood and adolescence is that adolescent boys (as well as girls) come to evaluate many stereotypically feminine traits highly favorably. This makes sense as boys are likely to have more satisfying social and romantic relationships with girls who possess feminine traits, such as warmth. In contrast, although stereotypically masculine traits prepare boys well for competition in school, at sports, and (later) on the job, these high power traits do not necessarily promote more satisfying heterosexual social and romantic relationships for girls when interacting with boys. Thus, the gendered interaction styles that were honed and reinforced in same-sex peer interactions in childhood suit women later to be more satisfying romantic partners for men (because of their social sensitivity) but help to ensure that men will be less satisfying romantic partners for women (because of their more competitive, dominance-oriented styles). In childhood, girls are able to solve the problem of boys' greater power by simply avoiding them. Once boys and girls begin to form romantic relationships in adolescence, however, their differing styles now have important consequences for cross-sex interactions.

Maccoby (1990) already suggested that cross-sex relationships tend to be less satisfying for girls who find they exercise less power than boys. We believe that this power difference may explain why college and adult women (in samples studied by Glick & Fiske, 1996, 1999a) show little benevolence toward men, whereas college and adult men (who experience the benefits of women's kinder, gentler social styles) exhibit a strong benevolence toward women. This may also be part of the reason why adolescence seems to be more stressful for girls, who are more likely to experience lower or decreasing self-esteem compared to adolescent boys (Chubb, Fertman, & Ross, 1997; Zimmerman, Copeland, Shope, & Dielman, 1997). Girls at this age realize that relationships with boys are (normatively speaking) supposed to be important, but they find themselves experiencing low power in these relationships. Further, their appearance increases in importance (in large part because of the value that boys place on girls' looks), which may create self-consciousness and anxiety (and contribute to the virtual epidemic of eating disorders among adolescent girls).

These pressures and the lower power position girls find themselves in when interacting with boys may foster a resentment among adolescent girls of their new interdependence with the other sex. Although we have argued that adolescent boys in some senses have it easier in their interactions with girls (leading them to feel benevolence toward the "fairer" sex), boys' former hostility does not disappear either but may be redirected toward those girls with whom they do not have satisfying relations. Glick et al. (1997) demonstrated that hostile sexism in college men is aimed at subtypes of women who are perceived not to possess stereotypically feminine traits (e.g., career women). These women are still viewed as competitors (e.g., for grades and, later, for jobs). Furthermore, adolescent boys' dependence on girls as romantic objects does lend girls a certain kind of power, that of being the gatekeeper to sexual intimacy (Rose & Frieze, 1993). Some of the items on the ASI hostile sexism scale (which cast women as sexual teases or as seeking to control men in romantic relationships) suggest that at least some men resent the power that accrues to women as a result of men's sexual dependence.

It is important to note here that ambivalent attitudes about the other sex and the tendency to classify gender groups into subtypes represent more complex, but not necessarily less prejudiced, attitudes toward the other sex. Although increasing attention has been paid to resolving the contradictory evidence concerning whether adolescence results in more or less flexibility in gender stereotyping (Alfieri, Ruble, & Higgins, 1996; Powlishta et al., 1994),[3] researchers have implicitly agreed on a questionable assumption— that greater flexibility in stereotypes indicates a reduction in gender prejudice. Our approach suggests that this is not necessarily correct. For example, placing women into subgroups that fulfill versus defy conventional roles and evaluating the former positively and the latter negatively is certainly more complex than disliking all girls, but in our view this "flexibility" is no less an example of prejudice. Indeed, such subtyping of and ambivalence toward women may be more effective in ensuring their continuing disadvantage in status and power.

---

[3]One resolution that has been suggested is that the age and flexibility relation is U-shaped (Alfieri et al., 1996), reflecting a developmental transition of the sort described by Ruble's (1994) phase model of transitions.

Benevolent sexist attitudes reward women for embracing conventional gender roles and behaving with deference toward men (Glick et al., 1997). The fear of losing these rewards and of being unattractive to men, coupled with the knowledge that competing directly with men often elicits hostile sexism, is an insidious combination that is likely to be more effective in keeping women "in their place" than would purely hostile attitudes (see Jackman, 1994). Even in our more egalitarian times when hostile forms of sexism are often decried, both women and men punish women who act in an overtly self-assertive manner, thus violating the prescription that women ought to be nice and accommodating (Rudman, 1998).

Similarly, changes in affective reactions or overall evaluations of the other sex (e.g., Powlishta et al., 1994) do not necessarily indicate prejudice reduction but may instead reflect a more nuanced, ambivalent form of prejudice. Increased flexibility in attitudes about violations of gender prescriptions (Galambos, Almeida, & Petersen, 1990; Levy, Taylor, & Gelman, 1995) seem more to the point in assessing whether there is a reduction of prejudice during adolescence. Unfortunately, although there is some evidence of a greater tolerance for such deviations, developmental researchers must consider social psychologists' findings that social desirability concerns may lead adolescents and adults to mask their prejudices when filling out self-report measures. As early as 1954, Allport suggested the possibility that an apparent decline in the endorsement of ethnic stereotypes from the 1930s to the 1950s might be due to a change in attitudes toward the social appropriateness of expressing open bigotry. There is strong evidence that people are loath to admit their prejudices (e.g., Gaertner & Dovidio, 1986; Swim et al., 1995). Young children may be less affected by or concerned with norms of at least pretending to be egalitarian, particularly when it comes to gender relations. Indeed, common observation suggests that children are expected to be sexist in their peer relations and that this is usually shrugged off as normal (for instance, only the most liberal parents are likely to insist that a young boy spend equal time playing with girls or worry that he is a rabid sexist for not wanting to do so). If egalitarian norms only begin to become important during adolescence, a decrease in sexist attitudes may be due at least in part to social desirability concerns (Brown, 1995; see also Aboud, 1988, for a similar view concerning ethnic prejudice).

Even when egalitarian norms are genuinely embraced, they are more likely to reduce the overt hostility boys express toward girls than the reverse. Because men are the dominant social group, negative attitudes toward them are not as likely to be classified as a form of prejudice or to be viewed as antiegalitarian. This too may help to account for the more consistently hostile attitudes of women toward men, untempered by the kind of benevolence evident in men's attitudes toward women. For men, benevolent sexism may serve as a more subtle and socially acceptable form of prejudice against women; even though benevolent sexism is antiegalitarian, it is often perceived simply as a form of niceness (Kilianski & Rudman, 1998).

In summary, the interdependence on the other sex that adolescent sexuality brings creates more paternalistic, benevolent attitudes on the part of men toward women. This benevolence, however, coexists with hostile, competitive attitudes and does not currently seem to be reciprocated fully by women toward men, perhaps because women continue to find themselves at a disadvantage in cross-sex relationships at a time when such relationships suddenly gain in importance. This disadvantage is caused by differences in male and female interaction styles that become ingrained during early childhood when cross-sex interactions are typically avoided—boys develop a direct, high-power style, whereas girls acquire a more indirect, polite style that works well with other girls but gives them less power in cross-sex interactions. Adolescent gender prejudice is further complicated by the tendency to use gender subtypes rather than a simple dichotomy in gender classification and by at least outward adherence to egalitarian norms. These changes during adolescence suggest increased complexity in gender-related attitudes; such complexity, however, does not necessarily mean a reduction in prejudice but rather a change in how it is manifested.

# ADULTHOOD: WORK, LOVE, AND AMBIVALENCE

The ambivalence and complexity of adolescent gender relations continues into adulthood. In this section we concentrate on how gender prejudice creates adult social realities that, in turn, institutionalize and perpetuate gender prejudice. Adult life, for many people, is dominated by work and marriage, both of which are greatly affected by and, in turn, help to shape gender-related attitudes. These adult institutions have long accommodated the ambivalence inherent in gender relations. To some extent, work outside the home has been a domain where the sexes have remained segregated (echoing the segregation of childhood peer interactions), whereas heterosexual intimacy has been compartmentalized within marriage. Although women have increasingly entered the paid workforce in many industrialized countries in recent years, they still tend to be segregated into occupational roles different from men's. Thus, the domains of work and marriage still roughly correspond to the two modes of prejudice: hostile (or at least competitive) and segregated in the work domain, benevolent and intimate within marriage. Although gender-related attitudes may become more complex with increasing adult experience, ambivalence on the part of each sex is maintained in adulthood as gender differences become *institutionalized* through work and marriage; sex differences in interaction styles are transformed in adulthood into differences in structural power and roles, which create social realities that reinforce and perpetuate gender-based prejudices.

In many countries, although women have increasingly been employed in jobs that were previously dominated by men, many occupations still remain highly sex segregated, in part because of continuing discrimination against women who seek employment in male-dominated jobs (Pratto, Stallworth, Sidanius, & Siers, 1997). Furthermore, women who do manage to enter male-dominated occupations may elicit hostile or competitive responses (including sexual harassment, see Fiske & Glick, 1995) from at least some men who view these women as invading their domain and competing for resources that properly belong to men. Sex segregation is also driven, however, by self-selection, as young adult men and women tend to be attracted to different kinds of jobs that match the gendered interaction styles each sex develops during childhood (Pratto et al., 1997). The preference of boys for competitions and dominance-hierarchies is reflected in the occupation choices of adult men. College men score higher on social dominance orientation (a preference for hierarchy) and also gravitate toward hierarchy-enhancing occupations—careers (e.g., in law and business) that reinforce current social hierarchies and the position of social groups (e.g., men and women, Whites and minorities) within them by keeping valued resources in the hands of those who traditionally have held power (Pratto et al., 1997; Sidanius et al., 1994). In contrast, the "linking," rather than "ranking" style evident in young girls (i.e., their preference to minimize hierarchy and to foster sympathetic connections with others), remains evident in young adult women's career preferences for hierarchy-attenuating occupations—jobs (e.g., in social services, health care, and education) that funnel resources downward to traditionally disadvantaged groups (Pratto et al., 1997).

As a result, men still tend to be overrepresented in occupations that restrict access to resources, as well as those that are highest in salary (Pratto et al., 1997). The "glass-ceiling" remains a problem as men compete strenuously for the most powerful and highest paid positions, making it difficult for women to gain access to these jobs. In short, occupational self-selection coupled with continuing discrimination helps to maintain a social structure in which men have more economic, governmental, and social power. This not only encourages the continuation of the hostile mode of prejudice to justify these differences, but also serves to institutionalize sex-based power differences and gender differentiation. Men come to be defined, stereotypically, by the traits, both positive (e.g., independent) and negative (e.g., arrogant), associated with powerful occupations; women, in contrast, are stereotyped as having traits, both positive (e.g., nurturant) and negative (e.g., subordinate), associated with a lack of power and with most female-dominated jobs (Cejka & Eagly, 1999; Eagly, 1987).[4] The reality of occupational segregation is accurately perceived by children at a relatively early age, affecting their occupational aspirations, which are strongly sex typed and tend to remain so even in adolescence (Gottfredson, 1984). The perception of occupational sex segregation also presumably reinforces the importance of gender as a social category in children's minds and encourages them to adopt gender stereotypes (Bigler, 1999).

At the same time, attitudes about men's and women's roles have become increasingly egalitarian in the United States (Spence & Buckner, in press; Twenge, 1997) and probably in many other Western nations over the past few decades as feminists have argued for equal rights and women have increasingly moved into the paid workforce. Although attitudes have no doubt become more sincerely egalitarian than before, hostile prejudice toward women has by no means disappeared. Feminist protest and women's movement into paid work have, for some, increased the sense of competition between women and men and fueled a backlash against women that emerges in antifeminist attitudes and hostility toward career-oriented women—both of which are predicted by scores on the hostile sexism scale (Glick et al., 1997; Glick & Fiske, 1996). Furthermore, men's sexist attitudes may become covert and masquerade as a form of egalitarianism in order to avoid the charge of being sexist. Swim et al.'s (1995) Modern Sexism Scale and Tougas, Brown, Beaton, and Joly's (1995) Neosexism Scale tap political attitudes that deny that women are currently discriminated against as a way of justifying hostile attitudes toward feminism and affirmative action. That these attitudes are not motivated by true egalitarianism, however, is revealed by their correlation with old-fashioned forms of sexism (Swim & Cohen, 1997).

How women's attitudes toward men have changed over these same decades has not been systematically studied, but we speculate that because women have increasingly taken on paid work to increase family incomes, whereas men have failed to share the burden of housekeeping and childrearing in an equitable manner (Biernat & Wortman, 1991), women's hostility toward men has been heightened. Increased interaction with men at work has also resulted in greater attention to the problem of sexual harassment, which may also fuel women's hostility toward men. Heterosexual attraction in the workplace, its permissibility and potential as a

---

[4]These stereotypes are supplemented by a variety of subtypes, such as the career woman who excels in a male-dominated occupation, that take account of the growing number of exceptions to the general rule. These subtypes reflect the sophistication and flexibility of adult minds and the manner in which stereotypes respond to experience. Nevertheless, the overall stereotypes of men and women remain strikingly intact today, in part because of the continuing segregation of "men's" and "women's" jobs.

form of harassment, has been one of the most divisive, difficult, and unresolved aspects of gender relations on the job.

Although sexuality can be a source of hostility toward the other sex for both women and men, it is also the source of their interdependence and emotional attachments. Traditionally, heterosexual intimacy has been institutionalized through marriage. Adult men's reliance on women for sexual gratification often expands to include dependence on women to fulfill the more generalized roles of wife and mother. Because of these dependencies, benevolent sexist attitudes (of protection, chivalry, adoration) on the part of men toward women continue in adulthood (Glick & Fiske, 1996). This male dependence on women, Glick and Fiske (1999b) argued, is why stereotypes about women are still *prescriptive* (specifying how women ought to be), not merely *descriptive* (describing what women are like). Although in many parts of the world beliefs about marriage have become increasingly egalitarian, the demands of childrearing and difference in men's and women's earnings outside the home often foster role divisions among couples. Wives who work full-time are still likely to do the bulk of the child care and housework, particularly when the husband earns relatively more money (Biernat & Wortman, 1991; Blair & Lichter, 1991). The greater money and power that men typically have outside the home translates to power within the marriage. Thus, as with work, marriage roles often reinforce power differences and gender differentiation.

In summary, although attitudes of adults toward members of the other sex may become increasingly more complex and less rigidly stereotypical (as they do from childhood to adolescence), adult choices about how to structure one's life—at work and in marriage—nevertheless remain highly gendered. These choices beget social structural facts—a sex-segregated job market in which men dominate the most powerful, high-salaried jobs and role divisions in marriage—that reinforce gender differentiation and power differences between men and women. What were once merely differences in interaction styles between boys and girls become structural differences in the social positions of men and women. These differences are one reason why gender-related attitudes are so resistant to change: Gender-related attitudes exaggerate, but also reflect (and help to reinforce), social realities.

## IMPLICATIONS FOR PREJUDICE REDUCTION

Our primary aim has been to provide an analytical framework for understanding the development of gender prejudice. Here we can do no more than merely sketch out (presuming that the framework outlined thus far is roughly correct) some general suggestions for thinking about prejudice-reduction efforts. In doing so, we are guided by not only the model presented here, but also Ruble's (1994) concept of social transitions—periods of increased flexibility when new concepts are being formed and may be most plastic and open to influence before attitudes are consolidated. It is during such transitions that interventions may most effectively be targeted. Two gender transitions may be particularly important: (a) the initial realization of gender as an important social category (beginning around 2½ years of age), before the development of gender constancy; and (b) the transition that begins around the time of puberty from simple childhood hostility to complex and ambivalent forms of gender prejudice. In suggesting potential interventions, we are guided by the pragmatic realization that most such efforts are likely to be made in day-care facilities and schools. Happily, these institutions are where much of children's and adolescents' interactions take place and therefore have the potential to be the sites of effective interventions.

The most important implication of our perspective for combating childhood gender prejudice is that interventions are likely to be ineffective unless they address the social-identity concerns that drive childhood sexism. The common approach of attacking gender stereotypes (e.g., stressing that "girls can be firefighters" and "boys can do housework") is unlikely to reduce gender-segregated behavior on the playground or hostility between the sexes because childhood gender prejudice is not caused by stereotypes so much as by simple group identification. Further, in the face of a contradictory social reality, such as children's observation that many occupations are indeed dominated by one sex, children are likely to trust their experiences more than their teachers (Bigler, 1999). Instead, interventions that directly reduce the salience or utility of gender as a category may be more effective (Bigler, 1999). Such techniques as the "jigsaw classroom" in which mixed-sex and mixed-ethnicity cooperative groups are created can promote positive cross-group interactions that can reduce hostility (Aronson, Stephan, Sikes, Blaney, & Snapp, 1978) and have generally been shown to be effective in reducing prejudice. But as gender prejudice also stems from stylistic differences in how boys and girls interact with peers, it may be important to go further and enforce norms of behavior that reduce this sex difference. Girls could be trained to be more interpersonally assertive when interacting with boys by showing them effective techniques to negotiate with boys rather than withdraw from them. Boys, in contrast, could be rewarded for behaving in less competitive ways when interacting with peers, though we suspect that it would be difficult indeed to inhibit completely their preference for competition and dominance hierarchies.

During adolescence, prejudice-reduction efforts must be informed by the complexity of adolescent gender prejudices and the new sexualized domain of cross-sex interaction. Once again, interventions may need to address sex differences in interaction style, as increased cross-sex interaction due to dating tends to slip into norms of male dominance and female passivity. Assertiveness training, or encouraging participation in activities that tend to encourage assertiveness, may help young women to deal more effectively with the other sex. School instruction classes that deal with issues of sexuality could be used critically to examine dating norms, which tend to reinforce male dominance through a benevolent sexism that may appear to be "romantic" to adolescents, but which insidiously perpetuates gender inequality. Discussions of dating scripts—where they come from and what effects they have—may be highly engaging to adolescents and may reduce unthinking adherence to these norms. In addition to addressing intimate relationships, the influence of sexist cultural norms on occupational aspirations could be addressed and counteracted by school counselors. Gottfredson (1984) found that young children eliminate whole occupational areas early on because they are associated with the other sex, subsequently failing to reconsider them seriously in adolescence when realistic job aspirations begin to be formed. School counselors, perhaps with the aid of interest inventories, might help children to reconsider occupations they may have summarily dismissed. Changing the occupational aspirations of adolescents and young adults is critical to lessening sex segregation in the workforce, which is a primary source of gender stereotypes (Eagly, 1987) and of male structural power in industrialized societies.

## CONCLUSION

We have conceptualized gender prejudice as developing from a simple form of childhood hostility exhibited by both boys and girls toward the other sex to a complex and ambivalent set of adult attitudes that combine, particularly for men, both hostile and benevolent forms of prejudice toward the other sex. We have attempted to piece together evidence from developmental and social psychology to support this model, but it remains a speculative one. Our aim has been to provide a way of viewing the development of gender prejudice that may guide researchers to fill the empirical gaps that have resulted from the compartmentalization of social and developmental research on gender relations. Although much is known about gender segregation and sex stereotypes in young children, relatively little is known about the transition in gender prejudice that occurs between childhood and adolescence. Our model suggests that future research would do well to focus on this transition to see how boys and girls reconcile their newfound interests in the other sex as potential romantic partners with their by then well-developed tendencies to segregate, compete with, tease, and disparage the other sex as a group. This transition may form a significant part of the well-documented difficulties experienced by adolescents, particularly for girls who may find it no longer desirable to avoid boys, but who may also experience a more radical shift in their identities as they begin to be treated as sexual objects. If our model is correct, understanding how gender-related attitudes change during adolescence is the key to fathoming how childhood hostility turns into adult ambivalence about the other sex.

# REFERENCES

Aboud, F. (1988). *Children and prejudice*. Oxford, England: Blackwell.

Alfieri, T., Ruble, D. N., & Higgins, E. T. (1996). Gender stereotypes during adolescence: Developmental changes and the transition to junior high school. *Developmental Psychology, 32*, 1129–1137.

Allport, G. W. (1954). *The nature of prejudice*. Reading, MA: Addison-Wesley.

Aronson, E., Stephan, C., Sikes, J., Blaney, N., & Snapp, M. (1978). *The jigsaw classroom*. London: Sage.

Ashmore, R. D., Del Boca, F. K., & Bilder, S. M. (1995). Construction and validation of the Gender Attitude Inventory, a structured inventory to assess multiple dimensions of gender attitudes. *Sex Roles, 32*, 753–785.

Ashmore, R. D., Del Boca, F. K., & Titus, D. (1984, August). *Types of women and men: Yours, mine, and ours*. Paper presented at the American Psychological Association Convention, Toronto, Ontario, Canada.

Banaji, M. R., & Hardin, C. (1996). Automatic stereotyping. *Psychological Science, 7*, 136–141.

Beere, C. A. (1990). *Gender roles: A handbook of tests and measures*. New York: Greenwood.

Bem, S. L. (1989). Genital knowledge and gender constancy in preschool children. *Child Development, 60*, 649–662.

Best, R. (1983). *We've all got scars: What boys and girls learn in elementary schools*. Bloomington, IN: University Press.

Biernat, M., & Wortman, C. B. (1991). Sharing of home responsibilities between professionally employed women and their husbands. *Journal of Personality and Social Psychology, 60*, 844–860.

Bigler, R. S. (1997). Conceptual and methodological issues in the measurement of children's sex typing. *Psychology of Women Quarterly, 21*, 53–69.

Bigler, R. S. (1999). Psychological interventions designed to counter sexism in children: Empirical limitations and theoretical foundations. In W. B. Swann, Jr., J. H. Langlois, & L. A. Gilbert (Eds.), *Sexism and stereotypes in modern society: The gender science of Janet Taylor Spence* (pp. 129–151). Washington, DC: American Psychological Association.

Bigler, R. S., Jones, L. C., & Lobliner, D. B. (1997). Social categorization and the formation of intergroup attitudes in children. *Child Development, 68*, 530–543.

Blair, S. L., & Lichter, D. T. (1991). Measuring the division of household labor: Gender segregation of housework among American couples. *Journal of Family Issues, 12*, 91–113.

Brown, R. (1995). *Prejudice: Its social psychology*. Oxford, England: Blackwell.

Bukowski, W. M., Gauze, C., Hoza, B., & Newcomb, A. F. (1993). Differences and consistency between same-sex and other-sex peer relationships during early adolescence. *Developmental Psychology, 29*, 255–263.

Cejka, M. A., & Eagly, A. H. (1999). Gender-stereotypic images of occupations correspond to the sex segregation of employment. *Personality and Social Psychology Bulletin, 25*, 413–423.

Chubb, N. H., Fertman, C. I., & Ross, J. L. (1997). Adolescent self-esteem and locus of control: A longitudinal study of gender and age differences. *Adolescence, 32*, 113–129.

Eagly, A. H. (1987). *Sex differences in social behavior: A social-role interpretation.* Hillsdale, NJ: Lawrence Erlbaum Associates.

Eagly, A. H., & Chaiken, S. (1993). *The psychology of attitudes.* Fort Worth, TX: Harcourt Brace Jovanovich.

Eagly, A. H., & Mladinic, A. (1994). Are people prejudiced against women? Some answers from research on attitudes, gender stereotypes, and judgments of competence. In W. Stroebe & M. Hewstone (Eds.), *European review of social psychology* (Vol. 5, pp. 1–35). New York: Wiley.

Fagot, B. I., & Leinbach, M. D. (1993). Gender-role development in young children: From discrimination to labeling. *Developmental Review, 13*, 205–224.

Fiske, S. T., & Glick, P. (1995). Ambivalence and stereotypes cause sexual harassment: A theory with implications for organizational change. *Journal of Social Issues, 51*(1), 97–115.

Gaertner, S. L., & Dovidio, J. F. (1986). The aversive form of racism. In J. F. Dovidio and S. L. Gaertner (Eds.), *Prejudice, discrimination, and racism* (pp. 61–89). Orlando, FL: Academic Press.

Galambos, N. L., Almeida, D. M., & Petersen, A. C. (1990). Masculinity, femininity, and sex role attitudes in early adolescence: Exploring gender intensification. *Child Development, 61*, 1905–1914.

Glick, P., Diebold, J., Bailey-Werner, B., & Zhu, L. (1997). The two faces of Adam: Ambivalent sexism and polarized attitudes toward women. *Personality and Social Psychology Bulletin, 23*, 1323–1334.

Glick, P., & Fiske, S. T. (1996). The Ambivalent Sexism Inventory: Differentiating hostile and benevolent sexism. *Journal of Personality and Social Psychology, 70*, 491–512.

Glick, P., & Fiske, S. T. (1999a). The Ambivalence toward Men Inventory: Differentiating hostile and benevolent beliefs about men. *Psychology of Women Quarterly, 23*, 519–536.

Glick, P., & Fiske, S. T. (1999b). Sexism and other "isms": Interdependence, status, and the ambivalent content of stereotypes. In W. B. Swann, Jr., J. H. Langlois, & L. A. Gilbert (Eds.), *Sexism and stereotypes in modern society: The gender science of Janet Taylor Spence* (pp. 193–221). Washington, DC: American Psychological Association.

Glick, P., & Fiske, S. T. (in press). Ambivalent stereotypes as legitimizing ideologies: Differentiating paternalistic and envious prejudice. In J. T. Jost & B. Major (Eds.), *The psychology of legitimacy: Emerging perspectives on ideology, justice, and intergroup relations.* New York: Cambridge University Press.

Gottfredson, L. S. (1984). Circumscription and compromise: A developmental theory of occupational aspirations. *Journal of Counseling Psychology Monograph, 28*, 545–579.

Guttentag, M., & Secord, P. F. (1983). *Too many women? The sex ratio question.* Beverly Hills, CA: Sage.

Hayden-Thompson, L., Rubin, K. H., & Hymel, S. (1987). Sex preferences in sociometric choices. *Developmental Psychology, 23*, 558–562.

Jackman, M. R. (1994). *The velvet glove: Paternalism and conflict in gender, class, and race relations.* Berkeley: University of California Press.

Kilianski, S. E., & Rudman, L. A. (1998). Wanting it both ways: Do women approve of benevolent sexism? *Sex Roles, 39*, 333–352.

Levy, G. D., Taylor, M. G., & Gelman, S. A. (1995). Traditional and evaluative aspects of flexibility in gender roles, social conventions, moral rules, and physical laws. *Child Development, 66*, 515–531.

Lott, B. (1995). Distancing from women: Interpersonal sexist discrimination. In B. Lott & D. Maluso (Eds.), *The social psychology of interpersonal discrimination* (pp. 12–49). New York: Guilford.

Lutz, S. E., & Ruble, D. N. (1995). Children and gender prejudice: Context, motivation, and the development of gender conceptions. *Annals of Child Development, 10*, 131–166.

Maccoby, E. E. (1988). Gender as a social category. *Developmental Psychology, 24*, 755–765.

Maccoby, E. E. (1990). Gender and relationships: A developmental account. *American Psychologist, 45*, 513–520.

Maccoby, E. E., & Jacklin, C. N. (1987). Gender segregation in childhood. In E. H. Reese (Ed.), *Advances in child development and behavior* (Vol. 20, pp. 239–287). New York: Academic Press.

Miller, C. L. (1983). Developmental changes in male/female voice classification by infants. *Infant Behavior and Development, 6*, 313–330.

Oakes, P. J., & Turner, J. C. (1980). Social categorization and intergroup behaviour: Does minimal intergroup discrimination make social identity more positive? *European Journal of Social Psychology, 10*, 295–302.

Petersen, A. C., Leffert, N., & Graham, B. L. (1995). Adolescent development and the emergence of sexuality. *Suicide and Life-Threatening Behavior, 25*, 4–17.

Powlishta, K. K. (1987, April). *The social context of cross-sex interactions.* Paper presented at the biennial meetings of the Society for Research in Child Development, Baltimore.

Powlishta, K. K. (1995a). Gender bias in children's perceptions of personality traits. *Sex Roles, 32*, 17–28.

Powlishta, K. K. (1995b). Intergroup processes in childhood: Social categorization and sex role development. *Developmental Psychology, 31*, 781–788.

Powlishta, K. K., Serbin, L. A., Doyle, A. B., & White, D. R. (1994). Gender, ethnic, and body type biases: The generality of prejudice in childhood. *Developmental Psychology, 30*, 526–536.

Pratto, F., Stallworth, L. M., Sidanius, J., & Siers, B. (1997). The gender gap in occupational role attainment: A social dominance approach. *Journal of Personality and Social Psychology, 72*, 37–53.

Rose, S., & Frieze, I. H. (1989). Young singles' scripts for a first date. *Gender and Society, 3*, 258–268.

Rose, S., & Frieze, I. H. (1993). Young singles' contemporary dating scripts. *Sex Roles, 28*, 499–509.

Ruble, D. N. (1994). A phase model of transitions: Cognitive and motivational consequences. In M. P. Zanna (Ed.), *Advances in experimental social psychology* (Vol. 26, pp. 163–214). San Diego, CA: Academic Press.

Rudman, L. A. (1998). Self-promotion as a risk factor for women: The costs and benefits of counterstereotypical impression management. *Journal of Personality and Social Psychology, 74*, 629–645.

Serbin, L. A., Sprafkin, C., Elman, M., & Doyle, A. B. (1984). The early development of sex differentiated patterns and social influence. *Canadian Journal of Social Science, 14*, 350–363.

Sidanius, J., Pratto, F., & Bobo, L. (1994). Social dominance orientation and the political psychology of gender: A case of invariance? *Journal of Personality and Social Psychology, 67*, 998–1011.

Six, B., & Eckes, T. (1991). A closer look at the complex structure of gender stereotypes. *Sex Roles, 24*, 57–71.

Smith, E. R. (1993). Social identity and social emotions: Toward a new conceptualization of prejudice. In D. M. Mackie & D. L. Hamilton (Eds.), *Affect, cognition, and stereotyping: Interactive processes in group perceptions* (pp. 297–316). San Diego, CA: Academic Press.

Spence, J. T. (1993). Gender-related traits and gender ideology: Evidence for a multifactor theory. *Journal of Personality and Social Psychology, 64*, 624–635.

Spence, J. T., & Buckner, C. E. (in press). Instrumental and expressive traits, trait stereotypes, and sexist attitudes: What do they signify? *Psychology of Women Quarterly.*

Swim, J. K., Aikin, K. J., Hall, W. S., & Hunter, B. A. (1995). Sexism and racism: Old-fashioned and modern prejudices. *Journal of Personality and Social Psychology, 68*, 199–214.

Swim, J. K., & Cohen, L. L. (1997). Overt, covert, and subtle sexism: A comparison between the Attitudes Toward Women and Modern Sexism scales. *Sex Roles, 21*, 103–118.

Tajfel, H. (1981). *Social identity and intergroup relations.* London: Cambridge University Press.

Tajfel, H., & Jahoda, G. (1966). Development in children of concepts about their own and other countries: A cross-national study. *Proceeds XVIII International Congress of Psychology.* Moscow, Symposium 36, 17–33.

Thompson, S. K. (1975). Gender labels and early sex role development. *Child Development, 46*, 339–347.

Thorne, B. (1986). Girls and boys together . . . but mostly apart: Gender arrangements in elementary schools. In W. W. Hartup & Z. Rubin (Eds.), *Relationships and development* (pp. 167–184). Hillsdale, NJ: Lawrence Erlbaum Associates.

Thorne, B. (1997). Children and gender: Constructions of difference. In M. M.Gergen & S. N. Davis (Eds.), *Toward a new psychology of gender: A reader* (pp. 185–201). London: Routledge.

Tougas, F., Brown, R., Beaton, A. M., & Joly, S. (1995). Neosexism: Plus ça change, plus c'est pareil. *Personality and Social Psychology Bulletin, 21*, 842–849.

Twenge, J. M. (1997). Attitudes toward women, 1970–1995: A meta-analysis. *Psychology of Women Quarterly, 21*, 35–51.

Yee, M., & Brown, R. (1994). The development of gender differentiation in young children. *British Journal of Social Psychology, 33*, 183–196.

Zalk, S. R., & Katz, P. A. (1978). Gender attitudes in children. *Sex Roles, 4*, 349–357.

Zimmerman, M. A., Copeland, L. A., Shope, J. T., & Dielman, T. E. (1997). A longitudinal study of self-esteem: Implications for adolescent development. *Journal of Youth and Adolescence, 26*, 117–141.

# 9

# Sexual Scripts and Heterosexual Aggression

## Barbara Krahé
*University of Potsdam*

The ability to engage in satisfying and responsible sexual relationships constitutes a major developmental goal in adolescence. The traditional restriction of sexual relationships to marriage has long become obsolete in most Western countries, and the age at which young people become sexually active has declined continuously (Moore & Rosenthal, 1993). At the same time, the number of sexual partners has increased, as has the range of sexual activities performed by adolescents. In a recent nationwide survey among German adolescents, 60% of all 14-year-old girls and 63% of all 14-year-old boys reported experience of kissing or cuddling a member of the opposite sex. At the age of 17, 65% of the girls and 59% of the boys had experienced sexual intercourse (Bundeszentrale für gesundheitliche Aufklärung [BZgA], 1998).

However, the sexual liberalism which these and many similar findings reflect, has a dark side to it. Evidence from a wide range of studies leaves no doubt about the fact that sexual aggression is a prevalent feature of adolescent dating relationships (e.g., Craig, 1990; Parrot & Bechhofer, 1991). In a survey of German female adolescents with a mean age of 17.7 years, 12% of the respondents reported experiences of kissing or petting through the use of physical force, 11% indicated that a man had tried to force them to have sexual intercourse by using physical means, and more than 6% reported a completed rape (Krahé, 1998). These findings concur with research from other Western countries showing similar patterns of both consensual and coercive sexual behaviors (see Miller, Christopherson, & King, 1993; Moore & Rosenthal, 1993).

Thus, it is clear that both consensual sexual contacts and the experience of aggression in dating relationships are significant constituents of adolescent sexuality. The present chapter addresses the link between the development of sexual relationships and the problem of heterosexual aggression in adolescence, focusing on the role of sexual scripts, that is, cognitive representations of both consensual and coercive sexual interactions.

The chapter is located at the interface of developmental and social psychology in that it refers to a central *developmental* task, the establishment of satisfactory sexual relationships, from a *sociocognitive* perspective, stressing the role of sexual scripts as guidelines of heterosexual behavior. More specifically, it deals with the way in which stereotypical representations of sexual encounters, shared among members of a given culture and learned by its individual members, pave the ground for unwanted sexual experiences and sexual aggression. *Sexual aggression* is defined here as any behavior involving the use of (verbal) coercion or (physical) force to obtain sexual contacts against the partner's will. Although this definition is open with regard to the sex of both perpetrators and victims, the present analysis will be limited to coercion and force used by men against women as the predominant form of sexual aggression (see, however, Hickson et al., 1994, for sexual aggression among homosexual men, and Struckman-Johnson, 1991, for female sexual aggression toward men).

Psychological research on sexual aggression is concerned to a large extent with explaining why men resort to coercive strategies to achieve their sexual interests (White & Kowalski, 1998). An inspection of the current landscape of theories dealing with this issue reveals three broad types of explanations:

1. Explanations that stress the *evolutionary* origins of sexual aggression as a potentially adaptive reproductive strategy. Rape is conceptualized as an optional, if high-risk, mating strategy when opportunities for reproduction through consensual sexual relationships are limited (Malamuth & Heilmann, 1998; see also Kenrick & Luce, chap. 2, this volume).

2. Explanations that focus on the *sociocultural environment* and locate the causes of sexual aggression in the cultural norms and practices of a given society, such as the availability of pornography and the way in which socially shared gender stereotypes and rape myths affect the definition and evaluation of sexual aggression (e.g., Sanday, 1981).

3. Explanations that focus on the cognitions, emotions, and behaviors of *individual persons* as they develop within a particular cultural framework. This category includes social learning theories, which explain the acquisition of sexually aggressive behaviors; social cognitive theories, which deal with the processing of social information pertinent to sexual aggression; and theories that refer to the affective processes involved in sexual aggression.

The perspective adopted in the present chapter draws upon evidence from the last two categories by examining the relationship between gender stereotypes and sociocognitive learning on the one hand and consensual sexual behavior and sexual aggression on the other. In particular, the focus is on the acquisition of sexual scripts, that is, prototypical representations of sexual interactions and their significance as guidelines for sexual behavior. As far as sexual aggression is concerned, it is argued that the use of aggressive tactics to obtain sexual contacts can be accommodated within a sexual script that reflects a traditional view of male sexuality and gender relationships (Simon & Gagnon, 1986).

## SCRIPTS AS GUIDELINES FOR SEXUAL BEHAVIOR

The general proposition underlying the present analysis is that both consensual sexual activities and sexual aggression are guided to a significant extent by cognitive scripts. Cognitive scripts consist of knowledge structures that describe "appropriate sequences of events in a particular context" (Schank & Abelson, 1977, p. 41). These knowledge structures are acquired through experience with the respective situations, either firsthand or vicariously, through observational learning. In his social cognitive approach, Huesmann (1988, 1998) proposed that social behavior in general, and aggressive behavior in particular, is controlled by behavioral repertoires acquired in the process of early socialization. They are developed into abstract cognitive representations containing characteristic features of the critical situations, expectations about the behavior of the participants involved, and an anticipation of the consequences of different behavioral options. Which script is activated and guides the person's behavior depends on the cognitive processing of the initial social information, which is conceptualized by Huesmann (1998) as a "heuristic search process to retrieve a script that is relevant for the situation" (p. 87). This process is broken down into a complex sequence of interpreting situational information against the background of emotional states associated with the situation, as outlined by Huesmann (1998). In his model, the critical link between scripts and behavioral performance is conceptualized as shown in Fig. 9.1.

The model shows that the implementation of scripts into overt behavior is mediated by normative beliefs that indicate whether or not a specific response is appropriate under the given circumstances. For example, if a child has activated an aggressive script following a provocation, the decision to behave in accordance with the script will be affected by the role relationship with the provoking person. An aggressive response is more likely to be considered appropriate (and subsequently enacted) if the provocation came from a peer than if it came from an adult in a position of authority. In the

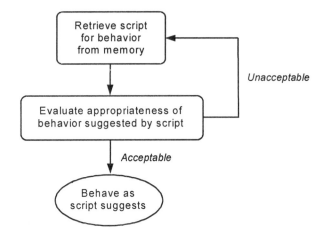

FIG. 9.1  The link between cognitive scripts and behavior. *Note.* From "The Role of Social Information Processing and Cognitive Schema in the Acquisition and Maintenance of Habitual Aggressive Behavior," by L. R. Huesmann, in *Human Aggression* (p. 88), by R. G. Geen and E. Donnerstein (Eds.), 1998, San Diego, CA: Academic Press. Copyright 1998 by Academic Press. Adapted with permission.

latter case, the child is likely to go back to the stage of script retrieval and search for alternative scripts, such as withdrawal or displacement. Failure to learn the normative restrictions imposed on the manifestation of a script will lead to the repeated performance of inappropriate responses, which—particularly in the case of aggression—may form the basis for long-term adjustment problems (Eron, 1987). Thus, scripts may be conceptualized as important cognitive antecedents of social behavior that contain information not only about typical behaviors in a given situation, but also about the normative evaluation of those behaviors.

It is important to stress that sexual scripts are inherently interactional in that they comprise the behaviors and characteristics of both the actor and his or her sexual partner. Scripted representations of the partner and his or her likely feelings and behaviors (e.g., "women like playing hard to get and don't really mean no when they say so") are critically important in the retrieval of scripts pertinent to a given heterosexual encounter as well as to the evaluation of the normative appropriateness of behavioral options suggested by the scripts (e.g., accepting or ignoring a woman's rejection of sexual advances).

As already noted, scripts regulating social behavior are assumed to be acquired through learning processes, first primarily by way of observation and imitation and then through positive reinforcement following the enactment of the observed behavior (Huesmann, 1998). This general proposition has also been applied to the development of scripts regulating sexual behavior (Moore & Rosenthal, 1993; Simon & Gagnon, 1986). Proposing that sexual behavior is shaped to a significant extent by cognitive scripts requires evidence that there is, indeed, a consensus within a particular cultural community as to the typical behavior of participants in a sexual encounter as well as shared normative beliefs about how these encounters should be conducted. Several studies are available that provide evidence of consensually shared sexual scripts. For example, Rose and Frieze (1989) found a high consensus among young adults as to the typical features of a first date. Respondents of both sexes agreed about a core of features typical of both male and female behavior on a first date. They also agreed about distinctive differences between the man's and the woman's script. The male dating script prescribed an active, initiating role, whereas the female script outlined a reactive, receptive role. In a subsequent study, Rose and Frieze (1993) compared respondents' scripts for a hypothetical date with their descriptions of an actual, self-experienced first date. They found a substantial overlap between the script for a hypothetical first date and the script for a first date from the respondents' personal experience, suggesting that dating behavior is, indeed, largely shaped by scripts. The findings further confirmed the strong impact of gender-specific role prescriptions (proactive male and reactive female) on dating scripts (see also Glick & Hilt, chap. 8, this volume, who analyze the link between traditional gender scripts and hostile as well as benevolent forms of gender prejudice).

## GENDER DIFFERENCES IN SEXUAL SCRIPTS

It is quite clear that heterosexual behavior, perhaps more than any other form of social behavior, is influenced by gender stereotypes assigning differential role behavior to male and female actors. These gender-specific role prescriptions are also part and parcel of socially shared representations, or scripts, of what is appropriate in sexual encounters. Several studies demonstrate that men and women conduct their sexual relationships on the basis of distinctly different scripts (Jackson, 1978).

Byers and Lewis (1988) asked their respondents to keep a dating diary in which they noted disagreements with their partner over the desired level of intimacy. The findings show that the most common form of disagreement is about the male partner desiring a higher level of intimacy than the female partner is prepared to engage in.

Clark and Hatfield (1989) demonstrated that men were much more receptive to sexual offers from a person of the opposite sex than women. When asked by a female confederate if they would go to bed with her that night, 75% of the male respondents in their 1978 study and 69% in their 1982 study agreed. In contrast, none of the female respondents approached by a male confederate with the same request agreed to it. These findings corroborate evidence from a variety of sources, including an extensive meta-analysis by Oliver and Hyde (1993), which show that compared to women, men's sexual behavior is guided to a far greater extent by the casual sex script. This script entails a positive evaluation of sexual intercourse without the requirement of an emotional commitment between the partners (see also Moore & Rosenthal, 1993). As far as the origins of this gender difference in sexual selectivity are concerned, Kenrick and Luce (chap. 2, this volume) offer an evolutionary account that refers to gender differences in parental investment to explain females' greater selectivity in choosing a partner.

Teasing apart gender differences in the perception of "good," "bad," and "typical" dates, Alksnis, Desmarais, and Wood (1996) found that both male and female respondents largely agreed about the typical features of a *good* and a *typical* date, including a high degree of overlap between the features named for both types of date. However, substantial gender differences emerged in the perception of the prototypical *bad* date. Here, women consensually named partner behaviors that were sexually suggestive as characteristic features (e.g., "Your date repeatedly tells you how sexy you look" or "Your date repeatedly touches you"). In contrast, the male respondents' script of sexually suggestive interactions on a bad date contained only one characteristic feature: "Your date rejects your sexual advances."

The evidence on gender differences in sexual scripts is directly relevant to the explanation of sexual violence in terms of gender roles that prescribe male behavior to be assertive and dominant and female behavior to be passive and submissive. According to Burt (1980), "rape is the logical and psychological extension of a dominant-submissive, competitive, sex-role stereotyped culture" (p. 229). In trying to explore the cultural antecedents of sexual aggression, the present analysis shifts the focus from the broad level of cultural scenarios to the more specific level of sexual scripts that translate general gender-role prescriptions into prototypical cognitive representations of sexual interactions. In this context, two lines of evidence are relevant that address the link between gender-role socialization and sexual interactions: (a) research on the miscommunication hypothesis, which claims that men often misunderstand women's nonverbal cues as being more sexually suggestive than they are actually meant to be; and (b) research on the so-called macho personality describing an extreme form of male sex typing conducive to sexual aggression.

It is part of the sexual script that sexual intentions are rarely communicated explicitly but conveyed implicitly through nonverbal and behavioral cues. Due to this reliance on implicit cues, misunderstandings are a common feature in heterosexual interactions. Abbey (1991) reported that two thirds of her respondents remembered at least one occasion where their friendliness had been misinterpreted as a sexual invitation, with women reporting misperception more frequently than men. In a recent German study, almost half of the female and more than a third of the male adolescents questioned indicated that a partner had misperceived the level of intimacy they desired (Krahé, Scheinberger-Olwig, & Waizenhöfer, 1999).

Beyond establishing prevalence rates for misperception from self-reports, gender differences in the interpretation of cues as suggesting sexual interests have been studied in response to videotaped depictions as well as live observations of heterosexual interactions (Abbey, 1991; Edmondson & Conger, 1995; Johnson, Stockdale, & Saal, 1991). These studies show a clear tendency for male observers to interpret female behavior in sexual terms, that is, to see a female actor as more sexually seductive, more promiscuous, and more sexually attractive than do female observers. Goodchilds, Zellman, Johnson, and Giarrusso (1988) showed for their adolescent sample that these gender differences tended to increase rather than decrease with age and sexual experience. Furthermore, Bridges (1991) found that men, compared to women, attributed greater desire for sexual intercourse to a woman experiencing unwanted sexual contacts in both acquaintance and stranger rape scenarios.

As Abbey (1991) noted, most misperceptions in heterosexual encounters are of a transient nature and are resolved either through explicit clarification or through indirect means. However, if misperceptions are allowed to persist, they may be a risk factor for sexual aggression. According to Abbey, Ross, McDuffie, and McAuslan (1996), women who had been raped reported more instances of having been misperceived than women who had experienced sexual coercion who, in turn, reported higher frequencies than women who had had only consensual sexual encounters (see also Muehlenhard & Linton, 1987). Thus, it seems that a divergence in sexual scripts, with men having a lower threshold for assigning sexual meaning to a partner's behavior than women, is responsible in large part for misunderstandings in the negotiation of sexual intimacy and may ultimately lead to sexual coercion.

Gender differences in sexual scripts and their impact on sexual aggression are further highlighted by a body of research that has focused on men characterized by the macho personality constellation (Mosher, 1991). These men show an extreme identification with the traditional male sex role and are therefore also referred to as hypermasculine (Mosher & Sirkin, 1984). As Mosher noted, "the ideological script of machismo is a hypermasculine variant of a traditional normative gender ideology that emphasizes destructive power rather than productive or integrative power" (p. 201). In their Hypermasculinity Inventory, through which macho men are typically identified, Mosher and Sirkin distinguished between three attitudinal components of the macho personality constellation: callous sexual attitudes, violence as manly, and danger as exciting. Callous sexual attitudes, that is, beliefs that women should be treated at the man's discretion to serve his sexual interests, provide an underpinning for sexually aggressive behavior. In accordance with this conceptualization, several studies have found a close link between the macho personality and sexual aggression (see Mosher, 1991, for a review). Moreover, macho men experienced less negative affect when asked to imagine committing a rape (Mosher & R. D. Anderson, 1986). Thus, macho men have developed a sexual script in which the use of force to gain sexual ends is contained as an integral element, and they are guided by this script in their heterosexual interactions.

## ENACTING SEXUAL SCRIPTS: AMBIGUOUS COMMUNICATION AND SEXUAL AGGRESSION

The idea that women should not—and generally do not—communicate their sexual intentions in an explicit and unambiguous way is deeply ingrained in traditional dating scripts: Men are expected to take the active role in initiating sexual contact and to persuade a seemingly reluctant woman to give in to their advances (Warshaw & Parrot, 1991). Implied in this script is the notion that women's rejections of a man's sexual advances do not necessarily represent genuine unwillingness but may reflect a kind of token resistance waiting to be overcome by the man's persistent efforts. Van Wie, Gross, and Marx (1995) asked their respondents to listen to an audiotaped sexual interaction in which, after an initial period of mutual kissing, the woman rejected the man's further sexual advances. The respondents were asked to indicate at which point in the interaction they thought the man should stop making further advances. One group was informed that the couple had had sexual contact before and that the woman had shown token resistance, that is, initial refusal, on that occasion. The other group was told there had been no resistance from the woman on the previous occasion. The findings revealed a strong effect of the token resistance information: Subjects who were told the woman had shown token resistance in the past thought the man should stop his sexual advances at a later point than subjects who were not informed about previous token resistance.

The question whether token resistance is purely a myth functioning to justify male sexual coercion or whether women do in fact use this strategy in negotiating sexual interactions was first addressed by Muehlenhard and Hollabaugh (1988). They defined token resistance as "a woman's indicating that she did not want to have sex even though she had every intention to and was willing to engage in sexual intercourse" (p. 872). In the researchers' sample of 610 female psychology undergraduates, 40% reported having shown token resistance at least once. Similar prevalence rates were found in subsequent studies (Krahé, 1998; Muehlenhard & McCoy, 1991; O'Sullivan & Allgeier, 1994; Shotland & Hunter, 1995; Sprecher, Hatfield, Cortese, Potapova, & Levitskaya, 1994, U.S. sample).

Concerning the attitudinal correlates of token resistance, Muehlenhard and Hollabaugh (1988) found that token resistance was associated with more traditional sex role stereotyping, higher acceptance of interpersonal violence and greater endorsement of the belief that women enjoy the use of coercion in a sexual relationship. These findings suggest that women who show token resistance are more committed to the traditional sexual script than women who do not use this strategy. Among the reasons for token resistance, fear of appearing promiscuous, desire to be the one in control, and situational constraints (e.g., no contraception) featured most prominently. Muehlenhard and Hollabaugh concluded that token resistance is most likely to imply negative consequences: It discourages honest communication, it makes women appear manipulative, and it encourages men to ignore women's refusals. These concerns are borne out by data from two studies by Shotland and Hunter (1995) and Krahé (1998) showing that token resistance was associated with a higher likelihood of sexual victimization.

Subsequent studies demonstrated, however, that token resistance is by no means limited to female courtship behavior. O'Sullivan and Allgeier (1994) as well as Sprecher et al. (1994) found that prevalence rates for token resistance were even higher for male respondents (43% vs. 25% in O'Sullivan & Allgeier; 47% vs. 38% in Sprecher et al., U.S. sample). O'Sullivan and Allgeier also challenged Muehlenhard and Hollabaugh's (1988) concerns about the negative consequences of token resistance. In their study, the majority of both men and women indicating token resistance rated the interaction with their partners as moderately or extremely pleasant.

Moreover, token resistance is not the only form of ambiguous communication in negotiating sexual intimacy. *Compliance*, that is, agreeing to sexual contacts without actually wanting them, is another type of sexual miscommunication closely linked to traditional sex-role stereotypes. In the Shotland and Hunter (1995) sample of women, 38% reported compliance. Sprecher at al. (1994) found prevalence rates of 55% for their female and 35% for their male respondents in the United States. (Interestingly, this gender ratio was reversed in their Japanese and Russian samples, where compliance rates were higher for men than for women.) Parallel to their findings on token resistance, Shotland and Hunter showed that women's compliance was also linked to an increased probability of experiencing sexual aggression.

Thus, there is evidence from several sources that both token resistance and compliance are frequently employed by both sexes in the negotiation of sexual intimacy. There is less consensus, however, about their potentially adverse effects on sexual relationships, in particular about their significance as risk factors of sexual victimization and aggression.

Krahé, Scheinberger-Olwig, Kolpin, and Waizenhöfer (1998) analyzed the link between ambiguous communication and sexual aggression in a sample of 526 sexually experienced male and female German adolescents. It was predicted that women using ambiguous communication in the form of either token resistance or compliance would be more likely to experience sexual victimization, that is, unwanted sexual contacts. Men reporting token resistance were predicted to be more likely to use coercion to pursue their sexual intentions. This prediction was based on the reasoning that men who use token resistance believe that saying "no" to a sexual advance does not necessarily mean "no" and are therefore more likely to show sexual aggression. Sexual aggression was measured by a German adaptation of the Sexual Experiences Survey (SES; Koss, Gidycz, & Wisniewski, 1987; Koss & Oros, 1982; see Krahé, Scheinberger-Olwig, Waizenhöfer, & Kolpin, 1999). Token resistance and compliance were measured in the format provided by Muehlenhard and Hollabaugh (1988). In addition to indicating whether or not they had ever shown token resistance and compliance, respondents who answered affirmatively were asked to write down their main reason for using the respective strategy.

Extending the scope of previous studies, men's perceptions of their female partner's token resistant and compliant behaviors were also elicited. If Muehlenhard and Hollabaugh (1988) were right in assuming that women's use of token resistance encourages men to ignore a woman's refusals, then one would expect a link between perceived token resistance and sexual aggression in men. More generally, it could be hypothesized that men who assume women conceal or are dishonest about their true intentions are more likely to pursue their sexual interests, ignoring female resistance. This would suggest that perceived compliance as well as perceived token resistance are associated with higher levels of sexual aggression.

It was found that female adolescents widely report the use of token resistance (51.6%) and compliance (33.2%). Both strategies were significantly related to higher levels of sexual victimization. A parallel finding was obtained for the male respondents: A substantial proportion of men reported the use of token resistance (46.1%), and there was a significant link between token resistance and self-reported sexual aggression. Moreover, perceived female token resistance (reported by 43.6% of the men) and perceived compliance (21.4%) were also related to higher sexual aggression scores in the male sample. The two sets of findings are reported in Figs. 9.2 and 9.3 (see Krahé, Scheinberger-Olwig, Waizenhöfer, & Kolpin, 1999, for a detailed description of the German version of the SES and how the SES items were converted into the four response categories).

The free-response reasons for engaging in token resistance facilitated a more fine-grained analysis of the motives underlying the use of token

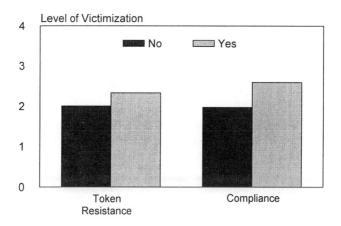

FIG. 9.2    Level of sexual victimization (female respondents) by type of ambiguous communication. Response scale: 1 = *Consensual sexual experiences only*, 2 = *Sexual experiences (except intercourse) through pressure/coercion*, 3 = *Attempted forced intercourse*, 4 = *Forced intercourse*.

resistance and their differential link to sexual victimization. The most severe sexual victimization was reported for those women who engaged in token resistance because of ambiguous feelings toward the sexual interaction (e.g., anxiety, fear of disappointment) and toward the partner. The lowest victimization scores were reported by those women who quoted external reasons unrelated to the relationship (e.g., no contraception, tiredness). For the male sample, ambiguous feelings toward the sexual interaction were linked to highest aggression scores, whereas the lowest aggression scores were found for men who reported token resistance because they had a steady relationship with another partner. The findings from these free-response data suggest a conceptual clarification of token resistance that differentiates between genuine ambiguity  as a high-risk factor and the rejection of a sexual advance for external reasons in the presence of feelings of regret (meaning "no, but would have liked to otherwise"). It is only token resistance in the form of genuine ambiguity that seems to be a risk factor for sexual aggression and victimization.

Shotland and Hunter (1995) found that true token resistance, that is, rejecting a  sexual advance while at the same time being willing to engage in sexual contacts, was shown by a relatively small proportion of their sample. More frequently, women reported a change in their sexual intentions in the course of a sexual episode from an initial "no" to a subsequent "yes." The issue of persistent deception versus change of intention is crucial for understanding  the functional  significance of token resistance from  the woman's

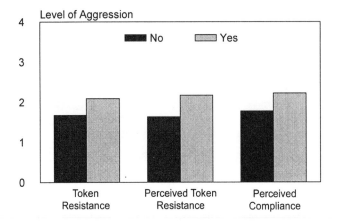

FIG. 9.3   Level of sexual aggression (male respondents) by type of ambiguous communication. Response scale: 1 = *Consensual sexual experiences only*, 2 = *Sexual experiences (except intercourse) through pressure/coercion*, 3 = *Attempted forced intercourse*, 4 = *Forced intercourse*.

point of view. It is, however, less pertinent to the issue of how token resistance may be related to sexual victimization, because in both instances women send out ambiguous signals to their sexual partners. This ambiguity—irrespective of whether it reflects manipulative goals or change of intention—may foster male convictions that a woman's "no" must not be accepted as such  and thus open up the way for pressure and even coercion on behalf of the man. Moreover, employed repeatedly or as a general strategy, token resistance may undermine a woman's ability to clearly and convincingly express genuine resistance.

The findings obtained by Krahé et al. (1998) support previous research trying to tease apart the different meanings attached to the concept of token resistance and thus to clarify the link between ambiguous communication and sexual aggression. The findings on perceived token resistance and compliance suggest that these perceptions may be used as potential justifications of male sexual aggression, highlighting the link between communication strategies and coercive power in heterosexual relationships.

## SEXUAL SCRIPTS AND THE "REAL RAPE" SCRIPT

Just as consensual sexual interactions can be crystallized into scripts, it is also possible to identify scripted representations of nonconsensual sexual encounters, or rape. Rape scripts define the types of situations which are, by general consensus, regarded as rape. Several authors have demonstrated the existence of a "real rape" script, which not only provides a descriptive framework for interpreting a given event as a rape incident, but also has a normative significance: To qualify as rape, a particular incident is required to meet the defining features of the script (e.g., Howard, 1984; Jackson, 1978). As shown in several studies, the prototypical or real rape script is generally considered to be a sexual assault by an unknown man, lurking on an unsuspecting victim in a dark lane, and using physical force to make the victim comply with his demands (Ryan, 1988). The more a specific rape incident deviates from the real rape script, for example, by involving previously acquainted participants or by the use of verbal coercion rather than physical threats, the lower the number of people who identify the incident as rape (Burt & Albin, 1981).

In a similar vein, Krahé (1991) found that students who were asked to generate prototypical representations of a "typical" rape and a "dubious" rape complaint defined the typical rape in accordance with the stranger rape script, that is, as involving an attacker unknown to the victim, who threatens to use force and has a weapon, with the victim showing physical resistance. In contrast, the prototypical descriptions of a dubious rape complaint contained many features of acquaintance rapes such as previous acquaintanceship between victim and assailant, the victim being slightly drunk and showing no resistance, the attack happening at either the victim's or the assailant's place. In addition, the two rape prototypes differed with respect to the assumed psychological consequences of the assault for the victim: Whereas the consequences of a typical rape were indicated as "serious," the consequences of the dubious complaint were rated as "slight." In their adolescent sample, Davis and Lee (1996) also found a convergence of the "typical" sexual assault with the stranger rape scenario.

This reduction of the rape script to stranger assaults not only affects the social perception of rape victims and assailants; it also affects women's self-identification as victims of rape. Kahn, Mathie, and Torgler (1994) elicited rape scripts from women who reported forced sexual experiences on a behavioral measure and identified themselves as rape victims on a direct question (acknowledged victims). A second group of women reported forced sexual experiences but answered "no" to the direct question of whether or not they had been raped (unacknowledged victims). Kahn et al. found that rape scripts provided by the acknowledged victims depicted the typical acquaintance rape scenario, involving a previously known assailant, an indoor location, and verbal protest rather than physical struggle on the victim's part. In contrast, the scripts generated by the unacknowledged victims corresponded to the typical blitz rape scenario, involving an unknown assailant, the use of weapons, and an outdoor location. It is important to note that the personal victimization experiences of all but one of the respondents had been acquaintance rapes. This suggests that unacknowledged victims failed to identify themselves as rape victims because their rape scripts were restricted to the stranger rape scenario and thus did not cover the particular events that had happened to them.

If the prevailing rape script is restricted to stranger assault involving the use of physical force, the majority of unwanted sexual encounters are not accommodated within that script. If they do not qualify as rape, then—the suggestion is—they are less serious or more dubious or both. Thus, the real rape script serves to deny the adverse nature of sexual aggression in dating relationships and between previously acquainted individuals (Bechhofer & Parrot, 1991). This implication is reflected in a number of studies that demonstrate significant differences in the social perception of stranger versus acquaintance rape.

In a study by Bridges and McGrail (1989), both male and female respondents attributed greater responsibility to the assailant in a stranger rape scenario than in an acquaintance rape scenario. Moreover, the psychological damage was rated as less serious by both men and women if the assault occurred with a steady date than if it happened with a stranger or on a first date (Bridges, 1991). Also relevant in this context are results by Stormo, Lang, and Stritzke (1997) who analyzed the effects of perceived alcohol consumption by the victim and the perpetrator in an acquaintance rape scenario on attributions of responsibility: The victim was attributed greater responsibility in the alcohol condition than in the no-alcohol condition, whereas the perpetrator was held less responsible when he had consumed alcohol than when he had not. However, the study also included a condition that involved a highly intoxicated victim and a moderately intoxicated perpetrator. In this case, the perpetrator was attributed more responsibility than in the case of an equally or less intoxicated victim, suggesting that observers attribute additional blame to men who are seen as exploiting an incapacitated victim (see also Norris & Cubbins, 1992).

Beyond these socially shared perceptions, several studies have identified systematic differences in the perception of acquaintance rape as a function of observers' sex, gender-role stereotypes, and acceptance of rape myths. As far as sex differences in applying the real rape stereotype are concerned, Sigler and Curry (1995) found that men rated stranger rape as more serious than date rape. The reverse pattern was found for women. However, these data are at odds with an earlier study by Tetreault and Barnett (1987) who found men and women to differ in the opposite direction.

In one of the early studies addressing individual differences in response to stranger versus acquaintance rape, Check and Malamuth (1983) analyzed responses to a consensual sexual interaction, an acquaintance rape depiction, and a stranger rape depiction as a function of observers' sex-role stereotyping. They found that respondents high on sex-role stereotyping were more likely to be sexually aroused by an acquaintance rape depiction than respondents low on sex-role stereotyping. Whereas low sex-role stereotyping was linked to significantly fewer individuals being sexually aroused by depictions of both acquaintance and stranger rape than by depictions of consensual sex, no such differential effect was found for high sex-role stereotyping individuals. In this group, the proportion of respondents reporting sexual arousal was in fact highest in response to the acquaintance rape depiction.

Sex-role stereotyping also affects women's perceptions of acquaintance rape: Women endorsing a traditional sex-role orientation were found to attribute less blame to the rapist than women holding nontraditional sex-role beliefs, even though no proportional increase in victim blame was found (Snell & Godwin, 1993). It must be noted, however, that other studies failed to confirm the effect of sex-role stereotypes on acquaintance rape perception, both for male and for female respondents (e.g., Bostwick & DeLucia, 1992; Muehlenhard, Friedman, & Thomas, 1985).

The tendency to restrict the negative evaluation of rape to the real rape script is further promoted by the widespread acceptance of rape-supportive attitudes, which also deny the adverse consequences of unwanted sexual encounters and stress the acceptability of coercion to obtain sexual contacts. Among the attitudinal foundations of the real rape script, the concept of *rape myth acceptance* has received particular attention. Rape myths refer to stereotyped or false beliefs about rape, rape victims, and rapists (Burt, 1991). An early study by Malamuth, Haber, and Feshbach (1980) found that subjects believed that as many as one in four women would derive some pleasure from being raped. They also believed that almost half the male population would rape a woman if they were certain they would not be caught and punished. The authors conclude: "These findings may be interpreted as providing some support for the contention that rape is an extension of normal attitudes and socialization practices in our society rather than totally the product of a sick, aberrant mind" (Malamuth et al., 1980, p. 134).

This conclusion is corroborated by evidence that shows that individuals who accept rape myths have more restrictive rape definitions, imposing the criteria of the stranger rape scenario in identifying an incident as rape. In addition, acceptance of rape myths by men has been found consistently to be related to the performance of sexually aggressive behavior (see K. B. Anderson, Cooper, & Okamura, 1997; Lonsway & Fitzgerald, 1994, for reviews). As shown by Davis and Lee (1996), the link between rape myth acceptance and stereotyped description of the typical sexual assault is already established in adolescence, as is the tendency for males to endorse rape myths to a greater extent than females. The authors stressed that there is a "need for intervention aimed at changing dysfunctional attitudes related to sexual assault" (p. 801).

# CONCLUSIONS AND
# IMPLICATIONS FOR INTERVENTION

The evidence reviewed in this chapter shows that heterosexual interactions among adolescents and young adults are still largely based on traditional gender-typed scripts in which men are expected to initiate sexual encounters and women to act as gatekeepers of sexual intimacy. Even though young men and women may regard less stereotyped behaviors as desirable, their actual dating interactions remain committed to the conventional sexual scripts. As Lawrance, Taylor, and Byers (1996) concluded after eliciting descriptions of ideal versus actual dating behaviors, "traditional gender role prescriptions continue to guide young men's and women's behavior in sexual interactions to a greater degree than these prescriptions guide their conceptions of ideal behavior" (p. 354).

Women who reject traditional gender roles and adopt more masculine self-descriptions show different patterns of sexual behavior compared to traditional women. In a study by Lucke (1998), these women reported a greater number of sexual partners over the past 12 months and were also more likely to use controlled substances with a recent nonsteady partner. Since both aspects refer to potentially high-risk dating behaviors, these findings point to drawbacks attached to the unilateral departure from the traditional female dating script and to the engagement in "masculine" patterns of sexual behavior. On the other hand, there can be no doubt that the adherence to traditional scripts equally entails serious adverse consequences. In particular, the close link between traditional sexual scripts and rape-supportive attitudes as well as sexually aggressive behavior in dating relationships has been established conclusively by a large body of research and poses a challenge for intervention and prevention. Moreover, Glick and Hilt (chap. 8, this volume) highlight the link between adherence to traditional dating scripts and the strength of gender prejudices, both in their hostile and their ambivalent varieties. This connection feeds into attitudinal and behavioral repertoires that are conducive to sexual aggression. Therefore, Glick and Hilt suggest that specific interventions should be directed at challenging the unthinking acceptance of those scripts.

There is a general consensus that intervention strategies need to be directed not only at the individual person but also at the more global social climate, entailing patriarchal power hierarchies, men's sexual entitlement, and acceptance of interpersonal violence, in which rape-supportive attitudes and aggressive behavior are allowed to flourish (Rozée, Bateman, & Gilmore, 1991). In terms of individual-centered strategies, changing rape-supportive attitudes of men and creating an awareness of violence-prone situations in women have been identified as important goals (Parrot, 1991). However, Lonsway and Fitzgerald (1994) pointed out that not all interventions directed at reducing rape myth acceptance in men were successful, some not obtaining the intended decrease, others even finding an increase in victim blame and identification with the perpetrator. As far as women are concerned, Anderson et al. (1997) noted that in their extensive meta-analysis, one expected finding failed to materialize, namely that women who had experienced sexual aggression or who had been in contact with a victim would express more negative attitudes about rape. The authors concluded from this negative evidence that intervention efforts should be directed at counteracting victims' self-blame tendencies. Moreover, their finding ties in with the study by Kahn et al. (1994) discussed earlier, which suggests that women who experience unwanted sexual contacts frequently fail to identify themselves as victims of sexual aggression because their victimization experience falls outside the boundaries of their rape scripts.

Thus, from a social cognitive perspective, dispelling the "real rape" stereotype in favor of a more comprehensive representation of sexual aggression and eliminating coercion and violence from socially shared sexual scripts are two objectives that should be high on the rape prevention agenda.

# REFERENCES

Abbey, A. (1991). Misperception as an antecedent of acquaintance rape: A consequence of ambiguity in communication between women and men. In A. Parrot & L. Bechhofer (Eds.), *Acquaintance rape: The hidden crime* (pp. 96–111). New York: Wiley.

Abbey, A., Ross, L. T., McDuffie, D., & McAuslan, P. (1996). Alcohol and dating risk factors for sexual assault among college women. *Psychology of Women Quarterly, 20,* 147–169.

Alksnis, C., Desmarais, S., & Wood, E. (1996). Gender differences in scripts for different types of dates. *Sex Roles, 34,* 321–336.

Anderson, K. B., Cooper, H., & Okamura, L. (1997). Individual differences and attitudes toward rape: A meta-analytic review. *Personality and Social Psychology Bulletin, 23,* 295–315.

Bechhofer, L., & Parrot, A. (1991). What is acquaintance rape? In A. Parrot & L. Bechhofer (Eds.), *Acquaintance rape: The hidden crime* (pp. 9–25). New York: Wiley.

Bostwick, T. D., & DeLucia, J. L. (1992). Effects of gender and specific dating behaviors on perceptions of sex willingness and date rape. *Journal of Social and Clinical Psychology, 11,* 14–25.

Bridges, J. S. (1991). Perceptions of date and stranger rape: A difference in sex role expectations and rape-supportive beliefs. *Sex Roles, 24,* 291–307.

Bridges, J. S., & McGrail, C. A. (1989). Attributions of responsibility for date and stranger rape. *Sex Roles, 21,* 273–286.

Bundeszentrale für gesundheitliche Aufklärung (Ed.). (1998). *Sexualität und Kontrazeption aus der Sicht der Jugendlichen und ihrer Eltern* [Sexuality and contraception as seen by adolescents and their parents]. Köln: BZgA.

Burt, M. R. (1980). Cultural myths and supports for rape. *Journal of Personality and Social Psychology, 38*, 217–230.

Burt, M. R. (1991). Rape myths and acquaintance rape. In A. Parrot & L. Bechhofer (Eds.), *Acquaintance rape: The hidden crime* (pp. 26–40). New York: Wiley.

Burt, M. R., & Albin, R. S. (1981). Rape myths, rape definitions, and probability of conviction. *Journal of Applied Social Psychology, 11*, 212–230.

Byers, S., & Lewis, K. (1988). Dating couples' disagreement over the desired level of sexual intimacy. *Journal of Sex Research, 24*, 15–29.

Check, J. V. P., & Malamuth, N. M. (1983). Sex role stereotyping and reactions to depictions of stranger versus acquaintance rape. *Journal of Personality and Social Psychology, 45*, 344–356.

Clark, R. D., & Hatfield, E. (1989). Gender differences in receptivity to sexual offers. *Journal of Psychology and Human Sexuality, 2*, 39–55.

Craig, M. E. (1990). Coercive sexuality in dating relationships: A situational model. *Clinical Psychology Review, 10*, 395–423.

Davis, T., & Lee, C. (1996). Sexual assault: Myths and stereotypes among Australian adolescents. *Sex Roles, 34*, 787–803.

Edmondson, C. B., & Conger, J. C. (1995). The impact of mode of presentation on gender differences in social perception. *Sex Roles, 32*, 169–183.

Eron, L. D. (1987). The development of aggressive behavior from the perspective of a developing behaviorism. *American Psychologist, 42*, 435–442.

Goodchilds, J. D., Zellman, G. L., Johnson, P. B., & Giarrusso, R. (1988). Adolescents and their perceptions of sexual interactions. In A. W. Burgess (Ed.), *Rape and sexual assault* (Vol. 2, pp. 245–270). New York: Garland.

Hickson, F. C. I., Davies, P. M., Hunt, A. J., Weatherburn, P., McManus, T. J., & Coxon, A. P. M. (1994). Gay men as victims of nonconsensual sex. *Archives of Sexual Behavior, 23*, 281–294.

Howard, J. A. (1984). The "normal" victim: The effects of gender stereotypes on reactions to victims. *Social Psychology Quarterly, 47*, 270–281.

Huesmann, L. R. (1988). An information processing model for the development of aggression. *Aggressive Behavior, 11*, 13–24.

Huesmann, L. R. (1998). The role of social information processing and cognitive schema in the acquisition and maintenance of habitual aggressive behavior. In R. G. Geen & E. Donnerstein (Eds.), *Human aggression: Theories, research, and implications for social policy* (pp. 73–109). San Diego, CA: Academic Press.

Jackson, S. (1978). The social context of rape: Sexual scripts and motivation. *Women's Studies International Quarterly, 1*, 27–38.

Johnson, C. B., Stockdale, M. S., & Saal, F. E. (1991). Persistence of men's misperceptions of friendly cues across a variety of interpersonal encounters. *Psychology of Women Quarterly, 15*, 463–475.

Kahn, A. S., Mathie, V. A., & Torgler, C. (1994). Rape scripts and rape acknowledgement. *Psychology of Women Quarterly, 18*, 53–66.

Koss, M. P., Gidycz, C. A., & Wisniewski, N. (1987). The scope of rape: Incidence and prevalence of sexual aggression and victimization in a national sample of higher education students. *Journal of Consulting and Clinical Psychology, 55*, 162–170.

Koss, M. P., & Oros, C. J. (1982). Sexual Experiences Survey: A research instrument investigating sexual aggression and victimization. *Journal of Consulting and Clinical Psychology, 50*, 455–457.

Krahé, B. (1991). Social psychological issues in the study of rape. In W. Stroebe & M. Hewstone (Eds.), *European review of social psychology* (Vol. 2, pp. 279–309). Chichester, England: Wiley.

Krahé, B. (1998). Sexual aggression among adolescents: Prevalence and predictors in a German sample. *Psychology of Women Quarterly, 22,* 537–554.

Krahé, B., Scheinberger-Olwig, R., Kolpin, S., & Waizenhöfer, E. (1998). *The role of ambiguous communication as a risk factor of sexual aggression and victimization.* Paper presented at the "East–West Meeting" on "Social Influence Processes" of the European Association of Experimental Social Psychology, Magdeburg, Germany.

Krahé, B., Scheinberger-Olwig, R., & Waizenhöfer, E. (1999). Sexuelle Aggression zwischen Jugendlichen: Eine Prävalenzerhebung mit Ost–West-Vergleich [Sexual aggression among adolescents: A prevalence study including an East–West comparison]. *Zeitschrift für Sozialpsychologie, 30,* 165–178.

Krahé, B., Scheinberger-Olwig, R., Waizenhöfer, E., & Kolpin, S. (1999). Childhood sexual abuse and revictimization in adolescence. *Child Abuse and Neglect, 23,* 383–394.

Lawrance, K., Taylor, D., & Byers, E. S. (1996). Differences in men's and women's global, sexual, and ideal-sexual expressiveness and instrumentality. *Sex Roles, 34,* 337–357.

Lonsway, K. A., & Fitzgerald, L. F. (1994). Rape myths: In review. *Psychology of Women Quarterly, 18,* 133–164.

Lucke, J. C. (1998). Gender roles and sexual behavior among young women. *Sex Roles, 39,* 273–297.

Malamuth, N. M., Haber, S., & Feshbach, S. (1980). Testing hypotheses regarding rape: Exposure to sexual violence, sex differences, and the "normality" of rapists. *Journal of Research in Personality, 14,* 121–137.

Malamuth, N. M., & Heilmann, M. F. (1998). Evolutionary psychology and sexual aggression. In C. B. Crawford & D. L. Krebs (Eds.), *Handbook of evolutionary psychology: Ideas, issues, and applications* (pp. 515–542). Mahwah, NJ: Lawrence Erlbaum Associates.

Miller, B. C., Christopherson, C. A., & King, P. K. (1993). Sexual behavior in adolescence. In T. P. Gulotta, G. R. Adams, & R. Montemayor (Eds.), *Adolescent sexuality* (pp. 57–76). Newbury Park, CA: Sage.

Moore, S., & Rosenthal, D. (1993). *Sexuality in adolescence.* London: Routledge.

Mosher, D. L. (1991). Macho men, machismo, and sexuality. *Annual Review of Sex Research, 2,* 199–249.

Mosher, D. L., & Anderson, R. D. (1986). Macho personality, sexual aggression, and reactions to guided imagery of realistic rape. *Journal of Research in Personality, 20,* 77–94.

Mosher, D. L., & Sirkin, M. (1984). Measuring a macho personality constellation. *Journal of Research in Personality, 18,* 150–163.

Muehlenhard, C. L., Friedman, D. E., & Thomas, C. M. (1985). Is date rape justifiable? The effects of dating activity, who initiated, who paid, and men's attitudes toward women. *Psychology of Women Quarterly, 9,* 297–309.

Muehlenhard, C. L., & Hollabaugh, L. C. (1988). Do women sometimes say no when they mean yes? The prevalence and correlates of women's token resistance to sex. *Journal of Personality and Social Psychology, 54,* 872–879.

Muehlenhard, C. L., & Linton, M. A. (1987). Date rape and sexual aggression in dating situations: Incidence and risk factors. *Journal of Counseling Psychology, 34,* 186–196.

Muehlenhard, C. L., & McCoy, M. L. (1991). Double standard/double bind: The sexual double standard and women's communications about sex. *Psychology of Women Quarterly, 15,* 447–461.

Norris, J., & Cubbins, L. A. (1992). Dating, drinking, and rape: Effects of victim's and assailant's alcohol consumption on judgments of their behavior and traits. *Psychology of Women Quarterly, 16,* 179–191.

Oliver, M. B., & Hyde, J. S. (1993). Gender differences in sexuality: A meta-analysis. *Psychological Bulletin, 114*, 29–51.

O'Sullivan, L. F., & Allgeier, E. R. (1994). Disassembling a stereotype: Gender differences in the use of token resistance. *Journal of Applied Social Psychology, 24*, 1035–1055.

Parrot, A. (1991). Institutional response: How can acquaintance rape be prevented? In A. Parrot & L. Bechhofer (Eds.), *Acquaintance rape: The hidden crime* (pp. 355–367). New York: Wiley.

Parrot, A., & Bechhofer, L. (Eds.). (1991). *Acquaintance rape: The hidden crime.* New York: Wiley.

Rose, S., & Frieze, I. H. (1989). Young singles' scripts for a first date. *Gender and Society, 3*, 258–268.

Rose, S., & Frieze, I. H. (1993). Young singles' contemporary dating scripts. *Sex Roles, 28*, 499–509.

Rozée, P. D., Bateman, P., & Gilmore, T. (1991). The personal perspective of acquaintance rape prevention: A three-tier approach. In A. Parrot & L. Bechhofer (Eds.), *Acquaintance rape: The hidden crime* (pp. 337–354). New York: Wiley.

Ryan, K. M. (1988). Rape and seduction scripts. *Psychology of Women Quarterly, 12*, 237–245.

Sanday, P. R. (1981). The socio-cultural context of rape: A cross-cultural study. *Journal of Social Issues, 37*(4), 5–27.

Schank, R., & Abelson, R. (1977). *Scripts, plans, goals, and understanding: An inquiry into human knowledge structures.* Hillsdale, NJ: Lawrence Erlbaum Associates.

Shotland, R. L., & Hunter, B. A. (1995). Women's "token resistant" and compliant sexual behaviors are related to uncertain sexual intentions and rape. *Personality and Social Psychology Bulletin, 21*, 226–236.

Sigler, R., & Curry, B. S. (1995). Perceptions of offender motivation in unwanted aggressive sexual advances. *International Review of Victimology, 4*, 1–14.

Simon, W., & Gagnon, J. H. (1986). Sexual scripts: Permanence and change. *Archives of Sexual Behavior, 15*, 97–120.

Snell, W. E., & Godwin, L. (1993). Social reactions to depictions of casual and steady acquaintance rape: The impact of AIDS exposure and stereotypic beliefs about women. *Sex Roles, 29*, 599–616.

Sprecher, S., Hatfield, E., Cortese, A., Potapova, E., & Levitskaya, A. (1994). Token resistance to sexual intercourse and consent to unwanted sexual intercourse: College students' dating experiences in three countries. *Journal of Sex Research, 31*, 125–132.

Stormo, K. J., Lang, A. R., & Stritzke, W. G. K. (1997). Attributions about acquaintance rape: The role of alcohol and individual differences. *Journal of Applied Social Psychology, 27*, 279–305.

Struckman-Johnson, C. (1991). Male victims of acquaintance rape. In A. Parrot & L. Bechhofer (Eds.), *Acquaintance rape: The hidden crime* (pp. 192–213). New York: Wiley.

Tetreault, P. A., & Barnett, M. A. (1987). Reactions to stranger and acquaintance rape. *Psychology of Women Quarterly, 11*, 353–358.

Van Wie, V. E., Gross, A. M., & Marx, B. P. (1995). Females' perception of date rape: An examination of two contextual variables. *Violence Against Women, 1*, 351–365.

Warshaw, R., & Parrot, A. (1991). The contribution of sex-role socialization to acquaintance rape. In A. Parrot & L. Bechhofer (Eds.), *Acquaintance rape: The hidden crime* (pp. 73–82). New York: Wiley.

White, J. W., & Kowalski, R. M. (1998). Male violence toward women: An integrated perspective. In R. G. Geen & E. Donnerstein (Eds.), *Human aggression: Theories, research, and implications for social policy* (pp. 203–228). San Diego, CA: Academic Press.

# IV

# GENDER, GROUP, AND CULTURE

# 10

# Gender, Communication, and Social Influence: A Developmental Perspective

Linda L. Carli
*Wellesley College*

Danuta Bukatko
*College of the Holy Cross*

In this chapter we examine the relation between gender differences in communication and gender differences in social influence across the life span. Although there is extensive research on gender differences in communication in a wide variety of domains as well as literature assessing the way language creates and maintains gender stereotypes,[1] in this chapter, we focus on those gender effects in communication that have been found to contribute

---

[1]Ruscher (1998) noted that the most common means of expressing stereotypes is through language. Her research indicates that when people talk about out-groups, they typically exaggerate the homogeneity of out-group members and emphasize information that is consistent with stereotypes about those out-groups, de-emphasizing inconsistent information. When discussing an individual who is a member of an out-group, people typically bring up examples of other out-group members who behave in a stereotypical manner; thus, stereotypes can be invoked even when the individual being discussed does not exhibit stereotypical behavior (Ruscher & Hammer, 1994). In addition, people present stereotype-congruent information in more abstract and general terms than stereotype-incongruent information (Maass, Milesi, Zabbini, & Stahlberg, 1995; Maass, Salvi, Arcuri, & Semin, 1989). For example, people might describe a woman generally as "emotional" but a man more concretely as "being upset." Research reveals that these and other forms of linguistic bias not only express stereotypes, but transmit, organize, and maintain them as well (Eckes, 1997; Maass & Arcuri, 1996).

to gender differences in social influence. In addition, we discuss several theoretical explanations for gender effects on communication and influence.

The life-span approach we present in this chapter has several advantages over past reviews that have focused primarily on either adults or children. First, by using this approach, we are able to show the consistency and pervasiveness of patterns of gender differences in communication and influence across much of the life span. Second, our discussion of theoretical explanations includes theories that have been applied to gender differences in children's behavior as well as those theories applied to gender differences in the behavior of adults. Consequently, we are able to assess in a comprehensive and integrated way the efficacy of these theories in accounting for gender differences across the life span and to point to gaps in the empirical literature.

# GENDER DIFFERENCES IN COMMUNICATION, INTERACTION, AND INFLUENCE

## Gender Differences in Communication

How do males and females differ in their communication style? Although the literature is quite extensive and the findings are somewhat mixed, when gender differences are reported, they generally reveal more competition, assertiveness, and authority by male speakers and more collaboration, agreeableness, and warmth by females (Carli, 1991).

Studies on children show that boys and girls begin to differ in their language as early as preschool. In interactions among same-sex peers, boys use talk to compete, exert control over peers, and play one-upmanship games—essentially creating a status hierarchy within their group; girls use talk to establish and maintain relationships, show awareness of others' feelings, and equalize differences among their peers (Maltz & Borker, 1982; Sheldon, 1990). During the preschool years, boys talk more than girls (Cook, Fritz, McCornack, & Visperas, 1985; Sadker & Sadker, 1994) and issue more directives than girls do (Serbin, Sprafkin, Elman, & Doyle, 1982). Moreover, research on children in preschool through middle school reveals that boys attempt to direct and try to gain the floor in conversations with other children by initiating new conversations and by using verbal and nonverbal attention-getters. Girls, in contrast, encourage the conversation of others by verbally reinforcing others and by following the ongoing theme of the conversation (Austin, Salehi, & Leffler, 1987). Girls use more mitigating language than boys; they hedge more than boys (Mulac, Studley, & Blau, 1990); and, in making requests of others or when trying to resolve conflicts, girls use speech devices such as tag questions and words like *let's* (Goodwin, 1997; Sachs, 1987). These devices suggest sensitivity to the conversation partner, as well as an orientation toward minimizing status differences.

Do the gender differences in conversation hold in situations involving disputes? Under such conditions, the situation may encourage both boys and girls to communicate in a more directive or dominant manner, thereby reducing gender differences in speech. However, research indicates that even when resolving disputes, girls communicate somewhat differently than boys. Among working-class African Americans in conflict situations, girls' communications are more directed toward maintaining connections than boys' are (Goodwin, 1980). In addition, when working out disputes, working-class African American girls avoid direct confrontation and instead discuss the conflict with third parties in order to form coalitions with other girls, whereas boys directly confront, insult, and attack other disputants (Goodwin, 1990). However, gender differences in communication tend to be smaller among African Americans than among Whites (Filardo, 1996).

The differences reported among children also occur among adults. Women's communications, more than men's, tend to create equality among group members and emphasize preserving relationships. In married couples, women work harder to maintain interactions and respond more to the interests of their partners than men do (DeFrancisco, 1991; Fishman, 1978). For example, women put greater effort into finding topics that appeal to others and talking about subjects that other people want to discuss. Research on college students (Carli, 1990; Leet-Pellegrini, 1980; Mulac & Bradac, 1995) and married couples (Fishman, 1978) revealed that women, like girls, also encourage others to speak by nodding and expressing verbal reinforcement, whereas men are more likely to ignore the contributions of others (Fishman, 1978; Leet-Pellegrini, 1980) and issue directives (Mulac & Gibbons, 1993, cited in Mulac, 1998).

Men's speech is not only less responsive to others, it is also more status asserting than women's speech. A review of the literature examining gender differences in talking in mixed-sex groups showed clear evidence that men talk more than women in all types of groups examined: structured task-oriented groups; less structured groups, such as those in college classrooms and faculty meetings; and informal conversation groups (James & Drakich, 1993). Findings on gender differences in interruption have been less clear. Some studies have reported greater interruptions by men than women; these results have been reported for a variety of settings: among college students (Mulac & Bradac, 1995; Mulac, Wiemann, Widenmann, & Gibson, 1988; West & Zimmerman, 1983), among college faculty (Eakins & Eakins, 1976), between couples in therapy (McCarrick, Manderscheid, & Silbergeld, 1981), and in interactions between male patients and their female physicians (West, 1984). However, a review of this literature revealed no consistent pattern of gender differences in interrupting, probably because many studies testing this effect have failed to distinguish between different types of interruptions (James & Clarke, 1993). For example, in some studies, verbal reinforcers (i.e., back channels) have been coded as interruptions even though these behaviors serve to encourage the other person in the conversation to speak and, therefore, do not represent an attempt to gain the floor or really interrupt the other person's speech.

Gender differences have also been found in the amount of mitigation or tentativeness in speech of adults. Examples of such speech include hedging (e.g., adding "sort of," "maybe," or "kind of" to statements), disclaiming expertise (e.g., qualifying one's opinions by saying "I'm no expert" or "I may be wrong"), and adding tag questions to the ends of statements (e.g., "Women speak differently than men, don't they?"). Although such mitigated speech can reflect uncertainty (Lakoff, 1975), it can also be a means to involve others in a conversation (Fishman, 1980) or an indirect influence strategy (Carli, 1990). Moreover, whereas a high amount of mitigating speech elements is perceived as incompetent and uncertain (Carli, 1990; Erickson, Lind, B. C. Johnson, & O'Barr, 1978; Geddes, 1992), modest amounts are perceived favorably (Geddes, 1992). Research on mitigated speech in studies conducted with different samples of subjects—college students, married couples, and the elderly—reveal that women hedge (Carli, 1990; Crosby & Nyquist, 1977; Fishman, 1980; Mulac & Gibbons, 1993, cited in Mulac, 1998; Preisler, 1986), disclaim expertise (Carli, 1990; Hartman, 1976), and add tag questions to the ends of statements (Carli, 1990; Crosby & Nyquist, 1977; Holmes, 1984; McMillan, Clifton, McGrath, & Gale; 1977; Mulac et al., 1988; Mulac & Lundell, 1986) more than men do. Some studies have found no gender differences in hedges (Mulac, Lundell, & Bradac, 1986; Mulac et al., 1988) or tag questions (Baumann, 1976), and some have revealed that men employ more hedges (Mulac & Bradac, 1995). But overall, women's speech appears more mitigated than men's.

Gender differences in nonverbal behavior also reflect women's greater other-directedness and men's greater power and authority. Women are generally more nonverbally warm than men are. For example, women smile and lean toward others during conversations more than men do (Ellyson, Dovidio, & Brown, 1992; Halberstadt & Saitta, 1987; J. A. Hall, 1984; Moskowitz, 1993). Gender differences have also been found in visual dominance, which is measured as the ratio of the amount of time that people maintain eye contact while talking to the amount of time that they maintain eye contact while listening to others (Ellyson & Dovidio, 1985). In general, individuals who are powerful maintain a relatively higher amount of eye contact while talking and less while listening than less powerful individuals. Men usually show more visual dominance than women do (Dovidio, Brown,

Heltman, Ellyson, & Keating, 1988; Dovidio, Ellyson, Keating, Heltman, & Brown, 1988).

Research indicates that an important variable in studies of gender differences in speech is not just subjects' gender, but also the sex composition of the group. Among preschoolers, both boys and girls communicate with and respond to same-sex more than opposite-sex peers (Fagot, 1985; Serbin et al., 1982). In mixed-sex interactions, however, typical gender-typed styles of interaction change to some degree. In the presence of girls, for example, boys increase their use of collaborative communications (Killen & Naigles, 1995; Leaper, 1991). Interestingly, girls more frequently use contradictions of other's statements—a typically masculine strategy—in groups where females are in the majority. When alone with two boys, though, or when they are in a same-sex group, girls revert to their typical pattern of using collaborative speech (Killen & Naigles, 1995). Children thus modulate their communication attempts, perhaps based on the way they "size up" the structure of the social group.

Among adults, gender differences in smiling occur more in same- than mixed-sex interactions; that is, men and women both smile more at women (J. A. Hall, 1984; C. Johnson, 1994). Similarly, in a study examining the vocal characteristics of men and women on television, pleasant warm voices were most characteristic of conversations between women and least characteristic of conversations between men, with subjects behaving more similarly in mixed-sex interactions (J. A. Hall & Braunwald, 1981). These results indicate that both men and women speak more warmly to women than to men. Carli (1990) found that the use of verbal reinforcement is, like smiling and vocal warmth, greatest in interactions among women and smallest in interactions among men, with no gender differences in mixed-sex interactions. The interaction between sex composition of the group and sex of subject reflects the greater use of verbal reinforcement in interactions with women. Although some studies have found no effect of sex composition of group (Mulac & Bradac, 1995), overall, it appears that the presence of women or girls in an interaction increases verbal and nonverbal warmth, whereas the presence of men or boys decreases it.

Quite different effects have been found for gender differences in mitigated and dominant communication. The gender difference in mitigated speech is greater in mixed-sex interactions; that is, women speak in a more mitigated manner primarily when talking to men (Carli, 1990; McMillan et al., 1977). Similarly, research on adults in business settings (Brouwer, Gerritsen, & de Haan, 1979) and on subjects between 60 and 80 years of age (Sayers & Sherblom, 1987) shows that men speak in a more mitigated manner when talking to other men than when talking to women. The gender difference in visual (i.e., nonverbal) dominance is also most pronounced in mixed-gender interactions; both men and women show less visual dominance to men and more to women (Ellyson et al., 1992). Finally, the review of gender differences in interrupting demonstrated that women are interrupted more than men are (James & Clarke, 1993). Given the lack of consistency in the way interruption has been defined, with some studies classifying verbal reinforcement as interruption and others defining interruptions as attempts to take the floor, the fact that women are interrupted more than men may reflect both the tendency for people to try to take the floor from women more often than from men and the tendency for them to be more verbally reinforcing when communicating with women than with men. Overall, then, both men and women are less mitigated or tentative and more nonverbally dominant or status-asserting when interacting with women than with men. On the other hand, as noted earlier, both men and women are warmer when interacting with women.

The results on mixed-sex interactions suggest that both men and women may have multiple agendas in social interactions; both sexes may be concerned, to varying degrees, with dominance and self-assertion, on the one hand, and warmth and collaboration, on the other hand. In fact, these may be two relatively independent dimensions of communication style. Certainly, both sexes are capable of using communication styles associated with each dimension. The blend of behaviors displayed by an individual may depend on the speaker's assessment of his or her relative power within a given social group and, thus, whether an assertive strategy is likely to be successful, along with the appropriateness of being affiliative. Furthermore, individuals' use of both affiliative and dominant behavior may be pragmatic, depending on their perceptions of what type of behavior will lead to increased effectiveness and influence in interactions with others. Mixed-sex interactions, in particular, may elicit more consideration of who holds power and, thus, may influence the particular blend of communication styles displayed by male and female speakers.

The importance of the relative power of interactants is evident in several studies. As noted earlier, girls more often use a somewhat more dominant style in their interactions with boys when another girl is present (Killen & Naigles, 1995; Leaper, 1991). Similarly, preschool-aged Chinese girls become bossy and argumentative with boys when enacting domestic scenes, a traditionally feminine domain in Chinese culture (Kyratzis & Guo, 1996). In this context, girls refuse to relent to boys' challenges, whereas boys defer to girls. Kyratzis and Guo pointed out that domestic roles have a high social value in Chinese culture, and women play a dominant and powerful role in this sphere. The preschool-aged boys and girls in this study seemed to have a clear appreciation for these larger culturally influenced power relationships as they reenacted them in their play.

Power also affects adult communication. Several studies have reported that powerful individuals interrupt more than less powerful individuals. For example, parents interrupt children more than children interrupt parents (Greif, 1980; West & Zimmerman, 1977); among romantic couples, the more powerful partner interrupts more than the less powerful partner (Kollock, Blumstein, & Schwartz, 1985); and university faculty members interrupt other faculty more when they possess higher rather than lower rank (Eakins & Eakins, 1976). In a study simulating an organizational setting, C. Johnson (1994) found that participants, regardless of gender, talked more and spoke less tentatively when they were assigned to a leadership position than to a subordinate position. Based on tape recordings of interactions in actual courtroom settings, O'Barr (1982) found that men and women possessing higher status or education speak less tentatively, using fewer hedges and tag questions, than lower status individuals. Although men show more visual dominance in gender-neutral tasks, both men and women show more visual dominance than the other gender when the task favors the expertise of their gender (Dovidio, Ellyson et al., 1988). Moreover, when working on a masculine sex-typed task, giving women specific training in that task eliminates the gender difference in visual dominance (Brown, Dovidio, & Ellyson, 1990). Research on the speech of male and female leaders reveals that the more authority they have, the more they communicate with subordinates using direct language (Hirokawa, Mickey, & Miura, 1991). Still, even for leaders, some gender differences in speech remain. For example, under conditions when leaders possess legitimate authority over subordinates, women leaders continue to speak less directly to subordinates than do men leaders (Hirokawa et al., 1991).

In summary, several themes emerge in the literature on gender and communication styles. First, there are notable gender differences in communication behaviors that are evident early in childhood and persist into adulthood. Males are generally more concerned with self-assertion and dominance, whereas females are generally more concerned with collaboration and responsiveness to others. What is striking is how early in childhood these gendered styles emerge and how persistent they are over the span of development. Second, these general orientations may not reveal some of the complexities that underlie male and female communication styles. Both sexes may, in fact, show varying amounts of dominance and collaboration, depending on the social situation. Research on mixed-sex interactions suggests that an important factor in the speaker's communication style is the speaker's perception of his or her relative power in the social group.

## Gender Differences in Group Interactions

Research on gender differences in verbal and nonverbal communication, as shown previously, typically focuses on the manner or style in which males and females communicate. A person, for example, could tell a friend to meet him or her for lunch in a direct manner (e.g., "Meet me at the restaurant at noon") or a more indirect manner (e.g., "I guess it would be best if you could meet me at the restaurant kind of around noon"). Research on group interaction, on the other hand, assesses the content or meaning of speech with the particular goal of determining how much of the speaker's communication is instrumental (i.e., directed at achieving some task goal) and how much is expressive (i.e., revealing of the speaker's emotions). A request to meet for lunch would be considered a task behavior, regardless of the style of speech used by the speaker.

Most studies examining gender differences in interaction have used Bales' (1950) *Interaction Process Analysis* to assess the proportion of task contributions, task-related questions, positive social behaviors, and negative social behaviors contributed by each person in the interaction. *Task contributions* are generally directed toward achieving the group's task by providing information, direction, or answers. *Questions* are requests for task-related information. *Positive social contributions* are directed toward maintaining good relationships among group members and showing agreement, whereas *negative social behaviors* express hostility, tension, or disagreement with other group members.

Formal studies of group interaction have typically used adult samples. Still, research on children, although not formally using Bales' (1950) coding scheme, has examined the amount of task-related behavior and positive and negative social behavior in children's interactions. This research reveals that boys engage in more task behavior, commanding and directing their peers, and in more negative social behaviors (e.g., issuing prohibitions, put-downs, and threats) than girls do (Goodwin, 1980; Leaper, 1991; Lever, 1976; McCloskey, 1996; Miller, Danaher, & Forbes, 1986; Sachs, 1987). Girls show higher amounts of positive social behavior (e.g., communicating friendliness and disclosing personal information), more conflict mitigation, and a greater amount of other-oriented speech than do boys (Haslett, 1983; Leaper, 1991; Miller et al., 1986). Even when they issue directives or prohibitions, or engage in conflict, girls offer explanations for their requests and assert their views in a less domineering manner (e.g., with less disagreement and other negative social behavior) and otherwise pay attention to the listener's point of view (Nohara, 1996; Sheldon, 1992). Observations of preschool-aged children in dyadic interactions also indicate that when boys approach girls to begin a social interaction, they use imperatives or simply join in their play without comment. Girls approaching boys are more likely to ask to join in, to help, or to offer information (Phinney & Rotheram, 1982).

Studies of adults in task-oriented groups have typically employed Bales' (1950) analysis or some variation of it. A meta-analytic review of these studies revealed moderate gender differences (Carli, 1981). Overall, men exhibit a higher percentage of task behaviors and direct disagreement than women do; women, on the other hand, exhibit a higher percentage of positive social behaviors than men do. Subsequent research has usually continued to reveal this pattern of findings (Carli, 1989; Craig & Sherif, 1986; Hutson-Comeaux & Kelly, 1996; C. Johnson, Clay-Warner & Funk, 1996; R. A. Johnson & Schulman, 1989; Mabry, 1985; Moskowitz, 1993; Wood & Karten, 1986). Because the analysis of group interaction is based on percentages of each behavior to control for overall talkativeness, these results do not mean that women do not make task contributions to groups. Instead, the results reveal that, compared with men, women contribute a relatively higher percentage of positive social behaviors and relatively lower percentage of negative social behaviors and task behaviors. Essentially, women are relatively more other-oriented. This is further reflected in women's greater willingness to share their positive emotions or disclose personal information than men's (Balswick, 1988; Lewis & McCarthy, 1988; Saurer & Eisler, 1990). Moreover, when women share their feelings and experiences, they often do so in a way that communicates empathy and mutual understanding, for example, by noting how their experience is similar to the person with whom they are speaking (D. Hall & Langellier, 1988). Overall, then, research on group interactions reveals that, compared with women and girls, the interactions of men and boys tend to focus more on the task and involve more disagreement and other negative social behavior. Compared with males, the interactions of women and girls tend to focus on the interpersonal needs of the group and to involve sharing feelings and emotions.

Although gender differences in interaction have been reported for both mixed- and same-sex interactions, there is some evidence that they tend to be larger in same-sex interactions (Aries, 1976; Carli, 1989; C. Johnson et al., 1996; Piliavin & R. R. Martin, 1978; Wheelan & Verdi, 1992), suggesting that both men and women are more warm and other-oriented when interacting with women. These results are similar to the gender differences in verbal and nonverbal warmth, but unlike the gender differences in verbal mitigation and visual dominance. Both men and women are relatively more warm and collaborative when interacting with women and more mitigating when interacting with men (Carli, 1989, 1990). The pattern of showing a greater interpersonal orientation toward women was also reported in a meta-analytic review of gender differences in self-disclosure (Dindia & Allen, 1992). In that review, gender differences were small to medium in size in same-sex interactions and extremely small in mixed-sex interactions. Moreover, both men and women self-disclosed more to women than to men.

Interestingly, just as was found in the research on children's verbal and nonverbal communications, the relative proportion of males and females also affects group interaction. In particular, in mixed-sex groups, stereotypical gender differences in making task contributions, with men making a higher percentage of task contributions than women, are most likely to occur when there is a lone woman in a group of men and least likely to occur when women are in the majority (R. A. Johnson & Schulman, 1989). Apparently, in mixed-sex groups, the absence of a same-sex ally inhibits men and women from contributing to a group.

Just as with gender differences in communication, gender differences in group interaction also depend on the relative power of interactants, such as their relative expertise or experience. When subjects interact on a stereotypically feminine task, women show proportionately more task behavior and less positive social behavior and men show proportionately more positive social behavior and less task behavior than for masculine tasks (Yamada, Tjosvold, & Draguns, 1983). Similarly, stereotypical gender differences in group interaction can also be reduced by giving women feedback that they have superior ability at the task (Wood & Karten, 1986) or by giving them extra experience at performing the task (Lockheed & K. P. Hall, 1976).

Do the gender differences in group interaction hold among male and female leaders? Perhaps men and women leaders behave more similarly than men and women do generally because formal leadership positions may prescribe particular behaviors, such as a high amount of task behavior. In fact, a person's relative power and status do affect his or her contributions to group interactions. In a study examining communications between third and first graders, McCloskey (1996) found that the older child, the leader in the interaction, produced most of the tutorial speech, that is, task contributions directed toward providing the younger child with information. Among college students, leaders exhibit more task behavior than subordinates do, regardless of gender (C. Johnson, 1993). With regard to gender differences, McCloskey (1996) found that girls in leadership positions actually contributed more tutorial speech than boys in the same position. In addition, Eagly and Johnson's (1990) meta-analytic review of gender differences in leadership style revealed no gender differences in task behaviors and only a very small difference in social behavior. Clearly, possessing a high-status position not only increases task behavior but also reduces stereotypic gender differences in interaction.

Nevertheless, even among leaders, some such differences remain. For example, the older boys in McCloskey's (1996) study exhibited more negative social behavior, such as insults and threats, than the older girls did, and the meta-analysis on adult leaders revealed that women leaders are more democratic and men leaders more autocratic than leaders of the opposite gender (Eagly & Johnson, 1990). Democratic leaders encourage collaboration and involve subordinates in decisions, reflecting a positive social orientation toward subordinates, whereas autocratic leaders are more directive and discourage participation by subordinates. Therefore, female leaders, although equally task-oriented, are also more other-directed than men.

In sum, as was the case with communication styles, there are gender-patterned styles of interaction in groups: males' communications emphasize task and negative social behaviors, whereas females' emphasize positive social behaviors. Once again, these are patterns that are evident in remarkably adultlike form from early childhood. As was the case with communication styles, gender-typed interaction in groups can change as a function of the gender composition of the group as well as perceived social power. Both genders display more positive social behavior in their interactions with females and more negative social behavior in their interactions with males. In addition, powerful individuals exhibit a relatively high amount of task behavior compared with less powerful individuals. These findings suggest that the particular pattern of interaction exhibited in groups depends on a complex interplay of factors, including each individual's standing in a social group as well as his or her perceptions about what behaviors would be both appropriate and effective, given the group task.

## Gender Differences in Social Influence

Research indicates that males are less influenced by females than females are by males. Resistance to female influence begins in early childhood. Jacklin and Maccoby's (1978) study of 33-month-old toddlers revealed that male toddlers were able to influence one another's behavior by issuing prohibitions; female toddlers were able to influence other girls, but were unable to influence boys, who simply ignored the influence attempts of girls.

Gender differences in social influence tend to become clearer as children become older; between 41 and 66 months of age, boys become generally more resistant to influence, whereas girls do not. Boys make more influence attempts than girls. Moreover, when using direct requests, in the form of imperatives or declaratives, boys are equally influential with male and female peers. However, even when girls use this seemingly powerful masculine style, they exert less influence over boys than over girls (Serbin et al., 1982). In mixed-sex interactions, girls (from a U.S. sample) exhibit more compliance (Kyratzis & Guo, 1996) or ask boys questions or for their opinions (Serbin et al., 1982).

Research on adults shows that men exert more influence than women in gender-neutral contexts (Pugh & Wahrman, 1983; Wagner, Ford, & Ford, 1986; Ward, Seccombe, Bendel, & L. F. Carter, 1985). Men resist influence by women more than women resist influence by men, even when there are no gender differences in the frequency or quality of the influence attempts.

Propp (1995) reported that when men and women interacted in the same group, information introduced by men was six times more likely to influence the group than the same information introduced by women; in fact, information introduced by women was usually ignored.

Just as with research on verbal and nonverbal communication and group interactions, the gender differences in social influence depend on the relative power of group members. In general, both males and females are more easily influenced in tasks that favor the interests or knowledge of the other gender (Eagly & Carli, 1981). For example, in the Kyratzis and Guo (1996) research mentioned earlier, Chinese girls exerted more influence than boys when the children were involved in a feminine task. Among adults, when tasks favor female expertise or are in a traditional female domain, women's ability to influence men increases (Pugh & Wahrman, 1983; Wagner et al., 1986).

Men's greater influence is also reflected in research on leadership attainment. Men attain leadership more often than women. In their meta-analytic review of gender differences in leader emergence, Eagly and Karau (1991) found that in initially leaderless groups, men emerged as leaders more often than women did, especially for task leadership and especially in groups that did not require complex social interactions among group members. Women's emphasis on positive social behavior in groups has resulted in their being characterized as the social leaders of groups (Bales, 1950); and Eagly and Karau (1991) found that women did, in fact, emerge more often than men as social leaders, although this effect was quite small. Nevertheless, it is task leadership (Stein & Heller, 1979) and total group participation (Mullen, Salas, & Driskell, 1989) that are generally associated with attaining a formal leadership position in groups, and as a result, it is men, more than women, who emerged as overall leaders of their groups (Eagly & Karau, 1991). Interestingly, although men are more likely to emerge as leaders than women are, a meta-analysis of leadership effectiveness revealed higher levels of effectiveness among male leaders only in military settings; women are as effective as men in businesses and in studies in involving college students and are actually more effective leaders than men in government and education organizations (Eagly, Karau, & Makhijani, 1995). The gender difference in leader emergence, then, is not a function of women's lower effectiveness but rather represents a bias against female leaders and resistance to their influence and leadership. Men, in particular, resist female leadership (Eagly, Makhijani, & Klonsky, 1992; Forsyth, Heiney, & Wright, 1997).

## Relation of Gender Differences in Communication and Interaction to Gender Differences in Social Influence

What is the relation of gender differences in communication to gender differences in social influence? Are women and girls less influential because they communicate in a more collaborative manner than men and boys? Are males influential because of their dominant, status-asserting, and powerful language? Although some researchers have argued that women and girls are disadvantaged because of their relatively powerless language (Lakoff, 1975), others claim that gender differences in speech may result from, rather than cause, gender differences in social influence (Carli, 1990).

Both male and female college students have been found to be more influential when using a communication style that is stereotypically associated with their gender than when using a style associated with the other gender (Burgoon, Dillard, & Doran, 1983; Buttner & McEnally, 1996). Research on hiring recommendations by managers indicates that women who communicate in a direct manner are less likely to be hired than men who speak directly or than women who communicate in a less stereotypically masculine manner (Buttner & McEnally, 1996). In particular, research on college students indicates that use of a masculine communication style is especially ineffective for women. For example, Carli (1990) reported a study showing that a woman speaker exerted greater influence over the opinions of male college students when she used somewhat tentative rather than very direct speech, whereas men speakers were equally influential with both males and females regardless of how they spoke. Men perceived the tentative woman to be less competent but more likable than her more direct counterpart. These results demonstrate not only that directness in language is less acceptable in women, but also that men have fewer constraints on their behavior when exerting influence over others. Other research reveals that women who are directive or demanding in their speech are perceived as unfeminine (Sterling & Owen, 1982). Based on these findings, it is clear that there is no one type of speech (e.g., assertive vs. tentative) that enhances influence; instead the effectiveness of a particular pattern of speech depends on the gender of both the speaker and the speaker's audience.

In research on nonverbal behavior, men who show high levels of visual dominance are more influential than men who show low levels; however, the relation of visual dominance to influence is reversed for women (Mehta et al., 1989, cited in Ellyson et al., 1992). The more visually dominant a woman is, the less she is able to influence others, perhaps because nonverbally dominant women are disliked more than nonverbally dominant men (Copeland, Driskell, & Salas, 1995). Similar effects have been found for other nonverbal behaviors. Carli, LaFleur, and Loeber (1995) reported that women who show a high degree of nonverbal competence (e.g., using rapid speech, few hesitations or stumbles, an upright posture, and moderate eye gaze) exerted less influence over male college students than male speakers using the same pattern of behavior. Although women students were equally influenced by the competent men and the competent women, men considered the competent women to be less likable and more threatening than their male counterparts. Female speakers were able to influence a male audience while conveying competence only when they also showed nonverbal warmth (e.g., by smiling, nodding, and leaning forward). These results again show that women exert little influence when they violate traditional gender role norms, whereas men have more freedom as to how they influence others.

Research has shown that men express more task behavior and disagreement and women more positive social behavior in groups. How do these gender differences in interaction relate to social influence? A number of theorists have argued that women must be collaborative and other-oriented to be influential because such behavior communicates little desire to exert influence or assert status over others (Lockheed & K. P. Hall, 1976; Meeker & Weitzel-O'Neill, 1985). In fact, women who exhibit positive social behaviors exert greater influence than women who do not; on the other hand, the amount of positive social behavior is unrelated to influence for male speakers (Carli, 1998; Ridgeway, 1982; Shackelford, Wood, & Worchel, 1996). These findings are comparable to the report noted previously that women influenced men more when they combined nonverbal warmth with competence than when they were merely competent (Carli et al., 1995). Similar findings have been reported from a meta-analysis of studies examining the evaluation of male and female leaders in a variety of settings: high school, college, graduate school, and business. Women are rated less favorably than men when they lead in an autocratic rather than a democratic or collaborative manner (Eagly, Makhijani, & Klonsky, 1992). Again, women must adhere more closely than men do to traditional sex-role norms in order to be influential. In addition, because exhibiting relatively high amounts of positive social behavior increases both men's and women's likableness (Carli, 1989), being likable appears to be more important to women's ability to influence others than to men's ability.

As noted earlier, task contributions are associated with leader emergence in groups. However, research indicates that the relation of task contributions to influence is stronger for men than for women. Women's task contributions are more likely to be ignored or to evoke negative reactions from others than men's contributions are (D. Butler & Geis, 1990; Ridgeway, 1982). In addition, although men's task contributions in mixed-sex groups predict their ability to influence other group members, women's task contributions are unrelated to influence (Walker, Ilardi, McMahon, & Fennell, 1996). Moreover, men, in particular, respond less favorably to women's task behavior than women do. Men rate task-oriented female leaders as less effective than task-oriented male leaders, whereas women rate male and female task leaders as equally effective (Rojahn & Willemsen, 1994).

Disagreement also has different effects on social influence for men and women. In a study involving dyadic interactions, Carli (1998) found that male confederates were equally influential and likable whether they agreed or disagreed with their partner, whereas female confederates who disagreed exerted less influence and were considered less likable than agreeable women. Furthermore, subjects showed increased antagonism and hostility toward female confederates who disagreed but did not show more hostility toward disagreeing male confederates. Again, women are more constrained than men in the kinds of behaviors that they can engage in and still be influential. For women to exert influence, they must exhibit traditionally feminine behaviors and ensure their likableness.

Other evidence that women must communicate in a traditionally feminine style in order to remain influential comes from research on modest versus self-promoting communications. Although speaking in a confident and self-promoting manner can benefit men, women receive greater recognition when they are modest than when they are self-promoting (Giacalone & Riordan, 1990; Wosinska, Dabul, Whetstone-Dion, & Cialdini, 1996). Self-promoting women are, for the most part, less influential and less likable than modest women (Rudman, 1998). Although women who self-promote may be perceived as more competent and confident than those who are modest, competence and confidence may be threatening when shown by women.

Unfortunately, this creates a double bind for women. In general, people are influential when they are perceived to be competent or expert, so communication that conveys a high degree of competence should enhance women's influence. However, as the research on self-promoting language shows, women can sometimes be too competent to be influential. Competent women are at a particular disadvantage with interacting with men. Men resist influence by women who appear highly competent, although women do not (Carli, 1990; Carli, LaFleur, & Loeber, 1995). For example, Foschi, Lai, and Sigerson (1994) conducted a study in which they manipulated the competence of male and female job candidates and then gave undergraduates the choice of hiring the man, the woman, or no one at all. Women preferred to hire the candidate with the better academic record, regardless of gender; men would hire the better male candidate, but preferred to hire no one at all to hiring a more competent woman.

Under what conditions do men defer to the influence of competent women? In general, men are less resistant to the influence of a woman when they stand to gain by her influence. Men are more influenced by a competent over a less competent woman when her ideas can help them achieve some goal, such as obtaining money or some other reward (Shackelford et al., 1996) and more influenced by a competent woman over a less competent man when the woman can help them improve their performance on a task (Pugh & Wahrman, 1983).

# THEORETICAL EXPLANATIONS FOR GENDER DIFFERENCES IN COMMUNICATION AND SOCIAL INFLUENCE

## Status Characteristics Theory

One explanation for gender differences in communication and social influence is that, in our culture, women and girls have lower status than men and boys (Berger, Fisek, Norman, & Zelditch, 1977; Carli, 1991; Meeker & Weitzel-O'Neill, 1985; Wagner & Berger, 1997). According to status characteristics theory (Berger et al., 1977), gender acts as a *diffuse status characteristic*, a general characteristic that is associated with an individual's relative status in society. Race, age, education, gender, and physical attractiveness all operate as diffuse status characteristics. Physical attractiveness, for example, is a status characteristic because being attractive is considered more desirable than being unattractive. In general, diffuse status characteristics, such as gender, operate in groups whose members differ with respect to that characteristic (e.g., in mixed-sex groups) but not in status-homogeneous groups (e.g., same-sex groups). Individuals of high diffuse status are assumed to be more competent than those of low diffuse status; consequently, in group interactions, high status individuals are encouraged to make contributions to the task, receive more positive reactions to their contributions, and exert greater influence than low status members (Berger et al., 1977). According to status theory, males would therefore be given more opportunities to contribute to the group task and would exert greater influence over other group members than females. Also, because those who make contributions to a group task enhance their status (Ridgeway, 1978; Wood & Karten, 1986) and increase their chances of emerging as group leaders (Hawkins, 1995; Stein & Heller, 1979), the expectation of greater male competence and influence can be self-fulfilling.

In fact, there is evidence that males are considered more competent than females. In gender neutral domains, men are generally considered more competent than women are (Carli, 1991; Wood & Karten, 1986). Research reveals a double standard in evaluating men and women. This means that women must perform better to be considered equally competent. This is true whether subjects are evaluating themselves (Foddy & Graham, 1987, cited in Foschi, 1992; Foschi, 1996) or their partners in group interactions (Biernat & Kobrynowicz, 1997; Bradley, 1981; Foschi, 1996).

According to status characteristics theorists, individuals' diffuse status not only affects their perceived competence and expectations about their future performance but also affects expectations about what constitutes appropriate behavior in the group. Low-status individuals do not have the *legitimacy* to act as leaders or influence agents in groups and are penalized for attempting to lead or influence the group (Meeker & Weitzel-O'Neill, 1985; Ridgeway & Berger, 1986). Behaviors that are associated with leadership and status are therefore acceptable when displayed by high-status individuals but unacceptable in those of low status because such behavior appears to represent an illegitimate attempt to gain status within the group. Consequently, whereas the contributions of high-status members are accepted and encouraged, enhancing their status further, the contributions of low-status individuals are often ignored or rejected, causing their status to drop even more (Meeker & Weitzel-O'Neill, 1985). According to this theory, people resist influence and leadership by women and girls more than by men and boys. In fact, in order to reduce this resistance, a female may have to convince others that she has little personal ambition to lead or control the group and that her contributions are motivated by a desire to help the other group members. One way to do this would be to use indirect forms of influence and to display increased amounts of warmth and positive social behaviors (Meeker & Weitzel-O'Neill, 1985; Ridgeway & Diekema, 1992).

## Social Role Theory

According to Eagly's (1987; Eagly, Wood, & Diekman, chap. 5, this volume) social role theory, gender differences in social influence and communication occur because men and women usually possess different social roles. Gender differences in behavior occur because the different roles that men and women possess typically demand very different behaviors. Moreover, both men and women adapt to their different role demands by developing different skills and by modifying their behaviors to fit the requirements of their respective roles.

In general, men possess occupational roles more than women do, and women possess domestic roles more than men. Even when women are employed, compared with men, they have more part-time employment and employment in relatively low-status jobs (Shelton, 1992). For example, men are more likely than women to be employed as upper level managers, a role that involves directiveness and leadership, whereas women are more likely than men to possess the role of primary caretaker, a role requiring nurturance and warmth. Sex-stereotyped behaviors displayed by men and women reflect their adaptation to their different social roles. In general, men's roles can be characterized as *agentic* and status-asserting, and women's roles can be characterized as *communal* and other-directed (Bakan, 1966; Pratto, Stallworth, Sidanius, & Siers, 1997; Wiggins, 1992).

Based on social role theory, as a consequence of the different distribution of men and women into life roles, the two genders often display different behaviors, leading people to expect these gender differences. Social role theory, like status characteristics theory, predicts that people would expect more agentic behavior, leadership, and influence from males than females and more communal behavior, deference, and warmth from females than males. Furthermore, because sex stereotypes can be self-fulfilling (Skrypnek & Snyder, 1982), these expectations can lead to gender differences in behavior.

In fact, knowledge of sex stereotypes is evident in children as young as 2 years and increases through elementary and middle school years (Kuhn, Nash, & Brucken, 1978; Serbin, Powlishta, & Gulko, 1993). In general, people do consider men to have more agentic qualities than women and women to have more communal qualities than men (Broverman, Vogel, Broverman, Clarkson, & Rosenkrantz, 1972; Ruble, 1983; Williams & Best, 1990). Women and girls are considered to be warmer, more sensitive, and more concerned with others, whereas men are considered to be more independent, competitive, and assertive. Furthermore, according to social role theory, gender differences in behavior, deriving from traditional gender roles, become not only expected but also demanded (Eagly, 1987). Sex-role norms require women to be more communal than men and men to be more agentic than women. Violations of these expectations can lead to penalties. Hence, both social role theory and status characteristics theory predict that women and girls should be less influential than men and boys when using a traditional masculine style of communication. Also, because influence and leadership are more congruent with male status and male roles, women and girls should be more disadvantaged than men and boys when violating gender-role expectations in leadership or influence contexts.

## Evidence Related to Status
## Characteristics and Social Role Theories

Clearly, many of the gender differences in communication and influence are consistent with both social role and status characteristics theories. Research on gender differences in communication overall does reveal more status-asserting or agentic language by males and more other-directed or communal language by females. Also consistent with both theories are the findings that men emerge more often as leaders and exert more influence over others than women do. Women, in general, are more constrained in the way they lead or influence than men are. In order to be effective, women must avoid traditionally masculine forms of communication and exhibit more other-directed speech. Furthermore, as described earlier, research on the effects of sex-role-norm violations in language indicates that women who are directive, commanding, or immodest in their speech receive more negative sanctions than do men.

According to status characteristics theory, gender is only one status characteristic. Other information about individuals' relative status in groups should also be used to infer overall status, including whether someone possesses a leadership position or special knowledge about the task. Gender differences in communication and influence would then be predicted by an individual's overall status. According to social role theory, people derive expectations about how they and others should behave based on the roles they possess. Therefore, people in leadership positions or who possess role-related expertise would be expected to exhibit more agentic behavior than those without such positions or expertise.

Support for status characteristics theory and social role theory, then, comes from research showing that gender differences in communication and influence depend on the relative power of interactants. Fewer gender differences in communication are found among leaders than among males and females in general. Gender differences in use of mitigating speech, visual dominance, and group interaction are reduced when females are more powerful, relative to males. Women and girls also communicate more assertively and exert more influence than men and boys when subjects are interacting in a feminine domain or one which favors the female's expertise.

Status theory, in particular, predicts that gender differences in behavior should be most pronounced in mixed-sex interactions, when gender acts as a diffuse status characteristic. This prediction has support from the research on gender differences in mitigated speech and visual dominance. In mixed-sex groups, women speak in a more mitigated manner and exhibit less visual dominance than men. However, contrary to predictions based on status theory, gender differences in verbal reinforcement, nonverbal warmth, and group interaction—especially for positive and negative social behaviors—appear to be more pronounced in same-sex interactions, as described earlier. Overall, both males and females are generally more warm in their interactions with females than males. A reasonable inference is that mixed-sex interactions enhance gender differences in status-related behaviors, behaviors conveying relative levels of dominance and power, because under such conditions males would possess higher status than females. However, displays of verbal and nonverbal warmth, although effective at reducing resistance to female influence in mixed-sex interactions, may also have a purely affiliative meaning, particularly in interactions among women or girls. That is, both males and females expect interactions with females to be more pleasant and warm and therefore they may themselves express greater warmth to females than males. Once warm behaviors are expressed they would likely encourage further warmth from other interactants, creating a snowball effect. This interpretation is congruent with social role theory, which posits that the particular behaviors displayed by men and women should be normative for the particular roles they are enacting. Perhaps, then, people interacting with women may take on a more informal social role than people interacting with men. One other possibility is that males may increase their interpersonal warmth when interacting with a female because they believe that she will respond favorably to it. Consequently, warm or affiliative behaviors may very well serve three purposes: Females may use them in interacting with males to reduce male resistance to female influence attempts, both males and females may exhibit them to be friendly and collaborative when such friendliness seems appropriate or expected (e.g., when they are interacting with a girl or woman), and males may exhibit them to elicit favorable reactions from a female—perhaps even with the goal of increasing their influence over her.

According to social role and status characteristics theories, gender differences in communication and influence are mediated by the expectation that women and girls are less agentic and competent than men and boys. That is, men and boys are perceived by others to have leaderlike characteristics and to possess high task abilities to a greater extent than women and girls. Of particular relevance to status characteristics theory and social role theory is research on perceived competence. In a study involving children, preschool boys and girls were asked to prepare a lunch for a group of younger children at their school (Carli, Werner, Alfonso, & Lau, 1997). Subjects were paired with same- or opposite-sex partners while they worked and then subsequently evaluated their performance at the task. In same-sex pairs, girls' actual performance was better than boys', but there were no gender differences in self-evaluation. Although objective raters found no gender differences in performance in the mixed-sex pairs, boys evaluated themselves more favorably in mixed-sex pairs than girls did. In addition, boys' self- evaluations were higher after interacting with a girl than after interacting with a boy.

Similar results were found in research on adults. In two studies of group interaction and self-evaluation in same- and mixed-sex pairs, undergraduate students discussed a topic upon which they disagreed and then later evaluated the quality and quantity of their ideas in the discussions (Carli, 1997a). Regardless of the sex composition of the pairs, independent raters found no gender differences in the quality or quantity of subjects' ideas. Nevertheless, in mixed-sex, but not same-sex pairs, men evaluated themselves more favorably than women evaluated themselves. Moreover, both men and women made more sex-stereotypical self-evaluations after mixed-gender than after same-gender interactions. These results, combined with those found with children, suggest that boys, men, and women all have more favorable self-evaluations after interacting with a female than a male. These findings confirm status characteristics and social role theories' prediction that people expect greater competency in males than in females, that these expectancies become heightened in the context of a mixed-sex interaction, and, further, that subjects' evaluations of their own behavior will tend to confirm these expectations.

In order to have strong explanatory power for the development of gender differences in communication and influence, status characteristics theory and social role theory should account for the fact that gendered communication, interaction, and influence styles occur early in development. As noted earlier, children's behavior in social interactions, even that of preschool-aged children, is in many ways consistent with both theoretical views. However, both theoretical positions call for certain forms of knowledge on the part of children. An implication of social role theory is that even pre-school-aged children have a fair amount of knowledge about the typical roles assumed by men and women and the characteristics associated with these roles. As mentioned earlier, research has confirmed that by the age of 2 or 3 years, children have a well-articulated understanding of stereotypical roles and traits. Status theory presumes two other aspects of children's behavior: first, that they are capable of responding on the basis of diffuse status characteristics and, second, that they have some understanding of the relative social standing of men versus women. There is some evidence that even preschool-aged children respond to others on the basis of diffuse status characteristics, for example, age and physical attractiveness. Preschoolers recognize that different types of speech are appropriate when speaking to young children as opposed to adults (Shatz & Gelman, 1973). In addition, preschoolers believe that attractive children are more friendly and intelligent than unattractive children (Dion & Berscheid, 1974; Langlois & Stephan, 1981). Young children also associate greater physical height and mature-looking faces (as opposed to baby faces) with greater power (Montepare, 1995; Montepare & Zebrowitz-McArthur, 1989). However, there is less information about children's knowledge of gender as a diffuse status characteristic. What exactly do they know about the status of males and females? Do they indeed believe that females have lower status than males? Some evidence shows that preschoolers, like adults, generally value the personality characteristics associated with females over those associated with males; however, they place higher value on stereotypical male occupations than female occupations (Bukatko, Fauth, & Lombard, 1997; Bukatko & Shedd, 1999). Thus, young children do possess evaluative beliefs about gender, some of which place males in higher status than females. The fact remains, though, that we have very little understanding of young children's knowledge about the status characteristics of males and females and how that knowledge might be related to their communication and influence styles.

## Gender Schema Theory

One important model for understanding gender-typing in the developmental psychology literature is gender schema theory, which emphasizes the role that a child's accumulating knowledge about gender plays in influencing behavior. According to gender schema theory, individuals tend to organize social information that surrounds them into cognitive frameworks that serve to guide future thinking and behavior. This is a general tendency of thinking beings, providing a way of dealing with information in a more efficient manner. Because gender is a highly salient social category, children begin to use this dimension to order their thinking about the social world as soon as they acquire gender identity. C. L. Martin and Halverson (1981) suggested that children first construct a broader, superordinate *same-sex/opposite-sex schema*, which is composed largely of stereotypes of the characteristics of males and females. A more elaborate and specific *own-sex schema* also develops, which consists of the various behaviors relevant to one's own sex.

Gender schemas influence which social information will be attended to in the first place and which information will be remembered. Children generally focus on and remember information that is consistent with their sex-stereotypical beliefs (D. B. Carter & Levy, 1988; Koblinsky, Cruse, & Sugawara, 1978). Gender schemas are so powerful that they may even lead to the distortion of information to make it consistent with one's gender schemata (C. L. Martin & Halverson, 1983; Signorella & Liben, 1984).

According to gender schema theory, once children reliably recognize their own gender, they behave in ways that are consistent with same-sex group membership; they positively evaluate individuals and behaviors associated with their own gender and negatively evaluate individuals and behaviors of the other gender. In some (but not all) research, gender schemas have been shown to influence children's behaviors. For example, children strongly prefer to play with toys labeled for their own sex as opposed to those labeled for the opposite sex (Bradbard & Endsley, 1983).

Although it has not explicitly done so, gender schema theory has the potential to explain differences in communication, interaction, and influence behaviors between boys and girls. Fagot and Leinbach (1993) pointed out that the phase between ages 2 and 4—a time when gender-typed discourse is already evident—is a period of accelerated acquisition of gender schemata; young children master gender labels for themselves and others, as well as gender stereotypes. Included in the base of information that children construct is not only explicit information, such as knowledge about stereotypes, but also tacit or abstract knowledge (Fagot & Leinbach, 1993; C. L. Martin, 1994). Tacit knowledge might include impressions or metaphorical knowledge, such as the ideas that "hearts" belong to girls and women and "something rough" belongs to boys and men (Fagot & Leinbach, 1993). It may very well be that speaking styles, task-orientation versus social-orientation, and more importantly, differential levels of power and status associated with males and females, including who resists and who gives in to influence, are part of that tacit knowledge. Presumably, the information that has been incorporated as part of these gender schemata directs the behaviors of the child. Questions remain as to the extent to which children acquire tacit beliefs about gender, the ages at which they do so, and further, whether these beliefs do, in fact, serve to influence subsequent behavior. In addition, it remains to be seen how gender schema theory can explain variations in children's social behaviors in response to changes in the composition of the social group (e.g., boys' increasing collaboration in the presence of girls). Unfortunately, very little research has been directed at identifying children's tacit or abstract knowledge about gender.

## Social Learning Theory

Social learning theory points to the role that modeling and reinforcement play in shaping gender-related behaviors in individuals (Mischel, 1966). Of particular importance are the behaviors of the same-sex parent and the differential reinforcements given to boys and girls. More recent versions of social learning theory acknowledge the role of several cognitive processes in socialization (Bandura, 1977, 1986; Perry & Bussey, 1979). First, children will produce gender-typed behaviors to the extent that they attend to the model's behaviors; children pay more attention to same-sex models and models that display sex-typical behavior. Second, children observe the frequency with which males and females as a group perform certain behaviors, resulting in the recognition (and memory) that certain behaviors are sex-typed. Third, motivational factors are involved; children's attempts to seek rewards and retain a sense of mastery influence their performance of gender-typed behaviors. Finally, self-regulation of gender-typed behaviors becomes important, especially as children grow older. According to social learning theory, then, the origins of sex differences in communication, interaction, and influence can be traced to the models children observe and the reinforcements they receive.

There is a good deal of evidence that parents may serve as models for gender-typed communication and interaction styles. Fathers use more directives—in some studies, twice as many—compared to mothers when speaking to their preschoolers (Bellinger & Gleason, 1982; Gleason, 1975;

Lindsey, Mize, & Pettit, 1997). They also interrupt more (Greif, 1980). Mothers use more supportive language (e.g., praise, approval, agreement, collaboration) with their children than do fathers (Mannle & Tomasello, 1987; Tomasello, Conti-Ramsden, & Ewert, 1990). A recent meta-analysis of parental speech to children concluded that many of the effect sizes associated with these findings are small but nonetheless still suggest a role for parental modeling of gender-typed speech (Leaper, Anderson, & Sanders, 1998). Thus, both boys and girls have opportunities to observe the characteristic speaking and interaction styles of both males and females. According to social learning theory, same-sex behaviors may be especially salient to children.

Research also shows that parents speak differently to their sons than to their daughters. Beginning when their children are around 2 years of age, mothers use more directives, prohibitions, and forceful commands with boys and more questions and supportive speech with girls (Cherry & Lewis, 1976; Cloran, 1989; Fagot, 1978; Gleason, 1975; Gleason, Ely, Perlmann, & Narasimhan, 1996). Parents interrupt girls more than they do boys (Greif, 1980). They use demeaning or disparaging names with boys such as *wiseguy* and *nutcake* (Gleason, 1975). Mothers also engage in almost twice as much emotion-talk with their 2- and 3-year-old daughters as with sons (Dunn, Bretherton, & Munn, 1987; Kuebli, S. Butler, & Fivush, 1995). Some of these differential patterns of adult speech to boys versus girls are associated with relatively small effect sizes. However, the effect sizes are larger in some contexts than others, such as situations where parents and children have more choice in their activities during an observation session (Leaper et al., 1998). Parental speech to their children tends to be more supportive and affiliative when they are participating in sociodramatic play, such as playing store, and is more task-oriented during focused situations, like toy construction tasks (Leaper & Gleason, 1996). Since girls are more likely to opt for sociodramatic play and boys are more likely to choose construction play, girls and boys may experience different types of parental speech and interactions styles because of the play activities they engage in. Thus, although the effects may be direct and/or mediated through type of play activities, it is tenable that the differential behaviors of parents toward boys versus girls provide children with information on how they themselves should speak and interact. The result is gender differences in children's language and interaction styles. In fact, observational research indicates that mothers' use of negative communications to their 2-year-old sons predicts their sons' use of coercive forms of social influence with peers at age 6 (Crockenberg & Lourie, 1996).

Finally, boys and girls, at least to some degree, receive differential reinforcement for the interactive styles they use. During the toddler years, girls' assertive behaviors are not attended to by teachers, for example, whereas boys' are (Fagot, Hagan, Leinbach, & Kronsberg, 1985). In contrast, mothers respond to supportive speech of daughters in the context of playing with toy food (Leaper, Leve, Strasser, & R. Schwartz, 1995). A meta-analysis of studies of parents' differential socialization of boys and girls showed that, in general, the magnitude of the effects is small. However, a significant effect was found for parental encouragement of sex-typed activities (Lytton & Romney, 1991). Differential reinforcement may thus not be the primary contributor to gender-typed behaviors, but probably does play some part in their emergence.

A stronger case could be made for the role that modeling and reinforcement play in influencing gender-typed behaviors if more data were available relating the behaviors of parents, teachers, and even siblings to the subsequent communication and interaction styles of boys and girls. At this point, very few longitudinal studies of this nature have been carried out. Moreover, in its emphasis on observational learning and differential reinforcement, social learning theory has the potential to explain gender-typed patterns of influence, as well as variations in interaction strategies as a function of the structure of the social group. Perhaps boys and girls have opportunities to see males' and females' influence attempts and their outcomes and to experience differential rewards for their own performance of and response to varying influence strategies. For example, fathers react positively to compliance from their daughters (Kerig, Cowan, & Cowan, 1993) but are less compliant themselves to daughters than to sons (Maccoby & Jacklin, 1983). Similarly, children may experience rewards for modulating their interaction styles in the presence of members of the opposite sex. Clearly, more research is needed to explore the implications of social learning theory for communication and influence behaviors.

## Gender Differences in Activity or Difficultness

It is possible that gender differences in communication and interaction are related to differences in temperament or to the general tempo of activity displayed by boys and girls. Although the data are not consistent, there is some evidence to suggest that boys are more active, irritable, and arousable as infants and toddlers than girls are (Eaton & Enns, 1986; Fabes, 1994; Kohnstamm, 1989; Prior, 1992). Active children may simply be predisposed to use a brusque, assertive interactional style. Alternatively, adults' responses to even small gender differences in activity and difficultness may mediate the relation of children's gender with gender differences in communication (Carli, 1997b). Active, irritable children elicit more negative parental reactions than children who are "easy," a pattern that is especially true for boys (Fagot & O'Brien, 1994). Active children and their parents get involved in more physical and verbal power struggles (Buss, 1981). This type of parent–child interaction may be set in motion at the time of the child's transition to upright locomotion, a developmental phase that is associated with greater conflicts between mothers and children. Mothers use more verbal and physical prohibitions at this time, especially with boys (Biringen, Emde, Campos, & Appelbaum, 1995). It is interesting to note that this is precisely the age at which children are also beginning to make rapid advances in language acquisition. It is reasonable to suggest, then, that active children—more likely boys—hear a more assertive, abrupt type of speech from their parents than less active children, providing a model for their own speech. Longitudinal research examining child activity levels, parental responses, and subsequent child behavior patterns is needed to substantiate these claims.[2]

---

[2]One theoretical model that has been used to account for gender differences in communication is speech accommodation theory (Giles, Mulac, Bradac, & P. Johnson, 1987). When conversing, people can either become more similar to one another, or *convergent*, in their speech or become more dissimilar to one another, or *divergent*, in their speech. According to speech accommodation theory, convergence typically reflects a desire for social approval and an identification or integration with the other person in the interaction, whereas divergence typically reflects a desire to maintain a separate identity and independence from others in the interaction (Giles et al., 1987). Research assessing speech accommodation theory has revealed that convergence in speech rate, accent, and response latencies is, in fact, as predicted by the theory, associated with being perceived as warm and cooperative (Feldman, 1968; Welkowitz & Kuc, 1973).

Although speech accommodation theory was not developed to explain gender differences in communication and influence, several studies examining gender differences in communication have been cited in support of the theory. According to the theory, in general, men are more divergent than women and women more convergent than men; that is, women tend to imitate the speech style of the people with whom they interact more than men do. This occurs, according to the theory, because women have lower status and power than men do and, as a result, are more inclined to want to emulate and seek the approval of others, especially when those others are male (Giles et al., 1987). Some research does indicate that, compared with same-sex interactions, in mixed-sex interactions, both men and women use more masculine speech (e.g., slang, a deep voice, and aggressive language) (Hogg, 1985), presumably reflecting women's convergence to stereotypically masculine speech and men's divergence from women's stereotypically feminine speech. Other research indicates that women show more convergence to men than to women in the amount that they switch from Spanish to English in bilingual conversations (Valdes-Fallis, 1977). However, for the behaviors examined in the present chapter, there does not appear to be consistent evidence that women are more convergent and men more divergent in communication. Both males and females speak in a less mitigated or tentative manner, are more nonverbally dominant or status-asserting, and are nonverbally and verbally warmer when interacting with females than with males. Men interacting with women, therefore, are in some ways divergent (i.e., more dominant and less tentative) and in others convergent (i.e., warmer). Similarly, women interacting with men are in some ways convergent (i.e., less warm) and in others divergent (i.e., less dominant and more tentative). Moreover, although convergence may generally reflect a desire for social approval and divergence reflect a desire for separateness, there undoubtedly are times when the opposite is true. For example, subjects tend to disagree in response to the disagreements of confederates

## CONCLUSION

Overall, research across the life span indicates that females' communications are more other-directed, warm, and mitigated, and less dominant, status-asserting, aggressive, and task-oriented than males' speech. Moreover, women and girls who exhibit traditionally masculine forms of speech, conveying high amounts of dominance or even competence, are often less influential and less likely to be accepted as leaders. Evidence suggests that gender differences in influence and in mitigated, dominant, and status-asserting speech are related to gender differences in power, status, and social roles. That is, these gender differences tend to be reduced and even reversed when females are in positions of authority or power relative to males. On the other hand, gender differences in other-directed or warm communications appear to depend more on the sex composition of groups than on the status or power of interactants. Both males and females show more warmth to women and girls than to men and boys. These results suggest that different social norms may be operating in interactions with females; perhaps in these instances people enact a more social role, or perhaps they are warm and affiliative because they believe females will find such behavior attractive and influential. Interestingly, other-directed speech can also be used by women in interactions with men to reduce male resistance to female influence. Clearly, the same type of communication can serve very different purposes in different contexts. Overall then, the patterns of communication and influence displayed by females and males—including children—are complex, but in general it appears that both genders exhibit behaviors that are expedient and likely to be most effective and influential, given their power, social roles, and relative position in their interactions with others.

Both status theory and social role theory make predictions that are consistent with the data on gendered styles of communication, interaction, and influence in adults and children. Somewhat problematic for status theory is the finding that males display more affiliative behaviors in the presence of females. According to social role theory, affiliation can be seen as part of the qualities that are associated with females and, so, are appropriate to display

---

(Carli, 1998). In this case, the convergence by subjects cannot be considered a reflection of their desire to gain the approval of the confederate. Instead, convergence here reflects an escalation of conflict.

Other theoretical explanations for gender differences have been proposed including sociobiology (Buss, 1989) and object relations theory (Chodorow, 1974). According to these perspectives, gender differences are based on fundamental differences in the personalities of males and females, which develop because of biological differences between the sexes or because of early interactions between children and primary caretakers. These perspectives have not been discussed in this chapter because they do not specifically address gender differences in communication.

in their presence. From a developmental perspective, there is a good deal of support for the idea that children have knowledge about social roles and the qualities that go with them. We simply do not have enough information yet on children's awareness of status. Many of the claims of status theory and social role theory overlap with gender schema theory, which states that children have knowledge about gender that guides their behavior. Perceptions of status and power relationships may be part of the tacit knowledge base that children build, although more empirical work is needed to explore these ideas. The data on parenting provide support for the social learning perspective. In addition, children may have physiological tendencies that elicit particular styles of parental interaction that, in turn, influence their own behaviors. More longitudinal studies are needed to evaluate these perspectives. One challenge facing developmental accounts of gendered styles of communication, interaction, and influence is to explain the emergence of the complex and nuanced behaviors that children, like adults, show in varying social situations.

# REFERENCES

Aries, E. (1976). Interaction patterns and themes of male, female, and mixed groups. *Small Group Behavior, 7*, 7–18.

Austin, A. M. B., Salehi, M., & Leffler, A. (1987). Gender and developmental differences in children's conversations. *Sex Roles, 16*, 497–510.

Bakan, D. (1966). *The duality of human existence: An essay on psychology and religion.* Chicago: Rand McNally.

Bales, R. F. (1950). *Interaction process analysis: A method for the study of small groups.* Cambridge, MA: Addison-Wesley.

Balswick, J. (1988). *The inexpressive male.* Lexington, MA: Lexington.

Bandura, A. (1977). *Social learning theory.* Englewood Cliffs, NJ: Prentice-Hall.

Bandura, A. (1986). *Social foundations of thought and action: A social cognitive theory.* Englewood Cliffs, NJ: Prentice-Hall.

Baumann, M. (1976). Two features of women's speech? In B. L. Dubois & I. Crouch (Eds.), *The sociology of the languages of American women* (pp. 33–40). San Antonio, TX: Trinity University Press.

Bellinger, D. C., & Gleason, J. B. (1982). Sex differences in parental directives to young children. *Sex Roles, 8*, 1123–1139.

Berger, J., Fisek, M. H., Norman, R. Z., & Zelditch, M., Jr. (1977). *Status characteristics and social interactions: An expectation states approach.* New York: Elsevier Science.

Biernat, M., & Kobrynowicz, D. (1997). Gender- and race-based standards of competence: Lower minimum standards but higher ability standards for devalued groups. *Journal of Personality and Social Psychology, 72*, 544–557.

Biringen, Z., Emde, R. N., Campos, J. J., & Appelbaum, M. I. (1995). Affective reorganization in the infant, the mother, and the dyad: The role of upright locomotion and its timing. *Child Development, 66*, 499–514.

Bradbard, M. R., & Endsley, R. C. (1983). The effects of sex-typed labeling on preschool children's information-seeking and retention. *Sex Roles, 9*, 247–260.

Bradley, P. H. (1981). The folk-linguistics of women's speech: An empirical examination. *Communication Monographs, 48,* 73–90.

Brouwer, D., Gerritsen, M., & de Haan, D. (1979). Speech differences between women and men: On the wrong track? *Language in Society, 8,* 33–50.

Broverman, I. K., Vogel, S. R., Broverman, D. M., Clarkson, F. E., & Rosenkrantz, P. S. (1972). Sex role stereotypes: A current appraisal. *Journal of Social Issues, 28*(2), 59–78.

Brown, C. E., Dovidio, J. F., & Ellyson, S. L. (1990). Reducing sex differences in visual displays of dominance: Knowledge is power. *Personality and Social Psychology Bulletin, 16,* 358–368.

Bukatko, D., Fauth, R., & Lombard, S. (1997, April). *Children's evaluations of masculine and feminine traits.* Paper presented at the biennial meeting of the Society for Research in Child Development, Washington, DC.

Bukatko, D., & Shedd, J. (1999, April). *Children's evaluation of masculine and feminine traits, activities, and occupations.* Paper presented at the biennial meeting of the Society for Research in Child Development, Albuquerque, NM.

Burgoon, M., Dillard, J. P., Doran, N. E. (1983). Friendly or unfriendly persuasion: The effects of violations of expectations by males and females. *Human Communication Research, 10,* 283–294.

Buss, D. M. (1981). Predicting parent–child interactions from children's activity level. *Developmental Psychology, 17,* 59–65.

Buss, D. M. (1989). Sex differences in human mate preferences: Evolutionary hypotheses tested in 37 cultures. *Behavioral and Brain Sciences, 12,* 1–49.

Butler, D., & Geis, F. L. (1990). Nonverbal affect responses to male and female leaders: Implications for leadership evaluations. *Journal of Personality and Social Psychology, 58,* 48–59.

Buttner, E. H., & McEnally, M. (1996). The interactive effect of influence tactic, applicant gender, and type of job on hiring recommendations. *Sex Roles, 34,* 581–591.

Carli, L. L. (1981, August). *Sex differences in small group interaction.* Paper presented at the 89th Annual Meeting of the American Psychological Association, Los Angeles.

Carli, L. L. (1989). Gender differences in interaction style and influence. *Journal of Personality and Social Psychology, 56,* 565–576.

Carli, L. L. (1990). Gender, language, and influence. *Journal of Personality and Social Psychology, 59,* 941–951.

Carli, L. L. (1991). Gender, status, and influence. In E. J. Lawler, B. Markovsky, C. Ridgeway, & H. A. Walker (Eds.), *Advances in group processes: Theory and research* (Vol. 8, pp. 89–113). Greenwich, CT: JAI.

Carli, L. L. (1997a, October). *Effect of gender composition on self-evaluation.* Paper presented at the meeting of the New England Social Psychological Association, Williams College, Williamstown, MA.

Carli, L. L. (1997b). No, biology does not create gender differences in personality. In M. R. Walsh (Ed.), *Women, men, and gender: Ongoing debates* (pp. 44–53). New Haven, CT: Yale University Press.

Carli, L. L. (1998, June). *Gender effects in social influence.* Paper presented at the meeting of the Society for the Psychological Study of Social Issues, Ann Arbor, MI.

Carli, L. L., LaFleur, S. J., & Loeber, C. C. (1995). Nonverbal behavior, gender, and influence. *Journal of Personality and Social Psychology, 68,* 1030–1041.

Carli, L. L., Werner, A., Alfonso, E., & Lau, D. (1997, April). *Gender differences in the self-evaluation of preschool boys and girls.* Paper presented at the biennial meeting of the Society for Research in Child Development, Washington, DC.

Carter, D. B., & Levy, G. D. (1988). Cognitive aspects of early sex-role development: The influence of gender schemas on preschoolers' memories and preferences for sex-typed toys and activities. *Child Development, 59,* 782–792.

Cherry, L., & Lewis, M. (1976). Mothers and two-year-olds: A study of sex-differentiated aspects of verbal interaction. *Developmental Psychology, 12,* 278–282.

Chodorow, N. (1974). Family structure and feminine personality. In M. Z. Rosaldo & L. Lamphere (Eds.), *Women, culture and society* (pp. 42–66). Stanford, CA: Stanford University Press.

Cloran, C. (1989). Learning through language: The social construction of gender. In R. Hasan, & J. R. Martin (Eds.), *Language development: Learning language, learning culture* (pp. 111–151). Norwood, NJ: Ablex.

Cook, A. S., Fritz, J. J., McCornack, B. L., & Visperas, C. (1985). Early gender differences in the functional use of language. *Sex Roles, 12,* 909–915.

Copeland, C. L., Driskell, J. E., Salas, E. (1995). Gender and reactions to dominance. *Journal of Social Behavior and Personality, 10,* 53–68.

Craig, J. M., & Sherif, C. W. (1986). The effectiveness of men and women in problem-solving groups as a function of group gender composition. *Sex Roles, 14,* 453–466.

Crockenberg, S. & Lourie, A. (1996). Parents' conflict strategies with children and children's conflict strategies with peers. *Merrill-Palmer Quarterly, 42,* 495–518.

Crosby, F. & Nyquist, L. (1977). The female register: An empirical study of Lakoff's hypothesis. *Language in Society, 6,* 313–322.

DeFrancisco, V. (1991). The sounds of silence: How men silence women in marital relations. *Discourse and Society, 2,* 413–423.

Dindia, K., & Allen, M. (1992). Sex differences in self-disclosure: A meta-analysis. *Psychological Bulletin, 112,* 106–124.

Dion, K. K., & Berscheid, E. (1974). Physical attractiveness and peer perception among children. *Sociometry, 37,* 1–12.

Dovidio, J. F., Brown, C. E., Heltman, K., Ellyson, S. L., & Keating, C. F. (1988). Power displays between women and men in discussions of gender-linked tasks: A multichannel study. *Journal of Personality and Social Psychology, 55,* 580–587.

Dovidio, J. F., Ellyson, S. L., Keating, C. F., Heltman, K., & Brown, C. E. (1988). The relationship of social power to visual displays of dominance between men and women. *Journal of Personality and Social Psychology, 54,* 233–242.

Dunn, J., Bretherton, I., & Munn, P. (1987). Conversations about feeling states between mothers and their young children. *Developmental Psychology, 23,* 132–139.

Eagly, A. H. (1987). *Sex differences in social behavior: A social-role interpretation.* Hillsdale, NJ: Lawrence Erlbaum Associates.

Eagly, A. H., & Carli, L. L. (1981). Sex of researcher and sex-typed communications as determinants of sex differences in influenceability: A meta-analysis of social influence studies. *Psychological Bulletin, 90,* 1–20.

Eagly, A. H., & Johnson, B. T. (1990). Gender and leadership style: A meta-analysis. *Psychological Bulletin, 108,* 233–256.

Eagly, A. H., & Karau, S. J. (1991). Gender and the emergence of leaders: A meta-analysis. *Journal of Personality and Social Psychology, 60,* 685–710.

Eagly, A. H., Karau, S. J., & Makhijani, M. G. (1995). Gender and the effectiveness of leaders: A meta-analysis. *Psychological Bulletin, 117,* 125–145.

Eagly, A. H., Makhijani, M. G., & Klonsky, B. G. (1992). Gender and the evaluation of leaders: A meta-analysis. *Psychological Bulletin, 111,* 3–22.

Eakins, B., & Eakins, R. G. (1976). Verbal turn-taking and exchanges in faculty dialogue. In B. L. Dubois & I. Crouch (Eds.), *The sociology of the languages of American women* (pp. 53–62). San Antonio, TX: Trinity University Press.

Eaton, W. O., & Enns, L. R. (1986). Sex differences in human motor activity level. *Psychological Bulletin, 100,* 19–28.

Eckes, T. (1997). Talking about gender: A social psychological perspective on language and gender stereotyping. In F. Braun & U. Pasero (Eds.), *Communication of gender* (pp. 30–53). Pfaffenweiler, Germany: Centaurus.

Ellyson, S. L., & Dovidio, J. F. (1985). Power, dominance, and nonverbal behavior: Basic concepts and issues. In S. L. Ellyson & J. F. Dovidio (Eds.), *Power, dominance, and nonverbal behavior* (pp. 1–27). New York: Springer.

Ellyson, S. L., Dovidio, J. F., & Brown, C. E. (1992). The look of power: Gender differences in visual dominance behavior. In C. L. Ridgeway (Ed.), *Gender, interaction, and inequality* (pp. 50–80). New York: Springer.

Erickson, B., Lind, E. A., Johnson, B. C., & O'Barr, W. M. (1978). Speech style and impression formation in a court setting: The effects of "powerful" and "powerless" speech. *Journal of Experimental Social Psychology, 14*, 266–279.

Fabes, R. A. (1994). Physiological, emotional, and behavioral correlates of gender segregation. In C. Leaper (Ed.), *Childhood gender segregation: Causes and consequences* (pp. 19–34). San Francisco: Jossey-Bass.

Fagot, B. I. (1978). The influence of sex of child on parental reactions to toddler children. *Child Development, 49*, 459–465.

Fagot, B. I. (1985). Beyond the reinforcement principle: Another step toward understanding sex role development. *Developmental Psychology, 21*, 1097–1104.

Fagot, B. I., Hagan, R., Leinbach, M. D., & Kronsberg, S. (1985). Differential reactions to assertive and communicative acts of toddler boys and girls. *Child Development, 56*, 1499–1505.

Fagot, B. I., & Leinbach, M. D. (1993). Gender-role development in young children: From discrimination to labeling. *Developmental Review, 13*, 205–224.

Fagot, B. I., & O'Brien, M. (1994). Activity level in young children: Cross-age stability, situational influences, correlates with temperament, and the perception of problem behaviors. *Merrill-Palmer Quarterly, 40*, 378–398.

Feldman, R. (1968). Response to compatriot and foreigner who seek assistance. *Journal of Personality and Social Psychology, 10*, 202–214.

Filardo, E. K. (1996). Gender patterns in African American and White adolescents' social interactions in same-race, mixed-gender groups. *Journal of Personality and Social Psychology, 71*, 71–82.

Fishman, P. M. (1978). Interaction: The work women do. *Social Problems, 25*, 397–406.

Fishman, P. M. (1980). Conversational insecurity. In H. Giles, W. P. Robinson, & P. M. Smith (Eds.), *Language: Social psychological perspectives* (pp. 127–132). New York: Pergamon.

Forsyth, D. R., Heiney, M. M., & Wright, S. S. (1997). Biases in appraisals of women leaders. *Group Dynamics: Theory, Research, and Practice, 1*, 98–103.

Foschi, M. (1992). Gender and double standards for competence. In C. L. Ridgeway (Ed.), *Gender, interaction, and inequality* (pp. 181–207). New York: Springer.

Foschi, M. (1996). Double standards in the evaluation of men and women. *Social Psychology Quarterly, 59*, 237–254.

Foschi, M., Lai, L., & Sigerson, K. (1994). Gender and double standards in the assessment of job applicants. *Social Psychology Quarterly, 57*, 326–339.

Geddes, D. (1992). Sex roles in management: The impact of varying power of speech style on union members' perception of satisfaction and effectiveness. *Journal of Psychology, 126*, 589–607.

Giacalone, R. A. & Riordan, C. A. (1990). Effect of self-presentation on perceptions and recognition in an organization. *Journal of Psychology, 124*, 25–38.

Giles, H., Mulac, A., Bradac, J. J., & Johnson, P. (1987). Speech accommodation theory: The first decade and beyond. *Communication Yearbook, 10*, 13–48.

Gleason, J. B. (1975). Fathers and other strangers: Men's speech to young children. In D. Dato (Ed.), *Developmental psycholinguistics: Theory and application* (pp. 289–297). Washington, DC: Georgetown University Press.

Gleason, J. B., Ely, R., Perlmann, R. Y., & Narasimhan, B. (1996). Patterns of prohibition in parent–child discourse. In D. I. Slobin, J. Gerhardt, A. Kyratzis, & J. Guo (Eds.), *Social interaction, social context, and language: Essays in honor of Susan Ervin-Tripp* (pp. 205–217). Mahwah, NJ: Lawrence Erlbaum Associates.

Goodwin, M. H. (1980). Directive/response speech sequences in girls' and boys' task activities. In S. McConnell-Ginet, R. Borker, & N. Furman (Eds.), *Women and language in literature and society* (pp. 157–173). New York: Praeger.

Goodwin, M. H. (1990). Tactical uses of stories: Participation frameworks within girls' and boys' disputes. *Discourse Processes, 13,* 33–71.

Goodwin, M. H. (1997). Crafting activities: Building social organization through language in girls' and boys' groups. In C. T. Snowdon & M. Hausberger (Eds.), *Social influences on vocal development* (pp. 328–341). Cambridge, England: Cambridge University Press.

Greif, E. B. (1980). Sex differences in parent–child conversations. *Women's Studies International Quarterly, 3,* 253–258.

Halberstadt, A. G., & Saitta, M. B. (1987). Gender, nonverbal behavior, and perceived dominance: A test of the theory. *Journal of Personality and Social Psychology, 53,* 257–272.

Hall, D. & Langellier, K. (1988). Story-telling strategies in mother–daughter communication. In B. Bate & A. Taylor (Eds.), *Women communicating: Studies on women's talk* (pp. 197–226). Norwood, NJ: Ablex.

Hall, J. A. (1984). *Nonverbal sex differences: Communication accuracy and expressive style.* Baltimore, MD: Johns Hopkins University Press.

Hall, J. A., & Braunwald, K. G. (1981). Gender cues in conversations. *Journal of Personality and Social Psychology, 40,* 99–110.

Hartman, M. (1976). A descriptive study of the language of men and women born in Maine around 1900 as it reflects the Lakoff hypothesis in *Language and women's place.* In B. L. Dubois & I. Crouch (Eds.), *The sociology of the languages of American women* (pp. 81–90). San Antonio, TX: Trinity University Press.

Haslett, B. J. (1983). Communicative functions and strategies in children's conversations. *Human Communication Research, 9,* 114–129.

Hawkins, K. W. (1995). Effects of gender and communication content of leadership emergence in small task-oriented groups. *Small Group Research, 26,* 234–249.

Hirokawa, R. Y., Mickey, J., & Miura, S. (1991). Effects of request legitimacy on the compliance gaining tactics of male and female managers. *Communication Monographs, 58,* 421–436.

Hogg, M. A. (1985). Masculine and feminine speech in dyads and groups: A study of speech style and gender salience. *Journal of Language and Social Psychology, 4,* 99–112.

Holmes, J. (1984). 'Women's language': A functional approach. *General Linguistics, 24,* 149–178.

Hutson-Comeaux, S. L., & Kelly, J. R. (1996). Sex differences in interaction style and group task performance: The process–performance relationship. *Journal of Social Behavior and Personality, 11,* 255–275.

Jacklin, C. N., & Maccoby, E. E. (1978). Social behavior at thirty-three months in same-sex and mixed-sex dyads. *Child Development, 49,* 557–569.

James, D., & Clarke, S. (1993). Women, men and interruptions: A critical review. In D. Tannen (Ed.), *Gender and conversational interaction* (pp. 231–280). New York: Oxford University Press.

James, D., & Drakich, J. (1993). Understanding gender differences in amount of talk: A critical review of research. In D. Tannen (Ed.), *Gender and conversational interaction* (pp. 281–312). New York: Oxford University Press.

Johnson, C. (1993). Gender and formal authority. *Social Psychology Quarterly, 56*, 193–210.

Johnson, C. (1994). Gender, legitimate authority, and leader–subordinate conversations. *American Sociological Review, 59*, 122–135.

Johnson, C., Clay-Warner, J., & Funk, S. J. (1996). Effects of authority structures and gender on interaction in same-sex task groups. *Social Psychology Quarterly, 59*, 221–236.

Johnson, R. A., & Schulman, G. I. (1989). Gender-role composition and role entrapment in decision-making groups. *Gender and Society, 3*, 355–372.

Kerig, P. K., Cowan, P. A., & Cowan, C. P. (1993). Marital quality and gender differences in parent–child interaction. *Developmental Psychology, 29*, 931–939.

Killen, M., & Naigles, L. R. (1995). Preschool children pay attention to their addressees: Effects of gender composition on peer disputes. *Discourse Processes, 19*, 329–346.

Koblinsky, S. G., Cruse, D. F., & Sugawara, A. I. (1978). Sex role stereotypes and children's memory for story content. *Child Development, 49*, 452–458.

Kohnstamm, G. A. (1989). Temperament in childhood: Cross-cultural and sex differences. In G. A. Kohnstamm, J. E. Bates, & M. K. Rothbart (Eds.), *Temperament in childhood* (pp. 483–508). Chichester, England: Wiley.

Kollock, P., Blumstein, P., & Schwartz, P. (1985). Sex and power in interaction: Conversational privileges and duties. *American Sociological Review, 50*, 34–46.

Kuebli, J., Butler, S., & Fivush, R. (1995). Mother–child talk about past emotions: Relations of maternal language and child gender over time. *Cognition and Emotion, 9*, 265–283.

Kuhn, D., Nash, S. C., & Brucken, L. (1978). Sex role concepts of two- and three-year-olds. *Child Development, 49*, 445–451.

Kyratzis, A., & Guo, J. (1996). "Separate worlds for girls and boys?" Views from U. S. and Chinese mixed-sex friendship groups. In D. I. Slobin, J. Gerhardt, A. Kyratzis, & J. Guo (Eds.), *Social interaction, social context, and language: Essays in honor of Susan Ervin-Tripp* (pp. 555–577). Mahwah, NJ: Lawrence Erlbaum Associates.

Lakoff, R. (1975). *Language and women's place*. New York: Harper & Row.

Langlois, J. H., & Stephan, C. W. (1981). Beauty and the beast: The role of physical attractiveness in the development of peer relations and social behavior. In S. S. Brehm, S. M. Kassin, & F. X. Gibbons (Eds.), *Developmental social psychology: Theory and research* (pp. 152–168). New York: Oxford University Press.

Leaper, C. (1991). Influence and involvement in children's discourse: Age, gender and partner effects. *Child Development, 62*, 797–811.

Leaper, C., Anderson, K. J., & Sanders, P. (1998). Moderators of gender effects on parents' talk to their children: A meta-analysis. *Developmental Psychology, 34*, 3–27.

Leaper, C., & Gleason, J. B. (1996). The relationship of play activity and gender to parent and child sex-typed communication. *International Journal of Behavioral Development, 19*, 689–703.

Leaper, C., Leve, L., Strasser, T., & Schwartz, R. (1995). Mother–child communication sequences: Play activity, child gender, and marital status effects. *Merrill-Palmer Quarterly, 41*, 307–327.

Leet-Pellegrini, H. M. (1980). Conversational dominance as a function of gender and expertise. In H. Giles, W. P. Robinson, & P. M. Smith (Eds.), *Language: Social psychological perspectives* (pp. 97–104). New York: Pergamon.

Lever, J. (1976). Sex differences in the games children play. *Social Problems, 23*, 478–487.

Lewis, E. T., & McCarthy, P. R. (1988). Perceptions of self-disclosure as a function of gender-linked variables. *Sex Roles, 19*, 47–56.

Lindsey, E. W., Mize, J., & Pettit, G. S. (1997). Differential play patterns of mothers and fathers of sons and daughters: Implications for children's gender role development. *Sex Roles, 37*, 643–661.

Lockheed, M. E., & Hall, K. P. (1976). Conceptualizing sex as a status characteristic: Applications to leadership training strategies. *Journal of Social Issues, 32*(3), 111–124.

Lytton, H., & Romney, D. M. (1991). Parents' differential socialization of boys and girls: A meta-analysis. *Psychological Bulletin, 109*, 267–296.

Maass, A., & Arcuri, L. (1996). Language and stereotyping. In C. N. Macrae, C. Stangor, & M. Hewstone (Eds.), *Stereotypes and stereotyping* (pp. 193–226). New York: Guilford.

Maass, A., Milesi, A., Zabbini, S., & Stahlberg, D. (1995). Linguistic intergroup bias: Differential expectancies or in-group protection? *Journal of Personality and Social Psychology, 68*, 116–126.

Maass, A., Salvi, D., Arcuri, L., & Semin, G. (1989). Language use in intergroup contexts: The linguistic intergroup bias. *Journal of Personality and Social Psychology, 57*, 981–993.

Mabry, E. A. (1985). The effects of gender composition and task structure on small group interaction. *Small Group Behavior, 16*, 75–96.

Maccoby, E. E., & Jacklin, C. N. (1983). The "person" characteristics of children and the family as environment. In D. Magnusson & V. Allen (Eds.), *Human development: An interactional perspective* (pp. 75–91). New York: Academic Press.

Maltz, D. N., & Borker, R. (1982). A cultural approach to male–female miscommunication. In J. J. Gumpertz (Ed.), *Language and social identity* (pp. 196–216). Cambridge, England: Cambridge University Press.

Mannle, S., & Tomasello, M. (1987). Fathers, siblings, and the bridge hypothesis. In K. E. Nelson & A. van Kleeck (Eds.), *Children's language* (Vol. 6, pp. 23–41). Hillsdale, NJ: Lawrence Erlbaum Associates.

Martin, C. L. (1994). Cognitive influences on the development and maintenance of gender segregation. In C. Leaper (Ed.), *Childhood gender segregation: Causes and consequences* (pp. 35–51). San Francisco: Jossey-Bass.

Martin, C. L., & Halverson, C. F. (1981). A schematic processing model of sex typing and stereotyping in children. *Child Development, 52*, 1119–1134.

Martin, C. L., & Halverson, C. F. (1983). Gender constancy: A methodological and theoretical analysis. *Sex Roles, 9*, 775–790.

McCarrick, A. K., Manderscheid, R. W., & Silbergeld, S. (1981). Gender differences in competition and dominance during married-couples group therapy. *Social Psychology Quarterly, 44*, 164–177.

McCloskey, L. A. (1996). Gender and the expression of status in children's mixed-age conversations. *Journal of Applied Developmental Psychology, 17*, 117–133.

McMillan, J. R., Clifton, A. K., McGrath, D., & Gale, W. S. (1977). Women's language: Uncertainty or interpersonal sensitivity and emotionality? *Sex Roles, 3*, 545–559.

Meeker, B. F., & Weitzel-O'Neill, P. A. (1985). Sex roles and interpersonal behavior in task-oriented groups. In J. Berger & M. Zelditch, Jr. (Eds.), *Status, rewards, and influence: How expectations organize behavior* (pp. 379–405). San Francisco: Jossey-Bass.

Miller, P. M., Danaher, D. L., & Forbes, D. (1986). Sex-related strategies for coping with interpersonal conflict in children aged five and seven. *Developmental Psychology, 22*, 543–548.

Mischel, W. (1966). A social-learning view of sex differences in behavior. In E. E. Maccoby (Ed.), *The development of sex differences* (pp. 56–81). Stanford, CA: Stanford University Press.

Montepare, J. M. (1995). The impact of variations in height on young children's impressions of men and women. *Journal of Nonverbal Behavior, 19*, 31–48.

Montepare, J. M., & Zebrowitz-McArthur, L. (1989). Children's perceptions of babyfaced adults. *Perceptual and Motor Skills, 69*, 467–472.

Moskowitz, D. S. (1993). Dominance and friendliness: On the interaction of gender and situation. *Journal of Personality, 61*, 387–409.

Mulac, A. (1998). The gender-linked language effect: Do language differences really make a difference? In D. J. Canary & K. Dindia (Eds.), *Sex differences and similarities in communication: Critical essays and empirical investigations of sex and gender in interaction* (pp. 127–153). Mahwah, NJ: Lawrence Erlbaum Associates.

Mulac, A., & Bradac, J. J. (1995). Women's style in problem solving interaction: Powerless, or simply feminine? In P. J. Kalbfleisch & M. J. Cody (Eds.), *Gender, power, and communication in human relationships* (pp. 83–104). Hillsdale, NJ: Lawrence Erlbaum Associates.

Mulac, A., & Lundell, T. L. (1986). Linguistic contributors to the gender-linked language effect. *Journal of Language and Social Psychology, 5*, 81–101.

Mulac, A., Lundell, T. L., & Bradac, J. J. (1986). Male/female language differences and attributional consequences in a public speaking situation: Toward an explanation of the gender-linked language effect. *Communication Monographs, 53*, 115–129

Mulac, A., Studley, L. B., & Blau, S. (1990). The gender-linked language effect in primary and secondary students' impromptu essays. *Sex Roles, 23*, 439–469.

Mulac, A., Wiemann, J. M., Widenmann, S. J., & Gibson, T. W. (1988). Male/female language differences and effects in same- and mixed-sex dyads: The gender-linked language effect. *Communication Monographs, 55*, 315–335.

Mullen, B., Salas, E., & Driskell, J. E. (1989). Salience, motivation, and artifact as contributions to the relation between participation rate and leadership. *Journal of Experimental Social Psychology, 25*, 545–559.

Nohara, M. (1996). Preschool boys and girls use *no* differently. *Journal of Child Language, 23*, 417–429.

O'Barr, W. (1982). *Linguistic evidence: Language, power, and strategy in the courtroom.* New York: Academic Press.

Perry, D. G., & Bussey, K. (1979). The social learning theory of sex differences: Imitation is alive and well. *Journal of Personality and Social Psychology, 37*, 1699–1712.

Phinney, J. S., & Rotheram, M. J. (1982). Sex differences in social overtures between same-sex and cross-sex preschool pairs. *Child Study Journal, 12*, 259–269.

Piliavin, J. A., & Martin, R. R. (1978). The effects of sex composition of groups on style of social interaction. *Sex Roles, 4*, 281–296.

Pratto, F., Stallworth, L. M., Sidanius, J., & Siers, B. (1997). The gender gap in occupational role attainment: A social dominance approach. *Journal of Personality and Social Psychology, 72*, 37–53.

Preisler, B. (1986). *Linguistic sex roles in conversation: Social variation in the expression of tentativeness in English.* Berlin, Germany: Mouton de Gruyter.

Prior, M. (1992). Childhood temperament. *Journal of Child Psychology and Psychiatry, 33*, 249–279.

Propp, K. M. (1995). An experimental examination of biological sex as a status cue in decision-making groups and its influence on information use. *Small Group Research, 26*, 451–474.

Pugh, M. D., & Wahrman, R. (1983). Neutralizing sexism in mixed-sex groups: Do women have to be better than men? *American Journal of Sociology, 88*, 746–762.

Ridgeway, C. L. (1978). Conformity, group-oriented motivation, and status attainment in small groups. *Social Psychology, 41*, 175–188.

Ridgeway, C. L. (1982). Status in groups: The importance of motivation. *American Sociological Review, 47*, 76–88.

Ridgeway, C. L., & Berger, J. (1986). Expectations, legitimation, and dominance behavior in task groups. *American Sociological Review, 51*, 603–617.

Ridgeway, C. L., & Diekema, D. (1992). Are gender differences status differences? In C. L. Ridgeway (Ed.), *Gender, interaction, and inequality* (pp. 157–180). New York: Springer.

Rojahn, K., & Willemsen, T. M. (1994). The evaluation of effectiveness and likability of gender-role congruent and gender-role incongruent leaders. *Sex Roles, 30*, 109–119.

Ruble, T. L. (1983). Sex stereotypes: Issues of change in the 1970s. *Sex Roles, 9*, 397–402.

Rudman, L. A. (1998). Self-promotion as a risk factor for women: The costs and benefits of counterstereotypical impression management. *Journal of Personality and Social Psychology, 74*, 629–645.

Ruscher, J. B. (1998). Prejudice and stereotyping in everyday communication. In M. P. Zanna (Ed.), *Advances in experimental social psychology* (Vol. 30, pp. 241–307). San Diego, CA: Academic Press.

Ruscher, J. B., & Hammer, E. D. (1994). Revising disrupted impressions through conversation. *Journal of Personality and Social Psychology, 66*, 530–541.

Sachs, J. (1987). Preschool boys' and girls' language use in pretend play. In S. U. Philips, S. Steele, & C. Tanz (Eds.), *Language, gender, and sex in comparative perspective* (pp. 178–188). Cambridge, England: Cambridge University Press.

Sadker, M., & Sadker, D. (1994). *Failing at fairness: How America's schools cheat girls.* New York: Scribner's.

Saurer, M. K., & Eisler, R. M. (1990). The role of masculine gender role stress in expressivity and social support network factors. *Sex Roles, 23*, 261–271.

Sayers, F., & Sherblom, J. (1987). Qualification in male language as influenced by age and gender of conversational partner. *Communication Research Reports, 4*, 88–92.

Serbin, L. A., Powlishta, K. K., & Gulko, J. (1993). The development of sex typing in middle childhood. *Monographs of the Society for Research in Child Development, 58* (2, Serial No. 232).

Serbin, L. A., Sprafkin, C., Elman, M., & Doyle, A. B. (1982). The early development of sex-differentiated patterns of social influence. *Canadian Journal of Behavioural Science, 14*, 350–363.

Shackelford, S., Wood, W., & Worchel, S. (1996). Behavioral styles and the influence of women in mixed-sex groups. *Social Psychology Quarterly, 59*, 284–293.

Shatz, M. & Gelman, R. (1973). The development of communication skills: Modification in the speech of young children as a function of listener. *Monographs of the Society for Research in Child Development, 38* (5, Serial No. 152).

Sheldon, A. (1990). Pickle fights: Gender talk in preschool disputes. *Discourse Processes, 13*, 5–31.

Sheldon, A. (1992). Conflict talk: Sociolinguistic challenges to self-assertion and how young girls meet them. *Merrill-Palmer Quarterly, 38*, 95–117.

Shelton, B. A. (1992). *Women, men and time: Gender differences in paid work, housework, and leisure.* New York: Greenwood.

Signorella, M. L., & Liben, L. S. (1984). Recall and reconstruction of gender-related pictures: Effects of attitude, task difficulty, and age. *Child Development, 55*, 393–405.

Skrypnek, B. J., & Snyder, M. (1982). On the self-perpetuating nature of stereotypes about women and men. *Journal of Experimental Social Psychology, 18*, 277–291.

Stein, R. T., & Heller, T. (1979). An empirical analysis of the correlations between leadership status and participation rates reported in the literature. *Journal of Personality and Social Psychology, 37*, 1993–2002.

Sterling, B. S., & Owen, J. W. (1982). Perceptions of demanding versus reasoning male and female police officers. *Personality and Social Psychology Bulletin, 8*, 336–340.

Tomasello, M., Conti-Ramsden, G., & Ewert, B. (1990). Young children's conversations with their mothers and fathers: Differences in breakdown and repair. *Journal of Child Language, 17,* 115–130.

Valdes-Fallis, G. (1977). Code-switching among bilingual Mexican American women: Towards an understanding of sex-related language alternation. *International Journal of the Sociology of Language, 17,* 65–72.

Wagner, D. G., & Berger, J. (1997). Gender and interpersonal task behaviors: Status expectation accounts. *Sociological Perspectives, 40,* 1–32.

Wagner, D. G., Ford, R. S., & Ford, T. W. (1986). Can gender inequalities be reduced? *American Sociological Review, 51,* 47–61.

Walker, H. A., Ilardi, B. C., McMahon, A. M., & Fennell, M. L. (1996). Gender, interaction, and leadership. *Social Psychology Quarterly, 59,* 255–272.

Ward, D. A., Seccombe, K., Bendel, R., & Carter, L. F. (1985). Cross-sex context as a factor in persuasibility sex differences. *Social Psychology Quarterly, 48,* 269–276.

Welkowitz, J., & Kuc, M. (1973). Interrelationships among warmth, genuiness, empathy, and temporal speech patterns in interpersonal attraction. *Journal of Consulting and Clinical Psychology, 41,* 472–473.

West, C. (1984). When the doctor is a "lady." *Symbolic Interaction, 7,* 87–106.

West, C., & Zimmerman, D. H. (1977). Women's place in everyday talk: Reflections on parent–child interaction. *Social Problems, 24,* 521–529.

West, C., & Zimmerman, D. H. (1983). Small insults: A study of interruptions in cross-sex conversations between unacquainted persons. In B. Thorne, C. Kramarae, & N. Henley (Eds.), *Language, gender, and society* (pp. 102–117). Rowley, MA: Newbury House.

Wheelan, S. A., & Verdi, A. F. (1992). Differences in male and female patterns of communication in groups: A methodological artifact? *Sex Roles, 27,* 1–15.

Wiggins, J. S. (1992). Agency and communion as conceptual coordinates for the understanding and measurement of interpersonal behavior. In W. M. Grove & D. Cicchetti (Eds.), *Thinking clearly about psychology* (pp. 89–113). Minneapolis, MN: University of Minnesota Press.

Williams, J. E., & Best, D. L. (1990). *Measuring sex stereotypes: A multinational study* (Rev. ed.). Newbury Park, CA: Sage.

Wood, W., & Karten, S. J. (1986). Sex differences in interaction style as a product of perceived sex differences in competence. *Journal of Personality and Social Psychology, 50,* 341–347.

Wosinska, W., Dabul, A. J., Whetstone-Dion, R. & Cialdini, R. B. (1996). Self-presentational responses to success in the organization: The costs and benefits of modesty. *Basic and Applied Social Psychology, 18,* 229–242.

Yamada, E. M., Tjosvold, D., & Draguns, J. G. (1983). Effects of sex-linked situations and sex composition on cooperation and style of interaction. *Sex Roles, 9,* 541–553.

# 11

# Gender-Role Socialization in the Family: A Longitudinal Approach

Jacquelynne S. Eccles
*University of Michigan*

Carol Freedman-Doan
*Eastern Michigan University*

Pam Frome
*University of Michigan*

Janis Jacobs
*Pennsylvania State University*

Kwang Suk Yoon
*University of Michigan*

Several researchers (e.g., Eccles, Jacobs, & Harold, 1990; Goodnow & Collins, 1990; Jacobs, 1987; Yee & Eccles, 1988) have suggested that parents' beliefs and stereotypes influence the expectations and goals parents develop for their children, parents' perceptions of their children's interests and talents, and the ways in which parents interact with their children. To the extent that these beliefs are influenced by gender-role-related stereotypes, they are likely to be a major influence on gender-role socialization. We explore this possibility in this chapter.

Previous studies have documented the positive impact of parents' confidence in their children's academic abilities on children's own self-perceptions and actual performance (e.g., Alexander & Entwisle, 1988; Eccles [Parsons], Adler, & Kaczala, 1982). These studies clearly indicate that parents' expectations for their children's performance in math and English have an impact on both children's subsequent performance in these subjects and their view of their own math and language arts abilities. By late elementary school this effect is stronger than the children's own current

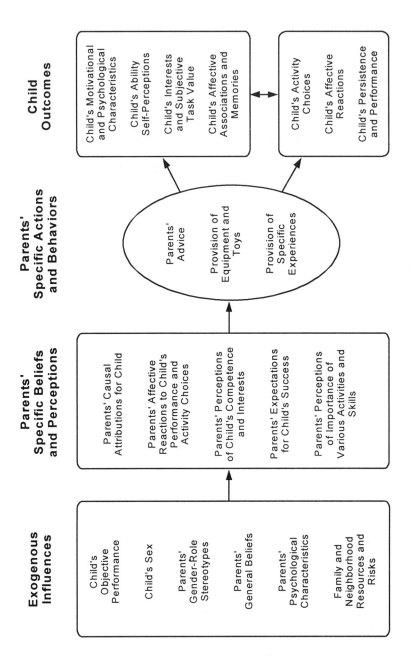

FIG. 11.1   Conceptual model of parental influences on children.

**Child Outcomes**

- Child's Motivational and Psychological Characteristics
- Child's Ability Self-Perceptions
- Child's Interests and Subjective Task Value
- Child's Affective Associations and Memories

- Child's Activity Choices
- Child's Affective Reactions
- Child's Persistence and Performance

**Parents' Specific Actions and Behaviors**

- Parents' Advice
- Provision of Equipment and Toys
- Provision of Specific Experiences

**Parents' Specific Beliefs and Perceptions**

- Parents' Causal Attributions for Child
- Parents' Affective Reactions to Child's Performance and Activity Choices
- Parents' Perceptions of Child's Competence and Interests
- Parents' Expectations for Child's Success
- Parents' Perceptions of Importance of Various Activities and Skills

**Exogenous Influences**

- Child's Objective Performance
- Child's Sex
- Parents' Gender-Role Stereotypes
- Parents' General Beliefs
- Parents' Psychological Characteristics
- Family and Neighborhood Resources and Risks

performance levels in these subject areas. But what factors are shaping parents' expectations for their children's performance potential in various activities? And how exactly are parents' beliefs actually affecting their children's self-perceptions, interests, and performance?

Using a theoretical framework first developed by Eccles and her colleagues (Eccles, 1993; Eccles et al., 1990; illustrated in Fig. 11.1), we discuss how gender is linked to parents' beliefs regarding their children's abilities, and then how these beliefs may affect both children's performance and involvement in various activities, and their perceptions of their own competence in these various activity domains. In this model, we assume that parents' views of their children's competencies across various activities are influenced by several factors. Primary among the social factors are both ascribed and achieved status characteristics of parents and children, and parents' interpretative belief systems. With regard to this chapter for example, we predict that parents' gender-role belief systems, in interaction with their child's gender, affect the inferences parents draw from their children's performance about their children's competence in various gender-role-stereotyped activity domains. These inferences, in turn, should affect parents' expectations for their children's future performance in these activities and should affect the opportunities these parents give their children to develop skills in these various activity domains. Over the past 20 years, we have gathered extensive longitudinal information from children and their families in two different studies directly relevant to these hypotheses. In this chapter, we summarize the major relevant results from these two studies.

## BACKGROUND FINDINGS AND NEW DATA SOURCES

In her earlier work, Eccles documented the fact that parents' perceptions of their children's math ability have a significant effect on the children's view of their own math ability—an effect that is independent of the impact of the child's actual performance on both the parents' and children's perceptions of the children's math ability (Eccles [Parsons] et al., 1982). We have replicated and extended this work in two new studies.

*The Michigan Study of Adolescent Life Transitions—MSALT* is a multiwave longitudinal study of adolescent development in the context of the family and the school. In 1983, approximately 2,000 sixth-grade, early adolescents were recruited into this study. About 1,000 of their families agreed to participate as well. These families have been participating in the study since that time. They represent a wide range of socioeconomic backgrounds. Parents were asked a series of questions regarding the perceptions of their child's competency and talent, the expectations for their child's future performance, and the importance they attach to competence in

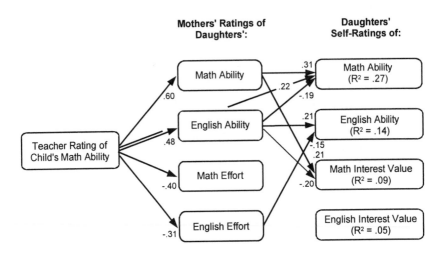

FIG. 11.2a  Relation of mothers' view of daughters to daughters' self-perception.

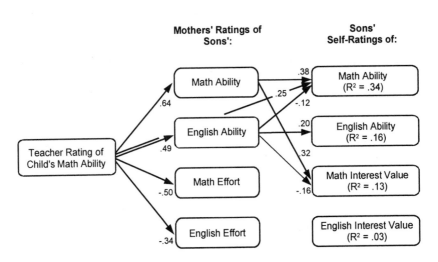

FIG. 11.2b  Relation of mothers' view of sons to sons' self-perception.

336

each of three domains (math, reading/English, and sports), using 7-point Likert-type response scales.[1] Due to limited space only the data from the mothers is summarized in this chapter. The father data, however, yield a very similar story.

First, we assessed whether parents' beliefs have any influence on children's self-perceptions, using standard path analytic techniques. Relevant findings are shown in Figs. 11.2a and 11.2b. Mothers' ratings of their children's abilities in math and English are related to the teacher's ratings of the children's math ability (we only had the teachers rate math ability due to limitations in the amount of time that teachers would spend filling out individual student ratings). But, more importantly, these results replicate Eccles' previous findings: Parents' views of their children's ability in both math and English have an important impact on the children's own self-perceptions (Eccles [Parsons] et al., 1982).

We next confirmed the causal order in this relation using cross-lagged, longitudinal structural equation modeling procedures as specified by Rogosa (1979). Such procedures allow one to compare the relative across-time impact of parents' beliefs on changes in children's self-perceptions versus the across-time impact of children's self-perceptions on changes in parents' beliefs. The results for both math and sports (see Fig. 11.3 for sports example) are consistent with the hypothesized causal direction. As one would expect, mother and child perceptions are reciprocally related at synchronous time points. Over time, however, mother's perceptions of their children's ability were more strongly related to change over time in the children's self-perceptions than vice versa, even when an independent indicator of the children's competence was included as a control. The adjusted goodness-of-fit indexes (AGFI) for both models were greater than .94—indicating a very good fit of both models to the data.

The path analyses shown in Figs. 11.2a and 11.2b suggest two other important conclusions. First, there is a negative effect of mothers' perceptions of their children's English ability on their children's perceptions of their own math ability. Individuals use a variety of information in deciding how good they are in various domains. We have suggested, for example, that individuals compare their relative performance across domains and generate a hierarchy of ability perceptions from these internal self-comparisons (e.g., they decide they are very good at math because they do better, and find it easier to do better, at math than at other school subjects; Eccles, 1987; Eccles [Parsons] et al., 1983; see also Marsh, 1990). The results depicted in Figs. 11.2a and 11.2b suggest that a similar phenomenon may characterize the impact of mothers' perceptions of their children's

---

[1]These items have good psychometric properties and factor into highly reliable scales (see Eccles [Parsons] et al., 1982, and Eccles et al., 1993, for details).

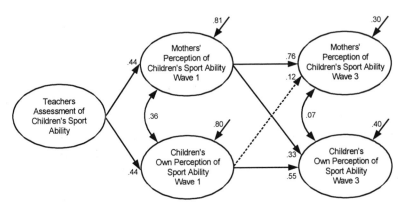

FIG. 11.3 Cross-lagged structural equation model of causal directions and medating influences of mothers' perceptions.

abilities on the development of the children's self-perceptions. The children in this study have a lower estimate of their math ability than one would predict given their teachers' and their mothers' rating of their math ability if their mothers think they are very good in English. Apparently, there are two consequences of having your mother think you are very good in English: (a) You also think you are good in English, and (b) you think you are less good in mathematics than your math teacher thinks you are. These results suggest that having a mother think you are very good in English undermines your estimates of your own math ability and interest. Such a situation is particularly likely to occur for daughters given the fact that parents typically rate daughters' English abilities higher than sons' and vice versa for mathematics.

Further, Figs. 11.2a and 11.2b illustrate the fact that mothers' perceptions of their children's math and English abilities also mediate the impact of performance (as rated by a teacher) on the children's interest in doing mathematics and English respectively. Thus, your mother's perception of your abilities affects your interest in particular subjects as well as your estimate of your own ability in these subjects.

These findings suggest two conclusions: (a) Parents form, and communicate, a hierarchical view of their children's relative abilities, and (b) where math falls in this hierarchy has an impact on the children's conclusions regarding their own math ability independent of their parents' absolute assessment of their children's math ability.

Next we wanted to pin down the long-term relation of parents' views of their children's abilities to lagged indicators of children's own self-concepts and expectations for success. In Frome and Eccles (1998), we ran a series of four structural equation models using LISREL 8 (Jöreskog & Sörbom, 1993)

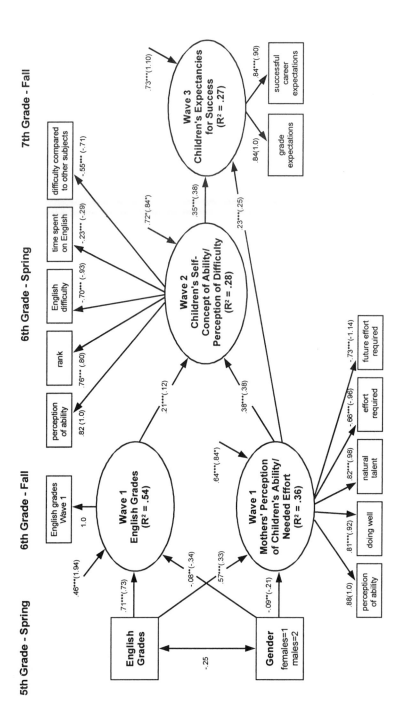

FIG. 11.4 Relation of children's gender to mothers' perceptions and to adolescents' self-perceptions in English. (* p < .05, ** p < .01, *** p < .001.) *Note.* From "Parents' Influence on Children's Achievement-Related Perceptions," by P. M. Frome and J. S. Eccles, 1998, *Journal of Personality and Social Psychology, 74,* p. 444. Copyright 1998 by the American Psychological Association. Reprinted with permission.

339

like the one illustrated in Fig. 11.4 (analyses were run separately for mothers and fathers for both math and English). In all four analyses, parents' estimates of their children's ability and effort needed to succeed partially mediated the impact of grades on children's own ability self-concepts. In addition, parents' gender-biased views of their children's English ability mediated the independent association of gender (i.e., controlling for actually performance differences) with children's own ability self-concepts and expectations for success.

Based on these findings, we have been studying the influences on parents' perceptions of their children's abilities. Clearly parents' perceptions in the academic domains are related to objective information provided by the school about how well their child is doing. But we are interested in identifying the other more subjective influences on parents' perceptions of

**TABLE 11.1**
**Sex-of-Child Effects on Parents' Perceptions**
**(Adolescent Transition Study)**

|  | Domains | | |
|---|---|---|---|
| Scales | Math | English/ Reading | Sports |
| Current Competence[a] | | | |
| Girls | 5.45 | 5.65*** | 4.84*** |
| Boys | 5.40 | 4.99 | 5.22 |
| Task Difficulty[b] | | | |
| Girls | 4.10*** | 3.73*** | 3.77*** |
| Boys | 3.80 | 4.24 | 3.47 |
| Natural Talent[c] | | | |
| Girls | 4.76* | 5.03*** | 4.22*** |
| Boys | 5.01 | 4.51 | 4.87 |
| Future Performance[d] | | | |
| Girls | 5.36 | 5.59*** | — |
| Boys | 5.34 | 5.02 | — |
| Performance in Career[d] | | | |
| Girls | 5.17*** | 5.41*** | — |
| Boys | 5.42 | 4.87 | — |
| Importance[e] | | | |
| Girls | 6.38** | 6.34 | 3.80*** |
| Boys | 6.50 | 6.34 | 4.10 |

*Note.* Ratings were made on 7-point scales: [a]1 = *not at all good*, 7 = *very good*. [b]1 = *not at all difficult*, 7 = *very difficult*. [c]1 = *much less talent than other kids*, 7 = *much more talent than other kids*. [d]1 = *not at all well*, 7 = *very well*. [e]1 = *not at all important*, 7 = *very important*.
*$p < .05$. ** $p < .01$. *** $p < .001$ (for sex differences within pairs).

their children's abilities. Gender is a very important organizing construct for addressing this question. We know in the academic domain, for example, that gender differences in performance in mathematics are small, don't emerge with great regularity prior to secondary school, and are not evident at any age in students' marks (Eccles, 1987; Hyde, Fennema, & Lamon, 1990). Nonetheless, our previous research showed that some parents believe there are innate gender differences in math talent (Yee & Eccles, 1988). We have replicated this effect in MSALT and extended it to other activity domains; namely, English and sports. The results are summarized in Table 11.1.

We have also replicated the results with a much younger sample, referred to as *The Michigan Study of Childhood and Beyond—CAB*. This is a multiyear longitudinal study of the development of elementary-school-age children in the context of the family and the school. In 1986, approximately 600 children and their families were recruited into this study. The children were in either kindergarten, first, or third grade at the start of the study. These families have been participating annually in the study since that time. The data summarized in this chapter were collected in the spring and summer of the first and third years of this study. Similar scales and items as used in MSALT were used in CAB. The gender-of-child effects on parents' estimates of their children's ability and interest in math, English, sports, and instrumental music for both of these waves are summarized in Table 11.2.

The expected gender-role-stereotypic differences are evident for both English and sports. Parents of daughters rated their child as more competent and more interested in English than parents of sons and vice versa for sports. Parents also rated daughters as more talented in instrumental music than sons. This is particularly interesting since few of the children had been

**TABLE 11.2**
**Parents' Ratings of Daughters' and Sons' Ability and Interest**
**(Childhood and Beyond Study—Grades 2, 3, and 5)**

| | Domains | | | |
|---|---|---|---|---|
| Scales | Math | English/ Reading | Sports | Instrumental Music |
| Ability[a] | | | | |
| Girls | 5.52 | 6.01* | 4.64* | 5.05* |
| Boys | 5.65 | 5.55 | 5.12 | 4.09 |
| Interest[b] | | | | |
| Girls | 4.65* | 6.10* | 4.83* | 4.92* |
| Boys | 5.09 | 5.37 | 5.78 | 3.79 |

*Note.* Ratings were made on 7-point scales: [a]1 = *not at all good,* 7 = *very good.* [b]1 = *not at all fun/enjoyable,* 7 = *very fun/enjoyable.*
*p < .05 (for sex differences within pairs).

provided the opportunity to learn a musical instrument. Nonetheless, the parents, and the children themselves, were quite willing to rate children's potential for learning a new musical instrument. Interestingly, teachers were also willing to make these ratings and they agreed with parents in rating girls' potential higher than boys'.

Because we were surprised by this finding, we asked a subset of our parents why parents and teachers might think that girls have higher potential for, and interest in, learning musical instruments than boys. At the time, we were in the process of doing qualitative interviews with all families who had more than one child in the study. We added this question to those interviews. Interestingly, the parents were also initially surprised by the finding. But they quickly offered a simple explanation: Learning a musical instrument takes patience and the ability to sit still for prolonged periods of time. Girls are more likely to have both of these characteristics than boys. So here we have an example of how gender-role stereotypes about temperamental characteristics can influence parents' beliefs about their children's ability to learn particular skills, which, in turn, can influence the opportunities they provide for their children during the elementary school years.

The story for mathematics was a bit more complicated: On the one hand, there was no gender-of-child effect for the parents' perceptions of their children's mathematical competence. On the other hand, there was a gender difference in parents' perceptions of their children's interest in math: Sons were seen as more interested in math than daughters. Finally, parents thought sons were most competent in math and most interested in sports; in contrast, they thought daughters were most competent and interested in reading. Given the results reported earlier about the influence of these hierarchical ratings on children's views of their own relative competencies across areas, it should not come as a surprise that the girls think they are much better at reading than math even though their teachers do not share this perception.

Why do parents hold these gender-differentiated perceptions of their children's competencies and interests in these domains? This is the one of the two questions that guide this chapter. The second question is the impact of parents' gender-differentiated perceptions on their own behaviors. We know, for example, that males are more likely to enroll in advanced math courses and to major in math-related fields in college, whereas females are more likely to major in languages and literature in college (see Eccles, 1987). There are also quite large gender differences in children's and adolescents' participation in various sport activities, especially competitive team sports (Eccles & Harold, 1991). Do these gender differences result from parents' gender-differentiated expectations for their daughters and sons?

# WHY DO PARENTS HOLD
# THESE GENDER-DIFFERENTIATED BELIEFS?

Many explanations have been offered to explain the gender-role stereotyping of people's ratings of males' and females' competencies in various domains. The most critical issue for this chapter is the extent to which parents' stereotypical perceptions of their children are either accurate or are a reflection of processes linked to perceptual bias (see Lee, Jussim, & McCauley, 1995). This is a very difficult issue because there is no consensus on what criteria should be used to assess the accuracy of gender-role stereotypes. Parents' perceptions of their children's competence in academic subjects are highly correlated with teacher's ratings of the children's competence and with various indicators of the children's performance and achievement, such as school grades and standardized test scores (Alexander & Entwisle, 1988; Eccles [Parsons] et al., 1982). But are their gender-role-stereotyped perceptions an accurate reflection of true gender differences in either talent or competence? This question is difficult to answer because females and males are treated differently by many people from infancy on. Consequently, it is impossible to get a good indicator of natural talent that is not influenced by the processes associated with gender-role socialization. For example, can it be concluded that parents' gender-role-stereotyped perceptions of their 6-year-old children's talent in sports are "accurate" if male children perform better than the female children on a standardized test of athletic skill at this age? Not really, because it is likely that girls and boys have already had different opportunities to develop their athletic skills. The best that can be done at this point is to use the strategy proposed by Jussim (1989). This strategy involves assessing the extent to which the perceiver's judgments are related to the variables of interest (in this case the child's gender) even after controlling for the possible association between the perceiver's judgment and more objective indicators of the children's actual performance level. If the judgments are related, then one can begin to identify the mediating cognitive processes that account for the biased portion of these perceptions (i.e., the portion not due to actual differences in the performance levels of girls and boys).

In both our own work (see Eccles & Jacobs, 1986; Eccles [Parsons] et al., 1982; Frome & Eccles, 1998) and the work of Alexander and Entwisle (1988), it is clear that parents' perceptions of their children's competence in mathematics are influenced by the children's gender, independent of the children's actual performance in mathematics. As noted earlier, it is also clear that there are gender-of-child effects on parents' ratings of older children's competence in mathematics in populations that do not evidence any significant differences in the performance of the female and male children on either grades or standardized test scores. Comparable patterns of results are now being reported in the domains of English and sports. For example, Jacobs and Eccles (1990) found that child's gender has an independent influence on parents' ratings of their sixth-grade child's athletic talent after controlling for the teachers' ratings of the children's athletic talent.

Similarly, as shown on Fig. 11.4, Frome and Eccles (1998) demonstrated that children's gender has an independent influence on mothers' (but not fathers') rating of their own children's math and English abilities, after actual performance indicators are controlled for.

Thus, it appears that something other than overt performance is influencing the formation of parents' perceptions of their children's competence in both math and sports. What might these factors be? The following three influences seem especially important to study: (a) true gender differences in the children's aptitude; (b) gender-biased attributions leading parents to make different inferences regarding their daughters' versus their sons' "talent"; and (c) generalizations by parents of their category-based, gender-role stereotypes to their target-based judgments of their own children's competence.

## Real Gender Differences in Children's Aptitude

The first influence—true gender differences—comes in two forms. First, in the domains of English and sports, there are measurable gender differences in children's performance by the time they enter school. Are these differences due to real gender differences in aptitude? As noted earlier, this is difficult to assess due to the fact that boys and girls are treated so differently from the time of birth. But even if there is a kernel of truth to the parents' perceptions in these domains, we know that the gender-of-child differences in parents' perceptions of their children in these domains continue to be significant even after independent indicators of the children's ability are included in the analyses as controls.

Second, in the domain of math, the differences in performance are very small, don't emerge until adolescence, and depend on the particular performance measure used. Nonetheless, there may be real gender differences in aptitude, and girls may compensate by working harder than boys in order to do so well. How does one evaluate the validity of this suggestion? One way is to compare the performance of females and males on a specific task that is considered more closely related to aptitude, and less closely related to effort, than school marks. If gender differences appear on this task in a population in which there are no gender differences in math course grades, then one might conclude that there is a true aptitudinal difference that is being overcome by a gender difference in effort. Evidence reported by Benbow and Stanley (1980) is consistent with this interpretation. They found that gifted boys score higher than gifted girls on standardized test scores and concluded that the boys have more natural aptitude for math than the girls. Unfortunately, they did not measure either effort or prior exposure to mathematics; thus, they cannot rule out the possibility that the gender differences on these aptitude tests are due to gender differences in either experience or test-taking strategies (see Eccles & Jacobs, 1986). In addition, although there is a reliable gender difference on standardized tests of math aptitude among the gifted, the evidence of such differences among more normally distributed samples is much less reliable, and the differences are much smaller whenever they are obtained (Hyde et al., 1990).

Furthermore, several findings from the Eccles (Parsons) et al. (1982) study cast doubt on the notion that girls compensate for lower levels of aptitude with hard work. First and foremost, there were no gender differences on either standardized tests of math aptitude or on school math grades. Second, there was not a significant gender difference in the amount of time the boys and girls reported spending on their math home- and schoolwork. Finally, the teachers of the boys and girls in this sample did not report any gender differences in these children's talent for mathematics. Nonetheless, there was still a significant gender-of-child effect on the parents' ratings of how difficult math was for their child. This pattern of findings makes it unlikely that the gender-of-child effects found for the parents' confidence in their children's competence in this study are due primarily to either a "real" gender difference in math talent or to "real" gender differences in the amount of work the children had invested in mastering mathematics. Although these explanations may be true in some populations, the Eccles (Parsons) et al. (1982) study suggests that a child's gender can affect parents' confidence in their child's math competence even when effort and ability are controlled. Similar processes could be going on for the English and sport domain. But, since comparable studies have not been done in the domains of English and sports, the validity of the compensation argument cannot be assessed at this point in these domains.

## Gendered Attributional Patterns

According to attribution theory (Weiner, 1974), perceptions of another's competence depends on the causal attributions made for the person's performance. If parents of boys make different attributions for their children's math performance than parents of girls, it would follow that these parents should develop different perceptions of their children's math competence. In a test of this hypothesis, Yee and Eccles (1988) found that parents of boys rated natural talent as a more important reason for their child's math successes than did parents of girls. In contrast, parents of girls rated effort as a more important reason for their child's math successes than did parents of boys. In addition, to the extent that the parents attributed their child's success in mathematics to effort, they also rated their child as less talented in mathematics. Conversely, to the extent that they attributed their child's success in mathematics to talent, they also rated their child as more talented in mathematics. Thus, it appears that the gender-role-stereotyped attributions parents make for their children's performance may be important mediators of the parents' gender-role-stereotyped perceptions of their children's math competence.

The data from MSALT provide a direct test of this conclusion. These mothers were asked to imagine a time when their child did very well in mathematics, reading, and sports and then to rate, on 7-point Likert scales, the importance of the following six possible causes in determining this success experience: natural talent, effort, task ease, teacher help, parent help, and current skill level. Significant gender-of-child effects were obtained on attributions of success to natural talent in each domain, and the pattern of these differences reflect the gender-role stereotyping of the domains. That is, parents were more likely to attribute their child's success to natural talent in math and sports if their child was a boy ($r = .13$ and $r = .09$ respectively, $p < .05$ in each case) and were more likely to attribute their child's success to natural talent in English if their child was a girl ($r = -.11, p < .05$).

To evaluate the mediation hypothesis we tested a series of path models using regression analyses on those mothers' perceptions that yielded a significant gender-of-child effect in each domain (see Table 11.1). According to Baron and Kenny (1986), support for a mediational hypothesis consists of demonstrating that the relation between variables $a$ and $c$ is reduced or eliminated when the hypothesized mediating variable $b$ is entered into the regression equation. The results for math are illustrated in Fig. 11.5. Consistent with the mediational hypothesis, the significant relation of child's gender to the relevant parent outcome variables (i.e., parents' perceptions of the child's natural math talent, the difficulty of math for their child, and their expectations regarding the child's likely future success in both math courses and a math-related career) disappeared once the relation between the child's gender and the parents' attributions for the child's math success to talent was controlled.

Comparable results for the talent attribution emerged in both the English and sport domains (see Fig. 11.6 for sports; Eccles et al., 1993). In each case, as predicted, children's gender influenced their mothers' causal attributions, which, in turn, influenced the mothers' perceptions of, and expectations for, their children. But in each of these domains, the direct effect of child's gender on parents' perceptions was still significant. The size of this effect,

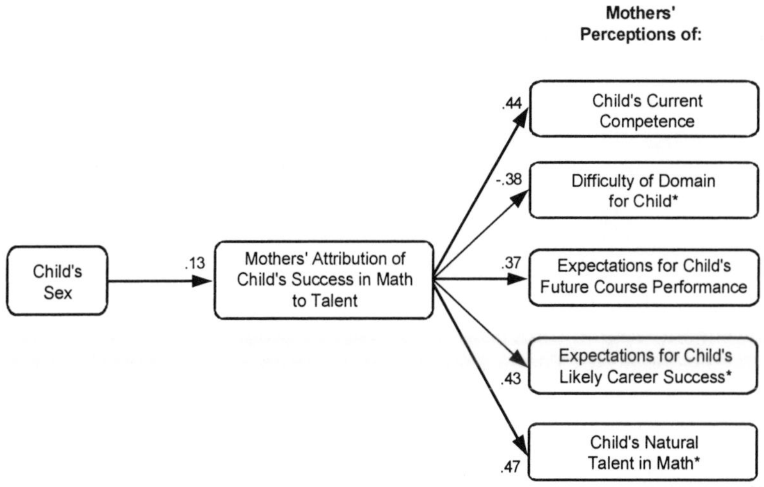

Mothers'
Perceptions of:
Child's Sex
.13
Mothers' Attribution of Child's Success in Math to Talent
.44
Child's Current Competence
-.38
Difficulty of Domain for Child*
.37
Expectations for Child's Future Course Performance
.43
Expectations for Child's Likely Career Success*
.47
Child's Natural Talent in Math*


FIG. 11.5 Mediational role of mothers' attribution of child's success in mathematics. (Asterisks refer to mothers' perceptions that yielded significant child sex differences in the main effect analyses.) *Note.* From "Parents and Gender-Role Socialization During the Middle Childhood and Adolescent Years," by J. S. Eccles, J. E. Jacobs, R. D. Harold, K. S. Yoon, A. Arbreton, & C. Freedman-Doan, in *Gender issues in contemporary society* (p. 71), by S. Oskamp and M. Costanzo (Eds.), 1993, Newbury Park, CA: Sage. Copyright 1993 by Sage Publications. Reprinted with permission.

Mothers'
Perceptions of:
Child's Sex
.09
Mothers' Attribution of Child's Success in Sports to Talent
.06
.32
Child's Current Competence
-.27
Difficulty of Domain for Child
.40
.13
Child's Natural Talent in Sports


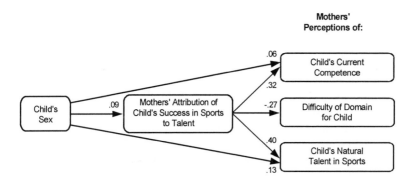

FIG. 11.6 Mediational role of mothers' attribution of child's success in sports.

however, was significantly reduced by including the parents' causal attribution in the path analysis; and thus, the results are consistent with our mediational hypothesis.[2]

These data provide good preliminary support for the hypothesized biasing effect of causal attributions on parents' perceptions of their children's competencies. However, it is important to note that these beliefs are all highly interrelated, and the data are correlational in nature. The consistency of the findings across domains indicates that the relations are reliable, but the actual causal direction of the relations is still at issue. We are just beginning the longitudinal analyses necessary to pin down the predominant causal directions of influence among these various beliefs. Preliminary analyses support the causal direction illustrated in these figures: Causal attributions at Time 1 predict parents' perceptions of their children's ability at Time 2 (1 year later) even after controlling for the parents' Time 1 perceptions of their children's abilities.

## Biasing Influence of Gender-Role Stereotypic Beliefs

Both Eccles and Jacobs (see Eccles et al., 1990; Jacobs & Eccles, 1985) hypothesized that parents' gender-role stereotypes regarding the extent to which males or females, in general, are likely to be more talented or more interested in a particular domain will impact on their perceptions of their own child's ability in this domain, leading to a distortion in the parents' perceptions of their children's ability in the gender-role-stereotyped direction. In other words, the impact of the child's gender on parents' perceptions of their child's ability in any particular domain should depend, in part, on the parents' gender-role stereotypes regarding ability in that domain. Furthermore, this effect should be significant even after entering an independent indicator of the children's actual level of competence in the domain as a control.

As reported earlier, parents do hold gender-differentiated views of their children's academic and nonacademic abilities when children are still very young, and these beliefs are more gender-differentiated than are objective indicators of the children's actual performance in these domains (e.g., Alexander & Entwisle, 1988; Eccles & Harold, 1991; Eccles et al., 1993; Jacobs & Eccles, 1985). These studies, however, did not look at the actual relation between parents' gender-role stereotypes and their perceptions of their own child's ability. The critical issue is not whether parents, on the average, give gender-differentiated estimates of their children's abilities.

---

[2]More complete details of these and other analyses summarized in this chapter have been reported elsewhere and can be obtained from the first author.

Instead, the issue is whether or not parents who endorse the culturally dominant gender-role stereotype regarding the distribution of talent and interest between males and females distort their perception of their own child's abilities in a direction that is consistent with the gender-role stereotype to a greater extent than parents who do not endorse the stereotype. Evidence from both MSALT and CAB support this hypothesis.

In CAB, mothers were asked at Time 1 who they thought was naturally better at mathematics, reading, and sports—boys, girls, or neither. They were also asked to rate how much natural talent their child had in each of these three domains, how difficult (or easy) each of these domains was for their child, and how important they thought it was to their child to be good in each domain on a 7-point Likert scale. In each domain  the significance of the interaction of the gender of one's child with the parents' gender-role stereotypes in predicting the parents' ratings of their own child's competency was tested. All nine interactions were significant (Eccles et al., 1993), indicating that the parents who endorsed the cultural gender-role stereotype regarding which gender is "naturally" better in each domain were more likely to rate sons and daughters differently than parents who did not endorse the cultural stereotype. Furthermore, in each domain the gender-of-child effect for the parents who endorsed the cultural stereotype was in the stereotypic direction; that is, among those parents who believed that boys in general were more talented in the domain, parents of sons rated their child's ability higher than the parents of daughters.

The results for mathematics are particularly interesting. As shown on Table 11.2, the gender of one's child was not significantly related as a main effect to the mothers' perceptions of their child's math talent. But, in another analysis, the gender of the child did affect parents' ratings of their child's competence in math when it was looked at in interaction with their gender-role stereotype of mathematical competence ($p < .05$). As predicted, mothers who believed that males were naturally more talented in mathematics evidenced a significant gender-of-child effect in their ratings of their children's math ability, and the direction of this effect was consistent with their stereotype; in contrast, the gender-of-child effect was not significant for the mothers who believed that neither males nor females were naturally more talented at mathematics.

Similar gender-role stereotypic effects characterize the mothers' reports on their children in sports and English. For example, in comparison to parents who did not endorse this cultural stereotype, parents who endorsed the stereotype that males are generally better at sports than females were more likely to rate sons' talent higher than daughters' talent. Similarly, parents who endorsed the cultural stereotype that females are naturally better at language arts than males were more likely than parents who did not endorse this stereotype to rate daughters' reading talent higher than sons'.

Although it is possible that these effects are due to the impact of target-based information on the mothers' category-based gender-role stereotypes, the extreme stability of gender-role stereotypes across time in a variety of populations makes this an unlikely alternative interpretation (Rothbart, 1989).

Jacobs and Eccles explored these effects in the domains of math and sports more fully with data from MSALT (Jacobs, 1987; Jacobs & Eccles, 1992). Using path analytic techniques, they tested the impact of the interaction of the gender of one's child and one's gender-role stereotypes on mother's perceptions of their child's ability, controlling for the effect of an independent indicator of the child's actual ability level (the teacher's rating of the child's ability). The interaction term was created so that a positive coefficient indicated that the mother was distorting her impression of her child in the gender-role stereotypic direction. That is, if she was talking about a boy child in a male activity domain like sports or mathematics, her perception of her child's ability was higher than what would have been predicted using only the teacher's rating; in contrast, if she was talking about a girl child, her perception was lower than what would have been predicted using only the teacher's rating.

The results for the sport domain are illustrated in Fig. 11.7. Once again the findings are consistent with our hypothesis. The interaction term was significant and the coefficient was positive. Thus, to the extent that these mothers endorsed the traditional gender-role stereotypic belief that males are naturally better in sports than are girls, they distorted their perception of their child's competence in these domains in the gender-role stereotypic direction. In addition, consistent with the findings of Eccles (Parsons) et al. (1982), the mothers' perceptions of their children's competence in each domain had a significant impact on the children's own self-perceptions even after the children's actual performance in each domain was controlled. Similar findings characterized the math and reading domains (Eccles et al., 1993; Jacobs & Eccles, 1992).

In summary, evidence from these studies suggests that parents' causal attributions for their children's successes as well as parents' gender-role stereotypes lead to perceptual bias in their impressions of their children's competencies in gender-role-stereotyped activity domains. Although parents' perceptions of their children's competencies in various domains are strongly related to independent indicators of their children's actual competence in these domains, the evidence clearly indicates that parents' perceptions of their children's competencies are also influenced by their children's sex and by the parents' gender-role-stereotypic beliefs about which sex is naturally more talented in these domains. Furthermore, the evidence supports the conclusion that these influences are independent of any actual differences that might exist in the children's competencies. Thus,

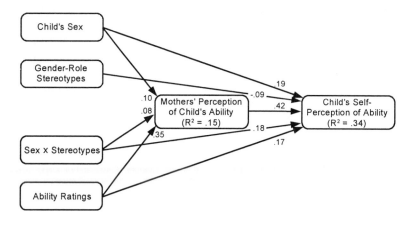

FIG. 11.7 Moderating role of mothers' gender-role stereotypes on their perceptions of children's sports ability.

our findings suggest that perceptual bias is operating in the formation of parents' impressions of their children's competencies in gender-role-stereotyped activity domains.

But they do not indicate how well the data fit the model we are proposing. To evaluate this fit, we tested a simplified model using LISREL analyses (Jöreskog & Sörbom, 1993) for each of these two domains, math and sports. Because the interaction of child gender and mother's gender-role stereotype was significant, we tested a two-group hierarchical LISREL model. The specified model assumed that a mother's stereotype influences her perception of her child's ability even after an independent indicator of the child's ability is entered as a control. It also tested whether the child's ability, as indicated by a teacher's rating of the child influences the mother's stereotype. The fit of the models to the data in both the math and sport domains was very good as indicated by the adjusted goodness-of-fit index (AGFIs > .96).

Let's consider the math domain first. In this domain, there was no significant relation between the teacher's rating of the child's ability and the mother's stereotype for math. In contrast, there was a very strong relation between the teacher's rating of the child's ability and the mother's rating of the child's ability. But most importantly for the present discussion, there was a small but significant positive relation between the mother's stereotype and her perception of her son's math ability and a marginally significant negative relation between the mother's stereotype and her perception of her daughter's math ability. Thus, as predicted, the more a mother stereotyped math as a male domain, the more she overestimated her son's math ability and underestimated her daughter's math ability relative to the level of ability indicated by the teacher's rating.

Similar results emerged in the sport domain. But in this domain, the daughter's sport ability, as rated by the teacher, was negatively related to the mother's gender-role stereotypes: Mothers with more sports-able daughters were less likely to stereotype sports as a male domain than other mothers. In addition, however, to the extent that the mothers stereotyped sport as a male domain, they also rated their daughters' sport ability lower than one would predict given the teacher's estimate of the girl's ability. This latter effect did not hold for sons. Apparently, mothers' endorsement of the cultural stereotype that males are naturally better at sports than girls only has a debilitating effect on their perceptions of daughters' sports ability. These LISREL analyses suggest that there was no enhancement effect for boys of mothers' holding the cultural stereotype in the sports domain.

These results provide support for the hypothesis that gender-role stereotypes bias parents' perceptions of their own children's competencies. Given the large amount of specific performance information parents get about their children as they grow up, we did not expect the biasing effects to be large, and they are not. Nevertheless, although the effects are not large, they are both reliable and consistent across two activity domains, and they do appear to influence the development of the children's own self-perceptions in a manner consistent with the self-fulfilling prophecy hypothesis.

## MEDIA INFLUENCES ON PARENTS' VIEWS

Scholars interested in gender-role socialization have long speculated that exposure to gender stereotypic media should reinforce and exacerbate people's gender-stereotyped beliefs (see Eccles & Hoffman, 1984). Rarely does one have a naturalistic opportunity to evaluate this hypothesis. Such an opportunity occurred shortly after the release of an article by Benbow and Stanley (1980) in *Science* that reported a major sex difference in the mathematical reasoning ability among gifted seventh-grade students.

The popular media coverage of this research report was extensive, including headlines such as "Do Males Have a Math Gene?" (Williams & King in *Newsweek*, 1980), "Are Boys Better at Math?" (in *The New York Times*, 1980), and "The Gender Factor in Math: A New Study Says Males May Be Naturally Abler than Females" (in *Time*, 1980). The text of the articles often implied that the sex difference was due to inherited or other biological factors. For example, in "Sex + Math = ?" *Family Weekly* (1981) reported that the Benbow and Stanley (1980) study had shown that males are born with more math ability than females; similarly *Time* magazine (1980) concluded that "males inherently have more mathematical ability than females" (p. 57).

Some publications included cartoons or other graphic representation of the implied gender difference. Typically these cartoons presented an extreme characterization of male superiority in mathematics and did not illustrate the fact that the Benbow and Stanley (1980) study contained only gifted children. These exaggerated depictions of the magnitude of sex differences in math ability are in stark contrast with the fact that gender rarely accounts for more than 4% of the variance in students' performance on standardized tests of math aptitude and virtually never accounts for any significant variance in mathematics course grades during the primary and secondary school years (Hyde et al., 1990).

Did exposure to this media campaign influence parents' views of their children's math ability? Did it influence their more general stereotypes about gender differences in math ability? Jacobs and Eccles (1985) were able to study these questions. We had assessed parents' general stereotypes as well as their views of their own children approximately 9 months before the media campaign in a sample of predominately middle-class parents living in southeastern Michigan. We reassessed those parents' beliefs approximately 3 months after the media campaign in the spring of 1981. In addition, the last page of the survey contained a question that described the media coverage of the research and asked if the parent had heard about it; approximately one quarter of the parents ($N = 57$) had. Of these people, 68% had seen a magazine article about it, 18% had read about it in the newspaper, and smaller numbers had heard about it on the radio, television, or from a friend. Many people indicated that they had heard about the report from several sources.

The beliefs of those who had heard about the Benbow and Stanley (1980) report from the media were compared with those who had not. For the sake of clarity, we refer to those who heard about the report as the exposed group and those who did not as the unexposed group. Analyses of variance performed on all pretest variables and on indicators of socioeconomic class indicated that exposed and unexposed parents did not differ in their perceptions of their children's math abilities, in their level of education, or in their socioeconomic status prior to media exposure.

Compared to other mothers, exposed mothers of daughters thought that their daughters had less math ability, were less likely to succeed in math in the future, found math more difficult, and had to work harder to succeed in math in the spring of 1981. Furthermore, the exposed mothers' estimates of their daughters had declined over time more than exposed mothers of sons or unexposed mothers of either daughters or sons. The change over time was particularly true for questions concerning the perceived difficulty of math for their child.

Father's responded differently. Generally, fathers of girls thought that their daughters had slightly less math ability compared to fathers of sons. However, exposed fathers of girls changed their beliefs in the direction of thinking their daughters had slightly more ability after hearing the media coverage, whereas unexposed fathers had become more gender stereotyped in their beliefs.

In contrast, we did find the predicted effect on fathers' more general gender-role stereotypes. Even though all fathers thought that math was more useful for males than females, fathers of sons endorsed this believe more than fathers of daughters. This difference was especially true for the exposed fathers: In the spring of 1981, exposed fathers endorsed the stereotype that males do better than females more strongly than unexposed fathers. In addition, exposed fathers of sons endorsed the stereotype that males do better than females in advanced math classes more strongly than any other group.

This study provides strong evidence that exposure to stereotyped media contributes to the acquisition and maintenance of gender stereotypic beliefs, even about one's own children. The study also provides support for a reactive effect. Fathers' came to the defense of their daughters even though the media had strengthened their own general stereotypic beliefs.

## BEHAVIORAL CONSEQUENCES OF PARENTS' BELIEFS

We have argued thus far that gender differentiation in parents' perceptions of their children's abilities in various domains results, in part, from processes associated with expectancy effects. In particular, we have presented evidence that both parents' causal attributions for their children's successes and parents' gender-role stereotypes lead to perceptual bias in their impressions of their children's competencies in gender-role-stereotyped activity domains. Although parents' perceptions of their children's competencies in math, English, and sports are strongly related to independent indicators of their children's actual competence in these domains, the evidence clearly indicates that parents' perceptions of their children's competencies in math, English, and sports are also influenced by their children's gender and by the parents' gender-role-stereotypic beliefs about which gender is naturally more talented and interested in these domains. Furthermore, the evidence is consistent with the conclusion that these influences are independent of any actual differences that might exist in the children's competencies. Thus, our findings suggest that perceptual bias is operating in the formation of parents' impressions of their children's competencies in gender-role stereotyped activity domains.

Proponents of a self-fulfilling prophecy view of the socialization of gender differences in children's competencies in various activity domains would argue that these differences in parents' perceptions of their children's competencies set in motion a chain of events that ultimately create the very differences that the parents originally believed to exist. We have already pointed to one mechanism through which such a process might be mediated, namely, parental influences on children's self-perceptions. We have argued elsewhere that children's self- and task-perceptions influence the choices children make about their involvement in various activities (see Eccles [Parsons] et al., 1983; Eccles & Harold, 1991). In particular, we have documented that children spend more time engaged in activities that they think they are good at and that they value and enjoy, and that gender differences in activity choice are mediated by gender differences in self-perceptions and subjective task value. For example, in math, we have demonstrated that decisions regarding course enrollment in high school are influenced by adolescents' confidence in their math ability and by the value they attach to math (Eccles [Parsons] et al., 1983; Updegraff, Eccles, Barber, & O'Brien, 1996). Similarly, in sports, we have demonstrated that the gender difference in the amount of free time sixth graders spend engaged in athletic activities is mediated by gender differences in both the adolescents' confidence in their athletic ability and the value they attach to athletic activities (Eccles & Harold, 1991).

Thus far in this chapter we have summarized evidence that gender differences in adolescents' self-perceptions are mediated, in part, by the gender-role stereotyped bias in their parents' perceptions of their competencies in various activities. Together these results support the conclusion that processes associated with the self-fulfilling prophecy phenomenon contribute to the socialization of gender differences in the domains of mathematics and sports. But exactly how do parents' gender-role-stereotyped perceptions of their children's competencies influence the children's self- and task-perceptions? We are just beginning to study this issue.

Guided by the theoretical perspective summarized in Fig. 11.1, we are testing the following sets of predictions: Parents' gender-role stereotypes, in interaction with their child's gender, affect the following parent beliefs and behaviors: the parents' emotional reaction to their children's performance in various activities, the importance parents attach to their child acquiring various skills, the advice parents provide their child regarding involvement in various skills, and the activities and toys parents provide for their children. In turn, these beliefs and behaviors influence the development of the following child outcomes across the various gender-role-stereotyped activity domains: children's confidence in their ability, children's interest in mastering various skills, children's affective reaction to participating in various activities, and, as a consequence of these self- and task-perceptions, the amount of time, and type of effort, the children end up devoting to mastering, and demonstrating, various skills.

Empirical work assessing these various causal links is now under way. Preliminary evidence looks very promising. For example, consider the link between the parents' perceptions of their children and the types of experiences they provide for their children. We are just beginning to explore this link with information gathered in CAB. In addition to asking the parents for their perceptions of their children's abilities and interests in several activity domains, we asked the parents in CAB to give us detailed reports of the types of activities and experiences they provide for their children in the various activity domains, the types of skills and activities they are encouraging their children to develop, and what they do with their children. As a first step in this process, we tested whether parents provide different types of experiences for girls and boys. They clearly do in several of the activity domains we are studying. The Wave 3 results are summarized in Table 11.3. For example, parents reported watching sports more often with

TABLE 11.3
Parents' Provision of Experiences for Daughters and Sons
(Childhood and Beyond Study—Grades 2, 3, and 5)

| Activity | Girls | Boys |
|---|---|---|
| Have child read to you | 3.10 | 2.90 |
| Play sports with child | 2.63 | 3.36 |
| Do active, outdoor activities with child | 3.20 | 3.56 |
| Take a child to a paid sporting event | 1.71 | 1.91 |
| Encourage child to do math or science-related activities at home | 4.01 | 4.35 |
| Encourage child to work on or play with a computer outside of school | 3.70 | 4.04 |
| Encourage child to read | 6.04 | 5.69 |
| Encourage child to play competitive sports | 3.58 | 4.43 |
| Encourage child to play noncompetitive sports | 4.54 | 4.94 |
| Encourage child to take dance lessons | 3.56 | 2.15 |
| Encourage child to take dancing for fun | 3.85 | 2.53 |
| Encourage child to watch sports on TV | 2.61 | 3.07 |
| Encourage child to take music lessons | 4.26 | 3.52 |
| Encourage child to play a musical instrument | 4.32 | 3.67 |
| Encourage child to build, make, or fix things | 3.83 | 4.67 |
| Encourage child to learn cooking and other homemaking | 4.01 | 3.59 |

*Note.* Ratings were made on 7-point scales: $1 = never$, $7 = almost\ everyday$, or $1 = strongly\ discourage$, $7 = strongly\ encourage$. All differences between girls' and boys' means are significant at $p < .05$.

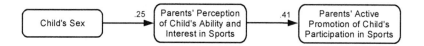

FIG. 11.8 Mediating role of parents' perceptions of their children in the relation between children's sex and parents' provision of opportunities to participate in sports.

sons, playing sports more often with sons, enrolling sons more often in sports programs, and encouraging sports participation more for sons than for daughters. Furthermore, these differences were already evident by the time the children were in kindergarten (Eccles et al., 1993).

But more importantly for the argument presented in this chapter, we used path analysis to determine whether the gender-of-child effects on the types of activities parents provide and encourage are mediated by the parents' perceptions of their children's ability and interests in each domain. The results are summarized in Fig. 11.8. Consistent with the mediational hypothesis, the gender-of-child effect on the types of experiences parents provide for their children became nonsignificant when the gender-of-child effect on parents' perceptions of their children's sport ability and interest was entered into the path analysis (Eccles et al., 1993). These results suggest the following conclusions: (a) Parents form an impression of their children's ability and interest in sports at a very young age, (b) this impression depends on the gender of their child to a greater extent than justified by objective evidence of gender differences in sport performance, and (c) this impression influences the types of experiences the parents provide for their children in the sport domain. If the processes associated with expectancy effects operate, this differential provision of experience should result over time in a pattern of gender differences in actual skills that is consistent with the cultural stereotypes.

How might exposure to toys and activities affect children's preferences and activity choices? Through the processes associated with channelization (Hartley, 1964), familiarity (Zajonc, 1968), and both operant and classical conditioning, children should come to prefer the toys and activities to which they are exposed.

But at a more specific level, exposure to different toys and activities also provides children with the opportunity to develop different competencies and a differentiated set of task values. We know that exposure to reading materials predicts later reading achievement (see, e.g., Hess & Holloway, 1984). Similarly, exposure to manipulative toys and large-space play activities appears to affect the development of such basic cognitive skills as spatial facility (Connor, Schackman, & Serbin, 1978). Without the opportunity to try a particular activity, children will never get a chance to find out if they are good at it or if they enjoy it.

## CONCLUSION

We have presented evidence of the influence of gender on parents' perceptions of their children's abilities in various activity domains. We have also presented evidence that parents' beliefs have an impact on children's developing self-concepts and on the experiences parents provide for their children in various activity domains. These relations are all likely to contribute to gender-role socialization. They also suggest possible routes to intervention. Because parents' beliefs appear to play a pivotal role in this system, interventions should be directed toward changing parents' beliefs and perceptions. We know in the math domain, for example, that teachers can convince parents that their daughters are talented in mathematics and can then enlist parents' help in encouraging young women to consider advanced math courses and occupations in math-related fields. Similar intervention efforts could be designed in other activity domains.

## ACKNOWLEDGMENTS

Work on this article was supported by grants to the first author from the National Institute of Child Health and Human Development, the National Science Foundation, and the Spencer Foundation. We would like to thank the school districts involved in these studies and the following people for their assistance at various stages in the projects outlined: Amy Arbreton, Bonnie Barber, Constance Flanagan, Toby Jayaratne, Allan Wigfield, and Doris Yee.

## REFERENCES

Alexander, K. L., & Entwisle, D. R. (1988). Achievement in the first two years of school: Patterns and processes. *Monograph of the Society for Research in Child Development*, *53*(2).

Are boys better at math? (1980, December). *The New York Times*, p. 102.

Baron, R. M., & Kenny, D. A. (1986). The moderator–mediator variable distinction in social psychological research: Conceptual, strategic, and statistical considerations. *Journal of Personality and Social Psychology*, *51*, 1173–1182.

Benbow, C. P., & Stanley, J. C. (1980). Sex differences in mathematical ability: Fact or artifact? *Science*, *210*, 1262–1264.

Connor, J. M., Schackman, M., & Serbin, L. A. (1978). Sex-related differences in response to practice on a visual-spatial test and generalization to a related test. *Child Development, 49*, 24–29.

Eccles, J. S. (1987). Gender roles and women's achievement-related decisions. *Psychology of Women Quarterly, 11*, 135–172.

Eccles, J. S. (1993). School and family effects on the ontogeny of children's interests, self-perceptions, and activity choice. In J. Jacobs (Ed.), *Nebraska symposium on motivation, 1992: Developmental perspectives on motivation* (pp. 145–208). Lincoln: University of Nebraska Press.

Eccles, J. S., & Harold, R. D. (1991). Gender differences in sport involvement: Applying the Eccles' expectancy-value model. *Journal of Applied Sport Psychology, 3*, 7–35.

Eccles, J. S., & Hoffman, L. W. (1984). Socialization and the maintenance of a sex-segregated labor market. In H. W. Stevenson & A. E. Siegel (Eds.), *Research in child development and social policy* (Vol. 1, pp. 367–420). Chicago: University of Chicago Press.

Eccles, J. S., & Jacobs, J. E. (1986). Social forces shape math attitudes and performance. *Signs, 11*, 367–380.

Eccles, J. S., Jacobs, J. E., & Harold, R. D. (1990). Gender role stereotypes, expectancy effects, and parents' socialization of gender differences. *Journal of Social Issues, 46*(2), 183–201.

Eccles, J. S., Jacobs, J. E., Harold, R. D., Yoon, K. S., Arbreton, A., & Freedman-Doan, C. (1993). Parents and gender-role socialization during the middle childhood and adolescent years. In S. Oskamp & M. Costanzo (Eds.), *Gender issues in contemporary society* (pp. 59–83). Newbury Park, CA: Sage.

Eccles, J. S., Wigfield, A., Flanagan, C. A., Miller, C., Reuman, D. A., & Yee, D. (1989). Self-concepts, domain values, and self-esteem: Relations and changes at early adolescence. *Journal of Personality, 57*, 283–310.

Eccles (Parsons), J., Adler, T. F., Futterman, R., Goff, S. B., Kaczala, C. M., Meece, J. L., & Midgley, C. (1983). Expectancies, values, and academic behaviors. In J. T. Spence (Ed.), *Achievement and achievement motives: Psychological and sociological approaches.* (pp. 75–146). San Francisco: Freeman.

Eccles (Parsons), J., Adler, T. F., & Kaczala, C. M. (1982). Socialization of achievement attitudes and beliefs: Parental influences. *Child Development, 53*, 310–321.

Eccles (Parsons), J., Adler, T., & Meece, J. L. (1984). Sex differences in achievement: A test of alternate theories. *Journal of Personality and Social Psychology, 46*, 26–43.

Frome, P. M., & Eccles, J. S. (1998). Parents' influence on children's acheivement-related perceptions. *Journal of Personality and Social Psychology, 74*, 435–452.

The gender factor in math: A new study says males may be naturally abler than females. (1980, December 15). *Time*, p. 57.

Goodnow, J. J., & Collins, W. A. (1990). *Development according to parents: The nature, sources, and consequences of parents' ideas.* Hillsdale, NJ: Lawrence Erlbaum Associates.

Hartley, R. E. (1964). A developmental view of female sex-role definition and identification. *Merrill-Palmer Quarterly, 10*, 3–16.

Hess, R. D., & Holloway, S. D. (1984). Family and school as educational institutions. In R. D. Parke (Ed.), *Review of child development and research: Vol. 17. The family* (pp. 179–222). Chicago: University of Chicago Press.

Hyde, J. S., Fennema, E., & Lamon, S. J. (1990). Gender differences in mathematics performance: A meta-analysis. *Psychological Bulletin, 107*, 139–155.

Jacobs, J. E. (1987). *Parents' gender role stereotypes and perceptions of their child's ability: Influences on the child.* Unpublished dissertation, University of Michigan, Ann Arbor.

Jacobs, J. E., & Eccles, J. S. (1985). Gender differences in math ability: The impact of media reports on parents. *Educational Researcher, 14*, 20–25.

Jacobs, J. E., & Eccles, J. S. (1992). The impact of mothers' gender-role stereotypic beliefs on mothers' and children's ability perceptions. *Journal of Personality and Social Psychology, 63,* 932–944.

Jöreskog, K. G., & Sörbom, D. (1993). *LISREL 8: Structural equation modeling with the SIMPLIS command language.* Hillsdale, NJ: Lawrence Erlbaum Associates.

Jussim, L. (1989). Teacher expectations: Self-fulfilling prophecies, perceptual biases, and accuracy. *Journal of Personality and Social Psychology, 57,* 469–480.

Lee, Y.-T., Jussim, L. J., & McCauley, C. R. (Eds.). (1995). *Stereotype accuracy: Toward appreciating group differences.* Washington, DC: American Psychological Association.

Marsh, H. W. (1990). A multidimensional, hierarchical model of self-concept: Theoretical and empirical justification. *Educational Psychology Review, 2,* 77–172.

Rogosa, D. (1979). Causal models in longitudinal research: Rationale, formulation, and interpretation. In J. R. Nesselroade & P. B. Baltes (Eds.), *Longitudinal research in the study of behavior and development* (pp. 263–302). New York: Academic Press.

Rothbart, M. (1989). *The stability of gender and ethnic stereotypes.* Talk given at the University of Colorado at Boulder.

Sex + Math = ? (1981, January 25). *Family Weekly.*

Updegraff, K. A., Eccles, J. S., Barber, B. L., & O'Brien, K. M. (1996). Course enrollment as self-regulatory behavior: Who takes optional high school math courses. *Learning and Individual Differences, 8,* 239–259.

Weiner, B. (Ed.). (1974). *Achievement motivation and attribution theory.* Morristown, NJ: General Learning Press.

Williams, D. A., & King, P. (1980, December 15). Do males have a math gene? *Newsweek,* p. 73.

Yee, D. K., & Eccles, J. S. (1988). Parent perceptions and attributions for children's math achievement. *Sex Roles, 19,* 317–333.

Zajonc, R. B. (1968). Attitudinal effects of mere exposure. *Journal of Personality and Social Psychology, 9* (Monograph Suppl., Pt. 2, 1–27).

# 12

# A Dual-Impact Model of Gender and Career-Related Processes

Andrea E. Abele
*University of Erlangen*

The 20th century has witnessed dramatic changes in women's workforce participation and also in the reasons for their participation. At the beginning of this century, women's workforce participation was mainly a question of status and family income. Women from upper classes, as well as wives of wealthy men, were not obliged to earn money through employment. In contrast, they were expected to fulfill their roles as wives and mothers and to stay at home even if they would have liked to do something else (Frevert, 1986, 1995; Kiernan, 1993). If women worked for money—and lots of them did so, of course—the predominant reason was economical necessity, or it was at least assumed that this was their only motive. These working women were usually poorly educated, had to work in low employment positions, and received a low income.

Education was generally sex segregated. Women were taught female-specific skills like housework and child care. It was very difficult for them to attain a higher education or to attend a university. In a country like Germany, for instance, it was not before 1896 that the first women passed the *Abitur* (i.e., the examination necessary for attending a university), and it was 1900 that women were allowed to enroll at universities as regular students. In the United States these developments were a little faster. In 1837, Oberlin College allowed female students to officially enroll, and by 1900, 30% of the students were female (Chamberlain, 1991). The few well-educated women usually had to choose between a career, for instance as a teacher or a medical doctor, or a family, because a combination of both was—with very few exceptions—impossible.

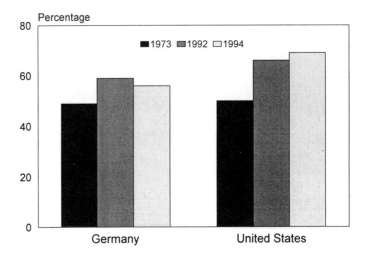

FIG. 12.1 Percentages of women's workforce participation in Germany and the United States. *Note.* From "Compatibility of Modernization and Family," by J. Künzler, 1999. Copyright 1999 by J. Künzler. Adapted with permission.

From that time until today, women's participation in the educational system has increased considerably. In Germany, for example, there are more women who pass the *Abitur* now than men who pass (52% women in 1998). The percentages of women and men studying at a university is equal. Also, women's workforce participation has become indispensable. Statistically speaking, the working woman is the norm (Hyde, 1985), and the pure homemaker is the exception. Figure 12.1 shows the  respective percentages in Germany and the United States.

It is also no longer expected that women work solely for monetary reasons; that is, having a satisfying occupation is now acknowledged to be important for both men and women (Abele, 1997; Teichler & Buttgereit, 1992).

In spite of these developments, however, there are still significant differences in the workforce participation of men and women. Several studies show that worldwide—and even within comparable positions—women earn only about two thirds of men's salaries (Major, 1994; Marini & Fan, 1997; U.S. Bureau of Census, 1998). These differences remain even when different occupational choices of men and women are considered (National Center for Education Statistics, 1998). Worldwide, women are harder hit by unemployment (Bundesanstalt für Arbeit, 1998; Künzler, 1999; U.S. Bureau of Census, 1998). There are also far more women in badly paid and badly insured part-time positions. The most striking difference, however, is that even though women are at least as well educated as men, more than 90% of all leading career positions are held by men. According to data reported by Gutek (1993), only 3.6% of all top-management positions in 159 United Nations Organization states are held by women. Estimates of the percentage of women in higher management positions vary between 2% (Bischoff, 1990) and 9% (Merkel, 1992).

The present chapter is concerned with these changes in women's workforce participation and their impact on gender as a developmental social psychological phenomenon. *Gender*—in contrast to *sex*, which refers to the demographic categories of female and male—is used here to refer to the social construction of the sexes. It is viewed as a context-dependent phenomenon, as a "dynamic construct that draws on and impinges upon processes at the individual, interactional, group, institutional, and cultural levels" (Deaux & LaFrance, 1998, p. 788). Gender entails a developmental component, both at the individual (socialization) and the cultural (cultural and societal change) level, as well as a social psychological component, again both at the individual (the gendered self) and the cultural level (gender-role expectations or gender stereotypes). Defining gender in such a way, it is evident that any changes in individual or societal life conditions should change the conceptualization of gender, too. It may, for instance, be asked how gender-related values, preferences, or behavioral enactments change with increasing education and increasing workforce participation of women. It may be asked how the gender category both from the perceiver and the target point of view has changed as a result of these societal processes. Or it may be asked how different self-conceptualizations in terms of gender relate to interests, choices, and behavioral enactments.

Here, some of these questions with respect to occupational choices and careers will be touched on. Against the background of the previously cited changes in women's workforce participation, early theories of occupational psychology are discussed and related to gender. Then, a theoretical framework for the analysis of gender in occupational contexts will be outlined, the *dual-impact model* of gender and career. It is rooted in the more general gender-in-context model as described by Deaux and Major (1987; see also Deaux & LaFrance, 1998). Three hypotheses are derived and tested in the *Erlangen Career Studies*. They are concerned with the impact of respondents' sex and gender-role orientation on occupational choice and behavior, as well as with the reciprocal impact of occupational development on gender-role orientation. The relative impact of respondents' sex versus gender-role orientation on career-related variables is especially important with respect to the social psychological focus on gender, whereas the reciprocal impact of career-related processes on a person's gender-role orientation is especially important with respect to the developmental focus on gender. Finally, some conclusions with respect to a developmental social psychology of gender are drawn.

# THEORIES AND FINDINGS FROM
# OCCUPATIONAL PSYCHOLOGY

Women's careers were completely neglected in occupational psychology until about 40 years ago when researchers started to think about this issue. In the early years, the principle focus was on the question of *why* women work, a question that has never been posed with respect to men (see, e.g., Lehr, 1969). Then, different career tracks of women were described (Myrdal & Klein, 1956; Super, 1957). It was assumed that women's workforce participation is a transitory stage before marriage (Myrdal & Klein, 1956) or in times of low family income (Oppenheimer, 1979). Continuous workforce participation was thought to be an alternative to marriage and children or—if a woman wanted to have both—was assumed to be characterized by conflict (see Houseknecht, Vaughan, & Stratham, 1987; Powell, 1988). Early empirical findings from longitudinal studies show that sex and marital status are better predictors of career development than intelligence. Terman and Oden (1959), for instance, analyzed the occupational development of highly gifted children (IQ above 135), who had first been tested in 1921–1922, and retested at the age of 44. At this age, 97% of the men had full-time positions, 86% of them were in high-status positions. The employment rate of unmarried women was exactly the same. However, only 19% of these unmarried women had leading positions. Married women were homemakers in 61% of the cases. Other researchers similarly showed a negative correlation of women's employment duration with their family status and number of children (Steel, Abeles, & Card, 1982; Stohs, 1991; Wolfson, 1976).

More detailed approaches to women's interest development and career choices were developed by Astin (1984); Betz and Fitzgerald (1987); Eccles (Parsons) et al. (1983; see also Eccles, Wigfield, & Schiefele, 1998; Eccles, Freedman-Doan, Frome, Jacobs, & Yoon, chap. 11, this volume); Farmer (1985); Fassinger (1985, 1990); and Gottfredson (1986; see also Phillips & Imhoff, 1997; Watkins & Subich, 1995). They all posited that being a man or a woman does not have a direct impact on career motivation, career choice, or career commitment, but that it does influence other variables that may be linked to career issues. Some of these other variables are socialization (Astin, 1984), sex-role attitudes (Betz & Fitzgerald, 1987; Fassinger, 1985, 1990), occupational self-esteem (Farmer, 1985), attitudes toward different life domains (Betz & Fitzgerald, 1987; Fassinger, 1985, 1990), expectations for success, gender-role stereotypes, the self-concept, and subjective task values (Eccles [Parsons] et al., 1983). Astin (1984) additionally suggested that being male or female has an impact on the structure of opportunity, like social support by parents and teachers and advantages or discriminations in the workforce. The career choice model developed by Betz and Fitzgerald (1987) and the model of achievement-related choices developed by Eccles (Parsons) et al. (1983) have been especially influential.

Betz and Fitzgerald (1987) were concerned with the *rationality* of women's career choice. According to these authors, a rational career choice is based on the congruency of abilities, aptitudes, values, and life plans with occupational choice and the affordances of the respective career. From an overview of empirical findings published up to 1986, they derive the following groups of variables that influence women's career decisions: person variables like abilities, gender-role attitudes, gender self-schema, self-esteem, and occupational self-concept; background variables like maternal employment, paternal support, educational status of the parents, female role models, experiences in the workforce, and non-gender-typed socialization; educational variables like degree of education, mathematical skills, and having been at a girls' school; and variables of the person's adult life like late or no marriage and few or no children. On the first level of this model, a rational career decision is advanced by perceived parental support, by adequate role models, by educational and academic success, and by previous work experiences. These factors influence the second level of the model with gender-role orientation, self-concept, and work attitudes as variables. These second-level variables, in turn, influence the third-level ones, such as lifestyle preferences and plans, which are related to the rationality of career choice. A recent review of the relevant literature published since then (Phillips & Imhoff, 1997) lends support to the basic premises of the model (see also Fassinger, 1985, 1990).

Eccles (Parsons) et al. (1983; see also Eccles et al., 1998; Eccles et al., chap. 11, this volume) developed a model of achievement-related choices. It is based on expectancy–value theory (Atkinson, 1964), which posits that behavioral enactments are the result of expectations for success and values attached to it. Gender-role stereotypes, the person's perceptions of gender roles, the self-concept, and subjective task values influence these factors. Eccles and colleagues assumed that achievement-related choices are a continuous process and are made in the context of a set of subjectively feasible choices—a considerably smaller set than the objective set that might exist in the person's environment. It is further assumed that one must also consider the choices not made in order to fully understand achievement-related behavior. The model has been tested with respect to task values, performance in different school subjects, and academic choice.

Occupational career models not directly related to women's careers usually treat gender as a background variable comparable to race or socioeconomic status. Background variables are assumed to influence many other variables, and some of these other variables have an impact on career issues, too. Current models stand mainly in the tradition of social learning theory (Bandura, 1994). They stress the importance of expectations and goals and analyze possible sex differences in these variables as related to career choice and career progress (see Lent, Brown, & Hackett, 1994). Quite a few studies, for instance, are concerned with possible sex differences in task-related self-efficacy beliefs (for overviews, see Bandura, 1994; Eccles et al., 1998; Phillips & Imhoff, 1997). The results of these studies clearly demonstrate that there are no simple sex differences, like women averaging higher or lower than men. Instead, there are more complex gender-role-related findings indicating differences between men and women if the respective task is strongly gender typed, and no differences if the task is neutral with respect to gender roles (see also Abele, Andrä, & Schute, 1999).

To sum up so far, a person's gender is one of the most important determinants of his or her occupational career. The status of gender in occupational career models usually is one of a background variable indirectly influencing career-related processes via other variables more or less related to gender.

# A DUAL-IMPACT MODEL OF GENDER AND CAREER

## Different Approaches to the Analysis of Gender

The focus of the sex differences approach is on the individual level of analysis (see Eckes & Trautner, chap. 1, this volume). It relates psychological differences between females and males to the biological sex categories. Interestingly, with respect to career-relevant cognitive skills hardly any differences between the sexes have been found (Alfermann, 1996; Eckes, 1991; Maccoby & Jacklin, 1974). As Anastasi summed up back in 1937, even when there are small mean differences, the overlap in the corresponding distributions may be considerable. It has further been shown that differences that existed some 40 years ago have diminished since then (Alfermann, 1996; Collaer & Hines, 1995). Generally speaking, the sex differences approach has been criticized as lacking a coherent theoretical basis and as neglecting gender as a context-dependent phenomenon (see, e.g., Ashmore, 1990).

A more recent approach builds on the evolutionary perspective (Bischof-Köhler, 1990; Buss, 1996). It suggests that sex differences are to be expected in those domains in which men and women have faced different adaptive problems over the course of evolutionary history, for instance in the domain of childrearing. Such an evolutionary perspective draws the attention to important aspects in gender research, particularly when it also considers cultural differences and culturally based historical changes (see Kenrick & Luce, chap. 2, this volume).

Social psychological and developmental approaches concerned with gender as a context-dependent phenomenon consider that every era and every culture has specific and usually divergent expectations and behaviors directed at boys and girls and men and women, and that these divergent expectations and behaviors are strongly tied to the roles men and women fulfill in society.

The gender-in-context model advanced by Deaux and Major (1987; see also Deaux & LaFrance, 1998) represents a general approach to the social psychological study of gender-related behavior. It emphasizes the larger system in which gender is enacted, as well as the dynamic character of gender itself. The model contains the three basic clusters of variables in social interaction, namely the *perceiver* (the acting person), the *target* (the reacting person), and the *situation* (the context of the interaction). Applied to the gender-in-context question, the perceiver is specified in terms of behavior influenced by his or her beliefs and expectations about gender in the interaction setting; the target is specified in terms of behavior influenced by the perceiver's behavior and by the target's self-conceptions and goals for the situation; and the situation specifies the conditions of the interaction, that is, whether gender is more or less salient. It is further proposed in this model that perceiver and target behavior have an impact on gender belief systems (perceiver) and self-systems (target). This model can be regarded as a general frame of reference for the integration of social psychological and—via the feedback loops—developmental findings on gender. The model can also be regarded as a framework for enlarging the analysis of gender.

Prominent related approaches are Eagly's (1987) social role theory (see also Eagly, Wood, & Diekman, chap. 5, this volume), and Bem's (1974, 1979, 1993) gender-schema theory. Eagly (1987) argued that differences between men and women (e.g., differences in empathy or risk-taking behavior) are not inherently biological or psychological differences, but primarily due to men's and women's different social roles. If, for instance, women work primarily as homemakers and men as income providers (Beck-Gernsheim, 1980), that is, if the roles of men and women are complementary, then the expectations directed at women and men reflect these complementary behaviors and roles. The different expectations, in turn, foster the complementarity of gender roles. If, however, the roles were not so clearly divided into male and female roles, then there would be fewer sex differences in social behavior. Supporting this assumption, Moskowitz, Suh, and Desaulniers (1994) showed that their participants' dominant or submissive behavior was not due to their being male or female but rather to the roles they fulfilled. People were dominant in supervisor roles and submissive in supervisee roles.

According to Bem (1974, 1979, 1993), every person possesses both stereotypically masculine and stereotypically feminine traits to varying degrees. Masculine traits are conceptualized as agentic (or instrumental) characteristics like ambitiousness, independence, assertiveness, initiative, and power (Ashmore, Del Boca, & Wohlers, 1986; Bakan, 1966; Broverman, Vogel, Broverman, Clarkson, & Rosenkrantz, 1972). Feminine traits are defined as communal (or expressive) characteristics like caring, sensitivity, and empathy

(Ashmore et al., 1986; Broverman et al., 1972). In contrast to gender stereotypes, which usually imply a gender polarization (i.e., a negative correlation between instrumental-agentic and expressive-communal traits), an individual's actual gender-role orientation is characterized by independent variation between both trait domains. The relative extent of masculine (instrumental-agentic) and feminine (expressive-communal) traits determines a person's psychological gender-role orientation. Aside from masculine persons (high in instrumental and low in expressive traits), and feminine persons (high in expressive and low in instrumental traits), there are also androgynous (high in both traits) and indifferent (low in both traits) persons (see also Spence & Helmreich, 1978). According to Bem (1974, 1979, 1993), androgynous persons should be the most flexible ones because they score high on both traits and should thus have a wider range of behavioral alternatives in novel situations.

## The Dual-Impact Model

The dual-impact model advanced here may be regarded as an application of the more general gender-in-context approach to the issue of occupational careers. It is not meant to be an exhaustive model, but it is especially devoted to the relationship of gender, gender-role orientations, gender-role expectations, gender stereotypes, and career. The model starts with four assumptions. First, gender is conceptualized as a social category (Deaux, 1984; Maccoby, 1988; see also Eckes & Trautner, chap. 1, this volume). Second, the social category of gender has both an inside perspective and an outside perspective. The inside perspective pertains to the respective actor, the outside perspective pertains to the interacting partner. Third, gender has a dual impact on behavior by influencing the actor on the one hand, and influencing the interacting partner on the other. And fourth, there is a reciprocal impact of the person's and his or her partner's behavior on the gender category, again both with respect to the inside and to the outside perspective.

*Impact of Categories.*    Categories are basic structures of information processing in that incoming stimuli are organized into meaningful categories. They are represented as prototypes or exemplars (see Schneider, 1991, for a discussion) and are characterized by particular attributes and fuzzy category boundaries. Categorizing persons has several consequences (see Abele & Petzold, 1998). One consequence is simplification. Persons sharing one attribute are put into one category even if they are quite different with respect to other attributes. Differences between persons sorted into the same category are diminished, which is called an assimilation effect. If, for instance, it is assumed that women in general are emotional, then the behavior of a specific woman may be regarded as emotional, too, even if it would not have been rated emotional when shown by a man. Women would thus be regarded as more similar to each other than they in fact are. This assimilation leads to a second consequence, namely the enhancement of differences between groups (i.e., accentuation). For instance, women and men are regarded as more different than they in fact are. A third consequence is enrichment, in which subjective knowledge and expectations regarding typical exemplars and extreme cases of the category are applied to the specific case. As an example, consider the stereotype of a typical woman, where emotionality may be connected with empathy. Observing an emotional behavior might lead to the (unproved) conclusion that this woman is also empathetic. Finally, a contrast effect may also result. A contrast effect means that a person who has been categorized into a group and has shown behavior inconsistent with the category-specific expectation may be evaluated more extremely than his or her behavior in fact suggests. For example, take a woman who speaks with a loud voice. If "speaking with a loud voice" does not match expectations, this woman will probably be rated as more aggressive than a man with a similar behavior. Since categorizing persons into men versus women is one of the most basic processes of person perception, the categorical expectations—or in their extreme form as stereotypes—directed at men and women are very powerful determinants of judgments about men and women, as well as of behavior toward them.

Gender categorizations vary with respect to an observer's perspective (i.e., how a particular observer conceptualizes male and female), with respect to their cross-situational stability versus variability, with respect to their width (i.e., broad categorizations of the groups of females and males vs. more narrow categorizations of subtypes of females or males), and with respect to their variability over time (i.e., how long it takes to change gender categorizations as a result of changes in women's and men's lives).

***Inside Perspective and Outside Perspective.*** We further distinguish between an inside perspective and an outside perspective of the gender category. The *inside perspective* describes the acting individual and his or her gendered self-conceptualization (see similarly the target perspective in the Deaux & Major model). One very important part of this gendered self-conceptualization is the person's gender-role orientation, that is, how he or she perceives the self in terms of instrumentality-agency and expressiveness-communion (for further aspects of the gendered self see, e.g., the content areas described by Ruble & Martin, 1998; see also Hannover, chap. 6, this volume). As outlined earlier, persons may perceive themselves—independently of their sex—as masculine, feminine, androgynous, or indifferent with respect to these instrumental–expressive traits. According to Bem (1974, 1979, 1993), Deaux and Major (1987), and Eagly (1987), self-conceptualization in terms of gender-role orientation is a central determinant of gender-typed behavior. Occupational career models also stress the importance of gender-role orientations (see Betz

& Fitzgerald, 1987; Eccles [Parsons] et al., 1983; Fassinger, 1985, 1990) for career-related processes. The psychological gender-role orientation is the result of the person's socialization experiences within a given time period and culture (Conway, Pizzamiglio, & Mount, 1996; Eagly, 1987; Martin, 1991; Perry & Bussey, 1984; Trautner, 1994, 1996).

The *outside perspective* pertains to the reacting other and his or her gendered conceptualization of other persons (similar to the perceiver perspective in the Deaux & Major model). This gendered conceptualization of other persons may be called gender-role expectation or, in its more extreme form, gender stereotype. The impact of gender stereotypes is widespread, pervasive, and in many cases automatic (Banaji, Hardin, & Rothman, 1993; Eckes, 1997; see Deaux & LaFrance, 1998, for a review; see also Zemore, Fiske, & Kim, chap. 7, this volume). Gender-role expectations and gender stereotypes influence information processing, generating differential interpretations of identical behaviors of men and women. Furthermore, gender-role expectations and gender stereotypes may have a direct impact on the actions a person takes toward another person categorized as female or male.

Inside and outside perspectives are interrelated in that every person holds both a gendered self-schema and a gendered conceptualization of other persons. However, there need not be a very strong relationship between both. Whereas persons may adhere to gender polarizations with respect to gender stereotypes, they may not do so with respect to their gendered self-orientation (Deaux & LaFrance, 1998). From an analytical point of view, the outside perspective stresses an intergroup differentiation between men and women, whereas the inside perspective is more closely related to an intragroup differentiation within each gender category.

***Dual and Reciprocal Impact.***   Based on this conceptualization of gender as a social category, with the gender-role orientation as the inside perspective and the gender-role expectation or stereotype as the outside perspective, a dual impact of being a man or a woman on behavior and achievement is posited. The first impact stems from the person's individual gender-role orientation, which should affect expectations, plans, and goals he or she pursues. The second impact stems from the gender-role expectations, stereotypes, and gender-differentiating behaviors of persons interacting with this particular man or woman. His or her structure of opportunity (Astin, 1984) varies according to these expectations and behaviors.

However, no learning or developing would be possible if there were no feedback loops from behavior back to the gender-role orientations and gender stereotypes. Thus, there must be a reciprocal dual impact of a person's behavior and achievement on the gender category (see also the dynamic conceptualization of gender in the Deaux & Major model). Categories reflect prior experiences, expectancies based on these prior experiences, and subjective knowledge. As a result of confirmatory processes, subjective knowledge and expectations regarding gender categories are stabilized. Disconfirmatory processes should have no impact if they occur only infrequently or in extreme situations. Frequent disconfirmatory processes, however, should lead to changes, especially to changes in one's gendered self-conceptualization. As an example of possible changes in the inside perspective (i.e., a person's gender-role orientation), take a woman in a career position, who—to a certain degree and almost automatically—might adapt her behavior and traits to the requirements of her work situation. Or take a man in a domestic position who— again to a certain degree and almost automatically—might also adapt his behavior and traits to the requirements of the family situation. The woman might become more instrumental; the man might become more expressive. Cross-sectional studies show that instrumental and expressive behaviors and traits are related to social roles (Conway et al., 1996; Eagly & Steffen, 1984; Moskowitz et al., 1994; see also Eagly et al., chap. 5, this volume). There are, however, very few studies that test the reciprocal impact of behavior on a person's gender-role orientation in a longitudinal perspective (Mummendey, 1990; Schallberger, Häfeli, & Kraft, 1984).

As to the outside perspective, changes in gender stereotypes are also conceivable. They are, however, much smaller and much slower than those in the inside perspective. In spite of the fact, for instance, that women in paid employment situations are the statistical norm today (see Fig. 12.1), gender stereotypes are still not up to date and have changed very little over time (Bergen & Williams, 1991; Broverman et al., 1972; Rosenkrantz, Vogel, Bee, Broverman, & Broverman, 1968; Williams & Best, 1990). Before stereotypes are changed on a broad scale, however, a more subtle form of change may emerge. This is called subtyping and represents a differentiation of the category into a number of subcategories. Six and Eckes (1991), for instance, showed that the category of women is subtyped into housewife, career woman, sexy woman, and feminist.

## Implications for Career-Related Processes

The dual-impact model of gender and career is graphically depicted in Fig. 12.2. Being a man or woman implies a gendered self-conceptualization, with the gender-role orientation as one important aspect (inside perspective). This gender-role orientation influences a number of other career-related psychological variables, for instance, self-efficacy expectations or goals, which have a direct impact on career-related behaviors and outcomes. On the other hand, being a man or a woman elicits different expectations and stereotypes regarding

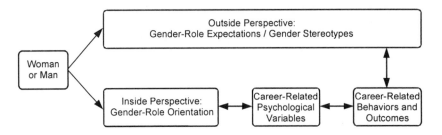

FIG. 12.2   A dual-impact model of gender and career-related processes.

men and women (outside perspective). These have a direct influence on the structure of opportunity, that is, the differential treatment of men and women in the context of career. Fig. 12.2 also shows the feedback-loops from career-related processes to both the inside and the outside gender category perspectives.

Several more specific predictions can be derived from this model. Three of these, which have been tested in our University of Erlangen career studies (see next section), are outlined in the following:

1.   Career-related psychological variables like career motivation, career self-efficacy, achievement motivation, and power motivation are more closely linked to psychological gender-role orientation than to respondents' sex. This prediction follows from the assumption that sex has an indirect impact via gender-role orientation on career-related psychological variables.

2.   Career-related behaviors and outcomes, like progress or stagnation in the career ladder, income, or occupational status, are both linked to sex and to gender-role orientation, with the concomitant career-related psychological variables. This prediction follows from the assumption of the dual impact of gender-role orientations and gender stereotypes on career-related processes.

3.   Progress and involuntary stagnation in career development have an impact on a person's gender-role orientation. Career progress should especially enhance a woman's instrumental traits; involuntary stagnation in career development should especially diminish a man's instrumental traits. This hypothesis regarding differential effects for women and men stems from our reasoning that there are different normative expectations (gender stereotypes) for men and women. Whereas the normative expectation for men is continuous employment and progress on the career ladder, the normative expectation for women is more flexible.

All three hypotheses are highly important for a developmental social psychological approach to gender. Hypothesis 1 is concerned with the individual level, the relative impact of one central social psychological aspect of gender (i.e., gender-role orientation) and respondent sex on career-related psychological variables. Hypothesis 2 is concerned with objective measures of career success and the social psychological aspect of gender as well as sex. Hypothesis 3 is especially related to the developmental perspective and is (to the author's knowledge) the first explicit statement of the reciprocity assumption, postulating a reciprocal impact of career processes on gender-role orientation.

# THE ERLANGEN CAREER STUDIES

## Cross-Sectional Studies on Sex, Gender-Role Orientation, and Career Motivation

In a first series of cross-sectional studies that we conducted in Erlangen, Hypothesis 1 was examined, predicting a stronger impact of gender-role orientation than respondents' sex on career-related psychological variables like career motivation (Abele, Weich, & Haussmann, 1994; Andrä, 1999). In order to analyze the stability of the findings across countries, these studies were conducted at two German universities (one located in former West Germany at Erlangen-Nürnberg; the other located in the former German Democratic Republic at Leipzig) and two American universities (Boston University; Massachusetts Institute of Technology). The participants were students with different majors in their third or fourth academic year. The Erlangen sample comprised 689 persons (50% women, 50% men; median age 24 years; majors: 15% arts/humanities, 15% future teachers, 14% medicine, 30% science and technical subjects, 13% law, 13% business); the Leipzig sample comprised 305 persons (58% women, 42% men; median age 22 years; 21% arts/humanities, 18% future physical education teachers, 15% medicine, 13% science, 33% business); and, finally, the Boston sample (from the two American universities) comprised 240 persons (49% women, 51% men; median age 20 years; 50% science, 34% engineering, 16% humanities). The participants were tested in groups. They were asked to fill out a questionnaire after class.

Aside from sociodemographic variables (sex, age, study major, academic year) and other variables not relevant in the present context, the questionnaire contained a measure of gender-role orientation and a measure of career orientation. Gender-role orientation was assessed by two scales of the Extended Personal Attributes Questionnaire (EPAQ; Spence & Helmreich, 1978) and its German adaptation (GEPAQ; Runge, Frey, Gollwitzer, Helmreich, & Spence, 1981). These were the positive expressiveness scale (eight items, 5-point rating scale each; examples: emotional, kind, understanding) and the positive instrumentality scale (seven items, 5-point rating scale each; examples: active,

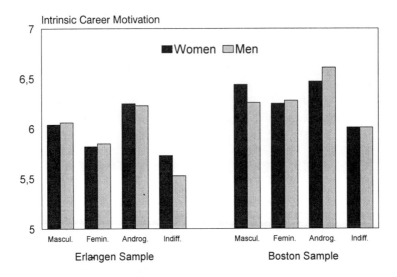

FIG. 12.3   Means for intrinsic career motivation in two samples by sex and gender-role orientation. *Note.* This figure is based on data reanalyzed from *Karriereorientierungen angehender Akademikerinnen und Akademiker: Eine Untersuchung an einer west- und einer ostdeutschen Universität,* by A. Abele, M. Weich, and A. Haussmann, 1994, Bielefeld, Germany: Kleine. Data used with permission.

independent, self-confident). Career orientation was assessed by two scales measuring intrinsic and extrinsic career orientation (Abele et al., 1994; see also Kraak & Nord-Rüdiger, 1984). Intrinsic career orientation is related to interest and self-fulfillment at work (eight items; 7-point rating scale each; examples: "I want to do highly qualified work"; "I am always interested in keeping my knowledge up to date"). Extrinsic career orientation refers to career motivation based on external rewards like money or success (eight items; 7-point rating scale each; examples: "I have chosen my major with respect to good opportunities at the labor market"; "In any case, I would like to earn a lot of money").

In order to test the hypothesis, we created four gender-role orientation types according to the criteria suggested by Spence and Helmreich (1978). Masculine persons are those high in instrumental traits and low in expressive traits, feminine persons are those high in expressive traits and low in instrumental traits, androgynous persons are high in both traits, and indifferent persons are low in both traits. Since there were no interactions between sex, gender-role orientation, and study major, we analyzed the data irrespective of study major.

In all three samples, the analyses for intrinsic career orientation resulted in a highly significant main effect of gender-role orientation: Erlangen sample, $F(3, 688) = 38.43$, $p < .01$; Leipzig sample, $F(3, 304) = 12.63$, $p < .01$; Boston sample, $F(3, 239) = 10.24$, $p < .01$. There were no effects of sex and no interactions (all $F$s, $ns$). Fig. 12.3 shows the findings for the Erlangen and Boston samples.

Women and men with androgynous and masculine gender-role orientation showed the highest intrinsic career motivation. Consistent with our hypothesis, the effect size for gender-role orientation was higher (Erlangen: $\eta^2 = 13.3\%$, Leipzig: $\eta^2 = 10.8\%$, Boston: $\eta^2 = 12.0\%$) than the effect size for sex (Erlangen: $\eta^2 = 0.1\%$, Leipzig: $\eta^2 = 0.4\%$, Boston: $\eta^2 = 0\%$).

Extrinsic career orientation also differed among the four gender-role orientation types (Erlangen: $\eta^2 = 3.2\%$, Leipzig: $\eta^2 = 1.8\%$, Boston: $\eta^2 = 3.7\%$), with higher scores for masculine and androgynous persons. Sex had no effect in the Leipzig and Boston samples, but there was an effect in the Erlangen sample with higher scores for men than for women ($\eta^2 = 0.9\%$).

To sum up, we found—consistent with Hypothesis 1—that career motivation is more strongly related to gender-role orientation than to sex. This effect is stable across different samples in different countries. Persons with high scores in instrumentality, that is, the masculine and the androgynous gender-role types, have both higher intrinsic and extrinsic career motivation than those with lower instrumentality scores, that is, the feminine and the indifferent gender-role types. These effects are—with one exception (extrinsic career motivation in the Erlangen sample)—independent of sex. Similar results were reported by Spence and Helmreich (1978) with respect to achievement motivation (see also Marshall & Wijting, 1980, and Bierhoff & Kraska, 1984, on fear of failure; Sieverding, 1990, on occupational self-esteem; and Betz, Heesacker, & Shuttleworth, 1990, on rational career choice). Thus, all these studies showed that gender-role orientation is a more important determinant of career-related psychological variables than sex.

## A Longitudinal Study on Sex, Gender-Role Orientation, and Career Development

After performing these cross-sectional studies, we started to run a longitudinal study on the career development of women and men (Abele, Andrä, & Schute, 1999; Abele, Schute, & Andrä, 1999; Abele, Stief, & Andrä, in press). The 1,500 participants (41% women, 59% men; median age 27 years; majors: 6% law, 16% business, 8% arts, 20% teachers, 33% science and technical subjects, 16% medicine) of this longitudinal study are graduates of the University of Erlangen-Nürnberg with various majors. They are representative for a graduate cohort of this university with respect to major, sex, and grade point average (GPA). The participants filled out the first questionnaire immediately after their graduation and the second questionnaire 18 months later. The third questionnaire was administered another 2 years later, and further questionnaires will follow. In the present context some of the data of the first and the second wave will be analyzed in order to further test our Hypothesis 1, and to get some results with respect to Hypotheses 2 and 3.

***The Impact of Sex and Gender-Role Orientation on Grade Point Average, Duration of Studies, Occupational Self-Efficacy, and Power and Achievement Motivation.*** In the first questionnaire of the longitudinal study we collected a number of variables that have been found to influence career development, like GPA, duration of studies, occupational self-efficacy, power motivation, and achievement motivation (Abele, Andrä, & Schute, 1999; Hackett & Betz, 1995; Jenkins, 1994; Marini & Fan, 1997; Phillips & Imhoff, 1997). We expected no differences between men and women and between the gender-role types with respect to achievement-related variables like GPA and duration of studies. In accord with our Hypothesis 1, however, we expected differences in occupational self-efficacy, power motivation, and achievement motivation. Occupational self-efficacy was measured using a newly developed scale (Berufliche Selbstwirksamkeit [BSW], Abele, Stief, & Andrä, in press; six items with 5-point rating scales each, internal consistency: $\alpha = .78$; example: "I know that I have the skills necessary for my job"). Power motivation as well as achievement motivation and—less important in the present context— affiliation motivation were measured using a semiprojective approach, the multimotive grid developed by Schmalt, Sokolowski, and Langens (1994).

An analysis of variance with sex, gender-role type, and study major as factors and GPA as the dependent variable resulted in a main effect of study major, which is irrelevant in the present context. There were no main effects of sex or gender-role orientation, and there were also no interactions. An equivalent analysis of variance (ANOVA) with duration of studies as the dependent variable again resulted in an effect of study major (which is irrelevant here). It also resulted in a main effect of gender-role orientation, $F(3, 1485) = 3.56$, $p < .02$ ($\eta^2 = 0.7\%$). Persons with a feminine gender-role orientation took longer to finish their studies, and persons with a masculine gender-role orientation needed less time to complete their studies than the other two groups. There was no main effect of sex, and there were also no interactions.

In accord with our prediction, occupational self-efficacy was highly related to gender-role orientation, $F(3, 1495) = 55.98, p < .01$ ($\eta^2 = 10.4\%$), and it was somewhat related to sex, $F(1, 1495) = 6.38, p < .02$ ($\eta^2 = 0.4\%$). Study major had no impact, and there were also no interactions (all $F$s, $ns$). Fig. 12.4 shows occupational self-efficacy in dependence on sex and gender-role orientation. Men and persons with high instrumentality (i.e., masculine and androgynous persons) had higher scores in occupational self-efficacy than women and persons low in instrumentality. The same result emerged with respect to power motivation. There were no effects of study major and no interactions (all $F$s, $ns$); there was a marginally significant effect of sex, $F(1, 1301) = 3.64$, $p <$

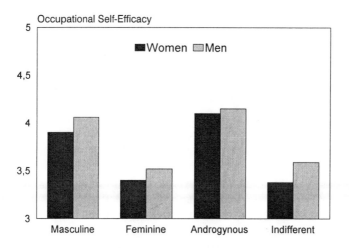

FIG. 12.4   Means for occupational self-efficacy by sex and gender-role orientation.

.06 ($\eta^2$ = 0.3%), and there was also a significant effect of gender-role orientation, $F(3, 1301) = 6.29, p < .01$ ($\eta^2 = 1.5\%$). Again, men and persons with high instrumentality had a higher power motivation than women and persons low in instrumentality. Regarding achievement motivation there was only an effect of gender-role orientation, $F(3, 1298) = 18.19, p < .01$ ($\eta^2 = 4.1\%$), with higher scores by masculine and androgynous types than feminine and indifferent ones.[1]

To sum up, initial testing of our longitudinal sample showed that sex had no impact on achievement-related variables, and in accord with Hypothesis 1 it had a smaller impact on psychological career-related variables like occupational self-efficacy, achievement motivation, and power motivation than did gender-role orientation. Persons with high instrumentality scores (i.e., masculine and androgynous types) were more convinced of their occupational self-efficacy and showed higher power and achievement motivation. The effects on occupational self-efficacy and power motivation, but not on achievement motivation, were more pronounced for men than for women.

**The Impact of Sex and Gender-Role Orientation on Early Progress in Career: Degree-Adequate Position and Income.**   Our second hypothesis stated that progress in the career ladder is both a question of a person's sex as instigating gender-role stereotypes and gender-discriminating behavior (i.e., the

---

[1]Affiliation motivation was also affected by gender-role orientation, $F(3, 1273) = 12.72, p < .01, \eta^2 = 2.9\%$, and by an interaction of sex with gender-role orientation, $F(3, 1273) = 3.54, p < .02, \eta^2 = 0.8\%$. Women and men both had the highest affiliation motivation when they were androgynous.

outside perspective) and of a person's gender-role orientation with its concomitant career-related psychological variables (i.e., the inside perspective). We analyzed this hypothesis in our longitudinal study by comparing the participants' career progress after 1½ years. There were 1,074 persons from the original sample who responded to the second questionnaire (response rate: 78%).

We tested the hypothesis with two "hard" career progress criteria, namely whether the participant received a position appropriate to his or her degree or not, and how much money he or she earned. We did not include in this analysis participants who had graduated in law, medicine, or as teachers, since those persons have to pass an obligatory second phase of training in Germany, and this training had not been completed at the time they filled out the second questionnaire. The subsample for the following analyses therefore consists of 595 persons who had majored in arts, science, business, and engineering. A *degree-adequate* position is defined as a position requiring the university education the person has achieved, for instance, an engineer who has passed an examination in engineering. A *degree-inadequate* position means that the person has either no job or a job for which the degree would not have been necessary, for instance, a secretary who has studied arts.

Independent of study major, women held a degree-adequate position less often (64.5% of the cases) than men (88.5% of the cases). A stepwise regression analysis with sex, GPA (adjusted for differences in study major), study duration (again adjusted for differences in study major), occupational self-efficacy, power motivation, achievement motivation, and instrumentality and expressiveness scores on having a degree-adequate position or not revealed the following. Sex was a more powerful predictor of having such a position ($\beta = .26, p < .01; R^2 = 7.8\%$) than occupational self-efficacy ($\beta = .16, p < .01; \Delta R^2 = 3.8\%$; higher self-efficacy, better chances,), study duration ($\beta = -.13, p < .01; \Delta R^2 = 2.6\%$; shorter duration, better chances), and GPA ($\beta = .10, p < .03; \Delta R^2 = 0.9\%$; better grades, better chances), $R = .39, p < .01$. Gender-role orientation, power motive, and achievement motive had no additional impact, because they were highly correlated with occupational self-efficacy. Occupational self-efficacy, in turn, was more strongly correlated with occupational status (having a degree-adequate position or not) than gender-role orientation, power motivation, and achievement motivation. The effect of a lower percentage of adequately employed women versus men was independent of their occupational self-efficacy, GPA, study duration, and study major (all $Fs < 1$).

We also computed this regression analysis without those 47 persons who had become parents since they had graduated (10 women, 6.2%; 37 men, 8.5%), in order to test whether the lower rate of degree-adequate positions of women may have been due to the fact that some of them had become mothers. This was not the case. The respective regression analysis again showed that sex was the most powerful predictor of having a degree-adequate position ($\beta = .22$,

$p < .01$; $R^2 = 6.6\%$), followed by study duration ($\beta = -.20$, $p < .01$; $\Delta R^2 = 4.8\%$) and occupational self-efficacy ($\beta = .15$, $p < .01$; $\Delta R^2 = 1.9\%$), $R = .37$, $p < .01$.

In analyzing the impact of gender-role orientation on occupying a degree-adequate position without considering occupational self-efficacy, we found that masculine persons (89.7% degree-adequate positions) and androgynous persons (82.8% degree-adequate positions) more often held a degree-adequate position than indifferent (78.9%) or feminine ones (75.0%), $\chi^2(3) = 12.42$, $p < .01$. This effect was independent of the person's study major and sex.

In order to study the effects of sex and gender-role orientation on income, we analyzed only those participants with a full-time degree-adequate position ($N = 407$). In a stepwise regression analysis, we again found that sex was the most powerful predictor of income ($\beta = .19$, $p < .01$; $R^2 = 3.9\%$; men more income), followed by degree of instrumentality ($\beta = .18$, $p < .01$; $\Delta R^2 = 3.4\%$; more instrumentality, higher income) and study duration ($\beta = -.11$, $p < .03$; $\Delta R^2 = 1.3\%$; shorter studies, higher income), $R = .29$, $p < .01$. Occupational self-efficacy, degree of expressiveness, and GPA did not have an additional impact. These effects were again independent of study major.

To sum up, examination of Hypothesis 2 showed that both sex and, to a smaller extent, gender-role orientation are predictors of hard career progress criteria. Women less often held a degree-adequate position; and if they did, they earned less money than men (see also Deaux & LaFrance, 1998; Major, 1994; Marini & Fan, 1997). These effects cannot be explained by having become a parent, by study major, GPA, study duration, occupational self-efficacy, power motivation, or achievement motivation. Persons with masculine and androgynous gender-role orientation more often had a degree-adequate position than persons with feminine or indifferent gender-role orientation. This effect is mainly due to the higher occupational self-efficacy of masculine and androgynous gender-role types, as well as to the shorter study duration of masculine gender-role types versus the longer duration of feminine ones.

***The Impact of Career Progress on Gender-Role Orientation of Men and Women.*** In the final step of the Erlangen career studies, we tested Hypothesis 3 concerning the reverse impact of career progress or stagnation on women's and men's gender-role orientations (Abele & Andrä, 1999; Andrä, 1998). We had postulated that career progress would lead to an enhancement of a person's instrumentality, especially a woman's instrumentality, whereas involuntary stagnation or even regression would lead to reduced instrumentality, especially of a man's instrumentality.

To study these questions we included a second measure of gender-role orientation in our second questionnaire. In addition to some filler variables, the participants again had to fill out the GEPAQ with the expressiveness scale and

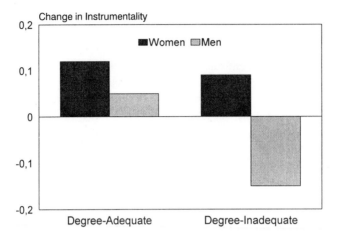

FIG. 12.5   Mean change in instrumentality by sex and occupational status.

the instrumentality scale (Runge et al., 1981). Dependent measures for the following analyses were the differences in the scores of these two scales (Time 2 minus Time 1), adjusted for their Time 1 value. The data of the same 595 persons that had already been analyzed with respect to career progress (see previous section on Hypothesis 2) were used.

We conducted analyses of covariance with gender, occupational status (holding a degree-adequate position or not), and study major as factors, instrumentality (or expressiveness) at Time 1 as covariate, and change in instrumentality (or change in expressiveness) as dependent measure. Since there were no effects of study major relevant in the present context we omitted this variable. With respect to changes in expressiveness we found only a significant effect of the covariate, revealing that change is dependent on the initial level. There was more change if the initial level was low ($r = -.46$). The analysis for changes in instrumentality showed again a significant effect of the covariate (more change with a lower initial level, $r = -.42$), a significant sex effect, $F(1, 594) = 7.22, p < .01$ ($\eta^2 = 1.2\%$), a significant effect of occupational status, $F(1, 594) = 16.08, p < .001$ ($\eta^2 = 2.7\%$), and a significant sex by occupational status interaction, $F(1, 594) = 5.16, p < .03$ ($\eta^2 = 0.9\%$). The respective means are graphically depicted in Fig. 12.5.

In accord with our Hypothesis 3, men showed a decrease in instrumentality when they did not have a degree-adequate position, whereas women did not. In contrast, the increase in instrumentality with a degree-adequate position is larger for women than for men. This is a clear confirmation of the dynamic conceptualization of sex and gender-role orientation, and it is, as far as we know, the first time that a reciprocal impact of career processes on gender-role orientation has been empirically demonstrated in a longitudinal study.

# CONCLUSIONS

The results of our studies revealed in accord with Hypothesis 1 that gender-role orientation is a more important determinant of career-related psychological variables than sex. There were similarities between the masculine and the androgynous gender-role types on the one hand and the feminine and indifferent types on the other. The androgynous and masculine gender types showed more intrinsic career motivation, more extrinsic career motivation, higher occupational self-efficacy, higher achievement motivation, and higher power motivation. Only with respect to power motivation and occupational self-efficacy did we find sex differences with higher scores for men. These effects were, however, much smaller than the effects of gender-role orientation. There were no sex effects at all in intrinsic career motivation and in achievement motivation: These findings support and extend previous studies in which gender-role orientation was also a more important determinant of career-related psychological variables than sex (Betz et al., 1990; Bierhoff & Kraska, 1984; Marshal & Wijting, 1980; Sieverding, 1990; Spence & Helmreich, 1978; see also Deaux & LaFrance, 1998; Eccles et al., 1998). Besides supporting our hypothesis derived from the dual-impact model, these data further suggest that the degree of instrumentality is the crucial factor for career-related psychological variables, whereas the degree of expressiveness is less important (see also Abele et al., 1994; Alfermann, 1996; Andrä, 1999).

As our analysis of academic success variables like GPA and study duration showed, there is no impact of sex on these variables, and gender-role orientation has only a small impact, with longer study duration of feminine gender-role types. These findings are in accord with several analyses on career-related cognitive skills, which usually do not find any significant differences between men and women (Alfermann, 1996; Eckes, 1991; Maccoby & Jacklin, 1974).

Even more important are the longitudinal findings on sex, gender-role orientation, and such hard criteria as occupational status and income level. In line with Hypothesis 2, and also consistent with previous results (described earlier), we found that women less often held a degree-adequate position than men. Sex explained 8% of the variance in occupational status, whereas achievement-related variables like GPA or study duration explained only 3.5%, and occupational self-efficacy 3.8%, of the variance. Gender-role orientation also had an impact, with more degree-adequate positions held by masculine and androgynous persons, which seemed to be due to these persons' higher occupational self-efficacy and shorter study duration. The disadvantage of women cannot be explained by different academic success (there was no difference); it cannot be explained by different occupational self-efficacy (there was no interaction of sex and occupational self-efficacy on occupational status) nor by different study majors or power motivation or achievement motivation (there were no interactions); and it also cannot be explained by family status, that is, whether the person had become a parent within the last 1½ years.

What do these findings imply with respect to the dual-impact model of gender and career? First of all, they suggest that sex is a more powerful predictor of career success than gender-role orientation. This finding points to the relevance of the outside perspective, that is, the impact of gender-role expectations and gender stereotypes on the differential structure of opportunity for men and women. Second, these findings must not, nevertheless, be misinterpreted to indicate that the lower percentage of women occupying a degree-adequate position solely reflects the outside perspective, that is, the less favorable structure of opportunity for women in the labor market. What we have shown is that neither the psychological variables (i.e., gender-role orientation, occupational self-efficacy, motivation, achievement variables) nor the variables of study major and family status (being a parent or not) can explain the gender gap at this stage of the career ladder. There are, however, further variables conceivable that may have an impact on career progress and that do not belong to the outside perspective but rather to the inside perspective or even to both. As an example, consider a woman who becomes gradually dissatisfied with her structure of opportunity in the workforce and who therefore disengages from high career goals. Third, we have also demonstrated the reciprocal impact of career progress on gender-role orientation. Our Hypothesis 3 suggested that career progress especially enhances instrumentality in women, whereas involuntary career stagnation especially reduces instrumentality in men. Our findings exactly revealed this pattern. Men became less instrumental when they did not occupy a degree-adequate position, and women became more instrumental in this case. These findings are important because they demonstrate the reciprocal impact of career progress or career stagnation on gender-role orientations in a longitudinal design.

What do these findings imply with respect to theorizing about occupational psychology of women as well as theorizing about gender? First of all, the importance of the gender-role orientation variable stressed in several gender-and-occupational-choice models (see Betz & Fitzgerald, 1987; Eccles [Parsons] et al., 1983; Fassinger, 1985, 1990) has again been demonstrated. Second, the data show that the impact of gender-role orientation is the same for women and men, which means that this variable may be fruitfully integrated into occupational choice models for women and men alike. Our data further demonstrate the importance of expectations, especially self-efficacy expectations, as has also been suggested in a number of career models (Bandura, 1994; Betz & Fitzgerald, 1987; Eccles [Parsons] et al., 1983; Hackett & Betz, 1995; Lent et al., 1994). There seems to be a strong link between gender-role orientation and occupational self-efficacy as measured by our newly developed instrument (Abele, Stief, & Andrä, in press). Feminine and indifferent persons hold lower occupational self-efficacy beliefs than masculine and androgynous persons.

This finding may be interpreted as indicating that occupational self-efficacy is still a gendered expectation, with traditionally less-masculine persons (i.e., feminine and indifferent ones) having less of it. Such an interpretation would also fit with the previously mentioned findings on sex differences in self-efficacy, which usually manifest themselves only when the respective task is gender-typed.

With respect to theorizing about gender in general our data strongly support a gender-in-context perspective, where gender is conceptualized as a dynamic construct varying with and changing through context conditions (Bem, 1974, 1979, 1993; Deaux & LaFrance, 1998; Deaux & Major, 1987; Eagly, 1987). What has been mainly demonstrated here, is the changeability of gendered self-conceptualizations (or gender-role orientation) through experience. Interestingly, these changes of gendered self-conceptualizations take place both in women and in men, but the critical incidents through which they are elicited seem to be partially different. Women become more instrumental with more career success but not less instrumental with less career success. Men become less instrumental with less career success but not more instrumental with more career success. Our data also suggest the importance of a longitudinal approach to the study of gender-in-context.

Finally, the proposed dual impact of gender and career as well as our data fit nicely with the more general theoretical orientation of a developmental social psychology of gender. Both aspects, the social psychological perspective of the gender category and its dynamic character, as well as the developmental aspect of individual and cultural changes in gender conceptualizations, are indispensable in understanding the similarities and differences between women and men.

## ACKNOWLEDGMENTS

The studies reported in the present chapter were supported by a grant from the Deutsche Forschungsgemeinschaft (grant no. Ab 45/8-1, 45/8-2). Miriam S. Andrä's helpful comments on a previous version of the manuscript are gratefully acknowledged.

## REFERENCES

Abele, A. (1997). Geschlechtsrollen, Geschlechtsrollenorientierungen und Geschlechterstereotype im Wandel [Changes in gender roles, gender-role orientations and gender stereotypes]. In E. Liebau (Ed.), *Das Generationenverhältnis: Über das Zusammenleben in Familie und Gesellschaft* (pp. 123–139). Weinheim, Germany: Juventa

Abele, A., & Andrä, M. (1999). *Changes in gender role orientation following job entrance: A longitudinal study.* Unpublished manuscript, University of Erlangen.

Abele, A., Andrä, M. S., & Schute, M. (1999). Wer hat nach dem Hochschulexamen schnell eine Stelle? Erste Ergebnisse der Erlanger Längsschnittstudie (BELA-E) [Who quickly receives a job after graduation? First results of the Erlangen longitudinal study]. *Zeitschrift für Arbeits- und Organisationspsychologie, 43,* 95–101.

Abele, A. E., & Petzold, P. (1998). Pragmatic use of categorical information in impression formation. *Journal of Personality and Social Psychology, 75,* 347–358.

Abele, A. E., Schute, M., & Andrä, M. S. (1999). Ingenieurin versus Pädagoge: Berufliche Werthaltungen nach Beendigung des Studiums [Female engineer versus male teacher: Work values of university graduates]. *Zeitschrift für Pädagogische Psychologie, 13,* 84–99.

Abele, A., Stief, M., & Andrä, M. S. (in press). Zur ökonomischen Erfassung beruflicher Selbstwirksamkeitserwartungen—Neukonstruktion einer BSW-Skala [An economical measure of occupational self efficacy—Construction of a new scale]. *Zeitschrift für Arbeits- und Organisationspsychologie.*

Abele, A., Weich, M., & Haussmann, A. (1994). *Karriereorientierungen angehender Akademikerinnen und Akademiker: Eine Untersuchung an einer west- und einer ostdeutschen Universität* [Career orientations of future university graduates: Data from an Eastern and a Western German university]. Bielefeld, Germany: Kleine.

Alfermann, D. (1996). *Geschlechterrollen und geschlechtstypisches Verhalten* [Gender roles and gender-typical behavior]. Stuttgart, Germany: Kohlhammer.

Anastasi, A. (1937). *Differential psychology: Individual and group differences in behavior.* New York: Macmillan.

Andrä, M. S. (1998). *Verändert sich die Geschlechtsrollenorientierung von Akademikerinnen und Akademikern durch den Berufseinstieg? Eine Längsschnittstudie* [Does gender-role orientation change as a function of job entry? A longitudinal study]. Hamburg, Germany: Kovac.

Andrä, M. S. (1999). Androgynie, berufliche Motivation und erfolgreicher Berufseinstieg: Ergebnisse der Erlanger Karrierestudien [Androgyny, career motivation, and successful job entry: Results from the Erlangen career studies]. In U. Bock & D. Alfermann (Eds.), *Androgynie: Vielfalt der Möglichkeiten* (pp. 156–172). Stuttgart, Germany: Metzler.

Ashmore, R. D. (1990). Sex, gender, and the individual. In L. A. Pervin (Ed.), *Handbook of personality: Theory and research* (pp. 486–526). New York: Guilford.

Ashmore, R. D., Del Boca, F. K., & Wohlers, A. J. (1986). Gender stereotypes. In R. D. Ashmore & F. K. Del Boca (Eds.), *The social psychology of female–male relations: A critical analysis of central concepts* (pp. 69–119). Orlando, FL: Academic Press.

Astin, H. S. (1984). The meaning of work in women's lives: A sociological model of career choice and work behavior. *Counseling Psychologist, 12,* 117–126.

Atkinson, J. W. (1964). *An introduction to motivation.* New York: Van Nostrand.

Bakan, D. (1966). *The duality of human existence. An essay on psychology and religion.* Chicago: Rand McNally.

Banaji, M. R., Hardin, C., & Rothman, A. J. (1993). Implicit stereotyping in person judgment. *Journal of Personality and Social Psychology, 65,* 272–281.

Bandura, A. (1994). *Self-efficacy: The exercise of control.* New York: Freeman.

Beck-Gernsheim, E. (1980). *Das halbierte Leben: Männerwelt Beruf, Frauenwelt Familie* [The bisected life: Men's world breadwinner, women's world homemaker]. Frankfurt/Main, Germany: Fischer.

Bem, S. L. (1974). The measurement of psychological androgyny. *Journal of Consulting and Clinical Psychology, 42,* 155–162.

Bem, S. L. (1979). Theory and measurement of androgyny: A reply to the Pedhazur–Tetenbaum and Locksley–Colten critiques. *Journal of Personality and Social Psychology, 37,* 1047–1054.

Bem, S. L. (1993). *The lenses of gender: Transforming the debate on sexual inequality.* New Haven, CT: Yale University Press.

Bergen, D. J., & Williams, J. E. (1991). Sex stereotypes in the United States revisited: 1972–1988. *Sex Roles, 24,* 413–423.

Betz, N. E., & Fitzgerald, L. F. (1987). *The career psychology of women.* Orlando, FL: Academic Press.

Betz, N. E., Heesacker, R. S., & Shuttleworth, C. (1990). Moderators of the congruence and realism of major and occupational plans in college students: A replication and extension. *Journal of Counseling Psychology, 37,* 269–276.

Bierhoff, H. W., & Kraska, K. (1984). Studien über Androgynie I: Maskulinität/Feminität in ihrer Beziehung zu Erfolgsstreben, Furcht vor Mißerfolg und Furcht vor Erfolg [Studies in androgyny I: The relation of masculinity–femininity to success striving, fear of failure, and fear of success]. *Zeitschrift für Differentielle und Diagnostische Psychologie, 5 ,* 183–201.

Bischoff, S. (1990). *Frauen zwischen Macht und Mann, Männer in der Defensive: Führungskräfte in Zeiten des Umbruchs* [Women between power and man, men in defense: Leaders in times of change]. Hamburg, Germany: Rowohlt

Bischof-Köhler, D. (1990). Frau und Karriere in psychobiologischer Sicht. *Zeitschrift für Arbeits- und Organisationspsychologie, 34,* 17–28.

Broverman, I. K., Vogel, S. R., Broverman, D. M., Clarkson, F. E., & Rosenkrantz, P. S. (1972). Sex role stereotypes: A current appraisal. *Journal of Social Issues, 28*(2), 59–78.

Bundesanstalt für Arbeit (1998). *Arbeitsmarktdaten 1998* [Labor force data 1998]. [On-line]. Available: Internet http://www.arbeitsamt.de

Buss, D. M. (1996). The evolutionary psychology of human social strategies. In E. T. Higgins & A. W. Kruglanski (Eds.), *Social psychology: Handbook of basic principles* (pp. 3–38). New York: Guilford.

Chamberlain, M. K. (1991). *Women in academe: Progress and prospects.* New York: Russell Sage Foundation.

Collaer, M. L., & Hines, M. (1995). Human behavioral sex differences: A role for gonadal hormones during early development? *Psychological Bulletin, 118,* 55–107.

Conway, M., Pizzamiglio, M. T., & Mount, L. (1996). Status, communality, and agency: Implications for stereotypes of gender and other groups. *Journal of Personality and Social Psychology, 71,* 25–38.

Deaux, K. (1984). From individual differences to social categories: Analysis of a decade's research on gender. *American Psychologist, 39,* 106–116.

Deaux, K., & LaFrance, M. (1998). Gender. In D. T. Gilbert, S. T. Fiske, & G. Lindzey (Eds.), *The handbook of social psychology* (4th ed., Vol. 1, pp. 788–827). Boston: McGraw-Hill.

Deaux, K., & Major, B. (1987). Putting gender into context: An interactive model of gender-related behavior. *Psychological Review, 94,* 369–389.

Eagly, A. H. (1987). *Sex differences in social behavior: A social-role interpretation.* Hillsdale, NJ: Lawrence Erlbaum Associates.

Eagly, A. H., & Steffen, V. J. (1984). Gender stereotypes stem from the distribution of women and men into social roles. *Journal of Personality and Social Psychology, 46,* 735–754.

Eccles, J., Wigfield, A., & Schiefele, U. (1998). Motivation to succeed. In W. Damon (Series Ed.) & N. Eisenberg (Vol. Ed.), *Handbook of child psychology: Vol. 3. Social, emotional, and personality development* (5th ed., pp. 1071–1095). New York: Wiley.

Eccles (Parsons), J., Adler, T. F., Futterman, R., Goff, S. B., Kaczala, C. M., Meece, J. L., & Midgley, C. (1983). Expectancies, values, and academic behaviors. In J. T. Spence (Ed.), *Achievement and achievement motives: Psychological and sociological approaches* (pp. 75–146). San Francisco: Freeman.

Eckes, T. (1991). Geschlechterstereotype: Der Stand der Forschung [Gender stereotypes: The state of the art]. In D. Frey (Ed.), *Bericht über den 37. Kongreß der Deutschen Gesellschaft für Psychologie in Kiel 1990* (Vol. 2, pp. 164–172). Göttingen, Germany: Hogrefe.

Eckes, T. (1997). *Geschlechterstereotype: Frau und Mann in sozialpsychologischer Sicht* [Gender stereotypes: Woman and man in social psychological perspective]. Pfaffenweiler, Germany: Centaurus.

Farmer, H. S. (1985). Model of career and achievement motivation for women and men. *Journal of Counseling Psychology, 32*, 363–390.

Fassinger, H. S. (1985). A causal model of college women's career choice. *Journal of Vocational Behavior, 27*, 123–153.

Fassinger, H. S. (1990). Causal models of career choice in two samples of college women. *Journal of Vocational Behavior, 36*, 225–248.

Frevert, U. (1986) *Frauen-Geschichte zwischen bürgerlicher Verbesserung und neuer Weiblichkeit: Sozialgeschichte der Frauen 1780–1986* [Women's history between civilian improvement and novel femininity: Social history of women 1780–1986]. Frankfurt/Main, Germany: Suhrkamp.

Frevert, U. (1995). *"Mann und Weib, und Weib und Mann": Geschlechter-Differenzen in der Moderne* ["Man and woman, and woman and man": Gender differences in modern time]. Munich, Germany: Beck.

Gottfredson, L. S. (1986). Special groups and the beneficial use of vocational interest inventories. In W. B. Walsh & S. H. Osipow (Eds.), *The assessment of interests* (pp. 127–198). Hillsdale, NJ: Lawrence Erlbaum Associates.

Gutek, B. A. (1993). Changing the status of women in management. *Applied Psychology: An International Review, 42*, 301–311.

Hackett, G., & Betz, N. E. (1995). Self-efficacy and career choice and development. In J. E. Maddux (Ed.), *Self-efficacy, adaptation, and adjustment: Theory, research, and application* (pp. 249–289). New York: Plenum.

Houseknecht, S. K., Vaughan, S., & Stratham, A. (1987). The impact of singlehood on the career patterns of professional women. *Wall Street Journal, 24*, 1–28.

Hyde, J. S. (1985). *Half the human experience: The psychology of women.* Lexington, MA: Heath.

Jenkins, S. R. (1994). Need for power and women's careers over 14 years: Structural power, job satisfaction, and motive change. *Journal of Personality and Social Psychology, 66*, 155–165.

Kiernan, K. (1993). The roles of men and women in tomorrow's Europe. In Bundesinstitut für Bevölkerungsforschung (Ed.), *Changing families in changing societies* (pp. 93–99). Wiesbaden, Germany: Sonderdruck.

Kraak, B., & Nord-Rüdiger, D. (1984). *Berufliche Motivation und berufliches Verhalten: Zur Frage geschlechtstypischer Unterschiede* [Occupational motivation and occupational behavior: The question of gender differences]. Göttingen, Germany: Hogrefe.

Künzler, J. (1999). *Compatibility of modernization and family.* Manuscript submitted for publication.

Lehr, U. (1969). *Die Frau im Beruf: Eine psychologische Analyse der weiblichen Berufsrolle* [Women in the laborforce: A psychological analysis of the female occupational role]. Frankfurt/Main, Germany: Athenäum.

Lent, R. W., Brown, S. D., & Hackett, G. (1994). Toward a unifying social cognitive theory of career and academic interest, choice, and performance. *Journal of Vocational Behavior, 45*, 79–122.

Maccoby, E. E. (1988). Gender as a social category. *Developmental Psychology, 24*, 755–765.

Maccoby, E. E., & Jacklin, C. N. (1974). *The psychology of sex differences.* Stanford, CA: Stanford University Press.

Major, B. (1994). From social inequality to personal entitlement: The role of social comparisons, legitimacy appraisals, and group membership. In M. P. Zanna (Ed.), *Advances in experimental social psychology* (Vol. 26, pp. 293–355). San Diego, CA: Academic Press.

Marini, M. M., & Fan, P. L. (1997). The gender gap in earnings at career entry. *American Sociological Review, 62*, 588–603.

Marshall, S. J., & Wijting, J. P. (1980). Relationships of achievement motivation and sex-role identity to college women's career orientation. *Journal of Vocational Behavior, 16*, 299–311.

Martin, C. L. (1991). The role of cognition in understanding gender effects. *Advances in Child Development and Behavior, 23*, 113–149.

Merkel, A. (1992). Frau in Beruf, Gesellschaft und Familie—Herausforderung für die Politik der Bundesregierung [Women in occupation, society and family—Challenge for the politics of the federal government]. In Bayerisches Staatsministerium für Wirtschaft, Verkehr und EG Kommission (Ed.), *Frau und Wirtschaft—Führen als Frau* (pp. 63–72). Stamsried, Germany: Vogel.

Moskowitz, D. W., Suh, E. J., & Desaulniers, J. (1994). Situational influences on gender differences in agency and communion. *Journal of Personality and Social Psychology, 66,* 753–761.

Mummendey, H. D. (1990). Selbstkonzept-Änderungen nach kritischen Lebensereignissen [Self-concept changes after critical life events]. In S.-H. Filipp (Ed.), *Kritische Lebensereignisse* (2nd ed., pp. 252–269). Munich, Germany: Psychologie Verlags Union.

Myrdal, A., & Klein, V. (1956). *Women's two roles: Home and work.* London: Routledge & Kegan Paul.

National Center for Education Statistics. (1998). *Findings from the Condition of Education 1998.* [On-line]. Available: Internet http://www.neces.ed.gov

Oppenheimer, V. (1979). Structural sources of economic pressure for wives to work: An analytical framework. *Journal of Family History, 4,* 177–197.

Perry, D. G., & Bussey, K. (1984). *Social development.* Englewood Cliffs, NJ: Prentice-Hall.

Phillips, S. D., & Imhoff, A. R. (1997). Women and career development: A decade of research. *Annual Review of Psychology, 48,* 31–59.

Powell, G. N. (1988). *Women and men in management.* Newbury Park, CA: Sage.

Rosenkrantz, P., Vogel, S., Bee, H., Broverman, I., & Broverman, D. M. (1968). Sex-role stereotypes and self-concepts in college students. *Journal of Consulting and Clinical Psychology, 32,* 278–295.

Ruble, D. N., & Martin, C. L. (1998). Gender development. In W. Damon (Series Ed.) & N. Eisenberg (Vol. Ed.), *Handbook of child psychology: Vol. 3. Social, emotional, and personality development* (5th ed., pp. 933–1016). New York: Wiley.

Runge, T. E., Frey, D., Gollwitzer, P. M., Helmreich, R. L., & Spence, J. T. (1981). Masculine (instrumental) and feminine (expressive) traits: A comparison between students in the United States and West Germany. *Journal of Cross-Cultural Psychology, 12,* 142–162.

Schallberger, U., Häfeli, K., & Kraft, U. (1984). Zur reziproken Beziehung zwischen Berufsausbildung und Persönlichkeitsentwicklung [The reciprocal relation between occupational training and personality development]. *Zeitschrift für Sozialisationsforschung und Erziehungssoziologie, 4,* 197–210.

Schmalt, H. D., Sokolowski, K., & Langens, T. (1994). *Die Entwicklung eines Verfahrens zur Messung der Motive Leistung, Macht und Anschluss mit der Gitter-Technik* [Construction of a measure of the achievement, power and affiliation motives by means of the grid technique]. Wuppertal, Germany: Bergische Universität.

Schneider, D. J. (1991). Social cognition. *Annual Review of Psychology, 42,* 527–561.

Sieverding, M. (1990). *Psychologische Barrieren in der beruflichen Entwicklung von Frauen: Das Beispiel der Medizinerinnen* [Psychological barriers in the occupational development of women: The case of medical doctors]. Stuttgart, Germany: Enke.

Six, B., & Eckes, T. (1991). A closer look at the complex structure of gender stereotypes. *Sex Roles, 24,* 57–71.

Spence, J. T., & Helmreich, R. L. (1978). *Masculinity and femininity: Their psychological dimensions, correlates, and antecedents.* Austin: University of Texas Press.

Steel, L., Abeles, R. P., & Card, J. J. (1982). Sex differences in the patterning of adult roles as a determinant of sex differences in occupational achievement. *Sex Roles, 8,* 1009–1024.

Stohs, J. (1991). Moving beyond women's career choices: Factors associated with career continuity among female former art students. *Journal of Career Development, 182,* 123–138.

Super, D. E. (1957). *The psychology of careers: An introduction to vocational development.* New York: Harper & Row.

Teichler, U., & Buttgereit, M. (1992). *Hochschulabsolventen im Beruf: Ergebnisse der dritten Befragung bei Absolventen der Kasseler Verlaufsstudie* [University graduates in their jobs: Results of the third survey of the Kassel longitudinal study]. Bad Honnef, Germany: Bock.

Terman, L. M., & Oden, M. H. (1959). *Genetic studies of genius: V. The gifted group at midlife.* Stanford, CA: Stanford University Press.

Trautner, H. M. (1994). Geschlechtsspezifische Erziehung und Sozialisation [Gender-typed education and socialization]. In K. A. Scheewind (Ed.), *Psychologie der Erziehung und Sozialisation* (pp. 167–195). Göttingen, Germany: Hogrefe.

Trautner, H. M. (1996). Die Bedeutung der Geschlechtskategorien im Jugendalter [The relevance of gender categories in adolescence]. In R. Schumann-Hengsteler & H. M. Trautner (Eds.), *Entwicklung im Jugendalter* (pp. 165–187). Göttingen, Germany: Hogrefe.

U.S. Bureau of Census. (1998). *Findings from the Condition of Education 1997.* [On-line]. Available: Internet http://www.neces.ed.gov

Watkins, C. E., & Subich, L. M. (1995). Annual Review, 1992–1994: Career development, reciprocal work/non-work, interaction, and women's workforce participation. *Journal of Vocational Behavior, 47,* 109–163.

Williams, J. E., & Best, D. L. (1990). *Measuring sex stereotypes: A multination study* (Rev. ed.). Newbury Park, CA: Sage.

Wolfson, K. P. (1976). Career development patterns of college women. *Journal of Counseling Psychology, 23,* 119–125.

# 13

# Gender Development in Cross-Cultural Perspective

## Judith L. Gibbons
*Saint Louis University*

Cross-cultural and international research has the potential to test the generality of psychological theories, to expand the range of variables available for study, and to identify phenomena that are widespread or universal (Lonner & Adamopoulos, 1997). With regard to gender development, cross-cultural research has made some important contributions. Cognitive theories about gender have been tested in various cultural settings to investigate their generalizability (e.g., De Lisi & Gallagher, 1991; R. H. Munroe, Shimmin, & Munroe, 1984). The range of naturally occurring variations has been used to explore the origins of gender-typed behaviors, as in studies of cultures that varied in the degree to which girls and boys were differentially assigned household tasks (Whiting & Edwards, 1988). Moreover, pancultural stereotypes about women and men, girls and boys, have been identified through cross-national research (Williams & Best, 1990a, 1990b). Nonetheless, to a great extent the potential of cross-cultural and international research remains unrealized, in part because of the methodological pitfalls in cross-cultural research and in part because of the lack of conceptual clarity in the study of gender development. In this chapter some of those pitfalls are identified and the conceptual distinctions are highlighted. Examples are drawn as much as possible from cross-cultural and non-Western research. Then, the literature on gender development in cross-cultural perspective is reviewed in three areas: (a) development of gender constancy and gender identity, (b) development of knowledge of gender stereotypes, and (c) adolescents' gender-related ideals.

# CULTURE AND PSYCHOLOGY:
# EMERGING FRAMEWORKS

Current notions about culture and culture's role in psychological development have been explicated well in recent reviews (C. R. Cooper & Denner, 1998; Fiske, Kitayama, Markus, & Nisbett, 1998; Greenfield, 1997; Lonner & Adamopoulos, 1997; Markus, Kitayama, & Heiman, 1996; Miller, 1997). Although contemporary psychologists studying culture seem to be less willing than in the past to advance a single definition of culture, Markus et al. (1996) have pointed to an emerging consensus on what culture is not: Culture is more than context, culture cannot be seen as separate from the individual, and cultures are not static but dynamic systems.

Although there have been a number of attempts at integration (e.g., Miller, 1997), there remain two distinct schools of thought on the relation of culture and human development: the cross-cultural perspective and the cultural perspective. The early cross-cultural researchers, especially, have seen culture as outside the individual, as a set of norms, beliefs, and values that influence a person's cognitive, emotional, physical, and social development. For example, Triandis (1994) wrote, "culture influences the way humans select, interpret, process, and use information" (p. 15). In this view culture serves as an antecedent to behavior, and comparisons between cultures are explicit or implied (Lonner & Adamopoulos, 1997). Researchers working from the cross-cultural framework have sought explanations for cultural differences in terms of cultural dimensions such as individualism and collectivism (Hofstede, 1980, 1983; Triandis, 1995) and have also explored mediating and moderating variables in the relation of culture and individual behavior (Lonner & Adamopoulos, 1997). Developmental studies derived from this perspective have included a number of tests of Piagetian developmental stages in international perspective (e.g., Dasen, 1994).

The second perspective, cultural psychology, has unfolded and blossomed in the past several decades. Of the researchers working in this framework, many trace their theoretical roots to Vygotsky and the sociohistorical approach to development (Vygotsky, 1981; Wertsch, del Rio, & Alvarez, 1995). According to the cultural perspective, the process of development is inherently social and cultural. Thinking is first developed through interactions with other persons, and consequently, thinking within individuals reflects cultural practices enacted in interpersonal interactions. Although cultural psychologists, more often than cross-cultural psychologists, focus on development within a single culture, the unicultural approach is not an essential feature of cultural psychology (Miller, 1997). Developmental researchers working in the cultural psychology framework have explored cognitive processes displayed in everyday activities such as mathematical understanding among child vendors (Saxe, 1991) or the process of learning to weave among Zinacantecan girls (Greenfield, 1993).

There are a variety of ways that gender development can be conceptualized within cultural and cross-cultural frameworks. Beliefs about gender can be seen as a component of culture, as in Díaz-Guerrero's (1975) notion of sociocultural premises. Díaz-Guerrero sees beliefs about women's and men's roles and responsibilities as part of the unstated assumptions embedded in the psyche of the Mexican people. Beliefs about gender have also been related to the processes of cultural change. Chia, Allred, and Jerzak (1997) proposed that cultural modernization brings with it more egalitarian attitudes about gender roles. The gender of the individual can also be seen as a factor that alters the contexts of socialization. For example, Schlegel and Barry (1991) in their study of adolescents in preindustrial societies found that boys spent more time in same-sex peer groups, whereas girls spent more time in mixed-age groups of women and girls. They suggested that the differences in the contexts of socialization might lead to gender differences in behavior such as greater social responsibility among girls and a greater propensity for delinquency among boys. Although cultural psychological approaches to gender development can be imagined (e.g., studying how parents and their children jointly talk about gender in a single culture or multiple cultures), no such studies were identified in the extant literature.

## METHODOLOGICAL CONSIDERATIONS IN CROSS-CULTURAL PSYCHOLOGY

A distinction often made in cross-cultural and international research is that between *emic* and *etic* approaches. The term *emic* refers to the culture-specific approach, an approach that emphasizes the indigenous meaning of constructs. *Etics* are those constructs or measures that are considered to be universal and can be applied cross-culturally. When a measure from one culture is heedlessly applied in a different cultural setting, the etic is said to be an imposed etic (with negative connotations), and when the measure is carefully extracted from within-culture studies, it is said to be derived (with positive connotations). One example of how similar findings may have different meanings when studied from an emic perspective comes from a study of adolescents' drawings of the ideal woman (Gibbons, Lynn, et al., 1993). In a variety of cultural settings, many adolescents drew the ideal woman as pursuing the activity of working in an office. However, when adolescents' drawings of women engaged in these activities were presented to their same-culture peers for interpretation, adolescents gave both pancultural and emic interpretations. In all countries studied, women working in offices were described as hardworking; but Guatemalan adolescents also saw them as working for the betterment of their families, Filipino adolescents saw them as sexy and adventurous, and U.S. adolescents saw them as bored with the routine of office work. So, although the image of women working in offices may serve as an etic, a construct that can be recorded across gender and culture, its meaning may best be understood from a consideration of the insider's or emic perspective.

One of the formidable methodological challenges in cross-cultural psychology especially with regard to gender is the issue of sampling. Sampling issues in comparative research have been discussed extensively in other volumes (e.g., Lonner & Berry, 1986; Van de Vijver & Leung, 1997). Here is presented an example of how culture and gender issues may interact. In gender-difference studies conducted internationally, samples are often drawn in a particular setting, such as colleges or universities, as a way of evoking equivalent samples. But college or university students do not reflect the population similarly in different countries, because the proportion of the population attending university differs widely internationally. Moreover, men attending a university may not be comparable to women attending the same university. This phenomenon was shown in a study by Sterzi (1989; see also Rabinowitz & Sechzer, 1993). The study was conducted among students attending a public university in New York City, and the findings were that Italian American women students had higher achievement motivation and were more academically successful than their male counterparts. Follow-up questions revealed that the brothers of the Italian American women in the sample were likely to be enrolled at private, more expensive colleges. The interpretation was that the population of Italian American students at a public, less expensive university represented women from families who highly valued education and sent their sons for expensive schooling, and men from less academically oriented families.

Another issue that is essential to address in cross-cultural comparisons is the identification of the cultural components or processes that contribute to cultural differences. A number of methodologists (e.g., Triandis, 1994; Van de Vijver & Leung, 1997) have pointed out that a finding of cross-cultural differences is virtually meaningless without an explanation as to the origin of the difference and that it is incumbent on the researcher to provide an interpretation or framework. Indeed, the editorial policy of the journal *Cross-Cultural Research* specifies that the proposed explanation for cultural differences must consist of a measured variable. Campbell (1988) noted that a comparison of only two cultures is usually nonproductive, and Triandis (1994) described eight rival hypotheses (causes other than a "real" cultural difference) that may account for a finding of a difference between samples.

The difficulty in interpreting a difference between two cultures can be seen in a study by Dickerscheid, Schwarz, Noir, and El-Taliawy (1988) on the development of gender constancy in the United States and Egypt. The authors originally hypothesized that children living in a society with more traditional gender roles (Egypt) would develop gender constancy at a younger age than children living in a society with more flexible gender roles (the United States). When the results appeared to be opposite to the prediction, the authors sought an interpretation. Among the rival hypotheses was that children in Egypt were less accustomed than children in the United States to answering adults' questions; another possibility is that the questioning procedure was less culturally appropriate in Egypt. This later interpretation is suggested by the failure of the Egyptian interviewer, despite training on the procedure, to ask counter questions (e.g., "Are you a girl?" after the child has just identified himself as a boy). In some cultures asking a question which requires a "no" answer would be considered rude. In sum, the origin of the detected difference was unknown and could have had a number of potential sources.

A proposed aid to interpretation is to sample at least four cultures (two high and two low on the proposed independent variable) and/or to make interpretations within a compelling theoretical framework; differences should emerge within a background of similarities (R. L. Munroe & Munroe, 1991; Triandis, 1994; Van de Vijver & Leung, 1997).

# GENDER DEVELOPMENT RESEARCH: SOME CONCEPTUAL CONSIDERATIONS

The present chapter focuses on children's and adolescents' cognitions—their knowledge, beliefs, and attitudes about gender—rather than gender differences in behavior. In reviewing the adult literature, Unger (1979) pointed out that gender differences in behavior that are revealed by empirical observation are generally of lesser magnitude than what people believe to be the case. An example from the child literature comes from a cross-cultural study of Dutch and Italian children that used stories having male or female protagonists (Zammuner, 1987). Zammuner found that there were more effects related to the gender of the story protagonist than to the gender of the child participant.

Although gender-related beliefs and knowledge are often treated as a unit, several distinctions may help to establish greater conceptual clarity and to reconcile some apparent discrepancies. These have been elaborated more fully in two articles appearing in a special issue of the *Psychology of Women Quarterly* (Bigler, 1997; Gibbons, Hamby, & Dennis, 1997) and have been described as well in earlier writings (e.g., Gibbons & Fisher, 1996; Signorella, Bigler, & Liben, 1993; Trautner, Helbing, Sahm, & Lohaus, 1989). There are at least five dimensions on which measures of gender-related thinking may differ: (a) the target of the attitudes or beliefs, specifically whether one is measuring beliefs about the self or about others; (b) whether the item is purely descriptive (represents knowledge of the stereotype) or has an evaluative component (expresses an attitude toward the stereotype); (c) the rigidity or flexibility of the belief; (d) whether the belief concerns traits (relatively enduring personality attributes) or specific roles and behaviors; and (e) the domain of gender-related behavior that is assessed (e.g., play activity, household task, or occupational role). See Table 13.1 for a visual representation of some dimensions of the conceptual framework as well as some ways that gender-related issues have been measured.

The most widely studied theories of gender development posit that knowledge about one's own gender precedes and influences thinking about the gender and gender-related behaviors of others (see Martin, chap. 4, this volume). However, the importance of target (self vs. others) in developmental studies of gender was further elaborated in a recent review by Bigler (1997). Bigler concluded that children's gender typing of the self is only sometimes correlated with gender typing of others and that these variables may be related to different predictor variables as well.

In the international literature, the differential consequences of targeting the self versus others can be seen in a study by Cheung Mui-ching (1986). In that study, secondary school students in Hong Kong responded to 100 adjectives four times; they described the typical male, the typical female, the self, and the ideal self. The results showed that the typical male and female were described more stereotypically than was the self. Urberg (1979) found that adolescents and adults in the United States also stereotyped others more than they did themselves. Moreover, children may show gender stability and gender consistency at younger ages for themselves than for others (Gouze & Nadelman, 1980; Leonard & Archer, 1989; Marcus & Overton, 1978).

The second dimension on which measures may differ concerns whether the items are purely descriptive or whether they have an evaluative component. Bigler (1997) made this distinction and pointed out that children can be asked either, "Who usually . . ." or "Who should . . ." perform various activities. The former question is descriptive and assesses knowledge of gender stereotypes, whereas the latter question is evaluative and assesses attitudes toward gender roles.

TABLE 13.1
**A Conceptual Framework and Measures for Studies of Gender Development**

| | Descriptive | Evaluative: Prescriptive or Proscriptive |
|---|---|---|
| | Part A. Others (Girls and Boys or Men and Women in General) | |
| Roles or activities | Story-telling doll game (Albert & Porter, 1986; e.g., fixes chair, helps hurt child), 28 gender-related actions (Zammuner, 1982; e.g., to comfort, to yell), Sex Role Learning Index (SERLI; Edelbrock & Sugawara, 1978) | Children's Occupation, Activity, and Trait-Attitude Measure (COAT-AM; Bigler, 1997; occupational and activity items), Attitudes Toward Women Scale for Adolescents (Galambos, Petersen, Richards, & Gitelson, 1985), Male Role Attitude Scale (MRAS; Pleck, Sonenstein, & Ku, 1993), Ideal man/ideal woman drawings (Stiles, Gibbons, & Schnellmann, 1990) |
| Traits | Sex Stereotype Measure II (Best & Williams, 1990a), Adjective Check List (Gough & Heilbrun, 1980) | Children's Occupation, Activity, and Trait-Attitude Measure (COAT-AM; Bigler, 1997; trait items), Ideal man/ideal woman ratings (Stiles, Gibbons, Hardardottir, & Schnell-mann, 1987) |
| | Part B. The Self | |
| Roles or activities | Children's Occupation, Activity, and Trait-Personal Measure (COAT-PM; Bigler, 1997; occupational and activity items applied to self), Sex Role Learning Index (SERLI; Edelbrock & Sugawara, 1978; sex-role preferences section), Offer Self-Image Questionnaire (Offer, Ostrov, & Howard, 1982) | no known instruments |
| Traits | Children's Occupation, Activity, and Trait-Personal Measure (COAT-PM; Bigler, 1997; trait items applied to self), Bem Sex-Role Inventory (Bem, 1974), Personal Attributes Questionnaire (Spence, Helmreich, & Stapp, 1974) | Bem Sex-Role Inventory (used for "ideal self"; Pettinati, Franks, Wade, & Kogan, 1987), Pancultural Adjective Checklist (Williams & Best, 1990a) as used for "ideal self" (Cheung Mui-ching, 1986) |

An example of how the mixing of evaluative and descriptive items can becloud the interpretation of results is provided by a study using the Historic-Sociocultural Premises scale (HSCP; Díaz-Guerrero, 1975). The HSCP comprises both evaluative items and descriptive items. One evaluative item is "It is not right for a married woman to work outside of her home." A descriptive item is "The majority of the men of my country feel superior to women." In a study of adolescents attending an international school in the Netherlands, students from individualist countries were more likely than students from collectivist countries to endorse an egalitarian ideology with respect to women's roles (Gibbons, Stiles, & Shkodriani, 1991). For example, the students from collectivist countries were more likely to agree that women should not work outside the home. However, the descriptive item about men feeling superior to women was an exception; there was an interaction with girls from individualist countries and boys from collectivist countries agreeing with the statement more than did the other two groups. Most likely they agreed for different reasons. Whereas boys from collectivist countries might have held the attitude that not only do men feel superior to women, but also that men are indeed superior, girls from individualist countries might have been, more than their male counterparts, detecting sexist beliefs.

A third orthogonal dimension along which gender-related beliefs can vary is that of rigidity and flexibility (Trautner et al., 1989). In a longitudinal study of German children from ages 4 through 10, rigidity in stereotyping peaked at about age 6 and then declined. Flexibility, first displayed at about age 8, increased with age. A recent study of adolescents in the United States has revealed that flexibility in gender-role attitudes increases when students make school transitions, regardless of the grade in which the transition occurs (Alfieri, Ruble, & Higgins, 1996).

Another distinction that may provide greater clarity in the literature on gender development is that between traits and roles. In the developmental literature, a good example of the importance of the distinction comes from the cross-cultural study by Zammuner (1993) of the gender-related knowledge of Dutch and Italian children. Zammuner found that 10-year-old children classified traits (e.g., strong, sensitive) more often than they classified activities (e.g., repair, sing) according to gender. Moreover, children's knowledge of gender-related personality traits may follow a different developmental course than their knowledge of occupations and activities (Ruble & Ruble, 1982; Serbin, Powlishta, & Gulko, 1993).

The domains assessed in studies of gender-related attitudes may differ greatly, and may account for different findings (Bigler, 1997; Gibbons, Hamby, & Dennis, 1997). Gender-role attitudes may be egalitarian in one domain, such as occupational choice, but differentiated in another, such as household responsibilities. In a study of school-age children in India, gender-role flexibility was assessed regarding toy preferences, activity preferences, and occupational aspirations (Bhogle, 1996). Correlations among the different domains were low and varied in direction and magnitude. Similar findings were reported by Trautner (1992).

In sum, some of the difficulty in assessing the international research on gender development stems from attempting to compare dissimilar measures. Further developmental studies are needed that address gender-related knowledge and beliefs about the self and others in domains that are culturally relevant. In addition, the study of gender belief development would be furthered by longitudinal studies, which consider as well the dimension of rigidity and flexibility in beliefs.

# CROSS-CULTURAL CONTRIBUTIONS TO THE STUDY OF GENDER DEVELOPMENT

In the past decade, there have been three reviews of the cross-cultural psychological literature on gender (Best & Williams, 1993, 1997; Gibbons, Hamby, & Dennis, 1997); however, none of those focused specifically on development. In the present chapter, we review three topics selected for their relation to development and for the availability of information. The first is exploration of the generality of the posited developmental pattern of gender constancy, including whether the developmental sequence of gender identity, gender stability, and gender consistency occurs universally. The second area concerns knowledge of gender trait stereotypes, including whether some aspects of gender stereotypes occur panculturally. The third issue derives from research on adolescents' views of the ideal man and the ideal woman; a cross-national commonality is identified and some differences in beliefs are linked to a dimension of culture.

## Development of Gender Constancy

One area of study to which international research has made a significant contribution is that of the development of gender constancy. According to the theory of Kohlberg (1966; see Martin, chap. 4, this volume), the development of thinking about gender is closely linked to cognitive development in general. The first stage of gender development is that of gender identity. A girl who has achieved gender identity is able to classify herself, dolls, and photographs as female. A girl who has achieved gender stability will also answer correctly that she was female at a younger age and will continue to be female in the future. A girl who has achieved gender consistency will recognize that despite changes in clothing and activities she will continue to be female.

Cross-cultural investigations of the development of gender constancy are essential because Kohlberg's (1966) theory was a major theory used to frame studies of gender development, and it is through cross-cultural studies that the generality of the theory can be evaluated. In addition, naturally occuring variations in circumstances provide natural experiments that will help to reveal factors that bring about the development of gender constancy in children, as well as the consequences of gender constancy.

There are two primary measures of gender constancy. In the Slaby and Frey (1975) procedure, children are interviewed about the gender identity, stability, and consistency of themselves, photographs, and dolls. In the Emmerich procedure (Emmerich, Goldman, Kirsh, & Sharabany, 1977), pictures of children are perceptually altered by changing hairstyles and clothing, and the children are queried about whether those changes produce changes in gender. Both procedures have been modified, however, by many researchers, often to make the stimuli more culturally relevant. According to the distinctions presented earlier, the gender constancy measure includes information about both the self and others, is descriptive rather than prescriptive, addresses the domains of clothing and play activities, and concerns activities and behaviors. Occasionally, trait measures have been added as well; for example, De Lisi and Gallagher (1991) asked Argentinian children, "If Suzanna were brave, would she be a girl or a boy?" (p. 502).

Studies of the development of gender constancy in different cultural settings, including American Samoa, Argentina, Australia, Belize, Canada, Egypt, Germany, Great Britain (both England and Wales), India, Israel, Kenya, Nepal, South Africa (among the Indian community), and the United States, have largely supported the invariance of the sequence of stages: gender identity, gender stability, and gender consistency (Bhana, 1984; Bhogle & Seethalakshmi, 1992; De Lisi & Gallagher, 1991; Dickerscheid et al., 1988; Eaton & Von Bargen, 1981; Gouze & Nadelman, 1980; Leonard & Archer, 1989; Lobel & Menashri, 1993; R. H. Munroe et al., 1984; Siegal & Robinson, 1987; Slaby & Frey, 1975; Trautner, 1992; Yee & Brown, 1994).

Because of differences in methodology, ages of child participants, and the reporting of results, it is impossible to directly compare across studies. In those studies in which the researchers simply reported the percentage of children at each age level who correctly answered each type of question, there seem to be some dips in performance, particularly among 7- and 9-year-olds. For example, a larger percentage of 5-year-olds (42%) than 7-year-olds (25%) and 9-year-olds (25%) in Belize responded correctly to the consistency questions (R. H. Munroe et al., 1984). Similar instances of higher percentages of correct responding among younger children have been reported in Nepal and Kenya (R. H. Munroe et al., 1984) and among 5-year-olds in Wales as compared to 7-year-olds (Yee & Brown, 1994). But because the design of those studies was cross-sectional, the results do not imply a reversal of the sequencing.

A more informative measure for the present purpose is whether (and if so, how many) children answered correctly the questions from higher stages, but failed the questions from the earlier stages. In the Slaby and Frey (1975) sample, only 2% of the children exhibited a pattern of responding that was inconsistent with the predicted sequence of stages. The percentage of reversals was similarly low in other studies: 10% in the four-culture study by R. H. Munroe et al. (1984), less than 2% in an Argentinian sample (De Lisi & Gallagher, 1991), less than 8% in another sample from the United States (Gouze & Nadelman, 1980), and less than 10% in a sample from Canada (Eaton & Von Bargen, 1981). In an extensive search of international and cross-cultural studies, none were found to report a large number of reversals in the sequencing (Bhana, 1984; Bhogle & Seethalakshmi, 1992; De Lisi & Gallagher, 1991; Dickerscheid et al., 1988; Eaton & Von Bargen, 1981; Gouze & Nadelman, 1980; Leonard & Archer, 1989; Lobel & Menashri, 1993; Martin & Halverson, 1983; R. H. Munroe et al., 1984; Newman, J. Cooper, & Ruble, 1995; Siegal & Robinson, 1987; Slaby & Frey, 1975; Trautner, 1992; Wehren & De Lisi, 1983; Yee & Brown, 1994). Thus, the literature overall supports the universality of Kohlberg's (1966) posited sequence for the development of gender constancy.

A second question is whether the typical age of achieving gender constancy shows cross-cultural variation. A review of the relevant studies suggested that the typical age for the achievement of gender constancy appears to vary in different studies and perhaps in different cultural settings. For example, the mean age for attaining gender constancy was approximately 8 years of age in four preindustrial societies (R. H. Munroe et al., 1984) and among middle-class Argentinian children (De Lisi & Gallagher, 1991), whereas mean ages for attaining gender constancy have been reported to be about 5 years of age for middle-class Canadians (Eaton & Von Bargen, 1981) and greater than 8 years of age among children of Indian descent living in South Africa (Bhana, 1984). The interpretation of those apparent differences is problematic because procedural and reporting differences among studies make direct comparisons and definitive conclusions impossible.

Furthermore, slight variations in procedure have been shown to produce large differences in children's responses. For example, Leonard and Archer (1989) asked children specifically about the possibility that a child who wore opposite-gender clothing may be pretending to be the opposite gender. Because all children who had first claimed that changes in clothing or hairstyle would alter gender responded that the person would be only pretending, all of the 3- to 4-year-olds were judged to exhibit gender constancy. Without the "pretending" question, only 37% to 67% would have been scored as having attained gender constancy. Martin and Halverson (1983), who originally raised the "pretending" issue, also showed significant differences in the results using the two types of tasks—the perceptual transformation task of Emmerich et al. (1977) and the verbal task of Slaby and Frey (1975). Moreover, Siegal and Robinson (1987) demonstrated that performance was greatly enhanced in children when the order of questions in the Slaby–Frey procedure was reversed. Finally, in part, because the probability of getting each question correct by chance is 50%, it may be useful to add questions that tap the reasoning behind the answers (Wehren & De Lisi, 1983).

Yet another contextual factor has been proposed to promote achievement of gender constancy—knowledge about anatomical genital differences (Bem, 1989, 1993; McConaghy, 1979). Although an early study showed gender constancy and knowlege about the genital basis of gender to be independent (McConaghy, 1979), a more recent study by Bem (1993) revealed that most of the sample of 3- to 5-year-olds from the United States who could correctly assign sex to photographs of babies on the basis of genitalia had achieved gender constancy. The hypothesis about the relation of knowledge of genital differences to gender constancy represents an ideal opportunity for cross-cultural exploration. Among the preindustrial societies in R. H. Munroe et al.'s (1984) four-culture study, children might be expected to exhibit more and earlier knowledge of genital differences because of children's increased observation of unclothed others and, especially for girls in Kenya and Nepal, greater involvement in the care of younger children; yet the children in that study typically achieved gender constancy at later ages (about 7 or 8 years of age).

Some other types of cross-cultural studies might address the generality of the developmental processes related to gender constancy. As Van Ijzendoorn (1990) persuasively argued with regard to the attachment literature, different distributions of responses across cultures do not address the question of universality of the theory. The studies that bear directly on the universality of the theory are those that address whether the antecedents, correlates, and consequences are similar in cross-cultural perspective. Cross-cultural studies that address the correlates of gender constancy are currently virtually unknown. Moreover, the correlates of gender constancy are controversial, with some studies suggesting that attainment of gender constancy acts as a motivational variable and influences such behaviors as gender-related toy preferences (e.g., Stangor & Ruble, 1989) and attitudes toward the use of computers (Newman et al., 1995). Other studies fail to find relationships between gender constancy and gender-related toy preferences (e.g., Lobel & Menashri, 1993; Trautner, 1992).

In conclusion, cross-cultural studies of gender constancy have revealed that the sequence of stages is relatively invariant. This conclusion is parallel to the findings of cross-cultural examination of Piagetian cognitive stages in general (Dasen, 1994). There is also an indication that the age of attaining the stages of gender constancy may vary. This finding is also similar to the result of evaluation of Piagetian stages cross-culturally (Dasen, 1994). Dasen has pointed out the importance of cultural and environment factors in cognitive development and has concluded that performance in a particular domain is dependent on one's experience in that domain. Although it is likely that this is also true for the development of gender constancy, the particular factors that lead to the achievement of gender constancy are unknown.

## Development of Gender Identity

Gender identity in its narrowest sense refers to one's sense of self as male or female (Unger & Crawford, 1996). Thus, the first item of the Slaby and Frey (1975) gender constancy measure, "Are you a boy or a girl?" is the basic measure of gender identity. Studies have shown that most children can identify themselves as male or female by the age of 3 (e.g., Slaby & Frey, 1975; Yee & Brown, 1994).

In the broader sense, however, gender identity can be construed as all of the gender-related measures that refer to the self, that is, the gender-related traits, preferences, and activities that one exhibits, as well as those that one ideally ought to exhibit. This broader view, involving the application of various gender-related concepts to the self, is sometimes called sex typing. One measure of sex typing, the Bem Sex-Role Inventory (BSRI; Bem, 1974), is the most widely used instrument in psychological research on gender issues. Beere (1990) found over 1,000 citations using the BSRI, and many additional studies have been published since Beere's review. With this instrument, participants rate themselves with regard to 20 masculine, 20 feminine, and 20 neutral qualities. The mean rating on the masculine items is the masculinity score, and the mean rating on the feminine items, the femininity score. Generally, participants who score above the median on both masculinity and femininity are considered androgynous and those who score below the median on both scales are considered undifferentiated. According to these distinctions, the BSRI measures descriptive gender traits as applied to the self, although on occasion, it has been used evaluatively in terms of the ideal self (e.g., Pettinati, Franks, Wade, & Kogan, 1987).

In a number of international studies researchers have attempted to ascertain the usefulness of the BSRI in cultures other than the United States. In many cases new instruments were developed using procedures similar to or identical with those of the BSRI; the items on those new instruments represented emic or culturally appropriate gender trait identity measures. For example, Kaschak and Sharratt (1984) developed the Latin American Sex-Role Inventory (LASRI) starting with 200 adjectives and identifying traits more often associated with females and those more often associated with males in Costa Rica. The LASRI does have some overlap with the BSRI; 11 of the LASRI masculinity and 10 of the LASRI femininity items duplicate the BSRI items. A measure was also developed in Hong Kong for Chinese adolescents, the Chinese Sex-Role Inventory (CSRI; Keyes, 1984); fewer items, however, overlapped with the BSRI. In addition, there exist a French version (the French BSRI; Gana, 1995) and a German version (Schneider-Düker & Kohler, 1988) of the BSRI. The BSRI was also evaluated in Mexico (Lara-Cantú & Navarro-Arias, 1987), in Malaysia and India (Ward & Sethi, 1986), and in Zimbabwe (Wilson et al., 1990). Overall, the necessity to create unique instruments in various cultural settings suggests that the items of the BSRI represent emic (culture-specific) constructs with respect to gender.

A different approach to understanding self-construals was taken by Kashima et al. (1995) in a study with a variety of instruments and careful attention to measurement issues. The self-descriptions of college students in five societies (Australia, the U.S. mainland, Hawaii, Japan, and Korea) could be differentiated by culture according to the dimensions of individualism and collectivism and by gender according to a measure of relatedness. Women, more than men in all five samples, expressed concern for others' feelings and worries; these gender differences were greatest in Australia and the United States. These results imply that there may be a widespread or universal gender difference in self-construal with the magnitude of the difference influenced by culture.

## Development of Knowledge of Gender Stereotypes

Despite a considerable increase in the understanding of stereotypes and their development (see Martin, chap. 4, this volume) there is relatively little cross-cultural research regarding stereotypes. Probably the most extensive international studies of gender stereotype development are those of Williams and Best and their collaborators (Best et al., 1977; Neto, Williams, & Widner, 1991; Tarrier & Gomes, 1981; Ward, 1985, 1990; Williams & Best, 1990a, 1990b; see also reviews by Best & Williams, 1993, 1997). The primary study (Williams & Best 1990a) addressed the development of children's knowledge of gender-related traits in 24 countries, including Australia, Brazil, Canada, Chile, England, Finland, France, Germany, India, Ireland, Italy, Japan, Malaysia, the Netherlands, New Zealand, Nigeria, Norway,

Pakistan, Peru, Spain, Taiwan, Thailand, the United States, and Venezuela. In terms of the distinctions made earlier, the topic was others rather than the self, traits rather than activities, and knowledge rather than prescriptions.

The measure used was the Sex Stereotype Measure II (SSM II), given in interview form to 5-year-olds and 8-year-olds. Researchers extracted 16 traits usually associated with females and 16 traits usually associated with males from a larger set of adjectives in studies with adults in the United States. The female traits were emotional, appreciative, weak, talkative, changeable, gentle, frivolous, fussy, meek, complaining, flirtatious, excitable, affectionate, softhearted, dependent, and affected. The male traits were aggressive, adventurous, independent, disorderly, enterprising, jolly, cruel, steady, boastful, coarse, severe, loud, dominant, confident, logical, and strong. In the test procedure, children were told a short story such as "One of these people is emotional. They cry when something good happens as well as when everything goes wrong. Which person is the emotional person?" (Williams & Best, 1990a, p. 154). The child then made a choice between a male silhouette figure and a female silhouette figure. Note that because the trait was defined in terms of behavior the measure was a mixture of activities and traits.

The findings indicated substantial knowledge of the gender trait stereotypes among 5-year-old children cross-culturally. Five-year-olds from 24 countries associated traits such as weak and softhearted with females and traits such as strong and aggressive with males. By age 8, even more traits were associated with females and males.

There was also some evidence of cross-cultural variation. The country with the highest percentage of gender differentiation of traits by both 5-year-olds and 8-year-olds was Pakistan. Gender differentiation was low for 5-year-olds in Italy, India, and France, and for 8-year-olds in Venezuela, Nigeria, and Thailand. The amount of common variance (variance shared with the other samples) was significantly correlated with "the percentage of Christians in a country, the percentage of the population that is urban, and the percentage of the school-age population attending school" (Best & Williams, 1993, p. 237). It seems likely that children who attend school and live in urban areas are more likely to learn gender stereotypes that are similar to the stereotypes held by children in other countries.

What these studies clearly demonstrated was that knowledge about gender-related traits increased panculturally between the ages of 5 and 8. Also, adjectives derived from studies of adults in the United States were often endorsed as stereotypic in 24 different countries. Thus, those studies provided empirical evidence that the 32 traits represented, to some degree, an etic in terms of their differential gender assignment.

Nonetheless, the measure, the SSM II, incorporated a forced choice procedure. Disagreement with the stereotype might not be distinguished from lack of knowledge. For example, a child who responded that the silhouette of a woman represents the person who is severe, and who frowns when things are done wrong, may have known the stereotype that men are more often severe but may have been expressing disagreement with the stereotype.

Another noteworthy contribution to the cross-cultural literature on knowledge of gender stereotypes, although of lesser scope, is the research by Zammuner (1982, 1987, 1993). As mentioned earlier, Zammuner incorporated knowledge of both traits and activities in her cross-cultural studies done in Italy and the Netherlands. Children (ages 5 through 12) assigned traits (such as affectionate or absent-minded) and activities (to reproach or to cure) as descriptive of either one or both sexes, by marking a sheet in response to printed cards. The application of multidimensional scaling techniques for Dutch and Italian children separately resulted in different solutions for the children of different nationalities. For example, the trait "lively" was highly associated with males for Italian children, but was a gender neutral term for Dutch children. These results are a good illustration of how gender stereotypes may differ cross-culturally, even within Western Europe.

Further cross-cultural research might address the correlates, antecedents, and consequences of knowledge of stereotypes. At least two possibilities for the factors contributing to stereotype knowledge are suggested by the literature. In a Canadian study, Serbin et al. (1993) provided evidence that knowledge of gender stereotypes is related to the child's general level of cognitive development. In a cross-cultural study in Cambridge, England, and Budapest, Hungary, children's stereotype knowledge was related to parents' gender attitudes and father's gender-typed behavior, in that the less the father engaged in nontraditional behaviors and the more traditional the parents' attitudes the greater the stereotype knowledge of children (Turner & Gervai, 1995).

In sum, the extant literature suggests that knowledge of gender stereotypes increases with age (at least until age 6 or 8) internationally (Williams & Best, 1990a). There appears to be some overlap of the gender stereotypes cross-culturally (Williams & Best, 1990a) as well as cultural variation in the structure of the stereotypes (Zammuner, 1987, 1993).

What is missing from the cross-cultural literature on knowledge of gender stereotypes is information on the cultural variables that are related to variations in the content of gender stereotypes and to the rate of development of knowledge of stereotypes. In addition, cross-cultural investigations of subtypes of gender stereotypes and their relation to the overall stereotypes (e.g., Deaux & Kite, 1993; Eckes, 1994), and studies of the cross-cultural development of flexibility in gender stereotyping (e.g., Katz & Ksansnak, 1994; Trautner, 1992), are few or absent.

## Adolescents' Gender-Related Ideals

With Deborah Stiles and other collaborators, I have been involved in studying adolescents' views of the ideal man and the ideal woman in cross-cultural perspective. In the basic task, participants rate the importance of 10 characteristics for the randomly assigned ideal man or woman and then draw a picture of the ideal person doing something (Stiles, Gibbons, Hardardottir, & Schnellmann, 1987; Stiles, Gibbons, & Schnellmann, 1990). The gender ideals of adolescents reflect not only their personal future aspirations as women and men (e.g., Gibbons, Stiles, Lynn, Collins, & Phylaktou, 1993) but also their culture's perspectives of appropriate gender roles and traits (Block, 1973). According to the distinctions presented earlier the ratings represent attitudes regarding women and men in general (not specifically the self), they are evaluative rather than descriptive, and they address traits rather than roles or activities. The drawings depict activities.

The findings have revealed many similarities among adolescents' views internationally. In Guatemala, Iceland, Mexico, the Netherlands, Puerto Rico, Singapore, Spain, and the midwestern United States adolescents rated the characteristic "she (or he) is kind and honest" as the most important trait for the ideal person to possess (Gibbons, Bradford, & Stiles, 1989; Gibbons, Brusi-Figueroa, & Fisher, 1997; Gibbons, Stiles, & Morton, 1989; Gibbons, Stiles, Schnellmann, & Morales-Hidalgo, 1990; Stiles et al., 1987; Stiles et al., 1990; Tay & Gibbons, 1998). Those findings were consistent with the results of a cross-national study of adolescent self-image (Offer, Ostrov, Howard, & Atkinson, 1988) in 10 countries—Australia, Bangladesh, Hungary, Israel, Italy, Japan, Taiwan, Turkey, West Germany, and the United States. Offer et al. found that the large majority of adolescent participants (ages 13 to 19) in all countries studied endorsed the values of helpfulness and truthfulness.

The widespread findings also contradicted the stereotype of adolescents as concerned with popularity and wealth, in that having a lot of money and being popular were given low ratings of importance in all samples (Gibbons, Bradford, & Stiles, 1989; Gibbons, Hamby, & Dennis, 1997; Gibbons, Stiles, & Morton, 1989; Gibbons et al., 1990; Stiles et al., 1987; Stiles et al., 1990; Tay & Gibbons, 1998).

In terms of cross-cultural variation, the gender-related ideals of adolescents have been linked to dimensions identified in the most extensive cross-national study ever undertaken (Hofstede, 1980, 1983, 1991, 1998). Hofstede surveyed the work values of IBM employees in more than 50 countries worldwide. Through factor analysis, he identified several dimensions on which cultures varied, including those he named individualism–collectivism (IC) and masculinity–femininity (MAS).

Individualism–collectivism, the extent to which the individual conscious-ness is governed by "I" versus "we," has been studied extensively as a cultural value and has been linked to a large number of variables (e.g., Kagitçibasi, 1997; Triandis, 1995). Adolescents' ratings of the qualities deemed to be desirable in the opposite-sex ideal have been shown to be related to this dimension. In a study of international students from 44 countries studying in the Netherlands, students from more individualistic countries attributed greater importance to the ideal being "fun" and "sexy" than did students from collectivist countries (Gibbons, Stiles, & Morton, 1989). In another study of adolescents living in four countries, similar findings were revealed (Gibbons, Richter, Wiley, & Stiles, 1996), in that adolescents from the more individualistic countries (Iceland and the United States) to a greater extent than students from the more collectivist countries (Guatemala and Mexico) ranked "fun" and "sexy" as important. These results are also in accord with the large-scale study by Buss et al. (1990) on the qualities desired in the ideal mate. Among university students from 37 countries, having an exciting personality was considered to be more impor-tant in the ideal mate by those from individualist countries.

Other aspects of adolescents' gender-related values may be linked with another of the dimensions identified by Hofstede (1980, 1983, 1998), that is, masculinity–femininity. The masculinity pole of the MAS (originally called Social/Ego) dimension represents the extent to which employees endorsed the importance of earnings, recognition, advancement, challenge, and use of skills and de-emphasized the relationship with the manager, cooperation, living in a desirable area, and security in the ideal job. Hofstede (1998) also proposed that the dimension is related to gender roles. He wrote that in feminine cultures, "women's liberation means that men and women should take equal shares both at home and at work," whereas in masculine cultures, "women's liberation means that women should be admitted to positions hitherto occupied only by men" (Hofstede, 1998, p. 17).

For a presentation at the 1994 annual meeting of the International Association for Cross-Cultural Psychology we looked again at some of the roles depicted in drawings of the ideal man and ideal woman in terms of their possible relation to the masculinity–femininity dimension (Gibbons, Stiles, Wood, & Biekert, 1994). Specifically, we reanalyzed data from nine countries, including those with high MAS scores according to Hofstede (1983)—Mexico, the Philippines, the United States, and India—and those with low (feminine) MAS scores such as Spain, Guatemala, the Netherlands, and Norway. Although the MAS score of Iceland had not been determined, we categorized it as "feminine" based on cultural and historical similarities to other "feminine" countries. Adolescent participants (12 to 15 years old, attending schools in urban areas) had been randomly assigned the ideal man or ideal woman version of the questionnaire. Among other measures, drawings of the ideal were scored for gender-role stereotyping of the depicted activity. Based on collaborators' comments, or those of cultural informants, the scoring for gender typing of the activity was adjusted to the local culture. For example, in Guatemala women traditionally weave using back strap looms, and men weave with foot looms. Thus, drawings of women depicted weaving on back strap looms were scored as traditional and those on foot looms as nontraditional. The scoring of the traditionality of the role had been shown to have an interrater reliability of .73 (Stiles et al., 1990).

The results showed that although there were differences by country for the amount of gender-role stereotyping in the drawings with some samples showing a great deal of gender-role stereotyping (e.g., Guatemala, Norway, and India) and others little (e.g., Netherlands, Spain, and the Philippines), the amount of stereotyping was not overall related to the MAS index.

However, when the percentage of drawings showing the ideal person in a nontraditional or a dual role was examined, a pattern emerged (see Fig. 13.1). In masculine countries, women were more likely to be drawn in nontraditional roles than were men. That is, women were depicted as successful business executives, presidents of companies, and managers. In feminine countries, men were more often drawn in nontraditional roles than were women. That is, men were drawn caring for children or engaging in housework. Those differences were significant in the United States, Iceland, and Mexico. There were trends toward significant differences in India and Norway. To summarize those results: In the masculine countries of Mexico, the United States, and India, the ideal woman was more often than the ideal man drawn in a nontraditional role. In the feminine countries of Norway and Iceland, the ideal man was more often than the ideal woman shown in a nontraditional role (Gibbons et al., 1994). In sum, cultural values appeared to interact with gender roles, in that persons were more likely to be shown in the opposite gender's traditional roles when those roles were consistent with cultural values.

There are many limitations to the studies of adolescents' views of the ideal woman and man. Specifically, the samples were samples of convenience and differed in a number of ways. The age range was too narrow to examine age-related changes. Finally, the cultural variables of IC and MAS were not directly assessed, so individual differences related to those dimensions within countries cannot be addressed. What has been revealed are some cross-cultural similarities in adolescents' ideals as well as some indications of gender-role ideals that vary in systematic ways.

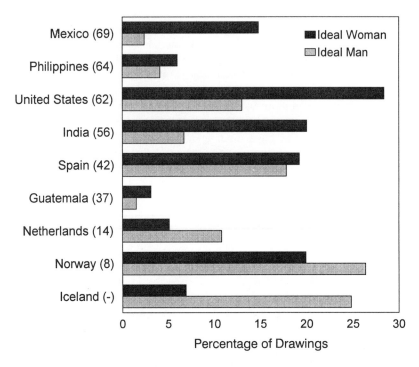

FIG. 13.1 Percentage of drawings of the ideal woman or man in a nontraditional role by country masculinity score (MAS according to Hofstede, 1983, in parantheses after country name). *Note.* From *Cultural Masculinity/Femininity and Adolescents' Drawings of the Ideal Man and Ideal Woman*, by J. L. Gibbons, D. A. Stiles, Y. Wood, and E. Biekert, 1994, paper presented in G. Hofstede (Chair), Masculinity/Femininity as a Cultural Dimension: 12th Congress of the International Association for Cross-Cultural Psychology, Pamplona, Spain. Used with permission.

# CONCLUSIONS

In this chapter, the potential for cross-cultural research in increasing the understanding of gender development has been underscored. Three areas of investigation were reviewed: the development of gender constancy and gender identity, the acquisition of stereotype knowledge, and adolescents' gender-related ideals. Other areas such as the development of gender schemas and gender role ideologies were omitted, either because of the scarcity of information or because they had been discussed in other recent reviews (e.g., Best & Williams, 1993, 1997). Two possible sources of children's gender-related thinking—gender segregation in children's play groups (Maccoby, 1998) and characteristic family interaction styles that are father-controlled, mother-controlled, or egalitarian (Wozniak, 1993)—could not be reviewed because of a scarcity of cross-cultural data.

Gender constancy appears to follow a developmental sequence that is widespread cross-culturally, although the ages at which the stages are achieved may vary. There may also be pancultural patterns in the development of knowledge about gender stereotypes as well as some overlap in the content of stereotypes. Finally, adolescents living in contemporary societies are more likely to endorse nontraditional roles for women and men when those roles are consistent with other cultural values.

Future cross-cultural research that acknowledges and addresses the conceptual issues outlined here is essential to explore the range of variation in gender development and to identify the antecedents, correlates, and consequences of gender development for individuals. Among the ways that culture may influence gender development is that culture itself comprises, in part, beliefs, norms, ideologies, and customs related to gender. In that sense, the end points of gender development are indisputably culture-specific. In addition, cultural traditions may provide settings that facilitate particular kinds of gender-related learning and development. Finally, the perspective of cultural psychology would suggest that gender beliefs and gender differentiated behaviors are engrained in intrapersonal processes on account of their derivation from interpersonal dialogue. The identification of the processes of development of gender-related beliefs and their relation to other developmental processes is an area that is ripe for further research.

# ACKNOWLEDGMENTS

The author would like to thank Deborah Stiles for her collaboration in many of the studies reviewed here, Lisa Kindleberger for pointing out the gender constancy literature, Paula Juelich for bibliographic searches, Karla Scott for comments on an earlier version of the manuscript, and the two editors Thomas Eckes and Hanns Martin Trautner for their helpful suggestions. The preparation of this chapter was supported, in part, by the Beaumont Faculty Development Fund of Saint Louis University.

# REFERENCES

Albert, A. A., & Porter, J. R. (1986). Children's gender role stereotypes: A comparison of the United States and South Africa. *Journal of Cross-Cultural Psychology, 17*, 45–65.

Alfieri, T., Ruble, D. N., & Higgins, E. T. (1996). Gender stereotypes during adolescence: Developmental changes and the transition to junior high school. *Developmental Psychology, 32*, 1129–1137.

410 GIBBONS

Beere, C. A. (1990). *Gender roles: A handbook of tests and measures.* Westport, CT: Greenwood.

Bem, S. L. (1974). The measurement of psychological androgyny. *Journal of Consulting and Clinical Psychology, 42,* 155–162.

Bem, S. L. (1989). Genital knowledge and gender constancy in preschool children. *Child Development, 60,* 649–662.

Bem, S. L. (1993). *The lenses of gender: Transforming the debate on sexual inequality.* New Haven, CT: Yale University Press.

Best, D. L., & Williams, J. E. (1993). A cross-cultural viewpoint. In A. E. Beall & R. J. Sternberg (Eds.), *The psychology of gender* (pp. 215–248). New York: Guilford.

Best, D. L., & Williams, J. E. (1997). Sex, gender, and culture. In J. W. Berry, M. H. Segall, & C. Kagitçibasi (Eds.), *Handbook of cross-cultural psychology* (2nd ed., Vol. 3, pp. 163–212). Boston: Allyn & Bacon.

Best, D. L., Williams, J. E., Cloud, J. M., Davis, S. W., Robertson, L. S., Edwards, J. R., Giles, H., & Fowles, J. (1977). Development of sex-trait stereotypes among young children in the United States, England, and Ireland. *Child Development, 48,* 1375–1384.

Bhana, K. (1984). The development of gender understanding in children. *South African Journal of Psychology, 14,* 10–13.

Bhogle, S. (1996). Multidimensionality in gender typing of Indian children. *Journal of the Indian Academy of Applied Psychology, 22,* 87–95.

Bhogle, S., & Seethalakshmi, R. (1992). Development of gender constancy in Indian children. *Journal of the Indian Academy of Applied Psychology, 18,* 49–56.

Bigler, R. S. (1997). Conceptual and methodological issues in the measurement of children's sex typing. *Psychology of Women Quarterly, 21,* 53–70.

Block, J. H. (1973). Conceptions of sex roles: Some cross-cultural and longitudinal perspectives. *American Psychologist, 28,* 512–526.

Buss, D. M., Abbott, M., Angleitner, A., Asherian, A., Biaggio, A., Blanco-Villasenor, A., Bruchon-Schweitzer, M., Ch'u, H.-Y., Czapinski, J., Deraad, B., Ekehammar, B., Lohamy, N. E., Fioravanti, M., Georgas, J., Gjerde, P., Guttman, R., Hazan, F., Iwawaki, S., Janakiramaiah, N., Khosroshani, F., Kreitler, S., Lachenicht, L., Lee, M., Liik, K., Little, B., Mika, S., Moadel-Shahid, M., Moane, G., Montero, M., Mundy-Castle, A. C., Niit, T., Nsenduluka, E., Pienkowski, R., Pirttila-Backman, A.-M., Ponce de Leon, J., Rousseau, J., Runco, M. A., Safir, M. P., Samuels, C., Sanitioso, R., Serpell, R., Smid, N., Spencer, C., Tadinac, M., Todorova, E. N., Troland, K., Van Den Brande, L., Van Heck, G., Van Langenhove, L., & Yang, K.-S. (1990). International preferences in selecting mates: A study of 37 cultures. *Journal of Cross-Cultural Psychology, 21,* 5–47.

Campbell, D. T. (1988). *Methodology and epistemology for social science.* Chicago: University of Chicago Press.

Cheung Mui-ching, F. (1986). Development of gender stereotype. *Educational Research Journal, 1,* 68–73.

Chia, R. C., Allred, L. J., & Jerzak, P. A. (1997). Attitudes toward women in Taiwan and China: Current status, problems, and suggestions for future research. *Psychology of Women Quarterly, 21,* 137–150.

Cooper, C. R., & Denner, J. (1998). Theories linking culture and psychology: Universal and community-specific processes. *Annual Review of Psychology, 49,* 559–584.

Dasen, P. R. (1994). Culture and cognitive development from a Piagetian perspective. In W. J. Lonner & R. Malpass (Eds.), *Psychology and culture* (pp. 145–150). Needham Heights, MA: Allyn & Bacon.

Deaux, K., & Kite, M. E. (1993). Gender stereotypes. In F. L. Denmark & M. A. Paludi (Eds.), *Psychology of women: A handbook of issues and theories* (pp. 107–139). Westport, CT: Greenwood.

De Lisi, R., & Gallagher, A. M. (1991). Understanding of gender stability and constancy in Argentinean children. *Merrill-Palmer Quarterly, 37*, 483–502.

Díaz-Guerrero, R. (1975). *Psychology of the Mexican: Culture and personality.* Austin: University of Texas Press.

Dickerscheid, J. D., Schwarz, P. M., Noir, S., & El-Taliawy, M. S. T. (1988). Gender concept development of preschool-aged children in the United States and Egypt. *Sex Roles, 18,* 669– 677.

Eaton, W. O., & Von Bargen, D. (1981). Asynchronous development of gender understanding in preschool children. *Child Development, 52,* 1020–1027.

Eckes, T. (1994). Explorations in gender cognition: Content and structure of female and male subtypes. *Social Cognition, 12,* 37–60.

Edelbrock, C., & Sugawara, A. I. (1978). Acquisition of sex-typed preferences in preschool-aged children. *Developmental Psychology, 14,* 614–623.

Emmerich, W., Goldman, K. S., Kirsh, B., & Sharabany, R. (1977). Evidence for a transitional phase in the development of gender constancy. *Child Development, 48,* 930–936.

Fiske, A. P., Kitayama, S., Markus, H. R., & Nisbett, R. E. (1998). The cultural matrix of social psychology. In D. T. Gilbert, S. T. Fiske, & G. Lindzey (Eds.), *The handbook of social psychology* (4th ed., Vol. 2, pp. 915–981). Boston: McGraw-Hill.

Galambos, N. L., Petersen, A. C., Richards, M., & Gitelson, I. B. (1985). The Attitudes Toward Women Scale for Adolescents (AWSA): A study of reliability and validity. *Sex Roles, 13,* 343–356.

Gana, K. (1995). Androgynie psychologique et valeurs socio-cognitives des dimensions du concept de soi [Psychological androgyny and sociocognitive dimensions of the self-concept]. *Cahiers Internationaux de Psychologie Sociale, 25,* 27–43.

Gibbons, J. L., Bradford, R., & Stiles, D. A. (1989). Madrid adolescents express an interest in gender roles and work possibilities. *Journal of Early Adolescence, 9,* 125–141.

Gibbons, J. L., Brusi-Figueroa, R., & Fisher, S. L. (1997). Gender-related ideals of Puerto Rican adolescents: Gender and school context. *Journal of Early Adolescence, 17,* 349–370.

Gibbons, J. L., & Fisher, S. L. (1996). El rol sexual como factor de estrés en la adolescencia [Sex roles as a stress factor in adolescence]. In J. Buendía (Ed.), *Psicopatología en niños y adolescentes* [Psychopathology in children and adolescents] (pp. 217–246). Madrid, Spain: Ediciones Pirámide.

Gibbons, J. L., Hamby, B. A., & Dennis, W. D. (1997). Researching gender-role ideologies internationally and cross-culturally. *Psychology of Women Quarterly, 21,* 151–170.

Gibbons, J. L., Lynn, M., Stiles, D. A., Jerez de Berducido, E., Richter, R., Walker, K., & Wiley, D. (1993). Guatemalan, Filipino, and U.S. adolescents' images of women as office workers and homemakers. *Psychology of Women Quarterly, 17,* 373–388.

Gibbons, J. L., Richter, R. R., Wiley, D. C., & Stiles, D. A. (1996). Adolescents' opposite-sex ideal in four countries. *Journal of Social Psychology, 136,* 531–537.

Gibbons, J. L., Stiles, D. A., Lynn, M., Collins, H., & Phylaktou, P. (1993). Matching future careers to possible selves: Adolescent girls' occupational alternatives in cross-national perspective. *Comenius, 52,* 390–409.

Gibbons, J. L., Stiles, D. A., & Morton, C. (1989). Conceptions of the ideal person by international students in the Netherlands. *Journal of Social Psychology, 129,* 859–861.

Gibbons, J. L., Stiles, D. A., Schnellmann, J. G., & Morales-Hidalgo, I. (1990). Images of work, gender, and social commitment among Guatemalan adolescents. *Journal of Early Adolescence, 10,* 89–103.

Gibbons, J. L., Stiles, D. A., & Shkodriani, G. M. (1991). Adolescents' attitudes toward family and gender roles: An international comparison. *Sex Roles, 25,* 625–643.

Gibbons, J. L., Stiles, D. A., Wood, Y., & Biekert, E. (1994, July). *Cultural masculinity/femininity and adolescents' drawings of the ideal man and ideal woman.*

Paper presented in G. Hofstede (Chair), Masculinity/femininity as a cultural dimension: 12th Congress of the International Association for Cross-Cultural Psychology, Pamplona, Spain.

Gough, H. G., & Heilbrun, A. B., Jr. (1980). *The Adjective Check List manual.* Palo Alto, CA: Consulting Psychologists Press.

Gouze, K. R., & Nadelman, L. (1980). Constancy of gender identity for self and others in children between the ages of three and seven. *Child Development, 51,* 275–278.

Greenfield, P. M. (1993). *Historical change and cognitive change: A two-decade follow-up study in Zinacantan, a Mayan community of Southern Mexico.* Paper presented in P. Greenfield (Chair), Sylvia Scribner Memorial Symosium: Culture, Activity, and Development, Society for Research in Child Development, New Orleans, LA.

Greenfield, P. M. (1997). Culture as process: Empirical methods for cultural psychology. In J. W. Berry, Y. H. Poortinga, & J. Pandey (Eds.), *Handbook of cross-cultural psychology* (2nd ed., Vol. 1, pp. 301–346). Boston: Allyn & Bacon.

Hofstede, G. (1980). *Culture's consequences: International differences in work-related values.* Beverly Hills, CA: Sage.

Hofstede, G. (1983). Dimensions of national cultures in fifty countries and three regions. In J. B. Deregowski, S. Dziurawiec, & R. C. Annis (Eds.), *Expiscations in cross-cultural psychology* (pp. 335–355). Lisse, Netherlands: Swets & Zeitlinger.

Hofstede, G. (1991). *Cultures and organizations: Software of the mind.* London: McGraw-Hill.

Hofstede, G. (1998). *Masculinity and femininity: The taboo dimension of national cultures.* Thousand Oaks, CA: Sage.

Kagitçibasi, C. (1997). Individualism and collectivism. In J. W. Berry, M. H. Segall, & C. Kagitçibasi (Eds.), *Handbook of cross-cultural psychology* (2nd ed., Vol. 3, pp. 1–50). Boston: Allyn & Bacon.

Kaschak, E., & Sharratt, S. (1984). A Latin American Sex Role Inventory. *Cross-Cultural Psychology Bulletin, 18,* 3–6.

Kashima, Y., Yamaguchi, S., Kim, U., Choi, S.-C., Gelfand, M. J., & Yuki, M. (1995). Culture, gender and self: A perspective from individualism–collectivism research. *Journal of Personality and Social Psychology, 69,* 925–937.

Katz, P. A., & Ksansnak, K. R. (1994). Developmental aspects of gender role flexibility and traditionality in middle childhood and adolescence. *Developmental Psychology, 30,* 272–282.

Keyes, S. (1984). Measuring sex-role stereotypes: Attitudes among Hong Kong Chinese adolescents and the development of the Chinese Sex-Role Inventory. *Sex Roles, 10,* 129–140.

Kohlberg, L. (1966). A cognitive-developmental analysis of children's sex-role concepts and attitudes. In E. E. Maccoby (Ed.), *The development of sex differences* (pp. 82–173). Stanford, CA: Stanford University Press.

Lara-Cantú, M. A., & Navarro-Arias, R. (1987). Self-descriptions of Mexican college students in response to the Bem Sex-Role Inventory and other sex role items. *Journal of Cross-Cultural Psychology, 18,* 331–344.

Leonard, S. P., & Archer, J. (1989). A naturalistic investigation of gender constancy in three- to four-year-old children. *British Journal of Developmental Psychology, 7,* 341–346.

Lobel, T. E., & Menashri, J. (1993). Relations of conceptions of gender-role transgressions and gender constancy to gender-typed toy preferences. *Developmental Psychology, 29,* 150–155.

Lonner, W. J., & Adamopoulos, J. (1997). Culture as antecedent to behavior. In J. W. Berry, Y. H. Poortinga, & J. Pandey (Eds.), *Handbook of cross-cultural psychology* (2nd ed., Vol. 1, pp. 43–83). Boston: Allyn & Bacon.

Lonner, W. J., & Berry, J. W. (Eds.). (1986). *Field methods in cross-cultural research*. Beverly Hills, CA: Sage.

Maccoby, E. E. (1998). *The two sexes: Growing up apart, coming together*. Cambridge, MA: Harvard University Press.

Marcus, D. E., & Overton, W. F. (1978). The development of cognitive gender constancy and sex role preferences. *Child Development, 49*, 434–444.

Markus, H. R., Kitayama, S., & Heiman, R. J. (1996). Culture and "basic" psychological principles. In E. T. Higgins & A. W. Kruglanski (Eds.), *Social psychology: Handbook of basic principles* (pp. 857–913). New York: Guilford.

Martin, C. L., & Halverson, C. F. (1983). Gender constancy: A methodological and theoretical analysis. *Sex Roles, 9*, 775–790.

McConaghy, M. J. (1979). Gender permanence and the genital basis of gender: Stages in the development of constancy of gender identity. *Child Development, 50*, 1223–1226.

Miller, J. G. (1997). Theoretical issues in cultural psychology. In J. W. Berry, Y. H. Poortinga, & J. Pandey (Eds.), *Handbook of cross-cultural psychology* (2nd ed., Vol. 1, pp. 85–128). Boston: Allyn & Bacon.

Munroe, R. H., Shimmin, H. S., & Munroe, R. L. (1984). Gender understanding and sex role preference in four cultures. *Developmental Psychology, 20*, 673–682.

Munroe, R. L., & Munroe, R. H. (1991). Results of comparative field studies. *Behavior Science Research, 25*, 23–54.

Neto, F., Williams, J. E., & Widner, S. C. (1991). Portuguese children's knowledge of sex stereotypes: Effects of age, gender, and socioeconomic status. *Journal of Cross-Cultural Psychology, 22*, 376–388.

Newman, L. S., Cooper, J., & Ruble, D. N. (1995). Gender and computers: II. The interactive effects of knowledge and constancy on gender-stereotyped attitudes. *Sex Roles, 33*, 325–351.

Offer, D., Ostrov, E., & Howard, K. I. (1982). *The Offer Self-Image for Adolescents: A manual*. Chicago: Michael Reese Hospital and Medical Center.

Offer, D., Ostrov, E., Howard, K. I., & Atkinson, R. (1988). *The teenage world: Adolescents' self-image in ten countries*. New York: Plenum.

Pettinati, H. M., Franks, V., Wade, J. H., & Kogan, L. G. (1987). Distinguishing the role of eating disturbance from depression in the sex role self-perceptions of anorexic and bulimic inpatients. *Journal of Abnormal Psychology, 96*, 280–282.

Pleck, J. H., Sonenstein, F. L., & Ku, L. C. (1993). Masculinity ideology and its correlates. In S. Oskamp & M. Costanzo (Eds.), *Gender issues in contemporary society* (pp. 85–110). Newbury Park, CA: Sage.

Rabinowitz, V. C., & Sechzer, J. A. (1993). Feminist perspectives on research methods. In F. L. Denmark & M. A. Paludi (Eds.), *Psychology of women: A handbook of issues and theories* (pp. 23–66). Westport, CT: Greenwood.

Ruble, D. N., & Ruble, T. L. (1982). Sex stereotypes. In A. G. Miller (Ed.), *In the eye of the beholder: Contemporary issues in stereotyping* (pp. 188–252). New York: Praeger.

Saxe, G. B. (1991). *Culture and cognitive development: Studies in mathematical understanding*. Hillsdale, NJ: Lawrence Erlbaum Associates.

Schlegel, A., & Barry, H. III. (1991). *Adolescence: An anthropological inquiry*. New York: The Free Press.

Schneider-Düker, M., & Kohler, A. (1988). Die Erfassung von Geschlechtsrollen: Ergebnisse zur deutschen Neukonstruktion des Bem Sex-Role-Inventory [The assessment of sex roles: Results of a German version of the Bem Sex-Role Inventory]. *Diagnostica, 34*, 256–270.

Serbin, L. A., Powlishta, K. K., & Gulko, J. (1993). The development of sex typing in middle childhood. *Monographs of the Society for Research in Child Development, 58* (2, Serial No. 232).

Siegal, M., & Robinson, J. (1987). Order effects in children's gender-constancy responses. *Developmental Psychology, 23*, 283–286.

Signorella, M. L., Bigler, R. S., & Liben, L. S. (1993). Developmental differences in children's gender schemata about others: A meta-analytic review. *Developmental Review, 13*, 147–183.

Slaby, R. G., & Frey, K. S. (1975). Development of gender constancy and selective attention to same-sex models. *Child Development, 46*, 849–856.

Spence, J. T., Helmreich, R. L., & Stapp, J. (1974). The Personal Attributes Questionnaire: A measure of sex-role stereotypes and masculinity–femininity. *JSAS Catalog of Selected Documents in Psychology, 4*, 43–44 (Ms. 617).

Stangor, C., & Ruble, D. N. (1989). Differential influences of gender schemata and gender constancy on children's information processing and behavior. *Social Cognition, 7*, 353–372.

Sterzi, G. (1989). Ethnicity, socialization, and academic achievement of Italian-American college students at the City University of New York. *Dissertation Abstracts International, 50* (05), 2209B.

Stiles, D. A., Gibbons, J. L., Hardardottir, S., & Schnellmann, J. (1987). The ideal man or woman as described by young adolescents in Iceland and the United States. *Sex Roles, 17*, 313–320.

Stiles, D. A., Gibbons, J. L., & Schnellmann, J. G. (1990). Opposite-sex ideal in the U.S.A. and Mexico as perceived by young adolescents. *Journal of Cross-Cultural Psychology, 21*, 180–199.

Tarrier, N., & Gomes, L. F. (1981). Knowledge of sex-trait stereotypes: Effects of age, sex, and social class on Brazilian children. *Journal of Cross-Cultural Psychology, 12*, 81–93.

Tay, L. S., & Gibbons, J. L. (1998). Attitudes toward gender roles among adolescents in Singapore. *Cross-Cultural Research, 32*, 257–278.

Trautner, H. M. (1992). The development of sex-typing in children: A longitudinal analysis. *German Journal of Psychology, 16*, 183–199.

Trautner, H. M., Helbing, N., Sahm, W. B., & Lohaus, A. (1989, April). *Beginning awareness–rigidity–flexibility: A longitudinal analysis of sex-role stereotyping in 4- to 10-year-old children.* Paper presented at the biennial meeting of the Society for Research in Child Development, Kansas City, MO.

Triandis, H. C. (1994). *Culture and social behavior.* New York: McGraw-Hill.

Triandis, H. C. (1995). *Individualism and collectivism.* Boulder, CO: Westview.

Turner, P. J., & Gervai, J. (1995). A multidimensional study of gender typing in preschool children and their parents: Personality, attitudes, preferences, behavior, and cultural differences. *Developmental Psychology, 31*, 759–772.

Unger, R. K. (1979). Toward a redefinition of sex and gender. *American Psychologist, 34*, 1085–1094.

Unger, R. K., & Crawford, M. (1996). *Women and gender: A feminist psychology* (2nd ed.). New York: McGraw-Hill.

Urberg, K. A. (1979). Sex role conceptualizations in adolescents and adults. *Developmental Psychology, 15*, 90–92.

Van de Vijver, F. J. R., & Leung, K. (1997). Methods and data analysis of comparative research. In J. W. Berry, Y. H. Poortinga, & J. Pandey (Eds.), *Handbook of cross-cultural psychology* (2nd ed., Vol. 1, pp. 257–300). Boston: Allyn & Bacon.

Van Ijzendoorn, M. H. (1990). Developments in cross-cultural research on attachment: Some methodological notes. *Human Development, 33*, 3–9.

Vygotsky, L. S. (1981). The genesis of higher mental functions. In J. V. Wertsch (Ed.), *The concept of activity in Soviet psychology* (pp. 144–188). Armonk, NY: Sharpe.

Ward, C. (1985). Sex trait stereotypes in Malaysian children. *Sex Roles, 12*, 35–45.

Ward, C. (1990). Gender stereotyping in Singaporean children. *International Journal of Behavioral Development, 13*, 309–315.

Ward, C., & Sethi, R. R. (1986). Cross-cultural validation of the Bem Sex-Role Inventory: Malaysian and South Indian research, *Journal of Cross-Cultural Psychology, 17*, 300–314.

Wehren, A., & De Lisi, R. (1983). The development of gender understanding: Judgments and explanations. *Child Development, 54*, 1568–1578.

Wertsch, J. V., del Rio, P., & Alvarez, A. (Eds.). (1995). *Sociocultural studies of mind.* New York: Cambridge University Press.

Whiting, B. B., & Edwards, C. P. (1988). *Children of different worlds: The formation of social behavior.* Cambridge, MA: Harvard University Press.

Williams, J. E., & Best, D. L. (1990a). *Measuring sex stereotypes: A multination study* (Rev. ed.). Newbury Park, CA: Sage.

Williams, J. E., & Best, D. L. (1990b). *Sex and psyche: Gender and self viewed cross-culturally.* Newbury Park, CA: Sage.

Wilson, D., McMaster, J., Greenspan, R., Mboyi, L., Ncube, T., & Sibanda, B. (1990). Cross-cultural validation of the Bem Sex Role Inventory in Zimbabwe. *Personality and Individual Differences, 11*, 651–656.

Wozniak, R. H. (1993). Co-constructive metatheory for psychology: Implications for an analysis of families as specific social contexts for development. In R. H. Wozniak & K. W. Fischer (Eds.), *Development in context: Acting and thinking in specific environments* (pp. 77–91). Hillsdale, NJ: Lawrence Erlbaum Associates.

Yee, M., & Brown, R. (1994). The development of gender differentiation in young children. *British Journal of Social Psychology, 33*, 183–196.

Zammuner, V. L. (1982). Sex role stereotypes in Italian children. *International Journal of Psychology, 17*, 43–63.

Zammuner, V. L. (1987). Children's sex-role stereotypes: A cross-cultural analysis. In P. Shaver & C. Hendrick (Eds.), *Review of personality and social psychology: 7. Sex and gender* (pp. 272–293). Newbury Park, CA: Sage.

Zammuner, V. L. (1993). Perception of male and female personality attributes and behaviors by Dutch children. *Bulletin of the Psychonomic Society, 31*, 87–90.

# V

# CONCLUSION

# 14

# Putting Gender Development Into Context: Problems and Prospects

Hanns M. Trautner
*University of Wuppertal*

Thomas Eckes
*University of Dresden*

In this book we have set out to overcome the compartmentalization of gender research into developmental and social psychological approaches. Rather than simply adding the two, we have aimed at an integrative account focusing on the dynamic interrelation between developmental change and social influence. To accomplish this task, we have chosen to adopt a multidimensional, multilevel conceptual framework that is based on the general view of gender as a social category. Thus, our main interest has not been in the classical question of sex differences research, asking whether, and how much, males and females differ in a number of psychological variables, but rather in the questions of how, when, and why it makes a difference to be male or female—seeking answers at the individual, the interpersonal, the group, and the cultural level.

Building on the premise that gender phenomena are just as much subject to developmental change as they are subject to social influence, the proposed framework draws attention to the mutual dependencies that exist between three broad dimensions of gender typing. These dimensions refer to content areas, developmental features or constructs, and levels of analysis. In addition, to account for processes of change over time, each cell in the matrix is implied to have its own, distinct temporal properties. We consider organizing the multitude of gender issues in a comprehensive taxonomy instrumental in planning studies the results of which may contribute to dissolving disciplinary lines.

In this chapter we want to summarize and review what appears to us to be significant advances in theorizing and research and point to open questions and directions for future research.

# ADVANCES IN THEORIZING AND RESEARCH

Looking back on the preceding 12 chapters, two main themes can be identified. First, evolutionary constraints, environmental input, cognitive processes, and social roles all seem to converge in pulling an individual's concepts or beliefs, sense of identity or self-perception, preferences, and behavioral enactment into a gendered direction. Second, gender processes cannot be adequately understood without making reference to their developmental history and to their permanent modulation through various social forces; that is, gender-related cognitions, attitudes, and behaviors change over time and interact with features of social contexts. In other words, developmental change and social influence do not merely coexist, rather they are viewed as fundamentally interdependent, as dynamically building on each other. Both themes, as well as their various ramifications that have been examined in the chapters of this book, provide a promising perspective on coming to terms with the bewilderingly large spectrum of sex differences and similarities that can be observed across context, time, and culture. It is to these themes that we now turn.

## Convergent Impact of Evolutionary Constraints, Environmental Input, Cognitive Processes, and Social Roles

Each of the four chapters addressing the theoretical foundations of an integrative approach (see part II, this volume) highlights a distinct set of factors accounting for developmental change and stability in gender differentiation. At first sight, each set of factors may seem sufficient to produce many of the gender effects identified in the literature; in addition, these factors seem to be only loosely, if at all, interconnected. Yet, from a more general point of view, one is struck by the underlying convergence of the various postulated forces pushing the individual into a gendered direction. Rather than being in conflict with each other, deeply rooted evolutionary forces, socialization processes, cognitive activities, and gender-typed social roles seem to complement one another in fostering gender differentiation.

Thus, gender differentiation seems to be a prime example of an *overdetermined* psychological process (Fagot, 1995). Even slight differences that are brought about by some factor in isolation are likely to become accentuated by some other factor or a combination of factors. For example, sex differences in competitive behavior displayed by preschool-age children that can be accounted for by higher degrees of same-sex competition in males' evolutionary history will be reinforced by expectations concerning competitive behavior in males and females, parents' differential encouragement of their sons and daughters to engage in competitive or cooperative social interaction, the self-perception of a masculine or feminine interpersonal orientation, and so forth. The impact one factor has on some other factor or set of factors may even take catalytic forms; that is, the presence of a particular factor is prerequiste for another factor to exert influence. Ultimately, the complex, yet convergent, interplay of various psychological and social forces may lead to the manifestation of substantial differences between the sexes in particular behavioral or cognitive domains (e.g., concerning males' and females' tendency to choose occupations requiring competitiveness or cooperativeness for being successful at work). It should also be noted that initially small gender effects may accumulate over time, that is, each factor can by itself gain in importance across an individual's life course inasmuch as boys and girls have increasingly different learning experiences (see Eisenberg, Martin, & Fabes, 1996).

As holds for the issue of psychological differences between individuals in general, the crucially important question is not "what" makes the difference or "how much" evolutionary, sociocultural, or cognitive influences per se contribute to the phenomenon under study. Rather, the question to be asked is how exactly the different factors *interact* in producing observed differences between females and males. Though most scholars in the field currently seem to share the basic assumption that biology, culture, and cognition have some role to play in the emergence of sex differences and similarities, there is an ongoing debate concerning each factor's contribution to this interaction and the specific kind of interplay between the factors involved (see, e.g., Archer, 1996; Eagly & Wood, 1999).

From the perspective of evolutionary psychology, in each domain where ancestral males and females have faced different adaptive problems or selection pressures over the course of evolutionary history (e.g., same-sex competition for access to mates, or differential parental investment), sex differences are to be expected to exist regardless of societal particulars. To the extent that the adaptive problems have been similar for both sexes (e.g., when forming long-lasting emotional bonds to one's spouse or to one's own children), gender similarities rather than differences should be observed. However, this reasoning does not rule out sex differences in the case of similar adaptive problems. Psychological differences between the sexes will become manifest whenever cultural norms or social-cognitive processes are specifically directed toward gender differentiation. On the other hand, different adaptive problems in the past are by no means bound to lead to sex differences given that they fail to get supported by extant cultural practices or local environments. A particularly intriguing conjecture of evolutionary psychology is that gender-linked evolutionary constraints function to *prepare* (or *sensitize*) women and men to have different learning experiences; that is, the sexes are hypothesized to differ, albeit only slightly and presumably in domain-specific ways, in the genetic predisposition to make associations between particular features of objects, persons, or events. This notion is succinctly worked out by Kenrick and Luce's evolutionary life-history model of sex differences and similarities (chap. 2, this volume).

Following the evolutionary rationale, in principle there should be some degree of *fit* between the preparedness to have learning experiences and the socialization practices prevailing in human societies. This fit would be larger for cultural practices that accommodate females' and males' differential preparedness, and it would be smaller in cultures that have settled on practices diverging to some extent from females' and males' genetic predispositions. Therefore, it should take less effort for girls and boys to learn gender-typical as compared to gender-atypical behaviors. Alternatively, at the cultural level, it should be easier to establish and promote cultural norms that are in accordance with females' and males' differentially evolved psychological dispositions as compared to those that contrast with these dispositions. To the extent that human cultures have been developing according to a "high-fit" strategy (i.e., accommodating females' and males' evolved dispositions), gender-differential socialization can be viewed as a coevolutionary process (Archer, 1996; see also Janicki & Krebs, 1998). However, much more should be known about the specifics of the connections between evolution and culture. The need to do more cross-cultural studies of differences in gender socialization seems obvious, as well.

It should also be noted that evolutionary accounts seek to find explanations for differences primarily existing *between* the two broad categories of (adult) females and males. This is done by referring to remote, ultimate causes. Differences *within* the sex categories that could be linked to proximate causes are not what most evolutionary psychologists are focusing on, thus running the risk of failing to pay sufficient attention to within-sex cultural diversity.

Furthermore, evolutionary approaches have difficulties accounting for the precise ways in which gender-differentiated cultural images, norms, and values are transmitted at the individual, the interpersonal, and the group level. In contrast, theories of socialization, cognitive approaches, and social role theory specifically address the processes involved in this transmission, highlighting the impact of various psychological factors (e.g., gender-schematic information processing, desire to act in accordance with a gendered self) and social factors (e.g., provision of gender-differentiated behavioral opportunities, self-fulfilling prophecies), as well as the interplay between these factors.

In spite of the discrepancies in the respective explanatory approaches taken, or perhaps because of these discrepancies, we think that socialization, cognitive, and social role perspectives lend themselves to being linked to the evolutionary perspective. Of course, this presupposes at least two assumptions. First, evolved mechanisms predispose individuals to learn some gender-related behaviors with less effort than others. Second, these dispositions become manifest only through complex gene–environment– cognition interaction; that is, in order to have impact on individuals' development they are themselves dependent on specific kinds of environmental stimulation, on the cognitive processing of this stimulation, and on a human culture that provides corresponding behavioral opportunities, fostering sex differences in some domains and tempering differences in others. More generally, evolved psychological mechanisms entail constraints that serve to facilitate, channel, and encourage particular kinds of gender-related learning in particular social contexts (see Gelman & Williams, 1998, for a detailed discussion of the view that constraints enable learning).

It is important to note, however, that the suggested linking of theoretical perspectives can go either way. Particularly, a point of convergence beginning to emerge concerns the seemingly disparate evolutionary and social role accounts of sex differences and similarities in human behavior. As pointed out by Eagly, Wood, and Diekman (chap. 5, this volume), social role theory needs to offer an explanation for two social-structural features that are common to all known human cultures—the sexual division of labor and gender hierarchy. Building on insights from anthropological studies, Eagly et al. trace the division of labor between the sexes back to physical sex differences, particularly to females' reproductive activities (i.e., pregnancy, lactation) and to males' greater size and strength. Additionally, in order to account for the origins of gender hierarchy (i.e., females' generally lower social power and status), Eagly et al. refer to demands of the socioeconomic system (e.g., demands that are typical of early agricultural societies). We do not think that evolutionists would disagree with this line of reasoning. At the same time, however, they would point out that the arguments of social role theory do not go far enough. Kenrick and Luce (chap. 2, this volume) make this point quite explicit when saying that physical sex differences are not the whole story but need themselves to be explained. That is, evolutionary psychologists would ask about the adaptive function of physical sex differences in the first place. And of course they would go about answering this question by referring to differing selection pressures, in particular sexual selection and parental investment. It is right here that social role and evolutionary accounts do not seem to be so far away from each other (see also Eagly & Wood, 1999).

Once again attesting to the overdetermined nature of gender differentiation, various sources of environmental input (parents, school, peers, media, etc.) appear to converge in pulling the individual toward gendered thinking, attitudes, and behaviors. Together these sources provide ample information about the importance of gender, through transmission of societal values, cultural norms, category-based expectations, role images, and gender-related responses directed toward the growing individual. Adding to this picture are multiple opportunities to observe male and female models, as well as the gender-differentiated structuring of social groups and group activities (see Fagot, Rodgers, & Leinbach, chap. 3, this volume).

The specifics of which aspects of behavior become gender-typed and which remain gender-neutral clearly are culturally defined and transmitted. As is shown throughout this book, the various social pressures and environmental influences to which girls and boys, women and men are subjected during their development are powerful and pervasive. Although in many respects parents treat sons and daughters in highly similar ways (see Lytton & Romney, 1991), within this pattern of overall similarity consistent trends toward gender differentiation turn up. For example, parents, especially fathers, appear to put more pressure on boys to be masculine than they put on girls to be feminine. It may well be that in doing so, fathers contribute to the emergence of asymmetries between boys' and girls' groups; that is, boys' groups are more exclusionary, more vigilant about within-group gender-boundary violations, and more separate from adult culture (see Maccoby, 1998, for more detail). Moreover, as Eisenberg et al. (1996) note, girls and boys may respond differently to the same parental behavior.

In discussing the relative impact of social factors, more and more weight is given to group influences. This is most clearly expressed in Harris' (1995) group socialization theory of development. In a word, the theory postulates that within-group and between-group processes, and not dyadic (e.g., child–parent) relationships, are responsible for the transmission of culture and for environmental modification of children's personality characteristics. Outside-the-home socialization taking place in the peer groups of childhood and early adolescence is claimed to exert great influence on the emergence and maintenance of segregation between boys' and girls' play groups. However, in our view, the role of parents in gender socialization should not be underestimated. Parents create and modify social environments mostly in gender-typical ways, and they are the first to transmit stereotypic beliefs about sex differences to their children (see chaps. 3 and 11, this volume). Yet, in a thoughtful discussion of this issue, and in accord with Harris' general line of reasoning, Maccoby (1998) points out that in-home socialization probably has a greater effect on the kinds of interaction styles characteristic of children in their same-sex groups than it has on the separation between these groups.

Rather than focusing on the environmental input as socialization approaches typically do, cognitive accounts of gender study the information-processing activities of individuals, that is, activities like encoding, storing, and remembering gender-related information. Proponents of cognitive theories emphasize functions of generic knowledge structures, their automatic or controlled activation, as well as their application to the interpretation or construction of environmental messages (see Martin, chap. 4, this volume). In other words, the meaning of information received from the environment is not so much seen to be constrained by stimulus characteristics as it is by the abilities of the individual to deal with environmental stimulation (e.g., categorization and inference skills). Basically, gender development is conceptualized as a transactional process. The role of the environment is to provide information about what it means to be male or female; this, in turn, stimulates the creation of gender theories or schemas, which then promote gender-related processing of newly incoming information. The more frequent and consistent the exposure to gender-linked information is, the more individuals will perceive their social environment through schematic lenses. Cumulative experience with social contexts, tasks, and other people's behavior that are prone to activate gender schemas gradually leads to an automatic use of the corresponding knowledge. More and more individuals will come to view themselves and others in terms of masculinity and femininity, taking stereotype-congruent distinctions between female and male for granted.

Moreover, the cognitive construction of gender exerts a motivational force; that is, gender schemas and gender stereotypes are not purely descriptive (i.e., specifying what is) but also prescriptive, in that they are used to evaluate the appropriateness of behavior (i.e., specifying what should be). As Martin (chap. 4, this volume) points out, these evaluations and the underlying gender schemas are finely tuned to various domains of experience (e.g., interacting with familiar vs. unfamiliar others).

Considering the mutual relations between evolutionary constraints, social-cultural influences, and cognitive processes, Maccoby (1998) aptly concluded:

> It may be that societies adopt the stereotypes and roles they do in part as an accommodation to biological forces. And biological forces are themselves sometimes responsive to social conditions. Gender cognitions, too, can hardly be independent of other factors. The content of stereotypes and scripts reflects, to some degree, the realities of social behaviors that emerge from biological and social forces, though gender cognitions can distort, magnify, or discount elements of social reality. All the elements of the explanatory web influence each other. (p. 78)

## Dynamic Interplay of Developmental
## Change and Social Influence

The second central theme running through the contributions of this book is that we will not be able to fully understand gender as a social category unless we closely attend to both the developmental history and the social factors involved in bringing about gender effects. This general proposition has several meanings and consequences. First, it means that gender-related constructs themselves are subject to change over time; for example, rigid gender concepts of young children tend to become more flexible during later childhood. Second, there are also systematic changes in the social contexts that developing individuals encounter and that they actively choose or avoid; for example, contexts may change in systematic ways from family to school or to the workplace, or from gender-segregated peer groups to intimate heterosexual relationships. Third, there are not only changing individuals in changing social contexts, but also changes in the impact of social contexts on individuals and in the mechanisms mediating between cognition, context, and behavior. In other words, there are changes in the match between psychological features of individuals and opportunities afforded them by the environment.

Whereas, for instance, differential parental reinforcement may be a main determinant of the acquisition of gendered behavior during early childhood, a few years later the child's striving for cognitive consistency with his or her gender identity and gender schemas, fostered by the interaction styles manifest in gender-segregated groups, becomes increasingly important. Reaching puberty, when boys and girls begin to face the developmental task of engaging in romantic and sexual relationships and, at the same time, experience stereotypic expectations concerning how to attract or approach members of the other sex, new adaptations of gender attitudes and gender-related behaviors ensue. On the adult level, cultural norms and values that regulate family processes and work-life, the perceived status and power differences between the sexes, the question of having children or not, and so forth gain steadily in importance when it comes to predicting the manifestation of gender-differentiated behavior.

Taking further into account that developmental factors may begin to exert influence only after extended periods of time, the complexity of describing and explaining the temporal qualities and social dynamics of gender processes becomes obvious. Whereas proximal factors of gender-typed cognition and behavior have been well documented in social psychological research, distal factors like genetic endowment, early levels of sexual hormones, young childrens' social experiences and their relation to sex differences and similarities observed in late adolescence and adulthood are much more difficult to analyze. The study and fine-grained analysis of distal factors and their changing impact over individuals' life course is one of the major challenges facing gender research.

The chapters of this volume are replete with examples demonstrating the complex nature of interrelationships between intraindividual changes, changes of social contexts, and changes in the relation between the two. For purposes of illustration, we want to highlight some particularly intriguing instances.

One important issue concerns the antecedents and consequences of developmental transitions in gender prejudice from childhood to adulthood (see Glick & Hilt, chap. 8, this volume). Although hostile attitudes toward the other sex characterize young children of both sexes and manifest themselves in the formation and maintenance of gender-segregated play groups, gender prejudice becomes increasingly complex during adolescence, reaching its most intricate form in adulthood. The change from predominately independent (i.e., gender-segregated) to interdependent (i.e., romantic, passionate, or communal) relationships stimulates the transition from hostile to ambivalent sexism. As a result, adolescents' and adults' gender prejudices often consist of a mixture of hostility and benevolence.

The consequences of ambivalent sexism can be seen at all levels of analysis, including individual efforts to deal with threats to cognitive consistency by splitting the global gender categories into subtypes with distinctly positive or negative evaluations, distancing behavior toward individual others who are perceived to belong to a negatively valued subtype, and benevolent beliefs about women or men in traditional roles (Eckes, 1997; Glick & Fiske, 1996). Ultimately, ambivalent sexism serves to justify and perpetuate a cultural system that promotes gender inequality (see Jost & Banaji, 1994, for an excellent discussion).

In light of the overdetermined nature of gender differentiation in human societies, the issue arises how, if at all, gender stereotypes and sexist attitudes in children can be countered effectively. When the development of stereotypic beliefs and gender-related attitudes is seen as the result of frequent exposure to social contexts that provide gendered information, with cumulative experiences of this kind gradually leading to automatic activation and use of cognitive gender categories, then changing children's gender-typed beliefs should be more successful at younger ages. However, there are several limitations to corresponding intervention strategies. First, young children's categorization skills are such that they tend to construct mutually exclusive categories and have difficulty assimilating stereotype-inconsistent information (see Martin, chap. 4, this volume; see also Markman, 1989). Second, children's gender-typed beliefs are enhanced by processes of social identification (Deaux, 1996); that is, activation and use of gender-typed beliefs foster defining oneself in terms of similarities to other members of the same-sex group and in terms of differences from the opposite-sex group, thus affirming a child's social identity. Third, from early ages on, children experience a strong societal emphasis on gender differentiation (e.g., through media influences) and observe adults in gender-differentiated social roles (e.g., family and occupational roles). Reviewing research on this topic, Bigler (1999) drew the following, fairly pessimistic conclusion: "Societal changes concerning the messages that children receive about the meaning and importance of gender may be necessary before psychological strategies for overcoming sex typing are likely to be highly effective" (p. 146). Thus, at the very least, effective intervention presupposes a combination of strategies, building on several different theoretical foundations (e.g., cognitive theories, social identification approaches, social-cultural accounts) and aiming at all levels at which gender differentiation is currently maintained.

The fundamental ambivalence inherent in adolescents' and young adults' gender-related attitudes strongly relates to the formation and quality of interpersonal relationships (see Krahé, chap. 9, this volume). Activated by sexual motives, guided by sexual scripts, and blinded by gender prejudice, adolescent males and females are drawn to each other in ways that more often than not end in sexual aggression of some kind or other, almost exclusively involving males as aggressors and females as victims. Indeed, ambivalent sexism can be hypothesized to form one major source contributing to the subtle, and at the same time pervasive, forms of miscommunication between females and males that underlie much of males' sexually aggressive action toward females. Generally speaking, research on heterosexual aggression has not only the potential to help remedy one of the most urgent problems in female–male relations, but can also inform attempts at reintroducing the concept of sexuality into accounts of gender development.

Actually, the lack of developmental studies addressing issues of gender prejudice noted earlier in this book is paralleled by a lack of studies concerning the development of sexual behavior, sexual attitudes, and sexual orientation. Considering the star status once ascribed to sexuality and to the adoption of sexual roles by psychoanalytic theorizing in the first half of the 20th century, it is puzzling to see these topics having led a shadowy existence in this century's second half. Although it seems pointless to speculate about the reasons for this neglect, it is mandatory that the study of sexual development and its relation to gender development is put on the research agenda of developmental social psychological analyses of gender.

The central role of sexuality in the fabric of female–male relations is highlighted not only by social psychological research on ambivalent sexist attitudes and heterosexual aggression but also by studies of the content and structure of late adolescents' and young adults' gender stereotypes and gender-stereotypic beliefs about female–male interaction. A case in point is

Holland and Skinner's (1987) research on cultural models of gender (i.e., the shared implicit knowledge about gender subtypes and about ways to talk about these types). College-age women were found to categorize males according to whether they are (a) likely to use their attractiveness to females for selfish purposes, (b) likable and competent, and (c) unusual in sexual appetites; college-age men tended to categorize females according to whether they are (a) sexy, (b) prestigious as a sexual companion, and (c) likable and nondemanding. Similarly, Eckes (1994) demonstrated that at least when subtyping men, female as well as male college students strongly associate sociability with a sexual behavior component; for example, subtypes such as macho, trendy, and playboy were judged high on properties like "outgoing" and "enjoys sex" (see also adolescents' opposite-sex ideal as described by Gibbons, chap. 13, this volume, p. 406).

Recently, an intriguing account of the development of both opposite-sex and same-sex attraction was advanced by D. J. Bem (1996). According to *EBE (Exotic Becomes Erotic) theory* (as it was dubbed by Bem), biological variables such as genes or prenatal hormones do not code for sexual orientation per se but for children's temperaments (e.g., activity level). These temperaments, in turn, predispose a child to enjoy some activities more than others (e.g., male-typical or female-typical play styles). Gender-conforming children (i.e., children preferring gender-typical activities and same-sex playmates) will feel different from opposite-sex peers, perceiving them as unfamiliar (or exotic); the same is presumed to happen with gender-nonconforming children in relation to same-sex peers. In each case, a child will experience heightened, nonspecific autonomous arousal to opposite-sex and same-sex peers, respectively. Finally, heightened arousal is transformed in later years into erotic or romantic attraction, leading to distinct kinds of sexual orientation (i.e., heterosexual, homosexual, bisexual, asexual). Though the specifics of EBE theory will have to be spelled out in more detail (e.g., the processes involved in transitions from one class of events to the next), and its core assumptions will have to be tested thoroughly in future research, the main thrust of its argument, that is, the postulate of a temporal sequence of events leading to a particular sexual orientation, is perfectly in line with an integrative, developmental social psychological approach to the topic.

Complex interrelations between developmental change and change in social contexts can also be observed in the development of gender stereotypes and the emergence and maintenance of a gendered self, as well as in the ways these stereotypes and gender-related self-construals influence behavior (see chaps. 4, 6, and 7, this volume). According to Ruble's (1994) phase model of transitions, cognitive–motivational orientations toward social information shift in systematic ways as individuals move through periods of major life changes. With respect to the gender transition, the three phases involved can be specified as follows. During *construction*, only rudimentary knowledge about what constitutes gender-typical versus gender-atypical behavior is available; the individual is actively seeking information in order to achieve mastery and understanding. Once such basic, still largely superficial knowledge—an overall in-group/out-group gender schema in Martin and Halverson's (1981) terms—has been acquired, the individual reaches the *consolidation* phase. Here, gender knowledge is more structured, abstract, and inferential; information seeking is increasingly focused on drawing conclusions about the applicability and relevance of this knowledge to the self—forming an own-sex schema, according to Martin and Halverson. In other words, whereas the construction phase means asking what it is that boys and girls typically do or do not do, the consolidation phase refers to preferring one category over the other and striving for consisteny of one's own behavior with the associated sets of category-based expectations. Finally, during *integration*, gender knowledge is highly differentiated and flexibly used depending on interaction goals and features of the immediate context; typically, both gender-congruent and gender-incongruent aspects of knowledge about the self and the social world are available to the individual.

Because individuals are typically more frequently exposed to social contexts that promote the activation of gender-congruent aspects of the self than to contexts in which gender-incongruent aspects appear applicable, a general tendency to act in accordance with a gendered self is to be expected. It is here that the distinction between situational (or immediate) and chronic sources of activation becomes important (see Hannover, chap. 6, this volume). That is, whenever an individual's gender-related self-construct is activated in a given situation, he or she will most likely behave in a gender-congruent manner, whereas gender-incongruent behavior is least likely to occur. With each situational activation the gender-related self-construct's chronic accessibility will increase, leading to a heightened probability of spontaneous activation at future occasions. In addition, as Zemore, Fiske, and Kim (chap. 7, this volume) convincingly show, the frequency with which an individual faces gender-relevant information is a critical factor in the formation and application of gender stereotypes. The repeated use of gender stereotypes, in turn, promotes their automatization, with the result that, in adulthood, gender stereotypes dominate processes of person perception and strongly influence interpersonal behavior.

Based upon research and theorizing addressing the development of a gendered self, gender stereotypes, and gender prejudice, the prevailing gender differentiation in all spheres of human social life can be seen as the cumulative result of lifelong processes during which individuals are consistently exposed to, and interact with, social contexts that foster primarily gender-congruent concepts and behavior. Adding to this picture, and once more stressing the overdetermination of gender phenomena, are broader societal conditions, particularly the sexual division of labor and gender hierarchy, giving rise to the formation of gender stereotypes, gender roles, and gender-differentiated behavior. As Eagly et al. (chap. 5, this volume) argued, gender roles exert direct influence on behavior through their descriptive and prescriptive (or injunctive) content (see also Zemore et al., chap. 7, this volume). Whereas the descriptive aspects of gender roles serve as a guideline to behave in ways that are gender-typical and thus would not elicit surprise in others, the prescriptive aspects (as mentioned previously) function to motivate an individual to behave in a way that would be met with approval from others. Since both kinds of social influence maintain and promote gender-congruent behaviors, and mostly do so in subtle ways, developing individuals have hardly any chance not to acquire or act out gender-typed behavioral tendencies.

Descriptive and prescriptive behavioral expectations exist in many different contexts or interaction settings; for example, in the family, at school, in peer groups, in close interpersonal relationships, and at work. In dyadic and group settings females' and males' verbal and nonverbal communication appears to be closely aligned to culturally shared gender-stereotypic expectations. For example, Carli and Bukatko (chap. 10, this volume) review research showing that sex differences in influence and in mitigated, dominant, and status-asserting speech relate to sex differences in power, status, and social roles. Importantly, these differences tend to be reduced and even reversed when descriptive and prescriptive expectations are based on females' positions of authority or power relative to males.

The influence of parents' gender-related expectations on a number of variables relating to their children's self-concept and performances in various domains has been worked out in admirable detail by Eccles in a series of longitudinal studies (see Eccles, Freedman-Doan, Frome, Jacobs, & Yoon, chap. 11, this volume). Parents' gender-stereotypic beliefs and belief-congruent behaviors have been shown to exert influence on girls' and boys' interest in various activity domains (e.g., math, English/reading, sports) and on their self-perceived competence in these domains, over and above what can be predicted on the basis of the children's actual performance level alone.

Another relevant setting where gender-stereotypic beliefs and expectations contribute to the maintenance of gender-differentiated behavior is the work context. As Abele (chap. 12, this volume) demonstrates, career-related psychological variables such as career motivation or self-efficacy are more strongly related to the gendered self-concept than to the sex of the individual, whereas sex seems to be a more powerful predictor of career-related outcomes (e.g., occupational status) than gender-role orientation. More importantly, there seems to exist a feedback loop from the actual career progress or stagnation to changes in gender-role orientation, once again attesting to the dynamic nature of the relation between developmental changes and social forces.

One issue that turns up in many chapters of this book, albeit rather implicitly, concerns the relation of developmental processes during childhood and adolescence to their outcomes in adulthood. At least two views on this point can be distinguished. According to the first, childhood is seen mainly as a preparatory period for adulthood, meaning that both evolutionary adaptations and socialization influences are geared toward reaching maturity. Alternatively, biological and social factors could be conceived of as being oriented toward coping with age-typical developmental tasks; in this view, it is not adequate to construe processes of change in childhood as a kind of preparation for adult roles.

With respect to this issue, evolutionary accounts focus on the ways in which individuals of the two sexes get predisposed to behave after they have reached reproductive maturity. Even a child's experiences in early socialization and their purported effects (e.g., on timing of maturation and puberty) are mainly discussed under the heading of reproductive strategy (see, e.g., Belsky, Steinberg, & Draper, 1991). More specifically, an evolutionary account highlights childhood's preparatory function in terms of three fundamental goals: to survive to reproductive age, to reproduce, and to rear one's offspring until they reach reproductive age. Accordingly, an extended childhood is claimed to provide individuals with an opportunity to develop complex behavioral, social, and cognitive competencies needed for success at survival, mating, and parenting (Geary, 1998). At this point, relevant questions immediately coming to mind are: What are the adaptive functions of different interaction and play styles in childhood? What is carried over from childhood to adulthood, and what are the specifics of such a transfer? Is there some kind of continuity between childhood behaviors and adult behaviors? What are the processes involved in the transition from largely gender-segregated peer groups to romantic or intimate heterosexual relationships or parents' close cooperation in child care?

Clearly, we need to know more about how childhood tendencies to separate into same-sex groups and to display gender-differentiated interaction styles and how the gendered self and the content and structure of gender stereotypes and gender-related preferences later manifest themselves in interaction contexts characterizing adulthood. Among the most relevant contexts are the choice of, and interaction with, heterosexual partners, the structuring of relationships at work, and the adoption of parental roles. As Maccoby (1998) argued, the interactive repertoires learned in children's same-sex groups are likely to be used, and are useful, when interacting with same-sex others throughout life. These learned repertoires, however, have to be modified to be sucessful in cross-sex interactions among adults.

Furthermore, the nature of the required modifications depends, at least in part, on whether an adult is interacting as lover, worker, or parent. An example of the behavioral modification in cross-sex interaction concerns the developmental history of hostility and aggression of some males toward females, and the concurrent developmental history of females that increases the likelihood of victimization—changes in behavioral tendencies over time that may eventually lead to gross misunderstandings in heterosexual relationships having adverse consequences.

Finally, an integrative developmental social psychological perspective stresses the importance of being more explicit about sources of gender differentiation that are located at the cultural level. Motivational and cognitive processes within individuals, the kind of interpersonal relationships individuals engage in, and the normative and informational social influence emanating from peer groups, work groups, and the like all depend on the broader cultural matrix in which social entities are embedded. As noted throughout this book, a typical feature of human culture is gender polarization—differences between the sexes are emphasized by imposing the female–male dichotomy on virtually every aspect of life (S. L. Bem, 1993; Deaux & LaFrance, 1998). Exemplary issues arising when the focus of research is directed toward the most inclusive or general level of analyzing gender include the following: How does a given culture produce the very mechanisms that serve to legitimize and perpetuate gender-polarizing images or representations of females and males? To what degree are these images influenced by, and do they influence, economical, political, and technological factors? How do gradual changes in the sexual division of labor, and possibly in gender hierarchy as well, feed back on culturally shared gender stereotypes, roles, and prejudices?

In addition, adopting a cross-cultural perspective allows one to pin down what changes and what remains unchanged, and why certain cultural features change or differ in the course of change processes. It is in these respects that comparing cultures varying on known parameters can yield important insights (see Gibbons, chap. 13, this volume). Generally speaking, the identification of cultural universals and specifics represents a prerequisite for testing basic assumptions about the underlying causes of continuing gender differentiation in all spheres of human social life. Particularly, the explanatory power of the evolutionary and social role accounts of human sex differences and similarities critically hinges on the compatibility of their propositions with findings from cross-cultural studies.

# CONCLUSION

As noted in the introductory chapter, the multidimensional, multilevel conceptual framework does not, and cannot, define all that may reasonably be asked about processes of gender differentiation. Yet it is meant to provide a coherent taxonomy that may raise new research questions promising to further our knowledge in the field. The chapters contained in this volume provide a wealth of insights, theoretical advances, and intriguing findings from empirical research that highlight various parts of our taxonomy, stimulating research probing into other parts as well.

Quite obviously then, there is much we need to learn about the kinds of interdependencies between developmental change and social forces. The issues emerging at the interface of developmental and social psychology certainly will increase the complexity of the tasks confronting gender researchers devoted to an integrative perspective. This heightened complexity is both a challenge and a source of continuing fascination.

Finally, we concur with Martin's (1999) conclusion that instead of thinking of gender as a puzzle with many pieces "Gender is better conceived of as being many puzzles, each with many pieces and the potential of having different origins" (p. 65). So let's start putting pieces together.

# REFERENCES

Archer, J. (1996). Sex differences in social behavior: Are the social role and evolutionary explanations compatible? *American Psychologist, 51,* 909–917.

Belsky, J., Steinberg, L., & Draper, P. (1991). Childhood experience, interpersonal development, and reproductive strategy: An evolutionary theory of socialization. *Child Development, 62,* 647–670.

Bem, D. J. (1996). Exotic becomes erotic: A developmental theory of sexual orientation. *Psychological Review, 103,* 320–335.

Bem, S. L. (1993). *The lenses of gender: Transforming the debate on sexual inequality.* New Haven, CT: Yale University Press.

Bigler, R. S. (1999). Psychological interventions designed to counter sexism in children: Empirical limitations and theoretical foundations. In W. B. Swann, Jr., J. H. Langlois, & L. A. Gilbert (Eds.), *Sexism and stereotypes in modern society: The gender science of Janet Taylor Spence* (pp. 129–151). Washington, DC: American Psychological Association.

Deaux, K. (1996). Social identification. In E. T. Higgins & A. W. Kruglanski (Eds.), *Social psychology: Handbook of basic principles* (pp. 777–798). New York: Guilford.

Deaux, K., & LaFrance, M. (1998). Gender. In D. T. Gilbert, S. T. Fiske, & G. Lindzey (Eds.), *The handbook of social psychology* (4th ed., Vol. 1, pp. 788–827). Boston: McGraw-Hill.

Eagly, A. H., & Wood, W. (1999). The origins of sex differences in human behavior: Evolved dispositions versus social roles. *American Psychologist, 54,* 408–423.

Eckes, T. (1994). Explorations in gender cognition: Content and structure of female and male subtypes. *Social Cognition, 12,* 37–60.

Eckes, T. (1997). *Geschlechterstereotype: Frau und Mann in sozialpsychologischer Sicht* [Gender stereotypes: Woman and man in social psychological perspective]. Pfaffenweiler, Germany: Centaurus.

Eisenberg, N., Martin, C. L., & Fabes, R. A. (1996). Gender development and gender effects. In D. C. Berliner & R. C. Calfee (Eds.), *Handbook of educational psychology* (pp. 358–396). New York: Macmillan.

Fagot, B. I. (1995). Psychosocial and cognitive determinants of early gender-role development. *Annual Review of Sex Research, 6*, 1–31.

Geary, D. C. (1998). *Male, female: The evolution of human sex differences.* Washington, DC: American Psychological Association.

Gelman, R., & Williams, E. M. (1998). Enabling constraints for cognitive development and learning: Domain specificity and epigenesis. In W. Damon (Series Ed.), D. Kuhn & R. S. Siegler (Vol. Eds.), *Handbook of child psychology: Vol. 2. Cognition, perception, and language* (5th ed., pp. 575–630). New York: Wiley.

Glick, P., & Fiske, S. T. (1996). The Ambivalent Sexism Inventory: Differentiating hostile and benevolent sexism. *Journal of Personality and Social Psychology, 70*, 491–512.

Harris, J. R. (1995). Where is the child's environment? A group socialization theory of development. *Psychological Review, 102*, 458–489.

Holland, D., & Skinner, D. (1987). Prestige and intimacy: The cultural models behind Americans' talk about gender types. In D. Holland & N. Quinn (Eds.), *Cultural models in language and thought* (pp. 78–111). Cambridge, MA: Cambridge University Press.

Janicki, M. G., & Krebs, D. L. (1998). Evolutionary approaches to culture. In C. B. Crawford & D. L. Krebs (Eds.), *Handbook of evolutionary psychology: Ideas, issues, and applications* (pp. 163–207). Mahwah, NJ: Erlbaum.

Jost, J. T., & Banaji, M. R. (1994). The role of stereotyping in system-justification and the production of false consciousness. *British Journal of Social Psychology, 33*, 1–27.

Lytton, H., & Romney, D. M. (1991). Parents' differential socialization of boys and girls: A meta-analysis. *Psychological Bulletin, 109*, 267–296.

Maccoby, E. E. (1998). *The two sexes: Growing up apart, coming together.* Cambridge, MA: Harvard University Press.

Markman, E. M. (1989). *Categorization and naming in children: Problems of induction.* Cambridge, MA: MIT Press.

Martin, C. L. (1999). A developmental perspective on gender effects and gender concepts. In W. B. Swann, Jr., J. H. Langlois, & L. A. Gilbert (Eds.), *Sexism and stereotypes in modern society: The gender science of Janet Taylor Spence* (pp. 45–73). Washington, DC: American Psychological Association.

Martin, C. L., & Halverson, C. F. (1981). A schematic processing model of sex typing and stereotyping in children. *Child Development, 52*, 1119–1134.

Ruble, D. N. (1994). A phase model of transitions: Cognitive and motivational consequences. In M. P. Zanna (Ed.), *Advances in experimental social psychology* (Vol. 26, pp. 163–214). San Diego, CA: Academic Press.

# Glossary

*Numbers in parantheses refer to chapters dealing with the concept.*[1]

**accessibility** the ease with which a construct (e.g., self-concept, stereotype, or attitude) is retrieved from memory. Constructs are accessible when they are recently, frequently, or chronically available to consciousness. Accessible knowledge significantly influences how people process relevant stimuli. For example, if the construct of hostility is accessible to a person, then that person may be especially likely to interpret another person's behavior as hostile. Accessible constructs may also affect mood and behavior. (6, 7)

**agency/communion** clusters of attributes that are stereotypically associated with the global categories of men (i.e., agentic or instrumental attributes) and women (i.e., communal or expressive attributes). For example, men are generally viewed as independent, competitive, and rational; women as dependent, submissive, and gentle. Agency characterizes the male gender role, communion the female gender role. (5, 7)

**ambivalent prejudice** prejudice that encompasses both subjectively benevolent and hostile attitudes toward the target group (e.g., paternalistic prejudice). Ambivalent sexism toward women, for example, combines hostile male attitudes that women are ill-suited to assume powerful male roles with subjectively benevolent attitudes of protectiveness and reverence toward women who embrace conventional roles. (8)

**androgyny** a balance or blending of masculinity and femininity within a person (see also "masculinity/femininity"). The androgyny construct resulted from reconceptualizing masculinity and femininity as independent and not opposite variables. Persons with high masculinity and high femininity scores are classified as androgynous. (4, 6, 12)

**associative network** a model of memory representation assuming that representations (e.g., beliefs or concepts) are constructed from discrete nodes (preexisting concepts or newly formed) connected by links varying in strength. A particular node can become activated by external stimulation or internal processes, with activation spreading to other nodes to which it is linked. The more links

---

[1]We would like to thank the authors of individual chapters who kindly suggested definitions of some of the glossary terms.

connecting to a particular node, and the stronger these links are, the greater its probability of retrieval. Long-term memory is viewed as a single large associative structure, short-term memory as the currently activated subset of this structure. (6)

**attitude** "a psychological tendency that is expressed by evaluating a particular entity with some degree of favor or disfavor" (Eagly & Chaiken, 1993, p. 1; italics omitted). These evaluations may be manifested in cognition, affect, and behavior. The cognitive, affective, and behavioral components of attitudes often have complex and variable relationships. (1, 8)

**attributional ambiguity** the uncertainty that stereotyped groups experience in attempting to understand the causes of their outcomes. For targets of social stereotypes, positive and negative behavioral outcomes can often be attributed to internal causes, or to people's reactions to their social category membership. For example, failing at a task can be attributed to personal deficiencies or to social discrimination. (7)

**automatic processing** information processing that occurs without conscious control. Automatic processing can develop in response to repeated experience with the same stimuli or environments, and it permits people to save the cognitive effort expended in more controlled responses. Automatic processes are unintentional, involuntary, and effortless; further, they operate outside of awareness and without conscious monitoring. (7)

**automatization** the transformation of conscious into automatic mental processes. Either through long-term frequency or recency of use constructs may eventually become automatized and capable of activation by the mere presence of relevant stimuli in the environment, regardless of the current focus of controlled information processing. For example, gender stereotypes become automatic through frequent use in early stages of development. (7)

**behavioral confirmation** a perception–interaction sequence in which a perceiver's expectation about someone causes that person to behave in ways that confirm the initial expectation (also called self-fulfilling prophecy). In behavioral confirmation, the perceiver's belief creates reality (i.e., the target's behavior). Perceivers are not necessarily aware of their expectations or of the processes by which they convey them to others; nor are the targets necessarily aware of others' influence on them. (5, 7, 11)

**benevolent prejudice** subjectively favorable attitudes (on the part of the prejudiced perceiver) that are nevertheless patronizing toward the targeted group and part of reinforcing that group's lower status (e.g., the view that women's sensitivity makes them ill-suited to having positions of power). Such beliefs are one component of ambivalent forms of prejudice, such as paternalistic prejudice. Benevolent sexism, for example, places women on a pedestal and offers them male protection as long as they fulfill conventional female roles. (8)

**biosocial interactionist perspective** the view that biology, culture, and cognition mutually construct and constrain one another. Instead of pitting evolutionary accounts of human behavior and social cultural accounts against each other, it is assumed that human genes, culture, and cognition interact with each other in complex and variable ways. (2)

**casual sex script** a sexual script that entails a positive evaluation of sexual intercourse without the requirement of an emotional commitment between the partners. Compared to women, men's sexual behavior is guided to a far greater extent by the casual sex script. (9)

**chronic sources of activation** cumulative situational influences on an individual persisting over extended periods of time and determining which self-constructs become part of the individual's working self. With each single situational activation the gender-related self-construct will be more likely to become activated spontaneously at future occasions, that is, the self-construct's activation will eventually become automatized. Processes of this kind may account for interindividual differences in the accessibility of gender-congruent versus gender-incongruent self-knowledge at later developmental stages. (6)

**cognitive developmental theory**   the view that children's understanding of gender emerges as part of general cognitive development (Kohlberg, 1966). Most importantly, children's understanding of gender, rather than their gender-typed behavior (as emphasized by learning theorists), is claimed to be the crucial feature of gender development. Once this understanding is reached, children become motivated to seek out information about what is appropriate for their own sex by observing the behaviors of those around them. (4)

**compliance**   a form of sexual miscommunication that entails agreeing to sexual contacts without actually wanting them. (9)

**controlled processing**   information processing that occurs with conscious control. Controlled processes are intentional, voluntary, and effortful; they occur with a sense of control and with a conscious monitoring of the control output. (7)

**correspondence bias**   the psychological tendency to assume correspondence between the type of actions people engage in and their inner dispositions (also called fundamental attribution error). Because perceivers often do not give much weight to situational constraints (e.g., social roles) in interpreting others' behavior, the correspondence tendency is likely to produce judgmental error. (5, 7)

**cultural/cross-cultural psychology**   theoretical perspectives on the relation of culture and human development. From the perspective of cultural psychology, human developmental processes are inherently social and cultural. Thinking develops through interactions with other persons, thus

reflecting cultural practices enacted in social contexts. According to the cross-cultural view, culture serves as an antecedent to behavior, and comparisons between cultures are explicit or implied. For example, researchers working from this perspective have sought explanations for cultural differences in terms of cultural dimensions like individualism and collectivism. (13)

**dating script**   a sexual script that refers to the initiation of sexual contact. Dating scripts entail the belief that men should take the active role in initiating sexual contact and to persuade a seemingly reluctant woman to give in to their advances. (9)

**discrimination**   in intergroup relations, the behavioral manifestation of prejudiced attitudes (i.e., social discrimination). In perception, the sorting of sensory input into distinct categories (i.e., perceptual discrimination). (3, 7, 8)

**disidentification**   a reaction to stereotype threat that entails detaching self-esteem from one's performance in a particular domain or context. Disidentification has the temporary effect of buffering self-esteem, but can also encourage confirmation of negative stereotypes. (7)

**dual-component models of stereotyping**   the view that stereotyping has two components: a controlled component and an automatic component (see "controlled processing" and "automatic processing"). These models claim that, at some level, people can control the tendency to stereotype others, at least after the first moments of interaction. However, controlled processes only attenuate or amplify what is happening at a more fundamental level, where stereotyping is driven by automatic processes. (7)

**dual-impact model of career development**   the view that women's and men's gendered self-conceptualization (or gender-role orientation) influences a number of career-related psychological variables (e.g., career motivation, self-efficacy) that, in turn, have impact on career-related behaviors and outcomes (e.g., income, occupational status); at the same time, gender stereotypes lead to differential career opportunities for women and men. Additionally, the model claims that career development has a reciprocal impact on females' and males' gender-role orientation. (12)

**dynamic systems approach** as applied to the study of gender, the view that behavior may organize itself in gender-typed forms during some parts of social interactions while moving to a less gender-typed from in other parts of interactions or with different partners. These dynamic changes in gender-related behavior may be moderated by situational demands. Quite in line with Deaux and Major's (1987) gender-in-context model, attention is shifted away from stability of gender-related behavior and onto the variability with which behavior is played out in social situations. (4)

**emic approach** a culture-specific approach emphasizing the indigenous meaning of constructs and measures. Characteristics unique to a culture are called "emics". (13)

**envious prejudice** prejudice directed at out-groups with higher status that mixes an implicit admiration for the powerful group with envy, fear, and a desire to undermine the other group's status. Women's prejudice toward men, which prominently features resentment of men's power, may be of this type. (8)

**etic approach** a cross-cultural approach emphasizing the universal meaning of constructs and measures. Universal aspects of cultures are called "etics". With regard to gender-related constructs, sexual division of labor, gender hierarchy, gender stereotypes, and the developmental sequence of acquiring gender constancy can be considered etics. (13)

**evolutionary psychology** a perspective emphasizing the similarities and differences in behavior across species and across cultures, with a focus on the adaptive significance of inherited behavioral tendencies. Just as human morphological features have been shaped by selection pressures, evolutionary psychologists assume that humans inherited mechanisms specially designed to solve recurrent problems in the ancestral world. Thus, evolutionary theorists do not expect females and males to differ on every possible psychological dimension. Instead, differences are expected only where ancestral females and males regularly faced different adaptive problems (e.g., direct care of young or within-sex competition for mates; see also "sexual selection"). (2)

**gender-as-a-personality-variable perspective** the view that gender is an essential quality of an individual's psychological makeup. Focus is on the constructs of masculinity and femininity that are interpreted as summarizing one's psychological maleness and femaleness. A major goal is testing these constructs' explanatory power with respect to individual differences in mental health, social adjustment, self-esteem, and a variety of gender-related behaviors. Accordingly, the analysis of gender within this perspective is primarily located on the individual level. (1)

**gender-as-a-social-category perspective** the view that an individual's thoughts, feelings, and behaviors are influenced by a large set of intertwined multilevel (i.e., individual, interpersonal, group, and cultural) factors associated with the categorical distinction between the sexes. These factors include the sexual division of labor and gender hierarchy, shared beliefs about the personal attributes of females and males, behavioral confirmation of gender-based expectations, and attitudes toward the sexes and toward gender-related issues. Adopting this view means asking how, when, and why it makes a difference to be female or male, not whether, and to which degree, the sexes differ in a particular attribute. (1)

**gender-as-a-subject-variable perspective** the approach that seeks to answer the seemingly simple question of whether, and to which degree, the sexes differ in a number of psychological measures concerning cognitive abilities, personality traits, social behaviors, and so forth (also called sex differences approach). Its focus is almost exclusively on the individual level of analysis. (1)

**gender concepts**    gender-related knowledge structures, the "building blocks" of an individual's gender knowledge. For example, gender concepts include knowledge about gender-typed toys, activities, and traits, about gender-appropriate interpersonal relations, and about different values attached to the sexes. (1, 4)

**gender constancy**    children's understanding that gender is a permanent characteristic and will not change with superficial alterations. Gender constancy is most likely achieved between the ages of 5 and 7. According to Kohlberg (1966), children acquire gender constancy in a developmental sequence involving three stages: gender identity (children categorize themselves and others as female or male), gender stability (the understanding that gender is stable over time), and gender consistency (the understanding that gender is unaffected by changes in appearance or activity). (4, 8, 13)

**gender hierarchy**    the traditional power difference between the sexes in human societies (also called patriarchy). Women typically have less power and status than men and control fewer resources. (5, 8)

**gender identity**    an individual's sense of being male or female. In cognitive-developmental accounts, gender identity refers to children's recognition of their own sex (i.e., self-labeling as "boy" or "girl"). More broadly, this term is used to characterize all aspects of the self that are relevant to gender (e.g., self-perception of gendered traits and behaviors, preferences, and social roles). (3, 4, 5, 6, 13)

**gender-in-context model**    the view that variability in gender-related behaviors is the

rule rather than the exception (Deaux & Major, 1987). According to this model, the extent to which an individual will display gender-typed behavior depends on a complex interplay between three components: first, the perceiver, bringing a set of beliefs about gender to the situation, second, the target person, entering the situation with particular self-conceptions and interaction goals, and, finally, features of the situation, making gender more or less salient. (1, 5, 12)

**gender labeling**    the ability to accurately label self and others as male or female (see "gender labeling test"). Gender labeling fosters organizing social stimuli along gender-stereotypic lines and accelerates the process of gender typing in behavioral preferences and interaction with peers. Most children do not show gender labeling before 2 years of age. (3)

**gender labeling test**    a test measuring gender labeling in children (Leinbach & Fagot, 1986). The test consists of 24 colored photographs each showing only the head and shoulders of a fully clothed boy or girl. Photographs are arranged as male–female pairs on facing pages of a looseleaf notebook. Children are asked to identify one member of each pair, the boy or the girl, by pointing to the appropriate picture. Passing the test requires correct discrimination on at least 10 of 12 trials. (3)

**gender preferences**    an individual's desire to possess gender-related attributes. For example, gender preferences include the wish to be male or female, preferences for gender-congruent toys, activities, or occupations, and gender-based social identification. (1, 4)

**gender prejudice**    prejudiced attitudes (i.e., the attitude that a group deserves lower social status) based on gender-related categorization. This prejudice can be directed at men as well as women. Gender prejudice can be based on the simple, dichotomous sex categories of "male" and "female" (such simple classification may be likely among young children), but, among adults, is more typically based on classifications of men and women into various subtypes (e.g., macho men, feminists, etc.). (1, 8)

**gender-related self-construct** the concept of one's own masculinity or femininity, viewed as an intersection in memory between the representation of (mostly) gender-congruent information and the self (i.e., agentic attributes for males, communal attributes for females). (6)

**gender roles** culturally shared expectations that apply to individuals on the basis of their socially identified sex. According to Eagly's (1987) social role theory, gender roles emerge from the activities carried out by individuals of each sex in their sex-typical occupational and family roles; the attributes required by these activities become stereotypic of women or men. Like other social roles, gender roles entail descriptive norms (i.e., beliefs about how women and men typically behave) and prescriptive (injunctive) norms (i.e., beliefs about how women and men should, or must not, behave). In general, men's gender role can be characterized as agentic and women's gender role as communal (see also "agency/communion"). (3, 5, 7, 11, 12)

**gender schema** an organized knowledge structure that contains information about the sexes. Gender schemas develop from children's basic tendency to classify and simplify informational input from their environment. Because gender is highly salient in human societies, children recognize its functional significance and use it for purposes of categorization, inference, and the self-regulation of behavior. (3, 4, 10)

**gender-schema theory** the view that gender schemas influence individuals' information processing and behavior. In Bem's (1981) social psychological account of gender schemas, emphasis is placed on the functional significance of gender categories within society and on individual

differences in gender-schematic processing. Martin and Halverson's (1981) account focuses on developmental change in gender schemas and on their functions and resulting biases (e.g., selective attention, biased encoding and retrieval). Other variants of gender schema theory have been proposed as well. (4, 10)

**gender scripts** children's and adults' understanding of the temporal sequences of activities and events related to their own sex as opposed to the other sex. Gender scripts influence, and are influenced by, gendered beliefs including views of self, gender stereotypes, and gender attitudes. Furthermore, situations may differ in the extent to which they elicit gender scripts. (4, 9)

**gender segregation** the tendency for children to prefer same-sex, and to avoid opposite-sex, social partners. Gender segregation emerges during the third year of life, and becomes progressively stronger between the ages of 3 and 6. A somewhat different meaning is implied when talking about gender segregation at later ages. Here, the term refers to gender-differentiated academic and occupational choices persisting despite efforts at affirmative action in schools and occupational settings. This kind of gender segregation is particularly marked in areas associated with mathematics, physical science, technology, sports, clerical/office work, and education. Occupational gender segregation reinforces the power difference between women and men. (3, 5, 8)

**gender stereotypes** cognitive structures or schemas that contain culturally shared beliefs about the personal attributes of men and women (see also "agency/communion"). Gender stereotypes are conceptualized as multicomponential, multilevel constructs. That is, they comprise multiple components such as personality traits, attitudes and beliefs, overt behaviors and behavioral preferences, and physical appearance; they also consist of well-articulated gender subtypes (e.g, career woman, intellectual) that often differ in significant ways from the global gender categories. Children begin to show first signs of gender stereotyping around the age of 3 years. ( 3, 4, 5, 6, 7, 11, 12, 14)

**gender stereotyping test** a test measuring children's knowledge of gender stereotypes (Leinbach, Hort, & Fagot, 1997). The test consists of a set of strongly sex-typed items, varying in the degree to which they are conventionally assigned to or are figuratively or metaphorically associated with one sex or the other. For example, a hammer (male) and a broom (female) are conventionally sex-typed, whereas a bear (male) and a butterfly (female) are metaphorically sex-typed. Children are asked to assign each item (e.g., a black-and-white drawing of a hammer) to one of two boxes, one for things that are "more for girls and women", the other for things that are "more for boys and men". (3)

**habituation technique** an experimental procedure designed to investigate category learning in infants. In the typical habituation study, infants are presented with multiple stimuli that are all members of the same category (e.g., female faces). After habituation, infants are shown a novel category member and a nonmember (e.g., a male face). Infants' increased attention to the nonmember is thought to reflect the formation of a category schema or prototype based on their previous experience with category members. (3)

**hostile prejudice** subjectively hostile attitudes toward a targeted group that serve to diminish that group's status or reinforce a preexisting low status. Hostile sexism toward women, for example, is directed against those women who seek powerful roles that have, in the past, been dominated by men. Such beliefs are one component of ambivalent forms of prejudice, such as paternalistic prejudice. (8)

**Huston matrix** a principled, taxonomic approach to the developmental analysis of gender advanced by Huston (1983), expressed as an arrangement of five content

areas (i.e., biological gender, activities and interests, personal-social attributes, gender-based social relationships, and stylistic and symbolic characteristics) by four constructs (i.e., concepts or beliefs, identity or self-perception, preference or attitudes, and behavioral enactment). Ruble and Martin (1998) updated this matrix by adding one more content area (i.e., gender-related values). (1, 4)

**levels-of-analysis approach** the view that the sexes relate to each other at four different but interconnected levels: the individual level, the interpersonal (or interactional) level, the group (or role) level, and the cultural (or societal) level. Gender as a social category has important implications at each level, with social influence originating from multiple sources and varying in intensity, direction, and temporal dynamics across levels. (1, 14)

**life history** a genetically organized plan for allocating energy to survival, growth, and reproduction across the lifespan. As used here, "plan" refers to a set of genetically encoded predispositions to respond in certain ways to the environment. (2)

**macho personality** a type of males who hold callous sexual attitudes, regard violence as manly, and danger as exciting. Callous sexual attitudes refer to the belief that women should be treated at the man's discretion to serve his sexual interests. Research has shown a close link between the macho personality and sexual aggression. (9)

**masculinity/femininity** sets of attributes commonly associated with men (i.e., masculine attributes) and women (i.e., feminine attributes). First considered a global personality trait, with masculinity and femininity as opposite ends of a single bipolar dimension, in the early 1970s masculinity and femininity were conceptualized as separate and orthogonal dimensions, giving rise to the construct of "androgyny." According to Spence's (1993) theory of gender identity, masculinity and femininity are each multidimensional concepts, the components of which (e.g., personality traits, abilities, physical attributes, preferences) are only loosely related to each other and have different developmental histories. (4, 6, 12)

**meta-analysis**   a method for quantitatively integrating results from individual empirical studies. Meta-analysis yields answers as to whether there exists a reliable sex difference in a particular psychological measure, how large the sex difference is, and whether the sex difference depends on, or is moderated by, other variables. (5)

**miscommunication hypothesis**   the claim that men often misunderstand women's nonverbal or behavioral cues as being more sexually suggestive than they are actually meant to be. It seems that men, as compared to women,   have a lower threshold for assigning sexual meaning to a partner's behavior. (9)

**mitigation in speech**   a class of tentative speech behavior, including   hedging, disclaiming expertise, and adding tag questions to the ends of statements. Mitigated speech can reflect uncertainty, but also the desire to involve others in a conversation. Overall, mitigation is more prevalent among women than it is among men. (10)

**model of achievement-related choices**   the view that expectations for one's success are important determinants of achievement-related behavioral choices such as course enrollment and career choice (Eccles [Parsons] et al., 1983). The model has two basic components: a psychological component and a socialization component. The first component predicts that expectations for success are directly influenced by individuals' ability self-concepts and estimates of task difficulty; the second component predicts that parents' perceptions of their children's ability are a major determinant of ability self-concepts, perceived task difficulty, and expectations for success. (6, 11, 12)

**modern sexism**   a prejudiced attitude toward women characterized by an overt rejection of traditional gender roles that coexists with negative feelings about women making economic and political demands. The central dimension of modern sexism is denial of continuing discrimination of women. (7, 8)

**module**   a cognitive mechanism sensitive to distinct inputs, operating according to specific decision-making rules. Evolutionary psychologists assume that an organism's brain is designed in a modular way, with a larger number of domain-specific, but functionally integrated, mechanisms (or modules), each fashioned to solve a particular problem of individual survival or reproduction. (2)

**multidimensional gender matrix**   a combination of six content areas, four constructs (see "Huston matrix"), and four levels of analysis (see "levels-of-analysis approach") that forms the basis for studying gender from a developmental social psychological perspective. This matrix also makes reference to the time axis, constituting a fourth dimension needed to account for processes of developmental change. (1, 14)

**naive social psychology**   a set of functionally significant intuitive ideas about the nature of humans in social situations. According to this view, children and adults form "theories" about the general nature of the sexes and their interrelations (e.g., why the sexes differ, why the same behavior is judged appropriate for girls and inappropriate for boys) that guide their behavior and thinking in social contexts. (4)

**parental belief system**   a multifaceted set of ideas parents have about their children. Parents' beliefs, attitudes, and expectations concerning childrens' ability in particular activity domains influence children's self-concepts, task perceptions, and expectations for success in these domains; that is, parents act as expectancy socializers. Moreover, parents' gender-related beliefs contribute to the emergence of gender-stereotypic differences in boys' and girls' self-concepts, task perceptions, and expectations; that is, parents also act as gender-role socializers. (6, 11)

**parental investment**    the contribution made by each sex to its offspring, at a cost to their ability to invest in other offspring. Parental investment can include direct physiological investment before birth (e.g., the nutrition contributed to the fetus); after birth, it can include the provision of food or other resources (e.g., protection from predators). In most species, the sexes differ largely in parental investment, with females investing more than males. (2)

**paternalistic prejudice**    a patronizing form of prejudice directed toward lower status out-groups, characterized by hostile condescension, but also patronizing affection. (8)

**phase model of transitions**    the view that different types of transitions (e.g., the gender transition) are characterized by three core phases representing changing cognitive-motivational orientations toward social information (Ruble, 1994). In the construction phase, only superficial knowledge about what constitutes gender-typical vs. gender-atypical behavior is available; during consolidation, gender knowledge becomes more structured, abstract, and inferential; integration is characterized by highly differentiated gender knowledge that is flexibly used depending on interaction goals and demands of the situation. (6, 14)

**power-based approach**    the view that stereotyping is inherently linked to power (Fiske, 1993). According to this view, stereotypes serve to establish, maintain, and justify superior power and status. Powerful individuals stereotype intentionally (or "by design") to further their position relative to others and to legitimize both the unequal division of resources and the social system more generally. Also, powerful individuals at times stereotype unintentionally (or "by default"), because they do not care much about the people that they control. In

contrast, less powerful individuals attend closely to the powerful, focusing on the most informative, nonstereotypic information. (7)

**prejudice**    the implicit or explicit attitude that a group deserves inferior social status. The cognitive, emotional, and behavioral aspects of prejudiced attitudes may (for the prejudiced perceiver) be subjectively favorable, unfavorable, or ambivalent in their orientation toward the target group, yet they all serve to promote or maintain that group's subordination. That prejudice may be "implicit" recognizes that the desire to subordinate another group may not be consciously recognized, may be covert or hidden. (8)

**preparedness**    a genetic predisposition to learn some associations more easily than others. According to this notion, evolved psychological differences between females and males need not be "hard-wired" at birth; instead, the sexes may simply be biologically "prepared" to have different learning experiences, and the societies constructed by adult members of their species may further reinforce, channel, and facilitate those experiences (see also "biosocial interactionist perspective"). (2)

**priming**    the facilitation of processing of a stimulus when the same or a similar stimulus has been previously encountered. Priming may have temporary or more durable effects on construct accessibility, depending on how frequently a construct is primed. When the same construct is primed repeatedly by the same (or highly similar) stimulus, the process is called repetition priming. Repetition priming plays an important role in the automatization of gender stereotypes. (6, 7)

**rape myth acceptance**    the endorsement of stereotypic beliefs about rape, rape victims, and rapists (e.g., "Women derive some pleasure from being raped"). Males holding these beliefs typically deny the adverse consequences of unwanted sexual encounters, accept coercion to obtain sexual contacts, and identify rape with the stranger rape script. (9)

**rape script**   a sexual script that specifies the types of situations and event sequences which are, by general consensus, regarded as rape. The prototypical or "real" rape script (also called the stranger rape script) implies the following constellation of features: a sexual assault by an unknown man, lurking on an unsuspecting victim in a dark lane and using physical force to make the victim comply with his demands. In contrast, an acquaintance rape script involves a previously known assailant, an indoor location, and verbal protest rather than physical struggle on the victim's part. (9)

**reproductive effort**   a life-history strategy that entails expending energy to mating, parental care, and investment in other kin. Investment in other kin has a genetic payoff because siblings, nieces, nephews, or cousins, like one's own offspring, share common genes. (2)

**self-promoting communication**   communicating with others in self-confident and self-asserting ways. While use of a self-promoting communication style usually benefits men, women receive greater recognition, are more likeable and influential when they are modest than when they are self-promoting. (10)

**self-regulation**   the process by which individuals regulate their own behavior based on gender-stereotypic self-construals. To the extent that individuals internalize and endorse gender-stereotypic qualities, they tend to adopt gender-typed norms as personal standards for evaluating and monitoring their own behavior. (5, 7)

**sex/gender**   the terms "sex" and "gender" are being used inconsistently in the literature. Some scholars tend to associate assumptions of causality with these terms, using "sex" for biologically based attributes and "gender" for socially based attributes, whereas others use both terms interchangea-

bly. Since the issue of causality is indeed far from being resolved, one may follow Ruble and Martin's (1998) suggestion and use "sex" to refer to classifications of people based on the demographic categories of female and male, and "gender" to refer to social judgments or inferences about the sexes (e.g., stereotypes or roles). Yet, even this distinction may not prove meaningful or applicable in each and every instance.

**sexism**   see "gender prejudice" (though conventional use of this term most often refers to prejudice directed toward women). (8)

**sexual aggression**   any behavior involving the use of (verbal) coercion or (physical) force to obtain sexual contacts against the partner's will. The predominant form of sexual aggression is coercion or force used by men against women. (9)

**sexual division of labor**   the traditional division between women's domestic labor and men's wage labor. Women typically perform more domestic work than men and spend fewer hours in paid employment. Further, women have lower wages than men, are concentrated in different occupations, and are only sparsely represented at the top levels of organizational hierarchies. (5)

**sexual script**   an abstract mental representation of sequences of events that are characteristic of, or appropriate in, particular kinds of sexual encounters. Sexual scripts are inherently interactional in that they comprise the behaviors and characteristics of both the actor and his or her sexual partner, including expectations about the behaviors and feelings of the participants involved and about the consequences of different behavioral options. (9)

**sexual selection**   the evolutionary principle dealing with the increase in reproductive success due to advantages in competing with one's own sex (intrasexual selection) or in attracting the opposite sex (intersexual, or epigamic, selection). Specifically, evolutionary psychologists assume that females and males faced different selection pressures in ancestral times, leading to different strategies for reproductive success: women (the more investing sex) chose their mates from among the available men, preferring those who provided resources like food, protection, and parental skills, while men (the less investing sex) competed with other men for sexual access to women, preferring healthy mates with high reproductive potential. (2)

**situational sources of activation** a particular situation's immediate influence on an individual, determining which self-constructs become part of the individual's working self. With respect to gender, situational sources of activation may refer to the sex composition of a social group, the gender-typedness of a particular task, or the enactment of gender-appropriate behavior. (6)

**social identity theory** the view that individuals use group membership as a source of self-esteem (Tajfel & Turner, 1986). Positive social identity for the in-group depends on favorable comparisons with a relevant out-group. The in-group (e.g., women) compares favorably to an out-group (e.g., men) only when it can demonstrate positive distinctiveness from the out-group. Positive distinctiveness is achieved through the use of stereotypes and the assignment of positive attributes to members of the in-group and negative attributes to members of the out-group. (4, 7, 8)

**social learning theory** the view that gender-typed behavior, like all other behavior, is shaped by environmental contingencies (i.e., reinforcement, punishment) and observational learning (Mischel, 1966). The revised version, labeled "cognitive social learning theory" (Bandura, 1986), emphasizes the role of cognitive factors (e.g., expectancies about behavioral consequences, self-regulatory processes) in mediating between situations and gender-typed behavior. (3, 4, 10)

**social role** a set of culturally shared expectations that apply to individuals who occupy a certain social position or are members of a particular social category. (5)

**social role theory** the view that sex differences in human behavior originate in the contrasting distributions of the sexes into social roles (Eagly, 1987). These differing role assignments are described in terms of two social structural characteristics: sexual division of labor and gender hierarchy. Women's and men's differing social roles give rise to the formation of gender roles, that is, shared expectations about how individuals of each sex typically behave or should behave. Gender-stereotypic expectations, in turn, produce sex differences in behavior, mainly through processes of behavioral confirmation and gender-based self-regulation (see also "gender roles"). (5, 7, 10)

**sociobiological fallacy** the misconception that humans (and other organisms) possess mechanisms with the goal of maximizing their inclusive fitness, that is, maxmizing their gene representation in subsequent generations relative to other individuals (Buss, 1995). Rather than viewing humans as "fitness maximizers", evolutionary psychologists assume that organisms inherit specific perceptual or motivational mechanisms designed to increase the probability of solving recurrent problems faced during ancestral live. These evolved mechanisms can be activated or executed in ways that may or may not lead to increased fitness in current environments. (2)

**somatic effort** a life-history strategy that entails expending energy toward building the body. (2)

**status characteristic** any valued attribute that implies task competence. Status characteristics vary from specific to diffuse, depending on the range of their perceived applicability. Gender is commonly treated as a diffuse status characteristic, meaning that it is viewed as relevant to a large, indeterminate number of different tasks.

Other diffuse status characteristics are race, age, and level of education. (5, 10)

**status characteristics theory**  the view that individuals' status characteristics (e.g., gender) affect their perceived competence, expectations about their future performance, and beliefs about what constitutes appropriate behavior in social interaction. For example, if a man perceives a given task as masculine, he will infer that he is better at this task than his female colleague. If no information as to the gender-typedness of the task is available, the theory predicts that he will consider the female to have inferior task competence—unless she demonstrates the opposite. (5, 10)

**stereotype**  an abstract mental representation, or cognitive schema, of a social category or group. A stereotype includes culturally shared beliefs about the characteristics of a social group (e.g., personality traits, expected behaviors, values, roles, and appearance), each associated in memory with the group label. Stereotypes can be viewed as the cognitive component of intergroup attitudes. (5, 7)

**stereotype threat**  a temporary state of apprehension caused by the experience of being in a situation where one faces judgment based on negative stereotypes about one's group. For stereotype threat to occur, the activating situation has to carry evaluative relevance for the self. Stereotype threat may affect the performance of individuals in ways that confirm stereotypes (e.g., lowering a girl's performance in math). (6, 7)

**token resistance**  a form of ambiguous communication in negotiating sexual intimacy: "a woman's indicating that she did not want to have sex even though she had every intention to and was willing to engage in sexual intercourse" (Muehlenhard & Hollabaugh, 1988, p. 872). (9)

**visual dominance**  the ratio of the amount of time that people maintain eye contact while talking to the amount of time that they maintain eye contact while listening to others. Men usually show more visual dominance than women do. (10)

**working self**  the configuration of temporarily activated self-constructs in short-term memory. Information contained in the working self can be retrieved and used more easily and efficiently than other information related to the self. (6)

# Author Index

*Numbers in italics refer to listings in the reference sections.*

## A

Abbey, A., 278, 279, *289*
Abele, A. E., 27, 362, 366, 368, 373, 374, 375, 376, 379, 381, 382, *383, 384*, 431
Abeles, R. P., 364, *387*
Abelson, R. P., 123, *161*, 275, *292*
Aboud, F., 255, 262, *269*
Adamopoulos, J., 389, 390, *412*
Adler, T. F., 333, *359*
Ageton, S. S., 219, *236*
Agronick, G. S., 158, *161*
Ahn, A., 148, *164, 168*
Aikin, K. J., 135, *172*, 209, *240*, 245, *272*
Ainley, J., 191, *202*
Aird, P., 211, *238*
Ajzen, I., 131, *166*
Albert, A. A., 409
Albin, R. S., 285, *290*
Alcock, J., 40, *59*
Alexander, K. L., 228, *237*, 333, 343, 348, 358
Alexander, R. D., 38, 42, *59*
Alfermann, D., 188, 198, *202, 205*, 366, 381, *384*
Alfieri, T., 261, *269*, 396, 409
Alfonso, E., 314, *323*
Alksnis, C., 278, *289*
Allen, M., 152, *164*, 303, *324*
Allen, V. L., 130, *171*
Allgeier, E. R., 281, *292*
Allport, G. W., 8, *29*, 92, *116*, 124, *161*, 213, 223, *235*, 244, 255, 256, 262, *269*
Allred, L. J., 391, *410*
Alpert, R., 67, *89*

Altemeyer, R. A., 147, *161*
Alvarez, M. M., 216, *238*
Amabile, T. M., 137, *171*
Anastasi, A., 366, *384*
Anderson, J. L., 41, *60*
Anderson, K. B., 152, *161*, 287, *289*
Anderson, K. J., 25, *31*, 318, *327*
Anderson, L. R., 152, *161*
Anderson, R. D., 280, *291*
Andrä, M. S., 366, 373, 375, 376, 379, 381, 382, *383, 384*
Antill, J. K., 111, *116*
Appelbaum, M. I., 320, *322*
Archer, J., 394, 398, 399, *412*, 421, 422, *434*
Arcuri, L., 295, *328*
Aries, E., 303, *322*
Aronson, E., 267, *269*
Aronson, J., 226, *240*
Astin, A. W., 158, *161*
Ashmore, R. D., 8, 10, 15, *29*, 95, 112, *116*, 124, 149, 152, *161, 172*, 209, 222, *235*, 247, *269*, 366, 367, 368, *384*
Astin, H. S., 364, 370, *384*
Atkinson, J. W., 365, *384*
Atkinson, R., 405, *413*
Austin, A. M. B., 296, *322*

## B

Bailey-Werner, B., 211, *238*, 246, *270*
Bakan, D., 126, *161*, 180, *202*, 312, *322*, 367, *384*
Bales, R. F., 124, 125, 144, *170*, 302, 306, *322*

Fritz, H. L., 133, *166*
Fritz, J. J., 296, *324*
Frodi, A. M., 37, *62*
Frodi, M., 37, *62*
Frome, P. M., 10, 27, 66, 195, *203*, 196, 226,
    338, 343, 344, *359*, 364
Frost, L. A., 27, *31*
Funk, S. J., 303, *327*
Fussell, S. R., 26, *31*

# G

Gabriel, S., 149, *166*
Gabrielidis, C., 38, *61*
Gaertner, S. L., 231, *237*, 245, 262, *270*
Gagnon, J. H., 275, 277, *292*
Galambos, N. L., 262, *270*, *411*
Gallagher, A. M., 389, 398, 399, *411*
Gale, W. S., 298, *328*
Galvan Millan, M. E., 72, *87*
Gana, K., 402, *411*
Gangestad, S. W., 47, 53, *60*
Garcia, J., 57, *60*
Gardner, W. L., 149, *166*
Garovich, L., 158, *169*
Gauthier, R., 81, *88*
Gautier, T., 110, *118*
Gauze, C., 252, *270*
Geary, D. C., 36, 37, 38, 44, 45, 48, 51, 52, 55,
    56, *60*, 432, *435*
Geddes, D., 298, *325*
Geis, F. L., 145, 147, *163*, *166*, 177, *203*, 308,
    *323*
Gelman, R., 315, *330*, 423, *435*
Gelman, S. A., 101, 102, 106, *118*, *121*, 214,
    215, *238*, 262, *271*,
Gerard, H. B., 131, 144, *164*
Gerritsen, M., 299, *323*
Gervai, J., 404, *414*
Gewirtz, J. C., 102, *118*
Giacalone, R. A., 309, *325*
Giarrusso, R., 279, *290*
Gibb, J., 43, *62*
Gibbons, F. X., 5, *29*
Gibbons, J. L., 28, 199, 391, 393, 394, 396,
    397, 405, 406, 407, 408, *411*, *414*, 429,
    *433*
Gibson, T. W., 297, *329*
Gilbert, D. T., 4, *30*, 137, *166*
Gilbert, L. A., 3, *32*
Giles, H., 320, *325*
Gilligan, C., 151, *167*
Gilligan, S. G., 179, *202*
Gilmore, T., 289, *292*
Gidycz, C. A., 282, *290*
Gitelson, I. B., *411*
Gjerde, P. F., 76, *87*

Gladding, S. T., 219, *238*
Glass, B., 133, *172*, 207, *240*
Gleason, J. B., 317, 318, *322*, *326*, *327*
Glick, P., 18, 25, *31*, 127, 136, 141, 146, 155,
    158, 159, *167*, 211, 212, 218, 219,
    222, *238*, 244, 245, 246, 249, 250,
    251, 257, 259, 260, 261, 262, 264,
    265, 266, *270*, 277, 288, 427, *435*
Godwin, L., 287, *292*
Goldman, K. S., 398, *411*
Gollwitzer, P. M., 373, *387*
Golombok, S., 180, *203*
Gomes, L. F., 402, *414*
Goodchilds, J. D., 279, *290*
Goodenough, F., 81, *87*
Goodnow, J. J., 5, 6, *31*, 198, *203*, 333, *359*
Goodwin, M. H., 297, 302, *326*,
Goodwin, S. A., 218, *238*
Gottfredson, L. S., 265, 268, *270*, 364, *386*
Gough, H. G., *412*
Gould, C. G., 38, *60*
Gould, J. L., 38, *60*
Gould, R. J., 148, *167*
Gouze, K. R., 394, 398, 399, *412*
Graham, B. L., 258, *271*
Gray, J., 223, *238*
Graziano, W. G., 50, *61*
Green, B. L., 52, *61*
Green, R., 111, *118*
Greenfield, P. M., 214, *236*, 390, 391, *412*
Greenwald, A. G., 222, *235*
Greif, E. B., 301, 318, *326*
Greve, W., 5, *32*
Griffiths, R. J., 220, *239*
Gross, A. M., 280, *292*
Gross, M. R., 43, *61*
Grossman, M., 131, 150, *167*
Groth, G., 36, 38, 51, *61*
Gubin, A., 218, *238*
Guo, J., 300, 305, 306, *327*
Gulko, J., 101, *119*, 312, *330*, 396, *413*
Gutek, B. A., 155, *167*, 362, *386*
Gutierres, S. E., 57, *61*
Guttentag, M., 55, *61*, 249, *270*

# H

Haber, S., 287, *291*
Haberfeld, Y., 147, *170*
Hackett, G., 366, 376, 382, *386*
Haddock, G., 135, 136, 147, *164*, *167*
Häfeli, K., 371, *387*
Hagan, R., 75, 78, 82, 83, *87*, 319, *325*
Hageman, M. B., 219, *238*
Hager, J. L., 57, *63*
Hahn, E. D., 158, *172*, 212, *240*
Halberstadt, A. G., 151, *167*, 298, *326*

# M

**463**

# Subject Index